"The conspectus of patristic exposition that this series offers has been badly needed for several centuries, and the whole Christian world should unite to thank those who are undertaking to fill the gap. For the ongoing ecumenical conversation, and the accurate appreciation of early Christian thought, and the current hermeneutical debate as well, the Ancient Christian Commentary on Scripture will prove itself to be a really indispensable resource."

J. I. PACKER
Board of Governors Professor of Theology
Regent College

"In the desert of biblical scholarship that tries to deconstruct or get behind the texts, the patristic commentators let the pure, clear waters of Christian faith flow from its scriptural source. Preachers, teachers and Bible students of every sort will want to drink deeply from the Ancient Christian Commentary on Scripture."

RICHARD JOHN NEUHAUS
President, Religion and Public Life
Editor-in-Chief, **First Things**

"The fathers of the ancient church were enabled, by the grace of God, to interpret the divine Scriptures in a way that integrates spirituality and erudition, liturgy and dogma, and generally all aspects of our faith which embrace the totality of our life. To allow the fathers to speak to us again, in our contemporary situation, in the way that you have proposed in your project, provides a corrective to the fragmentation of the faith which results from the particularization and overspecialization that exists today in the study of the Holy Bible and of sacred theology."

FR. GEORGE DRAGAS
Holy Cross Seminary

"This new but old Ancient Christian Commentary on Scripture takes us out of the small, closed-minded world in which much modern biblical scholarship is done into an earlier time marked by a Christian seriousness, by robust inquiry and by believing faith. This Commentary is a fresh breeze blowing in our empty, postmodern world."

DAVID F. WELLS
Andrew Mutch Distinguished Professor of Historical and
Systematic Theology, Gordon-Conwell Theological Seminary

"Composed in the style of the great medieval *catenae*, this new anthology of patristic commentary on Holy Scripture, conveniently arranged by chapter and verse, will be a valuable resource for prayer, study and proclamation. By calling attention to the rich Christian heritage preceding the separations between East and West and between Protestant and Catholic, this series will perform a major service to the cause of ecumenism."

AVERY CARDINAL DULLES, S.J.
Laurence J. McGinley Professor of Religion and Society
Fordham University

"The initial cry of the Reformation was *ad fontes*—back to the sources! The Ancient Christian Commentary on Scripture is a marvelous tool for the recovery of biblical wisdom in today's church. Not just another scholarly project, the ACCS is a major resource for the renewal of preaching, theology and Christian devotion."

TIMOTHY GEORGE
Dean, Beeson Divinity School, Samford University

"Modern church members often do not realize that they are participants in the vast company of the communion of saints that reaches far back into the past and that will continue into the future, until the kingdom comes. This Commentary should help them begin to see themselves as participants in that redeemed community."

ELIZABETH ACHTEMEIER
Union Professor Emerita of Bible and Homiletics
Union Theological Seminary in Virginia

"Contemporary pastors do not stand alone. We are not the first generation of preachers to wrestle with the challenges of communicating the gospel. The Ancient Christian Commentary on Scripture puts us in conversation with our colleagues from the past, that great cloud of witnesses who preceded us in this vocation. This Commentary enables us to receive their deep spiritual insights, their encouragement and guidance for present-day interpretation and preaching of the Word. What a wonderful addition to any pastor's library!"

WILLIAM H. WILLIMON
Dean of the Chapel and Professor of Christian Ministry
Duke University

"Here is a nonpareil series which reclaims the Bible as the book of the church by making accessible to earnest readers of the twenty-first century the classrooms of Clement of Alexandria and Didymus the Blind, the study and lecture hall of Origen, the cathedrae of Chrysostom and Augustine, the scriptorium of Jerome in his Bethlehem monastery."

GEORGE LAWLESS
Augustinian Patristic Institute and Gregorian University, Rome

"We are pleased to witness publication of the
Ancient Christian Commentary on Scripture. It is most beneficial for us to learn
how the ancient Christians, especially the saints of the church
who proved through their lives their devotion to God and his Word, interpreted
Scripture. Let us heed the witness of those who have gone before us in the faith."

METROPOLITAN THEODOSIUS
Primate, Orthodox Church in America

"Across Christendom there has emerged a widespread interest
in early Christianity, both at the popular and scholarly level. . . .
Christians of all traditions stand to benefit from this project, especially clergy
and those who study the Bible. Moreover, it will allow us to see how our traditions are
both rooted in the scriptural interpretations of the church fathers while at
the same time seeing how we have developed new perspectives."

ALBERTO FERREIRO
Professor of History, Seattle Pacific University

"The Ancient Christian Commentary on Scripture fills a long overdue need for scholars and
students of the church fathers. . . . Such information will be of immeasurable
worth to those of us who have felt inundated by contemporary interpreters and novel theories
of the biblical text. We welcome some 'new' insight from the
ancient authors in the early centuries of the church."

H. WAYNE HOUSE
Professor of Theology and Law
Trinity University School of Law

"Chronological snobbery—the assumption that our ancestors working without benefit of
computers have nothing to teach us—is exposed as nonsense by this magnificent
new series. Surfeited with knowledge but starved of wisdom, many of us are
more than ready to sit at table with our ancestors and listen to their holy
conversations on Scripture. I know I am."

EUGENE H. PETERSON
Professor Emeritus of Spiritual Theology
Regent College

"Few publishing projects have encouraged me as much as the recently announced Ancient Christian Commentary on Scripture with Dr. Thomas Oden serving as general editor.... How is it that so many of us who are dedicated to serve the Lord received seminary educations which omitted familiarity with such incredible students of the Scriptures as St. John Chrysostom, St. Athanasius the Great and St. John of Damascus? I am greatly anticipating the publication of this Commentary."

FR. PETER E. GILLQUIST
Director, Department of Missions and Evangelism
Antiochian Orthodox Christian Archdiocese of North America

"The Scriptures have been read with love and attention for nearly two thousand years, and listening to the voice of believers from previous centuries opens us to unexpected insight and deepened faith. Those who studied Scripture in the centuries closest to its writing, the centuries during and following persecution and martyrdom, speak with particular authority. The Ancient Christian Commentary on Scripture will bring to life the truth that we are invisibly surrounded by a 'great cloud of witnesses.'"

FREDERICA MATHEWES-GREEN
Commentator, National Public Radio

"For those who think that church history began around 1941 when their pastor was born, this Commentary will be a great surprise. Christians throughout the centuries have read the biblical text, nursed their spirits with it and then applied it to their lives. These commentaries reflect that the witness of the Holy Spirit was present in his church throughout the centuries. As a result, we can profit by allowing the ancient Christians to speak to us today."

HADDON ROBINSON
Harold John Ockenga Distinguished Professor of Preaching
Gordon-Conwell Theological Seminary

"All who are interested in the interpretation of the Bible will welcome the forthcoming multivolume series Ancient Christian Commentary on Scripture. Here the insights of scores of early church fathers will be assembled and made readily available for significant passages throughout the Bible and the Apocrypha. It is hard to think of a more worthy ecumenical project to be undertaken by the publisher."

BRUCE M. METZGER
Professor of New Testament, Emeritus
Princeton Theological Seminary

ANCIENT CHRISTIAN
COMMENTARY ON SCRIPTURE

NEW TESTAMENT
X

HEBREWS

EDITED BY

ERIK M. HEEN

PHILIP D. W. KREY

GENERAL EDITOR
THOMAS C. ODEN

InterVarsity Press
Downers Grove, Illinois

InterVarsity Press
P.O. Box 1400, Downers Grove, IL 60515-1426
World Wide Web: www.ivpress.com
E-mail: email@ivpress.com

InterVarsity Press® is the book-publishing division of InterVarsity Christian Fellowship/USA®, a student movement active on campus at hundreds of universities, colleges and schools of nursing in the United States of America, and a member movement of the International Fellowship of Evangelical Students. For information about local and regional activities, write Public Relations Dept., InterVarsity Christian Fellowship/USA, 6400 Schroeder Rd., P.O. Box 7895, Madison, WI 53707-7895, or visit the IVCF website at <www.intervarsity.org>.

Scripture quotations, unless otherwise noted, are from the Revised Standard Version of the Bible, *copyright 1946, 1952, 1971 by the Division of Christian Education of the National Council of the Churches of Christ in the U.S.A., and are used by permission.*

Selected excerpts from Fathers of the Church: A New Translation, copyright 1947-. Used by permission of The Catholic University of America Press. Full bibliographic information on individual volumes may be found in the Bibliography of Works in English Translation.

Selected excerpts from Bede the Venerable, Homilies on the Gospels, *translated by Lawrence T. Martin and David Hurst, Cistercian Studies 110 and 111, ©1991;* Pachomian Koinonia, *translated by Armand Veilleux, Cistercian Studies 45, 46 and 47, ©1980-1982; Evagrius Ponticus,* The Praktikos and Chapters on Prayer, *translated by John Eudes Bamberger, Cistercian Studies 4, ©1972. Used by permission of Cistercian Publications, Kalamazoo, Michigan.*

Selected excerpts from Augustine, The Literal Meaning of Genesis, *translated by John Hammond Taylor, Ancient Christian Writers 42, ©1982; Cassiodorus,* Explanation of the Psalms, *translated by P. G. Walsh, Ancient Christian Writers 52, ©1991; Origen,* An Exhortation to Martyrdom, Prayer and Selected Works, *translated by Rowan A. Greer, The Classics of Western Spirituality, ©1979; Symeon the New Theologian,* The Discourses, The Classics of Western Spirituality, *©1980; by Paulist Press, Inc., New York/Mahwah, N.J. Used with the permission of Paulist Press, www.paulistpress.com.*

Selected excerpts from Early Christian Fathers, *translated and edited by Cyril C. Richardson, The Library of Christian Classics 1, ©1953;* Christology of the Later Fathers, *edited by Edward Rochie Hardy, The Library of Christian Classics 3, ©1954;* Cyril of Jerusalem and Nemesius of Emesa, *edited by William Telfer, The Library of Christian Classics 4, ©1955. Used by permission of Westminster John Knox Press.*

Selected excerpts from The Works of Saint Augustine: A Translation for the 21st Century. *Copyright 1990-. Used by permission of the Augustinian Heritage Institute.*

Selected excerpts from Bede the Venerable, On the Tabernacle, *translated with notes and introduction by Arthur G. Holder, Translated Texts for Historians 18, ©1994. Used by permission of Liverpool University Press.*

Selected excerpts from Cyril of Alexandria, Origen and Theodore of Mopsuestia found in Rowan A. Greer, The Captain of Our Salvation: A Study in the Patristic Exegesis of Hebrews, *©1973. Used by permission of Mohr Siebeck Verlag, Tübingen, Germany.*

Selected excerpts from The Panarion of Epiphanius of Salamis, *translated by Frank Williams, Nag Hammadi and Manichaean Studies 36, ©1994;* Faith Gives Fullness to Reasoning: The Five Theological Orations of Gregory Nazianzen, *translated by Lionel Wickham and Frederick Williams. Used by permission of E. J. Brill.*

Selected excerpts from The Ascetical Homilies of Saint Isaac the Syrian, *edited by Dana Miller, ©1984. Used by permission of Holy Transfiguration Monastery, Brookline, Mass.*

Cover photograph: Scala/Art Resource, New York. View of the apse. S. Vitale, Ravenna, Italy.

Spine photograph: Byzantine Collection, Dumbarton Oaks, Washington D.C. Pendant cross (gold and enamel). Constantinople, late sixth century.

ISBN 978-0-8308-1495-4

Printed in the United States of America ∞

Library of Congress Cataloging-in-Publication Data

Hebrews/edited by Erik M. Heen and Philip D. W. Krey; general editor Thomas C. Oden.
    p. cm.—(Ancient Christian commentary on Scripture. New
    Testament; 10)
   Includes bibliographical references and indexes.
   ISBN 0-8308-1495-7 (cloth: alk. paper)
   1. Bible. N.T. Hebrews—Commentaries.   I. Heen, Erik M. II. Krey,
   Philip D., 1950-   III.Oden, Thomas C.   IV. Series.
   BS2775.53.H43 2005
   227'.87077'09—dc22
                                        2004025508

P	26	25	24	23	22	21	20	19	18	17	16	15	14	13	12	11	10	9	8	7	6	5	4	3
Y	28	27	26	25	24	23	22	21	20	19	18	17	16	15	14	13	12	11	10	09	08	07		

ANCIENT CHRISTIAN COMMENTARY PROJECT RESEARCH TEAM

GENERAL EDITOR
Thomas C. Oden

ASSOCIATE EDITOR
Christopher A. Hall

OPERATIONS MANAGER AND TRANSLATIONS PROJECT COORDINATOR
Joel Elowsky

RESEARCH AND ACQUISITIONS DIRECTOR
Michael Glerup

EDITORIAL SERVICES DIRECTOR
Warren Calhoun Robertson

ORIGINAL LANGUAGE VERSION DIRECTOR
Konstantin Gavrilkin

GRADUATE RESEARCH ASSISTANTS

Jeffrey Finch	*Hsueh-Ming Liao*
Steve Finlan	*Michael Nausner*
James A. Kellerman	*Alexei Khamine*
Joel Scandrett	*Vladimir Kharlamov*
Baek-Yong Sung	*Susan Kipper*
Elena Vishnevskaya	*Jeffery Wittung*

ADMINISTRATIVE ASSISTANT
Tod Bryant

In memory of

Bjørn Anders Loufman Heen

February 3, 2001—June 8, 2004

CONTENTS

General Introduction

The Ancient Christian Commentary on Scripture has as its goal the revitalization of Christian teaching based on classical Christian exegesis, the intensified study of Scripture by lay persons who wish to think with the early church about the canonical text, and the stimulation of Christian historical, biblical, theological and pastoral scholars toward further inquiry into scriptural interpretation by ancient Christian writers.

The time frame of these documents spans seven centuries of exegesis, from Clement of Rome to John of Damascus, from the end of the New Testament era to A.D. 750, including the Venerable Bede.

Lay readers are asking how they might study sacred texts under the instruction of the great minds of the ancient church. This commentary has been intentionally prepared for a general lay audience of nonprofessionals who study the Bible regularly and who earnestly wish to have classic Christian observation on the text readily available to them. The series is targeted to anyone who wants to reflect and meditate with the early church about the plain sense, theological wisdom and moral meaning of particular Scripture texts.

A commentary dedicated to allowing ancient Christian exegetes to speak for themselves will refrain from the temptation to fixate endlessly upon contemporary criticism. Rather, it will stand ready to provide textual resources from a distinguished history of exegesis that has remained massively inaccessible and shockingly disregarded during the last century. We seek to make available to our present-day audiences the multicultural, multilingual, transgenerational resources of the early ecumenical Christian tradition.

Preaching at the end of the first millennium focused primarily on the text of Scripture as understood by the earlier esteemed tradition of comment, largely converging on those writers that best reflected classic Christian consensual thinking. Preaching at the end of the second millennium has reversed that pattern. It has so forgotten most of these classic comments that they are vexing to find anywhere, and even when located they are often available only in archaic editions and inadequate translations. The preached word in our time has remained largely bereft of previously influential patristic inspiration. Recent scholarship has so focused attention upon post-Enlightenment historical and literary methods that it has left this longing largely unattended and unserviced.

This series provides the pastor, exegete, student and lay reader with convenient means to see what Athanasius or John Chrysostom or the desert fathers and mothers had to say about a particular text for preaching, for study and for meditation. There is an emerging awareness among Catholic, Protestant and Orthodox laity that vital biblical preaching and spiritual formation need deeper grounding beyond the scope of the historical-critical orientations that have governed biblical studies in our day.

Hence this work is directed toward a much broader audience than the highly technical and specialized scholarly field of patristic studies. The audience is not limited to the university scholar concentrating on the study of the history of the transmission of the text or to those with highly focused philological interests in textual morphology or historical-critical issues. Though these are crucial concerns for specialists, they are not the paramount interests of this series.

This work is a Christian Talmud. The Talmud is a Jewish collection of rabbinic arguments and comments on the Mishnah, which epitomized the laws of the Torah. The Talmud originated in approximately the same period that the patristic writers were commenting on texts of the Christian tradition. Christians from the late patristic age through the medieval period had documents analogous to the Jewish Talmud and Midrash (Jewish commentaries) available to them in the *glossa ordinaria* and catena traditions, two forms of compiling extracts of patristic exegesis. In Talmudic fashion the sacred text of Christian Scripture was thus clarified and interpreted by the classic commentators.

The Ancient Christian Commentary on Scripture has venerable antecedents in medieval exegesis of both eastern and western traditions, as well as in the Reformation tradition. It offers for the first time in this century the earliest Christian comments and reflections on the Old and New Testaments to a modern audience. Intrinsically an ecumenical project, this series is designed to serve Protestant, Catholic and Orthodox lay, pastoral and scholarly audiences.

In cases where Greek, Latin, Syriac and Coptic texts have remained untranslated into English, we provide new translations. Wherever current English translations are already well rendered, they will be utilized, but if necessary their language will be brought up to date. We seek to present fresh dynamic equivalency translations of long-neglected texts which historically have been regarded as authoritative models of biblical interpretation.

These foundational sources are finding their way into many public libraries and into the core book collections of many pastors and lay persons. It is our intent and the publisher's commitment to keep the whole series in print for many years to come.

Thomas C. Oden
General Editor

A Guide to Using This Commentary

Several features have been incorporated into the design of this commentary. The following comments are intended to assist readers in making full use of this volume.

Pericopes of Scripture

The scriptural text has been divided into pericopes, or passages, usually several verses in length. Each of these pericopes is given a heading, which appears at the beginning of the pericope. For example, the first pericope in the commentary on Hebrews is "1:1-4 The Prologue." This heading is followed by the Scripture passage quoted in the Revised Standard Version (RSV) across the full width of the page. The Scripture passage is provided for the convenience of readers, but it is also in keeping with medieval patristic commentaries, in which the citations of the Fathers were arranged around the text of Scripture.

Overviews

Following each pericope of text is an overview of the patristic comments on that pericope. The format of this overview varies within the volumes of this series, depending on the requirements of the specific book of Scripture. The function of the overview is to provide a brief summary of all the comments to follow. It tracks a reasonably cohesive thread of argument among patristic comments, even though they are derived from diverse sources and generations. Thus the summaries do not proceed chronologically or by verse sequence. Rather they seek to rehearse the overall course of the patristic comment on that pericope.

We do not assume that the commentators themselves anticipated or expressed a formally received cohesive argument but rather that the various arguments tend to flow in a plausible, recognizable pattern. Modern readers can thus glimpse aspects of continuity in the flow of diverse exegetical traditions representing various generations and geographical locations.

Topical Headings

An abundance of varied patristic comment is available for each pericope of these letters. For this reason we have broken the pericopes into two levels. First is the verse with its topical heading. The patristic comments are then focused on aspects of each verse, with topical headings summarizing the essence of the patristic comment by evoking a key phrase, metaphor or idea. This feature provides a bridge by which modern readers can enter into the heart of the patristic comment.

Identifying the Patristic Texts

Following the topical heading of each section of comment, the name of the patristic commentator is given. An English translation of the patristic comment is then provided. This is immediately followed by the title of the patristic work and the textual reference—either by book, section and subsection or by book-and-verse references.

The Footnotes

Readers who wish to pursue a deeper investigation of the patristic works cited in this commentary will find the footnotes especially valuable. A footnote number directs the reader to the notes at the bottom of the right-hand column, where in addition to other notations (clarifications or biblical cross references) one will find information on English translations (where available) and standard original-language editions of the work cited. An abbreviated citation (normally citing the book, volume and page number) of the work is provided. A key to the abbreviations is provided on page xv. Where there is any serious ambiguity or textual problem in the selection, we have tried to reflect the best available textual tradition.

Where original language texts have remained untranslated into English, we provide new translations. Wherever current English translations are already well rendered, they are utilized, but where necessary they are stylistically updated. A single asterisk (*) indicates that a previous English translation has been updated to modern English or amended for easier reading. The double asterisk (**) indicates either that a new translation has been provided or that some extant translation has been significantly amended. We have standardized spellings and made grammatical variables uniform so that our English references will not reflect the odd spelling variables of the older English translations. For ease of reading we have in some cases edited out superfluous conjunctions.

For the convenience of computer database users the digital database references are provided to either the Thesaurus Linguae Graecae (Greek texts) or to the Cetedoc (Latin texts) in the appendix found on pages 241-46.

Abbreviations

ACW	Ancient Christian Writers: The Works of the Fathers in Translation. Mahwah, N.J.: Paulist Press, 1946-.
AHSIS	Dana Miller, ed. *The Ascetical Homilies of Saint Isaac the Syrian*. Boston, Mass.: Holy Transfiguration Monastery, 1984.
ANF	A. Roberts and J. Donaldson, eds. Ante-Nicene Fathers. 10 vols. Buffalo, N.Y.: Christian Literature, 1885-1896. Reprint, Grand Rapids, Mich.: Eerdmans, 1951-1956; Reprint, Peabody, Mass.: Hendrickson, 1994.
CC	Richard A. Norris Jr., *The Christological Controversy*. Philadelphia: Fortress, 1980.
COS	Rowan A. Greer. *The Captain of our Salvation: A Study in the Patristic Exegesis of Hebrews.* Tübingen, Germany: J. C. B. Mohr (Paul Siebeck), 1973.
CS	Cistercian Studies. Kalamazoo, Mich.: Cistercian Publications, 1973-.
CSCO	Corpus Scriptorum Christianorum Orientalium. Louvain, Belgium, 1903-.
ECTD	C. McCarthy, trans. and ed. *Saint Ephrem's Commentary on Tatian's Diatessaron: An English Translation of Chester Beatty Syriac MS 709. Journal of Semitic Studies* Supplement 2. Oxford: Oxford University Press for the University of Manchester, 1993.
EHA	Marco Conti, trans. *Commentary on the Epistle to the Hebrews*. Works of Ephrem in Armenian. ACCS translation project.
FC	Fathers of the Church: A New Translation. Washington, D.C.: Catholic University of America Press, 1947-.
FGFR	F. W. Norris. *Faith Gives Fullness to Reasoning: The Five Theological Orations of Gregory Nazianzen.* Leiden and New York: E. J. Brill, 1991.
FSTR	Jean Daniélou. *From Shadows to Reality: Studies in Biblical Typology of the Fathers.* Translated by Wulstan Hibberd. London: Burns & Oates, 1960.
GCS	Die griechischen christlichen Schriftsteller der ersten drei Jahrhunderte. Berlin: Akademie-Verlag, 1897-.
GNLM	*Gregory of Nyssa: The Life of Moses.* Translated by A. J. Malherbe and E. Ferguson. Classics of Western Spirituality. New York: Paulist Press, 1978.
HCTM	Raymond Tonneau and Robert Devreesse, eds. and trans. *Les Homélies Catéchétiques de Théodore de Mopsueste.* Reproduction phototypique du ms. Mingana Syr. 561 (Selly Oak Colleges' Library, Birmingham). Studi e testi 145. Città del Vaticano: Biblioteca apostolica vaticana: 1949.
HM	Michael J. Walsh, ed. Heythrop Monographs. London: Heythrop College, 1976-.
HQG	Jerome. *Hebrew Questions on Genesis.* Translated with introduction and commentary by C. T. R. Hayward. Oxford Early Christian Studies. Oxford: Clarendon Press, 1995.
IHEGF	Bertrand de Margerie. *An Introduction to the History of Exegesis I: The Greek Fathers.* Petersham, Mass.: Saint Bede's Publications, 1993.
JCC	*John Cassian.* Conferences. Translated by Colm Luibheid. Classics of Western Spirituality. Mahwah,

	N.J.: Paulist, 1985.
LCC	J. Baillie et al., eds. The Library of Christian Classics. 26 vols. Philadelphia: Westminster, 1953-1966.
LCL	Loeb Classical Library. Cambridge, Mass.: Harvard University Press; London: Heinemann, 1912-.
NHMS	J. M. Robinson and H. J. Klimkeit, eds. Nag Hammadi and Manichaean Studies. Leiden: E. J. Brill, 1993-.
NPNF	P. Schaff et al., eds. A Select Library of the Nicene and Post-Nicene Fathers of the Christian Church. 2 series (14 vols. each). Buffalo, N.Y.: Christian Literature, 1887-1894. Reprint, Grand Rapids, Mich.: Eerdmans, 1952-1956. Reprint, Peabody, Mass.: Hendrickson, 1994.
NTA 15	K. Staab, ed., *Pauluskommentare aus der griechischen Kirche: Aus Katenenhandschriften gesammelt und herausgegeben* (Pauline commentary from the Greek church: collected and edited catena writings). NT Abhandlungen 15. Münster in Westfalen: Aschendorff, 1933.
OFP	Origen. *On First Principles.* Translated by G. W. Butterworth. London: SPCK, 1936.
OSW	*Origen: An Exhortation to Martyrdom, Prayer and Selected Writings.* Translated by Rowan A. Greer with Preface by Hans Urs von Balthasar. The Classics of Western Spirituality. New York: Paulist Press, 1979.
PDCW	*Pseudo-Dionysius: The Complete Works.* Translated by Colm Luibheid. The Classics of Western Spirituality. New York: Paulist Press, 1987.
PEP	P. E. Pusey, ed. *Cyril of Alexandria.* 7 vols. Oxford: 1868-77.
PG	J.-P. Migne, ed. Patrologia cursus completus. Series Graeca. 166 vols. Paris: Migne, 1857-1886.
PL	J.-P. Migne, ed. Patrologiae cursus completus. Series Latina. 221 vols. Paris: Migne, 1844-1864.
POG	Eusebius. *The Proof of the Gospel.* 2 vols. Translated by W. J. Ferrar. London: SPCK, 1920. Reprinted, Grand Rapids, Mich.: Baker, 1981.
SC	H. de Lubac, J. Daniélou et al., eds. Sources Chrétiennes. Paris: Editions du Cerf, 1941-.
SNTD	*Symeon the New Theologian: The Discourses.* Translated by C. J. de Catanzaro. Classics of Western Spirituality: A Library of the Great Spiritual Masters. New York: Paulist, 1980.
TCCLSP	Robert Charles Hill, trans. and ed. *Theodoret of Cyrus: Commentary on the Letters of St. Paul.* 2 vols. Brookline, Mass.: Holy Cross Orthodox Press, 2001.
TEM	H. B. Swete, ed. *Theodori episcopi Mopsuesteni: In epistolas b. Pauli commentarii.* 2 vols. Cambridge: Cambridge University Press, 1880, 1882.
TOB	James L. Kugel, *Traditions of the Bible: A Guide to the Bible as It Was at the Start of the Common Era.* Cambridge, Mass.: Harvard University Press, 1998.
TTH	G. Clark, M. Gibson and M. Whitby, eds. Translated Texts for Historians. Liverpool: Liverpool University Press, 1985-.
WSA	J. E. Rotelle, ed. *Works of St. Augustine: A Translation for the Twenty-First Century.* Hyde Park, N.Y.: New City Press, 1995.

INTRODUCTION TO HEBREWS

This volume on Hebrews in the ACCS project exhibits some unique characteristics that require explanation under the following rubrics: the reception of Hebrews in the early church; the rationale for anchoring the volume in Chrysostom's *On the Epistle to the Hebrews*; and the nature of the selections from other patristic commentators. The final section concludes with a discussion of genre and language issues embedded in this volume that complicate its use. The selections of comments from early Christian exegetes represent a variety of interpretive genres and stem from different times and contexts, facts that place demands upon the reader when moving from one text to the next. Further, the chronological distance from the original ancient languages of both the text of Hebrews (Greek) and those of the early Christian writers who commented upon it (e.g., Greek, Latin, Armenian) make particular claims upon the modern reader that deserve some comment.

The Reception of Hebrews

The epistle to the Hebrews occupies a distinctive place in the New Testament canon. It is, by tradition, associated with the Pauline corpus. Yet doubts regarding its authorship and authority surfaced early in its transmission and complicated its reception, particularly in the West (i.e., Latin-speaking areas), through the fourth century.[1] In the West, issues of church order came to dominate the interpretation of Hebrews. A rigorist interpretation of Hebrews 6:4-6, Hebrews 10:26-31 and Hebrews 12:17 claimed the impossibility of repentance for certain sins after baptism. This concern can be noted as early as the *Shepherd of Hermas* (120-140).[2] It is also apparent in Tertullian's (c. 160-c. 225) defense of Hebrews.[3] After the Decian persecution of 249-50, the rigorist Novatians used Hebrews to argue that those who had recanted the faith could not be forgiven and readmitted to the church. Cyprian, bishop of Carthage (fl. 248-258), himself a disciplined defender of the faith, declared that the lapsed could be reconciled with the church after rigorous penance. Still, Cyprian did not use Hebrews in his own constructive work. He never quotes from it.

In the Greek East, although issues related to Pauline authorship were also discussed, the "second repentance" passages were not construed as problematic in the same way as in the West, and the authority of Hebrews was never seriously questioned. The early Alexandrian exegetes Pantaenus and Clement accepted Pauline authorship, though Clement suggested that the stylistic differences in Hebrews are due to Luke translating Paul's letter from the original Hebrew to Greek, a tradition that was incorporated into the *glossa ordinaria* and became the

---

[1] Discussions regarding the reception and recognition of Hebrews in the East and West may be found in any in-depth commentary. See, e.g., William L. Lane, *Hebrews 1-8*, Word Biblical Commentary, vol. 47a (Dallas: Word, 1991), pp. cl-clv.

[2] The *Shepherd of Hermas*, which was critical of the rigorist position, was written in Greek but stems from Roman tradition, as does 1 Clement, which contains the earliest citation of Hebrews.

[3] *On Modesty* 20. Tertullian is illustrative of the ability of some Fathers to separate the issues of authorship and authority. He accepted the authority of the letter but attributed it to Barnabas, Paul's coworker.

traditional opinion of the medieval Western church.[4] Origen refined this notion to suggest that the final shape of the letter represented a different order of redaction from that of translation. Origen's comments on the authorship of Hebrews are representative of the Greek tradition in general. They come to us in an often-paraphrased text that is cited first by Eusebius and stems from Origen's now lost *Homilies on Hebrews*:

> But as for myself, if I were to state my own opinion, I should say that the thoughts are the apostle's, but that the style and composition belong to one who called to mind the apostle's teachings and, as it were, made short notes of what his master said. If any church, therefore, holds this epistle as Paul's, let it be commended for this also. For not without reason have the men of old time handed it down as Paul's. But who wrote the epistle, in truth God knows.[5]

In a papyrus manuscript that contains the earliest Greek collection of Paul's letters that has survived (c. A.D. 200), Hebrews follows Romans, an indication of its perceived importance and authority in the Eastern tradition. By comparison, Hebrews is missing from the Latin Muratorian canon, a list that may stem from the same period as P[46]. In the West, it is not until Jerome (c. A.D. 347-420) and Augustine (c. A.D. 354-430) that the work received its powerful advocates. This shift came, apparently, as a result of new knowledge of the deep appreciation the Greek tradition held for the epistle, as well as its proven value for the orthodox in the Arian controversy (e.g., the use of Heb 1:3 as a christological proof text). Neither of the great Latin fathers, however, produced extended commentary on the work, and both Jerome and Augustine remained circumspect with regard to the question of authorship.[6] Hebrews is also missing from the set of Pauline commentaries produced by Ambrosiaster (fl. c. A.D. 366-384). At the Council of Carthage in 397 the letter was officially recognized but placed at the end of the Pauline corpus—after the much shorter pastorals and Philemon—memorializing the West's earlier ambivalence regarding the letter's status.[7] Thus it is only from the late fourth century that an ecumenical consensus begins to develop that the epistle to the Hebrews derived from Paul and was of canonical stature. Once established, this ecumenical consensus regarding the apostolic origin and authority of the epistle lasted through the medieval period. With the rise of humanism in the late medieval and early Reformation period and its renewed interest in historical and literary issues, the questions regarding authorship resurfaced in the West (e.g., among Erasmus, Luther and Calvin). Luther, noting the theological distinctiveness of the letter as well as the elegance of the Greek and its expository style, suggested Apollos (1 Cor 1:12, 3:4-6) as the author of Hebrews, whom Acts 18:24 describes as Jewish, from Alexandria, "an eloquent man, well versed in the Scriptures." Today, the majority of biblical scholars trained in higher critical methods, like the earliest exegetes, recognize the difficulties of assigning authorship of the epistle to the Hebrews directly to Paul because of differences in form, style and theological emphases from the letters that make up the thirteen-letter Pauline corpus.[8]

---

[4]See Eusebius *Ecclesiastical History* 6.14.1-4.

[5]Eusebius *Ecclesiastical History* 6.25.13-14.

[6]Lane, *Hebrews 1-8*, p. cliv, suggests that Hilary of Poitiers, in 367, was the first Latin father to support the Pauline authorship of Hebrews. See the ACCS commentary at Hebrews 1:3 for its use in the Arian controversy.

[7]Before the standardization of canonical placement, Hebrews held many different positions within the Pauline collection. For a detailed discussion see William H. P. Hatch, "The Position of Hebrews in the Canon of the New Testament," *Harvard Theological Review* 29 (1936): 133-51.

[8]On the question of the authorship of Hebrews, see the extensive discussion by Donald Guthrie, *New Testament Introduction*, 4th ed. (Downers Grove, Ill.: InterVarsity Press, 1990), pp. 668-82. Guthrie concludes on p. 682, "An open verdict is clearly the safest course and in this the opinion of Origen can hardly be improved upon."

For the earliest period of patristic interpretation, the Greek exegetical responses to Hebrews dominate, as they do for all books of the Bible. This is simply because the postapostolic theological conversation was mainly carried out in Greek, even in Rome, the capital of the empire. In addition to the chronological priority of the Greek sources, there is less active interest in Paul in the West in the first four centuries.[9] The complicated reception history of Hebrews extends this silence forward in time. There is, for example, no extensive Latin commentary on Hebrews until Alcuin (c. A.D. 735-804), a work that relies heavily upon a mid-sixth-century translation of Chrysostom's *On the Epistle to the Hebrews*.[10] This ACCS volume reflects the imbalance in the source documents for the earliest centuries and has few representatives from the West. In addition we, the editors of this volume, within the Greek sphere have chosen to highlight responses to Hebrews that stem from the Antiochene tradition. This comes primarily as the result of our decision to give more space to the commentary of Chrysostom above other patristic sources. The justification for this strategy follows, but it may help first to comment on the exegetical differences and commonalities between the schools of Antioch and Alexandria.

There is a long tradition in scholarship that distinguishes between two schools of theological and hermeneutical thought in the Greek world, one based in Alexandria in Egypt and one based in Antioch in Syria. Both schools accepted the orthodox understanding that the Logos was divine and therefore immutable. The differences emerge in thinking through how the divine nature coexisted with the human nature in the incarnation. In christological matters, the Alexandrian school has been characterized as particularly eager to protect one incarnate Logos, truly and fully both God and human, as the Savior. Important scriptural passages were John 1:14, "The Word became flesh," and Hebrews 13:8, "Jesus Christ is the same yesterday and today and forever." As Jaroslav Pelikan has noted on this passage, "[Here] the subject of this passage was 'Jesus Christ,' not merely Christ or the Logos, and yet eternity and identity that were appropriate only to the Logos were predicated also of the human in whom the Logos dwelt."[11] Such a hermeneutical procedure protected the unity of Christ. However, it also tended to submerge the humanity of Christ into his divinity. Antiochene Christology, by contrast, was committed to preserving Christ's human involvement in order to protect the reality and the exemplary nature of Christ's experience and suffering. In order to do so, it was necessary to maintain a strict separation between the two natures, a view that, in turn, could undermine the unity of Christ.[12] The Antiochenes emphasized that the Son was the prototype of the redeemed, the new Adam, and consequently truly human like us. When Luke 2:52 says, "Jesus increased in wisdom and in stature, and in favor with God and man," they argued the text referred to the human nature

---

[9]Karlfried Froehlich, "Which Paul? Observations on the Image of the Apostle in the History of Biblical Exegesis," in *New Perspectives on Historical Theology*, ed. Bradley Nassif (Grand Rapids, Mich.: Eerdmans, 1996), p. 285, notes that there was a "'Renaissance of Paul' among Western theologians of the late fourth century and their opponents. The term refers to the phenomenon that, after a total Western silence during the earlier centuries, no fewer than six major Latin commentaries on the Pauline corpus were written during the fifty years between A.D. 360 and 410 those of Marius Victorinus, the so-called Ambrosiaster, Jerome, Augustine, Pelagius, and the Budapest *anonymous*."

[10]A study of the early medieval Latin commentaries is available in Eduard Riggenbach, *Historische Studien zum Hebräerbrief* (Leipzig: A. Deichert, 1907), pp. 19, 24.

[11]Jaroslav Pelikan, *The Emergence of the Catholic Tradition*, vol. 1, *The Christian Tradition: A History of the Development of Doctrine* (Chicago: University of Chicago Press, 1971), p. 255.

[12]For a discussion of these issues with respect to the exegesis of Hebrews, see Frances M. Young, "Christological Ideas in the Greek Commentaries on the Epistle to Hebrews," *Journal of Theological Studies* 20 (1969): 150-63, and Rowan A. Greer, *The Captain of Our Salvation: A Study in the Patristic Exegesis of Hebrews* (Tübingen: J. C. B. Mohr/Paul Siebeck, 1973).

of Jesus and not the divine because the divine cannot change or develop.

A difference has also been discerned in the ways the schools approached the interpretation of Scripture. The Alexandrian school has been seen to be more influenced by the traditions associated with neo-Platonism. For example, it favored the use of allegorical interpretation as had been developed by Philo and other Alexandrian Jewish scholars. Origen, the greatest example of the Alexandrian school, suggested a threefold sense of Scripture in analogy to the tripartite anthropology of the philosophers and of Paul: just as human beings consist of body, soul and spirit, so Scripture edifies by a literal, a moral and a spiritual sense.[13] Antioch, by comparison, has been seen as committed to a style of exegesis that is more indebted to rhetorical models than philosophical schools. It was more interested in the literal and historical aspects of the text, less focused on discovering allegorical, symbolic, or spiritual interpretations.

This characterization represents ideal types. In reality, the lines between the two traditions, understood in such categories, are blurred. Aspects of each tradition so understood may be found in both streams. Both traditions used the typological method in that they saw the Old Testament looking beyond itself for its interpretation. Old Testament referents prefigured New Testament events and figures or were types of Christ. Also, the secondary school training in basic exegetical skills members of both traditions received was similar.[14] One way of approaching the hermeneutical differences, then, is to note the tendency of the Antiochene tradition to respect the language and narrative of the biblical text as the medium through which true understanding and meaning comes, that is, for the purpose of moral and dogmatic teachings. The Alexandrian tradition at times had a tendency to approach the text as a symbol of the true realities that could be understood by means of allegorical interpretation and therefore gives only preliminary priority to the narrative coherence of the text.[15] Occasionally certain parts of the narrative were even considered to be historical fiction. Buried within the text are hidden senses of truth, so that the vital meaning must be most carefully sought out. For this school, Scripture is a means to an end, a guide for the soul on its way upward (anagogic meaning). Such a hermeneutic, for example, lies at the heart of Origen's soteriology.[16]

Chrysostom

After reviewing the extant exegetical material on the epistle to the Hebrews, we decided to base our volume of selections in *On the Epistle to the Hebrews*, composed by Chrysostom (c. 347-407) at the end of his career, probably while bishop in Constantinople (c. 403-404).[17] This decision was based on a variety of factors: the unique place the homilies hold in the history of interpretation of Hebrews in that they represent the first

---

[13]Karlfried Froehlich, *Biblical Interpretation in the Early Church*, Sources of Early Christian Thought, ed. William G. Rusch (Philadelphia: Fortress, 1984), p. 17.

[14]See K. Froehlich, "Which Paul?" pp. 280-81.

[15]For a discussion of such issues, see Frances M. Young, *Biblical Exegesis and the Formation of Christian Culture* (Cambridge: Cambridge University Press, 1997).

[16]Froehlich, *Biblical Interpretation in the Early Church*, p. 18. Others in the Alexandrian tradition are e.g., Clement of Alexandria, Gregory of Nyssa and Gregory of Nazianzus, and Basil of Cappadocia. The Greek commentaries that are most often consulted from the Antiochene tradition are those of Chrysostom, Theodoret of Cyr (c. 393-466) and Theophylact of Ohrid (c. 1050-c. 1108). Chrysostom's work is the most involved. Theodoret is brief yet comprehensive; Theophylact represents largely a paraphrase of Chrysostom.

[17]This is the reading of the evidence by Johannes Quasten, *Patrology*, vol. 3 (Westminster, Md.: Christian Classics, 1960), p. 450. Chrysostomus Baur, *John Chrysostom and His Time*, vol. 2 (Westminster, Md.: The Newman Press, 1960), pp. 94-95, is less certain of when or where the homilies were written.

comprehensive commentary on the epistle, their deep influence upon subsequent interpretation in the East and the West, and their rhetorical eloquence which has long been acknowledged. Our decision to highlight the homilies of Chrysostom was also influenced by our desire to imbue this ACCS volume with a certain continuity of voice. A few words on each point are in order.

Chrysostom's *On the Epistle to the Hebrews,* which follows closely and in sequence the text of Hebrews—almost line by line—provides the first comprehensive interpretation of the epistle to the Hebrews that has come down to us. An earlier commentary was written by Origen (c. 185-253/4), but, as already noted, this work has been largely lost. Chrysostom's contemporary, friend and fellow rhetor, Theodore of Mopsuestia (350-428), also wrote a commentary on Hebrews that, like Origen's, is preserved only in fragments. In addition, the influence upon the subsequent history of interpretation is much greater in the case of Chrysostom than that of Theodore. Indeed, of all the Fathers' work on Hebrews, it is Chrysostom's that was held in the highest regard through the Reformation, in the East and the West.[18] Cassiodorus (c. 485-c. 540) indicates that Chrysostom's homilies on Hebrews were already translated in Latin and in circulation in the West by the mid-sixth century.[19] It is this Latin translation that provides the foundation for the Western commentary tradition on the Epistle to Hebrews.

The current interest in rhetorical criticism, in biblical studies on Hebrews and in investigations of Chrysostom's work, reminds us that it is important to note the deep training in rhetoric—the art of persuasion—that Chrysostom received. He, along with Theodore, was a student of Libanius, the most famed rhetor in Antioch in the fourth century. Chrysostom's Greek prose is praised as among the finest examples coming from the revival of interest in the Greek language, known as the second sophistic. Contemporary scholars are drawn to Chrysostom in order to come to a better understanding of ancient rhetoric. This interest extends to biblical scholars who posit that an awareness of the rhetorical conventions of antiquity helps one understand aspects of the Epistle to Hebrews that might otherwise strike the modern reader as problematic.[20] Two related issues in particular will be addressed briefly, the rhetorical use of comparison (*synkrisis*) and invective (*psogos*).

As is well known, the epistle to the Hebrews describes the new that came in Christ by means of comparing it with wider Judaism, defined particularly in terms of Old Testament exegetical traditions associated with the cult of the tabernacle. Often this comparison has been read as taking place at the expense of Judaism. In antiquity, however, the rhetorical device of comparison (*synkrisis*) was understood to begin with what was construed as noble and good. The goal was not to disparage the basis of comparison but, assuming its goodness, to move the audience to accept the superiority of that which was being proposed as an alternative. Such *synkrisis* functioned within the encomium, a genre of rhetoric that was designed to honor

[18]See Kenneth Hagan, *A Theology of Testament in the Young Luther: The Lectures on Hebrews* (Leiden: E. J. Brill, 1974), p. 15.

[19]*Institutions* 1.8.3; English text available in Cassiodorus Senator, *An Introduction to Divine and Human Readings,* trans. Leslie Webber Jones (New York: Columbia University Press, 1946), p. 90.

[20]Recent exegetical investigations of Hebrews are much indebted to rhetorical criticism to understand the structure and communicative designs of the epistle. See, e.g., David A. deSilva, *Perseverance in Gratitude: A Socio-Rhetorical Commentary on the Epistle to the Hebrews* (Grand Rapids, Mich.: Eerdmans, 2000), and Craig R. Koester, *Hebrews,* The Anchor Bible, vol. 36 (New York: Doubleday, 2001). Two publications that have investigated the rhetorical aspects of Chrysostom's writings are Robert L. Wilken, *John Chrysostom and the Jews: Rhetoric and Reality in the Late 4th Century* (Berkeley: University of California Press, 1983), and Margaret M. Mitchell, *The Heavenly Trumpet: John Chrysostom and the Art of Pauline Interpretation* (Tübingen: Mohr Siebeck, 2000).

its object. In a reading of Hebrews that approaches its comparisons between Judaism and Christianity from such a perspective, far from being derided, Judaism is held in high esteem in order to argue for the greater value of the new that comes in Christ.[21] An appreciation of the rhetorical intent of *synkrisis* mitigates against a simple supersessionist understanding, which assumes a pejorative understanding of Judaism. In moving one's focus from Hebrews itself to the work of Chrysostom, it should be noted that Chrysostom's homilies have been interpreted as one grand encomium to Paul, where Paul—humble though he might have been in terms of origin and occupation—by the inspiration of the Spirit and by the grace of God was empowered to become superior to all those who have been trained either in rhetoric or in the art of virtue.[22]

A rhetorical device that cuts in the opposite direction to that of *synkrisis* is the use of invective (*psogos*).[23] Like the encomium, the invective was construed as a genre, yet it, in antithesis to the encomium, was used in order to vilify and defame its object. In the rhetorical schools one was trained not only to honor a person or object but also to use stereotyped images in order to discredit one's opponents. Chrysostom used such invective in his homilies in order to defame vital alternatives to his understanding of what was appropriate to the Christian life, including non-orthodox expressions of Christianity, Christians who were orthodox in belief but whom he considered were lax in moral fiber, and Judaism, whose worship life and halakic traditions remained attractive to many Christians in the fourth century. Exaggeration was a stock device of the invective (as well as the encomium), so one must be cautious how one reads these rhetorical constructions of Chrysostom. They are not to be taken as historically accurate descriptions of Chrysostom's various friends or opponents, perceived or real.

The careful reader will intuit that the devices of comparison and invective, *synkrisis* and *psogos*, might cancel one another out if applied to the same object. For example, Judaism might be seen in a highly favorable light if it were to provide the basis for the comparison of the new wrought in Christ. Judaism also might be the target of invective if it is perceived to be a threat to the authority or values of Christian community, either in the first or fourth century. As one reads Chrysostom reading Hebrews, one can sense a skilled rhetor who appreciates the eloquence of the Epistle to Hebrews. Yet one is also aware of a passionate defender of the faith who employs sophisticated rhetorical devices to fight his own battles. We caution the contemporary reader, then, that although the first-century author of Hebrews and the fourth-century Chrysostom may have shared similar training in the rhetorical arts, or at least breathed the same rhetorical air, this does not mean that Chrysostom can necessarily be relied upon to recover the epistle to the Hebrews' original communicative intent. The same holds true for other fathers of the church who received education in the rhetorical schools, which was the only education available in the high period of patristic exegesis.[24]

In defense of our choice to excerpt from Chrysostom's homilies at length, we also mention our desire to

---

[21]See Chrysostom's comment on the statement of Heb 9:23 "with better sacrifices than these" found on p. 143 in this volume: "What is 'better' is better than something else that is good." See also his comment on Heb 12:22 found on p. 223: "From the first, therefore, the Israelites were themselves the cause of God's being manifested through the flesh. . . . They who make comparison elevate the one side more that they may show the other to be far greater."

[22]Mitchell, *Heavenly Trumpet.*

[23]Wilken, *John Chrysostom and the Jews*, pp. 112-16.

[24]The exception to this rule may be found in monastic communities. Beginning in the fourth century, Pachomius instituted the rule that all should be able to read Scripture, which necessitated a form of Christian education. See H. I. Marrou, *A History of Education in Antiquity* (New York: Sheed and Ward, 1956), pp. 321-33. Interestingly, Chrysostom, in 375, advocated that the parents send their children to the monks who lived outside of Antioch for their education. This remained an impractical ideal. See Marrou, p. 332.

give this ACCS volume some continuity of voice. One of the glories of patristic exegesis is the conjoining of both close and imaginative readings of the Bible. This mix results in quite different understandings of the base text. Chrysostom's reading of Hebrews provides us with a kind of plumb line, against which other interesting comments may be compared. Also, if the reader were to become interested in Chrysostom's exegesis of Hebrews in particular, an old but adequate English translation of Chrysostom is readily available in the Nicene and Post-Nicene Fathers series.[25]

One final word regarding Chrysostom is in order. At the end of many of Chrysostom's discussions of Hebrews' texts, the exegete launches into a moral application of the pericope. To append a morality lesson to an exposition of a biblical text is characteristic of Chrysostom and other patristic writers. This *parenesis*, however, is often rather loosely tied, in terms of content, to the expository portion of the commentary that precedes it. This material provides a particular challenge within a volume that is arranged according to chapter and verse and addressed to those socialized into the conventions of modern commentaries where such material does not usually appear. In the end we decided to keep a few of these moral exhortations, for a couple of reasons. In the first place, this linkage of a moral imperative to scriptural exposition is so characteristic of Chrysostom that to remove it would distort Chrysostom's understanding of the role of exegesis in Christian community. Chrysostom's reading of Scripture was done not only to elucidate the mysteries of the faith. He was also deeply convinced that the truth of Scripture was lived out in the context of one's life. To excise the moral imperative from his exegesis is to lose the sense of how deeply practical and demanding he thought the application of exegesis to daily life was. Second, we have retained the moral injunctions so as to recover the social critique contained in it.[26] Chrysostom, for instance, is clear and passionate about the ability of material wealth to lure one away from the active display of the Christian virtues.[27] His words may have also a poignant currency as we, in the postmodern world, are approaching the extreme disparity between the rich and the poor that was characteristic of the ancient world.

Selections from the Other Patristic Authors

We have selected more and longer citations from Chrysostom for this volume than for any other author. Only in the occasional long passage can one discern the sweep of Chrysostom's rhetoric. In order that the Antiochene tradition does not dominate, we have also cited extensively from the Alexandrian tradition, but from a greater variety of sources. Clement of Alexandria (c. 150-215) sets an early precedent by much respecting Hebrews. As mentioned, he was willing to assign authorship of it to Paul. He quotes from it with some regularity. The first place of honor among the Alexandrian exegetes, however, goes to Origen, who was the first to explore the epistle systematically and integrate it fully into his theological thought.

---

[25]Chrysostom, *Homilies on the Gospel of St. John and The Epistle to the Hebrews*, vol. 14 of A Select Library of the Nicene and Post-Nicene Fathers of the Christian Church, ed. Philip Schaff (New York: The Christian Literature Co., 1890), pp. 363-522. On the history and biases of this translation series see Richard W. Pfaff, "The Library of the Fathers: The Tractarians as Patristic Translators," *Studies in Philology* 70 (1973): 329-44, and "Anglo-American Patristic Translations 1866-1900," *Journal of Ecclesiastical History* 28 (1977): 39-55.

[26]On Chrysostom's social ethic, see the exchange between Adolf Martin Ritter, "John Chrysostom as an Interpreter of Pauline Social Ethics," pp. 183-92, and Elizabeth A. Clark, "Comment: Chrysostom and Pauline Social Ethics," pp. 193-99, in the volume edited by William S. Babcock, *Paul and the Legacies of Paul* (Dallas: Southern Methodist University Press, 1990).

[27]One cluster of comments from Chrysostom on this matter occurs in this volume at 6:9-12. See also 10:12-13, 23-25, 30-34; 11:5-6; 12:2, 22-24.

Even with the loss of Origen's commentary on Hebrews, the extant citations of Hebrews in Origen far outnumber any other exegete of the first two centuries.[28] Origen's exegesis on Hebrews was influential, and his philosophical and allegorical interests may be taken as representative of the Alexandrian stream. In that Origen's commentary on Hebrews has not survived, in order to get at his comments on Hebrews, we have gone to other works in which he pulls in Hebrews while commenting on other portions of Scripture. This practice of intertextuality, however, is not limited to Origen. The patristic commentators regarded the whole of Scripture as a complexly interwoven document and often used Scripture to interpret Scripture. We have not limited ourselves, then, to selecting from commentaries on Hebrews but have searched for those passages in the Fathers that reveal how Hebrews was taken up into the larger, ongoing work of interpreting Scripture.

The way in which the verses of Hebrews were referenced among the early Christian exegetes are far from uniform. The early Christian writers could draw in the text of Hebrews to their exegesis in a variety of ways. Sometimes, if they started with the text of Hebrews (as Chrysostom did often in his *Homilies*), they would pursue a close reading of a particular verse or verses. Sometimes, however, they might begin with another biblical text, either from the Old Testament or the New, and a particular theme or theological or hermeneutical point raised in its exegesis might evoke a text or texts from Hebrews and/or passages from other portions of Scripture. A verse or a phrase or even an allusion to a phrase from Hebrews is all that surfaces in some of the selections we have chosen for this volume. Such selections have been retained not only because they illustrate how seamless a document the canon was to the early Christian writers but also because they reveal important aspects of patristic interpretative procedure or theology. Given the range of usage of the actual text of Hebrews represented by our selections, a certain deftness on the part of the reader is required to recognize the shifts in foci as one moves among the selections.

It has been our intention to balance the tendencies of the various streams of exegetical tradition from the early church. This may mean that the fathers we have chosen to comment on the same passage may have quite different understandings of the biblical text. This may also make a sequential reading of the selections difficult, since the theological interests of the Fathers may not, at first glance, seem to support one another. There is a greater unity, however, than that of agreement over the details and methods of interpretation that is expressed in this volume. That unity of vision is discovered not in a superficial agreement but in a common commitment to discover the appropriate meaning of Scripture—construed as the word (*logos*) of God spoken to the church—which found itself in an increasingly public role as it sought to shape the emergent Christian culture of late antiquity. Disagreements were common, but all were committed to the process and relied upon the Spirit of God to guide their work.

Outside of the representatives of the Greek and Latin traditions, we do have occasional citations from the other language groups that made up the great diversity of the early church. Of primary importance is the commentary of Ephrem the Syrian (b. c. 301; fl. 363-373). This work has been newly translated from the Armenian for this volume by Marco Conti and has been well used. It is a terse paraphrase of Hebrews

---

[28]See Pamela Bright, "The Epistle to the Hebrews in Origen's Christology," *Origeniana Sexta: Origèn et la bible/Origen and the Bible*, ed. Gilles Dorival and Alain le Boulluec (Louvain: Louvain University Press, 1995), pp. 559-65. For a list of references see the *Origène* volume in *Biblica Patristica: Index des Citations et Allusions Bibliques dans la Littérature Patristique*, ed. J. Allenbach et al. (Paris: Éditions du Centre National de la Recherche Scientifique, 1980), pp. 449-57.

with insightful explanatory comments.

Some portions of Hebrews attracted more interest and inspired more commentary than others among the Fathers, for a variety of reasons. For instance, the exordium (Heb 1:1-4) was heavily commented upon because the Fathers perceived in it careful christological constructions. This was especially true of Hebrews 1:3, "He reflects the glory of God and bears the very stamp of his nature," as it was seen to undercut the Arian claims. Theodoret notes, for example, that the Arians rejected Hebrews from their canon because of this particular text.[29] Other passages of Hebrews also became loci of ongoing theological discussions of various kinds. Where the ancient commentary is particularly thick, we have provided more citations from the Fathers to indicate both the diversity of opinions as well as the developing received tradition that a certain text would provoke. For example, commentary on Melchizedek, that mysterious figure from Genesis who serves as a type of Christ, takes up a large portion of the comments on Hebrews 7 in this volume.[30] Here we have included a lengthy passage from Epiphanius of Salamis's *Panarion,* "Against Melchizedekians." Epiphanius lists what he construes are heretical understandings of this elusive biblical figure. These sometimes bizarre interpretations show the rich and diverse theological interpretations of the early church and contemporary Judaism. In addition to the exordium and the figure of Melchizedek, the Fathers were also much interested in the epistle's texts that describe the Old Testament as a "shadow" of the New (Heb 8:4-5; 10:1) as well as the nature of God's discipline (Heb 12:5-7).

Occasionally we include a citation from an early Christian exegete because it reveals how very different his understanding of the world is from ours. These texts may strike the modern reader as odd or even offensive, but we have shied away from domesticating the patristic ethos so that it might conform to values that provide the norms of the post-Enlightenment epistemology and ethics.

Wherever the text does not indicate otherwise we have used the Revised Standard Version (RSV) for biblical citations. The Fathers, however, at times relied upon textual traditions that are not reflected in the surface text of the RSV. Also, the words of the original language (e.g., Greek, Latin, Syriac) often have a wider semantic range than the English equivalent used by the RSV suggests. When the Fathers are exploring this semantic range, the language of their citations or allusions to the text of Hebrews does not always match up with the RSV translation tradition. For instance, Hebrews 1:3, a critical passage for the Fathers, is translated by the RSV as "He reflects the glory of God and bears the very stamp of his nature." However, in the actual Greek of the biblical text, "God" (*theos*) is missing. The Greek text simply states rather that the Son is the *apaugasma tēs doxēs,* that is, the "radiance (or reflection) of glory." Also, in Hebrews 1:3b the Greek reads that the Son is *charaktēr tēs hypostaseōs,* that is, the "impress of his substance." The Greek *hypostasis,* which by the patristic era had become a technical term much used in the christological controversies, was subjected to a great deal of thought. Therefore, in the extensive selections from the Fathers that we have chosen at Hebrews 1:3, the allusions to the text in Hebrews extend beyond the necessarily restricted range of the RSV translation. *Apaugasma* may be "reflection" but more often "radiance" or "effulgence" or "brightness." Similarly, *hypostasis* may be translated by "nature" but also "substance" or "per-

---

[29]PG 82:681.

[30]Although the figure of Melchizedek is introduced in the epistle at Heb 5:6, 10 and 6:20, we have reserved the patristic comments on this theme until Heb 7.

son." Our resistance to limiting the Fathers' exploration of the meaning of the Greek text by artificially bringing their allusions to Hebrews into conformity with RSV language extends throughout this volume. This decision also places certain demands on the reader in that the citation or allusion to the Hebrews text, as known through the RSV translation tradition, may not always be immediately apparent. We have tried to alert the reader when this may be problematic by means of footnotes.

The variety of genres of biblical interpretation represented by this selection of patristic exegesis on the epistle to the Hebrews, as well as complex issues related to the translation of variant biblical texts and the patristic fathers' own Greek (and other languages) make the use of this volume, at times, challenging. We trust, however, that the benefits of an exposure to the variety and depth of early Christian commentary on Hebrews will be worth the effort required by the reader when it is presented in this format.

Many thanks are due to the people of the ACCS project that have assisted us in countless ways in this project under the direction of Dr. Thomas Oden, the general editor. Special thanks go to Joel Scandrett, Michael Glerup and Joel Elowsky. At the Lutheran Theological Seminary at Philadelphia three talented students, Sean Burke, Chris Duckworth and Anna Mercedes, have assisted us along the way. Rene Diemer, the registrar at the Lutheran Theological Seminary at Philadelphia, has taken time from her busy schedule to read through the volume at various points in the process. Ms. Diemer has been an invaluable resource in resolving the many issues of style and grammar we have confronted in this project. Her eye for detail has caught many mistakes.

In concluding our work on this volume, we simply invite the reader to enjoy the fruits of the Fathers' contemplation of Holy Scripture by means of an exhortation from Augustine:

> So let us hold on to the manner of exposition that we have taken up, with the help of the one who urges us to ask, to seek and to knock, in order to explain all those figures of things according to the Catholic faith, both those which pertain to history and those which pertain to prophecy. We do this without prejudice to a better and more careful treatment, whether God should deign to make it known through us or through others.[30]

Erik M. Heen and Philip D. Krey

---

[30]Augustine *On Genesis, Against the Manicheans* 2.2. For fuller citation, see below at Heb 5:14 under the rubric "The Help of Him Who Urges Us to Ask, Seek and Knock."

THE EPISTLE TO THE HEBREWS

OVERVIEW: When Pauline authorship was accepted in the East, it became necessary to explain why Paul's name is not appended to the actual text of Hebrews. Theodore of Mopsuestia and Severian of Gabala represent the received interpretation that, because Paul was an "apostle to the Gentiles," out of tact and appropriate deference to apostles called to the ministry to the historic people of Israel, Paul's authorship is not explicitly mentioned in the Epistle to the "Hebrews."

THE REASON PAUL DID NOT APPEND HIS NAME. THEODORE OF MOPSUESTIA:

Paul did not write as to unbelievers who had acquired an implacable hatred against him but to believers who have shared all things that it is necessary to share. He writes not to those who are simple in their faith but to those who are demonstrating in their works the solidity of their faith and the keenness of their virtue, as the contents of the epistle show. Consequently, the epistle must have been delivered to them as one of Paul's epistles, for if this were not the case the things written would not benefit them.

Again, in addition to these considerations the things written at the end of the epistle prove what I am stating: "I appeal to you, brethren" he says, "bear with my word of exhortation, for I have written to you briefly."[1] But to whom did he write, "I appeal to you" if those things were not the reason the letter was sent to them? Then he adds, "You should understand that our brother Timothy has been released with whom I shall see you if he comes soon."[2] Clearly you see that Timothy was the one who has delivered the epistle Paul wrote, with whom Paul clearly promises also to see them, if Timothy returns.

What then is the reason for Paul not appending his name? It is evident and very clear. Both Barnabas and Paul divided the preaching task with the disciples of the blessed Peter. [This was] not so that the former could teach some doctrines and the latter others—for there is one goal—but so that Paul and Barnabas might lead to faith some from the Gentiles while Peter and his disciples would lead some from the Jews to faith, deeming this division more expedient because at that time there was still a powerful rivalry due to

---

[1]Heb 13:22. [2]Heb 13:23.

the custom of the Jews (based on their law) who did not permit themselves to consort with Gentiles. Then some of the apostles had dealings with the Gentiles, while others with the circumcised. But those who had come to faith in all probability deemed the teachers and apostles to be shared by both communities. Thus, when Paul wrote to the Gentiles, he in all likelihood commands them as their apostle, but when he writes to the Hebrews, he does not. FRAGMENTS ON THE EPISTLE TO THE HEBREWS.[3]

THE EPISTLE IS PAUL'S. SEVERIAN OF GABALA: The heretics say that this epistle is not Paul's, and they offer as their first proof of this that his name is not superscribed as in the other epistles. Second, his vocabulary is different, that is, it is foreign to Paul's customary word choice and usage. One must know, however, that Paul was hated by the Jews on the grounds that he was teaching apostasy from the law, and having been endan-

gered for this reason in Jerusalem and having scarcely escaped, he was sent to Rome. Therefore, writing something useful to the Hebrews, he does not append his name, so that they might not lose any advantage they could have derived from the letter because of their hatred against him.

And he writes to them in the tongue of the Hebrews, which was also translated by one of his disciples—by Luke or more likely by Clement who also is mentioned. For this reason the vocabulary is different. And this has been investigated by previous generations, and Eusebius of Pamphilus, a historian of those things in preceding and contemporary generations, made mention of the investigation,[4] and it still seemed to our fathers, the predecessors of the bishops, that the epistle was Paul's. FRAGMENTS ON THE EPISTLE TO THE HEBREWS PROLOGUE.[5]

---

[3]NTA 15:200-201. [4]Eusebius *Ecclesiastical History* 6.25. [5]NTA 15:345.

1:1-4 THE PROLOGUE

In many and various ways God spoke of old to our fathers by the prophets; [2]but in these last days he has spoken to us by a Son, whom he appointed the heir of all things, through whom also he created the world. [3]He reflects the glory of God and bears the very stamp of his nature, upholding the universe by his word of power. When he had made purification for sins, he sat down at the right hand of the Majesty on high, [4]having become as much superior to angels as the name he has obtained is more excellent than theirs.

OVERVIEW: The first four verses of Hebrews 1 serve as an introduction to the whole epistle, and the Fathers saw them as anticipating the major doctrines of Christianity and guarding against some of the major heresies in the early church. (Note that the first passage by Theodoret of Cyr uses the prologue to summarize the content of

the whole epistle.) The different ways in which God spoke through the prophets announced a major theological theme in Hebrews, namely, the relation between the Old and New Testaments. The passage of Theodoret of Cyr states the difference: "For Moses gave the Old Testament but Christ the New, which was promised through the prophets of old. The former promised that Palestine would be given; the latter, the kingdom of heaven." Clement of Alexandria summarizes how the Scriptures are used to interpret Scripture. The heretics also use the Scriptures, he says, but they do not quote them entirely and wrest ambiguous passages from their contexts, gathering a few expressions here and there. Furthermore, they pay attention to mere words, not their sense. Although in the Old Testament God appeared under diverse guises (EPHREM), it was the Word of God that was operative in all those theophanies (EUSEBIUS). However, it is the Son who has the full knowledge of God the Father, and it is only who was able to make us partakers of the divine grace (CHRYSOSTOM). A later commentator, John of Damascus, concludes, citing Timothy, "To search the sacred Scripture is very good and most profitable for the soul."

The Fathers used these opening verses to comment on their doctrines of God, Christology and the nature of angels. Chrysostom interprets the last days as the time when there was no expectation of deliverance. The term *ages* may signify material and spiritual worlds (EPHREM) as well as temporal periods (JOHN OF DAMASCUS). Generally, in the third and fourth century the pericope was used to discuss the doctrine of God; in the late fourth and fifth centuries writers like Theodore of Mopsuestia, Cyril of Alexandria and Chrysostom addressed the two natures of Christ as human and divine. Augustine states that Christ "was both a sheep, because of his innocence and simplicity of soul, and a goat because of the likeness of sinful flesh." If the world could not hear God through the prophets, it should at least hear his crying from the cross (JEROME). Athanasius asks in the light of this passage how the Son of God can be made or be a creature when he made everything himself. The Son contains the whole and reflects the glory of God fully (ORIGEN, CHRYSOSTOM). Gregory of Nyssa explains the brightness imagery of this passage (not found in the RSV, which translates it as "he reflects the glory of God"), relating the role of the Son to the Father by explaining "the brightness of his glory" as his consubstantiality with the Father (THEODORET), which cannot be understood fully by the human mind (CHRYSOSTOM).

Since differing schools understood the two natures of Christ differently, the commentators did not always come to the same conclusions. Cyril of Alexandria emphasizes the union in God's becoming flesh so that the divine redeems the flesh, while Theodoret carefully protects the distinctions between the human and the divine natures in Christ. "Though God by nature, he became human while remaining God" (CYRIL OF ALEXANDRIA). "For the Lord Jesus Christ is heir of all things," not as God but as human" (THEODORET). The writer of Hebrews uses metaphorical language to address the role of Christ in relation to the Old Testament, God and the angels. He describes the Son as "heir of all things," the "stamp of his nature," "sitting at the right hand of God." Appointment of an heir refers to the profound mystery of relationship between the Father and the Son (PHOTIUS). The Fathers felt especially obliged to explain these metaphors to guard against misunderstandings of the text. Marius Victorinus and Cassiodorus comment on trinitarian allusions in Hebrews, Though we know these things in actuality as inexplicable and incomprehensible, some of the Fathers posit a parallel from physical and existent objects: in the sun we find three properties. The Son is begotten of the Father's will, and in him the Father rejoices (ORIGEN). The fact that the Son is truly God justifies the title of Mary "Theotokos," that is, God-bearer (THEODORET), since the divine nature has not been altered in the incarnation (NESTORIUS). The metaphor of the stamp of God's image applies to the Son of God (CYRIL OF ALEXANDRIA) and to all Christians who bear the image of God rather than that of the world (IGNATIUS OF ANTIOCH). The "image of God's substance" indicates the Son's unity and consubstantiality with the Father (ORIGEN, ATHANASIUS) and the Son's true divinity (ATHANASIUS), although the nature of the unity is a mystery (CYRIL OF JERUSALEM, GREGORY OF NYSSA). The Son shares with the Father creative and sustaining power (CHRYSOSTOM, GREGORY OF NYSSA). Cyril of Alexandria points out that the "image of the substance of God" is the foundation of the divine plan of salvation that culminates in our cleansing from sin through the sacrifice of the Lord (CHRYSOSTOM, EPHREM). The passage also prompted the Fathers to write brilliantly, as depicted in the *Life of Anthony* by Athanasius: "The fame of Anthony the first monk spread far and wide such that the emperor himself appealed to him for counsel. Anthony made nothing of the letters and emissaries sent to him and said, 'Do not be astonished if an emperor writes to us, for he is a man. Wonder rather that God wrote the law for men and has spoken to us through his own Son.'"

The nature of Christ's sitting at the right hand of the Father also was an image that required comment. Cyril of Jerusalem argued that one should not inquire too curiously into the precise nature of his sitting, for it surpasses our understanding. He argues that Christ did not begin sitting at the right hand of the Father only after his cross, resurrection and ascension. "He did not gain his throne by way of advancement, but from the time he is—and he is eternally begotten—he sits with the Father." Sitting on the right hand of the Father signifies the equality of dignity between the Father and his true Son (CHRYSOSTOM). It is through the Son that the eyes of our hearts have been opened and we have been enlightened (CLEMENT OF ROME). Although the Son is called "servant," he has preeminence over all created things (ATHANASIUS). Chrysostom uses the image of leading a child by degrees up a flight of stairs and down again to explain the theological images of the prologue. Frequently, because God had spoken already to the Israelites, they use Old Testament passages to explain what is not clear in Hebrews.

1:1 God Spoke to the People of Old

BETTER THAN ALL THE PROPHETS. THEODORET OF CYR: The divine apostle immediately in the prologue demonstrates that Christ is better than all the prophets. Beginning with the divine nature, he shows him to be eternal—coeternal with the Father and the Creator of all. Next, contrasting him with the angels, he turns to sacred Scripture, which openly teaches that Christ is Son and God, while angels are ministers and creatures. He proceeds to show that the dispensation of our Lord Christ is greater than that of Moses, for Moses gave the Old Testament but Christ gave the New, which was promised through the prophets of old. The former promised that Palestine would be given; the latter, the kingdom of heaven. He compares the priesthood after the order of Melchizedek with the Levitical priesthood and demonstrates its superiority and excellence. In addition, he shows that even those who lived before the law or under the law and were nourished by piety were distinguished because of their faith. He speaks of them and their sufferings and courage, encouraging his hearers, who were in grave danger. Then, reminding his hearers of their own struggles and exhorting them to stand steadfast to the end and weaving together moral exhortation with doctrine, he closes the epistle. INTERPRETATION OF HEBREWS 1.[1]

UNDER DIVERSE GUISES. EPHREM THE SYRIAN: "In many and various ways God spoke," in the first place, "to our fathers by the prophets." In fact, he evidently spoke in various and mutable manners to Noah, Abraham and Moses and to the people in the desert, appearing to them under the diverse guises of an old man, a giant and other characters. COMMENTARY ON THE EPISTLE TO THE HEBREWS.[2]

HE SET ALL TO RIGHTS. THEODORET OF CYR: The phrase "in many ways," of course, indicates the manifold dispensations, "various ways," the

---

[1]PG 82:676-77; TCCLSP 2:137-38. [2]EHA 197.

different kinds of divine visions. He appeared to Abraham in one way, to Moses in another, to Elijah in another, to Micaiah in another.[3] Isaiah, Daniel and Ezekiel saw him under different guises. To bring this out the God of all said, "It was I who multiplied visions, and took visible form at the hands of the inspired authors."[4] After all, the divine nature is not pluriform, but without either shape or appearance, simple and uncomplicated. It was, therefore, not the incomprehensible nature that they saw but guises of some kind, which the unseen God revealed as need required. The phrase "in many ways," of course, implies something else as well, that each of the inspired authors was entrusted with some particular dispensation, whereas their God—I mean Christ the Lord—did not provide for some single need, but by becoming man he set all to rights and secured the salvation of human beings. It became obvious, of course, that there is one lawgiver of the old and new. INTERPRETATION OF HEBREWS 1.[5]

IN DIFFERENT TIMES, IN DIFFERENT MANNERS.
SEVERIAN OF GABALA: "In many ways," that is, according to the differences of the times in which the promises concerning us were imparted, such as at the creation of Adam, at the time of Cain, in the days of Noah, at the time of Abraham, at the time before the law, at the time after the law. For many are the manners of God's administration on our behalf. And "in a variety of ways," because one commandment was given to Adam, another to Noah, yet another to Abraham, and another through Moses, and yet different ones through the prophets. FRAGMENTS ON THE EPISTLE TO THE HEBREWS 1.1-2.[6]

NO CONTRADICTION IS INVOLVED.
EUSEBIUS OF CAESAREA: Holy Scripture teaches that God was seen by Israel dimly, meaning the Word of God. In the book of Numbers Moses prays, saying, "Since you are the Lord of this people who is seen by them face to face."[7] . . . And it is said in Exodus, "Then Moses and Aaron, Nadab, and

Abihu and seventy of the elders of Israel went up, and they saw the God of Israel."[8] . . .

From the text, "No one has ever seen God,"[9] perhaps it might be thought that the above quotations contradict the Savior's words, implying that the invisible is visible. But if they are understood . . . as the Word of God, who was seen by the fathers "in many ways and various ways," no contradiction is involved. The God of Israel here seen is shown to be the same being who was seen by Israel, when he wrestled with the one who first changed his name from Jacob to Israel, saying, "You have striven with God."[10] And when also Jacob, appreciating God's divine power, called the place of the struggle the Sight of God, saying, "I have seen God face to face, and yet my life is preserved"[11] . . . this was no other than the Word of God. PROOF OF THE GOSPEL 5.18.[12]

COMPLETE EXHIBITION OF THE SCRIPTURES.
CLEMENT OF ALEXANDRIA: Those who are ready to toil in the most excellent pursuits will not desist from the search after truth until they have evidence from the Scriptures themselves. . . . Now all people have the same judgment. Some, following the Word, frame for themselves proofs. Others, giving themselves up to pleasures, wrest Scripture according to their lusts. . . . We have, as the source of teaching, the Lord, by the prophets, the gospel, and the blessed apostles "in many and various ways" leading from the beginning of knowledge to the end. . . . Thus we may not give our assent to people on a bare statement by them, who might equally state the opposite. . . . Rather, we establish the matter that is in question by the voice of the Lord, which is the surest of all demonstrations or rather is the only demonstration, in which knowledge those who have merely tasted the Scriptures are believers. On the other hand, those who have advanced further and have become correct expounders of the truth are

---

[3]1 Kings 22:19-22. [4]Hos 12:11 LXX. [5]PG 82:677, 680; TCCLSP 2:138*. [6]NTA 15:346. [7]Num 14:14. [8]Ex 24:9. [9]Jn 1:18. [10]Gen 32:28. [11]Gen 32:30. [12]POG 1:261-62*.

Gnostics. As, in what pertains to life, craftsmen are superior to ordinary people and model what is beyond common notions, so, consequently, we also persuade from faith by demonstration, giving a complete exhibition of the Scriptures from the Scriptures themselves. Those who follow heresies also venture to avail themselves of the prophetic Scriptures; however, they will not make use of all the Scriptures, and they will not quote them entirely, nor as the body and texture of prophecy prescribe. Instead, selecting ambiguous expressions, they wrest them to their own opinions, gathering a few expressions here and there. They do not look to the sense of the words but simply make use of the words themselves. For in almost all the quotations they make you will find that they attend to the names alone, while they alter the meanings. They neither know as they claim to nor use the quotations they cite according to their true nature. However, the truth is not found by changing the meanings—for so people subvert all true teaching—but in the consideration of what perfectly belongs to and becomes the sovereign God and in the corroboration of each point demonstrated in the Scriptures from similar Scriptures. STROMATEIS 7.16.[13]

CHRIST IS CALLED WISDOM. CLEMENT OF ALEXANDRIA: Christ is called Wisdom by all the prophets. This is he who is the teacher of all created beings, the fellow counselor of God who foreknew all things; and he from above, from the first foundation of the world, "in many and various ways" trains and perfects; hence it is rightly said, "Call no one your teacher on earth."[14] STROMATEIS 6.7.[15]

ALL WISDOM IS FROM THE LORD. CLEMENT OF ALEXANDRIA: And again, it is written expressly in the name of the Lord, "And speak to all that are wise in mind, whom I have filled with the spirit of perception."[16] Those who are wise in mind have a certain attribute of nature peculiar to themselves. And they who have shown themselves capable receive from the supreme Wisdom a spirit of per-

ception in double measure. For those who practice the common arts are highly gifted in what pertains to the senses: in hearing, those who are commonly called musicians; in touch, those who mold clay; in voice, the singers; in smell, the perfumers; in sight, the engravers of devices on seals. Those that are occupied in instruction train the sensibility according to which the poets are susceptible to the influence of measure; the sophists apprehend expression; the dialecticians, syllogisms; and the philosophers are capable of the contemplation of which they themselves are the objects. For sensibility finds and invents, since it persuasively exhorts to application. And practice will increase the application which has knowledge for its end. With reason, therefore, the apostle has called the wisdom of God "manifold," and it has manifested its power "in many and various ways"—by art, by knowledge, by faith, by prophecy—for our benefit. "All wisdom is from the Lord and is with him forever,"[17] as says the Wisdom of Jesus. STROMATEIS 1.4.[18]

BOTH SHEEP AND GOAT. AUGUSTINE: You see, those old sacrifices of the people of God also represented in a variety of ways this single one that was to come. Christ himself, I mean, was both a sheep, because of his innocence and simplicity of soul, and a goat because of "the likeness of sinful flesh."[19] And whatever else was foretold "in many and various ways" in the sacrifices of the old covenant refers to this single one which has been revealed in the new covenant. SERMON 228B.2.[20]

YOU HAVE BEEN MADE PARTAKERS. CHRYSOSTOM: Truly, as Paul says in Romans, "where sin increased, grace abounded all the more."[21] He intimates this here also, in the very beginning of his epistle to the Hebrews, for it was likely that they [the recipients of the law] were afflicted and worn out by evils, and, judging things from that perspective, they would think themselves worse

---

[13]ANF 2:550-51*. [14]Mt 23:8-10. [15]ANF 2:493. [16]Ex 28:3 LXX. [17]Sir 1:1. [18]ANF 2:305*. [19]Rom 8:3. [20]WSA 3 6:262. [21]Rom 5:20.

off than all other people. He shows here that they had rather been made partakers of a greater, even very exceeding, grace. Thus, with these words he arouses the hearer at the very opening of his discourse, saying, "God . . . in these last days . . . has spoken to us by a Son." ON THE EPISTLE TO THE HEBREWS 1.1.[22]

NONE OF THEM SAW GOD. CHRYSOSTOM: The apostle did well to begin, "In many and various ways," for he points out that not even the prophets themselves saw God. Nevertheless, the Son saw him. For the expression "in many and various ways" is the same as "in various ways." "It was I," says he, "who multiplied visions and through the prophets gave parables."[23] The excellence consists not in this alone, that to them prophets were sent, while to us was sent the Son. Rather, the excellence consists in that none of them saw God, but the only begotten Son saw God. The apostle does not at once assert this, but by what he says afterwards he establishes it, when he says, concerning Christ's human nature, "For to what angel did God ever say, 'You are my Son,'"[24] and, "Sit at my right hand?"[25] ON THE EPISTLE TO THE HEBREWS 1.1.[26]

FOR THE SAKE OF OUR SALVATION. JOHN OF DAMASCUS: The God proclaimed by the Old Testament and the New is the one who is celebrated and glorified in Trinity, for the Lord said, "I have come not to abolish the law, but to fulfill."[27] For he worked our salvation, for the sake of which all Scripture and every mystery has been revealed. Again, "Search the Scriptures, for it is they that bear witness to me."[28] And the apostle too says, "In many and various ways God spoke of old to our fathers by the prophets, but in these last days he has spoken to us by a Son." Through the Holy Spirit, then, both the law and the prophets, evangelists, apostles, pastors and teachers spoke. Therefore, "all Scripture is inspired by God and profitable,"[29] so that to search the sacred Scripture is very good and most profitable for the soul. ORTHODOX FAITH 4.17.[30]

1:2 God Has Spoken to Us by a Son

THEN WE WERE GIVEN MORE. CHRYSOSTOM: And the expressions "of old" and "in these last days" foreshadow some other meaning; when a long time had intervened, when we were on the edge of punishment, when the gifts had failed, when there was no expectation of deliverance, when we were expecting to have less than all—it was then that we were given more. ON THE EPISTLE TO THE HEBREWS 1.2.[31]

BOTH WORLDS. EPHREM THE SYRIAN: Paul says, "through whom he made the worlds,"[32] that is, both the spiritual and material worlds. COMMENTARY ON THE EPISTLE TO THE HEBREWS.[33]

HE CREATED THE AGES. THEODORET OF CYR: He spoke of the Son as "creator of the ages"[34] to bring out that he is eternal and to teach us that he was always beyond any temporal interval whatsoever. In these terms the Old Testament speaks of the God and Father as the one existing before the ages, that is, the one who always is.[35] INTERPRETATION OF HEBREWS 1.[36]

THE TERM *AGE* HAS SEVERAL MEANINGS. JOHN OF DAMASCUS: He made the ages who exists before the ages, of whom the divine David says, "From everlasting to everlasting you are"[37] and the divine apostle, "By whom he made the ages."[38]

Now one should note that the term *age* has several meanings, because it signifies a great many things. The span of life of every person is called an age, and a period of one thousand years is called an age. Moreover, this whole present life is called an age, and so is the age without end

---

[22]NPNF 1 14:366*. [23]Hos 12:10. [24]Heb 1:5. [25]Heb 1:13. [26]NPNF 1 14:366*. [27]Mt 5:17. [28]Jn 5:39. [29]2 Tim 3:16. [30]FC 37:373*. [31]NPNF 1 14:366. [32]The Greek text has a plural here (*aiōnas*, i.e., ages, eras, times), translated in RSV as "world" but as "worlds" in KJV. [33]EHA 197. [34]Literal translation of *tous aiōnas* is "the ages." RSV translates this phrase as "the world." [35]Ps 55:19 LXX. [36]PG 82:680; TCCLSP 2:139. [37]Ps 90:2 (89:2 LXX). [38]See n. 34.

to come after the resurrection.[39] Again, that is called an age which is neither time nor any division of time measured by the course and motion of the sun, that is, made up of days and nights; but it is coextensive with eternal things after the fashion of some sort of temporal period and interval. This kind of age is to eternal things exactly what time is to temporal things. ORTHODOX FAITH 2.1.[40]

CREATOR OF THE AGES. THEODORE OF MOPSUESTIA: "Through whom also he made the ages." An age is not a nature that is able to exist in substance but is understood to be a certain interval. This interval can be perceived from its having a beginning of existence until its end or until some other age has likewise taken its beginning. . . . The "creator of the ages" means nothing different than "everlasting, existing beyond every age, having his own limitless existence." For the maker exists before the things which are made, but an interval of time must be perceived by its having a beginning. . . . When blessed David says, "Who exists before the ages,"[41] he does not wish this to say that God exists before the latter ages, but that God has eternal existence, being earlier than every interval of time. When Paul says, "through whom God also made the ages," Paul does not wish God to be the creator of the later ages but to be eternal and the cause of all ages that have a beginning. FRAGMENTS ON THE EPISTLE TO THE HEBREWS 1.2-3.[42]

HE SPOKE TO US. CYRIL OF ALEXANDRIA: For at the end of the ages the Son himself spoke to us through himself. No longer through the mediation of a prophet or the voice of saints but through himself, the only begotten, by being born into our condition, spoke with us. And we say that the Father spoke in the Son, not as through a human being somehow established as a special kind of mediator or as one declaring a message to us which was not his own but another's. Rather, the Son spoke to us in his own voice through his own body. For the flesh belonged to the only

begotten and not to anyone else. Though God by nature, he became human while remaining God. COMMENTARY ON HEBREWS.[43]

THE END OF LABORS AND THE BEGINNING OF REST. CHRYSOSTOM: He said, "in these last days," for by this he both stirs up and encourages those despairing of the future. For as he says also in another place, "The Lord is at hand; have no anxiety about anything,"[44] and again, "For salvation is nearer to us now than when we first believed."[45] So also here. What then does he say? That whoever is spent in the conflict, hearing of the end of it, recovers his breath a little, knowing that it is the end indeed of his labors and the beginning of his rest. ON THE EPISTLE TO THE HEBREWS 1.2.[46]

HEIR OF ALL THINGS AS MAN. THEODORET OF CYR: "Whom he appointed heir of all things." The divine apostle began with human beings, and after speaking first of the lowlier things he thus lays hold of the greater. In other words, Christ the Lord is heir of all things, not as God, but as man: as God he is maker of all things, and the creator of all things is Lord of all by nature, whereas the heir is made master of what he was previously not lord. In like manner the believers are heirs of God and coheirs with Christ[47]: by grace they receive what they did not have before. INTERPRETATION OF HEBREWS 1.[48]

NOT CREATED AS AN HEIR, BUT APPOINTED. SEVERIAN OF GABALA: "He spoke to us in[49] his Son," instead of "by the Son." For he did not speak in him as an instrument but rather through him as one indwelling the flesh. . . . For when he had said, "He has spoken to us in his Son whom he appointed as an heir"—not "created as an heir"—he applied the word to his existence

---

[39]Mt 12:32. [40]FC 37:203*. [41]Ps 55:19. [42]NTA 15:201. [43]PEP 3:364; COS 322*. [44]Phil 4:5-6. [45]Rom 13:11. [46]NPNF 1 14:366*. [47]Rom 8:17. [48]PG 82:680; TCCLSP 2:138-39*. [49]En ("in") is translated in RSV as a marker of the instrumental dative, that is, "by."

before the ages. And he does this intelligently, now leading us up into theology, now bringing us down into the incarnation. FRAGMENTS ON THE EPISTLE TO THE HEBREWS 1.1-2.[50]

THE MYSTERY OF THE FATHER AND THE SON. PHOTIUS: "Whom he appointed the heir of all." Of what? Of all those who approach the undefiled divine nature. Indeed, the Son is the heir and partaker of the Father's nature, dominion and power. If the Son is the heir of the Father's attributes, it is necessary to explain, in what way. Through him, it says, he also created the ages [the world]. If the creation is a mutual deed of the Father and of the Son, then all that is in the world is also a shared property of the Father and the Son. If all in the spiritual universe belongs to both of them, then that is also true of what was created after the spiritual universe, that is, our world (*cosmos*) and everything in it. Yet in order that you would not dare to interpret "heir" as according to grace or favor rather than according to birth and nature, he adds, "who is the reflection of [God's] glory." The author had in mind to prevent you from a simpleminded yet ungodly conclusion after he stated that the Father *appointed* him an heir. I believe that "appointed" does not signify production or creation of the heir yet indicates relationship between the Son and the Father, who is the cause according to nature of their unity and convergence. [The writer does this] so that it would not appear as if the Son is deprived of the fatherly bond by his origin and hence the Father and the Son are two separate and unrelated entities. . . . He speaks in very clear terms, "the very stamp of his nature," that is he [the Son] shares the same nature and mode of existence, that is he is God, all-powerful, omnipotent, creator, and shares in all other attributes of the Father, except that the Father is always the Father and the Son is always the Son. Therefore, everything is created, sustained and directed by his almighty word. See, he is truly the heir, as the Father handed everything to him. FRAGMENTS ON THE EPISTLE TO THE HEBREWS 1.2-3.[51]

MAY THE WORLD HEAR HIM IN HIS CRYING. JEROME: He, who first spoke through patriarchs and prophets, afterwards spoke in his own person. As the Song of Songs says, "that he would kiss me with the kisses of his mouth."[52] He is saying, therefore, "Now, in my own person, I speak of him of whom I spoke through the prophets." The world could not hear him in his thundering, but may it hear him, at least, in his crying. HOMILIES ON THE PSALMS, ALTERNATE SERIES 66 (PSALM 88).[53]

BE ASTONISHED THAT GOD SPEAKS. ATHANASIUS: The fame of Anthony came even unto kings, for Constantine Augustus and his sons . . . wrote letters to him as to a father and begged an answer from him. He made nothing very much of the letters, nor did he rejoice at the messages; rather, he was the same as he had been before the emperors wrote to him. But when they brought him the letters, he called the monks and said, "Do not be astonished if an emperor writes to us, for he is a man. Wonder rather that God wrote the law for men and has spoken to us through his own Son." And so he was unwilling to receive the letters, saying that he did not know how to write an answer to such things. But at the urgings of the monks because the emperors were Christians and lest the emperors take offense on the ground that they had been spurned, he consented that the letters be read. And he wrote an answer approving of them because they worshiped Christ, and he gave them counsel on things pertaining to salvation: "not to think much of the present, but rather to remember the judgment that is coming, and to know that Christ alone was the true and eternal king." He begged them to be merciful and to give heed to justice and the poor. Having received the answer, they rejoiced. Thus he was dear to all, and all desired to consider him as a father. LIFE OF ST. ANTHONY 81.[54]

---

[50]NTA 15:346. [51]NTA 15:637-38. [52]Song 1:2. [53]FC 57:64*. [54]NPNF 2 4:217*.

SIGNIFYING BOTH SONSHIPS IN A SINGLE EXPRESSION. THEODORE OF MOPSUESTIA: He does not say, "God spoke to us in *the* Son" but simply "in a Son." By saying this and making no separation, he was able to signify both in a single expression. First of all, he signifies the true Son, and by true Son I mean the one who possesses sonship by his natural birth. In the second place, he also includes in this designation the one who shares truly in the dignity of sonship because of his union with God. FRAGMENTS ON THE TREATISE ON THE INCARNATION 12.1.[55]

FIRST SLAVES, THEN A SON. THEODORET OF CYR: He clearly brought out the difference between Christ the Lord and the prophets, calling him alone "Son." The opening resembles the parable of the Lord: in telling the parable about the vineyard to the Jews, the Lord showed that slaves were first sent to the wicked farmers, then after their murder a son arrived.[56] INTERPRETATION OF HEBREWS 1.[57]

1:3 The Stamp of God's Nature

THE SON REFLECTS THE WHOLE GLORY OF GOD. ORIGEN: In my opinion, the Son is the reflection of the total glory of God, according to Paul who said, "He reflects the glory of God," anticipating, however, a partial reflection on the rest of the rational creation from this reflection of the total glory. For I do not think that anyone except the Son can contain the whole reflection of the full glory of God. COMMENTARY ON THE GOSPEL OF JOHN 32.353.[58]

RADIANCE AS THE LIGHT OF THE WORLD. CHRYSOSTOM: "I am the light of the world."[59] Therefore the apostle uses the word *radiance*,[60] showing that this was said in the sense of "Light of Light." Nor is it this alone which he shows, but also that he has enlightened our souls. ON THE EPISTLE TO THE HEBREWS 2.2.[61]

THERE WOULD BE NO RAY WITHOUT THE SUN. GREGORY OF NYSSA: The majesty of the Father is expressly imaged in the greatness of the power of the Son, that the one may be believed to be as great as the other is known to be. Again, as the radiance of light sheds its brilliance from the whole of the sun's disk . . . so too all the glory which the Father has is shed from its whole by means of the brightness that comes from it, that is, by the true Light. Even as the ray is of the sun—for there would be no ray if the sun were not—the sun is never conceived as existing by itself without the ray of brightness that is shed from it. So the apostle delivered to us the continuity and eternity of that existence which the Only Begotten has of the Father, calling the Son "the brightness of God's glory." AGAINST EUNOMIUS 8.1.[62]

CHRIST PRESERVES AN ACCURATE REPRESENTATION. THEODORE OF MOPSUESTIA: "Who, being the radiance of glory and the exact representation of his substance." Quite appropriately he does not say "God" but "glory." In this way he does not allow us to meddle in the things of that nature when we are thunderstruck by his name, since of course the only "glory" worth mentioning is God's nature. Paul uses the analogy of "radiance" for that which he deemed most essential, and by the next phrase he explicates the point of the analogy. For he says that Christ preserves an accurate representation of God's nature, so that whatever you would think God's nature to be, so you must also think Christ's nature to be, inasmuch as Christ's nature bears the accurate representation of God's nature since Christ's nature does not differ from God's in the least. FRAGMENTS ON THE EPISTLE TO THE HEBREWS 1.2-3.[63]

IN THE SUN WE FIND THREE PROPERTIES.

---

[55]*TEM* 2:303; COS 260*. [56]Mt 21:33-41. [57]PG 82:677; *TCCLSP* 2:138*. [58]FC 89:408. [59]Jn 8:12. [60]Note that here and in subsequent comments "reflection" has been rendered as "brightness," "effulgence" or "radiance." "Radiance of glory" is a more literal translation of *apaugasma tēs doxēs* than RSV's "He reflects the glory." [61]NPNF 1 14:371. [62]NPNF 2 5:202*. [63]NTA 15:201.

CASSIODORUS: The Spirit in the essence of divinity is Father, Son and Holy Spirit and is rightly called one God. But in the distinction of persons there is peculiar to the Father the fact that, being by nature without a beginning, he begot the Son before time began. Peculiar to the Son is the fact that by nature he was begotten of the Father. Peculiar to the Holy Spirit is the fact that he proceeds from the Father and Son. Their consubstantial eternity and power, by an indescribable love and by their joint working, perform all that they wish in heaven and on earth. But though we know these things in actuality as inexplicable and incomprehensible, some of the Fathers posit a parallel from physical and existent objects: in the sun we find three properties. The first is the bodily substance itself, which is the sun; then there is its brightness, which abides in it; and third is the heat, which reaches us from its brightness. If any such parallel can be devised for so important a topic, I think it is to be assessed as follows. The bodily substance in the sun gives us some understanding of the person of the Father in the Trinity. The brightness in it can be a parallel to the person of the Son in the Trinity, as the apostle says: the "brightness of his glory." The heat in the sun is equivalent to the person of the Holy Spirit in the Trinity, as we read in Scripture, "Who hides himself from his heat?"[64] EXPOSITION OF THE PSALMS 50.14.[65]

THE BLASPHEMY IS EXCLUDED. THEODORET OF CYR: The "glory" is eternal. Therefore, the "brightness" is also eternal. Brightness is of the same nature as fire. Therefore, the Son is of the same nature as the Father. And since the metaphor of brightness so manifestly demonstrates their coeternity and consubstantiality, he allows an opportunity for those sick with the blasphemy of Sabellius and Photinus, according to which the brightness does not subsist by itself. By another metaphor he excludes this blasphemy, for he goes on to say "and the very stamp of his nature." INTERPRETATION OF HEBREWS 1.[66]

A SIMILARITY TO JOHN 1:1. THEODORE OF MOPSUESTIA: Indeed, there is a great deal of similarity [between the opening of John's Gospel and] the apostle's statement. After Paul calls him "the brightness of his glory," he adds, "the very stamp of his nature." With great care he turns from a statement of their distinction[67] to an indication of their perfect likeness.[68] COMMENTARY ON JOHN 1.1.1.[69]

RADIANCE AND IMAGE. SEVERIAN OF GABALA: Seeking to present more clearly that the Word was begotten of the essence of the Father, he makes mention of the "radiance." For the radiance is from the essence of that of which it is an efflux of light, and it is continuously conceived both from it and never apart from that of which it is the radiance. But since "radiance" implies a lesser nature than that of which it is the radiance and existence not in the same nature, he uses a different word and states that Christ is "the exact image of his nature." The first phrase ("radiance of his glory") demonstrates that Christ cannot be separated from the essence as God; the second phrase ("exact image of his nature") proves that he is not without God's nature. For just as John, calling Christ "the Word," adds, "he was with God and was God,"[70] so also Paul, having said "radiance," added, "and the exact image of his nature." FRAGMENTS ON THE EPISTLE TO THE HEBREWS 1.3.[71]

PAUL MIGHT HAVE SAID "GOD" OR "DIVINE NATURE." THEODORE OF MOPSUESTIA: He is the "Father of glory" in that Paul is accustomed to use the word *glory* to refer to the divine nature, because it is glorious and marvelous. So in Hebrews he says the Son is the "brightness of his glory." Instead of this he might have said "God"[72] or "divine nature." COMMENTARY ON EPHESIANS 1.16.[73]

---

[64]Ps 19:6 (17:7 LXX). [65]ACW 51:505*. [66]PG 82:681; *TCCLSP* 2:140*. [67]Cf. Jn 1:1. [68]Cf. Jn 1:1. [69]CSCO 115-16:16. [70]Jn 1:1. [71]NTA 15:346. [72]RSV has "glory of God," though "God" is not in the Greek text. [73]TEM 1:135-36; COS 244.

WHO HAS SEEN LIGHT WITHOUT RADIANCE?
ATHANASIUS: As the apostle, writing to the
Hebrews, says, "who being the brightness of his
glory and the stamp of his nature," and David too
in the eighty-ninth Psalm, "And the brightness of
the Lord be upon us,"[74] and "in your light shall we
see light."[75] Who has so little sense as to doubt
the eternity of the Son? For when did anyone see
light without the brightness of its radiance, that
one may say of the Son, "There was once when
he was not," or "Before his generation he was
not." And the words addressed to the Son in the
hundred and forty-fourth Psalm, "Your kingdom
is an everlasting kingdom,"[76] forbid anyone to
imagine any interval at all in which the Word did
not exist. FOUR DISCOURSES AGAINST THE ARI-
ANS 1.4.12.[77]

WE RECOGNIZE TWO NATURES IN CHRIST.
GREGORY OF NYSSA: Since we recognize two
natures in Christ, one divine and the other
human, the divine by nature but the human in
the incarnation, we accordingly claim for the
Godhead that which is eternal, and that which is
created we ascribe to his human nature. For as,
according to the prophet, he was formed in the
womb as a servant, so also, according to
Solomon, he was manifested in the flesh by
means of this servile creation. But when [the Ari-
ans] say, "If he was, he was not begotten, and, if
he was begotten, he was not," let them learn that
it is not fitting to ascribe to his divine nature the
attributes which belong to his fleshly origin. For
bodies that do not exist are generated, and God
makes those things to be that are not. But does
not he come into being from that which is not?
For this reason also Paul calls him "the brightness
of glory." He does this so that we may learn that,
just as the light from the lamp is of the nature of
that which sheds the brightness and is united
with it (for as soon as the lamp appears the light
that comes from it shines out simultaneously), in
like manner the Son is related to the Father, and
the Father is never without the Son. It is impossible that glory should be without radiance, as it is

impossible that the lamp should be without
brightness. It is clear that his being brightness is
a testimony to his being in relation with the glory,
for if the glory did not exist, the brightness shed
from it would not exist. Therefore, to say that the
brightness "once was not" is a declaration that
once the glory also was not, that is, when the
brightness was not, for it is impossible that the
glory should be without the brightness. As therefore it is not possible to say in the case of the
brightness, "If it was, it did not come into being,
and, if it came into being, it was not," so it is in
vain to say this of the Son, seeing that the Son is
the brightness. Let those who speak of "less" and
"greater," in the case of the Father and the Son,
learn from Paul not to measure things immeasurable. For the apostle says that the Son is the
express image of the person of the Father. It is
clear then that, however great the person of the
Father is, so great also is the express image of that
person, for it is not possible that the express
image should be less than the person contemplated in it. And this the great John also teaches
when he says, "In the beginning was the Word,
and the Word was with God."[78] For in saying that
he was "in the beginning" and not "after the
beginning," he showed that the beginning was
never without the Word. In declaring that "the
Word was with God," he signified the absence of
defect in the Son in relation to the Father, for the
Word is contemplated as a whole together with
the whole being of God. For if the Word were
deficient in his own greatness so as not to be
capable of relation with the whole being of God,
we are compelled to suppose that that part of
God which extends beyond the Word is without
the Word. But in fact the whole magnitude of the
Word is contemplated together with the whole
magnitude of God, and consequently, in statements concerning the divine nature, it is not
admissible to speak of "greater" and "less." ON
THE FAITH.[79]

---

[74]Ps 90:17 (89:17 LXX). [75]Ps 36:9 (35:10 LXX). [76]Ps 145:13 (144:13
LXX). [77]NPNF 2 4:313*. [78]Jn 1:1. [79]NPNF 2 5:337-38*.

WHEN OUR DISCOURSE FAILS THROUGH WEAKNESS. CHRYSOSTOM: We ought to receive all things with faith and reverence, and, when our discourse fails through weakness and is not able to set forth accurately the things that are spoken, then we ought especially to glorify God, in that we have such a God, surpassing both our thought and our conception. For many of our conceptions about God we are unable to express, and many things we express but do not have strength to conceive. For instance, that God is everywhere we know, but how we do not understand. That there is a certain incorporeal power, the cause of all our good things, we know, but how it is or what it is, we know not. We speak and do not understand! I said that he is everywhere, but I do not understand it. I said that he is without beginning, but I do not understand it. I said that he begot from himself, and again I know not how I shall understand it. And some things there are that we may not even speak—as, for instance, that thought conceives but cannot utter.

And to show you that even Paul is weak and does not put out his illustrations with exactness, and to make you tremble and refrain from searching too far, hear what he says, having called him Son and named him Creator, "who being the brightness of his glory and the express image of his person."[80] ON THE EPISTLE TO THE HEBREWS 2.1.[81]

IN WHOM HE REJOICED. ORIGEN: Now this Son was begotten of the Father's will, for he is the "image of the invisible God"[82] and the "effulgence of God's glory and the impress of God's substance." . . . Let those who dare to say, "There was a time when the Son was not"[83] understand that this is what they are saying: "Once wisdom did not exist, and word did not exist, and life did not exist." But it is not right, nor is it safe for us, in our weakness to rob God . . . of God's only begotten Word, who ever dwells with God, who is God's wisdom, in whom God rejoiced.[84] For if we do this, we shall think of God as not always rejoicing. ON FIRST PRINCIPLES 4.1.[85]

THE DIVINE NATURE HAS NOT BEEN ALTERED. NESTORIUS: That is why Paul also says, "Who is the radiance of his glory," lest someone who had heard the words "he was in the form of God"[86] should conjecture that his divine nature is transitory and has been altered. FIRST SERMON AGAINST THE *THEOTOKOS*.[87]

SHE IS THE BRIGHTNESS OF THE ETERNAL LIGHT. ORIGEN: The apostle Paul says, that the only begotten Son is . . . "the brightness of his glory, and the express image of his person." Now, we find in the treatise called the Wisdom of Solomon the following description of the wisdom of God: "For she is the breath of the power of God, and the purest emanation of the glory of the Almighty."[88] Nothing that is polluted can therefore come upon her, for she is the splendor of the eternal light, the stainless mirror of God's working and the image of his goodness. Now we say, as before, that Wisdom has her existence nowhere else but in him who is the beginning of all things, from whom also is derived everything that is wise, because he himself is the only one who is by nature a Son, and is therefore called the Only Begotten. ON FIRST PRINCIPLES 1.2.5.[89]

WE CALL THE HOLY VIRGIN THEOTOKOS. THEODORET OF CYR: I wish and I pray that I may follow the footprints of the holy fathers, and I earnestly desire to keep undefiled the evangelic teaching that was in sum delivered to us by the holy fathers assembled in council at the Bithynian Nicaea. I believe that there is one God the Father and one Holy Spirit proceeding from the Father. Also that there is one Lord Jesus Christ, only-begotten Son of God, begotten of the Father before all ages, brightness of his glory and express image of the Father's person, on account of

---

[80]The Greek *charaktēr* is translated in RSV as "stamp" but variously in ensuing comments as "impress" or "image." Similarly the Greek *hypostaseōs*, "nature" in RSV, is translated in such terms as "person," "substance" and "being." [81]NPNF 1 14:370*. [82]Col 1:15. [83]This was a position later taken by Arius. [84]Cf. Prov 8:30. [85]OFP 314-15*. [86]Phil 2:6. [87]CC 125. [88]Wis 7:25. [89]ANF 4:247*.

humanity's salvation incarnate and made human and born of Mary the virgin in the flesh. For so are we taught by the wise Paul . . . , "Concerning his Son who was descended from David according to the flesh and designated Son of God in power according to the Spirit of holiness."[90] On this account we also call the holy virgin "Theotokos"[91] and deem those who object to this appellation to be alienated from true religion. LETTER 83.[92]

THE SON EXISTS IN THE FORM OF GOD. CYRIL OF ALEXANDRIA: Does not the divine Word [Scripture] indicate to us that the Son exists in the form of God,[93] and does it not say that he is the image and stamp of the one who begot him? ON THE INCARNATION 686.[94]

TWO STAMPS. IGNATIUS OF ANTIOCH: There are two coinages, the one of God, the other of the world, and each has its own stamp impressed on it. Similarly, the unbelievers bear the stamp of this world, and the believers the stamp of God the Father in love through Jesus Christ. Unless we willingly choose to die through him in his passion, his life is not in us. LETTER TO THE MAGNESIANS 5.[95]

SIMILAR IN EVERY DETAIL. ORIGEN: In order . . . to more completely understand how the Savior is the figure of the person or subsistence of God, let us use an illustration. While it does not describe the subject of which we are treating either fully or appropriately, it may nevertheless be employed for this purpose only: to show that when the Son of God, who was in the form of God, emptied himself,[96] his object was to display to us by this very emptying the fullness of his deity. For instance, suppose that there were a statue of so enormous a size as to fill the whole world, and because of this could be seen by no one. If another statue were formed altogether resembling it in the shape of the limbs, and in the outline of features, and in form and material, but without the same immensity of size, then those

who were unable to behold the one of enormous proportions, should, on seeing the latter, acknowledge that they had seen the former, because it preserved all the features of its limbs and appearance, and even the very form and material, so closely as to be altogether undistinguishable from it. ON FIRST PRINCIPLES 1.2.8.[97]

AGAINST ARIUS. ATHANASIUS: Who that has heard the words of John, "In the beginning was the Word,"[98] will not denounce the saying of [Arius and his followers] that "there was a time when he was not"? Or who that has heard in the Gospel, "the only begotten Son" and "all things came into being through him,"[99] will not detest their declaration that he is "one of the things that were made"? For how can he be one of those things that were made by himself? Or how can he be the only begotten, when, according to them, he is counted as one among the rest, since he is himself a creature and a work? And how can he be "made of things that were not," when the Father says, "My heart has uttered a good Word,"[100] and "Out of the womb I have begotten you before the morning star"?[101] Or again, how is he "unlike in substance to the Father," seeing he is the perfect "image" and "brightness" of the Father, and that he says, "He who has seen me has seen the Father"?[102] And if the Son is the "Word" and "Wisdom" of God, how was there "a time when he was not"? It is the same as if they should say that God was once without Word and without Wisdom. And how is he "subject to change and variation" who says by himself, "I am in the Father, and the Father in me,"[103] and "I and the Father are one";[104] and who by the prophet says, "I the Lord do not change"?[105] For although one may refer this expression to the Father, yet it may

---

[90]Rom 1:3-4. [91]Literal translation of the Greek is "God-bearer." [92]NPNF 2 3:279*. [93]Phil 2:6. [94]SC 97:216; COS 322. [95]LCL 1:201*. [96]Phil 2:6-7. [97]ANF 4:248-49**. [98]Jn 1:1. [99]Jn 1:3, 14. [100]Ps 45:1 (44:1 LXX); RSV reads, "My heart overflows with a goodly theme." [101]Ps 110:3 (109:3 LXX); RSV reads, "From the womb of the morning like dew your youth will come to you." [102]Jn 14:9. [103]Jn 14:11. [104]Jn 10:30. [105]Mal 3:6.

now be more aptly spoken of the Word, that, though he has been made man, he has not changed. But as the apostle has said, "Jesus Christ is the same yesterday and today and for ever."[106] And who can have persuaded them to say that he was made for us, for Paul writes, "for whom and by whom all things exist"?[107] DEPOSITION OF ARIUS 3.[108]

HE IS TRUE GOD. ATHANASIUS: Therefore, he is true God, existing consubstantially (*homoousios*) with the true Father, while other beings to whom he said, "I say, 'you are gods,' "[109] have this grace from the Father only by participation in the Word through the Spirit. For he is the "very stamp" of the Father's "being," and "light" from "light," and the "power" and true "image" of the Father's substance. FOUR DISCOURSES AGAINST THE ARIANS 1.3.9.[110]

LET US NOT VENTURE WHERE SCRIPTURE DOES NOT LEAD. CYRIL OF JERUSALEM: Every grace is given by the Father through the Son, who also acts together with the Holy Spirit. There are not some graces that come from the Father and different graces from the Son and others again from the Holy Spirit. There is but one salvation, one giving of power, one faith; and yet there is one God the Father, our Lord, his only begotten Son, and one Holy Spirit, the Paraclete. Let us be content with this knowledge and not busy ourselves with questions about the divine nature or hypostasis. I would have spoken of that had it been contained in Scripture. Let us not venture where Scripture does not lead, for it suffices for our salvation to know that there is Father and Son and Holy Spirit. CATECHETICAL LECTURES 16.24.[111]

THE UNDERLYING ESSENCE OF BEING HE DISMISSED AS UNNAMABLE. GREGORY OF NYSSA: When he was asking how to give a name to what cannot be grasped in thought and did not discover a word expressing an interpretation of the incomprehensible, he called "glory" and "substance" whatever underlies all good and is not sufficiently known or spoken of. The underlying essence of being he dismissed as unnamable. However, interpreting the unity and inseparability of the Son and the Father, and the Son's being contemplated indefinably and invisibly with the indefinable and unseen Father, he addressed him as "radiance of glory" and "image of substance," indicating the unity of their nature by the word *radiance* and their equality by the word *image*. For, in connection with a radiant nature, there is no middle point in a beam of light, nor is there an inferior part of an image in connection with a substance determined by it. The observer of the radiant nature will know the radiance in its entirety, and the person comprehending the size of the substance measures it in its entirety with its accompanying image. ON PERFECTION.[112]

THE SUBSTANCE OF GOD. MARIUS VICTORINUS: The Greeks call "to be" *ousian* (substance) or *hypostasin*; we call it in Latin by one term, *substance*; and a few Greeks use *ousian* (substance) and rarely; all use *hypostasin* (hypostasis). Certainly one differs from the other, but for the moment let us omit this.

The divine Scripture has often used *hypostasin* in Greek, *substance* in Latin. And it has said of the substance of God in the prophet Jeremiah "that if they had stood in the substance of the Lord they would have seen my word."[113] But what is it "to stand in the substance"? To know the substance of God, which is "true light," which is infinite Spirit. If they had known that, they would have known the Logos of the Lord; that is, "they would have seen the word" of the Lord. And shortly after, the same Jeremiah uses the same words.

David says, "And my substance is in the lower regions of the earth."[114] He speaks also of God and says "substance." And it is clear what this is.

The apostle says to the Hebrews, "He who is the character of his substance." He said that

---

[106]Heb 13:8. [107]Heb 2:10. [108]NPNF 2 4:70*. [109]Ps 82:6 (81:6 LXX). [110]NPNF 2 4:311. [111]LCC 4:173. [112]FC 58:105-6*. [113]See Jer 23:18. [114]Cf. Ps 139:15-16.

Christ is the character of the substance of God. There are many other examples. But what is the point of all this? To show that the word *substance* is in Scripture and is used of the substance of God. On the Necessity of Accepting Homoousios 2.1b.[115]

To Hold the World Together Is No Less Than to Make It. Chrysostom: "God said," it is written, "Let there be light."[116] "The Father," says one [heretic], "commanded, and the Son obeyed." But here the Son acts by word for, says he, "upholding all things,"[117] that is, governing. He holds together what would fall to pieces, for to hold the world together is no less than to make it but even greater, if one must say a strange thing. For the one is to bring forth something out of things which are not; but the other, when things that have been made are about to fall back into nonexistence, is to hold and fasten them together, utterly at variance as they are with each other. This is indeed great and wonderful, and a certain proof of exceeding power. On the Epistle to the Hebrews 2.2.[118]

All Things Hang on His Voice. Theodore of Mopsuestia: He not only says that he is the maker of all things, but that he certainly also makes them by the great abundance of his power, for all things hang upon his voice, as it were. For this expression "who calls into existence the things that do not exist"[119] does not differ from the account of blessed Moses, who says, "And God said, 'Let there be light' and there was light . . . 'Let there be a firmament' and there was a firmament."[120] Fragments on the Epistle to the Hebrews 1.3.[121]

His Strong Works of Words. Severian of Gabala: This is what Jeremiah calls "his strong works of words."[122] Fragments on the Epistle to the Hebrews 1.3.[123]

All Things Have One Cause of Their Substance. Gregory of Nyssa: The Logos "upholds the universe by his word of power" from nonexistence to existence. For all things, as many as exist in connection with matter and as many as have received an immaterial nature, have one cause of their substance: the Word of unspeakable power. On Perfection.[124]

One Mystery, Many Images. Theodoret of Cyr: In this way the divine apostle in several terms brought out the reality of the begetting, the oneness in being and the shared eternity of the Father and the Son. Since the divinity transcends all understanding, and it is impossible to bring out in one single image the mystery of the true doctrine of God, the preachers of the truth are obliged to do so by means of many. . . . Blessed Paul called him "Son" to show him to be different from the Father in regard to personhood; he spoke of him "as creator of the ages" to bring out in these ways his eternity and called him also "effulgence of glory"[125] to indicate by this his shared eternity and the sameness of being, the effulgence being of the nature of the fire. He added that he is "stamp of his nature" to bring out both things at the same time, that he subsists of himself and that he reveals in himself the paternal characteristics. He adds also something else: "upholding all things by the word of his power."[126] He not only made everything but also directs and guides it. Interpretation of Hebrews 1.[127]

The Economy of the Incarnation. Cyril of Alexandria: He continues with the following words: "When he had made purification for sins, he sat down at the right hand of the Majesty on high, having become as much superior to angels as the name he has obtained is more excellent

---

[115]FC 69:306-7. [116]Gen 1:3. [117]RSV has "upholding *the universe*," though the Greek is *ta panta*, literally "all things." [118]NPNF 1 14:372*. [119]Rom 4:17. [120]Gen 1:3, 6. [121]NTA 15:202. [122]Jer 23:29. [123]NTA 15:247. [124]FC 58:106-7. [125]Literal translation of *apaugasma tēs doxēs*. RSV translates this as "he reflects the glory of God." [126]Greek *ta panta*, literally "all things." RSV translates this phrase as "the universe." [127]PG 82:681; *TCCLSP* 2:140*.

than theirs." Having demonstrated that he is the stamp of the Father's hypostasis and, indeed, the brightness of his glory, he necessarily passes over to the economy of the incarnation, through which we have been saved and enriched by the forgiveness of sins and sanctified through his blood. COMMENTARY ON HEBREWS.[128]

HE WAS NOT KEPT FAR FROM THE THRONE OF GOD. SEVERIAN OF GABALA: Even if the Word became flesh,[129] he nonetheless was in the glory and nature of divinity and was not kept far from the highest thrones of God the Father. And although "he was made a little lower than the angels"[130] because of the measure of his humanity—for human nature is subordinate to the glory of the angels—he was still "above every name that is named."[131] FRAGMENTS ON THE EPISTLE TO THE HEBREWS 1.3.[132]

ACCOMPLISHED THROUGH THE SON. CHRYSOSTOM: "By himself," says he, "having made purification for our sins, he sat down on the right hand of the majesty on high." He here sets down two very great proofs of his care: first the "purifying us from our sins," then the doing it "by himself."[133] And in many places you see him making very much of this—not only of our reconciliation with God, but also of this being accomplished through the Son. For the gift, being truly great, was made even greater by the fact that it was through the Son. For in saying "he sat down on the right hand" and "having by himself made purification for our sins," though he had put us in mind of the cross, he quickly added the mention of the resurrection and ascension. And see his unspeakable wisdom. He did not say "he was commanded to sit down" but "he sat down." Then again, lest you should think that he stands, he subjoins, "For to what angel has he ever said, Sit at my right hand." ON THE EPISTLE TO THE HEBREWS 2.2.[134]

BECAUSE OF THE FLESH. EPHREM THE SYRIAN: "He sat down at the right hand of the Majesty on high" because of the flesh he put on. COMMENTARY ON THE EPISTLE TO THE HEBREWS.[135]

LET US NOT TOO CURIOUSLY INQUIRE. CYRIL OF JERUSALEM: Recall also what I have often said regarding the sitting of the Son at the right hand of the Father, according to the sequence of the creed: "and he ascended into heaven, and sits at the right hand of the Father." Let us not too curiously inquire into the precise nature of this sitting, for it surpasses our understanding. Let us not endure those who perversely assert that it was only after his cross and resurrection and ascension into heaven that the Son began to sit at the right hand of the Father. For he did not gain his throne by way of advancement, but from the time he is—and he is eternally begotten—he sits with the Father. The prophet Isaiah, having beheld this throne before the coming of the Savior in the flesh, says, "I saw the Lord sitting upon a throne, high and lifted up."[136] For "no one has ever seen" the Father,[137] and he who then appeared to the prophet was the Son. The psalmist also says, "Your throne is established from of old; you are from everlasting."[138] There are many testimonies on this point, but we will content ourselves with these only, because of the lateness of the hour. CATECHETICAL LECTURES 14.27.[139]

EQUAL DIGNITY. CHRYSOSTOM: "He sat," says he, "on the right hand of the majesty on high." What is this "on high"? Does he enclose God in place? Away with such a thought! But just as when he says "on the right hand" he did not describe his outward form, but indicated his equal dignity with the Father, so, in saying "on high," he did not enclose him there but expressed his being higher than all things and having ascended up above all things. That is, he attained

[128]PEP 3:368-69; COS 323*. [129]Jn 1:14. [130]Heb 2:7, 9; Ps 8:5. [131]Eph 1:21. [132]NTA 15:347. [133]Chrysostom is here following a textual variant that includes *di' heautou* ("through himself"). [134]NPNF 1 14:373. [135]EHA 198. [136]Is 6:1. [137]Jn 1:18. [138]Ps 93:2 (92:2 LXX). [139]FC 64:50*.

even the very throne of the Father; as therefore the Father is on high, so also is he. For the "sitting together" implies nothing else than equal dignity. But if they say that God said, "Sit," we may ask them, What then? Did he speak to him standing? Moreover, he said not that he commanded, not that he enjoined, but that "he said," precisely that you might not think him without origin and without cause. That this is why he said it is evident from the place of his sitting, for had he intended to signify inferiority, he would not have said "on the right hand" but "on the left hand." ON THE EPISTLE TO THE HEBREWS 2.2.[140]

1:4 A Most Excellent Name

HE PRONOUNCES ALL THINGS INFERIOR. OECUMENIUS: Do not suppose the word "having become" applies to the flesh. So that you may not be thought to divide Christ, understand the word to apply to Christ who is worshiped in one nature with his flesh. For having once and for all undertaken his reign, he pronounces all things inferior without fear. FRAGMENTS ON THE EPISTLE TO THE HEBREWS 1.4.[141]

UNDERSTANDING SHOOTS UP INTO THE LIGHT. CLEMENT OF ROME: This is the way, dear friends, in which we found our salvation, Jesus Christ, the high priest of our offerings, the protector and helper of our weakness. Through him we fix our gaze on the heights of heaven. In him we see mirrored God's pure and transcendent face.[142] Through him the eyes of our hearts have been opened. Through him our foolish and darkened understanding springs up to the light. Through him the Master has willed that we should taste immortal knowledge. For, since "he reflects the glory of God," "he is as much superior to the angels as the name he has obtained is more excellent than theirs." For thus it is written: "He makes his angels winds, and his servants flames of fire."[143] But of his Son this is what the Master said: "You are my son, today I have begotten you. Ask of me, and I will make the nations your heri-

tage, and the ends of the earth your possession."[144] And again he says to him, "Sit at my right hand till I make your enemies your footstool."[145] Who are meant by "enemies"? Those who are wicked and resist his will. 1 CLEMENT 36.1-6.[146]

THE SON OF GOD BY NATURE. CHRYSOSTOM: Do you see that the name Son is intended to declare true relationship? And indeed if he were not a true Son—and "true" is nothing else than "of God"—how does he reason confidently from this? For if he is Son only by grace, he not only is not "more excellent than the angels" but is even less than they. ON THE EPISTLE TO THE HEBREWS 2.2.[147]

BETTER AND OTHER. ATHANASIUS: Both in the verse before us then and throughout he ascribes the word "better"[148] to the Lord, who is better and other than originated things. For better is the sacrifice through him, better the hope in him, and also the promises through him, not merely great as compared with small, but the one differing from the other in nature, because he who conducts this economy is "better" than things originated. FOUR DISCOURSES AGAINST THE ARIANS 1.13.59(8).[149]

SUPERIOR TO ANGELS. THEODORET OF CYR: This is spoken with reference to the humanity. As God he is maker of angels and Lord of angels, while as man he became superior to angels after the resurrection and ascension into heaven since he was also less than angels on account of experiencing death. . . . So just as he was less than angels as man, since they have an immortal nature whereas he endured the passion, so after

---

[140]NPNF 1 14:373. [141]NTA 15:462. [142]Cf. 2 Cor 3:18. [143]Heb 1:7; cf. Ps 104:4 (103:4 LXX). [144]Ps 2:7-8; cf. Heb 1:5. [145]Heb 1:13; Ps 110:1 (109:1 LXX). [146]LCC 1:60. [147]NPNF 1 14:373*. [148]Athanasius is referring here to the Greek term *kreittōn*, which is translated by RSV as "superior." *Kreittōn* and its cognates are much used in Hebrews to draw comparisons of various kinds. See the introduction to this volume. [149]NPNF 2 4:341*.

the ascension into heaven he became superior to the angels. INTERPRETATION OF HEBREWS 1.[150]

THE SON EXCELS A SERVANT. ATHANASIUS: Whereas the prophets ministered and the law was spoken by angels, the Son too came on earth in order to minister. The apostle was forced to add "become as much superior to angels," wishing to show that just as much as the Son excels a servant is the ministry of the Son better than the ministry of servants. Contrasting the old ministry and the new, the apostle then speaks freely to the Jews, writing and saying, "become as much superior to angels." This is why throughout he uses no comparison such as "become greater" or "more honorable," lest we should think of the Son and angels as one in kind, but "better" is his word, by way of marking the difference of the Son's nature from things originated. And we have proof of this from divine Scripture: David, for instance, saying in the psalm, "A day in your courts is better than a thousand,"[151] and Solomon crying out, "Take my instruction instead of silver, and knowledge rather than choice gold; for wisdom is better than jewels, and all that you may desire cannot compare with her."[152] Are not wisdom and stones of the earth different in essence and separate in nature? Are heavenly courts at all akin to earthly houses? Or is there any similarity between things eternal and spiritual and things temporal and mortal? . . . In like manner there is no relationship between the Son and the angels; thus the word *better* is not used to compare but to contrast, because of the difference of his nature from theirs. And so also the apostle himself, when he interprets the word *better,* places its force in nothing less than the Son's preeminence over things originated, calling the one Son and the other servants. The one, as a Son with the Father, sits on God's right; and the others, as servants, stand before God and are sent and serve. FOUR DISCOURSES AGAINST THE ARIANS 1.13.55(3).[153]

SEE BY HOW MANY STEPS HE LED THEM.

CHRYSOSTOM: One who leads a little child up to some lofty place, even reaching to the top of heaven, does this gently and by degrees, leading him upwards by the steps from below. Then, when he has set the child on high and encouraged him to gaze downwards, he sees the child turning giddy and confused and dizzy. He takes hold of him and leads him down to the lower stand, allowing him to take breath. Then, when the child has recovered, he leads him up again, and again brings him down. In the same way the blessed Paul has done, both with the Hebrews and everywhere, having learned it from his master. For even Jesus did so. Sometimes he led his hearers up high, and sometimes he brought them down, not allowing them to remain very long.

See here, then, by how many steps he led them up and placed them near the very summit of religion. See too that when they grow giddy and are seized with dizziness, he leads them down and allows them to take breath, saying, "God has spoken to us by a Son, whom he appointed the heir of all things." For the name of Son is so far common. . . . And see how he says, "who he appointed the heir of all things." The phrase "he appointed the heir" is humble. Then he placed them on the higher step, adding, "through whom also he created the world." Then he placed them on a higher step still, after which there is no other: "He reflects the glory of God and bears the very stamp of his nature." Truly he has led them to unapproachable light, to the very brightness itself. And before they are blinded, see how he gently leads them down again, saying, "upholding the universe by his word of power, when he had made purification for sins, he sat down at the right hand of the Majesty." He does not simply say "he sat down" but "when he had made purification, he sat down." For he has in these words touched on the incarnation, and his utterance is again lowly. ON THE EPISTLE TO THE HEBREWS 1.3.[154]

[150]PG 82:684; *TCCLSP* 2:141. [151]Ps 84:10 (83:11 LXX). [152]Prov 8:10-11. [153]NPNF 2 4:338-39**. [154]NPNF 1 14:367*.

1:5-14 THE SON AND THE ANGELS

[5]*For to what angel did God ever say,*
"Thou art my Son,
  today I have begotten thee"?
Or again,
  "I will be to him a father,
  and he shall be to me a son"?
[6]*And again, when he brings the first-born into the world, he says,*
  "Let all God's angels worship him."
[7]*Of the angels he says,*
  "Who makes his angels winds,
  and his servants flames of fire."
[8]*But of the Son he says,*
  "Thy throne, O God,[a] is for ever and ever,
  the righteous scepter is the scepter of thy[b] kingdom.
  [9]*Thou hast loved righteousness and hated lawlessness;*
  therefore God, thy God, has anointed thee
  with the oil of gladness beyond thy comrades."
[10]*And,*
  "Thou, Lord, didst found the earth in the beginning,
  and the heavens are the work of thy hands;
  [11]*they will perish, but thou remainest;*
  they will all grow old like a garment,
  [12]*like a mantle thou wilt roll them up,*
  and they will be changed.[c]
  But thou are the same,
  and thy years will never end."
[13]*But to what angel has he ever said,*
  "Sit at my right hand
  till I make thy enemies
  a stool for thy feet"?
[14]*Are they not all ministering spirits sent forth to serve, for the sake of those who are to obtain*
salvation?

a Or *God is thy throne* **b** Other ancient authorities read *his* **c** Other ancient authorities add *like a garment*

OVERVIEW: The early writers were intensely interested in the nature of angels (EPHREM), given that Christ is portrayed in Hebrews as superior to the angels (PHOTIUS). Gregory of Nazianzus catalogues them in Pauline terms as angels, arch-angels, thrones, dominions, princedoms, powers, splendors, ascents, intelligent powers, pure and unalloyed, immovable to evil. They are ministers of God's will, traveling through all space, readily present to all at any place through their zeal for ministry and agility of nature, guardians for different parts of the world or the universe. They are fellow ministers with us, our partners in service (CHRYSOSTOM). They are especially present when we apply ourselves to attending to the word of God, to prayer and to the mysteries (BEDE). According to Origen, though, Christ does not need the help of angels, being greater than the angels; indeed, the angels need the help of Jesus so as not to stumble.

According to Chrysostom, the statements of the epistle's opening questions are said of Christ, according to the flesh, for the flesh partakes of the high things, just as the Godhead of the lowly. In the incarnation the Lord was "brought into the world" in order to bring fallen humanity back to God (CHRYSOSTOM). "Christ" means "Anointed" by the oil of gladness. Eusebius further develops the uniqueness of Christ by noting that while the prophets and kings of the Old Testament were also anointed, only Christ, who is anointed with the Spirit, is worshiped; they were types of Christ. These "christs" signify him who saves us from our sins as the high priest reconciles us with the Father, and as kings give us the eternal kingdom of the Father (BEDE). Ephrem asserts that in the eschaton, all the works of creation will be renewed rather than annihilated.

Christ is also unique in that he stands and reigns on a lowly footstool, that is, the incarnation. "By taking on such lowliness he made it as lofty as it had earlier been insignificant in the world." Satan was overcome by the weakness of the flesh, and no other nature has been made one with Christ except that of our flesh, which he took and was glorified. Thus our miseries became strangers to us (CASSIODORUS). Christ offered human nature to the Father who

accepted the offering (PHOTIUS).

The Fathers address the issue of the role of angels in our salvation. Thus they assert that all ministering spirits are sent for our sake and for our salvation (AUGUSTINE, CHRYSOSTOM, BEDE). They may dwell in our hearts if they are adorned by the practice of virtue. There is an angel attached to every given soul to guard it (ORIGEN). The angels teach us the divine mysteries (ISAAC OF NINEVEH).

1:5-7 The Angels and the Son

ON ANGELS AND LUKE. ORIGEN: Let us see what the devil says to the Lord from the Scriptures: "It is written, 'He will give his angels charge of you; on their hands they will bear you up, lest you strike your foot against a stone.'"[1] See how crafty he is, even in the texts he quotes. For he wishes to diminish the Savior's glory, as if the Savior needed the help of angels. It is as if he would strike his foot unless he were supported by their hands. The devil takes this verse from Scripture and applies it to Christ. Yet it is written not of Christ but about the saints in general. Freely and in total confidence I contradict the devil. This passage cannot be applied to the person of Christ, for Christ does not need the help of angels. He is greater than the angels and obtained a better name than they by inheritance. For God never said to any of the angels, "You are my Son; today I have begotten you."[2] He has spoken to none of them as to a son. "He makes his angels winds, and his servants flames of fire."[3] But to his own Son he speaks properly and says countless things about him in the prophets.

As I say, the Son of God does not need the help of angels. No, devil; learn rather that unless Jesus helps the angels, they dash their feet. We have just heard a passage about the angels, "that we are to judge angels."[4] If any of the angels is seen to stumble, he stumbles because he did not

---

[1]Lk 4:9-11. [2]Ps 2:7. [3]Ps 104:4 (103:4 LXX). [4]1 Cor 6:3.

reach out his hand to Jesus. If Jesus had taken his hand, he would not have stumbled. For when someone trusts in his own strength and does not call upon the help of Jesus, he stumbles and falls. HOMILIES ON THE GOSPEL OF LUKE 31.4-5.[5]

CHRIST IS SUPERIOR TO THE ANGELS. PHOTIUS: When he introduces his only begotten, that is, when it was pleasing for him to reveal in the flesh his only begotten son to the inhabitants of the universe, he says, "Let all the angels who serve him, worship him," and "you will see the angels ascending and descending upon the Son of man."[6] FRAGMENTS ON THE EPISTLE TO THE HEBREWS 1.6.[7]

FIRSTBORN AND WORSHIP. THEODORET OF CYR: Both phrases, "brings the firstborn" and "let them worship," suggest the incarnation. Whence does he, the one who supports all things by the word of his power and is maker and creator of the ages, come into the world? How is he "firstborn" if he is only begotten? If even after the incarnation the angels adored him, did they not offer him this honor before the incarnation? He was everywhere as God, yet as man he came into the world. INTERPRETATION OF HEBREWS 1.[8]

ANGELS ARE NOT MATERIALLY FORMED. EPHREM THE SYRIAN: And it was never announced to any man, "Let all God's angels worship him." In fact, even though men are able to subject their fellow creatures, they will never force the angels to obey them. The angels are not materially formed. "He made," Paul says, "his angels spirits[9] and his ministers flames of fire." COMMENTARY ON THE EPISTLE TO THE HEBREWS.[10]

WE GET DIZZY ABOUT THIS SUBJECT. GREGORY OF NAZIANZUS: Since the Word knows the tabernacle of Moses to be a figure of the whole creation—I mean the entire system of things visible and invisible—shall we pass the first veil and,

stepping beyond the realm of sense, look into the holy place, the intellectual and celestial creation?[11] But not even this can we see in an incorporeal way, though it is incorporeal, since it is called—or is—fire and spirit. For he is said to make his angels spirits and his ministers flames of fire . . . though perhaps this "making" means preserving by that Word by which they came into existence. The angel then is called spirit and fire: spirit, as being a creature of the intellectual sphere; fire, as being of a purifying nature; for I know that the same names belong to the first nature.[12] But, relative to us at least, we must reckon the angelic nature incorporeal or, at any rate, as nearly so as possible. Do you see how we get dizzy over this subject and cannot advance to any point unless it be as far as this: that we know there are angels and archangels, thrones, dominions, princedoms, powers,[13] splendors, ascents, intelligent powers or intelligences, pure natures and unalloyed, immovable to evil or scarcely movable; ever circling in chorus around the first cause, or how should we sing their praises? Illuminated thence with the purest illumination or one in one degree and one in another, proportionally to their nature and rank . . . so conformed to beauty and molded that they become secondary lights and can enlighten others by the overflowing and largess of the first light?[14] They are ministers of God's will, strong with both inborn and imparted strength, traversing all space, readily present to all at any place through their zeal for ministry and agility of nature . . . different individuals of them embracing different parts of the world, or appointed over different districts of the universe, as knows the one who ordered and distributed it all. They combine all things in one, solely with a view to the consent of the Creator of all things. [They are] choristers of the majesty of the Godhead, eternally contemplating the eternal

---

[5]FC 94:127. [6]See Jn 1:51. [7]NTA 15:639. [8]PG 82:685; TCCLSP 2:142*. [9]The Greek is *pneumata*, meaning either "spirits" or "winds." [10]EHA 198. [11]Heb 9:1-3. [12]"First nature" refers to God. [13]Cf. Col 1:16; Rom 8:38. [14]"First light" refers to God.

glory, not that God may thereby gain an increase of glory, for nothing can be added to that which is full—to God, who supplies good to all outside God's self—but that there may never be a cessation of blessings to these first natures after God. If we have told these things as they deserve, it is by the grace of the Trinity and of the one Godhead in three persons, but if less perfectly than we have desired, yet even so our discourse has gained its purpose. For this is what we were laboring to show—that, if even the secondary natures[15] surpass the power of our intellect, much more then does the first and—for I fear to say merely—that which is above all the only nature. ON THEOLOGY, THEOLOGICAL ORATION 2(28).31.[16]

THE GODHEAD PARTAKES OF THE LOWLY.

CHRYSOSTOM: "For to what angel did God ever say, 'You are my Son, today I have begotten you'? Or again, 'I will be to him a father, and he shall be a son to me'"? For these things indeed are spoken with reference also to the flesh. . . . So also the word *today* seems to me to be spoken here with reference to the flesh. For when he has taken hold of it, he then speaks out boldly about everything. For indeed the flesh partakes of the high things, just as the Godhead partakes of the lowly. For he who did not disdain to become human and did not decline the reality, how should he have declined the expressions?

Seeing then that we know these things, let us be ashamed of nothing, nor have any high thoughts. For if he himself, being God and Lord and Son of God, did not decline to take the form of a slave, much more ought we to do all things, though they be lowly. For tell me, oh human, from where come your high thoughts? From things of this life? But these, as ever they appear, run by. Or from things spiritual? No, this is itself one spiritual essential: to have no high thoughts. ON THE EPISTLE TO THE HEBREWS 2.2.[17]

BIRTH IN THE FLESH. OECUMENIUS: Again let this also show how the Father accomplished the

birth of the Son in the flesh. For the word "I will be"[18] clearly is spoken about the incarnation. FRAGMENTS ON THE EPISTLE TO THE HEBREWS 1.5.[19]

PAUL CALLS IT A COMING IN. CHRYSOSTOM:

Our Lord Jesus Christ calls his coming in the flesh an exodus [or going out], as when he says, "The sower went out to sow."[20] And again, "I came from the Father and have come into the world."[21] And in many places one may see this. But Paul calls it a "coming in [or *eisodus*]," saying, "And again, when he brings the firstborn into the world," meaning by this "bringing in" his taking flesh.

Now why has he so used the expression? The things signified are manifest. . . . For Christ indeed calls it a "going out" justly, for we were out from God. For as in royal palaces, prisoners and those who have offended the king stand without, and he who desires to reconcile them does not bring them in but, himself going out, discourses with them until, having made them ready for the king's presence, he may bring them in, so also Christ has done. Having gone out to us—that is, having taken flesh—and having talked with us of the king's matters, so he brought us in, having purged the sins and made reconciliation. Therefore he calls it a "going out." But Paul names it a "coming in," from the metaphor of those who come into an inheritance and receive any portion or possession. For the saying, "and again, when he brings the firstborn into the world," means "when he puts the world into his hand." For when he was made known, then also he obtained possession of the whole of it. He says these things not concerning God the Word but concerning that which is according to the flesh. For if, according to John, "He was in the world, and the world came into being through him,"[22] how is he "brought in," other than in the flesh? ON THE EPISTLE TO THE HEBREWS 3.1.[23]

---

[15]"Secondary natures" refers to created beings. [16]LCC 3:158-59**. [17]NPNF 1 14:373**. [18]Cf. Ps 2:7. [19]NTA 15:462. [20]Mt 13:3. [21]Jn 16:28. [22]Jn 1:10. [23]NPNF 1 14:375*.

SCRIPTURE FORBIDS THE WORSHIP OF CRE-ATION. DIDYMUS THE BLIND: If all creation worships Christ—for by the name "angels" he denotes the higher rational beings, just as also in the passage "to what angel has he ever said, 'Sit at my right hand'?"[24] he himself is also above them—and the word of the Scriptures forbid us to worship creation in as much as it says, "Beware lest you lift up your eyes to heaven, and when you see the sun and the moon and the stars, all the host of heaven, you be drawn away and worship them."[25] Just as one is kept from worshiping the fixtures of the heavens, so also one is kept from worshiping other created beings, even if one happens upon a certain individual surpassing others. One must maintain firmly that Christ was the Creator, not a creation, even if for our sake he united himself to created flesh endowed with a reasonable and intellectual soul, and thus is worshiped as God by all creation. FRAGMENTS ON THE EPISTLE TO THE HEBREWS 1.6.[26]

THE SERVICE AND MINISTRY OF ANGELS. THEODORE OF MOPSUESTIA: The mention of the angels' "service" (wind) shows their quickness, while the mention of "ministry" (flames) shows their power. When he says that the angels have been made these things, he presents how they also have the ability to be these things. And he distinguishes them from the "Creator"[27] and "God" and "throne" and "scepter of the kingdom," all of which are symbols of his highest honor and worthiness. For also the phrase *God* reveals his highest nature, and *throne* and *scepter* set forth the certainty of this apart from human honors and worthiness. Then also the phrase "forever and ever" proves this, for the word *Creator* shows those things that have come into existence have their beginning in time, but this passage demonstrates the eternity of his kingdom. FRAGMENTS ON THE EPISTLE TO THE HEBREWS 1.7-8.[28]

HE WHO HAS AN ETERNAL THRONE. SEVERIAN OF GABALA: For just as in the matter of "radiance" and "exact image of his nature"[29] he imitated John, calling him "the Word" and saying that he was God,[30] so also here he imitated John. Just as John said, "This one was in the beginning, all things were created through him,"[31] so also does Paul, although he says, "these things were not" instead of saying, "This one was."[32] "To the angels is said, 'who makes them'; but to the Son, 'your throne.'" This proves the point: That which was made was not in existence previously, but he who has an eternal throne always was with his Father. FRAGMENTS ON THE EPISTLE TO THE HEBREWS 1.7-8.[33]

GOD'S ETERNAL THRONE. THEODORET OF CYR: "Your throne, O God, is forever." Through this he teaches us that the phrase "he sat down at the right hand of the majesty on high" was meant in human fashion. As God he has a throne that is eternal and a kingdom that is without beginning or end, but here human things are associated with it. INTERPRETATION OF HEBREWS 1.[34]

THINGS WILL NOT BE AS THEY ARE. CHRYSOSTOM: Lest upon hearing the words "and when he brings the firstborn into the world" you should think of it as a gift afterwards superadded to him, the apostle both corrected this beforehand and again further corrects, saying, "in the beginning." Not now, but from the first. See again how he strikes both Paul of Samosata and Arius a mortal blow, applying to the Son the things which relate to the Father. He has also intimated another thing, by the way, greater even than this. For surely he has incidentally pointed out as well the transfiguration of the world, saying, "they will all grow old like a garment; like a mantle you will roll them up, and they will be changed." That he also says in the Epistle to the Romans, that he shall transfigure the world.[35] And showing the facility thereof, he adds, as if a person should roll

---

[24]Cf. Ps 110:1. [25]Deut 4:19. [26]NTA 15:44-45. [27]*Ho poiōn*, translated "who makes" in RSV, can also be understood as "the one creating," that is, "Creator." [28]NTA 15:202. [29]Heb 1:3. [30]Jn 1:1-2. [31]Jn 1:3. [32]As in the rhetorical questions of Heb 1:5. [33]NTA 15:347. [34]PG 82:688; TCCLSP 2:143*. [35]Rom 8:20-21.

up a garment, so shall he both roll up and change it. But if he with so much ease works the transfiguration and the creation to what is better and more perfect, did he need another for the inferior creation? How far does your shamelessness go? Surely it is a very great consolation to know that things will not be as they are, but they all shall receive change, and all shall be altered; but he himself remains ever existing and living without end, "and your years," he says, "will never end." ON THE EPISTLE TO THE HEBREWS 3.3.[36]

1:8-10 *The Son and His Anointing*

SCRIPTURE FREQUENTLY USES THE PAST TENSE FOR THE FUTURE. JOHN OF DAMASCUS: It is when the Word was made flesh that we say he received the name of Christ Jesus. Since he was anointed with the oil of gladness[37]—that is to say, anointed with the Spirit by God the Father—he is called Christ, or Anointed. That the anointing was of the humanity no right-minded person would doubt. And the renowned Athanasius says to this effect, somewhere in his discourse, on the saving coming of Christ, "God (the Word), as existing before coming to dwell in the flesh, was not man but God with God, being invisible and impassible. But when he became man, he took the name Christ, because the passion and death are consequent upon this name."[38]

Now, even though sacred Scripture does say, "Therefore God, your God, has anointed you with the oil of gladness," one must know that sacred Scripture frequently uses the past tense for the future. [It says,] for example, "Afterwards, he appeared upon earth and lived among men,"[39] for God had not yet been seen by humanity nor had conversed with them when this was said. And again, "By the waters of Babylon, there we sat down and wept,"[40] for these things had not yet taken place. ORTHODOX FAITH 4.6.[41]

KING, PROPHET, PRIEST. EUSEBIUS OF CAESAREA: It was not only those that were honored

with the high priesthood and anointed for the sake of the symbol with prepared oil who were given tribute among the Hebrews with the name Christ. The kings too, at the bidding of God, were made Christs in a certain symbolism by the prophets who anointed them, inasmuch as they also bore in themselves the types of the royal and sovereign power of the only true Christ, the divine Logos who reigns over all. We have also received the tradition that some of the prophets themselves had by anointing already become Christs in type, seeing that they all refer to the true Christ—the divine and heavenly Logos, of the world the only high priest, of all creation the only king, of the prophets the only archprophet of the Father. The proof of this is that no one of those symbolically anointed of old, whether priests or kings or prophets, obtained such power of the divine virtue as our Savior and Lord, Jesus, the only real Christ, has exhibited. None indeed of them, though renowned in rank and honor for so many generations among their own people, ever gave the name of Christian to their subjects from the symbolic application to themselves of the name of Christ. The honor of worship was not paid to any of them by their subjects, nor did they hold them in such affection after their death as to be ready to die for him whom they honored.

For none of the men of those days was there such disturbance of all the nations throughout all the world, since the power of the symbol was incapable of producing such an effect among them as the presence of the reality manifested by our Savior; for he received from none the symbol and types of the high priesthood. Nor did he trace his physical descent from the race of priests; nor was he promoted to a kingdom by the armed force of men; nor did he become a prophet in the same way as those of old; nor did he hold any rank at all or precedence among the Jews. Yet with all these he

[36]NPNF 1 14:376*. [37]See Ps 45:7 (44:8 LXX). [38]Athanasius *Against Apollinaris* 2.1-2. [39]Bar 3:37 (3:38 LXX). RSV uses "she," meaning Wisdom. [40]Ps 137:1 (136:1 LXX). [41]FC 37:340-41*.

had been adorned, not in symbols, but in actual reality by the Father. Though he did not obtain the honors of which we have spoken before, he is called Christ more than any of them, and inasmuch as he is himself the only true Christ of God, he filled the whole world with Christians—his truly revered and sacred name. He no longer gave to his initiates types or images but the uncovered virtues themselves and the heavenly life in the actual doctrines of truth, and he has received the chrism—not that which is prepared materially, but the divine anointing itself with the spirit of God, by sharing in the unbegotten divinity of the Father. Again, Isaiah teaches this very point, for in one place he exclaims as if from Christ himself, "The Spirit of the Lord is upon me, because he has anointed me to preach good news to the poor, to proclaim release to the captives, and recovering of sight to the blind."[42]

And not only Isaiah but also David speaks with reference to him and says, "Your divine throne endures for ever and ever. Your royal scepter is a scepter of equity; you love righteousness and hate wickedness. Therefore God, your God, has anointed you with the oil of gladness above your fellows."[43] In this the text calls him God in the first verse, and in the second honors him with the royal scepter, and then goes on, after royal and divine power, to present him in the third place as having become Christ, anointed not with oil made of material substances but with the divine "oil of gladness."

And in addition to this he indicates his peculiar distinction and superiority to those who in the past had been more materially anointed as types. And in another place too the same David explains his position as follows: "The Lord says to my Lord, 'Sit at my right hand, till I make your enemies your footstool.'"[44] And "before the day-star I begot you from the womb. The Lord swore and will not repent, You are a priest forever according to the order of Melchizedek."[45] Now this Melchizedek is introduced in the sacred books as priest of the most high God, without having been so marked out by any material unction, or even as

belonging by racial descent to the priesthood of the Hebrews. For this reason our Savior has been called Christ and priest, on the authority of an oath, according to this order and not according to that of the others who received symbols and types. For this reason too the narrative does not relate that he was anointed physically by the Jews or even that he was of the tribe of those who hold the priesthood, but that he received his being from God himself before the day-star, that is to say, before the construction of the world, and holds his priesthood to boundless eternity, ageless and immortal. A weighty and clear proof of the immaterial and divine anointing effected on him is that he alone, out of all who have ever yet been until now, is called Christ among all men throughout the whole world. Under this title he is confessed and borne witness to by all and is mentioned thus by Jews, Greeks, and barbarians. Until this present day he is honored by his worshipers throughout the world as king, wondered at more than a prophet, and glorified as the true and only high priest of God, and above all, as the Logos of God, preexistent, having his being before all ages and having received the right of reverence from the Father, and he is worshiped as God. Strangest of all, we, who have been consecrated to him, honor him not only with our voices and with the sound of words but with the whole disposition of our soul, so as to value testimony to him more than our very life itself. ECCLESIASTICAL HISTORY 1.3.[46]

"JESUS" AND "CHRIST." BEDE: Jesus is the name of the son who was born of a virgin, and, as the angel explained, this name signified that he would save his people from their sins.[47] He who saves from sins is doubtlessly the same one who will save from the corruption of mind and body that happens as a result of sins. "Christ" is a term of priestly and royal dignity, for from "chrism"—that is, an anointing with holy oil—priests and

---

[42]Lk 4:18; cf. Is 61:1. [43]Ps 45:6-7 (44:7-8 LXX). [44]Ps 110:1 (109:1 LXX). [45]Ps 110:3-4 (109:3-4 LXX); cf. Heb 5:5-6. [46]LCL 153:31-35. [47]Mt 1:21.

kings were in the law called "christs," and they signified him who appeared in the world as true king and high priest and was anointed with the oil of gladness above those who shared with him.[48] From this anointing, that is, the chrism, he himself is called "Christ," and those who share this anointing, that is, spiritual grace, are called "Christians." In that he is Savior, may he deign to save us from sin. In that he is high priest, may he deign to reconcile us to God the Father. In that he is king, may he deign to give us the eternal kingdom of his Father. He is Jesus Christ our Lord, who with the Father and the Holy Spirit lives and reigns, God for all ages. Amen. HOMILIES ON THE GOSPELS 1.5.[49]

1:11-13 They Perish but You Remain

THE WORKS OF HEAVEN WILL BE RENEWED. EPHREM THE SYRIAN: Paul also said, "They will perish," and all the other things, and again the apostle took up the same words of David.[50] But if all the works of creation perish completely, then paradise, which is not perishable, will also perish. In truth, because of paradise, which does not cease, it is evident that all the works of creation will be renewed for us, as some assert, and they will not perish, as others have said. COMMENTARY ON THE EPISTLE TO THE HEBREWS.[51]

THE SAME. THEODORET OF CYR: He indicated creation's change for the better that was due to him, and his own lack of beginning or extinction. "You are the same, and your years will never end," he says, note, meaning, "You were not made, but you are, and you admit of no change, being always the same." This suggests also the impassibility of the divinity. If it suffered, how is it the same? After all, it would be changed, and if it passed three days in death, its years would fail. Both the prophet[52] and the apostle, however, the one writing the testimony and the other using it, emphasize that he is always the same and his years will not fail. INTERPRETATION OF HEBREWS 1.[53]

THE OLD TESTAMENT DOES NOT SPEAK ABOUT THE FATHER ALONE. THEODORE OF MOPSUESTIA: It is possible to see in a glance that whenever the Old Testament speaks about the divine nature, it does not speak distinctly about the Father alone, as the heretics suppose when they attempt to apply "I am God and there is no other besides me"[54] and similar passages to the Father alone. On the contrary, whatever it says concerning God as it expounds upon the divine nature, it says in such a way that those attributes may be joined together with the Son and the Holy Spirit, owing to the fellowship of their nature. Otherwise how has the apostle dragged in this second scriptural witness from it? . . . Has not Paul done the same in his epistle to the Romans, where he says, "For it is written, 'As I live,' says the Lord, 'every knee shall bow to me'"?[55] For no one would find here something that would clearly distinguish between them. FRAGMENTS ON THE EPISTLE TO THE HEBREWS 1.12.[56]

SHIFT TO THE HUMAN. THEODORET OF CYR: Having thus dealt with divine things, he shifts once more to the human. It is not to him as God that he says, "Sit at my right hand": how could it be, when "his throne is for ever and ever"? So as human he shared in this honor, having as God the eternal throne. INTERPRETATION OF HEBREWS 1.[57]

CHRIST AS SACRED FOOTSTOOL. CASSIODORUS: "He spoke to them in the pillar of the cloud, because they kept his testimonies and the commands which he gave them."[58] The words "in the pillar of the cloud" are not without point, for a pillar is always used in house building to add strength and beauty. So the Lord spoke to them in this shape, which announced the future fabric of the church. But whereas at that time he spoke

---

[48]Ps 45:7. [49]CS 110:50**. [50]Cf. Ps 102:26 (101:27 LXX). [51]EHA 198. [52]Ps 102:25-27 (101:26-28 LXX). [53]PG 82:688; TCCLSP 2:144*. [54]Is 45:21. [55]Rom 14:11; Is 45:23. [56]NTA 15:202. [57]PG 82:688; TCCLSP 2:144*. [58]Ps 99:7 (98:7 LXX).

to them through the cloud, he has deigned to speak and to appear to us more clearly by means of the sacred footstool, that is, through the incarnation. This footstool is loftier than all temples, much more preeminent than all spiritual creatures. As the apostle puts it, "But to what angel has he ever said, 'Sit at my right hand'?" Why is it surprising that he is called a stool, when he compared himself to a worm,[59] to the fuller's herb[60] and to a cornerstone,[61] not in lowly appearance but in humility of demeanor? By taking on such lowliness he made it as lofty as it had earlier been insignificant in this world. EXPOSITION OF THE PSALMS 98.7.[62]

HE MADE OUR MISERIES STRANGERS TO US. CASSIODORUS: We have listened to a psalm,[63] wondrous in its heavenly arrangement, in which it is clear that the power in his divinity is matched by the humility in his humanity. The sacred Word took on the nature of our weakness—the psalm heading says that it is "for them that shall be changed"—so that he might free us from a truly deserved death by the death which was not his due. He entered the confines of hell so that the lower regions could be opened up. Death was conquered by the arrival of the Savior and rightly forfeited its enduring darkness once it received the eternal light. He conquered the devil by means of the human nature that Satan held subject; in his strength Satan was overcome by the weakness of the flesh, when God raised above all creatures endowed with reason that which was feebler than all the spiritual powers. As the apostle remarked, "To what angel has he ever said, 'Sit at my right hand'?" No other nature has been made one with Christ except that of our flesh, which he took and which was glorified. Truly almighty, truly merciful is he who made blessed what was condemned, restored what was lost, freed what was subjugated, made our miseries strangers to us, and by his own death enabled man to live, when, though he was created immortal, the devil had caused him to die. Almighty God, we pray that, having deigned to suffer for us

in the flesh, you may bestow on us the crown of which you deign us worthy. EXPOSITION OF THE PSALMS 68.37.[64]

ANGELS WERE CREATED BUT HE WAS NOT. SEVERIAN OF GABALA: He does not say that a change of nature took place, but by way of comparison, that he permits these things to be destroyed and they do perish in contrast to the eternity of the Son. For also the Lord, when predicting his second coming, says "the stars will fall"[65] and there will no longer be sun or moon or heavens.

"But to what angel has he ever said?" Leaving aside all the rest of creation he speaks about that which is higher than the rest of creation, namely, the angels. For if the Son differed from the angels in that they were created but he was not, how much more does he differ from all invisible things? And one must demonstrate in addition that he revealed through the statement "but you are the same" Christ's eternal existence and the immutability of his nature. Through the phrase "Are they not all ministering spirits sent forth to serve" he shows that the Son is not a servant, but a fellow worker with God. FRAGMENTS ON THE EPISTLE TO THE HEBREWS 1.12-14.[66]

CHRIST ELEVATED HUMAN NATURE. PHOTIUS: He lifted up the first offering of our nature to the Father, and the Father marveled at this offering. And because of the high esteem of the one who offered it and because of the purity of the offering, he, as the father of the household shows him with his hand the place close to himself and also places the offering nearby and says, "sit at my right hand." FRAGMENTS ON THE EPISTLE TO THE HEBREWS 1.13.[67]

1:14 Angels for Our Sake

SENT TO SAVE. THEODORET OF CYR: Whereas

---

[59]Job 25:6. [60]Mal 3:2. [61]Ps 118:22 (117:22 LXX); Mt 21:42; Mk 12:10; Lk 20:17. [62]ACW 52:441. [63]Ps 68 (67 LXX). [64]ACW 52:160-61. [65]Mt 24:29; Mk 13:25. [66]NTA 15:347. [67]NTA 15:639.

he sits at the right hand [he is saying], they are sent as ministers of salvation for the sake of human beings. INTERPRETATION OF HEBREWS 1.[68]

THESE THINGS WERE DONE FOR OUR SAKE.
AUGUSTINE: Now certainly in the epistle to the Hebrews, when a distinction was to be made between the dispensation of the New Testament and the dispensation of the Old Testament in regard to the fitness of the ages and times, it was written most plainly that not only those visible things but also the word itself were wrought by the mediation of the angels. For it speaks as follows: "To what angel has he ever said, 'Sit at my right hand, till I make your enemies a stool for your feet'? Are they not all ministering spirits, sent forth to serve, for the sake of those who are to obtain salvation?" It is evident from this passage that all those things were not only done by angels but were also done for our sake, that is, for the people of God, to whom the inheritance of eternal life is promised. ON THE TRINITY 11.22.[69]

THIS IS THEIR MINISTRY. CHRYSOSTOM: What marvel says he if [angels] minister to the Son, when they minister even to our salvation? See how he lifts up their minds and shows the great honor that God has for us, since he has assigned to angels who are above us this ministration on our behalf. As if, one should say, for this purpose he says he employs them; this is the office of angels, to minister to God for our salvation. So that it is an angelic work to do all for the salvation of the brethren; or rather it is the work of Christ himself, for he indeed saves as Lord, but they as servants. And we, though servants, are yet angels' fellow servants. Why do you gaze so earnestly on the angels, says he? They are servants of the Son of God and are sent many ways for our sake and minister to our salvation. And so they are partners in service with us. Consider how he ascribes no great difference to the kinds of creatures. And yet the space between angels and humans is great. Nevertheless, he brings them down near to us, all

but saying, "For us they labor, for our sake they run to and fro. On us, one might say, they wait." This is their ministry, for our sake to be sent every way.

And of these examples the Old Testament is full, as well as the New. For when angels bring glad tidings to the shepherds or to Mary or to Joseph; when they sit at the sepulcher; when they are sent to say to the disciples, "Men of Galilee, why do you stand looking into heaven?";[70] when they release Peter out of the prison; when they discourse with Philip, consider how great the honor is. When God sends the angels for ministers as to friends; when an angel appears to Cornelius; when an angel brings forth all the apostles from the prison, and says, "Go and stand in the temple, and speak to the people all the words of this life."[71] And even to Paul himself an angel appears. Do you see that they minister to us on God's behalf and that they minister to us in the greatest matters? Thus Paul says, "All things are yours, whether life or death, or the world, or things present, or things to come."[72] Well then the Son was also sent, but not as a servant or as a minister, but as a Son and only begotten, desiring the same things with the Father. Indeed, he was not "sent," for he did not pass from place to place but took on him flesh, whereas these change their places, and, leaving those in which they were before, so come to others in which they were not. ON THE EPISTLE TO THE HEBREWS 3.4.[73]

GOD'S MINISTERS MUST FIND A PLACE IN US. ORIGEN: On this account our heart must be kept with all carefulness both by day and night, and no place be given to the devil. But every effort must be used that the ministers of God—those spirits who were sent to minister to those who are called to be heirs of salvation—may find a place within us, and be delighted to enter into the guest-chamber of our soul. And, dwelling within us [they] may guide us by their counsel; if, so,

---

[68]PG 82:689; TCCLSP 2:144. [69]FC 45:120*. [70]Acts 1:11. [71]Acts 5:20. [72]1 Cor 3:22. [73]NPNF 1 14:377*.

they shall find the habitation of our heart adorned by the practice of virtue and holiness. On First Principles 3.3.6.[74]

Where the Mysteries Are Being Enacted. Bede: It is no secret that angels are frequently present, invisibly, at the side of the elect, in order to defend them from the snares of the cunning enemy and uphold them by the great gift of heavenly desire. The apostle attests to this when he says, "Are they not all ministering spirits sent forth to serve for the sake of those who are to obtain salvation?" Nevertheless, we should believe that the angelic spirits are especially present to us when we give ourselves in a special way to divine services, that is, when we enter a church and open our ears to sacred reading, or give our attention to psalm singing, or apply ourselves to prayer, or celebrate the solemnity of the mass. Hence the apostle advises women to have a veil over their heads in church on account of the angels.[75] And a prophet says, "I will sing psalms to you in the sight of the angels."[76] We are not permitted to doubt that where the mysteries of the Lord's body and blood are being enacted, a gathering of the citizens from on high is present—those who were keeping such careful watch at the tomb where Christ's venerable body had been placed and from which he had departed by rising. Hence we must strive meticulously, my brothers, when we come into the church to pay the due service of divine praise or to perform the solemnity of the mass, to be always mindful of the angelic presence, and to fulfill our heavenly duty with fear and fitting veneration, following the example of the women devoted to God who were afraid when the angels appeared to them at the tomb, and who, we are told, bowed their faces to the earth. Homilies on the Gospels 2.10.[77]

They Are Allotted as Guards to Each One of Us. Origen: With respect to the fact that both good and evil angels attend to humans—a doctrine we have often taught fol-

lowing the Holy Scriptures—it is not by chance and without a divine judgment that a given angel is assigned to a given soul. For example, one is allotted to Peter and another to Paul. . . . Therefore, there can be no doubt that by a judgment of God, who sees clearly their worth and the quality of our soul, they are allotted as guards to each one of us by a mystical lot directed by the economy of Christ. Homilies on Joshua 23.3.[78]

Mysteries Transmitted by Angels. Isaac of Nineveh: Whenever the perception of the revelation of a mystery descends into the intellects of the saints, this is also from the angels. When it is permitted by God, a mystery is revealed from a higher angelic order to a lower one, even unto the lowest; and in the same manner, when it is permitted by the divine nod that a mystery should come even to human nature, it is transmitted by those angels who are wholly worthy of it. For by their intermediary the saints receive the light of divine vision, leading even to the glorious eternal Being, the mystery which cannot be taught. And the angels receive from one another, "for they are ministering spirits, sent forth to serve for the sake of those who are to obtain salvation," through the awareness of true intuitions that are proper to them. In the future age, however, this order of things will be abolished. For then one will not receive from another the revelation of God's glory unto the gladness and joy of his soul. But to each by himself the Master will give according to the measure of his excellence and his worthiness, and he will not receive the gift from his comrade as he does here. Then there will be no teacher and no pupil, nor one whose deficiency must be filled up by another. For one is the giver there, who gives without mediation to those who receive; and those who win joy procure it from him. For

---

[74]ANF 4:337*. [75]1 Cor 11:10. [76]Ps 138:1 (137:1 LXX). RSV reads, "before the gods I sing thy praise." [77]CS 111:91-92. [78]SC 71:460; COS 28; FC 105:199*.

they do not perceive him through diverse intellections but by direct revelation of him, without departing from him through thoughts. There the order of those who teach and those who learn ceases, and on that one alone hangs the ardent love of all. Ascetical Homilies 28.[79]

We Need to Know the Need for Assistance. Theodore of Mopsuestia: That the angels were "ministering spirits" he has established from previous testimony, but now he finally renews the image of their service, saying that they do everything in service for the things needful for our salvation. For it is not a small thing to know the need for the assistance of their service. Fragments on the Epistle to the Hebrews 1.14-2:1.[80]

---

[79]*AHSIS* 140. [80]NTA 15:203.

2:1-4 AN ADMONITION NOT TO DRIFT AWAY FROM SALVATION

Therefore we must pay the closer attention to what we have heard, lest we drift away from it. [2]For if the message declared by angels was valid and every transgression or disobedience received a just retribution, [3]how shall we escape if we neglect such a great salvation? It was declared at first by the Lord, and it was attested to us by those who heard him, [4]while God also bore witness by signs and wonders and various miracles and by gifts of the Holy Spirit distributed according to his own will.

Overview: The early writers were clear that what they heard was the word of salvation (2:1), namely, the message heard by their ancestors in faith through the angels as messengers both before and after the law. The angels are granted the divine enlightenment; theirs is a life of extraordinary intelligence. Having the first and most diverse participation in the divine, they thus provide the first and the most diverse revelations of the divine hiddenness. The law was given to us by the angels (Pseudo-Dionysius). Now, however, the message of salvation of the New Testament is spoken not by the angels but by the Lord (Augustine). This salvation is not deliverance from wars or the bestowal of the good things of the earth but the dissolution of death, the destruction of the devil and the kingdom of everlasting life (Chrysostom). How could we neglect so great a salvation? The Fathers admonish us not to drift away from salvation (Origen, Ephrem), because such disobe-dience brings about a recompense (Chrysostom). We should make every effort to be "lifted" to spiritual freedom (Symeon the New Theologian). The path of that spiritual ascent is the path of humility that facilitates the gifts of the Spirit bestowed individually. The word of salvation was not only delivered by word but also with signs and wonders and miracles. Thus it can be trusted (Chrysostom).

2:1-2 *Closer Attention*

KEEP YOUR HEART WITH ALL VIGILANCE.
ORIGEN: The design of Judas concerning the
betrayal of our Lord and Savior did not originate
in the wickedness of his mind alone. For Scripture
testifies that the "devil had already put it into his
heart to betray him."[1] On this account Solomon
rightly commanded, saying, "Keep your heart with
all diligence."[2] And the apostle Paul warns us:
"Therefore we ought to pay closer attention to the
things which we have heard, lest by chance we
drift away." ON FIRST PRINCIPLES 3.2.4.[3]

THE LAW WAS GIVEN TO US BY ANGELS.
PSEUDO-DIONYSIUS: Compared with the things
that merely are, with irrational forms of life and
indeed with our own rational natures, the holy
ranks of heavenly beings are obviously superior in
what they have received of God's largess. Their
thinking processes imitate the divine. They look
on the divine likeness with a transcendent eye.
They model their intellects on God. Hence it is
natural for them to enter into a more generous
communion with the deity, because they are forever marching towards the heights, because, as
permitted, they are drawn to a concentration of
an unfailing love for God, because they immateri-
ally receive undiluted the original enlightenment,
and because, ordered by such enlightenment,
theirs is a life of total intelligence. They have the
first and most diverse participation in the divine,
and they, in turn, provide the first and most
diverse revelations of the divine hiddenness. That
is why they have a preeminent right to the title of
angel or messenger, since it is they who first are
granted the divine enlightenment, and it is they
who pass on to us these revelations that are so far
beyond us. Indeed, the Word of God teaches us
that the law was given to us by the angels. Before
the days of the law and after it had come, it was
the angels who uplifted our illustrious ancestors
toward the divine. And they did so by prescribing
rules of conduct, by turning them from wandering and sin to the right way of truth, or by coming
to announce and explain sacred orders, hidden
visions, or transcendent mysteries, or divine

prophecies. CELESTIAL HIERARCHY 4.2.[4]

**THE MESSAGE DECLARED THROUGH THE
ANGEL IN SODOM.** EPHREM THE SYRIAN:
"Therefore we must pay the closer attention to
what we have heard" from the Son, "lest we drift
away" just like the former people. "If," because of
that message declared through the angel in
Sodom, those who did not want to listen to it
"received the penalty of punishment, then how
can we be saved, if we neglect so great a new life?"
COMMENTARY ON THE EPISTLE TO THE
HEBREWS.[5]

A JUST REWARD. CHRYSOSTOM: "And every
transgression or disobedience," he says. Not this
one or that one, but "every" one. Nothing, he
says, remained unavenged but "received a just
recompense of reward" instead of punishment.
Why does he speak like this? Such is the manner
of Paul, not to make much account of his phrases
but indifferently to put down words of evil
sound, even in matters of good meaning. As also
in another place he says, "Bringing into captivity
every thought to the obedience of Christ."[6] And
again he has put "recompense" for punishment,
as here he calls punishment "reward." ON THE
EPISTLE TO THE HEBREWS 3.6.[7]

2:3-4 Such a Great Salvation

THE DISSOLUTION OF DEATH. CHRYSOSTOM:
"How then shall we," Paul says, "escape if we
neglect so great a salvation?" Here he signifies
that the other salvation was no great thing. . . .
For it is not from wars, Paul says, that Christ will
now rescue us, nor will he bestow on us the earth
and the good things that are in the earth; rather it
will be the dissolution of death, the destruction
of the devil, the kingdom of heaven, everlasting
life. For all these things he has briefly expressed
by saying, "if we neglect so great a salvation." ON

---

[1]Jn 13:2. [2]Prov 4:23. [3]ANF 4:332**. [4]*PDCW* 156-57*. [5]EHA 199.
[6]2 Cor 10:5. [7]NPNF 1 14:378**.

THE EPISTLE TO THE HEBREWS 3.6.[8]

WHAT SALVATION? AUGUSTINE: Since the message was proclaimed in former times by angels but now by the Son, he draws [this] logical and obvious conclusion. . . . And, just as though you had asked, "what salvation?" he replied as follows, in order to show that he was referring to the salvation of the New Testament, that is, to the word not spoken by the angels but by the Lord. ON THE TRINITY 3.11.22.[9]

HE LEAVES IT IN THE FORM OF A QUESTION. CHRYSOSTOM: Why then ought we to "pay the closer attention"? Lest at any time, Paul says . . . we should fall away. And here he shows the grievousness of this falling away, in that it is a difficult thing for that which has fallen away to return again, inasmuch as it has happened through willful negligence. And he took this form of speech from the Proverbs. For Solomon says, "My son, take heed lest you fall away,"[10] showing both the easiness of the fall and the grievousness of the ruin. That is, our disobedience is not without danger. And while by his mode of reasoning he shows that the chastisement is greater, yet again he leaves it in the form of a question and not as a conclusion. For indeed this is to make one's discourse inoffensive, when one . . . leaves it in the power of the hearers to draw their own conclusions and thus be more greatly persuaded. The prophet Nathan does the same in the Old Testament[11] as Christ does in Matthew, saying, "What will he do to the tenants"[12] of that vineyard? In doing so he compels them to draw the conclusion themselves, for this is the greatest victory. ON THE EPISTLE TO THE HEBREWS 3.5.[13]

ENDEAVOR TO BE LIFTED UP. SYMEON THE NEW THEOLOGIAN: I urge you all . . . that no one of you neglect your own salvation but that you in every way endeavor to be lifted up even but a little from the earth. Should this wonderful thing happen, which would astound you, that you should float up from the earth into the air,[14] you

would not at all want to descend to the earth and stay there! But by "earth" I mean the fleshly mind, by "air" the spiritual. Once the mind is set free from evil thoughts and . . . we contemplate the freedom that Christ our God has bestowed on us,[15] we shall never again be willing to descend to our former slavery to sin and the fleshly mind. In accordance with the voice of Christ we shall not cease to watch and pray[16] until we depart for the bliss that lies beyond and obtain the promised blessings, by the grace and lovingkindness of our Lord Jesus Christ, to whom all glory is due forever and ever. Amen. DISCOURSE 5.25.[17]

THE HUMBLE RECEIVE A GIFT. CHRYSOSTOM: Even without a gift, the mere consciousness of a pure life would be sufficient to lift up a person; much more when the grace is added also. It was to the humble, to the simple, that it was given, and especially to the simple, for it is said, "with glad and generous hearts."[18] Hereby he urged them on, and, if they were growing negligent, gave them a spur. For the humble and those who imagine no great things concerning themselves become more earnest when they have received a gift, in that they have obtained more than they rightly deserve and think that they are not worthy of such a gift. But those who think they have done well, believing the gift to be something they deserve, are puffed up. This is why God dispenses this profitably, as one may see also in the church; for some have the word of teaching, while others do not have power to open their mouths. Let no one, he says, be grieved because of this. For "to each is given the manifestation of the Spirit for the common good."[19] For if the householder knows to whom he should entrust something, much more will God, who understands the mind of humans . . . One thing only is worthy of grief: sin; there is nothing else. Do not say, "Why am I not rich?" or "If I were rich,

[8]NPNF 1 14:379**. [9]FC 45:120*. [10]Prov 3:21. [11]2 Sam 12:1-13. [12]Mt 21:40. [13]NPNF 1 14:378**. [14]1 Thess 4:17. [15]See Gal 5:1. [16]Mt 26:41; Mk 14:38. [17]SNTD 118*. [18]Acts 2:46. [19]1 Cor 12:7.

I would give to the poor." You cannot know that you would not covet riches if you had any. For now indeed you say these things, but, if you were put to the test, you would be different. So also, when we are satisfied, we think that we are able to fast; but, when we have gone without food for a time, other thoughts come into us. Again, when we are away from strong drink, we think that we are able to master our appetite, but it is no longer so when we are caught by it.

Do not say, "Oh, that I had the gift of teaching," or "If I had it, I would have edified innumerable souls." You cannot know whether or not this gift of teaching would be to your condemnation. You cannot know whether envy or sloth would not have disposed you to hide your talent. On the Epistle to the Hebrews 3.8.[20]

God Gave the Spirit to Others. Chrysostom: You have a child, you have a neighbor, you have a friend, you have a brother, you have relatives. And, though publicly before the church you are not able to draw out a long discourse, to these you can exhort in private. Before them there is no need of rhetoric or elaborate discourse. Prove in this way that if you had skill of speech, you would not neglect it. But if in the small matter you are not faithful, how shall I trust you concerning the great?[21] That every person can do this, hear what Paul says, how he charged even lay people. "Build one another up," he says, "just as you are doing,"[22] and, "Comfort one another with these words."[23] God knows how God should distribute gifts to every person. Are you better than Moses? Hear how he shrinks from the hardship: "Am I," he says, "able to bear them? For you said to me, 'Carry them in your bosom, as a nurse carries the sucking child.' "[24] What then did God do? He took some of Moses' spirit and gave it to the others,[25] showing that, even when Moses bore them, the gift was not his own but was of the Spirit. On the Epistle to the Hebrews 3.9.[26]

What If Those Who Heard Were Forgers? Chrysostom: This is a great and trustwor-

thy thing, as Luke also says in the beginning of his Gospel: "As they were delivered to us by those who from the beginning were eyewitnesses and ministers of the word."[27] One may ask, "How then was it confirmed? What if those that heard were forgers?" Paul rejects this objection and shows that the grace was not human. If they had gone astray, God would not have borne witness to them; for Paul continued, "God also bore witness." Both they indeed bear witness and God bears witness too. How does God bear witness? Not by word or by voice, though this also would have been worthy of belief, but how? "By signs and wonders and various miracles." He appropriately said, "various miracles," declaring the abundance of the gifts, which was not so in the former dispensation—neither so great signs, nor so various. That is, we did not believe simply the eyewitnesses but signs and wonders; therefore, it is not they whom we believe, but God. On the Epistle to the Hebrews 3.7.[28]

Comparison and Exhortation. Theodoret of Cyr: Again he associated a comparison with the exhortation, showing the extent to which the gospel teaching surpasses the provisions of the law. The ministry of angels was involved in the giving of the law, whereas in this case the Lord in person was the first to propose the saving teaching, and those who were in receipt of the apostolic grace welcomed it. While the law gives us a glimpse of what has to be done, the Lord's teaching is the source of eternal salvation. . . . He also showed the new covenant to be resplendent with spiritual gifts: of old the inspired authors alone shared in the spiritual bounty, whereas now all the believers enjoy this grace. . . . While he said this to encourage them to give heed to the divine teaching more zealously, he brought out the difference between the former and the latter under the guise of exhortation. It was very

---

[20]NPNF 1 14:379-80**. [21]A paraphrase of Lk 16:10; 19:17. [22]1 Thess 5:11. [23]1 Thess 4:18. [24]Num 11:12. [25]Num 11:25. [26]NPNF 1 14:380**. [27]Lk 1:2. [28]NPNF 1 14:379**.

wise of him to say God witnesses to the message through miracles: the demonstration is beyond question, and the reliability of the witness indisputable. Interpretation of Hebrews 2.[29]

Many Outside the Faith Were Healed Through Us. Theodore of Mopsuestia: Paul showed that there is a very great difference between the old covenant and the new covenant, since he speaks about the "word" in the first covenant, but in this covenant he speaks of "salvation." For the first covenant was only a giving of customs and observances, whereas in this covenant there is also the grace of the Spirit and release from sins and the promise of the kingdom of heaven and the promise of immortality. Therefore, he also rightly says, "such a great salvation," showing by the epithet its greatness. In the first covenant it was given "through the angels," but now "through the Lord." And since there were marvels with the former covenant, so that the new covenant might not seem inferior to the old in this respect, he well appended the statement, "while God further testified with signs and wonders and various powers," saying this so that by its increase the fullness of grace might

appear beyond that of the law also in this matter. For there the wonders took place only according to the need, but here also many of those outside the faith were healed through us, from even whatsoever diseases happened to afflict them. For such was the abundance of healings among us. Also the dead were raised.... After comparing and contrasting the difference and showing the superiority in a various and manifold manner, he added a greater thing that did not happen to those in the law: "and by gifts of the Holy Spirit distributed." For that each of the believers should have their own share in the Spirit was a characteristic of those in grace. And well he adds in addition to all these things "according to his own will," that is, the will of God who fully wished once and for all to lavish us greatly so that his grace for us might not be repented of, and that the gifts of grace once given to us might not be changed along with the things of the previous covenant, as some might suspect. Fragments on the Epistle to the Hebrews 2.3-4.[30]

---

[29]PG 82:689; *TCCLSP* 2:144-45. [30]NTA 15:203.

2:5-9 ALL THINGS WILL BE SUBJECT TO THE SUFFERING CHRIST

[5]*For it was not to angels that God subjected the world to come, of which we are speaking. [6]It has been testified somewhere,*
"What is man that thou art mindful of him,
or the son of man, that thou carest for him?
[7]*Thou didst make him for a little while lower than the angels,*
thou hast crowned him with glory and honor,[d]
[8]*putting everything in subjection under his feet."*
Now in putting everything in subjection to him, he left nothing outside his control. As it is, we do not yet see everything in subjection to him. [9]But we see Jesus, who for a little while was made

lower than the angels, crowned with glory and honor because of the suffering of death, so that by the grace of God he might taste death for every one.

d Other ancient authorities insert *and didst set him over the works of thy hands*

Overview: It was apparent to the early writers that all things were not currently under the full subjection of Christ, especially given the evident suffering of the faithful, but that all things will be put under him. What is more consoling is that he under whom all things will be put in subjection has also died and submitted to innumerable sufferings. As we suffer, the early commentators remind us of the cross. Since the Scriptures call his cross "glory and honor," this glorifies our sufferings (Chrysostom). Christ's ultimate humiliation on the cross led to his ultimate triumph (Photius). Christ made those whose nature had previously become thorny through sin into a crown for himself, transforming the thorn through suffering into honor and glory (Gregory of Nyssa). It is as a human that he is mediator, for by deigning to share our humanity God shows us the shortest way to share in the divinity. Freeing us from mortality and misery, God leads us not to blessedness through the immortal and blessed nature of angels but to the Trinity, in communion with which even the angels are blessed (Augustine). "Until I make your enemies your footstool" signifies that the process is not immediate but takes place over time. When Jesus was placed on the cross as a fruit on a tree (Chrysostom), he tasted death for all (Origen). But he destroyed death because he was superior to it (Ephrem). It is important to observe that the writers from the school of Antioch in Syria, such as Theodore of Mopsuestia, were more concerned to emphasize the humanity of Christ and to distinguish between the divine and human natures. Theodore argues, "The man Jesus was like all humans and differed in no way from those whose nature he shares, save that to him grace was given." It shows how our souls are united with Christ's in the incarnation and raised up with him though dead (Symeon the New Theologian).

2:5-7 Through Christ's Sufferings

Only Three Days in Hades. Chrysostom: There is another consolation if indeed he, who is hereafter to have all put in subjection under him, has himself died and submitted to sufferings innumerable. "But," Paul says, "we see him who was made a little lower than the angels, even Jesus, for the suffering of death"—then turns immediately to the good things again—"crowned with glory and honor." Do you see how all things apply to him? For the expression "a little" would rather suit him, who was only three days in Hades, but not ourselves who are in corruption for a long time. Likewise also, the expression "with glory and honor" will suit him much more completely than us. Again Paul reminds them of the cross, thereby effecting two things, both showing Christ's care for them and persuading them to bear all things nobly, looking to the master. For, he would say, if he who is worshiped by angels endured for your sake to have a little less than the angels, much more ought you, who are inferior to the angels, to bear all things for his sake. Then Paul shows that the cross is "glory and honor," as Christ himself always calls it, saying, "that the Son of man may be glorified"[1] and "the Son of man is glorified."[2] If then he calls his sufferings for his servants' sake "glory," much more should you endure sufferings for the Lord. On the Epistle to the Hebrews 4.3.[3]

The Ultimate Humiliation and the Ultimate Honor. Photius: Why does he bring up the quote, "what are human beings that you are mindful of them?" He purports to prove, from the contrary, the following statement, that Christ is far superior to the angels. "A little while lower

[1]Jn 11:4. [2]Jn 12:23. [3]NPNF 1 14:383**.

than the angels," he brings . . . up in order to disprove the opposite proposition. He means that he was made lower through the suffering of death, "we saw him, but he had no form nor beauty."[4] Therefore, it was appropriate to say that about the Lord, because he was exalted; again, it was appropriate to exhort them [angels] to "put everything in subjection under his feet." FRAGMENTS ON THE EPISTLE TO THE HEBREWS 2.6-9.[5]

PLACED IN THE MIDDLE OF THE MASTER'S CROWN. GREGORY OF NYSSA: When, according to the prophetic word, people were alienated from the life-giving womb through sin and went astray from the womb in which they were fashioned, they spoke falsehood instead of truth.[6] Because of this, the Mediator, assuming the first fruit of our common nature, made it holy through his soul and body, unmixed and unreceptive of all evil, preserving it in himself. He did this in order that, having taken it up to the Father of incorruptibility through his own incorruptibility, the entire group might be drawn along with it because of their related nature, in order that the Father might admit the disinherited to "adoption"[7] as children and the enemies of God to a share in the Godhead. And just as the first fruit of the dough[8] was assimilated through purity and innocence to the true Father and God, so we also as dough in similar ways will cleave to the Father of incorruptibility by imitating, as far as we can, the innocence and stability of the Mediator. Thus, we shall be a crown of precious stones for the only begotten God, having become an honor and a glory through our life. For Paul says, "Having made himself a little lower than the angels because of his having suffered death, he made those whose nature had previously become thorny through sin into a crown for himself, transforming the thorn through suffering into honor and glory." And yet, once he has "taken away the sins of the world"[9] and taken upon his head a crown of thorns in order to weave a crown of "honor and glory," there is no small danger that someone may be discovered to be a burr and a

thorn because of his evil life, and then be placed in the middle of the Master's crown because of sharing in his body. The just voice speaks directly to this one: "How did you get in here without a wedding garment?[10] How were you, a thorn, woven in with those fitted into my crown through honor and glory?" ON PERFECTION.[11]

HE WILLED TO TAKE THE NATURE OF A SLAVE. AUGUSTINE: The fact that he is the Word is not the reason why he is a mediator, for certainly the Word at the summit of immortality and the apex of beatitude is far removed from miserable mortals. Rather, he is a mediator because he is human and, as a human, shows us that to attain that supreme good, blessed and beatific, we need not seek other mediators to serve like rungs on a ladder of ascent. For the blessed God who makes us blessed by deigning to share our humanity showed us the shortest way to sharing in his divinity. Freeing us from mortality and misery, he leads us, not to the immortal blessed angels so as to become immortal and blessed by sharing in their nature, but to that Trinity in communion with which even the angels are blessed. When, then, in order to be mediator, he willed to take "the form of a servant"[12] below the angels, he remained in the form of God above the angels, being simultaneously the way of life on earth and life itself in heaven. CITY OF GOD 9.15.[13]

2:8 Everything in Subjection

THAT THEY MUST BE MADE SUBJECT IS EVIDENT. CHRYSOSTOM: He said, "Until I make your enemies your footstool."[14] But it was likely that his hearers would still be grieved . . . so he added this testimony in confirmation of the subjection. That they might not say, "How is it that he has put his enemies under his feet, when we have suffered so much?" He did . . . hint at this in the

[4]Is 53:2. [5]NTA 15:639-40. [6]See Ps 58:3 (57:4 LXX). [7]See Gal 4:5; Eph 1:5. [8]Rom 11:16. [9]Jn 1:29. [10]Mt 22:12. [11]FC 58:116-17*. [12]Phil 2:7. [13]FC 14:100-101*. [14]Heb 1:13.

former place, for the word *until* showed not what should take place immediately, but over the course of time. Nevertheless, here he follows it up. For do not suppose, he says, that because they have not yet been made subject, they are not to be made subject; for that they must be made subject is evident. It is on this account that the prophecy was spoken. "For," he says, "in that he has put all things under him, he left nothing not put under him." How then is it that all things have not been put under him? Because they are hereafter to be put under him. ON THE EPISTLE TO THE HEBREWS 4.2.[15]

2:9 We See Jesus

THE MAN JESUS. THEODORE OF MOPSUESTIA: Jesus is a man. For "what is man that you are mindful of him?"[16] Yet the apostle asserts that this passage refers to Jesus, for he says, "We see him who was made a little lower than the angels, Jesus." What then do we conclude? The man Jesus was like all humans and differed in no way from those whose nature he shares, save that to him a grace was given. The grace that was given does not change his nature. But after death was destroyed, "God gave him the name which is above every name."[17] The one who gave is God. The one to whom it was given is the man Jesus Christ, the first fruits of those who are raised. For he is the "firstborn from the dead."[18] Therefore, he ascended and sits at the right hand of the Father and is above all. FRAGMENTS ON THE TREATISE ON THE INCARNATION 2.[19]

WHO IS THE MAN? SEVERIAN OF GABALA: He calls it the age to come. Then he adds at last, "we do not yet see everything in subjection to him. But we see Jesus made lower than the angels." Then he applies to Jesus the question, "What is man that you are mindful of him?"[20] For the things common to humanity belong to him. But as the Son himself says, "Out of the mouths of babes and sucklings I will establish praise for the sake of your enemies" and "I will

see the heavens, the works of your fingers."[21] No one would say that the man God remembered had made "the praise established from the mouth of babes and infants for the sake of your enemies" and "I will see the heavens, the works of your fingers."[22] This one remembered humanity and lowered himself a little lower than the angels. But who is the "man"? Jesus. Because of the suffering of his death, "he was made a little lower than the angels." FRAGMENTS ON THE EPISTLE TO THE HEBREWS 2.5-9.[23]

THE TEXT READS "BY THE GRACE OF GOD." OECUMENIUS: Note that the Nestorians stumble against the Scripture and so they read "so that without God he tasted death for all," constructing the argument that Christ had an indwelling of the Word of God but not union with it, because he did not have his divinity when he was crucified. For they say that it is written "without God he tasted death." But see how a certain orthodox man answered. First, the text reads "by the grace of God."[24] Moreover, even if we understand it to read "apart from [without] God," it ought to be understood in the sense that Christ died for all the other beings except for God, for he died not only for humanity but also for the powers above, that "he might break down the dividing wall"[25] and unite the lower beings with the higher ones. Similar to this is that statement which is said elsewhere, "But when it says, 'All things are put in subjection under him,' it is plain that the One is excepted who put all things under him." FRAGMENTS ON THE EPISTLE TO THE HEBREWS 2.9.[26]

THEY CHANGE "WITHOUT GOD" TO "BY THE GRACE OF GOD." THEODORE OF MOPSUESTIA: Some suffer something very laughable here, changing "without God"[27] and making it to read

---

[15]NPNF 1 14:383**. [16]Ps 8:4 (8:5 LXX). [17]Phil 2:9. [18]Col 1:18. [19]TEM 2:291-92; COS 252*. [20]Heb 2:6; Ps 8:4. [21]Mt 21:16; Ps 8:2-3. [22]Ps 8:3. [23]NTA 15:348. [24]This textual variant in Heb 2:9 is noted in modern critical editions of the New Testament, i.e., "by grace" (*chariti*) or "apart from" (*chōris*)." [25]Eph 2:14. [26]NTA 15:462. [27]Regarding this textual variant, see n. 24 above.

"by the grace of God," not following the Scripture's train of thought. Owing to their failure to understand that he once said, "without God," they erase it to no profit and put in what seems satisfactory to their opinion. Yet what notion would be suggested by Paul inserting "by the grace of God"? And what train of thought would lead him to this? For it is not his custom to append "by the grace of God" capriciously, but always there is some logical train of thought involved. For example, he talks about grace when he, talking about his experience, adds, "by the grace of God I am what I am."[28] Or when it is his task to speak concerning God's love for humankind and that God has done all things, even though we are not worthy to obtain them, as is contained in his statement, "By grace you have been saved,"[29] . . . he appends, "And this not of your own doing, it is the gift of God, not because of works, lest any one should boast."[30] Clearly he shows through this, that he is speaking concerning the grace of God, which he showed on behalf of all people. But in Hebrews Paul is discussing what is being set forth by him concerning Christ, what sort of person he is and how he differs from the angels (the starting point of his discussion), and in what respect he seems to be lower than them because of his death. What need was there then for him to say, "by the grace of God"? It is out of place for him to speak concerning his goodness concerning us.

Instead, the line of argument shows this to be the case when he says, "without God he tasted death," since his divinity was not hindered in this respect, and therefore he showed a diminution "for a short time" from his usual state. He appears also here to share the honor because of his connection with the other nature. It is most natural that those who have heard these things would think that the indwelling of the Word of God would be spectacular at the time of his suffering, even though this does not correspond with the things that have been set forth. Yet "without" God he tasted the trial of death, he adds, "For it was fitting for him, on whose

account all things exist and through whom all things exist, having led many sons into glory while he was the originator of their salvation to be made perfect through suffering." It is not that his divinity was not a contributor, he says. For the usual things "were fitting." . . . For, let me tell you, the fact of suffering in no way was appropriate for it. But clearly this "it was fitting" confirms the notion of "without God." For although it was not fitting, Paul himself says that it is fitting, showing at the same time also what sort of things he once did, and what they were. "For it was fitting for him, because of whom and through whom all things exist." Quite clearly he is speaking about the divine Word, inasmuch as he shared with many his sonship and led them into this glory. He is the "originator" of everybody's "salvation," our Lord and Savior Jesus Christ, the one who is said flatly to have been accepted as a perfect man through his sufferings, so that also Christ's nature and God's grace might be made manifest. FRAGMENTS ON THE EPISTLE TO THE HEBREWS 2.9-10.[31]

APART FROM GOD, HE TASTED DEATH FOR ALL. ORIGEN: We understood the Christ to be the creator, but the Father is greater. He, indeed, who is such great things as "the advocate," "the expiation," "the propitiatory,"[32] because he showed compassion "on our weaknesses" in experiencing temptation "in all things" human "in our likeness, without sin,"[33] is a "great high priest"[34] who offered himself as the sacrifice offered once for all,[35] not for humans alone, but also for every spiritual being. For "apart from God he tasted death for all." This appears in some copies of the epistle to the Hebrews as "by the grace of God."[36]

But whether "apart from God he tasted death for all," he died not only for humans but also for the rest of the spiritual beings, or "by the grace of God he tasted death for all," he died for all apart

---

[28]1 Cor 15:10. [29]Eph 2:8. [30]Eph 2:9. [31]NTA 15:204. [32]1 Jn 2:1-2; Heb 2:17; Rom 3:25. [33]Heb 4:15. [34]Heb 4:14. [35]Cf. Heb 9:28; 7:27; Rom 6:10. [36]Regarding this textual variant, see n. 24 above.

from God, for "by the grace of God he tasted death for all." And, indeed, it would be strange to declare that he tasted death for human sins but not also for any other creature, besides man, that happened to be in sin—for instance, for the stars, since not even the stars are absolutely pure before God. As we have read in Job, "And the stars are not clean in his sight,"[37] unless this was said hyperbolically.

For this reason he is a "great high priest," since he restores all things to the kingdom of the Father, causing the things that are lacking in each of the creatures to be supplied, that they may be able to receive the Father's glory. COMMENTARY ON THE GOSPEL OF JOHN 1.255-58.[38]

SONSHIP BY GRACE. THEODORE OF MOPSUESTIA: In this account of the sonship, the apostle appears to include the man who was assumed with the "many," not because, like them, he received the sonship by grace, since the Godhead alone possesses the sonship by nature. FRAGMENTS ON THE TREATISE ON THE INCARNATION 12.2.[39]

ASSIMILATED TO THE SUFFERINGS OF THE LORD. SYMEON THE NEW THEOLOGIAN: But, if you will, let us look and carefully examine . . . the mystery of that resurrection of Christ our God which takes place mystically in us at all times, if we are willing, and how Christ is buried in us as in a tomb and how he unites himself to our souls and rises again and raises us with himself. Such is the aim of our discourse.

Christ our God was hanged on the cross and nailed on it the sin of the world.[40] He tasted death and went down to the uttermost depths of hell.[41] Again, he returned from hell into his own spotless body, from which he had in no way been separated as he descended there, and immediately he arose from the dead. After that he ascended into heaven with great glory and power.[42] So likewise, as we have now come out of the world and entered into the tomb of repentance and humiliation by being assimilated to the sufferings of the

Lord,[43] he himself comes down from heaven and enters into our body as into a tomb. He unites himself to our souls and raises them up, though they were undoubtedly dead, and then grants to them who have thus been raised with Christ that they may see the glory of his mystical resurrection. DISCOURSE 13.2.[44]

THE FRUIT OF THE CROSS. CHRYSOSTOM: Do you see the fruit of the cross, how great it is? Fear not the matter, for it seems to you indeed to be dismal, but it brings forth innumerable good things. From these considerations he shows the benefit of trial. Then he says, "that by the grace of God he might taste death for every one." "That by the grace of God," he says. And he indeed suffered these things because of the grace of God toward us. "He who did not spare his own Son," he says, "but gave him up for us all."[45] Why? He did not owe us this but has done it of grace. And again, in the epistle to the Romans he says, "Much more have the grace of God and the free gift in the grace of that one man Jesus Christ abounded for many."[46] This occurred "that by the grace of God he might taste death for every one," not for the faithful only, but even for the whole world, for he indeed died for all. But what if all have not believed? He has fulfilled his own part. Moreover, he said rightly, "taste death for every one"; he did not say "die." For as if he really was tasting it, when he had spent a little time in the grave, he immediately arose. ON THE EPISTLE TO THE HEBREWS 4.3.[47]

CHRIST TASTING DEATH. CHRYSOSTOM: By saying then "because of the suffering of death," he signified real death, and by saying, "superior to angels," he declared the resurrection. For as a physician, though not needing to taste the food prepared for a sick person, tastes it first himself so that he may persuade the sick person to eat

---

[37]See Job 25:5. [38]FC 80:85-86*. [39]TEM 2:303; COS 247. [40]See Col 2:14. [41]See Eph 4:9. [42]Mt 24:30. [43]Rom 6:5; 2 Cor 1:5; Phil 3:10. [44]SNTD 182*. [45]Rom 8:32. [46]Rom 5:15. [47]NPNF 1 14:383-84*.

with confidence, so also, since all people were afraid of death, . . . he tasted it himself, though he did not need it himself. "For," he says, "the ruler of this world comes and has no power over me."[48] So both the words "by grace" and "might taste death for every one" establish this. ON THE EPISTLE TO THE HEBREWS 4.3.[49]

SUPERIOR TO DEATH BY HIS NATURE. EPHREM THE SYRIAN: God "tasted death for every one," but, because his immortal nature could not die in the flesh in which he died, he who was dead, as it is, did not die. He did not die because of his nature; he nominally clothed himself with death for his love to us. Since he was superior to death by his nature, death could not approach him. COMMENTARY ON THE EPISTLE TO THE HEBREWS.[50]

ALL THINGS NEEDED THE REMEDY. THEODORET OF CYR: Since Paul called him both maker and Lord of the angels, and this seemed somehow beyond belief to those being taught that the nature of the angels is immortal and yet hearing of the passion of Christ the Lord, he was obliged to offer instruction on this as well. He was made less than the angels not in the divine nature but in his suffering humanity; this shared in divine glory after the resurrection. Of course, he endured the suffering for all: everything in possession of created nature needed this healing. He said as much, in fact, "so that apart from God he would taste death for everyone,"[51] only the divine nature is without need (he is saying); all other things needed the remedy of the incarnation. By becoming man God the Word destroyed the power of death; in destroying it he promised us resurrection, to resurrection he linked incorruptibility and immortality, and visible things also will share in incorruptibility. INTERPRETATION OF HEBREWS 2.[52]

---

[48]Jn 14:30. [49]NPNF 1 14:384**. [50]EHA 200. [51]Regarding this textual variant, see n. 24 above. [52]PG 82:692-93; TCCLSP 2:146.

2:10-18 THE PIONEER OF OUR SALVATION

[10]*For it was fitting that he, for whom and by whom all things exist, in bringing many sons to glory, should make the pioneer of their salvation perfect through suffering.* [11]*For he who sanctifies and those who are sanctified have all one origin. That is why he is not ashamed to call them brethren,* [12]*saying,*

"*I will proclaim thy name to my brethren,*
in the midst of the congregation I will praise thee."
[13]*And again,*
"*I will put my trust in him.*"
And again,
"*Here am I, and the children God has given me.*"
[14]*Since therefore the children share in flesh and blood, he himself likewise partook of the same nature, that through death he might destroy him who has the power of death, that is, the devil,*

15and deliver all those who through fear of death were subject to lifelong bondage. 16For surely it is not with angels that he is concerned but with the descendants of Abraham. 17Therefore he had to be made like his brethren in every respect, so that he might become a merciful and faithful high priest in the service of God, to make expiation for the sins of the people. 18For because he himself has suffered and been tempted, he is able to help those who are tempted.

OVERVIEW: Christ is the pioneer or captain of salvation. He is the Savior; we are the saved. He is the cause of our salvation. Perfection in suffering here means that the one who suffers for another becomes more glorious, but this is no addition to Christ. All are unified in the purpose of Christ's sufferings, namely, to redeem the world from suffering, which is a "far greater thing than making the world and bringing it out of things that are not" (CHRYSOSTOM). Those sufferings made his divine nature as well as God's grace evident (THEODORE). The one who made all things to exist cannot himself be a creature (ATHANASIUS). He is the Son of God by nature; we are God's sons by grace (THEODORET), and thus are the Lord's siblings by grace (CHRYSOSTOM, PHOTIUS, AUGUSTINE, THEODORET). He incorporates us into his own body (THEODORE). Cyril of Alexandria emphasizes the unity of the two natures in the person of Christ in the economy of salvation: "For existing essentially as life, the only begotten Word of God united himself to earthly and mortal flesh in order that death, which was pursuing it like some wild beast, might thereafter relax its hold."

Ambrose asserts that Christ is both the victim and the high priest. Maximus the Confessor explains that Christ destroys death through death by casting at the devil the weapon of the flesh that had vanquished Adam; the flesh became poison to the devil in order that he might vomit up all those whom he had swallowed up in death. In high rhetorical style, Eusebius shows how Christ pursued death from behind and drove it on until he burst the eternal gates of its dark realms and made a return road back to life for the dead in bondage there. Chrysostom uses the same image of pursuit to refer to human nature: "For

when human nature was fleeing from him (and fleeing far away . . .), he pursued after and overtook us."

In his baptism, Jesus imparted grace and dignity on those baptized (CYRIL OF JERUSALEM). When he surrendered his life to receive it again, he destroyed death, liberated us from the bondage of the devil (CHRYSOSTOM) and restored our nature to incorruption (CYRIL OF ALEXANDRIA). Through his death, Christ annihilated fear of death (PHOTIUS). When the veil in the temple was torn, the things of heaven were revealed (GREGORY OF NAZIANZUS). Cyril of Alexandria insists on the organic and indivisible unity of human and divine in Christ. That Jesus shares our humanity makes us his brothers. His incarnation, death and resurrection were real, not illusory (CHRYSOSTOM). Ephrem summarizes what all of the Fathers are agreed upon, namely, that because Christ experienced passions and temptations by being connatural with us, he was able to help those who are infirm and victims of temptation. The Lord took hold of us and wrought innumerable good things. In doing so, he sympathized with our sufferings. His overcoming temptations teaches us to overcome our daily temptations (CHRYSOSTOM, PHOTIUS).

2:10 *Bringing Many to Glory*

HE ALWAYS HAD THAT GLORY BY NATURE.
CHRYSOSTOM: By saying "to make perfect through suffering," he shows that the one who suffers for someone not only helps him but becomes himself more glorious and more perfect. . . . But when I say he was glorified, do not suppose there was an addition of glory to him; for he always had that glory by nature and received

nothing in addition. ON THE EPISTLE TO THE HEBREWS 4.4.[1]

PERFECT THROUGH SUFFERINGS. THEODORE OF MOPSUESTIA:

And the pioneer of all men's salvation, our Lord and Savior Jesus Christ, the man assumed by him, is declared perfect through sufferings in such a way that both his own nature and God's grace are made evident. COMMENTARY ON HEBREWS 2.9-10.[2]

GREATER THAN CREATING THE WORLD. CHRYSOSTOM:

Sufferings are a perfecting and a cause of salvation. Do you see that to suffer affliction is not the fate of those who are utterly forsaken, if indeed it was by leading him through sufferings that God first honored his Son? And truly, his taking flesh to suffer what he suffered is a far greater thing than creating the world out of things that are not. This is indeed a token of his lovingkindness, but the other far more. ON THE EPISTLE TO THE HEBREWS 4.4.[3]

WE WERE MADE FOR HIM. ATHANASIUS:

If all things made by the will of God were made by God, how can God be one of the things that were made? And since the apostle says, "for whom and by whom *all* things exist," how can these men say we were not made for him, but he for us? LETTER TO THE BISHOPS OF EGYPT 2.15.[4]

TOGETHER WITH THE SON, YET SEPARATE. CHRYSOSTOM:

God has done what is worthy of God's love toward humankind in showing the firstborn to be more glorious than all and in setting him forth as an example to the others, like some noble wrestler who surpasses the rest.

Paul says, "The pioneer of their salvation," that is, the cause of their salvation. Do you see what a vast difference there is between the two? He is a Son, and we are sons and daughters; but he saves, and we are saved. Do you see how Paul both brings us together and then separates us? By saying, "bringing many sons to glory," he brings us together; by saying, "the pioneer of their salva-

tion," he separates us. ON THE EPISTLE TO THE HEBREWS 4.4.[5]

2:11-12 Not Ashamed to Call Us Siblings

WE ARE SONS AND DAUGHTERS BY GRACE. THEODORET OF CYR:

"The one who sanctifies and those who are sanctified have all one origin." This is a reference to the humanity of the one who sanctifies, for the assumed nature is created. The creator of him and of us is one. We are sanctified through him. Now if the heretics wish to understand this of the divine nature, let them not do so in such a way as to lessen the glory of the only begotten. For both we and he have one Father; but it is clear that he is Son by nature, we by grace. The fact that it says, "He sanctifies, but we are sanctified," teaches us this difference. INTERPRETATION OF HEBREWS 2.[6]

CLOTHED AS OUR SIBLING. CHRYSOSTOM:

"He is not ashamed to call them brethren." Do you see how again he shows the superiority? For by saying, "he is not ashamed," he shows that the whole comes not of the nature of the thing but of the loving affection of him who was "not ashamed" of anything, yes, of his great humility. For though we are "of one origin," yet he sanctifies and we are sanctified, and great is the difference. Moreover "he" is of the Father as a true Son, that is, of his substance; "we" as created, that is, brought out of things that are not, so that the difference is great. Therefore he says, "He is not ashamed to call them brethren, saying, 'I will declare your name to my brothers and sisters.'"[7] For when he clothed himself with flesh, he clothed himself also with his siblings, and at the same time came in human form. ON THE EPISTLE TO THE HEBREWS 4.5.[8]

GOD BY NATURE, BROTHER BY GRACE. PHO-

---

[1]NPNF 1 14:384**. [2]PG 66:957; COS 236*. [3]NPNF 1 14:384**. [4]PG 25:572; COS 75; NPNF 2 4:231. [5]NPNF 1 14:384**. [6]PG 82:693; TCCLSP 2:147. [7]Ps 22:22 (21:23 LXX). [8]NPNF 1 14:384*.

tius: "He will not be ashamed." He highlighted the difference. Even though he is truly human, he is our brother not according to nature but according to his love toward humankind, as he remains truly God. Fragments on the Epistle to the Hebrews 2.11.[9]

Born unto God's Grace. Augustine: Insofar as he is the only begotten, he is without sibling, but insofar as he is the "firstborn" he has deigned to call all those his siblings who, subsequent to and in virtue of his being first, are born again unto God's grace through filial adoption, in accordance with the teaching of the apostle. On Faith and the Creed 4.6.[10]

Clothed with Our Nature. Theodoret of Cyr: How would it be possible to name him our brother or to call us sons and daughters properly if it were not for the nature—the same as ours—with which he was clothed? . . . And it was especially necessary for Paul to say "in the same way" so that he might refute the reproach of making the incarnation a fantasy. He makes all of these points in order to teach those who suppose that the Son was lower than the angels that he endured suffering for a necessary reason. He explains this more clearly in what follows. Interpretation of Hebrews 2.14-15.[11]

2:13 Children God Has Given

He Makes Us His Own Body. Theodore of Mopsuestia: He [Christ] has given us in holy baptism regeneration, and by this he makes us his own body, his own flesh, his offspring—as it is written, "Here am I, and the children God has given me."[12] Catechetical Homilies 16.25.[13]

Masters and Slaves, Brethren and Children. Theodoret of Cyr: The phrase "he is not ashamed" suffices to bring out the difference in sonship. Speaking of masters and slaves we are accustomed to bring out the humility of masters by saying, "He is not afraid to eat and drink with his servants, to sit with them and personally to tend those of them who are ill." So this is what he is implying here as well, that the one who for our sakes accepted suffering is not ashamed to call "brethren" those for whom he endured the suffering—and not only "brethren," he also calls them "children." Likewise the Lord in the sacred Gospels said to the divine apostles, "Little children, yet a little while I am with you," and again, "Children, have you any fish?"[14] He also shows that what is said in lowly fashion is said in reference to the incarnation: to the phrase "he is not ashamed" he linked "I shall have trust in him," that is, he is not ashamed on account of the salvation of humankind even to use language at variance with his own dignity. Interpretation of Hebrews 2.[15]

2:14 Destroying the Power of Death

Some Wild Beast. Cyril of Alexandria: For existing essentially as life, the only begotten Word of God united himself to earthy and mortal flesh in order that death, which was pursuing it like some wild beast, might thereafter relax its hold . . . Indeed, if the only begotten Word of God did not become human, but rather united to himself the external form [prosōpon] of a man, as is the opinion of those who define the union only by good pleasure and by an inclination of will, how would he be likened to "his brethren in all respects"? . . . How would he have "shared in blood and flesh" unless these had become his own as they are ours? Commentary on Hebrews.[16]

Rising Like Dough. Maximus the Confessor: He destroys the tyranny of the evil one who dominated us by deceit. By casting at him as a weapon the flesh that was vanquished in Adam, he overcame him. Thus what was previously captured for death conquers the conqueror and

---

[9]NTA 15:640. [10]FC 27:323**. [11]PG 82:696; COS 301-2**. [12]Is 8:17-18. [13]HCTM 575*. [14]Jn 13:33, 21:5. [15]PG 82:693-696; TCCLSP 2:147*. [16]PEP 3:394-95; COS 343.

destroys his life by a natural death. It became poison to him in order that he might vomit up all those whom he had swallowed when he held sway by having the power of death. But it became life to the human race by impelling the whole of nature to rise like dough to resurrection of life.[17] It was for this especially that the Logos, who is God, became human—something truly unheard of—and voluntarily accepted the death of the flesh. THE LORD'S PRAYER 348.[18]

THE LAWS OF LOVE. EUSEBIUS OF CAESAREA: Now the laws of love summoned him even as far as death and the dead themselves, so that he might summon the souls of those who were long dead. And so, because he cared for the salvation of all for ages past, and in order that "he might destroy him who has the power of death," as Scripture teaches, here again he underwent the dis-pensation in his mingled natures. As a man, he left his body to the usual burial, while as God he departed from it. For he cried with a loud cry and said to the Father, "I commend my spirit,"[19] and departed from the body free, in no way waiting for death, who was lagging as if in fear to come to him. Nay, rather, he pursued death from behind and drove him on, trodden under his feet and fleeing, until he burst the eternal gates of his dark realms, making a road of return back again to life for the dead there bound with the bonds of death. Even his own body was raised up, and many bodies of the sleeping saints arose and came together with him into the holy and real city of heaven, as rightly is said by the holy words.[20] . . .

The Savior of the universe, our Lord, the Christ of God, called victor, is represented in the prophetic predictions as reviling death and releasing the souls that are bound there, by whom he raises the hymn of victory. And he says these words: "From the hand of Hades I will save them, and from death I will ransom their souls. O Death where is your victory? O Death, where is your sting?"[21] "The sting of death is sin, and the power of sin is the law."[22] PROOF OF THE GOSPEL 4.12.[23]

BAPTISM DRAWS DEATH'S STING. CYRIL OF JERUSALEM: Jesus sanctified baptism when he himself was baptized. If the Son of God was baptized, can anyone who scorns baptism pretend to piety? Not that he was baptized to receive the remission of sins—for he was without sin—but, being sinless, he was nevertheless baptized that he might impart grace and dignity to those who receive the sacrament. For, "since the children share in flesh and blood, he himself likewise partook of the same nature," that we, sharing his incarnate life, might also share his divine grace. Thus Jesus was baptized that we, in turn, so made partakers with him, might receive not only salvation but also the dignity. The dragon, according to Job, was in the water, he who received the Jordan in his maw.[24] When, therefore, it was necessary to crush the heads of the dragon,[25] descending into the water, he bound the strong one, that we might receive the "power to tread upon serpents and scorpions."[26] It was no ordinary beast, but a horrible monster. No fishing ship could last under a single scale of his tail; before him stalked destruction, ravaging all in her path.[27] But life came running up, that that maw of death might be stopped and all we who were saved might say, "O death, where is your sting? O grave, where is your victory?"[28] Baptism draws death's sting. CATECHETICAL LECTURES 3.11.[29]

THE WORD BECAME FLESH. CYRIL OF ALEXANDRIA: We say that he partook of blood and flesh in accordance with the meaning established by the interpreters of God. By "he" we do not mean the one who was in flesh and blood by his own nature and could not exist otherwise, but rather the one who never existed in this way and was of a nature different from ours. . . . For the Word became flesh, only not sinful flesh. . . . He was God and human at the same time. ON THE UNITY OF CHRIST 744.[30]

---

[17]Cf. Rom 11:15-16; 1 Cor 5:6-7. [18]PG 90:880-81. [19]Lk 23:46. [20]Eusebius refers to Is 25:7-8. [21]Hos 13:14; 1 Cor 15:54-55. [22]1 Cor 15:56. [23]POG 1:186-87*. [24]Job 40:15-23; 7:12. [25]Ps 74:13 (73:13 LXX). [26]Lk 10:19. [27]See Job 41:2, 31-33. [28]1 Cor 15:55; Hos 13:14. [29]FC 61:115*. [30]SC 97:402; COS 346.

The Veil Is Rent. Gregory of Nazianzus: He surrenders his life, yet has the power to take it again.[31] Yes, the veil is rent, for things of heaven are being revealed, rocks are being split, and dead men have an earlier awakening.[32] He dies but he brings to life,[33] and by death he destroys death. He is buried, yet he rises again. He goes down to hades, yet he leads souls up,[34] ascends to heaven, and will come to judge the quick and dead. On the Son, Theological Oration 3(29).20.[35]

Jesus Christ Must Not Be Divided. Cyril of Alexandria: Therefore, the one Lord Jesus Christ must not be divided into two sons. The correct expression of the faith is not assisted by taking this line, even when some allege that there is a union of persons, for Scripture says not that the Logos united to himself the person of the human being but that he became flesh. And for the Logos to become flesh is nothing other than for him to "share flesh and blood as we do," to make his own a body from among us, and to be born of a woman as a human being. He did not depart from his divine status or cease to be born of the Father; he continued to be what he was, even in taking on flesh. This is what the correct teaching of the faith everywhere proclaims. And this is how we shall find the holy fathers conceived things. Accordingly, they boldly called the Virgin "God's mother" (*Theotokos*) not because the nature of the Logos or the deity took the start of its existence in the holy Virgin, but because the holy body which was born of her possessed a rational soul to which the Logos was hypostatically united and was said to have had a fleshly birth. Second Letter to Nestorius.[36]

Priest and Victim Are One. Ambrose: See in what way the writer calls him created: "In so far as he took upon him the seed of Abraham," plainly asserting the begetting of a body. How else, indeed, but in his body did he expiate the sins of the people? In what did he suffer, except in his body—even as we said above: "Christ having suffered in the flesh"? In what is he a priest, except in that which he took to himself from the priestly nation? It is a priest's duty to offer something, and, according to the law, to enter into the holy places by means of blood. Seeing then that God had rejected the blood of bulls and goats, this High Priest was indeed bound to make passage and entry into the holy of holies in heaven through his own blood in order that he might be the everlasting propitiation for our sins. Priest and victim, then, are one; the priesthood and sacrifice are, however, exercised under the conditions of humanity, for he was led as a lamb to the slaughter, and he is a priest after the order of Melchizedek. On the Christian Faith 3.11 [86-87].[37]

The Likeness Is in the Flesh. Chrysostom: "Since therefore the children," he says, "share in flesh and blood," do you see where he says the likeness is? It is in reference to the flesh that "he himself likewise partook of the same." Let all the heretics be ashamed, let those hide their faces who say that he came in appearance and not in reality. For he did not say, "he took part of these" only and then say no more, although, had he said thus, it would have been sufficient. Rather he asserted something more, adding "likewise"— not in appearance, he means, or by an image, but in reality, showing his brotherhood with us. On the Epistle to the Hebrews 4.5.[38]

Strong Weapon Against the World. Chrysostom: Next he sets down also the cause of the economy of salvation, "that through death," he says, "he might destroy him who has the power of death, that is, the devil." Here [Paul] points out the wonder that, by that through which the devil prevailed, [the devil] was himself overcome. By the very thing that was [the devil's] strong weapon against the world—death— Christ struck him. In this Christ exhibits the

---

[31]Jn 10:17-18. [32]Mt 27:51-52. [33]Jn 5:21. [34]Eph 4:8-9; Ps 68:18 (67:19 LXX). [35]*FGFR* 260. [36]CC 134-35. [37]NPNF 2 10:255. [38]NPNF 1 14:385*.

greatness of the conqueror's power. Do you see what great goodness death has wrought? ON THE EPISTLE TO THE HEBREWS 4.6.[39]

SIN IS THE POWER OF DEATH. OECUMENIUS: And how does he rule over death? Since he rules over sin from which death has its power, he also rules over death. Sin, at any rate, is the power of death. Then having a sacrifice for sin and being the agent of the sacrifice, he has the power over death. . . . Through his own death he rendered sin ineffective and held the devil under his power, who is the strength and power of death. For if sin had not had power over humankind, death would not have entered the world. FRAGMENTS ON THE EPISTLE TO THE HEBREWS 2.14.[40]

CHRIST CONQUERED THE FEAR OF DEATH. PHOTIUS: Human beings had been afraid of death because they are held in slavery. The slavery of death means to be a subject of sin. "The sting of death is sin."[41] Now, by his death Christ destroyed "the one who has the power of death, that is, the devil," the inventor and the leader of sin. Sin became a disease. However, as we have been released from the oppression of that slavery, so we have been also delivered from the fear of death. And that is evident from the following illustrations. Before we feared and tried to avoid death as the supreme and invincible evil, but now we perceive it as prelude transition into the superior life and accept it joyously from those who persecute us for the sake of Christ and his commandments. FRAGMENTS ON THE EPISTLE TO THE HEBREWS 2.14-15.[42]

2:15 Lifelong Bondage

NO SENSE OF PLEASURE. CHRYSOSTOM: But what does it mean that "through fear of death were subject to lifelong bondage"? He either means that he who fears death is a slave and submits to all things rather than die; or that all people were slaves of death and were held under death's power because he had not yet been done

away. Or [it means] that people lived in continual fear, ever expecting that they should die, and, being afraid of death, could have no sense of pleasure while this fear was present with them. ON THE EPISTLE TO THE HEBREWS 4.6.[43]

YOKE OF MORTALITY. THEODORET OF CYR: How is it possible, he is saying, for Christ to style himself our brother or call us really children unless he bears the same nature? Hence on assuming it he overcame the influence of death and did away with the dread besetting us. We lived ever in the dread of death because we were forced to haul the yoke of mortality. Now, it was very necessary for him to use the phrase "likewise" so as to refute the calumny of mere appearance. INTERPRETATION OF HEBREWS 2.[44]

THOSE WHOM THE FEAR OF DEATH RULED. EPHREM THE SYRIAN: "Since therefore the children," summoned through his promise, "share in flesh and blood," that is sin, as signified by flesh, "and he himself likewise partook of the same nature" in the likeness of flesh, he was mingled with them, so that he might become for them a model of goodness. He consigned himself to death, so that through his death "he might destroy him who has the power of death, that is, the devil," who instilled death into living creatures when the fruit was eaten. So he died in order "to free," through his death, those over whom the fear of death ruled and "who were, for all their lives, subject to the slavery of eternal death." You do not receive the medicine that vivifies your life from angels, but from the seed itself of Abraham, to whom it was said, "In your seed all nations will be blessed."[45] "So he had to become similar in everything . . ." to the children of Abraham, "in order to become as merciful" as Moses, who, as an image of the Son, devoted himself to the salvation of the children of his nation. And [he had to be-

---

[39]NPNF 1 14:385*. [40]NTA 15:462-63. [41]1 Cor 15:56. [42]NTA 15:640. [43]NPNF 1 14:385*. [44]PG 82:696; TCCLSP 2:147-48. [45]Gen 22:18.

come similar] also in order to become faithful and save all the nations from death, like Aaron, who in the mystery of the Son repelled death from the children of his generation by using the censor, which he received to oppose death.[46] God appointed him high priest not for those things which are generously given to us through sacrifices, as through Eleazar,[47] but for those which are spiritually granted to us in him: that is, in order that he becomes the propitiator through baptism and not through aspersion.

"Because he himself has suffered and been tempted"—that is, he was tempted through his becoming connatural with us—he is able to assist those who are infirm in their weakness and victims of temptation. In fact, he is now made aware of . . . the weakness of flesh and knows humans more fully after clothing himself with flesh. COMMENTARY ON THE EPISTLE TO THE HEBREWS.[48]

LAUGHING DEATH TO SCORN. CHRYSOSTOM: He shows not only that death has been put to an end, but also that thereby he who is ever showing that war without truce against us—I mean the devil—has been brought to nothing; since he fears that death is not out of reach of the devil's tyranny. "Skin for skin! All that a man has he will give for his life."[49] When anyone has determined to disregard even this, of what then will he be the slave? He fears no one, he is in terror of no one, he is higher than all and freer than all. For he who disregards his own life will much more disregard all other things. And when the devil finds a soul such as this, he can accomplish in it none of his works. Why? Tell me, shall he threaten with loss of property and degradation and banishment from one's country? But these are small matters to him who "counts not even his life dear,"[50] according to the blessed Paul. You see that, in casting out the tyranny of death, he also overthrew the strength of the devil. For him who has learned to study innumerable truths concerning the resurrection, why should he fear death? Why should he shudder any more?

Therefore, do not be grieved, saying, "Why do we suffer such and such things?" For so the victory becomes more glorious. And it would not have been glorious unless by death he had destroyed death; but the most wonderful thing is that he conquered him by the very means by which he was strong, showing at every point the abundance of his means and the excellence of his plans. Let us not then prove false to the gift bestowed on us. "For God," he says, "did not give us a spirit of timidity, but a spirit of power and love and self-control."[51] Let us stand then nobly, laughing death to scorn. ON THE EPISTLE TO THE HEBREWS 4.6-7.[52]

2:16 The Descendants of Abraham

REALLY AN INCARNATION. CYRIL OF ALEXANDRIA: For if it was a shadow and an appearance and not really an incarnation, then the Virgin did not give birth, nor did the Word from God the Father assume "the seed of Abraham,"[53] nor did he become "like his brothers." . . . Therefore, if the Word did not become flesh, neither was he tested by what he suffered so as to be able to help those who are tested. ON THE INCARNATION 681.[54]

SEED OF ABRAHAM. THEODORET OF CYR: It was very wise of the divine apostle to use the proper name instead of a generic name: he did not say, "He takes hold of human seed," but "He takes hold of Abraham's seed,"[55] reminding them also of the promise made to Abraham. INTERPRETATION OF HEBREWS 2.[56]

GREAT THINGS CONCERNING THE HUMAN RACE. CHRYSOSTOM: Paul, wishing to show the great kindness of God toward humans and the love which God had for the human race, after saying, "Since therefore the children share in flesh

---

[46]Num 16:46-48. [47]Num 20:25-28. [48]EHA 200-201. [49]Job 2:4. [50]Acts 20:24. [51]2 Tim 1:7. [52]NPNF 1 14:385*. [53]*Spermatos Abraam*, "seed [singular] of Abraham," is translated as "descendants of Abraham" in RSV. [54]SC 97:198; COS 345. [55]See n. 53 above. [56]PG 82:696; TCCLSP 2:148.

and blood, he himself likewise partook of the same," follows up the subject in this passage. For do not regard lightly what is spoken, or think it a trifle, that he takes on our flesh. . . . "For truly he does not take hold of angels, but rather of the seed of Abraham." What is it that he says? He took on not an angel's nature, but humanity's. But what is "he takes hold of"? . . . Why did he not say, "he took on him," but "he takes hold of"? It is derived from the image of persons pursuing those who turn away from them, doing everything to overtake them as they flee and to take hold of them as they are bounding away. For when human nature was fleeing from him (and fleeing far away, for we "were far off,")[57] he pursued after and overtook us. He showed that he has done this only out of kindness and love and tender care. When he says, "Are they not all ministering spirits, sent forth to serve for the sake of those who are to obtain salvation,"[58] he shows his extreme interest in behalf of human nature and that God makes great account of it. So also in this place he sets it forth much more by a comparison, for he says, "he does not take hold of angels." For indeed it is a great and a wonderful thing and full of amazement that our flesh should sit on high and be adored by angels and archangels, by the cherubim and the seraphim. For having oftentimes thought upon this myself, I am amazed at it and imagine to myself great things concerning the human race. On the Epistle to the Hebrews 5.1.[59]

Improving Our State. Cyril of Alexandria: The Only Begotten operated not through his own nature, for that would in no way have improved our state, or through the nature of angels; but he operated through "the seed of Abraham," as Scripture has it. For in this way and no other could the race, fallen into corruption, be restored to salvation. On the Incarnation 684.[60]

He Paid Humankind's Debt. Theodoret of Cyr: If he had assumed the nature of angels, he would have proved superior to death; but since what he assumed was human, through the passion he paid humankind's debt, while through the resurrection of the body that had suffered he demonstrated his own power. Interpretation of Hebrews 2.[61]

2:17 High Priest

Ways Beyond Number. Chrysostom: He that is so great, he that is "the brightness of his glory," he that is "the express image of his person," he that "made the worlds," he that "sits on the right hand of the Father,"[62] he was willing and earnest to become our sibling in all things, and for this cause did he leave the angels and the other powers and come down to us; he took hold of us and wrought innumerable good things. He destroyed death, he cast out the devil from his tyranny, he freed us from bondage. Not as a sibling alone did he honor us, but also in other ways beyond number. For he was willing also to become our high priest with the Father; for he adds, "that he might become a merciful and faithful high priest in things pertaining to God." For this cause, he means, he took on himself our flesh, only for love to humankind, that he might have mercy upon us. For neither is there any other cause of the economy, but this alone. For he saw us cast on the ground, perishing, tyrannized over by death, and he had compassion on us. On the Epistle to the Hebrews 5.1-2.[63]

2:18 Able to Help Those Who Are Tempted

The Flesh Itself Suffered Many Fearful Things. Chrysostom: "For," he says, "because he himself has suffered and been tempted, he is able to help those who are tempted." This seems altogether low and mean and unworthy of God— to suffer and be tempted. "For because he himself has suffered," he says. But it is of him who was

---

[57]Eph 2:13. [58]Heb 1:14. [59]NPNF 1 14:388*. [60]SC 97:208; COS 344. [61]PG 82:696; TCCLSP 2:148. [62]Heb 1:2-3. [63]NPNF 1 14:389**.

made flesh that he here speaks. This was said for the full assurance of the hearers and on account of their weakness. That is, he would say, he went through the very experience of that which we have suffered. Now he is not ignorant of our sufferings, not only because as God he knows them, but also because as man he knows them through the trial with which he was tested. Since he suffered many things, he knows how to sympathize with suffering. It is certainly true that God is impassible, but the statement here is made of the incarnation, as though it were said, "The flesh of Christ itself suffered many fearful things." He knows what tribulation is. He knows what temptation is, not less than we who have suffered, for he himself also has suffered. ON THE EPISTLE TO THE HEBREWS 5.2.[64]

HE EXTENDS ASSISTANCE TO THOSE UNDER ATTACK. THEODORET OF CYR: He presented his saving death as an offering: the body he had assumed he offered for the whole of creation. He included something else as well for their consolation: having learned by experience the weakness of human nature in living under the law and under grace, he extends assistance to those under attack. This is said in respect of humanity: he is our high priest not as God but as human; he suffered not as God but as human; it was not as God that he learned our condition, but as God and creator he has a clear grasp of everything. INTERPRETATION OF HEBREWS 2.[65]

AFFLICTIONS THAT BEFALL US EVERY DAY. CHRYSOSTOM: Even if there is no persecution or tribulation, still there are other afflictions that befall us every day, and if we do not bear these, we should scarcely endure those. "No temptation has overtaken you," it is said, "that is not common to man."[66] Let us then indeed pray to God that we may not come into temptation; but if we come into it, let us bear it nobly. For it is indeed a trait of prudent people not to throw themselves upon dangers; but this is the trait of noble persons and true philosophers. Let us not lightly cast

ourselves upon dangers, for that is rashness; but, if we are led into them and called by circumstances, let us not yield, for that is cowardice, and, if indeed the gospel calls us, let us not refuse. In a simple case, when there is no reason or need or necessity that calls us in the fear of God, let us not rush in, for this is mere display and useless ambition. But should any of those things which are injurious to religion occur, then, though it be necessary to endure ten thousand deaths, let us refuse nothing. Do not risk trials when you find things that concern godliness prospering as you desire. Why draw down needless dangers that bring no gain?

These things I say because I wish you to observe the laws of Christ, who commands us to "pray that we may not enter into temptation"[67] and commands us to "take up the cross and follow" him.[68] For these things are not contradictory; rather, they are exceedingly in harmony. Do be prepared like a valiant soldier. Be continually in your armor, sober, watchful and ever looking for the enemy. Do not, however, breed wars, for this is not the act of a soldier but of a mover of sedition. But if . . . the trumpet of godliness calls you, go forth immediately and make no account of your life, and enter with great eagerness into the contests, break the phalanx of the adversaries, bruise the face of the devil, set up your trophy. If, however, godliness is in nowise harmed, and if no one lays waste to our doctrines (those, I mean, which relate to the soul) or compels us to do anything displeasing to God, do not be meddlesome. ON THE EPISTLE TO THE HEBREWS 5.7.[69]

THE POWER OF JESUS IS THE POWER OF THE CROSS. PHOTIUS: "He is able to help those who are tempted" . . . should be interpreted as follows. As the sinless body of the Lord was subjected to the evil and the temptations of suffering befell it . . . therefore, having the sinless body, having been tried and having suffered, he has the

[64]NPNF 1 14:389**. [65]PG 82:696-97; *TCCLSP* 2:148. [66]1 Cor 10:13. [67]Mt 26:41. [68]Mt 16:24. [69]NPNF 1 14:392*.

just and blessed power over evil, can deliver humans who are dying under sin from the temptations that fall on them, and he can defend from the temptations. If the Lord had righteous and blessed power over the audacious evil that tempted his sinless body, he also is able to release those who are subject to sin and temptations and to be the helper of those who are tempted. FRAGMENTS ON THE EPISTLE TO THE HEBREWS 2.18.[70]

---

[70]NTA 15:640-41.

3:1-6 CHRIST IS SUPERIOR TO MOSES

Therefore, holy brethren, who share in a heavenly call, consider Jesus, the apostle and high priest of our confession. [2]He was faithful to him who appointed him, just as Moses also was faithful in[e] God's house. [3]Yet Jesus has been counted worthy of as much more glory than Moses as the builder of a house has more honor than the house. [4](For every house is built by some one, but the builder of all things is God.) [5]Now Moses was faithful in all God's house as a servant, to testify to the things that were to be spoken later, [6]but Christ was faithful over God's[f] house as a son. And we are his house if we hold fast our confidence and pride in our hope.[g]

e Other ancient authorities insert *all*   f Greek *his*   g Other ancient authorities insert *firm to the end*

OVERVIEW: Basil was concerned that this text implied that Jesus was made an apostle and high priest, but he explains it metaphorically, noting that he was made a way, a door, a shepherd, a messenger, a sheep, a high priest and an apostle, "different names given according to the different conceptions." As apostle, Jesus is God's envoy to humanity (JUSTIN MARTYR). As high priest, he enters God's presence to bring humanity close to God, first by his resurrection from the dead and then by sitting at the right hand of God. He becomes the pledge for our ascension into heaven (THEODORE). It is clear to the Fathers that the author of Hebrews carefully proclaims Jesus much more worthy than Moses. Ephrem summarizes this concept: "Since he said, 'as Moses,' do not think that he is as Moses. . . . The honor of the Lord and the Son is greater than that of the ser-

vant Moses. In truth, Christ is not a faithful servant like Moses, but 'as a son' he was faithful, and not over the shrine of the temple, but over the souls of people." The figure of Moses highlights Jesus' humanity and divinity (PHOTIUS).

3:1 Consider Jesus

COMPARISON WITH MOSES. THEODORET OF CYR: After having in this fashion completed the comparison with the angels, he makes a parallel with the mighty Moses, greater than all the prophets, so that after showing the difference to be infinite, he may show at the same time the contrast between the covenants, the promises and of course the priests. Once again he mingles exhortation with the comparison lest he seem to be doing it on purpose rather than under pressure of a kind of necessity. INTERPRETATION OF HEBREWS 3.[1]

DOOR, SHEPHERD, MESSENGER, SHEEP, PRIEST AND APOSTLE. BASIL THE GREAT: According to the words of the wise Solomon in the Proverbs,[2] he was created. "The Lord," he says, "created me." And he is called "the beginning of the evangelical way" which leads us to the kingdom of heaven, since he is not a creature in substance but was made the "way" in the divine dispensation. For "being made" and "being created" have the same meaning. In fact, as he was made a way, so also was he made a door, a shepherd, a messenger, a sheep, and, in turn, a high priest and apostle, different names given according to the different conceptions. LETTER 8.[3]

GIVING CLOSENESS TO GOD. THEODORE OF MOPSUESTIA: Because it is also the work of a high priest to enter God's presence first and then to bring the others close to him, he [Paul] quite rightly calls him high priest, because he did this in fact. Blessed Paul calls him this because by the resurrection of the dead he ascended into heaven and sat down at the right hand of God, and by these events he gave us, too, closeness to God and participation in the good things. CATECHETICAL HOMILIES 15.16.[4]

APOSTLE AFTER THE INCARNATION. THEODORET OF CYR: For if he were high priest as God, he would be so before the incarnation. As it is, that he became the apostle of our confession after the incarnation is taught us by the epistle to the Galatians: "But when the time had fully come, God sent forth his Son, born of a woman."[5] INTERPRETATION OF HEBREWS 3.1-2.[6]

HEAVENLY THINGS WERE MADE ACCESSIBLE. THEODORE OF MOPSUESTIA: But once for all heavenly things were made accessible to humans, when one of us humans was assumed and, according to the law of human nature, died and was raised from the dead in a marvelous fashion and, because immortal and incorruptible by nature, ascended into heaven. And he became high priest for the rest of humankind and the pledge for their ascension into heaven. CATECHETICAL HOMILIES 12.4.[7]

3:2-5 Faithful in God's House

THE WORD OF GOD IS ALSO CALLED ANGEL AND APOSTLE. JUSTIN MARTYR: The Word of God . . . is also called "angel"[8] and "apostle" for as angel he announces what it is necessary to know, and as apostle he is sent forth to testify to what is announced. As our Lord himself said, "He that hears me hears him that sent me."[9] This can be made clear from the writings of Moses, in which this is to be found: "And the angel of the Lord spoke to Moses in a flame of fire out of the bush and said, 'I am he who is, God of Abraham, God of Isaac, God of Jacob, the God of your fathers; go down to Egypt and bring out my people.' "[10] . . . But these words were uttered to demonstrate that Jesus Christ is the Son of God, an apostle, who was first the Word and appeared, now in the form of fire, now in the image of the bodiless creatures. . . . The Jews, continuing to think that the Father of the universe had spoken to Moses when it was the Son of God, who is called both angel and apostle, who spoke to him, were rightly censured both by the prophetic Spirit and by Christ himself, since they knew neither the Father nor the Son. . . . What was said out of the bush to Moses, "I am he who is the God of Abraham and the God of Isaac and the God of Jacob and the God of your fathers," was an indication that they, though dead, still existed and were Christ's own people. For they were the first of all people to devote themselves to seeking after God, Abraham being the father of Isaac, and Isaac of Jacob, as Moses also recorded. FIRST APOLOGY 63.[11]

---

[1]PG 82:697; TCCLSP 2:148. [2]Prov 8:22. [3]FC 13:33. [4]HCTM 489. [5]Gal 4:4. [6]PG 82:697. [7]HCTM 329*. [8]Ex 3:2. [9]Lk 10:16; Jn 14:24. [10]Ex 3:2-6. [11]LCC 1:284-85*.

A HIGH ESTEEM FOR MOSES. CHRYSOSTOM: Being about to place him before Moses in comparison, Paul led his discourse to the law of the high priesthood; for they all had a high esteem for Moses. . . . Therefore he begins from the flesh and goes up to the Godhead, where there was no longer any comparison. He began from the flesh, from his human nature, by assuming for a time the equality, and says, "as Moses also was faithful in all God's house." Nor does he at first show his superiority, lest the hearers should start away and straightway stop their ears. For although they were believers, yet nevertheless they still had strong feeling of conscience as to Moses. ON THE EPISTLE TO THE HEBREWS 5.4.[12]

MOSES AND CHRIST. THEODORET OF CYR: As great as is the difference between creature and creator, he is saying, so great is the difference between Moses and Christ. INTERPRETATION OF HEBREWS 3.[13]

CREATOR AND CREATION. PHOTIUS: "One who has been worthy of much more glory." He discussed in what ways Moses is equal to Christ, now he talks about Christ's superiority. "Of much more." Who is that? Christ, who is the Word incarnate. "More glory than Moses, just as the builder of a house has more honor than the house itself." Now he talks about the highest superiority of God over human beings. He says Moses was a faithful ruler over the whole household, that is, over the whole people, yet Moses himself was one of them. Therefore, the humanity of Christ is worthy of so much more honor than the honor of Moses, as the creator is superior to the creation, "just as the builder of a house has more honor than the house itself." By "house" he means the people who were with Moses, yet Moses was one of them while Christ was the one who created the house. FRAGMENTS ON THE EPISTLE TO THE HEBREWS 3.3.[14]

FAITHFUL SERVANTS. CLEMENT OF ROME: The apostles received the gospel for us from the Lord Jesus Christ. Jesus, the Christ, was sent from God. Thus Christ is from God and the apostles from Christ. In both instances the orderly procedure depends on God's will. And so the apostles, after receiving their orders and being fully convinced by the resurrection of our Lord Jesus Christ and assured by God's Word, went out in the confidence of the Holy Spirit to preach the good news that God's kingdom was about to come. They preached in country and city and appointed their first converts, after testing them by the Spirit, to be the bishops and deacons of future believers. Nor was this any novelty, for Scripture had mentioned bishops and deacons long before. For this is what Scripture says somewhere: "I will appoint their bishops in righteousness and their deacons in faith."[15]

And is it any wonder that those Christians whom God had entrusted with such a duty should have appointed the officers mentioned? For the blessed Moses too, "who was a faithful servant in all God's house,"[16] recorded in the sacred books all the orders given to him, and the rest of the prophets followed in his train by testifying with him to his legislation. Now, when rivalry for the priesthood arose and the tribes started quarreling as to which of them should be honored with this glorious privilege, Moses asked the twelve tribal chiefs to bring him rods, on each of which was written the name of one of the tribes. These he took and bound, sealing them with the rings of the tribal leaders; and he put them in the tent of the testimony on God's table. Then he shut the tent and put seals on the keys, just as he had on the rods. And he told them, "Brothers, the tribe whose rod puts forth buds is the one God has chosen for the priesthood and for his ministry."[17] Early the next morning he called all Israel together, six hundred thousand strong, and showed the seals to the tribal

---

[12]NPNF 1 14:390*. [13]PG 82:697; *TCCLSP* 2:149. [14]NTA 15:641. [15]See Is 60:17 LXX; "deacons in faith" is not in the text of Scripture. It was common for early Christian authors to give a quotation or even a paraphrase of a scriptural passage from memory; giving the exact text and reference was often not their primary concern. [16]See Num 12:7. [17]See Num 17:1-10.

chiefs and opened the tent of testimony and brought out the rods. And it was discovered that Aaron's rod had not only budded but was actually bearing fruit. What do you think, dear friends? Did not Moses know in advance that this was going to happen? Why, certainly. But he acted the way he did in order to forestall anarchy in Israel and so that the name of the true and only God might be glorified. To him be the glory forever and ever. Amen.

Now our apostles, thanks to our Lord Jesus Christ, knew that there was going to be strife over the title of bishop. It was for this reason and because they had been given an accurate knowledge of the future that they appointed the officers we have mentioned. Furthermore, they later added a codicil to the effect that, should these die, other approved men should succeed to their ministry. In the light of this, we view it as a breach of justice to remove from their ministry those who were appointed either by them (i.e., the apostles) or later on and with the whole church's consent, by others of the proper standing, and who, long enjoying everybody's approval, have ministered to Christ's flock faultlessly, humbly, quietly and unassumingly. For we shall be guilty of no slight sin if we eject from the episcopate men who have

offered the sacrifices with innocence and holiness. 1 CLEMENT 42-44.[18]

3:6 Faithful as a Son

FAITHFUL OVER OUR SOULS. EPHREM THE SYRIAN: But since he said, "as Moses," do not think that he is as Moses; "the glory of this" high priest "is greater than that of Moses inasmuch as the maker of a house has greater honor than the house." Similarly the honor of the Lord and the Son is greater than that of the servant Moses. "Every house was built by someone," but "he who created Moses" and "built all things is God. And Moses was certainly faithful," but as an assistant, "as a servant was faithful to testify to the things that were to be spoken later." In truth Christ is not a faithful servant like Moses, but "as a son" he was faithful, and not over the shrine of the temple but over the souls of people. In fact, "we are his house if we stand firm in his confidence" and are not brought into disorder while "in the glory of his hope." But if we transgress, we cause his suffering. COMMENTARY ON THE EPISTLE TO THE HEBREWS.[19]

---

[18]LCC 1:62-64. [19]EHA 202.

3:7-19 WARNING AND EXHORTATION

[7]Therefore, as the Holy Spirit says,
"Today, when you hear his voice,
[8]do not harden your hearts as in the rebellion,
on the day of testing in the wilderness,
[9]where your fathers put me to the test
and saw my works for forty years.
[10]Therefore I was provoked with that generation,

and said, 'They always go astray in their hearts;
they have not known my ways.'
[11]As I swore in my wrath,
'They shall never enter my rest.'"

[12]*Take care, brethren, lest there be in any of you an evil, unbelieving heart, leading you to fall away*
from the living God. [13]*But exhort one another every day, as long as it is called "today," that none*
of you may be hardened by the deceitfulness of sin. [14]*For we share in Christ, if only we hold our*
first confidence firm to the end, [15]*while it is said,*

"Today, when you hear his voice,
do not harden your hearts as in the rebellion."

[16]*Who were they that heard and yet were rebellious? Was it not all those who left Egypt under the*
leadership of Moses? [17]*And with whom was he provoked forty years? Was it not with those who*
sinned, whose bodies fell in the wilderness? [18]*And to whom did he swear that they should never*
enter his rest, but to those who were disobedient? [19]*So we see that they were unable to enter*
because of unbelief.

OVERVIEW: For the early writers the word *today* in this passage clearly meant for all time. "For as we must not talk of a beginning of the days of Christ, so never suffer anyone to speak of an end of his kingdom" (CYRIL OF JERUSALEM). Hardness of heart causes unbelief (CHRYSOSTOM). "Today" means that they might never be without hope, even if they have sinned. Even if there is unbelief, as long as we are in this world, the "today" is in season (CYRIL OF JERUSALEM, CHRYSOSTOM). Moreover, "today" means that we are called to listen to spiritual advice every day (CASSIODORUS). The evil of unbelief is the ultimate evil as it separates us from the living God (PHOTIUS).

In the Spirit, we have become partakers of Christ, who gives us faith and confidence (CHRYSOSTOM, THEODORE). The sin of "unbelief in the word of God" prevented Hebrew people from entering the promised land under the leadership of Moses (EPHREM). However, that entrance is granted to the Christians under the leadership of Jesus (JEROME).

3:7-13 Do Not Harden Your Hearts

HE REMINDS THEM OF THE HISTORY. CHRY-SOSTOM: From hardness comes unbelief. As in bodies the parts that have become callous and hard do not yield to the hands of the physicians, so also souls that are hardened yield not to the Word of God. For it is probable that some even disbelieved those things which had already been done; hence he says, "Take heed." . . . Because the argument from the future is not so persuasive as from the past, he reminds them of the history in which they had lacked faith. For if your fathers, he says, because they did not hope as they ought to have hoped, suffered these things, much more will you. To them also is this word addressed, for "today," he says, is "ever," so long as the world lasts. Therefore, "exhort one another daily, as long as it is called 'today.'" That is, edify one another, raise yourselves up, lest the same things should befall you. "Lest any one of you be hardened by the deceitfulness of sin." Do you see that sin produces unbelief? For as unbelief brings forth an evil life, so also a soul, "when it is come into a depth of evils, becomes contemptuous"[1] and, having become contemptuous, it endures not even to believe, in order thereby

---

[1]Prov 18:3.

to free itself from fear. ON THE EPISTLE TO THE HEBREWS 6.3-4.[2]

SEPARATION FROM THE LIVING GOD. PHOTIUS: Many have evil, unbelieving hearts. To have an evil, unbelieving heart means to have no faith. Evil is the love of property, wantonness, alcohol, and the like. . . . Beware that your heart may not become evil and unbelieving; unbelief, he says, is separation from the living God. FRAGMENTS ON THE EPISTLE TO THE HEBREWS 3.12.[3]

THEY HAVE RECEIVED PHYSICAL FELLOWSHIP WITH CHRIST. THEODORE OF MOPSUESTIA: This word comes to ones who have already come to faith, as I understand it. So that it is fitting for you to praise the same things so that you might remain in the same opinions once and for all. This then Paul says, because those who believe and who have received the Spirit "share" in the substance of Christ, since they have received some physical fellowship with him. Then finally it remains to guard thoroughly this beginning with an uncontaminated mind. FRAGMENTS ON THE EPISTLE TO THE HEBREWS 3.12-14.[4]

3:13 As Long as It Is Today

TODAY CLEARLY MEANS FOR ALL TIME. CYRIL OF JERUSALEM: Take also another like expression. "To this day whenever Moses is read a veil lies over their minds."[5] Does "to this day" mean "up to the time that Paul wrote the words and no longer"? Does it not mean until this present day and indeed to the very end? And if Paul should say, "We are come all the way to you with the gospel of Christ, having hope, when your faith is increased, to preach the gospel in lands beyond you,"[6] you can see clearly that the phrase "all the way" sets no limit but indicates what lies beyond. With what meaning, therefore, ought you to recall the words "till he has put all enemies"? Just the same as in another saying of Paul, "But exhort each other daily, as long as it is called

'today,'" which clearly means for all time. For as we must not talk of a beginning of the days of Christ, so never suffer anyone to speak of an end of his kingdom. For Scripture says, "his kingdom is an everlasting kingdom."[7] CATECHETICAL LECTURES 15.32.[8]

BY "THIS DAY" HE MEANS DAILY. CYRIL OF JERUSALEM: "Give us this day our superessential[9] bread." Ordinary bread is not "superessential," but this holy bread is superessential in the sense of being ordained for the essence of the soul. Not of this bread is it said that it "passes into the stomach and is discharged into the drain."[10] No, it is absorbed into your whole system to the benefit of both soul and body. By "this day" he means "daily," as in Paul's "while it is called 'today.'" MYSTAGOGICAL LECTURES 5.15.[11]

SAVING ADVICE MUST BE LISTENED TO CONTINUALLY. CASSIODORUS: "Today"[12] signifies always, for he who offers saving advice must be listened to continually. The apostle powerfully expressed the force of these words: "But exhort one another every day, while it is called 'today.'" EXPOSITION OF THE PSALMS 94.7.[13]

THAT THEY MIGHT NEVER BE WITHOUT HOPE. CHRYSOSTOM: He said "today," that they might never be without hope. "Exhort one another daily," he says. That is, even if persons have sinned, as long as it is "today," they have hope; let them not then despair so long as they live. Above all things indeed, he says, "Let there not be an evil, unbelieving heart." But even if there should be, let no one despair, but let that one recover; for as long as we are in this world, the "today" is in season. ON THE EPISTLE TO THE HEBREWS 6.8.[14]

---

[2]NPNF 1 14:394*. [3]NTA 15:641. [4]NTA 15:205. [5]2 Cor 3:15. [6]2 Cor 10:14-16. [7]Dan 7:27. [8]LCC 4:166-67*. [9]The Greek is the elusive hapaxlegomenon *epiousios*, traditionally translated as "daily" (cf. Mt 6:11). [10]Mt 15:17. [11]FC 64:200*. [12]Ps 95:7 (94:7 LXX). [13]ACW 52:412. [14]NPNF 1 14:396**.

The Present Age Is One Day. Severian of Gabala: He introduces the present age as one day.[15] Fragments on the Epistle to the Hebrews 3.13.[16]

3:14 We Share in Christ

We Have Come to Be Through Faith. Chrysostom: What is the beginning of confidence? It means faith, through which we subsisted and have come to be and have been made to share in being. On the Epistle to the Hebrews 6.4.[17]

Baptism Is Our First Confidence. Theodoret of Cyr: We shared in death with Christ the Lord through all-holy baptism, and after being buried with him we prefigured the resurrection, provided of course we kept faith firm. He referred to this by the phrase "first confidence." Through it we were renewed, we were joined to Christ the Lord, and we shared the grace of the all-holy Spirit. Interpretation of Hebrews 3.[18]

Partakers in Christ's Hypostasis. Theodore of Mopsuestia: He says that those who have believed and shared in the Spirit have become partakers in Christ's "hypostasis" in that they have received a certain natural communion with him. Now there remains the task of preserving this foundation with a pure resolve. Commentary on Hebrews 3.12-13.[19]

3:17-19 Unable to Enter

They Died in the Desert. Jerome: They died, for they could not enter the promised land. They merely looked over toward the land of promise, but they could not enter it. The Jews beheld the promised land but could not enter it. They died in the desert. . . .We, their children, under the leadership of Jesus, have come to the Jordan and entered the promised land. Homilies on the Psalms 10 (Psalm 76).[20]

God Brought in Their Children. Theodoret of Cyr: God urged them to leave for the promised land, but some spoke in opposition, citing fear and the multitude of the enemy. Hence God consumed them all individually in the desert and brought in their children in place of them. Interpretation of Hebrews 3.[21]

A Similar Situation. Theodore of Mopsuestia: He wishes to show that all who went out through Moses perished because of their unbelief, so that these might fear all the more since they were in a similar situation to those against whom he was making the argument. Fragments on the Epistle to the Hebrews 3.16-18.[22]

Because They Did Not Believe. Ephrem the Syrian: "To whom did he swear that they should never enter his rest?" To those who did not want to obey Moses, Aaron, Joshua and Caleb . . . "So we see that they were unable to enter" the land promised to them, not because of their evil actions, even though they were wicked, but "because of unbelief" in the Word of God. Commentary on the Epistle to the Hebrews.[23]

---

[15]Cf. Ps 90:4 (89:4 LXX). [16]NTA 15:348. [17]NPNF 1 14:394*. [18]PG 82:701; TCCLSP 2:151. [19]PG 66:957; COS 237. [20]FC 48:77. [21]PG 82:701; TCCLSP 2:151. [22]NTA 15:205. [23]EHA 203.

4:1-13 THE REST WHICH GOD PROMISED

Therefore, while the promise of entering his rest remains, let us fear lest any of you be judged to have failed to reach it. [2]For good news came to us just as to them; but the message which they heard did not benefit them, because it did not meet with faith in the hearers.[h] [3]For we who have believed enter that rest, as he has said,

"As I swore in my wrath,

'They shall never enter my rest,"'

although his works were finished from the foundation of the world. [4]For he has somewhere spoken of the seventh day in this way, "And God rested on the seventh day from all his works." [5]And again in this place he said,

"They shall never enter my rest."

[6]Since therefore it remains for some to enter it, and those who formerly received the good news failed to enter because of disobedience, [7]again he sets a certain day, "Today," saying through David so long afterward, in the words already quoted,

"Today, when you hear his voice,

do not harden your hearts."

[8]For if Joshua had given them rest, God[i] would not speak later of another day. [9]So then, there remains a sabbath rest for the people of God; [10]for whoever enters God's rest also ceases from his labors as God did from his.

[11]Let us therefore strive to enter that rest, that no one fall by the same sort of disobedience. [12]For the word of God is living and active, sharper than any two-edged sword, piercing to the division of soul and spirit, of joints and marrow, and discerning the thoughts and intentions of the heart. [13]And before him no creature is hidden, but all are open and laid bare to the eyes of him with whom we have to do.

h Other manuscripts read *they were not united in faith with the hearers*   **i** Greek *he*

OVERVIEW: Again the early writers expand upon the apostle's point of admonition that the generation in the wilderness was destroyed by unbelief, and we need to be careful lest we also do not understand in faith what is promised (THEODORE, EPHREM). There are three rests mentioned: the sabbath, Palestine and the kingdom of heaven. The third is the one focused on here (CHRYSOSTOM). It is only in God that the human heart can rest (AUGUSTINE). The Fathers made distinctions in the same way that Hebrews does between the imperfect and war-plagued rest that Joshua provided the Israelites and the future sabbath rest for the people of God that God will provide. This rest is more like the rest that God took when he rested from his works (EPHREM). Lack of faith prevents us from rest in God (CHRYSOSTOM). From a mystical perspective, Isaac of Nineveh explains a process from tears to rest that is attested to, he says, by the whole church. This process begins with unceasing tears in the stillness of God during one's transition to the revelation of heavenly mysteries and finally to peace of thought.

The violent image of the Word of God being sharper than a two-edged sword and the bodily image of all creatures being naked to God calls for an explanation (Chrysostom). The double-edged sword of the Word of God signifies a distinction between the two Testaments (Augustine) or between the soul and the body, or between the physical and spiritual parts of a human being (Origen). That sword cuts off the doubts concerning belief in the crucified and risen Lord (Basil). Cassiodorus comments that this is part of God's condescension because of the weakness of hearers who need milk and not strong meat. The holy depth of Scripture is expressed in such common language that everyone immediately takes it in, but buried within it are hidden senses of truth, so that the vital meaning must be most carefully sought out. Ambrose relates the image to our desire to hide ourselves and our sins from God. "But God, who is the 'discerner of thoughts and intentions of the heart, piercing to the division of soul and spirit,' says, 'Adam, where are you?'" Symeon the New Theologian relates this image to the lusts of the heart (see Mt 5:28).

4:1-11 *Strive to Enter That Rest*

After Fear, Hope and Rest. Theodoret of Cyr: After making this digression to scare them[1] and to cause them to look forward to the hope given them, he then gives attention to the "rest," bringing out that in times past the inspired David foretold it to us. Interpretation of Hebrews 4.[2]

They Were Not Joined to the Things Promised. Theodore of Mopsuestia: It was fitting for them to be afraid, he says so that they might not be found lacking because of the depravity of their opinion, when they themselves had received the promise of access into the rest. For let no one suppose that the promise of the things to come are sufficient for him, just as it was not sufficient for them. For they were not joined to

the things promised in accordance with faith. Therefore, one ought to read as follows, "They did not attach themselves in faith to the things that they heard," namely, the promises that were made to them from God through Moses. Fragments on the Epistle to the Hebrews 4.1-2.[3]

We May Be Found Lacking. Theodore of Mopsuestia: We ought to be afraid . . . lest we, too, who have received the promise of the entrance into the rest, may be found lacking through a wickedness of purpose. For let no one think that the promise of things to come suffices him any more than it did them. Indeed, they did not understand in faith what had been promised. Commentary on Hebrews 4.1-2.[4]

The Message Met with Faith. Theodoret of Cyr: Hearing the words does not suffice for salvation; accepting it in faith is necessary, and holding it firm. After all, what benefit was God's promise to those who received it, but did not receive it faithfully, trust in the power of God or, as it were, associate closely with God's words? Interpretation of Hebrews 4.[5]

Law Mixed with Faith. Ephrem the Syrian: We also had the promise to enter into the kingdom through our faith and spiritual way of life, as well as those who accepted the command through the law so that . . . they might possess the land granted to them. "But the message" of the law "which they heard did not benefit them because it did not meet with faith" in the hearers. "We who have believed" in Christ and his gifts "enter" faithfully "that rest." They, on the other hand, did not enter into that rest in consequence of the vow made through David, who said, "I swore in my anger that they should not enter my rest."[6] Commentary on the Epistle to the Hebrews 4.[7]

---

[1]Heb 3:7-19. [2]PG 82:701; *TCCLSP* 2:151. [3]NTA 15:205-6. [4]PG 66:960; *COS* 236. [5]PG 82:701, 704; *TCCLSP* 2:151-52. [6]See Ps 95:11 (94:11 LXX). [7]EHA 203.

FAITH JOINS US TOGETHER. PHOTIUS: He says, "Not having joined themselves[8] to the things they heard," that is, the things they believed. How was it possible for them to be joined to those things? "By faith," he says, that is, through faith. For if the latter had believed as the former had, they would have been joined together into one, since their faith would have joined them together and blended them together. FRAGMENTS ON THE EPISTLE TO THE HEBREWS 4.2.[9]

REST IN GOD. AUGUSTINE: Our heart is restless until it rests in you. CONFESSIONS 1.1.[10]

ORDER OF TEARS TOWARD ENTERING REST. ISAAC OF NINEVEH: I am speaking of that order of tears which belongs to those who shed tears unceasingly both night and day. Whoever has found the reality of these things truly and accurately has found it in stillness. The eyes of such a person become like fountains of water for two years' time or even more, that is, during the time of transition, I mean, of mystical transition. But afterwards you enter into peace of thought; and from this peace of thought you enter into the rest of which St. Paul has spoken, but only in part and to the extent that nature can contain it. From that peaceful rest your intellect begins to behold mysteries. And thereupon the Holy Spirit begins to reveal heavenly things to you, and God dwells within you and raises up the fruit of the Spirit in you. And from this you perceive dimly . . . the change nature is going to undergo at the renewal of all things. . . . When you enter into that region which is peace of thought, then the multitude of tears is taken away from you, and afterwards tears come to you in due measure and at the appropriate time. This is, in all exactness, the truth of the matter as told in brief, and it is believed by the whole church. ASCETICAL HOMILIES 14.[11]

REST THAT IS THE KINGDOM OF HEAVEN. CHRYSOSTOM: He says that there are "three" rests: one, that of the sabbath, in which God rested from works; the second, that of Palestine, in which, when the Jews had entered, they would be at rest from their hardships and labors; the third, that which is rest indeed, the kingdom of heaven, where those who obtain it do indeed rest from their labors and troubles. Of these three then he makes mention here.

And why did he mention the three, when he is speaking only of the one? That he might show that the prophet is speaking concerning this one. For he did not speak, he says, concerning the first. For how could he, when that had taken place long before? Nor yet again concerning the second, that in Palestine. For how could he? For he says, "They shall not enter into my rest." It remains, therefore, that it is this third. ON THE EPISTLE TO THE HEBREWS 6.1.[12]

SABBATH REST FOR THE PEOPLE OF GOD. PHOTIUS: Just as the first "rest" did not prevent there being a second rest, so neither does the existence of a second rest prevent the existence of a third and more perfect rest. . . . Then it is clear that there is a certain other rest beyond those rests which have been spoken of, and that this rest is hallowed not for any who happen to chance upon it, but rather "for the people of God." But truly the people of God are "those who believe" in him and who keep his commandments. FRAGMENTS ON THE EPISTLE TO THE HEBREWS 4.3-11.[13]

THREE RESTS. THEODORET OF CYR: He wants to make clear three rests mentioned in the divine Scripture: first, the seventh day, on which God finished creating; second, the land of promise; and third, the kingdom of heaven. He provides proof of this from the inspired testimony: If there is no other rest (he is saying), why on earth does he also urge those in receipt of the second kind not to harden their hearts, threaten punishment

---

[8]*Synkerannymi*, which means "blend," "unite" or "join," is translated in RSV as "meet." [9]NTA 15:642. [10]NPNF 1 1:45*. [11]*AHSIS* 83**. [12]NPNF 1 14:393*. [13]NTA 15:642.

and make mention of those who spurned the second kind? He cites them in order, and firstly the rest on the seventh day. INTERPRETATION OF HEBREWS 4.[14]

THERE REMAINS THE SABBATH OF GOD.

EPHREM THE SYRIAN: In fact, if Joshua, the son of Nun, who allowed them to inherit the land, had settled them and given them rest, they still would not speak at all about the "other day of rest." Indeed, Joshua made them rest, because he gave them the land as an inheritance, but they did not rest in it perfectly, as God perfectly rested from God's works, for they lived in toils and wars. If that rest was not a true rest, since Joshua himself, the giver of their rest, was urged by the wars, if this is their condition, I say, there still remains the sabbath of God, who gives rest to those who enter there, as God rested from God's works, that is, from all the works which God made. COMMENTARY ON THE EPISTLE TO THE HEBREWS 4.[15]

THE KINGDOM OF HEAVEN IS A SABBATH

REST. OECUMENIUS: "Sabbath rest." Sabbath is translated "rest." Then a certain third rest remains, that of the kingdom of heaven. And he calls it a sabbath rest from the archetype of the rest of the sabbath, on which "God rested from his works."[16] FRAGMENTS ON THE EPISTLE TO THE HEBREWS 4.9-10.[17]

FOR YOU ALSO. CHRYSOSTOM: But what is "after

the same example of unbelief"? As if one should say, why did they of old not see the land? They had received clear evidence of the power of God; they ought to have believed. But yielding too much to fear and imagining nothing great concerning God and being faint-hearted, they perished. And there is also something more to be said, as, that after they had accomplished the greatest part of the journey, when they were at the very doors, at the haven itself, they were sunk into the sea. This I fear, he says, for you also. This is the meaning of "after the same example of unbelief." ON THE EPISTLE TO THE HEBREWS 7.3.[18]

WHOEVER ENTERS GOD'S REST. THEODORET

OF CYR: As the God of all on the sixth day completed the whole of creation, and on the seventh he rested from creating, so those departing this life and moving to that one will be rid of the present labors. INTERPRETATION OF HEBREWS 4.[19]

"REST" IS NOT RUNNING TO THE OLD. THE-

ODORE OF MOPSUESTIA: This is the work of true "rest," namely, not having to run again to the old things, while enduring transition and change. For just as God is said to rest from his creation of the world, having completed its foundation,[20] so it is fitting that also the one who has entered "into rest"[21] not run back again to the old things, viewing with contempt the labors required by the law's virtuous ordinances to restrain transgression. For out of necessity change and a removal from the old institution follows these things. FRAGMENTS ON THE EPISTLE TO THE HEBREWS 4.4-7.[22]

EACH DAY IS "THE DAY" SPOKEN TO US.[23]

THEODORE OF MOPSUESTIA: "Today" is neither an indefinite period of time, nor can it be predicated of an interval outside of "days" as if "today" were joined with each day. This should be stated not only for the sake of apostolic perspicuity but also for the sake of those who wish to understand, in the matter of the origin of the Only Begotten, the "I have begotten you today"[24] by flatly asserting that the "today" is an indefinite period of time. They cannot perceive that if this were the case one would not be able to speak of a "today" since there was then not yet a day. The apostle has made clear that he would not say that "today" is an indefinite period of time when he said, "Again speaking in David he marks off a day." Also in another passage, "Comfort them every day until it will be called 'the Day.' "[25] First

---

[14]PG 82:704; TCCLSP 2:152. [15]EHA 204. [16]Gen 2:2. [17]NTA 15:463. [18]NPNF 1 14:399*. [19]PG 82:705; TCCLSP 2:153. [20]Gen 2:2. [21]Ps 95:11. [22]NTA 15:206. [23]See also the discussion regarding "today" at Heb 3:13. [24]Ps 2:7. [25]Heb 3:13. Here *achris* is translated "until" rather than RSV's "as long as."

he showed that the "today" is not being spoken of outside of "days," by his saying "every day," and so appending "until it will be called 'the Day.'" Then in the matter of the "day" it does not appear as if he were talking about an indefinite period of time which might be applied both to the time that has already passed and the time that is about to come. For what does he say? Deeming "each day" to be "the Day" which is spoken to we should give heed to remaining in the faith. For as "the Day" indicates the present day, he advises them to make full use of the day for that which is useful for exhortation. FRAGMENTS ON THE EPISTLE TO THE HEBREWS 4.4-7.[26]

4:12-13 No Creature Is Hidden

SHARPER THAN ANY SWORD. CHRYSOSTOM: Do not then, when hearing the Word, think of it lightly. For "he is sharper," he says, "than any sword." Observe God's condescension, and hence consider why the prophets also needed to speak of saber and bow and sword. "If a person does not repent," it is said, "God will whet his sword; he has bent and strung his bow."[27] For if even now, after so long a time and after their being perfected, he cannot smite down by the name of the Word alone, but needs these expressions in order to show the superiority arising from the comparison of the gospel with the law, much more was this true of old. . . .

He judges the inner heart, for there he passes through, both punishing and searching out. "And why do I speak of men?" he says. "For even if you speak of angels, of archangels, of the cherubim, of the seraphim, even of any "creature" whatsoever, all things are laid open to God's eye. All things are clear and manifest. There is nothing able to escape it. "All are open and laid bare to the eyes of him with whom we have to do." But what is meant by "open"? The metaphor comes from the skins which are drawn off from the prey. . . . When one has killed them and drawn aside the skin from the flesh, he lays open all the inward parts and makes them manifest to our eyes; so

also do all things lie open before God. And observe, I ask you, how he constantly needs bodily images, which arise from the weakness of the hearers. For that they were weak he made plain when he said that they were "dull" and "had need of milk, not solid food."[28] ON THE EPISTLE TO THE HEBREWS 7.2.[29]

TWO EDGES, TWO TESTAMENTS. AUGUSTINE: He did not come "to bring peace on earth . . . but a sword,"[30] and Scripture calls the Word of God a "two-edged sword" because of the two Testaments. CITY OF GOD 20.21.[31]

DIVISION OF SOUL AND SPIRIT. SEVERIAN OF GABALA: He says, "division of soul and spirit." The soul has a special feeling for the body, but the grace of the Holy Spirit draws against the body to the heavenly things. FRAGMENTS ON THE EPISTLE TO THE HEBREWS 4.12.[32]

DISCERNER OF OUR THOUGHTS. AMBROSE: Therefore, the dread of divine power returns to the soul when we are eager to hide ourselves. Then, placed as we are by the thought of our sins in the midst of the trees of Paradise, where we committed sin, we are desirous of concealing ourselves and thinking hidden things which God does not demand of us. But God who is "the discerner of our thoughts and intentions of our hearts," "piercing to the division of soul and spirit," says, "Adam, where are you?"[33] ON PARADISE 14.68.[34]

THAT THE SOUL MAY GIVE ITSELF TO THE SPIRIT. ORIGEN: The mouth of the Son of God is a sharp sword because "the Word of God is living and active, sharper than any two-edged sword." . . . The metaphor is especially appropriate, since he did not come to bring peace on earth—that is, on the things which are corporeal and perceived by the senses—but a sword.[35] And

[26]NTA 15:206. [27]Ps 7:12 (7:13 LXX). [28]Heb 5:11-12. [29]NPNF 1 14:398-99*. [30]Mt 10:34. [31]FC 24:308-9. [32]NTA 15:348. [33]Gen 3:9. [34]FC 42:347. [35]Mt 10:34.

since he cuts, so to speak, the harmful association of soul and body that the soul may give itself to the Spirit, which wars against the flesh, and become a friend of God. This is why, according to the prophetic word, he has a mouth which is a "sword" or "like a sharp sword."[36] COMMENTARY ON THE GOSPEL OF JOHN 1.229.[37]

THE PRIZE OF PEACE. ORIGEN: Jesus once endured the cross, despising the shame, and therefore is seated at the right hand of God.[38] And those who imitate him by despising the shame will be seated with him and will rule in heaven[39] with him, who came to bring peace not to earth but to the souls of his disciples and to bring a sword on earth.[40] For since "the Word of God is living and active, sharper than any two-edged sword, piercing to the division of soul and spirit, of joints and marrow, and discerning the thoughts and intentions of the heart," this Word especially now awards our souls the prize of the peace that passes all understanding, which he left to his apostles.[41] And he draws a sword between the image of the person of dust and the image of the person of heaven,[42] so that, by taking our heavenly part at this time, he may later make us entirely heavenly, if we are worthy of not being cut in two. EXHORTATION TO MARTYRDOM 37.[43]

LAID BARE. THEODORET OF CYR: He used the phrase "laid bare to the eyes of him" as a metaphor from sacrificed beasts, which lie completely mute, the slaughter doing away with their life, and along with their life their cries. In similar manner, he is saying, when we also are judged, we behold everything done by us in ungodly or lawless fashion, whereas we receive the sentence of punishment in silence, realizing as we do its justice. INTERPRETATION OF HEBREWS 4.[44]

THE THOUGHTS OF THE HEART. SYMEON THE NEW THEOLOGIAN: Do you not tremble when you hear God day by day saying to you through the whole of sacred Scripture, "Let no evil talk come out of your mouths"?[45] In truth I tell you,

"You will render account for every careless word,"[46] and receive a reward even for the gift of a drink of cold water.[47] Have you not heard that God is judge "of the thoughts and intentions of the heart"? What is said? "He who looks at a woman lustfully has already committed adultery with her in his heart."[48] Do you see how one who looks at someone's face with lust is judged as an adulterer? Know then for sure that one who is ruled by lust of money is judged covetous, even though that one possesses nothing at all. One who lusts after many and costly dishes is a glutton, even though that one on account of poverty feeds on nothing but bread and water. And those are whoremongers who attach themselves to imaginations and so are defiled, even though they have never seen the face of anyone. So too, those who say in their hearts, "This has been badly done and has not turned out right," and "Why has this and that happened? Why did that not happen?"—let them not deceive themselves. They are slanderers and will be judged as those who condemn, even though they utter not a word with their tongues and no one hears their voices. DISCOURSE 3.6.[49]

CONFIRMING OUR HEARTS IN FAITH. BASIL THE GREAT: And Scripture calls by the name of "sword" the Word which has the power of trying and of discerning thoughts and which "extends even to the division of soul and spirit, of joints and marrow." . . . Every soul at the time of the passion was subjected to a sort of test, as it were, according to the words of the Lord, who said, "You will all fall away because of me."[50] Simeon prophesies concerning Mary that, standing beside the cross and looking at what was happening and hearing his words[51]—even after the testimony of Gabriel,[52] after the secret knowledge of her divine conception,[53] after the great showing of mira-

---

[36]Cf. Rev 1:16; Is 49:2. [37]FC 80:79*. [38]Heb 12:2. [39]See 2 Tim 2:12. [40]Mt 10:34. [41]Phil 4:7; cf. Jn 14:27. [42]See 1 Cor 15:49. [43]OSW 68-69*. [44]PG 82:705; TCCLSP 2:153. [45]Eph 4:29. [46]Mt 12:36. [47]See Mt 10:42; Mk 9:41. [48]Mt 5:28. [49]SNTD 66**. [50]Mt 26:31. [51]See Jn 19:25-27. [52]See Lk 1:31-33. [53]Lk 1:35.

cles—"Even you will flee," he says, "a certain per-plexity about your soul."[54] For the Lord must taste of death for the sake of all, and, being made a propitiation for the world, he must justify all people in his blood.[55] Therefore, some doubt will touch even you yourself who have been taught from above concerning the Lord. That is the sword. "That the thoughts of many hearts may be revealed,"[56] meaning that, after the scandal which happened at the cross of Christ to both the disciples and to Mary herself, some swift healing will follow from the Lord, confirming their hearts in their faith in him. Thus we see that even Peter, after having stumbled, clung more firmly to his faith in Christ. What was human, therefore, was proved unsound in order that the power of the Lord might be manifested. LETTER 260.[57]

HIDDEN SENSES OF TRUTH. CASSIODORUS: "The word of God is . . . sharper than any two-edged sword." Now the holy depth of divine Scripture is expressed in such common language that everyone immediately takes it in. But buried within it are hidden senses of truth, so that the vital meaning must be most carefully sought out. What contributes most of all to our understanding that it is really divine is the fact that ignorant persons are known to have been able to explain most subtle things, and mortal humans eternal things, but only when filled with the divine Spirit. EXPOSITION OF THE PSALMS, PREFACE 15.[58]

---

[54]See Lk 2:35. [55]Jn 11:50-52. [56]Lk 2:35. [57]FC 28:231-32*. [58]ACW 51:37*.

4:14—5:10 JESUS OUR HIGH PRIEST

[14]*Since then we have a great high priest who has passed through the heavens, Jesus, the Son of God, let us hold fast our confession.* [15]*For we have not a high priest who is unable to sympathize with our weaknesses, but one who in every respect has been tempted as we are, yet without sin.* [16]*Let us then with confidence draw near to the throne of grace, that we may receive mercy and find grace to help in time of need.*

5 *For every high priest chosen from among men is appointed to act on behalf of men in relation to God, to offer gifts and sacrifices for sins.* [2]*He can deal gently with the ignorant and wayward, since he himself is beset with weakness.* [3]*Because of this he is bound to offer sacrifice for his own sins as well as for those of the people.* [4]*And one does not take the honor upon himself, but he is called by God, just as Aaron was.*

[5]*So also Christ did not exalt himself to be made a high priest, but was appointed by him who said to him,*

"Thou art my Son,
 today I have begotten thee";
[6]*as he says also in another place,*

"Thou art a priest for ever,

after the order of Melchizedek."

⁷In the days of his flesh, Jesus^j offered up prayers and supplications, with loud cries and tears, to him who was able to save him from death, and he was heard for his godly fear. ⁸Although he was a Son, he learned obedience through what he suffered; ⁹and being made perfect he became the source of eternal salvation to all who obey him, ¹⁰being designated by God a high priest after the order of Melchizedek.

j Greek *he*

OVERVIEW: To understand this passage in the light of Jesus' resurrection or his passing through the heavens, Origen points out that Christ is everywhere and runs through all things, and we are no longer to think of him as being confined to a body as he was on earth. This view of the risen Christ's ubiquity would not have been accepted by the Antiochene school. Origen believed that the saints, in departing this life, would ascend according to the purity of their spirits through the spheres and heavens to a clearer understanding of the mysteries. Nevertheless, as we become "friends of God" in this life, we will not learn by enigmas, but we will see and understand things clearly. This was Paul's experience when he was caught up to the third heaven, but we can know even more than Paul and not have to come down from the third heaven as he did, if we take the cross and follow Jesus, who has passed through the heavens. As sons of the Father adopted through the Logos, we glorify the Father (CLEMENT OF ALEXANDRIA) and learn about him not through the types and enigmas but through the Son himself (ORIGEN).

All the Fathers were clear that Christ took on the form of sinful flesh and assumed all our weaknesses but without sin. He became fully human to procure our salvation by offering himself, the high priest and consecrator as a perfect sacrifice (HIPPOLYTUS, THEODORET, PSEUDO-DIONYSIUS). Furthermore, he suffered all our afflictions and endured grievous sorrows even to the point of death. However, every person of the Trinity plays a role in the mystery of salvation (LEO THE GREAT). God thus compassionately identifies with the weak and the poor, whom the world rejects. Therefore, the Lord's throne is a throne of grace and mercy, not a throne of judgment (CHRYSOSTOM, EPHREM). "God, who is served by myriads of powers without number, who 'upholds the universe by his word of power,' whose majesty is beyond anyone's endurance, has not disdained to become the father, the friend, the brother of those rejected ones" (SYMEON). What was not agreed upon until the famous Council of Chalcedon in 451 was how to speak about the two natures of Christ, the divine and human, in relation to these afflictions.

There is no consensus in these passages on the christological debate. Theodoret of Cyr states emphatically that no one could be so foolish as to attribute Hebrews 5:7-9 to the divinity; Chrysostom reiterates that point. How would it be possible, he argues, for God the Word to fear death, since he is the creator of the ages, unchangeable, immutable, and free of passion? (See also the comments of Nestorius, Theodore's student, on Hebrews 1:3 and Hebrews 7:3.) Theodore asserts that Jesus' suffering and even his cry from the cross ascertain the reality and fullness of his human nature. Cyril of Alexandria, by contrast, sees this as a divine drama performed by the divine nature for our edification: "He wept ... to suppress our tears. He experienced fear ... to fill us with courage." He is keen to assert that the Logos did not suffer according to his divine nature. According to Ephrem, salvation is bestowed by the Lord only upon those who obey him.

Using the word *intermingling* with respect to

Christ's two natures, Gregory of Nazianzus argues that he comes down to our level in the form of a servant and receives an alien "form" to bear "the whole of me, along with all that is mine." It is appropriate that a selection from Leo the Great ends the comments on this pericope. Pope Leo sent a famous letter from Rome to the emperor Flavian at the Council of Chalcedon that helped to settle the controversy. At the council, rules were established in the form of a definition, namely, that one could say things about the person of Christ that one would not say about the natures. In other words, Christ suffered, but not the divine nature. Jesus was God, but human nature is not divine. Mary was the mother of God, but one would not say that of her nature as a woman. Some of the following sentences from his letter, although not referring directly to Hebrews, help to see the consensus to which the great pope contributed: "Since, therefore, the characteristic properties of both natures and substances are kept intact and come together in one person, lowliness is taken on by majesty, weakness by power, mortality by eternity, and the nature which cannot be harmed is united to the nature which suffers, in order that the debt which our condition involves may be discharged. In this way, as our salvation requires one and the same mediator between God and human beings, the human being who is Jesus Christ can at one and the same time die in virtue of the one nature and in virtue of the other be incapable of death. That is why true God was born in the integral and complete nature of a true human being, entire in what belongs to him and entire in what belongs to us.... Each nature retained its characteristic without defect.... Each 'form' carries on its proper activities in communion with the other. ... Because of this unity of person, which must be understood to subsist in a twofold nature, we read that the Son of man came down from heaven, ... and conversely we say that the Son of God was crucified and buried."[1] According to Pope Leo the Great, the "mystery of great compassion" filled the whole world.

4:14 Let Us Hold to Our Confession

A COMPARISON WITH MELCHIZEDEK. THEODORET OF CYR: In what has been commented on before, he made the comparison of the different kinds of rest and brought out that the rest promised to us is better than that pledged to Jews: to them he pledged the land of promise, whereas to us heaven. Here on the other hand he now develops the contrast of high priesthood and brings out that the high priesthood according to the order of Melchizedek is far better and greater than the levitical kind. Adopting once again exhortatory mode, he makes the comparison lest he seem to those still embracing the way of life according to the law to be hostile to the law and not rather defending the truth.... The apostolic verses also teach us this: they present him as having passed through the heavens, whereas the divinity of Christ the Lord has an uncircumscribed nature, is present everywhere and is near to everyone. The Lord himself also taught us this, "No one has ascended to heaven except the one who descended from heaven, the Son of man, who is in heaven."[2] Though being here below and conversing with human beings, he claimed also to be on high. It is therefore necessary for us to realize that some names are appropriate to the divinity, some to the incarnation. INTERPRETATION OF HEBREWS 4.[3]

A SCHOOL FOR SAINTS. ORIGEN: I think that the saints, as they depart from this life, will remain in some place situated on the earth that the divine scripture calls "paradise."[4] This will be a place of instruction and, so to speak, a lecture room or school for souls, in which they may be taught about all that they had seen on earth. They may also receive some indications of what is to follow in the future, just as ... in this life they had obtained certain indications of the future,

---

[1]CC 148-51. [2]Jn 3:13. [3]PG 82:705-8; *TCCLSP* 2:153-54*. [4]Lk 23:43; cf. Gen 2:8 where the LXX uses *paradeisos* to refer to the Garden of Eden.

seen indeed "through a glass darkly" and truly "in part,"[5] which are revealed more clearly and brightly to the saints in their proper times and places. If any are "pure in heart"[6] and of unpolluted mind and well-trained understanding, they will make swifter progress and quickly ascend to the region of the air until they reach the kingdom of the heavens, passing through the series of those "rooms,"[7] if I may so call them, which the Greeks have termed spheres, that is, globes, but which the divine Scripture calls heavens. In each of these they will first observe all that happens there and then learn the reason why it happens; and thus they will proceed in order through each stage, following him who has "passed through the heavens, Jesus the Son of God," and who has said, "I desire that they also may be with me where I am."[8] Further, he alludes to this diversity of places when he says, "In my Father's house are many rooms."[9] He himself, however, is everywhere and runs through all things. And we are no longer to think of him as being confined within those narrow limits in which he once lived for our sakes, that is, in that circumscribed condition which was his when he dwelt on earth among humans in a body like ours, so that it was then possible to think of him as being enclosed in some one place. On First Principles 2.11.6.[10]

FULLY ESTABLISHED AS DAUGHTERS AND SONS. CLEMENT OF ALEXANDRIA: The greatest possible likeness to the Logos, the hope of being established fully as adopted sons of the Father— this is our goal, a sonship that constantly glorifies the Father through "the great high priest" who deigned to call us "brothers"[11] and "fellow heirs."[12] STROMATEIS 2.22.134.[13]

VISIONS THAT NO BODILY NATURE CAN COMPREHEND. ORIGEN: You will know the accurate interpretation of Scripture ... if you desire in Christ to learn and to go beyond instruction by an enigma and so hasten to him who calls you. Then you will know as friends of the Father and teacher in heaven, since you have

never before known face to face. For friends learn not by enigmas but by a form that is seen or by wisdom bare of words, symbols and types; this will be possible when they attain to the nature of intelligible things and to the beauty of truth. If, then, you believe that Paul was caught up to the third heaven and was caught up into paradise and heard things that cannot be told, which one may not utter, you will consequently realize that you will presently know more and greater things than the unspeakable words then revealed to Paul, after which he came down from the third heaven. But you will not descend if you take up the cross and follow Jesus, whom we have as a great high priest who has passed through the heavens. And if you do not shrink from what following him means, you will pass through the heavens, climbing above not only earth and earth's mysteries but also above the heavens and their mysteries. For in God there are treasured up much greater visions than these, which no bodily nature can comprehend, if it is not first delivered from everything corporeal. And I am convinced that God stores up and keeps ... much greater visions than the sun, the moon and the chorus of the stars have seen, indeed than the holy angels have seen, whom God made wind and a flame of fire.[14] God's purpose is to reveal them "when the whole creation is set free from its bondage to decay and obtains the glorious liberty of the children of God."[15] EXHORTATION TO MARTYRDOM 13.[16]

4:15 In Every Way Tempted as We Are

HE SYMPATHIZES WITH OUR WEAKNESSES. PHOTIUS: From both ways he establishes that "he will sympathize with our weaknesses": first, because he is great and mighty, being the Son of God and very God himself, and, second, because he also as very man suffered and endured the testing of afflictions and the weakness of the flesh.

[5]1 Cor 13:12. [6]Mt 5:8. [7]Jn 14:2. [8]Jn 17:24. [9]Jn 14:2. [10]ANF 4:299; OFP 152-53**. [11]Heb 2:11. [12]Eph 3:6. [13]FC 85:247*. [14]Cf. Ps 104:4 (103:4 LXX); Heb 1:7. [15]See Rom 8:21. [16]OSW 50-51*.

For both these reasons he is in every respect made a partaker of our weaknesses. FRAGMENTS ON THE EPISTLE TO THE HEBREWS 4.15.[17]

TRIUNE WORK OF OUR RESTORATION. LEO THE GREAT: By the saving cooperation of the indivisible divinity, whatever the Father, whatever the Son, whatever the Holy Spirit accomplishes in a particular way is the plan of our redemption. It is the order of our salvation. For if human beings, made in the image and likeness of God, had remained in the honor of their own nature and, undeceived by the devil's lies, had not deviated from the law placed over them for their lusts, the Creator of the world would not have become a creature. The eternal would not have undergone temporality, and God the Son, equal to God the Father, would not have assumed the "form of a servant"[18] and the "likeness of sinful flesh."[19]

Since, however, "through the devil's envy death entered the world"[20] and because captive humanity could only be freed in one way, namely, if that one would undertake our cause who, without the loss of his majesty, would become true man, and who alone had no contagion of sin,[21] the mercy of the Trinity divided for itself the work of our restoration so that the Father was appeased, the Son was the appeaser, and the Holy Spirit enkindled the process. It was right that those to be saved should do something for themselves, and, when their hearts were turned to the Redeemer, that they should cut themselves off from the domination of the enemy. In regard to this, the apostle says, "God has sent the Spirit of his Son into our hearts crying, 'Abba! Father!' "[22] "Where the Spirit of the Lord is, there is freedom."[23] "No one can say 'Jesus is Lord' except by the Holy Spirit."[24] SERMON 77.[25]

THE WORD SAVED THE FALLEN ADAM. HIPPOLYTUS: So let us in the future believe, blessed brethren, in accordance with the tradition of the apostles, that God the Word came down from the heaven into the holy virgin Mary. . . . Once he had taken flesh out of her and taken a soul of the human kind—a rational one, I mean—and had become everything that a human is, sin excepted, he might save fallen Adam and procure incorruption for such as believe in his name. AGAINST NOETUS 17.2.[26]

THE ONE IN WHOM HUMAN NATURE WAS INNOCENT. LEO THE GREAT: What has been instilled in our hearts, if not that we should be "renewed" through them all "after the image"[27] of that one who, remaining "in the form of God,"[28] condescended to become "the form of sinful flesh"?[29] He assumed all those weaknesses of ours that come as a result of sin, though "without" any part in "sin." Consequently, he lacked none of the afflictions due to hunger and thirst, sleep and weariness, sadness and tears. He endured grievous sorrows even to the point of death. No one could be released from the fetters of mortality unless he, in whom alone the nature of all people was innocent, should allow himself to be killed by the hands of wicked persons.

Our Savior, the Son of God, gave both a mystery and an example to all who believe in him, so that they might attain to the one by being reborn and arrive at the other by imitation. Blessed Peter the apostle teaches this, saying, "Christ also suffered for you, leaving you an example, that you should follow in his steps. He committed no sin; no guile was found on his lips. When he was reviled, he did not revile in return; when he suffered, he did not threaten; but he trusted to him who judges justly. He himself bore our sins in his own body on the tree, that we might die to sin and live to righteousness."[30] SERMON 63.[31]

UNITED TO THE WORD. THEODORET OF CYR: It was the nature assumed from us for our sake that experienced our passions without sinning, not the one who took our nature for our salvation.

---

[17]NTA 15:642. [18]Phil 2:7. [19]Rom 8:3. [20]Wis 2:24. [21]Cf. Jn 8:46; 2 Cor 5:21. [22]Gal 4:6. [23]2 Cor 3:17. [24]1 Cor 12:3. [25]FC 93:342. [26]HM 2:4. [27]Col 3:10. [28]See Phil 2:6. [29]Cf. Rom 8:3; Phil 2:7. [30]1 Pet 2:21-24. [31]FC 93:274-75.

And in the beginning of this section Paul teaches us by saying, "Consider Jesus, the apostle and high priest of our confession, faithful to him who made him."[32] . . . No one of orthodox conviction would call a creature the uncreated and unmade, God the Word, coeternal with the Father. Rather the one from the seed of David, who existed free from all sin, became our high priest and sacrifice by offering himself to God for us, having the Word . . . united to himself and joined inseparably. IN CYRIL OF ALEXANDRIA'S LETTER TO EUOPTIUS, ANATHEMA 10.[33]

FRIEND OF THE REJECTED. SYMEON THE NEW THEOLOGIAN: Nearly all reject the weak and the poor as objects of disgust; an earthly king cannot bear the sight of them, rulers turn away from them, while the rich ignore them and pass them by when they meet them as though they did not exist; nobody thinks it desirable to associate with them. But God, who is served by myriads of powers without number, who "upholds the universe by his word of power,"[34] whose majesty is beyond anyone's endurance, has not disdained to become the father, the friend, the brother of those rejected ones. He willed to become incarnate so that he might become "like unto us in all things except for sin" and make us to share in his glory and his kingdom. What stupendous riches of his great goodness! What an ineffable condescension on the part of our master and our God! DISCOURSE 2.4.[35]

HE WILL TAKE OUR WEAKNESS INTO ACCOUNT. THEODORET OF CYR: The believers at that time were subjected to constant billowing by trials; so he consoles them by bringing out that our high priest not only knows as God the weakness of our nature but also as man had experience of our sufferings, remaining unfamiliar with sin alone. Understanding this weakness of ours, he is saying, he both extends us appropriate help and when judging us he will take our weakness into account in delivering sentence. INTERPRETATION OF HEBREWS 4.[36]

4:16 *The Throne of Grace*

LET US COME BOLDLY. CHRYSOSTOM: Of what "throne of grace" is he speaking? That royal throne concerning which it is said, "The Lord says to my Lord, Sit at my right hand."[37]

What is "let us come boldly"? We come boldly because "we have a sinless high priest" contending with the world. For he says, "Be of good cheer, I have overcome the world";[38] for this is to suffer all things and yet to be pure from sins. Though we are under sin, the apostle means, yet the High Priest is sinless.

How is it that we should "approach boldly"? Because now it is a throne of grace, not a throne of judgment. Therefore, boldly, "that we may obtain mercy," even such as we are seeking. For the affair is one of munificence, a royal largess.

"And may find grace to help in time of need." He said well, "for help in time of need." If you approach now, he means, you will receive both grace and mercy, for you approach "in time of need." . . . Now he sits granting pardon, but when the end is come, then he rises up to judgment. For it is said, "Arise, O God, judge the earth."[39] "Let us come boldly" or, he says again, having no "evil conscience," that is, not being in doubt, for such a one cannot "come with boldness." On this account it is said, "At the acceptable time I have listened to you, and helped you on the day of salvation,"[40] since even now, for those who sin after baptism, to find repentance is grace.

But lest when you hear he is High Priest, you should think that he stands, Paul immediately goes on to the "throne." A priest does not sit but stands. Do you see that for him to be made High Priest is not of nature but of grace and condescension and humiliation?

Thus is it seasonable for us also now to say, "Let us draw near," asking "boldly"; let us only bring faith, and he gives all things. Now is the

---

[32]Heb 3:1-2. [33]PG 76:437; COS 300*. [34]Heb 1:3. [35]SNTD 50*. [36]PG 82:708-9; TCCLSP 2:154. [37]Ps 110:1 (109:1 LXX). [38]Jn 16:33. [39]Ps 82:8 (81:8 LXX). [40]2 Cor 6:2.

time of the gift; let no one despair. Then will be the time of despairing, when the bridechamber is shut, when the king is come in to see the guests, when they who will be accounted worthy will have received as their portion the patriarch's bosom;[41] but now it is not as yet so. For still are the spectators assembled, still is the contest, still the prize is in suspense. On the Epistle to the Hebrews 7.6.[42]

The Throne of Grace and Lovingkindness. Theodoret of Cyr: As God, Christ the Lord has kingship by nature, an eternal throne: "Your throne, O God, is forever," Scripture says, remember. But as man, high priest and apostle of our confession he hears the words "Sit at my right hand"; it is to this the divine apostle referred by "throne of grace." In my view he hints also at the lovingkindness he will employ in judging, adding the comment, "so as to receive mercy and find grace by way of timely assistance": making our approach in the present life and giving evidence of unalloyed and sincere faith, we shall on the day of judgment attain lovingkindness. Interpretation of Hebrews 4.[43]

Let Us Imitate Him. Ephrem the Syrian: Let us imitate him so that we may be "without sin" like him, so that "we may approach with confidence the throne of his grace" in the hour of retribution. "Let us obtain his mercy," for instance, through prayers, so that he may be with us in the hour of our fight with the devil. Commentary on the Epistle to the Hebrews 4.[44]

5:1-6 Acting on Our Behalf

A Proof for the Weak. Chrysostom: The blessed Paul wishes to show that this covenant is far better than the old. He does this by first laying down remote considerations . . . just as in the epistle to the Romans, having argued that faith effects that which the labor of the law or the sweat of the daily life could not, an argument of

which they were not easily persuaded . . . so now here also he opens out the other path of the priesthood, showing its superiority from the things which happened before. And as, in the matter of punishment, he brings before them not hell alone, but also what happened to their ancestors, so now here also, he first establishes this position from things present. For it were right indeed that earthly things should be proved from heavenly, but when the hearers are weak, the opposite course is taken. On the Epistle to the Hebrews 8.1.[45]

He Did Not Usurp the Priesthood. Ephrem the Syrian: And in consequence of his weakness Jesus "felt a proper compassion" for sins, because he had clothed himself with the flesh of sin. And he had the duty "to offer a sacrifice both for his people and for himself and his sins." He did not obtain the high priesthood by usurpation, but just like Aaron, whom God elected with the leafy staff. Commentary on the Epistle to the Hebrews 5.[46]

Not an Angel but a Human Being. Theodoret of Cyr: Even under the law it was not an angel that was appointed to act as priest for human beings but a human being for human beings, with the same nature, affected by the same passions, understanding the weakness of nature, assigning pardon to the recalcitrant, offering a hand to sinners, treating what affects the neighbor as his own. This is the very reason he is appointed to offer sacrifices not for the people alone but also for himself. Interpretation of Hebrews 5.[47]

He Is Called By God as Aaron Was. Theodoret of Cyr: The one receiving appointment from God is the lawful high priest; this was the way Aaron, the first high priest, received the

---

[41]See Lk 16:22. [42]NPNF 1 14:400**. [43]PG 82:709; TCCLSP 2:155*. [44]EHA 205. [45]NPNF 1 14:403*. [46]EHA 205. [47]PG 82:709; TCCLSP 2:155.

honor. The divine apostle said this, of course, not intending to inform us now of the norms for high priesthood, but to lay the groundwork for a treatment of the Lord's high priesthood. INTERPRETATION OF HEBREWS 5.[48]

JESUS DID NOT EXALT HIMSELF. PSEUDO-DIONYSIUS: The rites of consecration and those being consecrated denote the mystery that the performer of consecration in love of God is the exponent of the choice of the divinity. It is not by virtue of any personal worth that the hierarch summons those about to be consecrated, but rather it is God who inspires him in every hierarchic sanctification. Thus Moses, the consecrator in the hierarchy of the law, did not confer a clerical consecration on Aaron, who was his brother, whom he knew to be a friend of God and worthy of the priesthood, until God himself commanded him to do so, thereby permitting him to bestow, in the name of God who is the source of all consecration, the fullness of a clerical consecration.[49] And yet our own first and divine consecrator—for Jesus in his endless love for us took on this task—"did not exalt himself," as Scripture declares. Rather, the consecrator was the one "who said to him . . . 'You are a priest for ever after the order of Melchizedek.'" ECCLESIASTICAL HIERARCHY 5.3.5.[50]

BECAUSE OF YOUR SALVATION. GREGORY OF NAZIANZUS: He whom presently you scorn was once transcendent over even you. He who is presently human was incomposite. He remained what he was; what he was not he assumed. No "because" is required for his existence in the beginning,[51] for what could account for the existence of God? But later he came into being because of something, namely, your salvation, yours who insult him and despise his Godhead for that very reason, because he took on your thick corporeality. Through the medium of the mind he had dealings with the flesh, being made that God on earth which is human. Human and God blended;

they became a single whole, the stronger side predominating, in order that I might be made God to the same extent that he was made man. He was begotten[52]—yet he was already begotten—of a woman.[53] ON THE SON, THEOLOGICAL ORATION 3(29).19.[54]

"FOREVER" REFERS TO PRESENT SACRIFICING PRIESTS. OECUMENIUS: The word makes clear that if Christ himself offered a sacrifice not unstained with blood—for he offered his own blood—then in contrast the priests who derive their office from him (whomever God and the high priest deem worthy to be priests) will bring a sacrifice untainted by blood. For the phrase *forever*[55] reveals this. For he did not speak to the sacrifice and offering made once and for all when he said "forever," but he had in mind the present sacrificing priests, by means of whom Christ sacrifices and is sacrificed, who also gives to those in the mystic supper the character of such a sacrifice. FRAGMENTS ON THE EPISTLE TO THE HEBREWS 5.6.[56]

5:7-10 *With Loud Cries and Tears*

HE STILL HAS THE FLESH. OECUMENIUS: It was not for this reason that he called "days of his flesh" the days when the Lord was upon the earth visibly, as if now he had put off the flesh. Perish the thought! For he still has the flesh, even if it is now imperishable. But he calls "the days of his flesh" the days in his fleshly life. FRAGMENTS ON THE EPISTLE TO THE HEBREWS 5.7.[57]

HIS CRUCIFIERS MAY LIVE. EPHREM THE SYRIAN: Jesus' prayers were granted, but how were his prayers granted if he had demanded to be delivered from death? To be sure, he was not saved. He wanted to fulfill in himself the will of

---

[48]PG 82:709; TCCLSP 2:155. [49]Ex 28:1-4; 29:4-9. [50]PDCW 241*. [51]Jn 1:1. [52]Mt 1:16. [53]Gal 4:4. [54]FGFR 257*. [55]Ps 110:4. [56]NTA 15:464. [57]NTA 15:464.

the Father. And for this reason it was evident that he was the Son of God, because in behalf of human creatures he exposed his own soul for the rest of the soul of the one who sent him, and his obedience was made evident by the hands of those who crucified him. If, therefore, the crucifiers testify that his prayers were granted, if it is so, I say, he certainly wanted to die, and he demanded that the will of his Father was fulfilled. He offered supplications with loud claims to the one who was able to save him from death; he who was about to die did not ask for delivery from death nor demand to be resurrected after his death because this had been promised to him earlier, but he prayed for his crucifiers lest they might die in him. And his prayers were granted, because the door was opened so that his crucifiers might live in him. And the one who did these things, that is, the one who abased himself to such humility and suffering for his murderers is the Son of God; and from this it was evident that he was satisfied in those sufferings which he endured. In fact, some of his murderers were converted, and through their repentance they were the heralds of his resurrection. COMMENTARY ON THE EPISTLE TO THE HEBREWS.[58]

JESUS FELT FEAR. THEODORE OF MOPSUESTIA: Even if he [the Word] gave a certain exceptional cooperation to the one who was assumed, this does not mean that the divinity took the place of the mind. If the divinity did take the place of his mind in the assumed man, as you say, how is it that he felt fear in his passion? Why did he need strong prayers in the face of necessity, the strong prayers that he offered to God with a loud voice and many tears, according to blessed Paul? TREATISES AGAINST APOLLINARIS 3.4.[59]

HE WAS OFTEN SAD. CHRYSOSTOM:[60] Our affairs, both our business and our politeness, are turned into laughing; there is nothing steady, nothing grave. I do not say these things only to people of the world, but I know those whom I am hinting at. For the church has been filled with

laughter. Whatever clever thing one may say, immediately there is laughter among those present, and the marvelous thing is that many do not leave off laughing even during the very time of the prayer.

Everywhere the devil leads the dance; he has entered into all and is master of all. Christ is dishonored, is thrust aside; the church is made no account of. Do you not hear Paul saying, "Let there be no filthiness, nor silly talk, nor levity"?[61] He places "levity" along with "filthiness," and do you laugh? What is "silly talk"? That which has nothing profitable. And do you, solitary one, laugh at all and relax your countenance? You that are crucified, you that are a mourner, tell me, do you laugh? Where do you hear of Christ doing this? Nowhere, but that he was sad, indeed oftentimes. For even when he looked on Jerusalem, he wept; and when he thought on the traitor, he was troubled; and when he was about to raise Lazarus, he wept; and do you laugh? If he who grieves not over the sins of others deserves to be accused, of what consideration will he be worthy who is without sorrow for his own sins and even laughs at them? This is the season of grief and tribulation, of bruising and of conflicts, and do you laugh? Do you not see how Sarah was rebuked? Do you not hear Christ saying, "Woe to you that laugh now, for you shall weep"?[62] You chant these things every day, for, tell me, what do you say? "I have laughed"? By no means; but what? "I am weary with my moaning."[63]

But perhaps there are some persons so dissolute and silly as even during this very rebuke to laugh, because we discourse thus about laughter. For, indeed, such is their derangement, such their madness, that it does not feel the rebuke. ON THE EPISTLE TO THE HEBREWS 15.8.[64]

LOUD CRIES. CHRYSOSTOM: Do you see that Paul sets forth nothing else than Christ's care and

[58]EHA 206. [59]TEM 2:315; COS 251*. [60]Chrysostom is here commenting on Heb 9:14. [61]Eph 5:4. [62]Lk 6:25. [63]Ps 6:6 (6:7 LXX). [64]NPNF 1 14:441-42*.

the exceptional greatness of his love? For what does the expression "with loud cries" mean? The gospel nowhere says this, nor that he wept when praying, nor that he uttered a cry. Do you see that it was condescension? ON THE EPISTLE TO THE HEBREWS 8.3.[65]

BEARING THE WHOLE OF ME. GREGORY OF NAZIANZUS: Connected with this general view are the facts that he "learned obedience through what he suffered," his "loud cries and tears," the fact that he "offered up prayers," that he "was heard" and he was "God-fearing." These things are marvelously constructed drama dealing with us. As Word, he was neither obedient nor disobedient—the terms apply to amenable subordinates or inferiors who deserve punishment. But as the "form of a servant"[66] he comes down to the same level as his fellow servants; receiving an alien "form," he bears the whole of me, along with all that is mine, in himself, so that he may consume within himself the meaner element, as fire consumes wax or the sun ground mist, and so that I may share in what is his through the intermingling. ON THE SON, THEOLOGICAL ORATION 4(30).6.[67]

WOULD ANYONE SAY THESE THINGS OF GOD? CHRYSOSTOM: Let the heretics who deny the flesh be ashamed. What do you mean? The Son of God was "heard for his godly fear"? What more would anyone say of the prophets? And what sort of logical connection is there between "he was heard for his godly fear" and "although he was a Son, he learned obedience through what he suffered"? Would anyone say these things of God? Why, who would be so insane? And who, even if he were beside himself, would have said this? ON THE EPISTLE TO THE HEBREWS 8.3.[68]

HOW CAN HE SAY HE WAS HEARD? PHOTIUS: Two things are most in need of investigation here. First, how can he say, "He was heard,"[69] and yet he himself begged not to enter into death? He did not avoid death, for he was crucified and died.

Second, on the basis of what sort of "godliness"[70] was he heard? And third, to what should the phrase "although he was a Son" be adjoined? Does it belong to the clause "he was heard because of his godliness" or to the clause that follows, so that it would read, "although he was a Son, he learned obedience from the things he suffered"? For it is not a small difference between those two. FRAGMENTS ON THE EPISTLE TO THE HEBREWS 5.7-9.[71]

FIRST: HIS PETITION NOT TO ENTER DEATH. PHOTIUS: Now as regards the first matter we say that he did not make one petition but a twofold one. For the one petition asked to avoid death, the other petition asked for death. For he also says in the same prayer and petition, "However, not my will but yours be done."[72] And John, showing this more clearly, says that the Son prayed by saying, "Father, glorify your Son, in order that your Son may glorify you,"[73] calling the cross and death glory, as is clear. So the excellent Paul says quite well, "He was heard."[74] FRAGMENTS ON THE EPISTLE TO THE HEBREWS 5.7-9.[75]

SECOND: "ON THE BASIS OF GODLINESS." PHOTIUS: The phrase "on the basis of his godliness" comes closer to being understood from the things that have already been spoken. For we said that there were two petitions, the petition to be delivered from the death, and the petition of consent, which was really of much "godliness," namely, the petition, "however, not my will, but yours, be done." Therefore, Christ was heard not on the basis of his prayer to avoid death but on the basis of his "godliness," that is, that petition of his came to pass, not the petition that sought to avoid death but the godly petition. Therefore, he says, "And having been made perfect," that is, he was acknowledged as perfect and good beyond

---

[65]NPNF 1 14:404. [66]Phil 2:7. [67]FGFR 265. [68]NPNF 1 14:404*. [69]Photius has *eisēkousthē* for *eisakoustheis*. [70]*Eulabeia* is translated "godly fear" in RSV. [71]NTA 15:643. [72]Mt 26:39; Lk 22:42. [73]Jn 17:1. [74]Photius has *eisēkousthē* for *eisakoustheis*. [75]NTA 15:643.

description and loving of humankind through his sufferings and cross and death. And he also hinted at this above, when he said, "petitions and supplications," speaking rather enigmatically by doubling the petition. Then also when he said, "petitions and supplications," he did not append the words about avoiding death but rather "to the One who was able to save him from death." [He added this] well and very wisely, in order that whenever you think of him who was crucified and buried, you may not think that he endured this owing to the helplessness of his Father but because it was the common will (of the Father and the Son) that the Christ suffer these things for the salvation of the world. And this can be said also because of his resurrection. For the excellent Paul having uttered rather humble things in many places, says that the Father raised Christ. Therefore, having raised him, he rescued and delivered him from death. This is how these things are understood in my opinion. FRAGMENTS ON THE EPISTLE TO THE HEBREWS 5.7-9.[76]

THIRD: "ALTHOUGH BEING A SON." PHOTIUS: Now as far as the phrase "although being a Son" is concerned, if someone should understand it as a transposition—and such a trope is uncustomary for the excellent apostle—the natural reading of the passage would be something like this: "Who in the days of his flesh, although being a Son, made petitions and supplications," etc. That is, although having the very great advantage of being a Son, which enabled him to do all things by his own autocratic opinion without any petition or request, even as the Father does,[77] nonetheless, since he was in the days of the flesh, he offered petitions and supplications. And according to this understanding it can also be understood how the phrase was soon joined to "and being heard because of his godliness," inasmuch as he says that he was heard, although being a Son, and not asking to be heard, inasmuch as he made his will concurrent to his Father's will and it was fulfilled without any petition. But if you conjoin this clause with

what follows, the understanding will also be guided in the right way in the manner that I will show. But first we ought to examine the meaning of the clause "he learned obedience from the things which he suffered." It really cannot be that he himself learned from the things he suffered to obey his Father and that by testing he acquired knowledge of how to obey him, can it? Or is it not rather that by testing he learned such was the greatness of the obedience, with which the Father hearkened to him, in that he was crucified and died and rose and exalted the human race to be at the right hand of the Father and to save our race? For these sort of things pertain to that obedience which took place when he said, "Father, glorify your Son."[78] Christ, being the Son and God just as much as the Father, already knew this obedience and how great it was, even before he rendered obedience to the Father, but "having been heard" he learned it through the things he suffered and through the testing he underwent. Then, however one wishes to understand it—although to me the second way of understanding seems particularly well suited—the phrase "although being a Son" presents no difficulty. FRAGMENTS ON THE EPISTLE TO THE HEBREWS 5.7-9.[79]

EXTREME HUMILIATION. THEODORET OF CYR: How would it be possible for God the Word to fear death, since he is the Creator of the ages, unchangeable, immutable, free of passion? Certainly it would be the height of folly to go on at length about the point. For the extreme humiliation that marks the theme of the passage compels even those who blaspheme the divinity to recognize that none of these things are suitable to the divinity. INTERPRETATION OF HEBREWS 5.[80]

PERSUADED TO OBEDIENCE. CHRYSOSTOM: If he, though the Son, gains obedience from his sufferings, how much more shall we? Do you see

---

[76]NTA 15:643. [77]Jn 5:19. [78]Jn 17:1. [79]NTA 15:644. [80]PG 82:712; TCCLSP 2:156*.

how many things Paul says about obedience in order to persuade them to obedience? . . . "Through what he suffered" he continually "learned" to obey God, and he was "made perfect" through sufferings. This, then, is perfection, and by this means we must arrive at perfection. For not only was he himself saved; he also became an abundant supply of salvation to others. ON THE EPISTLE TO THE HEBREWS 8.3.[81]

MORE THAN APPEARANCE. THEODORET OF CYR: For the divinity allowed the humanity to suffer this so that we might learn that he truly became man and assumed a human nature and that the mystery of the incarnation was not perfected in appearance or seeming. INTERPRETATION OF HEBREWS 5.[82]

A FINE AND USEFUL EXAMPLE. CYRIL OF ALEXANDRIA: It was not while bare and not participating in the limits of his emptying that God the Word became our model, but "in the days of his flesh." Then, quite legitimately, he could employ human limits and pray insistently and shed tears and even appear somehow to need a savior and learn obedience, though a Son. The inspired author is, so to speak, stupefied by the mystery that the Son, existing by nature truly and endowed with the glories of divinity, should so abase himself that he endured the low estate of our impoverished humanity. But this was for us, as I have said, a fine and useful example. ON THE UNITY OF CHRIST 755.[83]

IN JESUS WE SEE HUMAN NATURE PURIFIED. CYRIL OF ALEXANDRIA: Consider the fact that the only begotten spoke these words only when he had become man and insofar as he was one of us and spoke on our behalf. It was just as though he had said, "The first man sinned by falling into disobedience; he paid no attention to the command which had been given. . . . But you have established me as a second beginning for those on earth, and I have been named a second Adam. In me you see human nature purified,

established sinless, holy and pure. From now on bestow the good things of your mercy, loose despair, rebuke corruption, and put an end to the effects of your wrath. I have conquered even Satan, the ancient ruler, for he found in me absolutely nothing of his own." ON THE UNITY OF CHRIST 757.[84]

CHRIST WAS TRULY SON. CYRIL OF ALEXANDRIA: For he gave voice to a strong cry and supplication when he became like us; and he was heard because he did not disobey, since by nature he was truly Son. LETTER TO PULCHERIA AND EUDOXIA.[85]

FIRE IS NOT HARMED WHEN STRUCK. CYRIL OF ALEXANDRIA: Iron or any other like material, when joined to the impact of fire, receives it and nourishes the flame. If then it happens to be struck by someone, the material receives damage, but the nature of the fire is in no way harmed by the one who strikes. In the same way, you may understand the Son can be said to suffer in the flesh but not to suffer in his divinity. ON THE UNITY OF CHRIST 776.[86]

HIS LIFE WAS A MODEL OF SAINTLY EXISTENCE. CYRIL OF ALEXANDRIA: He wept in a human manner in order to suppress your tears. He experienced fear in virtue of the economy, at times allowing his flesh to feel what is proper to it in order to fill us with courage. . . . He slept in order that you might learn not to sleep in times of temptation but rather to apply yourself to prayer. Offering his life as a model of saintly existence to be used by earthly beings, he took on the weaknesses of humanity, and what was his purpose in doing this? That we might truly believe that he became man, although he remained what he was, namely, God. LETTER TO EUOPTIUS, ANATHEMA 10.[87]

[81]NPNF 1 14:404. [82]PG 82:712; TCCLSP 2:156. [83]SC 97:436. [84]SC 97:444**. [85]PEP 7:308; COS 341. [86]SC 97:506. [87]PG 76:441.

LIFE IS GIVEN TO THOSE WHO OBEY. EPHREM THE SYRIAN: "He became the source of our eternal salvation" by replacing Adam, who had been the source of our death through his disobedience. But as Adam's death did not reign in those who did not sin, so life reigns in those who do not need to be absolved. Even though he is a liberal giver of life, life is given to those who obey, not to those who fall away from him. COMMENTARY ON THE EPISTLE TO THE HEBREWS.[88]

MADE PERFECT. THEODORET OF CYR: By "being made perfect" he referred to resurrection and immortality, this being the completion of the incarnation. INTERPRETATION OF HEBREWS 5.[89]

SALVATION ACCOMPLISHED. LEO THE GREAT: Our origin, corrupted right after its start, needed to be reborn with new beginnings. A victim had to be offered for reconciliation, a victim that was at one and the same time both related to our race and foreign to our defilement. In this way alone could the plan of God—wherein it pleased him that the sin of the world should be wiped away through the birth and passion of Jesus Christ—in this way alone could the plan of God be of any avail for the times of every generation. Nor would the mysteries—as they pass through various developments in time—disturb us. Instead, they would reassure us, since the faith by which we live would not have differed at any stage.[90]

Let them stop complaining, those who speak up against the divine arrangements with a disloyal murmuring and object to the lateness of our Lord's nativity—as if that which was done in the last age of the world was not applied to previous eras as well. For the incarnation of the Word accomplished by being about to take place the very same thing that it did by having taken place—as the mystery of human salvation never ceased to be active in any earlier age. What the apostles preached, the prophets had also announced. Nor was it too late in being fulfilled, since it has always been believed.

But the wisdom and "kindness of God"[91]—by this delay in his salvific work—has made us better disposed to accept his calling. That way, what had been foretold through so many ages by numerous signs, numerous words and numerous mysteries would not be open to doubt in these days of the gospel. That way, the birth of the Savior—which was to exceed all wonders and the whole measure of human intelligence—would engender in us a faith all the more steadfast, the more often and the earlier it had been proclaimed beforehand.

No, indeed, it is not that God has just recently come up with a plan for attending to human affairs, nor that it has taken him this long to show compassion. Rather, he laid down from the very "foundation of the world"[92] one and the same "cause of salvation" for all. For the grace of God—by which the entire assembly of saints has always been justified—was not initiated at the time when Christ was born, but augmented. This "mystery of great compassion,"[93] with which the whole world has now been filled, was so powerful even in its prefigurations that those who believed it when promised attained to it no less than those who received it when actually given. SERMON 23.3-4.[94]

---

[88]EHA 206-7. [89]PG 82:713; *TCCLSP* 2:157. [90]Heb 2:4; 10:38; cf. Rom 1:17. [91]Tit 3:4. [92]Eph 1:4. [93]1 Tim 3:16; RSV reads "the mystery of our religion." [94]FC 93:90-91.

5:11—6:3 LET US GO ON TO MATURITY

[11]*About this we have much to say which is hard to explain, since you have become dull of hearing.* [12]*For though by this time you ought to be teachers, you need some one to teach you again the first principles of God's word. You need milk, not solid food;* [13]*for every one who lives on milk is unskilled in the word of righteousness, for he is a child.* [14]*But solid food is for the mature, for those who have their faculties trained by practice to distinguish good from evil.*

6 *Therefore let us leave the elementary doctrine of Christ and go on to maturity, not laying again a foundation of repentance from dead works and of faith toward God,* [2]*with instruction*[k] *about ablutions, the laying on of hands, the resurrection of the dead, and eternal judgment.* [3]*And this we will do if God permits.*[l]

k Other ancient manuscripts read *of instruction*   l Other ancient manuscripts read *let us do this if God permits*

OVERVIEW: The first four chapters are about the elementary doctrine of Christ, and the writer does not want to lay again the foundation. "Solid food is for the mature." Origen uses this image to list the parts of the Bible that can be harmful for beginners in the faith: the beginning of Genesis, the first four chapters of Ezekiel, the end of Ezekiel and the Song of Songs. Chrysostom emphasizes that unceasing distribution of the same spiritual food in the church edifies the faithful. Ephrem associates milk with hope in the promises of earthly law and solid food with the word of righteousness in the crucifixion of our flesh.

The early writers recognized that to assimilate the correct affirmations and reject the rest is not a product of simple faith; it requires learning, virtue and education (CLEMENT OF ALEXANDRIA). The Bible is not always easy to understand. The Fathers understood that it was best when the Bible could be understood literally, if that interpretation harmonized with the catholic faith, but frequently it could not be, because it was filled with figures and enigmas. Thus, especially with regard to the Old Testament, we are urged by Christ "to seek and knock," to practice zeal combined with spiritual sobriety and discernment in order to explain all these figures according to the catholic faith

(AUGUSTINE, SYMEON, CHRYSOSTOM). Difficult passages of Scripture are always best interpreted by clear scriptural passages. But divine inspiration is not dependent on our understanding because the treasure of divine wisdom is hidden in the baser and rude vessel of words (ORIGEN). Tertullian points out that even tradition without the written word is acceptable when it is a long-standing practice, such as the mixture of milk and honey given to the newly baptized.

5:11-13 *Milk, Not Solid Food*

FIRST PRINCIPLES OF GOD'S WORD. THEODORET OF CYR: To those still lacking perfect faith the heralds of the truth propose only things to do with the humanity. This is the way followed by blessed Peter in addressing Jews. He accommodated his teaching to the limitations of the listeners, saying, "Jesus of Nazareth, a man attested to you by God," and so on in keeping with this theme. The divinely inspired Paul in proposing the message to the Athenians called Christ the Lord not God but a man.[1] INTERPRETATION OF HEBREWS 5.[2]

---

[1]Acts 2:22; 17:31. [2]PG 82:713; TCCLSP 2:157.

MILK FOR SIMPLE-MINDED FOLK. ORIGEN: For we do everything in our power to see that our gathering consists of intelligent people, and we dare to bring forward in common discourse at the time of our gathering our most noble and divine beliefs when we have an intelligent audience. But we conceal and pass over the more profound truths whenever we see that the meeting consists of simple-minded folk who are in need of that teaching which is figuratively called milk. AGAINST CELSUS 3.52.[3]

OUR LABORS ARE ALL FOR YOUR PROFIT. CHRYSOSTOM: I am afraid that this might fitly be said to you also, that "though by this time you ought to be teachers," you do not hold fast to the rank of learners. Ever hearing the same things on the same subjects, you remain still in the same condition as if you heard no one. If any person should question you, no one will be able to answer, except a very few who may soon be counted. This is no trifling loss. For oftentimes, when the teacher wishes to go on further to touch on higher and more mysterious themes, the want of attention in those who are being taught prevents it. If a boy, though hearing continually the basic elements, does not master them, a grammar master will continually din the same things into the boy and will not leave off teaching until the boy has learned them accurately, for it is great folly to lead him on to other things without having put the first well into him. So too in the church, if, while we constantly say the same things, you learn nothing more, we shall never cease saying the same things.

For if our preaching were a matter of display and ambition, it would have been right to jump from one subject to another and change about continually, taking no thought for you but only for your applauses. But since we have not devoted our zeal to this, but our labors are all for your profit, we shall not cease discoursing to you on the same subjects, till you succeed in learning them. ON THE EPISTLE TO THE HEBREWS 9.1.[4]

CRUCIFIXION OF OUR FLESH. EPHREM THE SYRIAN: "Every one who lives on milk" as food . . . whose hope of salvation is in the promises of the earthly law, is "unskilled in the word of righteousness," that is, in the crucifixion of our flesh, by which the righteousness of God is proclaimed. COMMENTARY ON THE EPISTLE TO THE HEBREWS 5.[5]

5:14 Distinguish Good from Evil

SOLID FOOD OF THE PASSION. EPHREM THE SYRIAN: "Solid food is for the mature," that is, the passion written in the new gospel, and about them it was written, "make ready for the Lord a people prepared."[6] In their own taste, thanks to the right measure of their faith, "they have been trained to distinguish good from evil," that is, by themselves and not by the law. COMMENTARY ON THE EPISTLE TO THE HEBREWS.[7]

FAITH ENGAGED IN LEARNING. CLEMENT OF ALEXANDRIA: Just as we say that it is possible to have faith without being literate, so we assert that it is not possible to understand the statements contained in the faith without study. To assimilate the right affirmations and reject the rest is not the product of simple faith but of faith engaged in learning. Ignorance involves a lack of education and learning. It is teaching that implants in us the scientific knowledge of things divine and human. It is possible to live uprightly in poverty. It is also possible in wealth. We admit that it is easier and quicker to track down virtue if we have a preliminary education. It can be hunted down without these aids, although even then those with learning, "with their faculties trained by practice," have an advantage. STROMATEIS 1.6.35.[8]

SONG OF SONGS. ORIGEN: In the words of Song of Songs may be found that food of which the

---

[3]ANF 4:485*. [4]NPNF 1 14:408-9**. [5]EHA 207. [6]Lk 1:17. [7]EHA 207. [8]FC 85:47.

apostle says, "But solid food is for the mature" and requires such people as listeners who "have their faculties trained by practice to distinguish good from evil." Thus, if those we have called "little ones" come to these places in Scripture, it can happen that they receive no profit at all from this book or even that they are badly injured either by reading what has been written or by examining what has been said to interpret it. But for one who is mature according to the flesh, no little risk and danger arises from this book of Scripture [Song of Songs]. For if he does not know how to listen to the names of love purely and with chaste ears, he may twist everything he has heard from the inner man to the outer, fleshly man and be turned away from the Spirit to the flesh. Then he will nourish in himself fleshly desires, and it will seem because of the divine Scriptures that he is impelled and moved to the lusts of the flesh. For this reason I give warning and advice to everyone who is not yet free of the vexations of flesh and blood and who has not withdrawn from the desire for corporeal nature that he completely abstain from reading this book and what is said about it. Indeed, they say that the Hebrews observe the rule that, unless someone has attained a perfect and mature age, he is not even permitted to hold this book in his hands. Moreover, we also accept the observance of the following rule from them—it is their custom that all the Scriptures should be given to children by the teachers and the wise, and that at the same time those passages which they call *deuterōseis* should be held back to the last. There are four of them: the beginning of Genesis, in which the creation of the world is described; the first chapters of Ezekiel the prophet, in which mention is made of the cherubim; the end of Ezekiel, which includes the building of the temple; and this book, Song of Songs. COMMENTARY ON THE SONG OF SONGS, PROLOGUE.[9]

THE HELP OF HIM WHO URGES US TO ASK, SEEK AND KNOCK. AUGUSTINE: If anyone wanted to take everything that was said according to the letter . . . and could avoid blasphemies and explain everything in harmony with the Catholic faith, we should not only bear him no hostility but also regard him as a leading and highly praiseworthy interpreter. But if there is no way in which we can understand what has been written in a manner that is pious and worthy of God without believing that these things have been set before us in figures and in enigmas, we have the apostolic authority by which so many enigmas from the books of the Old Testament are solved. So let us hold on to the manner of exposition that we have taken up, with the help of him who urges us to ask, to seek and to knock, in order to explain all those figures of things according to the Catholic faith, both those that pertain to history and those that pertain to prophecy. We do this without prejudice to a better and more careful treatment, whether God should deign to make it known through us or through others. ON GENESIS, AGAINST THE MANICHEANS 2.2.3.[10]

CONDUCIVE FOR SAVING US. SYMEON THE NEW THEOLOGIAN: We must carefully discern the thoughts that come on us and set them against the testimonies from the divinely inspired Scriptures and from the teaching of the spiritual teachers, the holy Fathers, so that, if we find them to agree with these witnesses and correspond to them, we may with all our might hold these thoughts fast and boldly act on them. But if they are not in harmony with "the word of truth"[11] we must expel them from us with much anger, as it is written, "Be angry, but sin not."[12] As from something defiling and from the sting of death, so must we flee from the interior assault of passionate thoughts. Accordingly, we need great soberness, great zeal and much searching of the divine Scriptures. The Savior has shown us their usefulness by saying, "search the Scriptures."[13] Search them and hold fast to what they say with great exactitude and faith, in order that

---

[9]*OSW* 218-19. [10]FC 84:95-96*. [11]Eph 1:13; Col 1:5. [12]Ps 4:4. [13]Jn 5:39.

you may know God's will clearly from the divine Scriptures and be able infallibly to distinguish good from evil and not believe every spirit[14] or be carried away with harmful thoughts.[15] Be assured, my brethren, that nothing is so conducive for saving us as the following of the divine precepts of the Savior. Nevertheless, we shall need many tears, much fear, much patience and persistent prayer, if the full meaning of even one single saying of the master is to be revealed to us, in order that we may know the great mystery hidden in small words and lay down our lives unto death even for a single dot of God's commandments. For the word of God is "like a two-edged sword,"[16] which cuts off and separates the soul from every bodily lust and feeling. Even more, it becomes like a burning fire[17] in that it kindles the zeal of the soul. It causes us to despise all life's painful experiences and to count as joy every trial that assails[18] and to desire and embrace death, which is so frightening to others, as life and the cause of life. DISCOURSE 3.8.[19]

FACULTIES BECOME EXERCISED BY EXPERIENCE OF THE SCRIPTURES. CHRYSOSTOM: He is not speaking now concerning life conduct when he says "to distinguish good from evil," for this is possible and easy for every person to know, but concerning doctrines that are wholesome and sublime and those that are corrupted and low. The babe knows not how to distinguish bad and good food. Oftentimes, at least, it even puts dirt into its mouth and takes what is hurtful, and it does all things without judgment; but not so the full-grown person. Such babes are they who lightly listen to everything and give up their ears indiscriminately, which seems to me to blame these Hebrews also, as being lightly "carried away" and giving themselves now to these, now to those. This he also hinted near the end of the epistle, saying, "Do not be led away by diverse and strange teachings."[20] This is the meaning of "to distinguish good from evil." "For the mouth tastes meat, but the soul tries words."[21]

Let us then learn this lesson. Do not, when

you hear that someone is not a heathen or a Jew, straightway believe him to be a Christian, but examine also all the other points; for even Manichaeans and all the heresies have put on this mask in order to deceive the more simple. But if we "have the faculties" of the soul "trained to distinguish good from evil," we are able to discern such teachers.

But how do our "faculties" become "trained"? By continual hearing and by experience of the Scriptures. For when we set forth the error of those heretics and you hear today and tomorrow and prove that it is not right, you have learned the whole, you have known the whole; and even if you should not comprehend today, you will comprehend tomorrow. "Who have," he says, their "faculties trained." You see that it is needful to exercise our hearing by divine studies, so that they may not sound strangely. "Trained," says he, "to distinguish," that is, to be skilled. One person says that there is no resurrection, and another looks for none of the things to come; another says there is a different God; another that he has his beginning from Mary. And see at once how they have all fallen away from want of moderation, some by excess, others by defect. ON THE EPISTLE TO THE HEBREWS 8.7-8.[22]

6:1-3 *Leaving the Elementary Doctrine*

HE CALLED THOSE THINGS A FOUNDATION. SEVERIAN OF GABALA: The beginning of Christ was from within Judaism—for he lived as a Jew according to the law. He says because of this, "Leaving this behind, let us be borne to that maturity," knowing that the one about to be a high priest apart from the law must be a priest "according to the order of Melchizedek."[23]

"Dead works and faith in God, ritual washing." For Christians the earthly things are dead.

---

[14]1 John 4:1. [15]See Eph 4:14. [16]Heb 4:12. [17]Jer 20:9; 23:29. [18]Jas 1:2. [19]*SNTD* 67-68*. [20]Heb 13:9. [21]Job 34:3. RSV reads, "For the ear tests words, as the palate tastes food." [22]NPNF 1 14:406-7*. [23]Heb 5:10; Ps 110:4.

Therefore he says that it is out of place that they neglect the way of life based on faith and the mortification of all things and return to ablutions according to the law. When the Lord came, he preached repentance, saying, "Repent, for the kingdom of God has drawn near,"[24] but it was "a repentance from dead works." . . . This, then, is what he says: it is not necessary to run back to the law, leaving behind the repentance from dead works and faith in God and baptism[25]— which he named in the plural because of the multitude of those deemed worthy. And he spoke of baptisms and the teaching and the laying on of hands through which are the elections, and the hope of the resurrection and the rest. And he has prepared this beforehand, since the priests in the law uphold the law with a vengeance, but Melchizedek was outside the law. Not coming from the levitical priesthood, he followed "the order of Melchizedek."[26] He says that it was not necessary to leave behind the priest in the order of Melchizedek to pursue those who are priests under the law, so that the things written in the law might stand. But he called those things in the law a "foundation," since it has become a preamble of godliness for men. FRAGMENTS ON THE EPISTLE TO THE HEBREWS 6.1-2.[27]

MANY DIFFERENT BAPTISMS UNDER THE LAW. OECUMENIUS: These people, thinking in a more Jewish fashion because there were many different baptisms under the law,[28] wished also to be baptized often with the baptism of the new covenant, the baptism that bestows the new birth, because they wished to be deemed worthy frequently of the forgiveness of sins. FRAGMENTS ON THE EPISTLE TO THE HEBREWS 6.2.[29]

ELEMENTS OF THE BEGINNING OF THE ORACLES OF GOD. PHOTIUS: Although you ought to be teachers, not only are you not teachers, but also you cannot even learn anything except the rather rudimentary and elementary and simple

things, and even these things not absolutely but weaker than the beginning of the oracles of God. He does not say the "elements of the oracles," but the elements of "the beginning" of the oracles. Most likely the elements of the oracles of God would be the words about the incarnation, but the elements of the "beginning" of the oracles are the things about which he goes on to say, "not laying again a foundation," etc.

The argument of the arrangement is this: "Therefore, leaving behind the word of the beginning of Christ, let us be carried to perfection, and we will do this, if God permits."

"The Word of Christ."[30] What sort of word? The word of teaching that it is necessary to lay down a foundation of repentance from dead works, the word of teaching that it is necessary to believe in God, the word of teaching that one must be baptized, the word of teaching that one must be deemed worthy of the Holy Spirit, the word of teaching that there will be a resurrection and that there will be a judgment. For the word and the teaching have a common origin in every respect. FRAGMENTS ON THE EPISTLE TO THE HEBREWS 6.1-3.[31]

LEAVING BEHIND ELEMENTARY MATTERS. PHOTIUS: When he says to leave behind the elementary matters concerning Christ and to leave behind the word which stops any progress at the beginning and to be carried "to perfection,"[32] he does not simply say perfection in its proper sense, but the perfection, as it were, that exists between the rudiments of the oracles of God and the heavenly perfection. For the "elements of the beginning of the oracles of God" consist of renouncing Satan and his works, believing in God, being baptized, receiving the Holy Spirit, knowing about the resur-

---

[24]Mt 4:17. [25]RSV translates *baptismōn* ("baptisms") as "ablutions." [26]Ps 110:4. [27]NTA 15:348-49. [28]Cf. Lev 15:5-6; Num 19:7-8, 31:24; Gen 30:18-20. [29]NTA 15:464. [30]*Ton tēs archēs tou Christou logon* is translated "elementary doctrine of Christ" in RSV. A more literal translation is "the word of the beginning of Christ." [31]NTA 15:644-45. [32]*Teleiotēs* is translated as "maturity" in RSV.

rection of the dead and believing that there is a judgment. These things are the elements of the beginning of the oracles of God. But the "elements of the oracles of God"—not merely the beginning of the oracles of God—is to know that Christ suffered on our behalf, that he removed our sins, that he wrought our salvation for us, that he has become our high priest, that he offered himself on our behalf, and such other things. And "perfection" in renouncing Satan and his cohorts consists of advancement in the virtues and endurance amid tribulations, persecutions and periods of testing. And heavenly "perfection" is the exact apprehension concerning the divine teaching of Christ, insofar as is humanly possible. So first we believe and are baptized, then we know what sort of things Christ underwent for our sake and what sort of things he did in his human nature, then we are perfected in the virtues, then we are deemed worthy of the knowledge which is in accordance with divine wisdom. FRAGMENTS ON THE EPISTLE TO THE HEBREWS 6.1-3.[33]

DRAWN TO FAITH AND TRUST. ORIGEN: But just as the doctrine of providence is not at all weakened because of those things which are not understood by those who have once honestly accepted it, so neither is the divine character of Scripture, which extends to the whole of it, lost because our weakness cannot discover in every expression the hidden splendor of the doctrines concealed in common and unattractive style. For "we have the treasure in earthen vessels, that the exceeding greatness of the power of God may shine forth"[34] and may not be reckoned as coming from us who are but human beings. . . . Therefore, since a celestial or even a supercelestial power compels us to worship the only Creator, let us leave the doctrine of the beginning of Christ, i.e., the elements, and "endeavor to go on to perfection," in order that the wisdom spoken to the perfect may be spoken also to us. ON FIRST PRINCIPLES 4.1.7.[35]

ON TO MATURITY. TERTULLIAN: Now, how long shall we saw away along the same line on this question [i.e., what is permitted], when we have a long-standing practice which by anticipation has all but settled the question? Even though no scriptural passage prescribes it, it is strengthened by a custom that certainly arose from tradition. How can anything become normal practice if it has not first been handed down to us? But, you tell me, "You must always have a written source if you are going to plead the force of tradition."

Let us look into the matter, then, of whether or not a tradition without a written source should be accepted. The answer will certainly be no if we cannot adduce examples of other observations which are without written source in Scripture and rest solely on the basis of tradition and yet have come to have the force of custom. To begin, for instance, with baptism: When we are about to enter the water, and, as a matter of fact, even a short while before, we declare in the presence of the congregation before the bishop that we renounce the devil, his pomps and his angels. After that, we are immersed in the water three times, making a somewhat fuller pledge than the Lord has prescribed in the gospel.[36] After this, having stepped forth from the font, we are given a taste of a mixture of milk and honey[37] and from that day, for a whole week, we forego our daily bath. We also receive the sacrament of the Eucharist that the Lord entrusted to all at the hour for supper, at our early morning meetings, and then from the hand of none but the bishops. Further, we make offerings for the dead on their anniversary to celebrate their birthday of eternal life.

We consider fasting or kneeling during service on Sundays to be unlawful, and we enjoy the same privilege from Easter until Pentecost. We also are upset if any of our bread or wine falls to the earth at the Lord's Supper. Lastly, we make

---

[33]NTA 15:644-45. [34]See 2 Cor 4:7. [35]ANF 4:354-55**. [36]See Mt 28:19. [37]Cf. 1 Cor 3:2; 1 Pet 2:2.

the sign of the cross on our foreheads at every turn, at our going in or coming out of the house, while dressing, while putting on our shoes, when we are taking a bath, before and after meals, when we light the lamps, when we go to bed or sit

down, and in all the ordinary actions of daily life. The Chaplet 3.1-4.[38]

---

[38]FC 40:236-37*.

6:4-12 GOD IS NOT UNJUST

[4]*For it is impossible to restore again to repentance those who have once been enlightened, who have tasted the heavenly gift, and have become partakers of the Holy Spirit,* [5]*and have tasted the goodness of the word of God and the powers of the age to come,* [6]*if they then commit apostasy, since they crucify the Son of God on their own account and hold him up to contempt.* [7]*For land which has drunk the rain that often falls upon it, and brings forth vegetation useful to those for whose sake it is cultivated, receives a blessing from God.* [8]*But if it bears thorns and thistles, it is worthless and near to being cursed; its end is to be burned.*

[9]*Though we speak thus, yet in your case, beloved, we feel sure of better things that belong to salvation.* [10]*For God is not so unjust as to overlook your work and the love which you showed for his sake in serving the saints, as you still do.* [11]*And we desire each one of you to show the same earnestness in realizing the full assurance of hope until the end,* [12]*so that you may not be sluggish, but imitators of those who through faith and patience inherit the promises.*

Overview: In the earliest tradition, especially in the Latin West, and among rigorists like the later Tertullian, the sense of Hebrews 6:4 that it is impossible to repent from sins after baptism was taken literally. Gradually, however, the tradition interpreted this text to mean that baptism, with its symbols of crucifixion, death and life, was a once-and-for-all event that was unrepeatable. Thus, according to Ephrem, while baptism cannot be repeated, the door of repentance is always open to the penitents. Repentance is always possible, however, because what is impossible with humans is possible with God. There is always hope of forgiveness (Ambrose). Origen compares those who need to repent after apostasy to Laz-

arus in the tomb, who needs to hear the voice of Jesus to live again. Chrysostom is most concerned that this passage not become an occasion for Christians to become judgmental, and he defines what it is to be a saint: Every believer is a saint in that he is a believer. Faith makes saintship. In fact, Chrysostom argues that everyone in affliction needs help; we are not to become judgmental and overly curious about the state of a person in need. The person in need is God's, whether he is heathen or Jew; even an unbeliever in need still needs our aid. Repentance, like baptism, signifies rising from spiritual death to new life (Origen, Chrysostom).

Jerome interprets the rain as the life-giving

water of the Word of God. However, Origen points out that the fruits of the divine Word may weather and turn into thistles if stifled by the thorns of worldly passions. It is by uprooting the thorns of passions and vices that we pursue the path of spiritual life (CHRYSOSTOM). The soil of one's heart may harden because of persistence in evil (ORIGEN). It is assurance of hope that carries us through the periods of trouble and tribulations (CHRYSOSTOM). By practicing hope and faith we imitate Christ (CLEMENT OF ALEXANDRIA), which is carried to perfection by the works of unconditional charity to saints and sinners. Indeed, those in need and suffering have an important ministry, for they give us a chance to practice charity. Lent is a special time for practicing kindness, forgiveness and mercy (CHRYSOSTOM).

6:4-6 Impossible to Restore

THE LIMIT FOR DIVINE BAPTISM. THEODORET OF CYR: It is out of the question, he is saying, for those who have approached all-holy baptism, shared in the grace of the divine Spirit and received the type of the eternal goods to make their approach again and be granted another baptism. This is no different, in fact, from fixing the Son of God to the cross again and besmirching him again with the dishonor already shown. As he in his own case endured the passion once, we too likewise ought share the passion with him once. We are buried with him in baptism, and we rise with him; so it is not possible for us to enjoy the gift of baptism again. . . . Our former self was crucified with him in baptism by receiving the type of death. By "goodness of the Word of God" he meant the promise of good things; "powers of the age to come" is the term he used of baptism and the grace of the Spirit: through them it is possible to attain the promised goods.

Now, the apostle said this to teach the believers from Jews not to think all-holy baptism is like the Jewish baptisms: they did not wash away sins, but cleansed the body of apparent defilement—hence they were applied many times and fre-

quently. This baptism of ours, on the contrary, is one only, for the reason that it involves the type of the saving passion and resurrection and prefigures for us the resurrection to come. The followers of Novatian use these words to contest the truth, failing to understand that the divine apostle, far from prohibiting the remedies of repentance, set the limit for divine baptism. . . . After all, his writings to the Corinthians and the Galatians testify to the fact that he preaches repentance everywhere, and he disseminates these teachings everywhere. INTERPRETATION OF HEBREWS 6.[1]

WHAT CAN THE COMING AGE DO? PHOTIUS: "And the powers of the age to come," which is to say, "having learned what things the coming age is capable of." For "having tasted" means "having learned" or "having been instructed," as it commonly means, being taken in a figurative manner. But what can the coming age do? And what are its needs and work? In that age each one finds the reward for the things one did; that neither the punishment nor the blessing in that age has an end; that then whatever deed was not unmindful of the judge but was righteous will appear, etc. He says that for those who have learned these things with others and then have fallen away, it is impossible to bring to repentance. FRAGMENTS ON THE EPISTLE TO THE HEBREWS 6.5.[2]

THE DOOR OF MERCY IS OPEN FOR REPENTANTS. EPHREM THE SYRIAN: "It is impossible to restore again to repentance" through a second baptism "those who have once been baptized,[3] who have tasted the heavenly gift" through the medicine which they received, "have become partakers of the Holy Spirit" through the gifts received from the Spirit, "have tasted the goodness of the Word of God" in the new gospel and were armed with the power of the age to come in the promises prepared for the pious ones, but

---

[1]PG 82:717; *TCCLSP* 2:159-60. [2]NTA 15:645. [3]RSV reads "enlightened."

now "have fallen away" again. Those who propose two baptisms ask for the crucifixion again of the Son of God and for his dishonor. But crucifixion was performed once and will not be performed once more, and baptism was conceded as an "absolver" and is not conceded a second time to the sinner. . . . After the apostle said these words and discouraged them from sinning and being in want of propitiation, he changed his tone and encouraged them, as if to say, "If there is no second baptism to purify you, your deeds and charity are to be an eternal baptism for you." "Though," he says, "we speak thus" and close the door of mercy before the just ones lest they may sin, nevertheless the door of mercy is open for penitents. "God is not so unjust as to overlook your work," that is, your gift, "and the love" which you have for the saints and the poor who are in Jerusalem. COMMENTARY ON THE EPISTLE TO THE HEBREWS.[4]

A SECOND BAPTISM IS AN ACT OF RIDICULE.
SEVERIAN OF GABALA: The apostles raised the dead. And this was the power of the resurrection. He said, "hold him up to contempt," because if baptism is a mystery, it suffices once and for all. And if the matter happens a second time, it is an act of despising and ridicule. FRAGMENTS ON THE EPISTLE TO THE HEBREWS 6.6.[5]

WE HAVE BEEN CRUCIFIED THROUGH BAPTISM. PHOTIUS: What does it mean, "crucifying for themselves anew[6] the Son of God and holding him up to contempt"? He says that they crucify him again for themselves and dishonor him. This is what he means here: Christ was crucified once and for all, and we have been crucified together with him through baptism.[7] Then he says that such a one, imagining that there is a second baptism, like their [first] baptism into him, crucifies the Lord again. For what else does the one do who intends to be crucified a second time with him than to deem that Christ has been crucified a second time through the things he does? But he says that to crucify Christ a second time (insofar as it applies to him) is nothing other than to ridicule and dishonor him. For having died once and for all he is immortal thereafter, but the one who crucifies him anew posits this lie, inasmuch as he reproaches him as a liar when he says that he died once and for all. FRAGMENTS ON THE EPISTLE TO THE HEBREWS 6.6.[8]

THINGS IMPOSSIBLE FROM A HUMAN POINT OF VIEW ARE POSSIBLE WITH GOD. AMBROSE: Could Paul teach in opposition to his own act? He had at Corinth forgiven sin through penance; how could he himself speak against his own decision? Since, then, he could not destroy what he had built, we must assume that what he says was different from, but not contrary to, what had gone before. For what is contrary is opposed to itself; what is different has ordinarily another meaning. Things that are contrary are not such that one can support the other. Inasmuch, then, as the apostle spoke of remitting penance, he could not be silent as to those who thought that baptism was to be repeated. And it was right first of all to remove our anxiety and to let us know that, even after baptism, if any sinned, their sins could be forgiven them, lest a false belief in a reiterated baptism should lead astray those who were destitute of all hope of forgiveness. And second, it was right to set forth in a well-reasoned argument that baptism is not to be repeated. . . .

So, then, that which he says in this epistle to the Hebrews, that it is impossible for those who have fallen to be "renewed unto repentance, crucifying again the Son of God and putting him to open shame," must be considered as having reference to baptism, wherein we crucify the Son of God in ourselves that the world may be by him crucified for us. We triumph, as it were, when we take to ourselves the likeness of his death. We put to open shame upon his cross principalities and powers and triumphed over them, that in the likeness of his death we, too, might triumph over

---

[4]EHA 208. [5]NTA 15:349. [6]*Palin* ("again") is not present in RSV translation. [7]Rom 6:4. [8]NTA 15:646.

the principalities whose yoke we throw off. But Christ was crucified once and died to sin once, and so there is but one, not several baptisms. . . .

And indeed I might also say to anyone who thought that this passage spoke of repentance, that things which are impossible from the human point of view are possible with God. God is able whenever God wills to forgive us our sins, even those which we think cannot be forgiven. And so it is possible for God to give us that which it seems to us impossible to attain. For it seemed impossible that water should wash away sin, and Naaman the Syrian[9] thought that leprosy could not be cleansed by water. But that which was impossible, God who gave us such great grace made to be possible. Similarly it seemed impossible that sins should be forgiven through repentance, but Christ gave this power to his apostles, which has been transmitted to the priestly office. That, then, has become possible which was impossible. But by true reasoning, the apostle convinces us that the reiteration by anyone of the sacrament of baptism is not permitted. Concerning Repentance 2.2.7-12.[10]

The Medicine of Repentance. Chrysostom: What then is the medicine of repentance, and of what does it consist? First, of the condemnation of our own sins. . . . Second, of great humbleness of mind, for it is like a golden chain; if one grasps firmly the beginning, all will follow. Because if you confess your sin as one ought to confess, the soul is humbled, for conscience, turning it on itself, causes it to be subdued.

Other things too must be added to humbleness of mind if it is to be such as the blessed David knew when he said, "A broken and contrite heart, O God, you will not despise."[11] For that which is broken does not rise up, does not strike, but is ready to be ill-treated and does not strike back. Such is contrition of heart. Though it is insulted, though it be evilly treated, it is quiet and is not eager for vengeance.

And after humbleness of mind, there is need of intense prayers, of many tears, tears by day and

tears by night, for, he says, "I am weary with my moaning; every night I flood my bed with tears; I drench my couch with my weeping."[12] And again, "For I eat ashes like bread and mingle tears with my drink."[13] And after prayer this intense, there is need of much almsgiving, for thus it is which especially gives strength to the medicine of repentance. . . . For hear what the divine Scripture says, "Give alms, and all things shall be clean."[14] And again, "By almsgiving and acts of faithfulness sins are purged away."[15] And "Water extinguishes a blazing fire; so almsgiving atones for sin."[16]

Next, do not be angry with any one, not bearing malice, forgiving all their trespasses. For it is said, "Does a man harbor anger against another and yet seek healing from the Lord?"[17] "Forgive that you may be forgiven."[18]

Also, converting our brethren from their wandering. For it is said, "Go, and convert your brethren, that your sins may be forgiven."[19] Remain in close relation with the elders, so if one has "committed sins, he will be forgiven."[20] Stand forward in defense of those who are wronged. Do not retain anger. Bear all things meekly. On the Epistle to the Hebrews 9.8.[21]

Repentance and Humility. Chrysostom: But let us all humble our own souls by almsgiving and forgiving our neighbors their trespasses, by not remembering injuries or avenging ourselves. If we continually reflect on our sins, no external circumstances can make us elated, neither riches, nor power, nor authority, nor honor. Even if we should sit in the imperial chariot itself, we shall sigh bitterly. For even the blessed David was a king, and yet he said, "Every night I flood my bed"[22] . . . and he was not at all hurt by the purple robe and the diadem. He was not puffed up, for he knew himself to be a man, and inasmuch as his heart had been made contrite, he continued mourning. On

---

[9]See 2 Kings 5:11-12. [10]NPNF 2 10:345-46. [11]Ps 51:17 (50:19 LXX). [12]Ps 6:6 (6:7 LXX). [13]Ps 102:9 (101:10 LXX). [14]Lk 11:41. [15]Prov 16:6 LXX. RSV reads, "By loyalty and faithfulness iniquity is atoned for." [16]Sir 3:30. [17]Sir 28:3. [18]Mk 11:25. [19]Cf. Jas 5:19-20; Lk 22:32. [20]Jas 5:15. [21]NPNF 1 14:411-12*. [22]Ps 6:6 (6:7 LXX).

THE EPISTLE TO THE HEBREWS 9.9.[23]

REPENTANCE IS LIFE FROM THE DEAD. ORIGEN: Now we ought to be aware that there are some Lazaruses even now who, after having become friends of Jesus, have become sick and died. As dead persons they have remained in the tomb and the land of the dead with the dead. . . . Consider the one who has fallen away from Christ and returned to the Gentiles' life after he has received knowledge of the truth. He has been enlightened and tasted the heavenly gift and become a partaker of the Holy Spirit . . . yet now is in hades with the shades and the dead and to be in the land of the dead or the tombs.

Whenever, therefore, on behalf of such a person, Jesus comes to his tomb and, standing outside it, prays and is heard, he asks that there be power in his voice and words, and he cries out with a loud voice to summon him who was his friend to the things outside the life of the Gentiles and their tomb and cave. COMMENTARY ON THE GOSPEL OF JOHN 28.54-56.[24]

FORGETTING THE FORMER GRACE. CHRYSOSTOM: "They crucify," he says, "the Son of God on their own account and hold him up to contempt." What he means is this. Baptism is a cross, and "our old self was crucified with him,"[25] for we were "united with him in a death like his"[26] and again, "we were buried therefore with him by baptism into death."[27] Therefore, it is not possible that Christ should be crucified a second time, for that is to "hold him up to contempt." For if "death no longer has dominion over him,"[28] if he rose again, by his resurrection becoming superior to death, if by death he wrestled with and overcame death, and then is crucified again, all those things become a fable and a mockery. He then that baptizes a second time crucifies him again. . . .

For as Christ died on the cross, so do we in baptism, not as to the flesh but as to sin. Behold two deaths. He died as to the flesh. In our case, the old self was buried and the new self arose, made conformable to the likeness of his death. If,

therefore, it is necessary to be baptized again, it is necessary that this same Christ should die again. For baptism is nothing else than the putting to death of the baptized and his rising again. And he well said, "crucify on their own account," for he that does this, having forgotten the former grace and ordering his own life carelessly, acts in all respects as if there were another baptism. It behooves us therefore to take heed and to make ourselves safe. ON THE EPISTLE TO THE HEBREWS 9.6.[29]

6:7-8 Land That Has Drunk the Rain

RAIN. THEODORET OF CYR: By "rain" he referred metaphorically to instruction. INTERPRETATION OF HEBREWS 6.[30]

SPIRITUAL RAIN. JEROME: Would you like to know in what way the faithful are compared with clouds in holy writ? Isaiah says, "I will also command the clouds that they rain no rain upon them."[31] Moses was speaking as if he were a cloud when he said, "May my teaching drop as the rain."[32] The letters of the apostles are spiritual rain for us. As a matter of fact, what does Paul say in his letter to the Hebrews?: "For land which has drunk the rain that often falls upon it," and again, "I planted, Apollos watered."[33] HOMILIES ON THE PSALMS, ALTERNATE SERIES 73 (PSALM 96).[34]

THE SAME RAIN MAY BEAR THISTLES OR FRUIT. ORIGEN: Our earth, that is, our heart, receives blessings if it receives "the rain" of the doctrine of the law "that often falls upon it" and brings forth the fruit of works. But if it does not have a spiritual work but "thorns and thistles," that is, cares of the world or the desire of pleasures and riches, "it is worthless and near to being cursed; its end is to be burned." For that

---

[23]NPNF 1 14:412*. [24]FC 89:303-4*. [25]Rom 6:6. [26]Rom 6:5; cf. Phil 3:10. [27]Rom 6:4. [28]Rom 6:9. [29]NPNF 1 14:410-11**. [30]PG 82:717-720; TCCLSP 2:160. [31]Is 5:6. [32]Deut 32:2. [33]1 Cor 3:6. [34]FC 57:112.

reason, each one of the hearers, when he assembles to hear, receives "the shower" of the Word of God; and, if one indeed brings forth the fruit of a good work, one will obtain "a blessing." But if a person disdains the received Word of God and frequently neglects to hear it and subjects himself to the care and passion of secular affairs, as one who would suffocate the Word "with thorns," he will procure "a curse" for a blessing, and, instead of receiving a blessing, his "end is to be burned." Therefore, he says, "I will give you your rains in their season."[35] HOMILIES ON LEVITICUS 16.2.4-6.[36]

WE FARM TO PLEASE GOD. PHOTIUS: "It is cultivated" manifestly for their salvation and the enjoyment of those producing fruit. And if "the Father is the vinedresser,"[37] just as the Lord says, and again the Son is also the sower, "the one sowing the good seed,"[38] if the crop is suitable for them, that is, if the fruit appears—for we also ought to bear fruit for God, as he says somewhere, "but now having become slaves to God, produce your fruit for sanctification"[39]—then if this is the case, we farm manifestly because of God, in order that we may please him with a virtuous life. Therefore we also will be deemed worthy of his blessing. FRAGMENTS ON THE EPISTLE TO THE HEBREWS 6.7.[40]

NEAR TO BEING CURSED. CHRYSOSTOM: "Worthless," he says, "and near to being cursed." Oh, how great consolation in this word! For he said "near to being cursed," not "cursed." Now he that has not yet fallen into a curse but has come to be near to it, may he then come to be far off from it. And not by this only did he encourage them, but also by what follows. For he did not say . . . "which shall be burned," but what? "Its end is to be burned," if he continues in this way to the end, he means. Thus if we cut out and burn the thorns, we shall be able to enjoy those good things innumerable and become approved and partake of blessing. ON THE EPISTLE TO THE HEBREWS 10.3.[41]

IT IS NOT GOD'S PURPOSE TO HARDEN. ORIGEN: Let us see then whether by an illustration used by the apostle in the epistle to the Hebrews, we are able to prove that by one operation God has mercy upon one while he hardens another. It is not God's intent to harden, but while having a good purpose, hardening follows as a result of the inherent principle of wickedness in such persons, so that he is said to harden him who is hardened.[42] . . . As regards the rain there is one operation, but the ground which is cultivated produces fruit, while that which is neglected and is barren produces thorns. ON FIRST PRINCIPLES 3.1.10.[43]

6:9-12 *In Your Case*

HOPE RECOVERS US. CHRYSOSTOM: This is the admirable part of Paul's wisdom. . . . For when he says, "We desire each one of you," it is as if one should say, "I wish you always to be in earnest and, such as you were before, to be also now and for the time to come." For this made his reproof more gentle and easy to be received. And he did not say, "I will," which would have been expressive of the authority of a teacher, but what is expressive of the affection of a father and what is more than "willing," "we desire." He is all but saying, "Pardon us, even if we say what is distasteful."

"We desire each one of you to show the same earnestness in realizing the full assurance of hope until the end." Hope, he means, carries us through. It recovers us again. So do not despair, lest your hope be in vain. For one that works for good hopes also for good and never despairs of himself. ON THE EPISTLE TO THE HEBREWS 10.5.[44]

IMITATING CHRIST. CLEMENT OF ALEXANDRIA: "We," according to the good apostle, "wait for the

---

[35]Lev 26:4. [36]FC 83:265**. [37]Jn 15:1. [38]Mt 13:24. [39]Rom 6:22. [40]NTA 15:646-47. [41]NPNF 1 14:414*. [42]Origen is writing here specifically about the hardening of Pharaoh. [43]ANF 4:310**. [44]NPNF 1 14:415*.

hope of righteousness, for in Christ neither circumcision nor uncircumcision is of any avail, but faith working through love."[45] "We desire each one of you to show the same earnestness in realizing the full assurance of hope," and so on to, "having become a high priest forever, after the order of Melchizedek."[46] Wisdom, full of every virtue, uses similar words to Paul's: "Anyone who listens to me will live safely, trusting in hope."[47] The establishment of hope and hope itself are spoken of interchangeably. That is why he has done admirably to add the word *trusting* to "will live safely." He is showing that the sort of person who has hold of the hope he hoped for is at peace. This is why he adds, "And he will be tranquil, without fear, free from all evil."[48] The apostle speaks openly in the first letter to the Corinthians when he says expressly, "Be imitators of me, as I am of Christ,"[49] to bring this about. If you imitate me and I imitate Christ, then you are imitating Christ as he is representing God. So he establishes a target for faith in "the likeness to God so far as possible in justice and holiness combined with practical wisdom,"[50] and the goal in the actualization of the promise on the basis of faith. STROMATEIS 2.22.136.[51]

VISIT IN PRISON SAINT AND SINNER. CHRYSOSTOM: Hearing these things, let us, I beseech you, "minister to the saints." For every believer is a saint in that he is a believer. Though he remains a person living in the world, he is a saint. "For," he says, "the unbelieving husband is sanctified through the wife, and the unbelieving wife through the husband."[52] See how the faith makes the saint. If then we see even a secular person in misfortune, let us stretch out a hand to him. Let us not be zealous only for those [ascetics] who dwell in the mountains; they are indeed saints both in manner of life and in faith; these others, however, are saints by their faith, and many of them also in manner of life. Let us not refuse to visit one in prison if he is unholy but go visit him if he is a saint. Whether he is a saint or brother, visit him. Suppose then you ask, but if he is unclean and polluted? Listen to

Christ saying, "Judge not, that you be not judged."[53] Act for God's sake. What am I saying? Even if we see a heathen in misfortune, we ought to show kindness to him, and to every one without exception who is in misfortunes, and all the more to a believer who is in the world. Listen to Paul saying, "Do good to all men, and especially to those who are of the household of faith."[54] But I know not where this notion has come from or how this habit has prevailed. For if one actively seeks after the solitaries and is willing to do good to them alone, but with regard to others, on the contrary, is overcurious in his inquiries and says, "unless he be worthy, unless he be righteous, unless he work miracles, I will not stretch out my hand"—such a one has taken away the greater part of charity. In time he will in turn destroy the charity itself. If it is truly charity, it is shown toward sinners, toward the guilty. For this is charity, not to pity those who have done well, but those who have done wrong. ON THE EPISTLE TO THE HEBREWS 10.7.[55]

A JUST CLAIM ON YOUR AID. CHRYSOSTOM: So then also, if you see anyone in affliction, do not be curious to inquire further. His being in affliction involves a just claim on your aid. For if, when you see an ass choking, you raise him up without curiously inquiring whose he is, much more about a man one ought not to be overcurious in inquiring whose he is. He is God's, whether heathen or Jew. Even if he is an unbeliever, still he needs help. If the office is committed to you to judge or inquire, then you might well have inquired. But, as it is, his misfortune as such does not permit you to search out these things. Even about people in good health it is not right to be overcurious, nor to be a busybody in other people's matters; even less about those that are in affliction. ON THE EPISTLE TO THE HEBREWS 10.8.[56]

---

[45]Gal 5:5-6. [46]Heb 6:20. [47]Prov 1:33. [48]Prov 1:33. [49]1 Cor 11:1. [50]Plato *Theatetus* 176B. [51]FC 85:248-49. [52]1 Cor 7:14. [53]Mt 7:1. [54]Gal 6:10. [55]NPNF 1 14:416-17*. [56]NPNF 1 14:417*.

SHOW LOVE FOR GOD'S SAKE. CHRYSOSTOM: The poor perform needful services for you. What are these? Don't they serve you well? Suppose then I show an especially poor man who performs needful services for you far greater than they do. He will stand by you in the day of judgment. Will he deliver you from the fire? Will all your servants deliver you likewise? When Tabitha died, who raised her up? The servants who stood around or the poor? But you—you are not even willing to put the freeman on an equality with your servants. The frost is hard, and the poor man is cast out in rags, well-nigh dead, with his teeth chattering. Both by his looks and his air you should be moved. And yet, you pass by, warm and full of drink. How do you expect that God should deliver you when in misfortune? And often you will say to yourself, "If I had found one that had done many wrong things, I would have forgiven him, so won't God forgive me?" Do not say this. You neglect the one who has done you no wrong, yet you would be able to help. How shall he forgive you when you are sinning against him? Is not this deserving of hell? . . . Oftentimes you adorn with innumerable vestments of varied colors and gold decorations a dead body, insensible, that can no longer even perceive the honor. Meanwhile one who is in pain and lamenting and tormented and racked by hunger and frost, you neglect and give more to vainglory than to the fear of God.

And it does not even stop here. Immediately accusations are brought against the applicant. For why does he not work, you say? And why is he to be maintained in idleness? But, tell me, is it by working that you have what you have? Did you not receive it as an inheritance from your fathers? And even if you work, is this a reason why you should reproach another? Do you not hear what Paul says? For after saying, "If anyone will not work, let him not eat,"[57] he says, "Do not be weary in well doing."[58] But what do they say? He is an impostor. What do you say, O man? Do you call him an impostor for the sake of a single loaf or of a garment? But, you say, he will sell it immediately. And do you manage all your affairs well?

But what? Are all poor through idleness? Is no one so from shipwreck? None from lawsuits? None from being robbed? None from dangers? None from illness? None from any other difficulties? If, however, we hear any one bewailing such evils and crying out aloud and looking up naked toward heaven, with long hair and clad in rags, at once we call him, "The impostor! The deceiver! The swindler!" Are you not ashamed? Whom do you call impostor? Do not accuse the man or give him a hard time. But, you say, he has means and pretends. This is a charge against yourself, not against him. He knows that he has to deal with the cruel, with wild beasts rather than with rational persons. He knows that even if he tells his pitiable story, no one pays any attention. And on this account he is forced to assume even a more miserable guise, that he may melt your soul. If we see a person coming to beg in a respectable dress, "This is an impostor," you say, "and he comes in this way that he may be supposed to be of good birth." If we see one in the contrary guise, we reproach him too. What then are they to do? Oh, the cruelty, Oh, the inhumanity!

And why, you say, do they expose their maimed limbs? Because of you. If we were compassionate, they would have no need of these artifices. If they persuaded us at the first application, they would not have contrived these devices. Who is there so wretched as to be willing to cry out so much, as to be willing to behave in an unseemly way, as to be willing to make public lamentations, with his wife destitute of clothing, with his children, to sprinkle ashes on himself? How much worse than poverty are these things? Yet, on account of them, not only are they not pitied, but they are even made subject to our accusations. ON THE EPISTLE TO THE HEBREWS 11.7-8.[59]

IT IS THE SEASON OF KINDNESS. CHRYSOSTOM: "Give to him who begs from you, and do not refuse him who would borrow from you."[60] Stretch out your hand; let it not be closed up. We

---

[57]2 Thess 3:10. [58]2 Thess 3:13. [59]NPNF 1 14:420-21*. [60]Mt 5:42.

have not been constituted examiners into others' lives, for then we should have compassion on no one. When you call upon God, why do you say, "Remember not my sins"? So, even if that person is a great sinner, make this allowance in his case also, and do not remember his sins. It is the season of kindness, not of strict inquiry; of mercy, not of account. He wishes to be maintained; if you are willing, give; but if not willing, send him away without raising doubts. Why are you wretched and miserable? Why do you not pity

him yourself, but even turn away those who would as well? For when such a one hears from you, "This person is a cheat; that a hypocrite; and the other lends out money," he neither gives to the one nor to the other, for he suspects all to be such. For you know that we easily suspect evil, but good, not so easily. On the Epistle to the Hebrews 11.9.[61]

---

[61]NPNF 1 14:421-22*.

6:13-20 THE SECURE BASIS FOR HOPE IS GOD'S PROMISE

[13]*For when God made a promise to Abraham, since he had no one greater by whom to swear, he swore by himself,* [14]*saying, "Surely I will bless you and multiply you."* [15]*And thus Abraham,^m having patiently endured, obtained the promise.* [16]*Men indeed swear by a greater than themselves, and in all their disputes an oath is final for confirmation.* [17]*So when God desired to show more convincingly to the heirs of the promise the unchangeable character of his purpose, he interposed with an oath,* [18]*so that through two unchangeable things, in which it is impossible that God should prove false, we who have fled for refuge might have strong encouragement to seize the hope set before us.* [19]*We have this as a sure and steadfast anchor of the soul, a hope that enters into the inner shrine behind the curtain,* [20]*where Jesus has gone as a forerunner on our behalf, having become a high priest for ever after the order of Melchizedek.*

m Greek *he*

Overview: The Fathers were most impressed that God took an oath in making the promise to Abraham, "even though it be unworthy of him that he should not be believed." The oath of God never fails, as God and his Word cannot lie (Athanasius, Clement of Rome, Ephrem). But this was promised as much for us as for Abraham (Chrysostom). Jesus our forerunner did not go just into the shrine of the tabernacle like Moses but into the inner part of the veil of

heaven. As our high priest he offered fitting sacrifice for all nations, after the pattern of Melchizedek (Ephrem). While we are still in the world we are already living among the promises. Through hope we are already in heaven. Hope is like an anchor for us in the storms of life (Chrysostom).

6:13-20 The Unchangeable Character of God's Purpose

HE SWORE BY HIMSELF. CHRYSOSTOM: Do you see that God regards not his own dignity, but more so how he may persuade people, even though God bears with having unworthy things said of himself. His wish is to impart full assurance. In the case of Abraham, indeed, the apostle shows that the whole promise was of God, not of [Abraham's] patient endurance, since God was even willing to add an oath—for it was by him by whom men swear that God also "swore," that is "by himself." People swear by one greater. God swore not by one greater, for there was none greater, yet he did it. It is not the same thing for man to swear by himself as for God, for man is not the final authority over himself. You see then that this is said no more for Abraham than for ourselves: "that we who have fled for refuge," he says, "might have strong encouragement to seize the hope set before us." Here too again, "having patiently endured, he obtained the promise." . . .

He did not say, "when he swore." One shows the seriousness of an oath by speaking of swearing by one greater. But since the race of humanity is hard of belief, he condescends to communicate on our level. So then for our sake he [so to speak] swears, even though it be unworthy of him that he should not be believed. So also in this sense the apostle made that other statement, "He learned obedience through what he suffered,"[1] because people think going through experience to be more worthy of reliance. ON THE EPISTLE TO THE HEBREWS 11.2.[2]

OATH AS WITNESS. THEODORET OF CYR: As God has no one superior to him (he is saying), his oath was witness; he swore by himself, in fact. Yet though making a promise and doing it with an oath, he did not immediately fulfill the promise; instead, the patriarch needed great patience, and only with the passage of a great length of time did he thus see the realization of the promise. INTERPRETATION OF HEBREWS 6.[3]

GOD'S PROMISE WILL NEVER BE CHANGED.

EPHREM THE SYRIAN: "Through this" oath "God desired to show more convincingly to the heirs of the promise" that God's promise, because indeed it is God's, will never be changed. God's oath was infallible in its being interposed, that is, between God, the angel and Abraham. COMMENTARY ON THE EPISTLE TO THE HEBREWS.[4]

HEAVEN IS THE CURTAIN. THEODORET OF CYR: By "curtain" he referred to heaven: the Lord promised to give the kingdom of heaven to those believing in him. INTERPRETATION OF HEBREWS 6.[5]

NOTHING IS IMPOSSIBLE TO GOD, SAVE LYING. CLEMENT OF ROME: With this hope, then, let us attach ourselves to the one who is faithful to promises and just in judgments. The one who bids us to refrain from lying is all the less likely to lie. For nothing is impossible to God, save lying. 1 CLEMENT 27.1-2.[6]

SCRIPTURES DO NOT LIE. ATHANASIUS: Through Moses God gave commandments about sacrifices, and the whole book of Leviticus is taken up with acceptable ways for them to be carried out. The Lord, through the prophets, found fault with those who contemptuously misstated these things, calling them disobedient to the commandment. He told them, "I have not asked you to do these things! . . . Neither did I speak to your fathers about sacrifices, nor give them commands about whole burnt offerings."[7]

Some have put forth the opinion that either the Scriptures do not agree or that God, who gave the commandment, is a liar. But in this there can be no disagreement—far from it. The Father, who is truth, cannot lie, "for it is impossible for God to lie," as Paul affirms. Actually, these things are plain to those who accept the writings of the

---

[1]Heb 5:8. [2]NPNF 1 14:419*. [3]PG 82:720; *TCCLSP* 2:161. [4]EHA 209-10. [5]PG 82:721; *TCCLSP* 2:161-62. [6]LCL 1:56; FC 1:31*. [7]Cf. Is 1:11-13; Jer 7:22.

law with faith and look at them in the right way. Here is my explanation, and may God grant by your prayers that I am not too far from the truth. It does not appear to me that God gave the commandments and the law concerning sacrifices right away when he led them out of Egypt. Nor did he who gave the law really pay any attention to the whole burnt offerings, as such. He was looking ahead to those things that were prefigured and pointed out by them. "For the law has but a shadow of the good things to come."[8] And "Those regulations were set forth until the time of reformation."[9]

That is why the whole law did not deal with sacrifices, although it did include commands concerning them. By means of these commands it began to teach people, calling them away from idols and drawing them to God, giving them proper teaching for the times in which they lived. So you see, God did not give the people those commands about sacrifices and offerings when he brought them out of Egypt, nor even when they first came to Mount Sinai. God is not like people, that he should want those things for himself. No, he gave the commandment so that they might know him and his Word (the Son)—and forget about those so-called gods that do not really exist but appear to do so because of the show people put on. FESTAL LETTERS 19.4.[10]

GOD'S PURPOSE. SEVERIAN OF GABALA: When he said above, "the full assurance of the hope,"[11] he made clear that God furnished to Abraham "full assurance," not that which belonged to his conduct through works but that which belonged to him through God's redemptive plan. FRAGMENTS ON THE EPISTLE TO THE HEBREWS 6.17.[12]

TWO UNCHANGEABLE THINGS. THEODORE OF MOPSUESTIA: "Through two unchangeable things," namely, that God would never be able to lie about what had been promised and that he made the promise with an oath. FRAGMENTS ON THE EPISTLE TO THE HEBREWS 6.18.[13]

THE WORD FOR ALL NATIONS. EPHREM THE SYRIAN: "Through two unchangeable things" . . . the former is that he swore by himself. The latter is that David said, "The Lord has sworn and will not change his mind, that you are a priest forever after the order of Melchizedek."[14] It is by this means that we who have been made coheirs of his promise "might have strong encouragement." We "have fled for refuge" in order to protect ourselves, not for God's justice, in order that God may draw and drive us away from the evils of this world, and may open for us the way "into the inner shrine behind the curtain." We do not go in first. We do not go into the shrine of the tabernacle, where Moses went, but into the inner shrine in heaven, "where Jesus has gone as a forerunner, having become a high priest forever," not in order to offer the victims of sacrifices, like Aaron, but to offer the word for all nations, like Melchizedek. COMMENTARY ON THE EPISTLE TO THE HEBREWS.[15]

THE ANCHOR OF HOPE. CHRYSOSTOM: Paul shows that while we are still in the world and not yet departed from this life, we are already living amid God's promises. For through hope we are already in heaven. . . . As the anchor, dropped from the vessel, does not allow it to be carried about even if ten thousand winds agitate it but, being depended upon, makes it steady, so also does hope.

Note what a fitting image he has chosen. He did not speak of a foundation, which would not be suitable, but of an anchor. For that which is on the tossing sea and seems not to be very firmly fixed stands on the water as upon land and is shaken and yet is not moved. For in regard to those who are very firm and who love the truth, Christ with good reason spoke of one who "has built his house on a rock."[16] But in respect of those who are giving way and who ought to be

---

[8]Heb 10:1. [9]Heb 9:10. [10]NPNF 2 4:546**. [11]Heb 6:11. [12]NTA 15:349. [13]NTA 15:206. [14]Ps 110:4 (109:4 LXX), cf. Heb 6:20. [15]EHA 210. [16]Mt 7:24.

carried through by hope, Paul has more suitably set down this metaphor. For the surge and the great storm toss the boat, but hope does not permit it to be carried back and forth, although winds innumerable agitate it, so that, unless we had this hope we should long ago have been sunk. Nor is it only in things spiritual, but also in the affairs of this life, that one may find the power of hope great. Whatever it may be, in merchandise, in husbandry, in a military expedition, unless one sets this before him, he would not even touch the work. But he said not simply "anchor," but "sure and steadfast," not shaken. ON THE EPISTLE TO THE HEBREWS 11.3.[17]

FORERUNNER. THEODORET OF CYR: He augmented their confidence with the name forerunner: if he is our forerunner and has gone up for us, we too must follow and be granted ascent. INTERPRETATION OF HEBREWS 6.[18]

HIGH PRIEST NOT AS SACRIFICE BUT AS MEDIATOR. THEODORET OF CYR: He is a high priest forever, not in offering sacrifices (having offered his own body once), but in being a mediator leading the believers to the Father; through him (he says, remember) we both have had access to the Father. The Lord himself says in the sacred Gospels, "No one comes to the Father except through me."[19] We must be aware, of course, that the divine apostle made mention of the oaths sworn to Abraham so that the unchanging character of the divine will should be brought out; it endures in advance the stability of high priesthood according to the order of Melchizedek, the oath being linked to the word at this place. INTERPRETATION OF HEBREWS 6.[20]

THE HOPE OF THE RESURRECTION. THEODORE OF MOPSUESTIA: Paul added that "Christ" has become "an eternal high priest" for us, in that Christ leads all those believing through him in each generation to God based on the hope of the resurrection. FRAGMENTS ON THE EPISTLE TO THE HEBREWS 6.20.[21]

---

[17]NPNF 1 14:419*. [18]PG 82:721; TCCLSP 2:162. [19]Jn 14:6. [20]PG 82:721, 724; TCCLSP 2:162. [21]NTA 15:207.

7:1-10 MELCHIZEDEK, PRIEST OF THE MOST HIGH GOD

For this Melchizedek, king of Salem, priest of the Most High God, met Abraham returning from the slaughter of the kings and blessed him; ²and to him Abraham apportioned a tenth part of everything. He is first, by translation of his name, king of righteousness, and then he is also king of Salem, that is, king of peace. ³He is without father or mother or genealogy, and has neither beginning of days nor end of life, but resembling the Son of God he continues a priest for ever.

⁴See how great he is! Abraham the patriarch gave him a tithe of the spoils. ⁵And those descendants of Levi who receive the priestly office have a commandment in the law to take tithes from the people, that is, from their brethren, though these also are descended from Abraham. ⁶But this man who has not their genealogy received tithes from Abraham and blessed him who had the promises.

⁷It is beyond dispute that the inferior is blessed by the superior. ⁸Here tithes are received by mortal men; there, by one of whom it is testified that he lives. ⁹One might even say that Levi himself, who receives tithes, paid tithes through Abraham, ¹⁰for he was still in the loins of his ancestor when Melchizedek met him.

OVERVIEW: A major theme of this epistle and especially this pericope is the superiority of Christ over all creatures and the preeminence of his mediatorial office over all other ministries. The story of Abraham and Melchizedek from Genesis 14 provides the pattern. The mortal Levite priest usually receives the tithes, but here, according to the author of Hebrews, the immortal one, the eternal priest from Salem, Melchizedek, for whom there is no mention of a father or mother, receives the tithes from Abraham who will one day father Levi (EUSEBIUS, AUGUSTINE, SEVERIAN). Melchizedek is here compared with the perfect Jesus, who descended not from Levi but from Judah. There was a diversity of speculation about Melchizedek in the early church. These speculations are often discovered in the writings against the heretics, who depicted him as a divine or angelic being. Christ is prefigured by Melchizedek (LEO THE GREAT, CYPRIAN, EPIPHANIUS) whose name points to his kingship and his priesthood (CLEMENT OF ALEXANDRIA, GREGORY OF NAZIANZUS, EPHREM). However, on the basis of the same facts Ambrose concludes that it is Melchizedek who is modeled after Christ.

Melchizedek receives tithes from Abraham and witnesses to Abraham (EPHREM). Anticipating Christ, he is a priest forever (EUSEBIUS, BEDE), the Word without a mother (THEODORE, NESTORIUS), who offers sacrifice for all (BEDE, EPHREM), whose priesthood is not derived from Aaron but from above (AUGUSTINE). Justin finds theological significance in the fact that Melchizedek, the priest of those without circumcision, blessed Abraham, who was in circumcision. The name of Melchizedek, interpreted by the Fathers as "righteous king" or "king of justice," signifies Christ (GREGORY OF NAZIANZUS, EPHREM, CLEMENT OF ALEXANDRIA). Jerome and Ephrem allow for a possibility that Melchizedek was Shem. Chrysostom and Eusebius, however, believe that Melchizedek's superiority over human nature signifies divinity of Christ that surpasses his humanity (EPHREM).

Christ is both alike and different from Melchizedek (CHRYSOSTOM), who points to the mystery of the twofold birth of Christ (JOHN CASSIAN). The priesthood of Melchizedek lasts forever, not in Melchizedek himself but in the Lord of Melchizedek (EPHREM). A passage from Gregory of Nazianzus captures the poetry of Melchizedek's mysterious role: "The old has passed away, / Behold all things have been made anew.... / The laws of nature are abrogated / that the cosmos above be brought to perfection."

7:1 *Priest of the Most High God*

A PRIEST FOREVER. EUSEBIUS OF CAESAREA: An ancient priest of the Mosaic order could only be selected from the tribe of Levi. It was obligatory without exception that he should be of the family descending from Aaron and do service to God in outward worship with the sacrifices and blood of irrational animals. But he that is named Melchizedek, which in Greek is translated "king of righteousness," who was king of Salem, which would mean "king of peace," without father, without mother, without line of descent, not having, according to the account, "beginning of years or end of life," had no characteristics shared by the Aaronic priesthood. For he was not chosen by humans, he was not anointed with prepared oil, he was not of the tribe of those who had not yet been born; and, strangest of all, he was not even circumcised in his flesh, and yet he blesses Abraham, as if he were far better than he. He did not act as priest to the Most High God with sacrifices and libations, nor did he minister at the temple in Jerusalem. How could he? It did not yet exist. And he was such, of course, because there was going to be no similarity between our Savior Christ and Aaron, for he was neither to be designated priest after a period when he was not priest, nor was he to become priest, but be it. For we should notice carefully in the words, "You are a priest forever," he does not say, "You shall be what you were not before," any more than, "You were that before which you are not now"—but by him who said, "I am who I am,"[1] it is said, "You are, and remain, a priest forever." . . .

And the fulfillment of the oracle is truly wondrous to one who recognizes how our Savior Jesus, the Christ of God, now performs through his ministers even today sacrifices after the manner of Melchizedek's. For just as he, who was priest of the Gentiles, is not represented as offering outward sacrifices but as blessing Abraham only with wine and bread, so in exactly the same way our Lord and Savior himself first, and then all his priests among all nations, perform the spiritual sacrifice according to the customs of the church and with wine and bread darkly express the mysteries of his body and saving blood. This by the Holy Spirit Melchizedek foresaw and used the figures of what was to come, as the Scripture of Moses witnesses, when it says, "And Melchizedek, king of Salem, brought out bread and wine; he was priest of God Most High, and he blessed Abraham."[2] And thus it followed that to him only was the addition of an oath, "The Lord God has sworn and will not change his mind, 'You are a priest forever after the order of Melchizedek.' "

The psalm too, continuing, even shows in veiled phrase the passion of [Christ], saying, "He will drink from the brook by the way; therefore he will lift up his head."[3] And another psalm shows "the brook" to mean the time of temptations: "Our soul has passed through the brook; yes, our soul has passed through the deep waters."[4] He drinks, then, in the brook, that cup of which he darkly spoke at the time of his pas-

sion, when he said, "Father, if it be possible, let this cup pass from me."[5] And also, "If this cannot pass unless I drink it, your will be done."[6]

It was, then, by drinking this cup that he lifted up his head, as the apostle says, for when he was "obedient unto death, even death on a cross, therefore," he says, "God has highly exalted him,"[7] raising him from the dead and setting him at his right hand, far above all rule and authority and power and dominion and every name which is named, not only in this world but in that which is to come. And he has put all things in subjection under his feet, according to the promise made to him, which he expresses through the psalmist, saying, "Sit at my right hand, till I make your enemies your footstool. . . . Rule in the midst of your foes."[8]

It is plain to all that today the power of our Savior and the word of his teaching rule over all them that have believed in him, in the midst of his enemies and foes. PROOF OF THE GOSPEL 5.3.[9]

NOT IN THE LINE OF AARON. AUGUSTINE: On receiving this promise[10] Abraham moved on and stayed in another place in the same land, Hebron, near the Oak of Mamre. . . . But he received at the same time a public blessing from Melchizedek, who was "a priest of the Most High God."[11] Many important things are written about Melchizedek in the epistle entitled "To the Hebrews," which the majority attribute to the apostle Paul, though many deny the attribution. Here we certainly see the first manifestation of the sacrifice which is now offered to God by Christians in the whole world, in which is fulfilled what was said in prophecy, long after this event, to Christ who was yet to come in the flesh: "you are a priest forever, after the order of Melchizedek."[12] Not, it is observed, in the line of Aaron, for that line was to be abolished when the events prefigured by these shadows came to the light of day. CITY OF GOD 16.22.[13]

[1]Ex 3:14. [2]Gen 14:18. [3]Ps 110:7 (109:7 LXX). [4]Ps 124:4 (123:4 LXX). [5]Mt 26:39. [6]Mt 26:42. [7]Phil 2:9. [8]Ps 110:1-2 (109:1-2 LXX). [9]POG 1:241-43*. [10]Gen 13:15. [11]Gen 14:18. [12]Ps 110:4 (109:4 LXX). [13]FC 14:526*.

MELCHIZEDEK'S PRIESTHOOD. SEVERIAN OF GABALA: It is for a reason that we are reminded how Melchizedek met with Abraham after his victory over the Assyrians and gave him one-tenth of all the spoils. This indicates that Melchizedek, the priest, was a forefather of the tribe of the Levites. However, the priesthood without the law is greater than that under the law. FRAGMENTS ON THE EPISTLE TO THE HEBREWS 7.1-2.[14]

PRIEST OF THOSE IN UNCIRCUMCISION. JUSTIN MARTYR: And Melchizedek was priest of those who were in uncircumcision, and he blessed Abraham who was in circumcision, who offered him tithes. Thus God has shown that his eternal priest, also called "Lord" by the Holy Spirit, would become priest of those in uncircumcision. DIALOGUE WITH TRYPHO 33.[15]

INSTITUTED THE SAME TYPE OF SACRIFICE THAT WAS TO COME. BEDE: Just as our Redeemer, when he appeared in the flesh, deigned to become like a king to us by bestowing a heavenly kingdom, so too did he become a high priest by offering himself for us as a sacrifice to God with an odor of sweetness. Hence it is written, "The Lord has sworn and will not change his mind, 'You are a priest forever according to the order of Melchizedek.'"[16] Melchizedek, as we read, was a priest of the Most High God long before the time of the priesthood of the law, and he offered bread and wine to the Lord. Our Redeemer is said to be a priest "after the order of Melchizedek" because he put aside the sacrificial victims stipulated by the law and instituted the same type of sacrifice to be offered in the new covenant in the mystery of his own body and blood. HOMILIES ON THE GOSPELS 2.19.[17]

THE ONE PREFIGURED BY MELCHIZEDEK. LEO THE GREAT: We therefore confess, dearly beloved, not rashly but with faith, that the Lord Jesus Christ is present in the midst of believers. Although he "sits at the right hand" of God the Father "until he makes of his enemies a footstool,"[18] the high priest has not left the assembly of his priests.

Fittingly does this chant rise up to him from the mouth of the whole church and from that of all priests, "The Lord has sworn, and he will not change his mind, 'You are a priest forever after the order of Melchizedek.'"[19] He himself is the true and eternal bishop whose ministry can neither change nor end. He is the one prefigured by the high priest Melchizedek.

Attached to oaths among human beings are certain conditions that have been made irrevocable by permanent guarantees. Surety for the divine oath can therefore be found in promises that have been fixed by immutable decrees. Since regret implies a change of will, God does not regret what, according to his eternal good pleasure, he cannot want to be otherwise than how he has wanted it. SERMON 5.3.[20]

MELCHIZEDEK BORE A TYPE OF CHRIST. CYPRIAN: Also in the priest Melchizedek we see prefigured the sacrament of the sacrifice of the Lord, according to what divine Scripture testifies and says, "And Melchizedek, king of Salem, brought out bread and wine."[21] Now he was a priest of the Most High God and blessed Abraham. And that Melchizedek bore a type of Christ, the Holy Spirit declares in the psalms, saying from the person of the Father to the Son, "Before the morning star I begat you; you are a priest forever, after the order of Melchizedek."[22] That order is assuredly this, coming from that sacrifice and thence descending, that Melchizedek was a priest of the Most High God; that he offered wine and bread; that he blessed Abraham. For who is more a priest of the Most High God than our Lord Jesus Christ, who offered a sacrifice to God the Father and offered that very same thing which Melchizedek had offered, that is, bread and wine, to wit,

---

[14]NTA 15:350. [15]ANF 1:211. [16]Ps 110:4 (109:4 LXX). [17]CS 111:189. [18]Ps 110:1 (109:1 LXX). [19]Ps 110:4 (109:4 LXX). [20]FC 93:31. [21]Gen 14:18. [22]Cf. Ps 110:4 (109:4 LXX).

his body and blood? And with respect to Abraham, that blessing going before belonged to our people. For if Abraham believed in God and it was accounted unto him as righteousness, assuredly whosoever believes in God and lives in faith is found righteous and already is blessed in faithful Abraham and is set forth as justified. This the blessed apostle Paul proves, when he says, "Abraham 'believed God, and it was reckoned to him as righteousness.' So you see that it is people of faith who are the children of Abraham. And the Scripture, foreseeing that God would justify the Gentiles by faith, preached the gospel beforehand to Abraham, saying, 'In you shall all the nations be blessed.' So then, those who are of faith are blessed with Abraham who had faith."[23] Thus in the Gospel we find that "children of Abraham are raised from stones, that is, are gathered from the Gentiles."[24] And when the Lord praised Zacchaeus, he answered and said, "Today salvation has come to this house, because he too is a son of Abraham."[25] In Genesis, therefore, that the benediction, in respect of Abraham by Melchizedek the priest, might be duly celebrated, the figure of Christ's sacrifice precedes, namely, as ordained in bread and wine. The Lord, completing and fulfilling, offered bread and the cup mixed with wine, and so he who is the fullness of truth fulfilled the truth of the image prefigured. LETTER 62.4.[26]

THE THINGS THEY IMAGINE ABOUT
MELCHIZEDEK. EPIPHANIUS OF SALAMIS: Some sectarians honor Melchizedek, who is mentioned in the Scriptures and regard him as a sort of great power. He is on high in places that cannot be named and in fact is not just a power; indeed, they claim in their error that he is greater than Christ. Based, if you please, on the literal wording of, "You are a priest for ever *after the order* of Melchizedek," they believe that Christ has merely come and been given the order of Melchizedek. Christ is thus younger than Melchizedek, they say. For if his place were not somehow second in line, he would have no need of Melchizedek's rank.

Of Melchizedek himself they say that he has come into being "without father or mother or genealogy"—as they would like to show from St. Paul's epistle to the Hebrews. They also fabricate spurious books for their own deception.

Their refutation comes from the texts themselves. When David prophesies that the Lord will be a priest after the order of Melchizedek,[27] the sacred Scripture is saying in the same breath that Christ will be a priest. But we find that Paul says at once, "resembling the son of God, Melchizedek continues a priest forever." Now if he *resembles* the Son of God, he is not *equal* to the Son of God. How can the servant be the master's equal? For Melchizedek was a man. "Without father or mother" is not said because he had no father or mother but because his father and mother are not explicitly named in the sacred Scripture. . . .

In fact Melchizedek's father and mother are mentioned by some authors, though this is not based on the canonical, covenanted Scriptures. . . .

And of how many others is the ancestry not expressly given? Daniel, Shadrach, Meshach, Abednego, Elijah the Tishbite—neither their fathers nor their mothers are found anywhere in any of the covenanted Scriptures. . . .

Will they too—Shadrach, Meshach and Abednego—delude us into drawing wrong inferences, wondering far too much about each one's lineage and concluding that they have no fathers and mothers? Let's hope not! Apostolic tradition, holy Scriptures and successions of teachers have been made our boundaries and foundations for the upbuilding of our faith, and God's truth has been protected in every way. No one need be deceived by worthless stories. PANARION 4, AGAINST MELCHIZEDEKIANS 1.1—3.8.[28]

MELCHIZEDEK NOT PART OF THE HEAVENLY
ORDER. EPIPHANIUS OF SALAMIS: But to return to the subject, the things they imagine about Melchizedek. It is plain that this righteous man

---

[23]Gal 3:6-9. [24]Cf. Mt 3:9. [25]Lk 19:9. [26]ANF 5:359*. [27]Ps 110:4 (109:4 LXX). [28]NHMS 36:77-80*.

was holy, a priest of God, and the king of Salem, but he was no part of the order in heaven and has not come down from heaven. "No one has ascended into heaven but he who descended from heaven, the Son of man,"[29] says the holy divine Word who tells no lies.

For when the sacred Scripture proclaimed, and the Holy Spirit expressly taught, the order of Melchizedek, they indicated the removal of the priesthood from the ancient synagogue and the physical nation to a nation which is the finest and best and which is not united by a common physical descent. For this holy Melchizedek had no successors, but neither did he have his priesthood abolished. He remained a priest himself throughout his life and is still celebrated as a priest in the Scripture, since no one either succeeded him or abolished the priesthood during the time of his service. So our Lord—though he was not a man but the holy divine Word of God, God's Son begotten without beginning and not in time, and was with the Father but became man for our sakes, of Mary and not of a man's seed—our Lord took the clay from his manhood, received the priesthood and made his offering to the Father. He had taken his substance from man so as to be made a priest for us after the order of Melchizedek, which has no succession. For he abides forever to offer gifts for us—after first offering himself by the cross, to abolish every sacrifice of the old covenant by presenting the more perfect, living sacrifice for the whole world. He himself is temple, sacrifice, priest, altar, God, man, king, high priest, lamb, sacrificial victim— become all in all for us that life may be ours in every way and to lay the changeless foundation of his priesthood forever, no longer allotting it by descent and succession but granting that, in accordance with his ordinance, it may be preserved in the Holy Spirit. PANARION 4, AGAINST MELCHIZEDEKIANS 4.1-7.[30]

MELCHIZEDEK AS HOLY SPIRIT? EPIPHANIUS OF SALAMIS: Others in their turn imagine and say other things about this Melchizedek. Since they lack a spiritual understanding of the things the holy apostle said in his same epistle to the Hebrews, they have been condemned by a fleshly sentence. The Egyptian heresiarch Hieracas believes that Melchizedek is the Holy Spirit because of "resembling the Son of God he continues a priest forever," as though this is to be interpreted by the holy apostle's "The Spirit intercedes for us with sighs too deep for words."[31] But one who understands the Spirit's mind knows that he intercedes for the elect with God.[32] But Hieracas too has departed entirely from the prescribed path. The Spirit never assumed flesh, and, not having assumed flesh, he could not be king of Salem and priest of anywhere. PANARION 4, AGAINST MELCHIZEDEKIANS 5.1-4.[33]

MELCHIZEDEK AS SHEM? EPIPHANIUS OF SALAMIS: But how many other fancies others have about this Melchizedek! Samaritans believe that he is Noah's son, Shem, but it will be found that they too are absurd. The sacred Scripture, which safeguards everything with due order, has confirmed the truth in every way; not for nothing has it listed the time periods and enumerated the years of each patriarch's life and succession. For when Abraham was eighty-eight or even about ninety, Melchizedek met him and served him loaves and wine,[34] prefiguring the mysteries through types—types of the Lord's body, since our Lord himself says, "I am the living bread," and of the blood which flowed from his side for the cleansing of the defiled and the sprinkling and salvation of our souls. . . .

And the Shem we spoke of, whom the Samaritans imagine to be Melchizedek, fathered Arpachshad[35] in the hundred second year of his life, and altogether there were 1,241 years until the time of Abraham, when he met Melchizedek on his return from the slaughter of the kings,[36] Amraphel, Arioch, Chedorlaomer and Tidal. . . . Thus on no account can Shem have lived until

---

[29]Jn 3:13. [30]NHMS 36:80-81*. [31]Rom 8:26. [32]Rom 8:27. [33]NHMS 36:81*. [34]Gen 14:18. [35]Gen 10:22. [36]Gen 14:1, 15.

Abraham's time, to be thought of as Melchizedek. And the Samaritans' jabber is likewise all wrong. PANARION 4, AGAINST MELCHIZEDEKIANS 6.1-11.[37]

MELCHIZEDEK A SON OF A HARLOT? EPIPHANIUS OF SALAMIS: In their turn, the Jews say that Melchizedek was righteous, good and the priest of the Most High, as the sacred Scripture says. But they say that his mother's name is not recorded because he was the son of a harlot, and his father is unknown. But their silly assertion too has failed. Rahab was a harlot, and she is in Scripture.[38] Zimri's name is recorded although he committed fornication, and Cozbi's with his, even though she was a foreigner and not of Israelite descent.[39] For the Savior receives harlots, if only they repent through him. And as the holy Gospel said, "Who does not enter by the door is a thief and not a shepherd."[40] PANARION 4, AGAINST MELCHIZEDEKIANS 7.1-2.[41]

MELCHIZEDEK THE SON OF GOD? EPIPHANIUS OF SALAMIS: But some who are members of the Church make various assertions about this Melchizedek. Some suppose that he is the actual Son of God and that he appeared to Abraham then in the form of a man. But they too have left the path; no one will ever "resemble" himself. As the sacred Scripture says, "*resembling* the Son of God, he continues a priest for ever." Indeed, "this man who has not their genealogy received tithes from Abraham"; for, since his descent is not counted from the Israelites themselves, it is counted from other people. . . .

And how worthless all the sects' notions are! See here, these too have denied their master who "bought them with his own blood"[42]—whose existence does not date from Mary as they suppose, but who, as every Scripture says, is the divine Word ever with the Father and begotten of the Father, without beginning and not in time. It was to him, not to Melchizedek, that the Father said, "Let us make man in our image and after our likeness."[43] For even though

Melchizedek was priest of God Most High in his own generation and had no successors, he did not come down from heaven. The Scripture said not that he brought bread and wine *down*, but that he brought them *out*,[44] as though from his palace, to Abraham and his companions, when he received the patriarch as he passed through the country. And he blessed Abraham for his righteousness, faithfulness and piety. For though the patriarch had been tried in everything, in nothing had he lost his righteousness, but here too he had God's assistance against the kings who had attacked Sodom like bandits and carried off his nephew, the holy Lot. And he brought him back, with all the booty and spoil.[45]

Where can we not find proof that the Son was always with the Father? For "In the beginning was the Word, and the Word was with God, and the Word was God";[46] it did not say, "In the beginning was Melchizedek" or "And Melchizedek was God. . . ." PANARION 4, AGAINST MELCHIZEDEKIANS 7.3—9.6.[47]

MELCHIZEDEK THE FATHER OF JESUS? EPIPHANIUS OF SALAMIS: Again, I have heard that some, who are the furthest afield of all and are incited by further pride of intellect, have dared to resort to an unthinkable idea and arrive at a blasphemous notion, saying that this same Melchizedek is the Father of our Lord Jesus Christ. What careless minds people have and what deceived hearts, with no place for truth! Since the apostle says that Melchizedek has no father and mother and is without lineage, these people have gone wrong because of the sublimity of the expression, have foolishly supposed that what is said of Melchizedek corresponds with the Father of all, and have imagined a blasphemous imposture. For because God the almighty, the Father of all, has no father, mother, beginning of days or end of life—

---

[37]NHMS 36:81-82*. [38]Josh 2:1-21; cf. Jas 2:25; Heb 11:31. [39]Num 25:14-15. [40]Jn 10:1. [41]NHMS 36:82-83*. [42]Rev 5:9. [43]Gen 1:26. [44]Gen 14:18. [45]Gen 14:11-16. [46]Jn 1:1. [47]NHMS 36:83-84*.

everyone admits this—they have fallen into the foolish blasphemy of likening Melchizedek to him because the apostle has spoken of Melchizedek like that, but have not noticed the other things that are said about him. For it is said of Melchizedek that "he was *priest of* God Most High."[48] Now, assuming that Melchizedek is the Most High and the Father, then, as the priest of another "Most High," he cannot be the Father of all himself. He serves another Most High as priest.

Such confusion on people's part, that will not perceive truth but is bent on error! To give the final solution of the entire problem, the holy apostle said, "He whose descent is not counted from them"—obviously not; but it was counted from others—"received tithes from Abraham." And again, he said, who "in the days of his flesh, offered up prayers and supplications to him who was able to save him"[49]—but it is plain that the Father did not assume flesh.

But now that we have discussed them sufficiently too, let us leave this sect, for we have struck it with the firm faith at its foundation, as though we had hit a mousing viper with a rock and avoided its deadly poison. For they say that the mousing viper does no immediate harm to the one it bites, but that in time it destroys his body and infects its victim with leprosy in every limb. Similarly, if this heresy is implanted in their minds, it does people no apparent harm when they first hear of these things. But the long-term effect of the words is to sink into their minds, raise questions, and, as it were, cause the destruction of those who have not happened on the remedy of this antidote—the refutation of this heresy and the counterargument to it which I have given.

The mousing viper is not readily seen; it is active at night and does its harm at that time, especially in Egypt. Thus those who do not know the beast must realize that, when I compared it with the harm that is done by this sect, I did not bring up the subject of the beast lightly or as a slander; it does this sort of injury. PANARION 4,

AGAINST MELCHIZEDEKIANS 9.11-18.[50]

7:2 The Name of Melchizedek

A TYPE OF CHRIST. THEODORET OF CYR: Now, the comparison he had frequently gone to great trouble to develop he develops in the present case. Firstly, he recalls the story of Melchizedek. While he seems to conduct his treatment in narrative style, he is laying the groundwork for his thesis. The reason, you see, that he showed Abraham giving a blessing and offering a tenth of the spoils was to show the patriarchy yielding precedence even in type. Then he brings out his importance also from the names. This name, Melchizedek, in the Hebrew and Syriac language means "king of righteousness"; he ruled over Salem, and the word *Salem* is translated as peace. His intention, therefore, is to present him in this way as a type of Christ the Lord: according to the apostle he is our peace, and according to the Old Testament author he is our righteousness. INTERPRETATION OF HEBREWS 7.[51]

TRANSLATION OF HIS NAME. GREGORY OF NAZIANZUS: Using the principles of pastoral science, he gathers us into his heavenly fold.[52] He is called "sheep,"[53] because he was sacrificed, a "Lamb,"[54] because he was without blemish.[55] He is the "high priest" because he presented the offering. "Melchizedek," because on the transcendent level he had no mother, on the human level no father, and his high estate is without genealogy. "Who," it says, "can recount his generation?"[56] He is "Melchizedek" too, as king of Salem or peace, as king of righteousness, and because he tithes the patriarchs who prevailed over evil powers. ON THE SON, THEOLOGICAL ORATION 4(30).21.[57]

IN THIS NAME THE MYSTERY WAS INSCRIBED.

---

[48]Gen 14:18. [49]Heb 5:7. [50]NHMS 36:85-86*. [51]PG 82:724; TCCLSP 2:162-63. [52]Is 40:11. [53]Is 53:7. [54]Is 53:7. [55]Ex 12:5. [56]Is 53:8. [57]FGFR 278.

Ephrem the Syrian: Now the interpretation of the name Melchizedek is "king of justice" and "king of peace." The apostle indeed demonstrated that in this name the mystery of the grace and justice of the Son, Lord of Melchizedek, was inscribed. Commentary on the Epistle to the Hebrews.[58]

RIGHTEOUS KING. Clement of Alexandria: For Salem is, by interpretation, peace; of which our Savior is enrolled King, as Moses says, Melchizedek king of Salem, priest of the Most High God, who gave bread and wine, furnishing consecrated food for a type of the Eucharist. And Melchizedek is interpreted "righteous king"; and the name is a synonym for righteousness and peace. Stromateis 4.25.[59]

7:3 Resembling the Son of God

MELCHIZEDEK SIGNIFIES PRIESTHOOD. Severian of Gabala: Without father, without mother, without genealogy, according to the Scripture. Later, among the Levites it is always clear who were the parents of a priest. They also had allotted times and periods of service, and the total length of their service and of their life is known. All these data exist for each priest under the law, even if not for every year. However, it is said that Melchizedek is without father, without mother, without genealogy, having no beginning and no end of life according to the word of Scripture. He does not belong to a priestly family; we do not know when he started his priesthood or what kind of a priest he was, or whether he was a priest all his life. We do not know any information that is available for those priests under the law. It is said that, likened to the Son of God, he continues his priesthood forever. And how does Melchizedek remain a priest? Here is a solution to that question. As Moses sometimes signifies the law, so Melchizedek, a human being, signifies the priesthood. Now, if he is likened [to the Son of God] through the priesthood in Christ, he remains forever, not as a mortal man but as a pat-tern of the priesthood. Fragments on the Epistle to the Hebrews 7.3.[60]

LIKENESS AND DIFFERENCE. Chrysostom: And what does Paul say? "For this Melchizedek, king of Salem, priest of the Most High God." And, what is especially noteworthy, he shows the difference to be great by the type itself. For as I said, he continually confirms the truth from the type, from things past, on account of the weakness of the hearers. "You are a priest forever, after the order of Melchizedek," whereas Melchizedek was dead and was not "priest forever," see how he explained it mystically. . . .

"And who can say this concerning a man?" He does not assert this, in fact, Paul says; the meaning is that we do not know when or what father he had, nor what mother, nor when he received his beginning, nor when he died. And what of this, one says? For does it follow, because we do not know it, that he did not die, or had no parents? You say well; he both died and had parents. How then was he "without father or mother"? How, "having neither beginning of days nor end of life"? How? From its not being expressed. And what of this? That as this man is, from his genealogy not being given, so is Christ from the very nature of the reality. . . .

Where is the likeness to the Son of God? That we know not of the one or of the other either the end or the beginning. Of the one because they are not written; of the other, because they do not exist. Here is the likeness. But if the likeness were to exist in all respects, there would no longer be type and reality; but both would be type. Here then, just as in representations by painting or drawing, there is something that is like and something that is unlike. By means of the lines, indeed, there is a likeness of features, but when the colors are put on, then the difference is plainly shown, both the likeness and the unlikeness. On the Epistle to the Hebrews 12.2-3.[61]

---

[58]EHA 210. [59]ANF 2:439. [60]NTA 15:350. [61]NPNF 1 14:423-24*.

WITHOUT MOTHER, FATHER, GENEALOGY.
THEODORET OF CYR: Christ the Lord, of course, has each of these by nature and in reality: while as God he is "without mother," being begotten only of the Father, as man he is "without father," being born only of a mother—the Virgin, I mean. As God he is "without genealogy": the one of the unbegotten Father does not require a family tree. "Without beginning of days": the begetting was eternal. "Without end of life": he has an immortal nature.

This was the reason he likened not Christ the Lord to Melchizedek, but Melchizedek to Christ the Lord: one was type of the other, and the other the realization of the type. In respect of the priesthood, of course, Melchizedek did not imitate Christ the Lord; rather, Christ the Lord is a priest forever according to the order of Melchizedek: being a priest belongs to a human being, whereas accepting offerings belongs to God. Yet by becoming incarnate the only begotten Son of God also became our high priest according to the order of Melchizedek, not by aggregating to himself the position but by concealing the divine status and accepting the lowly condition for the sake of our salvation. This is why he was called lamb, sin, curse, way, door, and many other names like that. INTERPRETATION OF HEBREWS 7.[62]

MELCHIZEDEK MODELED ON CHRIST.
AMBROSE: Let no one claim Divinity resides in an order established by human beings when he encounters such an order. For the church does not consider even Melchizedek, by whose office Abraham offered sacrifice, an angel (as some Jewish interpreters do). It rather considers him a holy man and priest of God who, *prefiguring* our Lord, is described as "without father or mother, without history of his descent, without beginning and without end." It does this in order to show beforehand the coming into this world of the eternal Son of God who was likewise incarnate and then brought forth without any father, begotten as God without mother, and was without history of descent. For it is written: "Who shall declare his generation?"[63]

This Melchizedek, then, we have received as a priest of God based upon the model of Christ. However, the one we regard as the type, the other as the original. Now, a type is a shadow of the truth. We have accepted the royalty of the one [Melchizedek] in the name of a single city [Jerusalem], but that of the other [Jesus] as shown in the reconciliation of the whole world. For it is written: "God was in Christ, reconciling the world to himself,"[64] that is to say, the eternal Godhead was in Christ. Or, if the Father is in the Son, even as the Son is in the Father, then their unity in both nature and operation is plainly not denied. ON THE CHRISTIAN FAITH 3.11 [88-89].[65]

ADVOCATE FOR THE HEAVENLY POWERS. TERTULLIAN: The heretic Theodotus . . . says that the human being Christ was conceived and born of the Holy Spirit and the virgin Mary, but that he was inferior to Melchizedek because it is said of Christ, "You are a priest forever after the order of Melchizedek."[66] For this Melchizedek, he says, by special grace is a heavenly power, and what Christ does for human beings, having been made their intercessor and advocate, Melchizedek does for the heavenly angels and powers. For to such a degree, he says, he is better than Christ that he is fatherless, motherless, without genealogy, of whom neither the beginning nor the end has been comprehended, nor can be comprehended. AGAINST ALL HERESIES 8.[67]

THE PRIESTHOOD OF ALL NATIONS. EPHREM THE SYRIAN: Some say that this Melchizedek was actually Shem, son of Noah; in fact, they say the book of Genesis clearly shows that he lived in the days of Abraham and Isaac and Jacob. Moreover, from the sortitions of those tribes who inherited the land of the house of Shem, it looks clear that

---

[62]PG 82:724-25; *TCCLSP* 2:163-64. [63]Is 53:8. [64]2 Cor 5:19. [65]NPNF 2 10:255*. [66]Ps 110:4 (109:4 LXX). [67]ANF 3:654.

he lived in Salem in his own inheritance.

Not only Melchizedek but also the name Melchizedek are "without father, and mother and without genealogy" because neither the name Melchizedek nor the name Israel were written in the genealogy, whereas Shem and Jacob had father and mother, and a beginning and an end, and were inscribed in the genealogy. But the names of Melchizedek and Israel did not have any of these things. God glorified them both with names equally imposed by him. He "was made similar to the Son of God" through his priesthood, so that the priesthood of Melchizedek might last forever, not in Melchizedek himself but in the Lord of Melchizedek.

And the apostle highly praises the priesthood of all nations rather than that of his people, when he says, "Consider how great this man is to whom even our patriarch Abraham gave the tenth part of everything." COMMENTARY ON THE EPISTLE TO THE HEBREWS.[68]

HE HAD A FAMILY TREE. THEODORET OF CYR: He commented also on the term "without a genealogy." He said Melchizedek was not of their family tree. So it is clear that he was not really without a family tree but only to provide a type. INTERPRETATION OF HEBREWS 7.[69]

WAS MELCHIZEDEK SHEM? JEROME: The Jews say that Melchizedek was Shem, Noah's son, and, counting up the total years of his lifetime,[70] they demonstrate that he would have lived up to the time of Isaac; and they say that all the firstborn sons of Noah were priests before Aaron performed the priestly office. Also, by "king of Salem" is meant the king of Jerusalem, which was formerly called Salem. And the blessed apostle writing to the Hebrews makes mention of Melchizedek as "without father or mother" and refers him to Christ and, through Christ, to the church of the Gentiles, for all the glory of the head is assigned to the members. . . . While he was uncircumcised, he blessed Abraham who had been circumcised; and in Abraham he blessed

Levi; and through Levi he blessed Aaron from whom the priesthood afterwards descended. For this reason, he maintains, one should infer that the priesthood of the church, which is uncircumcised, blessed the priesthood of the synagogue, which is circumcised. And as to the Scripture which says, "You are a priest forever after the order of Melchizedek," our mystery is foreshown in the word *order*; not at all, indeed, in the sacrifice of nonrational victims through Aaron's agency, but when bread and wine, that is, the body and blood of the Lord Jesus, were offered in sacrifice. HEBREW QUESTIONS ON GENESIS 14.18-19.[71]

THE WORD IS WITHOUT MOTHER. THEODORE OF MOPSUESTIA: God the Word was not generated from a woman; the one generated from a woman was the one fashioned in her by the power of the Holy Spirit. The one who is of one essence with the Father was not born from her womb, for he is "without mother," as blessed Paul's phrase has it. It was rather the one fashioned in his mother's womb by the power of the Holy Spirit who came in the last times. For this reason he is also called "without father." TREATISES AGAINST APOLLINARIS 3.1.[72]

HIS HUMANITY AND HIS DIVINE ESSENCE. THEODORE OF MOPSUESTIA: When Paul wished to show that Christ was a high priest after the order of Melchizedek,[73] he speaks those things that pertain to him, not explaining his nature but putting forth the explanation about him found in the divine Scripture and demonstrating the similarity between Melchizedek and Christ from the Scripture.

Thus, he calls him "fatherless" and "motherless," on the grounds that the divine Scripture does not narrate his genealogy. Then he adds, "being without genealogy," showing that he is not

---

[68]EHA 210-11. [69]PG 82:725; TCCLSP 2:164. [70]Eight hundred years, according to Gen 11:11. [71]HQG 47. [72]TEM 2:314; COS 259. [73]Heb 6:20.

talking about the nature of the man but rather the account of the divine Scripture. Then he further connects in the thought "neither having a beginning of days nor an end of life"—not in his nature but in the divine Scripture. And since it was possible to also say these about another person—for the divine Scripture does not remember to note the parents of many people or to set forth their genealogy, especially as many as we have learned were born outside the Israelite race—he does well to add, "being likened to the Son of God, he remains a priest forever." For no longer does this apply to the rest as it does to him. And he makes clear from this explanation of the Scripture how Christ has this property as well as the rest. For Christ was "without father" in the begetting of his humanity, and "without mother" in the origin of his divine essence, and really "without genealogy." For what genealogy would there be of him who exists from his Father alone? And it is also clear that "he has neither beginning of days nor an end of life." In the case of Christ it is actually the case, whereas in the case of Melchizedek it is what we find (or do not find) in the Scripture's account of him. Christ received his "priesthood forever" from the divine Scripture where it said, "You are a priest forever according to the order of Melchizedek,"[74] even as Melchizedek acts as priest eternally. And he calls him an "eternal" priest on the grounds that he has not passed on the priesthood to successors, which happened to be the case under Mosaic law. Therefore he also said, "Having been likened to the Son of God," and yet it was appropriate to say that the Son had been made like Melchizedek— for the first is not made like the second. Yet the truth took place in connection with Christ, but no such thing took place beforehand with Melchizedek. So he says that Melchizedek was made like Christ by the way that he appears in the narrative, since the divine Scripture wished to show to us in its narration of the life of Melchizedek the similarity with the one who was to be. FRAGMENTS ON THE EPISTLE TO THE HEBREWS 7.3.[75]

MELCHIZEDEK SPRANG FROM CURSED SEED. PHOTIUS: He calls Melchizedek "without genealogy" because he was not from the seed of Abraham nor was he given a genealogy by Moses, but his race was Canaanite and he sprang from that cursed seed. He was pronounced righteous in regards to his deeds. Yet because he had not sprung from righteous forebears or from some righteous seed, it was not proper to give the genealogy of this man who inclined to the epitome of righteousness. Now Melchizedek demonstrates that he was of Canaanite origin and it also can be proved positively from those regions that he ruled and reigned over and the regions with which he was associated. For he was a neighbor of Sodom, and he was very close to Abraham when he lived near "the oak of Mamre."[76] And one must also reckon that he happens to be king of that "Salem,"[77] which is Jerusalem. FRAGMENTS ON THE EPISTLE TO THE HEBREWS 7.3.[78]

DOES GOD HAVE A MOTHER? NESTORIUS: Does God have a mother? A Greek without reproach introducing mothers for the gods! Is Paul then a liar when he says of the deity of Christ, "without father or mother or genealogy"? Mary, my friend, did not give birth to the Godhead, for what "is born of flesh is flesh."[79] A creature did not produce him who is uncreatable. The Father has not just recently generated God the Logos from the Virgin, for "in the beginning was the Logos," as John says.[80] FIRST SERMON AGAINST THE THEOTOKOS.[81]

HE CONTINUES FOREVER. THEODORET OF CYR: The text said of Melchizedek, of course, that "he continues a priest forever" since he did not transmit the priesthood to his children, like Aaron, Eleazar and Phineas; the one transmitting it to another as an heirloom seems somehow to be deprived of the position when someone else is performing it. It has another sense as well: just as we

[74]Ps 110:4. [75]NTA 15:646-47. [76]Gen 14:13. [77]Gen 14:18. [78]NTA 15:646. [79]Jn 3:6. [80]Jn 1:1. [81]CC 124.

refer to Moses not just as the lawgiver but as the law itself, so too we use the name Melchizedek both of the person and the thing, namely, priesthood. Christ the Lord has it, enjoying eternal life. Interpretation of Hebrews 7.[82]

The Twofold Birth of Christ. John Cassian: Listen, you heretic, to the passage you have garbled: hear in full and completely, what you quoted mutilated and hacked about. The apostle wants to make clear to every one the twofold birth of God. In order to show how the Lord was born [both] in the Godhead and in flesh, he says, "Without father, without mother." The one belongs to the birth of divinity, the other to that of the flesh. For, as he was begotten in his divine nature "without mother," so he is in the body "without father." Though he is neither without father nor without mother, we must believe in him "without father and without mother." For, if you regard him as begotten of the Father, he is without mother. If you regard him as born of his mother, he is without father. And so in each of these births he has one [parent]: in both [births] together he is without each. For, the birth of divinity had no need of mother; and for the birth of his body, he was himself sufficient, without a father. Therefore says the apostle "Without [father or] mother, without genealogy." Incarnation of the Lord, Against Nestorius 7.14.[83]

The Shadows Flee, the Truth Breaks In. Gregory of Nazianzus: The old has passed away,

> behold all things have been made anew.
> The letter withdraws, the Spirit advances.
> The shadows flee, the truth breaks in.
> Melchizedek is summed up; the motherless
> becomes fatherless.
> The first without a mother,
> The second without a father,
> The laws of nature are abrogated
> that the cosmos above be brought to
> perfection.

On the Birth of Christ, Oration 38.2.[84]

7:4 See How Great He Is

The Superiority of Melchizedek. Chrysostom: "Now consider," Paul says, "how great this man is to whom even the patriarch Abraham gave the tenth of the spoils." Up to this point he has been applying the type; henceforward, he boldly shows Melchizedek to be more glorious than the Aaronic priesthood. But if he who bears a type of Christ is so much better not merely than the priests, but even than the forefather himself of the priests, what should one say of the reality? You see how superabundantly he shows the superiority. . . . Have you seen the superiority? Have you seen how great is the interval between Abraham and Melchizedek, who bears the type of our High Priest? And he shows that the superiority had been caused by authority, not necessity. For the one paid the tithe, which indicates the priest; the other gave the blessing, which indicates the superior. This superiority passes on also to the descendants. On the Epistle to the Hebrews 12.4.[85]

From Shem to Rebekah. Ephrem the Syrian: This Melchizedek is Shem,[86] who became a king due to his greatness; he was the head of fourteen nations. In addition, he was a priest. He received this from Noah, his father, through the rights of succession. Shem lived not only to the time of Abraham, as Scripture says, but even to the time of Jacob and Esau, the grandsons of Abraham. It was to him that Rebekah went to ask and was told, "Two nations are in your womb, and the elder shall serve the younger."[87] Rebekah would not have bypassed her husband, who had been delivered at the high place, or her father-in-law, to whom revelations of the divinity came continually, and gone straight to ask Melchizedek

---

[82]PG 82:725; TCCLSP 2:164. [83]NPNF 2 11:611-12*. [84]NPNF 2 7:345*. [85]NPNF 1 14:424*. [86]Ephrem is commenting on Gen 14:18-20. [87]Gen 25:23.

unless she had learned of his greatness from Abraham or Abraham's son. Abraham would not have given him a tenth of everything unless he knew that Melchizedek was infinitely greater than himself. Would Rebekah have asked one of the Canaanites or one of the Sodomites? Would Abraham have given a tenth of his possessions to any one of these? One ought not even entertain such ideas.

Because the length of Melchizedek's life extended to the time of Jacob and Esau, it has been stated, with much probability, that he was Shem. His father Noah was dwelling in the east, and Melchizedek was dwelling between two tribes, that is, between the sons of Ham and his own sons. Melchizedek was like a partition between the two, for he was afraid that the sons of Ham would turn his own sons to idolatry. COMMENTARY ON GENESIS 11.2.2-4.[88]

HIGHER THAN HUMANITY. EUSEBIUS OF CAESAREA: So far, then, we have learned that they who are called "Christs" in the highest sense of the term are anointed by God, not by people, and anointed with the Holy Spirit, not with a prepared unguent.

It is now time to see how the teaching of the Hebrews shows that the true Christ of God possesses a divine nature higher than humanity. Hear, therefore, David again, where he says that he knows an eternal priest of God and calls him his own Lord and confesses that he shares the throne of God Most High in the one hundred ninth psalm.[89] . . . And note that David in this passage, being king of the whole Hebrew race and, in addition to his kingdom, adorned with the Holy Spirit, recognized that the being of whom he speaks, who was revealed to him in the Spirit, was so great and surpassingly glorious, that he called him his own Lord. He said, "The Lord said to my Lord," for he knows him as eternal high priest, priest of the Most High God, and throned beside almighty God and his offspring. Now it was impossible for Jewish priests to be consecrated to the service of God without

anointing, which is why it was usual to call them Christs. The Christ, then, mentioned in the psalm will also be a priest, for how could he have been witnessed to as priest unless he had previously been anointed? It is also said that he is made a priest forever. Now this would transcend human nature, for it is not in humanity to last forever, since our race is mortal and frail. Therefore, the priest of God described in this passage, who by the confirmation of an oath received a perpetual and limitless priesthood from God, was greater than human. "For the Lord has sworn," he said, "and will not change his mind, 'You are a priest after the order of Melchizedek.' " . . . The object of the psalmist's prophecy, therefore, is presented distinctly as an eternal priest and Son of the Most High God, begotten by the Most High God and sharing the throne of his kingdom. . . .

Thus I think I have clearly proved that the essential Christ was not man, but Son of God, honored with a seat on the right hand of his Father's Godhead, far greater not only than human and mortal nature, but greater also than every spiritual existence among things begotten. PROOF OF THE GOSPEL 4.15.[90]

7:5-10 Tithes from Abraham

A WITNESS FOR ABRAHAM. EPHREM THE SYRIAN: Through Abraham, who gave him the tenth part, the house of Levi, which had to be generated by him, took the tenth part in him. The Levites, even though they took the tenth part, did not take it from strangers but received the tenth part from themselves; in fact, they took the tenth part from their brothers, the sons of Abraham. Therefore, Abraham, to whom the promise of priesthood was made, gave the tenth part to Melchizedek, who was not inscribed in the Levitic generation. And to Abraham it had been promised that all nations would have been blessed in him. So why did he need the blessing of

---

[88]FC 91:151. [89]See Ps 110:1-5. [90]POG 1:197-99*.

an uncircumcised man?[91] Does not this show and prove that, if Abraham had not been inferior to Melchizedek, he would not have demanded to be blessed by him? And so the mortal sons receive the tenth part, and in the same manner Melchizedek, who was mortal, lived at that time to be a witness for Abraham, for the indisputably true Melchizedek's blessing destined to the seed of Abraham. COMMENTARY ON THE EPISTLE TO THE HEBREWS.[92]

THE TYPE IS GREATER THAN ABRAHAM. PHOTIUS: He says, "even though they have come out of the loins of Abraham."[93] Although the Levites are in all other respects equal in rank with the other tribes, nonetheless because the other tribes give tithes while the Levites receive them, the Levites are clearly superior. But if this is the case, then clearly also the same principle applies to Abraham and Melchizedek, the giver and recipient, respectively.[94] Consequently, the type of Christ [Melchizedek] is greater than the patriarch Abraham. But if he is greater than Abraham, he is much greater than the priests. And if the type is greater than Abraham, what would anyone say concerning Christ himself? FRAGMENTS ON THE EPISTLE TO THE HEBREWS 7.5.[95]

HE WHO RECEIVES TITHES WAS MADE TO TITHE. PHOTIUS: He says, that because Abraham paid tithes, also Levi "who receives tithes himself was made to tithe," that is, he gave a tithe. We must underscore the phrase "through Abraham," so that the meaning does not suffer violence. For because Abraham was made to tithe, in a certain sense also Levi, being still "in his loins" has been made to tithe. FRAGMENTS ON THE EPISTLE TO THE HEBREWS 7.9-10.[96]

ACCORDING TO THE FLESH, IN THE LOINS OF ABRAHAM. AUGUSTINE: What is significant about the marked distinction between the priesthood of Christ and the priesthood of Levi on the basis of the fact that Levi paid tithes to Melchizedek since he was in the loins of Abraham?

Christ was there also, and hence they both paid tithes. But the point is that we must understand that Christ was not there in a certain sense. Yet who would deny that he was there according to the flesh? Therefore, it was according to the soul that he was not there. The soul of Christ, therefore, was not transmitted from the soul of Adam who sinned; otherwise it also would have been there. . . .

Now, Levi was there according to the seminal reason by which he was destined to enter his mother on the occasion of carnal union; but not by such a reason was the flesh of Christ there, although the flesh of Mary was there according to such a reason. Therefore, neither Levi nor Christ was in the loins of Abraham according to the soul. According to the flesh, both Levi and Christ were there, but Levi according to carnal concupiscence, Christ solely according to his corporeal substance. Since in a seed there are both the visible corporeal germ and the invisible formative principle, both of these came from Abraham, or even from Adam, to the body of Mary, which was conceived and born in that manner. Christ, however, assumed the visible substance of the flesh from the flesh of the Virgin; the formative principle of his conception, however, was not from the seed of a man but came from above in a far different way. Consequently, in respect of what he received from his mother, he was also in the loins of Abraham.

Levi paid tithes, therefore, in Abraham, since he was in Abraham's loins, although it was according to the flesh alone, just as Abraham himself was in his father's loins. In other words, he was born of this father Abraham as Abraham was born "with the law of the mind"[97] and through an invisible concupiscence, although the chaste and honorable rights of marriage do not allow that law of the members to prevail except

---

[91]See Gen 14:19. [92]EHA 211-12. [93]Num 18:21. This is also a literal translation of Heb 7:5, which RSV paraphrases as "descended from Abraham." [94]Gen 14:20. [95]NTA 15:647. [96]NTA 15:647. [97]Rom 7:23.

insofar as they can provide for the continuation of the race through it.

But tithes were not paid through Abraham by him whose flesh received from that source not a festering wound but the material that would heal. For since this tithing belonged to the foreshadowing of the remedy, tithes were paid in the flesh of Abraham by him who was healed, not by him who was the source of the healing. For the same flesh—not only of Abraham but also of the first and earthly man—had both the wound of sin and the remedy for that wound: the wound of sin in the law of the members at war with that of the mind, a law transmitted thence by a seminal reason to all generations of descendants. And at the same time the remedy of the wound [was] in the body taken from the Virgin, from which source alone came the corporeal matter, without the working of concupiscence, but through a divine causal principle of conception and formation, for the purpose of sharing with humanity the necessity of dying without any taint of sin and of giving them the hope of resurrection without any fear of disappointment. . . .

The soul of Christ is from the original soul only on the condition that it has not contracted the taint of sin; but if it could not be from that source without the guilt of sin, it has not come from that soul. ON THE LITERAL INTERPRETATION OF GENESIS 10.19.34-21.37.[98]

WHY BAPTIZE CHILDREN OF THE BAPTIZED? AUGUSTINE: We now advance in reply to those who argue that one who is born of a baptized man ought himself to be regarded as already baptized. "For why," they ask, "could he not have been baptized in the loins of his father, when, according to the epistle to the Hebrews, Levi was able to pay tithes in the loins of Abraham?" They who propose this argument ought to observe that it was not because he had paid tithes already in the loins of Abraham that Levi did not subsequently pay tithes, but because he was ordained to the office of the priesthood in order to receive tithes, not pay them. Otherwise, neither would his brethren, who all contributed their tithes to him, have been tithed—because they too, while in the loins of Abraham, had already paid tithes to Melchizedek. ON THE MERITS AND FORGIVENESS OF SINS AND ON INFANT BAPTISM 2.39.[99]

---

[98]ACW 42:121-26. [99]NPNF 1 5:60*.

7:11-28 A CHANGE IN THE PRIESTHOOD

[11]*Now if perfection had been attainable through the Levitical priesthood (for under it the people received the law), what further need would there have been for another priest to arise after the order of Melchizedek, rather than one named after the order of Aaron?* [12]*For when there is a change in the priesthood, there is necessarily a change in the law as well.* [13]*For the one of whom these things are spoken belonged to another tribe, from which no one has ever served at the altar.* [14]*For it is evident that our Lord was descended from Judah, and in connection with that tribe Moses said nothing about priests.*

[15]*This becomes even more evident when another priest arises in the likeness of Melchizedek,* [16]*who has become a priest, not according to a legal requirement concerning bodily descent but by the power of an indestructible life.* [17]*For it is witnessed of him,*

"Thou art a priest for ever,

after the order of Melchizedek."

[18]*On the one hand, a former commandment is set aside because of its weakness and uselessness* [19]*(for the law made nothing perfect); on the other hand, a better hope is introduced, through which we draw near to God.*

[20]*And it was not without an oath.* [21]*Those who formerly became priests took their office without an oath, but this one was addressed with an oath,*

"The Lord has sworn

and will not change his mind,

'Thou art a priest for ever.'"

[22]*This makes Jesus the surety of a better covenant.*

[23]*The former priests were many in number, because they were prevented by death from continuing in office;* [24]*but he holds his priesthood permanently, because he continues for ever.* [25]*Consequently he is able for all time to save those who draw near to God through him, since he always lives to make intercession for them.*

[26]*For it was fitting that we should have such a high priest, holy, blameless, unstained, separated from sinners, exalted above the heavens.* [27]*He has no need, like those high priests, to offer sacrifices daily, first for his own sins and then for those of the people; he did this once for all when he offered up himself.* [28]*Indeed, the law appoints men in their weakness as high priests, but the word of the oath, which came later than the law, appoints a Son who has been made perfect for ever.*

OVERVIEW: This pericope contrasts the priesthood of the Old Testament law with the priesthood of Christ, of which Melchizedek is a type. Under a perfect priesthood, the further priesthood of Christ would be unnecessary. The law did not present the perfect sacrifice (CHRYSOSTOM). Melchizedek was a high priest of his people, but the Lord made the offering for the salvation of the whole of the human race (THEODORET). With the change in priesthood, the law is changed too; now there is no need of sacrificial law. The law was of use, but not to make humans perfect. While before it was necessary to have many priests, because death would take them, now there is no other high priest than our Lord, "who lives forever . . . and makes intercession for us," not in sacrifices but in prayers (EPHREM). He does not need a ransom, for he himself is the propitiation (BASIL). The only Son who became man is our priest forever (BASIL,

AUGUSTINE, EPHREM). Earthly lineage does not obtain this anointing (LEO THE GREAT). Our Lord was appointed and accepted the priesthood by the power of a life that is not broken down by death (EPHREM). Humans can be high priests according to the order of Aaron, but only Christ according to the order of Melchizedek (ORIGEN). By this better hope in Christ, our intercessor, we draw near to God (ORIGEN, CHRYSOSTOM). He intercedes for us as a man and as the appointed Son (ORIGEN, GREGORY OF NAZIANZUS, CHRYSOSTOM). Speech is surpassed by grace in attempting to understand this sacrifice celebrated in the Eucharist (BRAULIO, BEDE).

7:11-12 *If Perfection Had Been Attainable*

EARTHLY LINEAGE DOES NOT OBTAIN THE ANOINTING. LEO THE GREAT: When I compare the impoverishment of my insufficiency with the

---

greatness of the gift I have received,[1] I too should cry out in those words of the prophet, "Lord, I have heard your word and was afraid; I have considered your works and trembled."[2] What indeed could instill as much anxiety and fear as labor for the frail, elevation for the lowly, dignity for the undeserving? Yet we do not despair or give up, since we do not depend on ourselves but on the one "who works in us."[3] . . . So we have chanted with one voice the psalm of David, dearly beloved, not for our own exaltation but for the glory of Christ the Lord.

He it is of whom it was said in prophetic manner, "You are a priest for ever after the order of Melchizedek," that is to say, "not according to the order of Aaron," whose priesthood passed down through the descent of his offspring and was a temporary ministry that ceased with the law of the Old Testament, but "after the order of Melchizedek," in whom the office of eternal high priest was prefigured. Since there is no mention of the parents he came from, he must be understood as standing for the one "whose genealogy cannot be told."[4]

Finally, since the mystery of this divine priesthood also extends to its implementation by people, it does not pass down through the course of generations. It is not what flesh and blood have created that is chosen. Rather, the privileges of paternity give way, and the social positions of families are disregarded, as the church accepts for its rulers those whom the Holy Spirit has prepared. Among the people of God's adoption, which is priestly and kingly when taken as a whole, the prerogative of earthly lineage does not obtain the anointing. SERMON 3.1.[5]

THE LAW COMES TO AN END. THEODORET OF CYR: If the priesthood according to the law contained perfection, he is saying, on the grounds that through it everything according to the law was fulfilled, why is the giving of another one intended? Why on earth is the promise made to give it not according to the order of Aaron but according to the order of Melchizedek? Actually, all

the law's requirements were fulfilled in the former one: it offered sacrifices, it gave purification from defilement, through it the commandments about festivals were fulfilled, the text says, "for under it the people received the law."

After thus demonstrating the change of priesthood, he shows also the cessation of the law. The law was liked to the priesthood; so with priesthood coming to an end, the law also suffered the same fate. INTERPRETATION OF HEBREWS 7.[6]

JUDAH BECOMES PRIESTLY. THEODORET OF CYR: The mystery of the divine plan is worthy of admiration: as Christ the Lord, eternal king as he is, was styled our high priest, so the tribe of Judah, which was formerly kingly, attained the priesthood through the Lord. INTERPRETATION OF HEBREWS 7.[7]

7:13-15 Another Priest in the Likeness of Melchizedek

CHRIST AN ARCHETYPE OF MELCHIZEDEK CONCERNING THE HUMAN NATURE. THEODORET OF CYR: Orth.—[C]all to mind the words used of Melchizedek in the epistle to the Hebrews. Eran.[8]—What words? Orth.—Those in which the divine apostle, in comparing the levitical priesthood with that of the Christ, likens Melchizedek in other respects to the Lord Christ and says that the Lord had the priesthood after the order of Melchizedek. Eran.—I think the words of the divine apostle are as follows—"For this Melchizedek, king of Salem, priest of the Most High God who met Abraham returning from the slaughter of the kings and blessed him; to whom also Abraham gave a tenth part of all; first being by interpretation king of righteousness, and after that also king of Salem, which is king of peace; without father, without mother,

---

[1]The priesthood. [2]Hab 3:2. [3]1 Cor 12:6. [4]Cf. Is 53:8. [5]FC 93:21. [6]PG 82:728; TCCLSP 2:165. [7]PG 82:729; TCCLSP 2:166. [8]Theodoret presents a dialogue between two parties, Orthodox (Orth.) and Eranistes, that is, Questioner (Eran.).

without descent, having neither beginning of days, nor end of life; but made like unto the Son of God; remains a priest continually."[9] I presume you spoke of this passage.

Orth.—Yes, I spoke of this; and I must praise you for not mutilating it but for quoting the whole. Tell me now, does each one of these points fit Melchizedek in nature and reality? *Eran.*—Who has the audacity to deny a fitness where the divine apostle has asserted it? *Orth.*—Then you say that all this fits Melchizedek by nature? *Eran.*—Yes. *Orth.*—Do you say that he was a man, or assumed some other nature? *Eran.*—A man. *Orth.*—Begotten or unbegotten? *Eran.*—You are asking very absurd questions. *Orth.*—The fault lies with you for openly opposing the truth. Answer then. *Eran.*—There is one only unbegotten, who is God and Father. *Orth.*—Then we assert that Melchizedek was begotten? *Eran.*—Yes. *Orth.*—But the passage about him teaches the opposite. Remember the words which you quoted a moment ago, "Without father, without mother, without descent, having neither beginning of days nor end of life." How then do the words "Without father and without mother" fit him; and how the statement that he neither received beginning of existence nor end, since all this transcends humanity?

Eran.—These things do in fact overstep the limits of human nature. *Orth.*—Then shall we say that the apostle told lies? *Eran.*—God forbid. *Orth.*—How then is it possible both to testify to the truth of the apostle and apply the supernatural to Melchizedek? *Eran.*—The passage is a very difficult one and requires much explanation. *Orth.*—For any one willing to consider it with attention it will not be hard to attain perception of the meaning of the words. After saying "without father, without mother, without descent, having neither beginning of days nor end of life," the divine apostle adds "made like unto the Son of God, he abides as a priest continually." Here he plainly teaches us that the Lord Christ is archetype of Melchizedek in things concerning the human nature. And he speaks of Melchizedek as

"made like unto the Son of God." *Orth.*—Now let us examine the point in this manner. Do you say that the Lord had a father according to the flesh? *Eran.*—Certainly not. *Orth.*—Why? *Eran.*—He was born of the holy Virgin alone. *Orth.*—He is therefore properly styled "without father"? *Eran.*—True. DIALOGUE 2.[10]

MADE LIKE UNTO THE SON OF GOD. THE-ODORET OF CYR: *Orth.*—Do you say that according to the divine nature [the Lord] had a mother? *Eran.*—Certainly not. *Orth.*—For he was begotten of the Father alone before the ages? *Eran.*—Agreed. *Orth.*—And yet, as the generation he has of the Father is ineffable, he is spoken of as "without descent." "Who," says the prophet, "shall declare his generation?"[11] *Eran.*—You are right. *Orth.*—Thus it becomes him to have neither beginning of days nor end of life; for he is without beginning, indestructible, and, in a word, eternal, and coeternal with the Father.

Eran.—This is my view too. But we must now consider how this fits the admirable Melchizedek. *Orth.*—As an image and type. The image, as we have just observed, has not all the properties of the archetype. Thus to the Savior these qualities are proper both by nature and in reality; but the story of the origin of the race has attributed them to Melchizedek. For after telling us of the father of the patriarch Abraham, and of the father and mother of Isaac, and similarly of Jacob and of his sons, and exhibiting the pedigree of our first forefathers, it records neither the father nor the mother of Melchizedek. It also does not teach that he traced his descent from any one of Noah's sons, to the end that he may be a type of him who is in reality without father and without mother. And this is what the divine apostle would have us understand, for in this very passage he says further, "But he whose descent is not counted from them received tithes of Abra-ham, and blessed him that had the promises."[12]

Eran.—Then, since holy Scripture has not

---

[9]Heb 7:1-3. [10]NFPF 2 3:187-88*. [11]Is 53:8. [12]Heb 7:6.

mentioned his parents, can he be called without father and without mother? *Orth.*—If he had really been without father and without mother, he would not have been an image, but a reality. But since these are his qualities not by nature, but according to the dispensation of the divine Scripture, he exhibits the type of the reality. *Eran.*—The type must have the character of the archetype.

Orth.—Is man called an image of God? *Eran.*—Man is not an image of God but was made in the image of God.[13] *Orth.*—Listen then to the apostle. He says, "For a man indeed ought not to cover his head, forasmuch as he is the image and glory of God."[14] *Eran.*—Granted, then, that he is an image of God.

Orth.—According to your argument then he must have plainly preserved the characters of the archetype, and he must have been uncreated, uncompounded and infinite. He ought also to have been able to create out of the nonexistent, he ought to have fashioned all things by his word and without labor. In addition to this, he ought to have been free from sickness, sorrow, anger and sin, to have been immortal and incorruptible and to possess all the qualities of the archetype. *Eran.*—Man is not an image of God in every respect. *Orth.*—Although he is truly an image in the qualities in which you would grant him to be so, you will find that he is separated by a wide interval from the reality. *Eran.*—Agreed.

Orth.—Consider now too this point. The divine apostle calls the Son the image of the Father; for he says, "Who is the image of the invisible God?"[15] *Eran.*—What then; does not the Son have all the qualities of the Father? *Orth.*—He is not Father. He is not uncaused. He is not unbegotten. *Eran.*—If he were he would not be Son. *Orth.*—Then does not what I said hold true; the image does not have all the qualities of the archetype? *Eran.*—True. *Orth.*—Thus too the divine apostle said that Melchizedek is made like unto the Son of God. DIALOGUE 2.[16]

HAVING NO BEGINNING, NO ENDING. THEODORET OF CYR: *Eran.*—Suppose we grant that [Melchizedek] is without Father and without mother and without descent, as you have said. But how are we to understand his having neither beginning of days nor end of life?

Orth.—The holy Moses when writing the ancient genealogy tells us how Adam being so many years old begat Seth,[17] and when he had lived so many years he ended his life.[18] He writes the same of Seth, of Enoch, and of the rest. But he mentions neither beginning of existence nor end of life when speaking about Melchizedek. Thus as far as the story goes he has neither beginning of days nor end of life, but in truth and reality the only begotten Son of God never began to exist and shall never have an end. *Eran.*—Agreed. *Orth.*—Then, so far as what belongs to God and is really divine is concerned, Melchizedek is a type of the Lord Christ; but as far as the priesthood is concerned, which belongs rather to man than to God, the Lord Christ was made a priest after the order of Melchizedek.[19] For, Melchizedek was a high priest of the people, and the Lord Christ has made the right holy offering of salvation for everyone.

Eran.—We have spent many words on this matter. *Orth.*—Yet more were needed, as you know, for you said the point was a difficult one. DIALOGUE 2.[20]

7:16 The Power of an Indestructible Life

NOT BROKEN DOWN BY DEATH. EPHREM THE SYRIAN: Paul says, "If perfection had been attainable" through the Levitic house, "for under it the people received the law"—that is, through its agency the law of the people was declared—"what further need would there have been" to elevate another priest from another place, "rather than one named after the order of Aaron," who was the patriarch of those priests, "but after the

---

[13]See Gen 1:27. [14]1 Cor 11:7. [15]Col 1:15. [16]NFPF 2 3:188-89*. [17]Gen 4:25. [18]Gen 5:5. [19]Heb 6:20. [20]NPNF 2 3:189**.

order of" the uncircumcised "Melchizedek"?

After thus proving the necessity to change priesthood, Paul begins again to prove that, with this change in the priesthood, the law is changed too. "When there is a change in the priesthood," he says, "there is necessarily a change in the law as well." Is there need of a sacrificial law, if sacrifices and priesthood have been abolished?

So Melchizedek, "of whom these things are spoken" even though he was from that generation, came "from another tribe from which no one has ever served at the altar," and the one who received his priesthood was certainly not from the Levites, lest he might be estranged from Melchizedek because of his origin.

In fact, "it is evident that our Lord" Jesus Christ "was descended from Judah, and in connection with that tribe Moses said nothing about priests."

For this reason Uzziah was stricken with leprosy,[21] because he wanted to transfer priesthood by his action and move it to the house of Judah, before Jesus, who was from Judah, came and took it in his hour.

"This becomes even more evident" because "another priest arises in the likeness of Melchizedek, who has become a priest not according to a legal requirement concerning bodily descent," that is, not by being appointed before the people through the aspersion, sanctification, and blood and anointment of priesthood, and through its garments. Our Lord, on the contrary, was appointed and accepted the priesthood "by the power of a life" which is not broken down by death.

He accepted the priesthood through the oath proffered by David, "You are a priest forever after the order of Melchizedek." Therefore, "a former commandment is set aside," as well as the previous priesthood, "because of its weakness and uselessness" as a rule. COMMENTARY ON THE EPISTLE TO THE HEBREWS.[22]

NOT BY BODILY DESCENT. THEODORET OF CYR: He is saying it is possible to bring out the likeness between the one and the other: as one did not have successors to his priesthood, so neither did the other transmit it to another—which he referred to as "bodily descent" because the law required on account of the mortality of human beings that after the death of the high priest his son would succeed to the priesthood. Now, in my view this phrase[23] has another meaning as well: the priests cleansed the body in particular, sprinkling and washing it; they offered sacrifices for it. In other words, it was not for murderers or wreckers of others' marriages that they were in the habit of performing sacrifices, but for menstruating women, lepers and people who touched the bones of the dead. INTERPRETATION OF HEBREWS 7.[24]

7:17 A Priest Forever, in the Order of Melchizedek

AARON AND MELCHIZEDEK AS PRIESTLY TYPES. ORIGEN: Just as the people of old, who were called the people of God,[25] were divided into twelve tribes plus the levitical order, and this order itself, which engaged in service of the Divine, was divided into additional priestly and levitical orders, so, I think, all the people of Christ according to "the hidden person of the heart,"[26] who bear the name "Jew inwardly" and who have been circumcised "in spirit," possess the characteristics of the tribes in a more mystical manner. . . .

Most of us who approach the teachings of Christ, since we have much time for the activities of life and offer a few acts to God, would perhaps be those from the tribes who have a little fellowship with the priests and support the service of God in a few things. But those who devote themselves to the divine Word and truly exist by the service of God alone will properly be said to be Levites and priests in accordance with the excel-

---

[21]2 Chron 26:16-20. [22]EHA 212. [23]The Greek phrase, *entolēs sarkinēs*, which RSV translates "bodily descent," is more literally translated as "fleshly ordinance." [24]PG 82:729; TCCLSP 2:166. [25]Num 27:17. [26]1 Pet 3:4.

lence of their activities in this work.

And, perhaps, those who excel all others and who hold, as it were, the first places of their generation will be high priests according to the order of Aaron, but not according to the order of Melchizedek. If someone should object to this, thinking that we are impious when we prescribe the title of high priest for humans, since Jesus is proclaimed as great priest in many places—for we have "a great high priest who has passed through the heavens, Jesus, the Son of God"[27]—we would have to say to him that the apostle indicated this when he said that the prophet said of Christ, "You are a priest forever after the order of Melchizedek," and not after the order of Aaron. On this basis, we too say that humans can be high priests according to the order of Aaron, but only the Christ of God according to the order of Melchizedek. COMMENTARY ON THE GOSPEL OF JOHN 1.1, 1.10-11.[28]

THE TRUE PONTIFF, JESUS CHRIST. BRAULIO OF SARAGOSSA: It is better to be in doubt about hidden matters than to quarrel about what is uncertain. Let us turn to what is true and firm, to what most assuredly keeps any Christian and good Catholic from doubting or quibbling. That is, through the sacrament, bread and wine offered to God become for us the true body and blood of Christ, according to the words of the Lord himself and the sacred Scriptures composed by the Holy Spirit. This sacrament the Catholic church offers daily on its altar "after the order of Melchizedek" by the true pontiff, Jesus Christ, with mystical understanding and an ineffable dearth of speech, because surpassing grace goes beyond everything. LETTER 42.[29]

THE MYSTERY OF HIS SACRIFICE IS REENACTED IN THE EUCHARIST. BEDE: And in the Apocalypse, John the apostle . . . says, "Who loved us and washed from us our sins in his blood."[30] Not only did he wash away our sins in his blood when he gave his blood for us on the cross, or when each of us was cleansed in his baptism by the mystery of his most sacred passion.

But he also takes away every day the sins of the world and washes us of our daily sins in his blood, when the memory of his blessed passion is reenacted on the altar, when a created thing, bread and wine, is transformed by the ineffable sanctification of the Spirit into the sacrament of his flesh and blood. Thus his body and blood is not poured forth and slain by the hands of the unfaithful to their own ruin, but he is taken by the mouth of the faithful to their salvation.

The lamb in the law of Passover rightly shows us a type of him, since, having once liberated the people from their Egyptian servitude, it sanctified the people every year by being immolated in memory of their liberation, until he came, to whom such a sacrificial offering gave testimony. When he was offered to the Father for us as a sacrificial offering and for a sweet savor, he transformed, by the lamb that was offered, the mystery of his passion into a created thing, bread and wine, having been made "a priest forever after the order of Melchizedek." HOMILIES ON THE GOSPELS 1.15.[31]

7:18-19 *We Draw Near to God*

THROUGH FREEDOM FROM MATERIAL POSSESSIONS. EPHREM THE SYRIAN: Because of their earthly voluptuousness and desire for pleasure, which the former priests showed, and because of their infirmity, through which they made their people infirm before their cupidities, they did not bring any of them to that perfection, thanks to which we got rid of all our material goods. In fact, "the introduction" of the gospel made for the hope which surpassed what was previously preached to us, was also made for the introduction of this precept: through our own freedom from material possessions "we approach God," whereas through the voluptuousness and pleasures of the law we were rejected and removed from God. COMMENTARY ON THE EPISTLE TO THE HEBREWS.[32]

---

[27]Heb 4:14. [28]FC 80:31, 33-34*. [29]FC 63:94. [30]Rev 1:5. [31]CS 110:149*. [32]EHA 212-13.

FOR PERFECTION THE LAW WAS OF NO USE.
CHRYSOSTOM: Was the law then of no use? It was indeed of use and of great use, but to make humans perfect it was of no use. For in this respect he says, "the law made nothing perfect." All were figures, all shadows: circumcision, sacrifice, sabbath. Therefore they could not reach through the soul, and thus they pass away and gradually withdraw. But "a better hope is introduced, through which we draw near to God." ON THE EPISTLE TO THE HEBREWS 13.4.[33]

THE LAW WAS INCAPABLE OF PROVIDING THE PERFECT BENEFIT. THEODORET OF CYR: The law ceases to have effect, he is saying, and the hope of better things is introduced. It ceases to have effect, not for being evil (the frenzied view of the heretics), but for being ineffective and incapable of providing the perfect benefit. It must be noted, of course, that he refers to the obsolete prescriptions of the law as ineffective and useless—circumcision, sabbath observance and similar things; the New Testament also bids us observe to a greater extent the commandments, you shall not kill, you shall not commit adultery, and suchlike things. In place of the former, therefore, we receive the hope of the good things to come: it relates us to God. INTERPRETATION OF HEBREWS 7.[34]

THE INTRODUCTION OF A BETTER HOPE. ORIGEN: We may also ask what it means when it says in the law that Moses' face was shining with glory, though covered with a veil,[35] while his hand when put "into his bosom" became "leprous as snow."[36] In this it seems to me the form of the whole law is quite fully described. For his "face" is the word of the law, and by "hand" are described the works of the law. "For no human being will be justified by works of the law."[37] Nor could the law lead anyone to "perfection." In the same way the "leprous" hand of Moses was hidden in his bosom, since it could not perform any perfect work; but his face shone, though covered with a veil, since his word has the glory of knowl-

edge, but a hidden glory. HOMILIES ON EXODUS 12.3.[38]

7:20-22 An Oath and Surety

THIS PRIESTHOOD WILL NOT END. THEODORET OF CYR: Since he was the one who under the law appointed priests but brought them to an end and declared another in their place, he was obliged to say that he appointed them without taking an oath, but in his case included an oath as well. Do not think, then, that this priesthood will cease to have effect like that one, or that another one will take its place; the taking of an oath excludes such a false impression. INTERPRETATION OF HEBREWS 7.[39]

HIS RESURRECTION CONFIRMS OUR HOPE.
THEODORET OF CYR: Since the New Covenant promised us the kingdom of heaven, resurrection from the dead and life everlasting, though none of these is in sight, he had to call the Lord Jesus its "surety," who through his own resurrection confirmed the hope of our resurrection, on the one hand, and on the other continued to give his own resurrection through the miracles worked by the apostles. INTERPRETATION OF HEBREWS 7.[40]

PRIESTS NEED TO CEASE BEING PRIESTS.
THEODORE OF MOPSUESTIA: He says that it shows the difference between Christ and Aaron in that Christ received the priesthood with an oath. For those who became priests without oaths became so because of their need to cease being priests at some time, but Christ entered the priesthood with oaths, since he intended to remain based on his rank. He shows his rank is far greater than those under the law, since he intended also to furnish a greater high priest to those coming to him. For in this way he says he becomes "a surety" . . . for being the first to rise,

[33]NPNF 1 14:428-29*. [34]PG 82:729-732; TCCLSP 2:166-67. [35]Ex 34:29-35. [36]Ex 4:6. [37]Rom 3:20. [38]FC 71:370**. [39]PG 82:732; TCCLSP 2:167. [40]PG 82:732; TCCLSP 2:167.

just as he also calls him a "high priest," so he pledges to us a similar resurrection. FRAGMENTS ON THE EPISTLE TO THE HEBREWS 7.20-22.[41]

7:25 He Always Lives to Make Intercession

HE STANDS BEFORE THE ALTAR. ORIGEN: Jesus now stands "before the face of God interceding for us."[42] He stands before the altar to offer a propitiation to God for us. As he was about to approach that altar, moreover, he was saying, "I shall not drink again of this fruit of the vine until I drink it anew with you."[43] Therefore, he expects us to be converted, to imitate his example, to follow his footsteps, that he may rejoice with us and "drink wine with us in his Father's kingdom." For now, because "the Lord is merciful and gracious,"[44] he "weeps with those who weep and desires to rejoice with those who rejoice"[45] with greater feeling than this apostle. And how much more "this one mourns over many of those who sinned before and have not repented."[46] For we must not think that Paul is mourning for sinners and weeping for those who transgress, but Jesus my Lord abstains from weeping when he approaches the Father, when he stands at the altar and offers a propitiatory sacrifice for us. This is not to drink the wine of joy "when he ascends to the altar" because he is still bearing the bitterness of our sins. He, therefore, does not want to be the only one to drink wine "in the kingdom" of God. He waits for us, just as he said, "Until I shall drink it with you."[47] Thus we are those who, neglecting our life, delay his joy. HOMILIES ON LEVITICUS 7.2.3.[48]

AS MAN HE INTERCEDES. GREGORY OF NAZIANZUS: Petition does not imply here, as it does in popular parlance, a desire for legal satisfaction; there is something humiliating in the idea. No, it means interceding for us in his role of mediator, in the way that the Spirit too is spoken of as "making petition" on our behalf.[49] "For there is one God, and there is one mediator between God and men, the man Christ Jesus."[50]

Even at this moment he is, as human, interceding for my salvation, until he makes me divine by the power of his incarnate humanity. "As human," I say, because he still has with him the body he assumed, though he is no longer "regarded as human,"[51] meaning the bodily experiences, which, sin aside, are ours and his. This is the "advocate"[52] we have in Jesus—not a slave who falls prostrate before the Father on our behalf. Get rid of what is really a slavish suspicion, unworthy of the Spirit. It is not in God to make the demand, nor in the Son to submit to it; the thought is unjust to God. No, it is by what he suffered as man that he persuades us, as Word and encourager, to endure. That, for me, is the meaning of his "advocacy." ON THE SON, THEOLOGICAL ORATION 4(30).14.[53]

HE THAT HAS ALL JUDGMENT ALSO INTERCEDES. CHRYSOSTOM: You see that he says this in respect of that which is according to the flesh. For when he appears as priest, then he also intercedes. Wherefore also, when Paul says, "who indeed intercedes for us,"[54] he hints the same thing; the high priest makes intercession. For he that "raises the dead and gives them life"[55] and does so "as the Father," how is it that, when there is need to save, he "makes intercession"? He that has "all judgment,"[56] how is it that he "makes intercession"? He that "sends his angels"[57] that they may "throw" some into "the furnace" and save others, how is it that he "makes intercession"? Wherefore, he says, "he is able to save." For this cause then he saves, because he dies not. Inasmuch as "he always lives," he has, he means, no successor; and if he has no successor, he is able to aid all people. For there under the law indeed, the high priest, although he were worthy of admiration during the time in which he was high priest as Samuel, for instance, and any other

---

[41]NTA 15:208. [42]Cf. Heb 9:24. [43]Mt 26:29. [44]Ps 103:8 (102:8 LXX). [45]Cf. Rom 12:15. [46]2 Cor 12:21. [47]Mt 26:29. [48]FC 83:134-35. [49]Cf. Rom 8:26. [50]1 Tim 2:5. [51]2 Cor 5:16. [52]1 Jn 2:1. [53]FGFR 272. [54]Rom 8:34. [55]Jn 5:21. [56]Jn 5:22. [57]Mt 13:41-42.

such, but, after this, no longer; for they were dead. But here it is not so, but "he" saves "to the uttermost." What is "to the uttermost"? He hints at some mystery. Not here only, he says, but there also he saves them that "draw near to God through him." How does he save? "Since he always lives," he says, "to make intercession for them." Do you see the humiliation? Do you see the manhood? For he says not that he obtained this by making intercession once for all, but continually and whenever it may be needful to intercede for them. "To the uttermost." What is it? Not for a time only, but there also in the future life. On the Epistle to the Hebrews 13.6.[58]

From His Incarnation He Advocates for Us. Oecumenius: He intercedes as "we have him as an advocate with the Father."[59] He says that from his incarnation itself he advocates for us and exhorts the Father to have mercy on us. Fragments on the Epistle to the Hebrews 7.25.[60]

7:26-28 The Appointed Son

Is It Reasonable to Call God Crafty? Chrysostom: You see that the whole passage is said of the humanity. But when I say the humanity, I mean the humanity having divinity, not dividing one from the other, but leaving you to suppose what is suitable. . . . He says, "such a high priest also became us, who is holy, blameless." "Blameless"—what is that? Without wickedness, about which another prophet says, "there was no deceit in his mouth."[61] That is, he is not crafty. Could any one say this concerning God? And is one not ashamed to say that God is not crafty, nor deceitful? Concerning him, however, in respect of the flesh, it might be reasonable to say it. On the Epistle to the Hebrews 13.7.[62]

He Became Us. Basil the Great: Although we are not his brothers but have become his enemies by our transgressions, he who is not mere man, but God, after the freedom that he bestowed on us, also calls us his brothers. "I will

tell of your name," he says, "to my brethren."[63] Now, he who has redeemed us, if you examine his nature, is neither brother nor man; but if you examine his condescension to us through grace, he calls us brothers and descends to our human nature. He does not need a ransom, for he himself is the propitiation. Homilies on the Psalms 19.4 (Psalm 48).[64]

The Only Son of God. Augustine: Who then is so just and holy a priest as the only Son of God, who had no need of a sacrifice for the washing away of his own sins, neither original sins nor those that are added from human life? And what could be so fittingly chosen by men to be offered for them as human flesh? And what so suitable for this immolation as mortal flesh? And what so clean for cleansing the vices of mortals as the flesh born in the womb without the contagion of carnal concupiscence, and coming from a virginal womb? And what could be so acceptably offered and received as the flesh of our sacrifice made the body of our priest? Four things are to be considered in every sacrifice: by whom it is offered, to whom it is offered, what is offered, and for whom it is offered. On the Trinity 4.14.19.[65]

He Is a Priest Forever. Ephrem the Syrian: In the house of Levi, because "they became priests without an oath," they did not last; he, on the contrary, lasts forever. In fact, it cannot happen that he speaks falsely about the oath, because he said, "The Lord has sworn and will not change his mind, 'You are a priest forever' " of the priests according to the order of Melchizedek. And "Jesus Christ" was "a much better" mediator than the former priests in that thing, which he promised us through the New Testament.

While before it was necessary that the priests were many, because death interrupted the older ones in the course of their office and they did not last forever, now there is no other high priest

---

[58]NPNF 1 14:429*. [59]1 Jn 2:1. [60]NTA 15:464. [61]Is 53:9. [62]NPNF 1 14:430. [63]Ps 22:22 (21:23 LXX). [64]FC 46:318-19*. [65]FC 45:155*.

with our Lord, "who lives forever to make intercession for us," not in the victims of the sacrifices but in prayers.

"And he is able for all time to save us," not in the earthly delights, which nourish us for a few days, but "when we draw near to God through him" in eternity.

"It was fitting that we should have such a high priest, holy, blameless, unstained, separated from sinners . . . who had no need, like those high priests, to offer sacrifices first for his own sins and then for those of the people; he did this once for all when he offered up himself," not for him but for the sins of humankind.

"The law appointed" weak "men as high priests" who certainly needed to offer sacrifices for their sins. "The word of the oath," however, "which" was provided in David "later than the law, appointed the Son" who remains "perfect forever." COMMENTARY ON THE EPISTLE TO THE HEBREWS.[66]

---

[66]EHA 213.

8:1-13 WE HAVE SUCH A HIGH PRIEST

Now the point in what we are saying is this: we have such a high priest, one who is seated at the right hand of the throne of the Majesty in heaven, [2]a minister in the sanctuary and the true tent" which is set up not by man but by the Lord. [3]For every high priest is appointed to offer gifts and sacrifices; hence it is necessary for this priest also to have something to offer. [4]Now if he were on earth, he would not be a priest at all, since there are priests who offer gifts according to the law. [5]They serve a copy and shadow of the heavenly sanctuary; for when Moses was about to erect the tent," he was instructed by God, saying, "See that you make everything according to the pattern which was shown you on the mountain." [6]But as it is, Christ° has obtained a ministry which is as much more excellent than the old as the covenant he mediates is better, since it is enacted on better promises. [7]For if that first covenant had been faultless, there would have been no occasion for a second.

[8]For he finds fault with them when he says:
"The days will come, says the Lord,
when I will establish a new covenant with the house of Israel
and with the house of Judah;
[9]not like the covenant that I made with their fathers
on the day when I took them by the hand
to lead them out of the land of Egypt;
for they did not continue in my covenant,
and so I paid no heed to them, says the Lord.
[10]This is the covenant that I will make with the house of Israel

after those days, says the Lord:
I will put my laws into their minds,
and write them on their hearts,
and I will be their God,
and they shall be my people.
[11]And they shall not teach every one his fellow
or every one his brother, saying, 'Know the Lord,'
for all shall know me,
from the least of them to the greatest.
[12]For I will be merciful toward their iniquities,
and I will remember their sins no more."

[13]In speaking of a new covenant he treats the first as obsolete. And what is becoming obsolete and growing old is ready to vanish away.

n Or *tabernacle*   o Greek *he*

Overview: The sense of this pericope for the early writers is that the ancient religious institutions like the priesthood, the tabernacle and the Mosaic laws and covenant were shadows and symbols or patterns of the institutions of the church. The testament that is always new, or the "eternal gospel," is in heaven, declared first in the people of Israel but fulfilled in Christ (Origen). These ancient religious institutions were shadows and symbols of the coming *ecclesia* (Ephrem). Christ, who himself is the sacrifice (Chrysostom), is minister in the tabernacle of truth (Ephrem), worthy of the heavens (Chrysostom). Christ's sitting on the right hand signifies his equality of honor with the Father (Basil). Christ, the perfect priest and perfect victim, sacrificed his own flesh for us (Theodoret) so that he may lead humans to God (Athanasius, Augustine, Lactantius). It was through the resurrection that the disciples believed (Origen). The author of the law, himself born under the law,[1] took away from the law its barrenness (Bede). The end consists in a return (Origen) that reveals the ultimate spiritual reality (Origen, Chrysostom, Augustine). The law, the prophets, and even the name of Jesus are but shadows of that eschatological reality (Eusebius, Origen). The Holy Spirit addresses the faithful through Scripture, which must be rightly interpreted according to its intention (Origen). All things are better in the Lord (Athanasius). It is clear to the early writers that the new covenant, the Christian community, fulfills the old (Chrysostom, Bede, Ephrem), but the old covenant is not to be treated as useless (Lactantius). Paul here used a familiar form of speech, as if one should say that a house is not faultless because it has some defect or decay. Paul here uses a rhetorical device, according to Chrysostom, to show that what was good has become better (see the introduction). The old human nature is consumed by the new creation in Christ (Gregory of Nyssa). The new covenant is written in the heart (Chrysostom, Clement of Alexandria). The meekness of the Lord overshadowed the harshness of the law (Leo the Great).

8:1-2 *The True Tent*

It Is Fitting for This Minister to Sit.
Photius: When he serves and ministers, it is for this purpose: to cleanse humans from their sins and to make them holy. For it is fitting for the minister and creator of the saints to sit at the

[1]Gal 4:4.

right hand of the Father as true God and his Son.[2] FRAGMENTS ON THE EPISTLE TO THE HEBREWS 8.1.[3]

HIS MINISTRY IS SALVATION OF HUMAN BEINGS. THEODORET OF CYR: He left till last the greatest honor, presenting him seated at the right hand of the throne of majesty. Aaron, the forebear of priests, remember, who was the first to receive the role of high priesthood, entered the divine sanctuary with fear and trembling, whereas this person has a seat at the right hand. He included the word *minister*, of course, because he is speaking of a high priest. What ministry does he discharge after offering himself once and for all, and no longer offering a further sacrifice? How is it possible for him at one and the same time to be seated and to minister? Only if you were to say the ministry is the salvation of human beings, which he procures in lordly fashion. INTERPRETATION OF HEBREWS 8.[4]

SERVANT OF THE SAINTS. EPHREM THE SYRIAN: "The point in what we are saying," that is, the discussion which we have undertaken with regard to priesthood and the law, is now presented to you according to what I have said above. "We have such a high priest" of the high priests, who does not stand before the ark of alliance but "who," by ascending, "is seated at the right hand of the throne of the majesty in heaven."

Moreover, he, who was so entirely praised, was "a minister in the sanctuary" in the very tabernacle of truth—that is, either in the kingdom of heaven, as he promised, or in this world, as he actually did by washing the feet of his disciples. COMMENTARY ON THE EPISTLE TO THE HEBREWS.[5]

THE FLESH OF THE LORD IS THE TRUE TENT. ARETHAS OF CAESAREA: He calls the heavens "the tent" in this passage. In my opinion he seems to then call the flesh of the Lord "the true tent," which also the Lord himself fashioned when he

was not yet man, considering that immaculate flesh did not come into existence by human coupling but by the Holy Spirit. FRAGMENTS ON THE EPISTLE TO THE HEBREWS 8.2.[6]

TENT AS HEAVEN. THEODORET OF CYR: By "tent" he referred to heaven, where the apostle said he was ministering as man, though being its creator. INTERPRETATION OF HEBREWS 8.[7]

SITTING AT THE RIGHT HAND INDICATES HONOR. BASIL THE GREAT: If one assigns to the Father the upper place by way of precedence and asserts that the only begotten Son sits below, he will find that all the consequent conditions of body attach to the creature of his imagination. And if these are the imaginations of drunken delusion and frenzied insanity, can it be consistent with true religion for people taught by the Lord himself that "he that honors not the Son honors not the Father"[8] to refuse to worship and glorify with the Father him who in nature, in glory and in dignity is conjoined with him? What shall we say? What just defense shall we have in the day of the awful universal judgment of all creation, if, when the Lord clearly announces that he will come "in the glory of his Father";[9] when Stephen beheld Jesus standing at the right hand of God;[10] when Paul testified in the Spirit concerning Christ "that he is at the right hand of God";[11] when the Father says, "Sit at my right hand"[12]; when the Holy Spirit bears witness that he has sat down on "the right hand of the majesty" of God—what defense shall we have when we attempt to degrade him, who shares the honor and the throne, from his condition of equality to a lower state? Standing and sitting, I apprehend, indicate the permanence and entire stability of the nature, as Baruch, when he wishes to exhibit the immutability and immobility of the divine

[2]Cf. Jn 17:3; 1 Jn 5:20; Mk 16:19. [3]NTA 15:647. [4]PG 82:733-736; TCCLSP 2:169. [5]EHA 214. [6]NTA 15:661. [7]PG 82:736; TCCLSP 2:169. [8]Jn 5:23. [9]Mt 16:27. [10]Acts 7:55. [11]Rom 8:24. [12]Ps 110:1 (109:1 LXX).

mode of existence, says, "For you sit forever and we perish utterly."[13] Moreover, the place on the right hand indicates, in my judgment, equality of honor. It is rash, then, to attempt to deprive the Son of participation in the doxology, as though worthy only to be ranked in a lower place of honor. ON THE SPIRIT 6.15.[14]

CHRIST SENT TO FOUND A NEW TEMPLE. LACTANTIUS: Let people therefore learn and understand why the Most High God willed that he should be clothed with mortal flesh, afflicted with torture and sentenced to death when he sent his ambassador and messenger to instruct mortals with the precepts of his righteousness. For since there was no righteousness on earth, he sent a teacher, as it were, a living law to found a new name and temple so that, by his words and example, he might spread throughout the earth a true and holy worship. However, in order that people might know for sure that he was sent by God, it was fitting that he should not be born as human beings are born, composed of a mortal on both sides. Rather, so that it might appear that he was heavenly even in the form of man, he was born without the office of a father. For he had a spiritual Father—God. And, as God was the Father of his spirit without a mother, so a virgin was the mother of his body without a father. He was therefore both God and man, being placed in the middle between God and man. From which the Greeks call him *Mesitēs*,[15] that he might be able to lead humankind to God—that is, to immortality. For if he had been God only (as we have before said), he would not have been able to afford to people examples of goodness; if he had been man only, he would not have been able to compel people to righteousness, unless there had been added an authority and virtue greater than that of man. DIVINE INSTITUTES 4.25.[16]

8:3 Appointed to Offer Gifts and Sacrifices

THE WORD OF GOD SACRIFICED HIS FLESH FOR OUR SALVATION. ATHANASIUS: I am very much surprised how they have ventured to entertain the idea that the Word became man in consequence of his nature. For, if this were so, the commemoration of Mary would be superfluous. For nature has no conception of a virgin bearing apart from a man. By the good pleasure of the Father, being true God, and Word and Wisdom of the Father by nature, he became man in the body for our salvation in order that, having something to offer for us he might save us all, "as many as through fear of death were all their lifetime subject to bondage."[17] For it was not some man that gave himself up for us; since every man is under sentence of death, according to what was said to all in Adam, "earth you are and unto earth you shall return."[18] Nor yet was it any other of the creatures, since every creature is liable to change. But the Word himself offered his own body on our behalf that our faith and hope might not be in man, but that we might have our faith in God the Word himself. LETTER 61, TO MAXIMUS 3.[19]

THERE IS NO PRIEST WITHOUT A SACRIFICE. CHRYSOSTOM: That you may understand that he used the word *minister* of humanity, observe how he again indicates it: "For," he says, "every high priest is appointed to offer gifts and sacrifices; hence it is necessary for this priest also to have something to offer." Do not now, because you hear that he sits, suppose that his being called high priest is mere idle talk. For clearly the former—his sitting—belongs to the dignity of the Godhead, but this [his being a priest] to his great lovingkindness and his tender care for us. On this account, he repeatedly urges this very thing and dwells more upon it, for he feared lest the other truth should overthrow it. Therefore, he again brings his discourse down to this, since some were inquiring why he died. He was a priest. But there is no priest without a sacrifice. It is necessary then that he also should have a sacri-

---

[13]Bar 3:3 LXX. [14]NPNF 2 8:9-10*. [15]Mediator, someone who stands between two parties in order to bring them together. [16]ANF 7:126*. [17]Cf. Heb 2:15. [18]Gen 3:19 LXX. [19]NPNF 2 4:579*.

fice. ON THE EPISTLE TO THE HEBREWS 14.2.[20]

CHRIST THE PERFECT PRIEST, PERFECT VICTIM. AUGUSTINE: They do not understand that not even the proudest of spirits could themselves rejoice in the honor of sacrifices unless a true sacrifice was due to the one true God in whose place they desire to be worshiped. This sacrifice cannot be rightly offered except by a holy and righteous priest, and it also must be received by those for whom it is offered. And it also has to be without fault, so that it may be offered for cleansing those with faults. This is at least what everyone does who wants a sacrifice to be offered for themselves to God. Who then is so righteous and holy a priest as the only Son of God who had no need to purge his own sins by sacrifice, neither original sins nor those that are added by human life? And what could human beings more appropriately choose to be offered for themselves than human flesh? And what could be more fitting for this immolation than mortal flesh? And what could be cleaner for cleansing the faults of mortals than the flesh born in and from the womb of a virgin without any infection of carnal desires? And what could be more acceptably offered and taken than that the flesh of our sacrifice be the body of our priest? And so, where four things are to be considered in every sacrifice—(1) to whom it is offered, (2) by whom it is offered, (3) what is offered, (4) for whom it is offered—the same one and true mediator himself, reconciling us to God by the sacrifice of peace, might remain one with him [the Father] to whom he offered, might make those one in himself for whom he offered, and he himself might be in one both the offerer and the offering. ON THE TRINITY 4.14.1 [19].[21]

HE OFFERED OUR NATURE FOR US. THEODORET OF CYR: It is proper for a high priest to offer gifts to the God of all. For this reason, the only begotten, when he was made man and assumed our nature, offered it for us. INTERPRE-

TATION OF HEBREWS 8.3.[22]

8:4-6 *Shadow of the Heavenly Sanctuary*

HE WAS NOT CRITICIZING THE LAW. THEODORET OF CYR: He mentioned this by way of defense to stress that he was not criticizing the law but regarding it also as venerable for containing the type of the heavenly things. This was the reason he said it was pointless to refer to him as a priest while living on earth, there being priests according to the law discharging the worship prescribed by the law. So if the priesthood according to the law also came to an end, and the high priest according to the order of Melchizedek offered sacrifice and made further sacrifices unnecessary, why do the priests of the New Covenant perform the sacramental liturgy? It is clear to those versed in divine things, however, that it is not another sacrifice we offer; rather, we perform the commemoration of the one, saving sacrifice. The Lord himself, remember, required this of us, "Do this in memory of me,"[23] so that we should recall with insight the type of the sufferings undergone for us, kindle love for the benefactor and look forward to the enjoyment of the good things to come. INTERPRETATION OF HEBREWS 8.[24]

SHADOWS OF THE CHURCH. EPHREM THE SYRIAN: Since they were in the darkness without a model, they managed their office according to a general affinity in divine matters. That is, all those ancient religious institutions were shadows and symbols of this institution of the church, which is established in its spirituality and divinity before him. And to Moses himself it was ordered, when he was about to build the tabernacle of the hour, "See that you make everything according to the pattern which was shown you on the mountain." COMMENTARY ON THE EPISTLE TO THE HEBREWS.[25]

---

[20]NPNF 1 14:433**. [21]NPNF 1 3:79*. [22]PG 82:736. [23]Lk 22:19; 1 Cor 11:24. [24]PG 82:736; *TCCLSP* 2:169-70. [25]EHA 214.

The End Consists of a Return. Origen: Now if we correctly understand it, this is the statement Moses writes in the beginning of his book, when he says, "In the beginning God created the heavens and the earth."[26] For this is the beginning of all creation: to this beginning the end and consummation of all things must return. That is, that heaven and earth may be the dwelling place and rest of the pious, so that all the saints and the meek may first obtain an inheritance in that earth, for this is the teaching of the law and the prophets and the gospel. In that earth I believe there exist, the true and living forms of worship which Moses handed down under the shadow of the law. For it is said that "they serve as a copy and shadow of the heavenly sanctuary"—that is, those who were in subjection in the law. To Moses himself it was also said, "See that you make everything according to the pattern which was shown you on the mountain."[27] It seems to me, therefore, that on this earth the law was a kind of schoolmaster to those who by it were to be led to Christ[28] and to be instructed and trained in order that, after the training of the law, they might more easily receive the more perfect precepts of Christ. So also that other earth, which receives into it all the saints, may first imbue and mould them by the precepts of the true and everlasting law, that they may more easily gain possession of those perfect precepts of heaven, to which nothing can be added. And in heaven there will truly be what is called the "eternal gospel"[29] and that testament that is always new, which shall never grow old. On First Principles 3.6.8.[30]

Shadow of Heavenly Things. Theodoret of Cyr: The divine apostle, by "shadow of the heavenly things"[31] referred to the worship according to the law and confirms his statement with a scriptural testimony. Interpretation of Hebrews 8.[32]

Worthy of the Heavens. Chrysostom: Here we must apply our minds attentively and consider the apostolic wisdom. For again he shows the difference of the priesthood, "who," he says, "serve a copy and shadow of heavenly things." What are the heavenly things he speaks of here? The spiritual things. For although they are done on earth, yet nevertheless they are worthy of the heavens. For when our Lord Jesus Christ lies slain as a sacrifice, when the Spirit is with us, when he who sits on the right hand of the Father is here, when sons are made by the washing, when they are fellow citizens of those in heaven, when we have a country and a city and citizenship there, when we are strangers to things here, how can all these be other than "heavenly things"? But what! Are not our hymns heavenly? Do not we also who are below utter in concert with them the same things that the divine choirs of bodiless powers sing above? Is not the altar also heavenly? How? It has nothing carnal. All spiritual things become the offerings. The sacrifice does not disperse into ashes or into smoke or into steamy savor. It makes the things placed there bright and splendid. How again can the rites that we celebrate be other than heavenly? For when he says, "If you forgive the sins of any, they are forgiven them; if you retain the sins of any, they are retained,"[33] when they have the keys of heaven, how can all be other than heavenly? On the Epistle to the Hebrews 14.3.[34]

Angels Serve Not Shadow but Reality. Origen: But who could more properly speak to us about who God is than the Son? "For no one knows the Father except the Son."[35] We too aspire to know how God is Spirit as the Son reveals it and to worship God in the Spirit that gives life and not in the letter that kills.[36] We want to honor God in truth and no longer in

---

[26]Gen 1:1. [27]Ex 25:40. [28]See Gal 3:24. [29]Rev 14:6. [30]ANF 4:347-48**. [31]RSV translates *tōn epouraniōn* as "of the heavenly sanctuary." A more literal translation is "of the heavenly things." [32]PG 82:736; TCCLSP 2:170. [33]Jn 20:23. [34]NPNF 1 14:433-34**. [35]Mt 11:27. [36]See 2 Cor 3:6.

types, shadows and examples, even as the angels do not serve God in examples and the shadow of heavenly realities but in realities that belong to the spiritual and heavenly order, having a high priest of the order of Melchizedek[37] as leader of the saving worship for those who need both the mystical and secret contemplation. COMMENTARY ON THE GOSPEL OF JOHN 13.146.[38]

JESUS AS DELIVERER. EUSEBIUS OF CAESAREA: It is now time to show that the very name of Jesus, and especially that of Christ, had already been honored by the ancient God-loving prophets. Moses himself, having been the first to make known the name of Christ as being especially revered and glorious, having handed down the types and symbols of heavenly things and the mysterious images according to the oracle which said to him, "See that you make everything according to the pattern which was shown you on the mountain,"[39] and having consecrated a man high priest of God insofar as it was at all possible, calls this man Christ.[40] That is, to this dignity of the high priesthood, which surpassed all preeminence among humans, he attaches for additional honor and glory the name of Christ. Thus, then, he indeed knew Christ as a being divine. And the same Moses by divine inspiration foresaw the name Jesus very clearly and again also endowed this with special privilege. The name of Jesus, which had never been uttered among people before it was made known to Moses, Moses applied first to this one alone,[41] whom he knew, again as a type and a symbol, would receive the rule over all after his death. His successor . . . had never before used the title Jesus but had been called by another name, Hoshea, which his parents had bestowed upon him. He himself [the successor] proclaims Jesus, as a privilege of honor far greater than a royal crown, giving him the name because Jesus, the son of Nun, himself bore a remembrance to our Savior, who alone, after Moses and the completion of the symbolic worship transmitted by him, received the rule of the true and pure religion. And in this way Moses bestowed the name of our Savior Jesus Christ as a mark of the greatest honor upon the two men who in his time surpassed all the rest of the people in virtue and glory—the high priest and him who would rule after him. ECCLESIASTICAL HISTORY 1.3.[42]

THE LAW AND OUR LIFE ARE SHADOWS OF GREATER THINGS. ORIGEN: The apostle says with reference to the law that they who have circumcision in the flesh "serve as the copy and shadow of heavenly things." And in another place, "is not our life on earth a shadow?"[43] If then both the law that is on the earth is a "shadow" and all our life that is on the earth is the same, and we live among nations under the "shadow of Christ," we must consider whether the truth of all these shadows will be learned in that revelation when, no longer "through a mirror and darkly," but "face to face"[44] all the saints shall be counted worthy to behold the glory of God and the causes and truth of things. And the pledge of this truth being already received through the Holy Spirit,[45] the apostle said, "Even if we have known Christ after the flesh, yet now henceforth we know him no more."[46] ON FIRST PRINCIPLES 2.6.7.[47]

BELIEVE THE WORD AS INTENDED. ORIGEN: Since, however, "when he was raised from the dead, his disciples remembered that he had said this, and they believed the Scripture and the word which Jesus had spoken,"[48] we must admit, as far as the literal meaning is concerned, that, after the Lord was raised from the dead, the disciples understood that the things said about the temple refer to his passion and resurrection, and they recalled that the saying, "in three days I will raise it up"[49] indicated the resurrection. It was then that "they believed both the Scripture and the word which Jesus had spoken," since there is no earlier testimony that they had believed the

---

[37]Heb 5:6; 7:17. [38]FC 89:99. [39]Ex 25:40. [40]See Lev 4:5, 16; 6:22. [41]Num 13:16. [42]FC 19:46-47*. [43]See Job 8:9. [44]See 1 Cor 13:12. [45]2 Cor 5:5. [46]2 Cor 5:16. [47]ANF 4:284**. [48]Jn 2:22. [49]Jn 2:19.

Scripture or this word which Jesus spoke. For faith is, strictly speaking, the acceptance with one's whole soul of the object of faith at baptism. But as for the anagogical meaning, since we previously mentioned the resurrection from the dead of the whole body of the Lord, we must know that the disciples—once they were reminded through the fulfillments of the Scripture which they had not thoroughly understood when they were in this life and once it was brought before their eyes and made manifest that it contained an example and shadow of certain heavenly things—believed what they formerly did not believe, and believed the word of Jesus as he who spoke it intended, which they had not understood before the resurrection.

For how can one be said to believe the Scripture in the proper sense, when one does not perceive the meaning of the Holy Spirit in it which God wants to be believed, rather than the intent of the letter? According to this, we must say that none of those who walk according to the flesh[50] believe in the spiritual meanings of the law, whose first principle they do not even imagine. COMMENTARY ON THE GOSPEL OF JOHN 10.298-300.[51]

MUCH MORE EXCELLENT. THEODORET OF CYR: He concisely brought out the superiority: whereas the Old Covenant had corporeal promises associated with it—a land flowing with milk and honey, olive groves and vineyards, big families and suchlike things—the New had an eternal and heavenly kingdom. INTERPRETATION OF HEBREWS 8.[52]

8:6-9 The Mediator of a Better Covenant

EVERYTHING IS BETTER IN THE LORD. ATHANASIUS: "It was therefore necessary that the patterns of things in the heavens should be purified with these; but the heavenly things themselves with better sacrifices than these."[53] Both in the verse before us, then, and throughout, does he ascribe the word better to the Lord, who is better and other than originated things. For better is the sacrifice through him, better the hope in him and also the promises through him, not merely as great compared with small, but the one differing from the other in nature, because he who conducts this economy, is better than things originated. FOUR DISCOURSES AGAINST THE ARIANS 1.13.8 [59].[54]

AN EARTHLY AND A HEAVENLY PROPHECY. AUGUSTINE: Prophetic utterances are of three kinds: (1) some relating to the earthly Jerusalem; (2) some to the heavenly Jerusalem; (3) and some to both simultaneously. I think it proper to prove what I say by examples. The prophet Nathan was sent to convict King David of heinous sin and predict what future evils would happen to him because of his sin. Who can question that this pertains to the earthly city? There are other instances, sometimes addressed to the public at large for their safety and benefit, and sometimes addressed to someone in private who merited an utterance from God in order to know in advance about some event to guide his temporal life.

The following prophecy, however, without a doubt references the heavenly Jerusalem. "Behold, the days are coming, says the Lord, that I will make for the house of Israel, and for the house of Judah, a new testament: not according to the testament that I settled for their fathers in the day when I laid hold of their hand to lead them out of the land of Egypt; because they continued not in my testament, and I regarded them not, says the Lord. For this is the testament that I will make for the house of Israel: after those days, says the Lord, I will give my laws in their mind, and will write them upon their hearts, and I will see to them; and I will be to them a God, and they shall be to me a people." Here, God himself is Jerusalem's reward. Its chief and entire good is to possess him and to be possessed by him.

Both cities are indicated when the city of God

[50]See Rom 8:4. [51]FC 80:322*. [52]PG 82:736; TCCLSP 2:170. [53]Cf. Heb 7:19, 22; 9:23. [54]NPNF 2 4:341*.

is called Jerusalem and when it is prophesied that the house of God shall one day be in Jerusalem. This prophecy seems to be fulfilled when King Solomon builds that most noble temple. For these things both happened in the earthly Jerusalem, as history shows, and were types of the heavenly Jerusalem. This kind of prophecy, as it were, blending both the others in the ancient canonical books devoted to historical narratives, is very common. It has exercised and continues to exercise greatly the talents of those who search holy Scripture. CITY OF GOD 17.3.[55]

WORDS OF JEREMIAH FULFILLED WITH THE APOSTLES. LEO THE GREAT: [The Lord] ascended into the retirement of a neighboring mountain and called his apostles to him there. From the height of that mystical seat he could instruct them in the loftier doctrines, signifying from the very nature of the place and act that it was he who had once honored Moses by speaking to him. He spoke with Moses then, indeed, with a more terrifying justice, but now with a holier mercy in order that what had been promised might be fulfilled when the prophet Jeremiah says, "Behold, the days are coming when I will complete a new covenant for the house of Israel and for the house of Judah. After those days, says the Lord, I will put my laws in their minds, and in their heart will I write them."[56] He therefore who had spoken to Moses, spoke also to the apostles, and the swift hand of the Word wrote and deposited the secrets of the new covenant in the disciples' hearts. There were no thick clouds surrounding him as of old, nor were the people frightened off from approaching the mountain by frightful sounds and lightning.[57] Rather, quietly and freely his discourse reached the ears of those who stood by. In this way the harshness of the law might give way before the gentleness of grace, and "the spirit of adoption" might dispel the terrors of bondage. SERMON 95.1.[58]

8:10-11 Written on Their Hearts

THE APOSTLES RECEIVED NOTHING IN WRITING. CHRYSOSTOM: "No longer," he says, "shall the covenant be in writings, but in hearts." Let the Jew, in that case, show if this was ever carried into effect, but he could not, for it was made a second time in writings after the return from Babylon. But I show that the apostles received nothing in writing, but received it in their hearts through the Holy Ghost. Therefore also Christ said, "When he comes, he will teach you all things and bring to your remembrance all that I have said to you."[59] ON THE EPISTLE TO THE HEBREWS 14.5.[60]

HOW TO WITHDRAW FROM PROPER RELIGION? OECUMENIUS: For that this is the case is clear from this reason: Who would have easily persuaded someone in the Old Testament to withdraw from the proper religion? To the contrary Israel, being full of unbelief, changed their knowledge of God for error. FRAGMENTS ON THE EPISTLE TO THE HEBREWS 8.10.[61]

ALL SHALL KNOW ME. THEODORET OF CYR: This does not happen in this life, but will happen in that: those still beset with the gloom of unbelief will see the truth there, and will be smitten, in keeping with the divine oracle. INTERPRETATION OF HEBREWS 8.[62]

A HOLY RENTAL AGREEMENT. CLEMENT OF ALEXANDRIA: [He bestows] on us the truly great, divine and inalienable inheritance of the Father, deifying us by heavenly teaching, putting his laws into our minds and writing them on our hearts. What laws does he inscribe? "That all shall know God, from small to great"; and, "I will be merciful to them," says God, "and will not remember their sins." Let us receive the laws of life, let us comply with God's exhortations; let us become acquainted with him, that he may be gracious. And

---

[55]NPNF 1 2:338-39**. [56]Cf. Jer 31:31-33. [57]Cf. Heb 12:18. [58]NPNF 2 12:202-3*. [59]Jn 14:26. [60]NPNF 1 14:435*. [61]NTA 15:464. [62]PG 82:737; TCCLSP 2:171.

though God needs nothing, let us give him the grateful compensation of a thankful heart and of a holy life as a kind of rental payment for our dwelling here below. EXHORTATION TO THE HEATHEN II.[63]

8:12-13 A New Covenant

WE ARE ALSO NEW. CHRYSOSTOM: So then we also are new, or rather we were made new, but now have become old; therefore we are "near to vanishing away," and to destruction. Let us scrape off this old age. It is indeed no longer possible to do it by washing, but by repentance it is possible here in this life. If there be in us anything old, let us cast it off; if any "wrinkle," if any stain, if any "spot," let us wash it away and become fair,[64] that "the king may desire our beauty."[65] ON THE EPISTLE TO THE HEBREWS 14.8.[66]

WHAT IS GROWING OLD? BEDE: For what is the meaning of John's being born to elderly parents? Was it not to indicate the earthly birth of the one who was soon to follow, since by bringing forward the hidden spiritual mysteries of the new covenant, he would teach that the fleshly observance of the law and the priesthood of the old covenant were now to be brought to an end? For "what is becoming obsolete and growing old is ready to vanish away." And what does it mean that our Lord's precursor came from a father who was mute, a leader of the priests of that time? Is it not that, by the time our Lord appeared, the tongue of the ancient priesthood had to a large extent become mute as regards the spiritual sense of the law's teaching, since the scribes and those learned in the law were only concerned with teaching the keeping of the letter of the law? Moreover, in a number of instances, they were even falsifying the letter of the law by substituting their own traditions, as is proven by our Lord's having rebuked them more than once in the Gospels. And what does it mean that he was born to a barren mother? Is it not that the law, which was ordered to beget spiritual issue for

God with the help of the priestly office, led no one to perfection,[67] undoubtedly because it was unable to open up the gates of the kingdom to its followers? The author of the law himself, born under the law,[68] took away from the law the opprobrium of its barrenness, for he pointed out that it was to be understood spiritually; and he taught that in it was formerly prefigured and, as it were, conceived, the gift of happiness from on high which now shines out clearly in the gospel. HOMILIES ON THE GOSPELS 2.20.[69]

NEW IN PART. CHRYSOSTOM: A covenant might be said to be "new" when it is different and shows some advantage over the old. Surely one might say it is new also when part of it has been taken away and part not. For instance, when an old house is ready to fall down, if a person, leaving the whole, has patched up the foundation, we say he has made it new when he has taken some parts away and brought others into their place. For even the heaven also is thus called "new," when it is no longer "of brass"[70] but gives rain; and the earth likewise is new when it is not unfruitful, not when it has been changed; and the house is likewise new, when portions of it have been taken away and portions remain. . . . But, do you see how this interpretation breaks down? I maintain that this covenant must be called "new" in the proper sense of the word.[71] . . . In calling it new, Paul says, "he treats the first as obsolete, and what is becoming obsolete and growing old is ready to vanish away." . . . Therefore it is done away with and is perishing and no longer exists.

Paul here used a familiar form of speech, as if one should say, the house is not faultless; that is, it has some defect, it is decayed. The garment is not faultless, that is, it is coming to pieces. He does not, therefore, here speak of the old covenant as evil, but only as having some fault and

---

[63]ANF 2:203-4*. [64]Eph 5:26-27. [65]Ps 45:11 (44:12 LXX). [66]NPNF 1 14:436*. [67]Heb 7:19. [68]Gal 4:4. [69]CS 111:205-6. [70]Deut 28:23. [71]Is 65:17.

deficiency. ON THE EPISTLE TO THE HEBREWS 14.6-7.[72]

NOT UNCLEANNESS BUT SIN. EPHREM THE SYRIAN: "For I will be merciful" to them, not with regard to their impurity but "toward their iniquities," not with regard to the uncleanness of nocturnal dreams but to the sins which are performed in them through the power of the devil.

Therefore in the new covenant that Jeremiah announced, "The first has become old. Now what decayed and became old is near to vanishing away." COMMENTARY ON THE EPISTLE TO THE HEBREWS.[73]

PRAYER IS A GREAT WEAPON. CHRYSOSTOM: How does it happen that wickedness is transcended in forgetfulness? From the remembrance of good things, from the remembrance of God. If we continually remember God, we cannot remember those things also. For, the psalmist says, "When I remembered you upon my bed, I thought upon you in the morning dawn."[74] We ought then to have God always in remembrance, but then especially, when thought is undisturbed and when by means of that remembrance one is able to condemn himself, when one can retain things in memory. For in the daytime, indeed, if we do remember, other cares and troubles, entering in, drive the thought out again; but in the night it is possible to remember continually, when the soul is calm and at rest; when it is in the harbor and under a serene sky. "The things which you say in your hearts are grieved for on your beds," the psalmist says.[75] For it were indeed right to retain this remembrance through the day also. But inasmuch as you are always full of cares and distracted amidst the things of this life, at least then remember God on bed. At the morning dawn meditate upon God. If at the morning dawn we meditate on these things, we shall go forth to our business with much security. If we have first made God propitious by prayer and supplication, going forth thus we shall have no enemy. Or if you should, you will laugh him to scorn, having

God propitious. There is war in the marketplace; the affairs of every day are a fight, they are a tempest and a storm. We therefore need arms, and prayer is a great weapon. We need favorable winds; we need to learn everything, so as to go through the length of the day without shipwrecks and without wounds. For every single day the rocks are many, and oftentimes the boat strikes and is sunk. Therefore have we especially need of prayer early and by night. ON THE EPISTLE TO THE HEBREWS 14.9.[76]

CHRIST THE TESTATOR OF THE NEW TESTAMENT. LACTANTIUS: All Scripture is divided into two Testaments. What preceded the advent and passion of Christ—that is, the law and the prophets—is called the Old [Testament]; but what was written after his resurrection is named the New Testament. The Jews make use of the Old, we of the New. Yet, they are not dissonant. The New Testament is the fulfilling of the Old, and in both there is the same testator, even Christ who suffered death for us and made us heirs of his everlasting kingdom. . . . When, therefore, we who were in time past as it were blind, and as it were shut up in the prison of folly, were sitting in darkness, ignorant of God and of the truth, we have been enlightened by him, who adopted us by his testament; and having freed us from cruel chains, and brought us out to the light of wisdom, he admitted us to the inheritance of his heavenly kingdom. DIVINE INSTITUTES 4.20.[77]

THE OLD MAN VANISHES IN CHRIST. GREGORY OF NYSSA: Mighty Paul knew that the only begotten God, who has the preeminence in all things, is the author and cause of everything that is good. Paul witnesses to the fact that the creation of all that exists was formed by the only begotten God. On top of this he also testifies that when the original creation of man had decayed and vanished away (to use his own language), and another new

[72]NPNF 1 14:435-36. [73]EHA 215. [74]See Ps 63:6 (62:7 LXX). [75]See Ps 4:4 (4:5 LXX). [76]NPNF 1 14:437**. [77]ANF 7:122-23*.

creation was formed in Christ, in this too no other than he [the only begotten God] took the lead. But he is himself the firstborn of all that new creation of human beings which is effected by the gospel. AGAINST EUNOMIUS 2.8.[78]

NEW FOREVER. THEODORET OF CYR: The law is suited to mortals, whereas the New Covenant

guarantees us eternal life. It was therefore right for the former one to grow old, while the latter remains new forever in being associated with the ages that do not grow old. INTERPRETATION OF HEBREWS 8.[79]

---

[78]NPNF 2 5:112*. [79]PG 82:737; *TCCLSP* 2:171.

9:1-10 AN EARTHLY SANCTUARY

Now even the first covenant had regulations for worship and an earthly sanctuary. [2]For a tent[p] was prepared, the outer one, in which were the lampstand and the table and the bread of the Presence;[q] it is called the Holy Place. [3]Behind the second curtain stood a tent[p] called the Holy of Holies, [4]having the golden altar of incense and the ark of the covenant covered on all sides with gold, which contained a golden urn holding the manna, and Aaron's rod that budded, and the tables of the covenant; [5]above it were the cherubim of glory overshadowing the mercy seat. Of these things we cannot now speak in detail.

[6]These preparations having thus been made, the priests go continually into the outer tent,[p] performing their ritual duties; [7]but into the second only the high priest goes, and he but once a year, and not without taking blood which he offers for himself and for the errors of the people. [8]By this the Holy Spirit indicates that the way into the sanctuary is not yet opened as long as the outer tent[p] is still standing [9](which is symbolic for the present age). According to this arrangement, gifts and sacrifices are offered which cannot perfect the conscience of the worshiper, [10]but deal only with food and drink and various ablutions, regulations for the body imposed until the time of reformation.

p Or *tabernacle*   q Greek *the presentation of the loaves*

OVERVIEW: The author of Hebrews now turns his attention to the tabernacle and the things in it, in order to show how these also have passed away with the abrogation of their law. These religious institutions were mere shadows of the true ministry, which will endure. Even though these things had their proper places in the history of salvation, they were nonetheless sym-

bolic shadows of the heavenly ministry (CHRYSOSTOM). Since the truth has now come, it is not necessary anymore that we deal with shadows (EPHREM). The laws are like models of clay that anticipate a later reality (ORIGEN), the intellectual, spiritual creation (GREGORY OF NAZIANZUS). The ark can also be taken figuratively as the soul (JOHN CASSIAN), or the holy church, which is constructed from incorruptible wood (that is, from holy souls). The golden urn in the ark holding the manna is the holy soul in Christ that contains in itself all the fullness of divinity (BEDE). Each believer becomes a tabernacle; each one can supplicate through the Mediator (ORIGEN) who offered his blood once for all (CHRYSOSTOM) and opened to the Gentiles the entrance into the inner tabernacle (PACHOMIUS). Extended throughout the four quarters of the world, with faith in the holy gospel, the church expects from God the eternal crown of life (BEDE). The present age referred to in the text is the age that anticipates the age to come through the power of Christ (ORIGEN, CHRYSOSTOM).

9:1-5 A Tent Was Prepared

TABERNACLE CALLED TEMPLE, SANCTUARY.
THEODORE OF MOPSUESTIA: He begins to say how there were symbols in the law and the types of things in the era of grace and how it was possible to see clearly the things of the new covenant glimpsed beforehand in the things of the old covenant, even as he shows in comparison what sort of preeminence the new covenant things have over those of the old covenant. He makes this the beginning of the exposition of his teaching. Then he says that also the first testament had bounds and commandments of ritual that were obligated to be offered to God. The phrase "regulations for worship" refers to the commandments concerning these things.

"And an earthly sanctuary." Most likely he calls the temple "the sanctuary" because the liturgy is rendered in it to God, or also he calls the tabernacle "the sanctuary," since they had this in service before the temple. For in a similar manner he called the tabernacle "the temple," inasmuch as God happened to be present in it, while the later temple was built by Solomon. "And Samuel sat in the temple of the Lord where the ark of God was,"[1] although the temple had not yet been built by Solomon. And just as when God commanded Moses to erect the tabernacle

as a symbol of the world according to a certain plan, God ordered him to make an enclosure out of curtains that would divide the middle from the rest,[2] so also the temple was made according to the same plan. FRAGMENTS ON THE EPISTLE TO THE HEBREWS 9.1-2.[3]

THE WHOLE OLD COVENANT COMPARED WITH THE NEW. PHOTIUS: I think that the phrase "also the first one had regulations for worship"[4] refers to the old covenant and not the tabernacle. For he did not compare the tabernacle with the new covenant but the whole old covenant with the new one, and he showed the superiority of the latter over the whole former covenant. "For behold," he says, "the days are coming and I will effect a new covenant on the house of Israel and on the house of Judah, not like the covenant which I established for their fathers,"[5] and again, "When he says 'new' he has already made the first old."[6] And he adds these things and says, "Now the first one had." . . . Therefore it is clear that the discussion is still concerning the covenant. For since he struck it down in comparison with the new covenant, in order that no one may say then that it was rejected as worthless, he anticipates the argument and says that even that covenant had "regulations for worship," laws and order and fitting conformity with the service of God. And having spoken broadly of the whole law, that "it had regulations of worship," he also proceeds part by part, beginning with the tent. It had, he says, "the earthly sanctuary." Then after the earthly sanctuary (which was accessible to all), he had again another tabernacle placed in front of the yet more mystical and holier tabernacle. And in the more outward tabernacle there was "the lampstand and the showbread," which tabernacle is not called "the earthly sanctuary," as is the tabernacle in

---

[1] 1 Sam 3:3. [2] Ex 26:33. [3] NTA 15:208. [4] RSV translation supplies "covenant," which is not in the Greek. [5] Heb 8:8-9; Jer 31:31-34. [6] Heb 8:13. The Greek *palaioō* can simply mean "become old" rather than "obsolete" (RSV).

front of all the other tabernacles, but it is simply called "the Holy Place." FRAGMENTS ON THE EPISTLE TO THE HEBREWS 9.1-2.[7]

PARTS OF THE TABERNACLE. OECUMENIUS: The "first" part of the tabernacle was that portion near the "Holy of Holies," since it technically was not the first but the middle part of the tabernacle. For the first part of the tabernacle was where the bronze altar was for sacrifices and whole burnt offerings, while the second part was that of which he says, "In it was the lampstand and the showbread on the table," and the third part was "the golden altar of incense" and "the ark of the covenant." FRAGMENTS ON THE EPISTLE TO THE HEBREWS 9.1-4.[8]

THE INTELLECTUAL CREATION. GREGORY OF NAZIANZUS: Since the Word knows the tabernacle of Moses to be a figure of the whole creation—I mean the entire system of things visible and invisible—shall we pass the first veil and, stepping beyond the realm of sense, shall we look into the holy place, the intellectual and celestial creation? ON THE DOCTRINE OF GOD, THEOLOGICAL ORATION 2.31.[9]

AN EARTHLY SANCTUARY. THEODORET OF CYR: This is the term he used of the tabernacle, which represents a type of the whole world: it is divided into two down the middle by a veil, one part of it called Holy, the other Holy of Holies. While the Holy represented the way of life on earth, the Holy of Holies represented life in heaven. The veil itself performed the function of the firmament. . . . Accordingly, just as he separates what is below from what is above, so the veil stretched out in the middle of the tabernacle divided the Holy of Holies from the Holy. INTERPRETATION OF HEBREWS 9.[10]

IT IS NOT NECESSARY TO DEAL WITH SHADOWS. EPHREM THE SYRIAN: Now "even the first covenant had" in it some rules in addition to "regulations" of the ministry of "worship," be-

cause sin exacted the punishment of the sword. However, this sanctification—this law that sanctifies us by means of water—does not pass away like those rules; in fact, it remains forever hereafter, because Jesus rejected that law for a new covenant, which was earlier proclaimed through Jeremiah.

Then Paul turns his attention to the temporary tabernacle and to all the things which were in it in order to prove and reveal that they also have passed away, together with the abrogation of their law. It could not happen that they remained after the cessation of the law, because they also were shadows and symbols of this true ministry, which will last. Therefore, he begins again to deprive of its authority the service of the ministry held in the temporary tabernacle, of which the priests were proud in their overconfidence, by saying, "The first tent was prepared" so, because "in it were the lampstand and the table" and the other things. In the inner tent, "called the Holy of Holies," under its veil, there was placed one "golden altar of incense and the ark covered on all sides with gold," together with the other things. However, is there now any need to describe these objects in detail, one by one? In fact, even though each of these things had been set in their proper place for the service of religious ministry, they were nonetheless symbolic shadows of this heavenly ministry; since the truth has now come, it is not necessary anymore that we deal with shadows. COMMENTARY ON THE EPISTLE TO THE HEBREWS.[11]

EACH ONE A TABERNACLE. ORIGEN: Each one of us can build a tabernacle for God in himself. For if, as some before us have said, this tabernacle represents a figure of the whole world, and if each individual can have an image of the world in oneself, why should not each individual be able to fulfill the form of the tabernacle in oneself? . . . For that part within you which is most valuable

---

[7]NTA 15:647-48. [8]NTA 15:465. [9]LCC 3:158. [10]PG 82:737-40; TCCLSP 2:171-72. [11]EHA 215-16.

of all can act the part of priest—the part which some call the first principle of the heart, others the rational sense or the substance of the mind or whatever other name one wishes to give to that part of us which makes us capable of receiving God. Homilies on Exodus 9.4.[12]

Your Soul Will Become the Ark of God's Testament. John Cassian: If you wish to achieve true knowledge of Scripture, you must hurry to achieve unshakable humility of heart. This is what will lead you not to the knowledge that puffs a person up[13] but to the love which illuminates through the achievement of love. It is impossible for the unclean of heart to acquire the gift of spiritual knowledge. Therefore be very careful that your zeal for scriptural reading does not, because of empty pretentiousness, prove to be a cause of perdition instead of being for you the source of knowledgeable light and of the endless glory promised to the one enlightened by knowledge.

Then, having banished all worldly concerns and thoughts, strive in every way to devote yourself constantly to the sacred reading, so that continuous meditation will seep into your soul and, as it were, will shape it to its image. Somehow it will form that "ark" of the Scriptures and will contain the two stone tablets, that is, the perpetual strength of the two Testaments. There will be the golden urn that is a pure and unstained memory and which will preserve firmly within itself the everlasting manna, that is, the eternal, heavenly sweetness of spiritual meanings and of that bread which belongs to the angels. The branch of Aaron is the saving standard of our exalted and true high priest, Jesus Christ. It leafs out forever in the greenness of undying memory. This is the branch that was cut from the root of Jesse and which after death comes more truly alive.

Now all of these things are covered over by the two cherubim, that is, by the plentitude of historical and spiritual lore. "Cherubim" means knowledge in abundance. They provide an everlasting protection for that which appeases God, namely,

the calm of your heart, and they will cast a shadow of protection against all the attacks of malignant spirits.

And thus your soul will not only become the ark of God's testament, but it will be carried forward into a priestly realm. And, by its unfailing love of purity, its concentration upon the disciplines of the spirit, it will implement the priestly command imposed by the lawgiver, "He will not emerge from the holy place, lest he profane the sanctuary of God."[14] That is, he will not depart from his own heart, where the Lord promised to live continuously when he said, "I will live and walk among them." Conference 14.10.[15]

Gentiles in the Inner Tabernacle. Pachomius: The brothers assembled at evening as was their custom. For in all seasons, when they had finished their modest meal, it was their habit to assemble and for each one to pronounce what he knew of the holy Scriptures. . . . The brother who had returned from the north spoke and said, "Allow me, my brothers, to tell you the saying and its commentary which I heard from a righteous man. It was while returning south that I passed by Tabennesi and was put up there at Abba Pachomius's monastery. Toward evening Pachomius seated himself and spoke the Word of God to the brothers gathered around him. He spoke of the tabernacle and of the Holy of Holies, applying them to two peoples. The first people is the outer tabernacle, whose service consisted in sacrifices and visible loaves; the Holy of Holies, on the other hand, is the Gentiles' calling, which, according to the gospel, is the fulfillment of the law. And all the objects that are found in this inner tabernacle are filled with glory. For instead of animal sacrifices, there is the altar of incense; instead of the table, the ark containing the spiritual loaves, that is, the fullness of the law and all that is to be found there; and instead of the light of the

---

[12]FC 71:340-43*. [13]1 Cor 8:1. [14]Lev 21:12. RSV reads "neither shall he go out of the sanctuary, nor profane the sanctuary of his God." [15]JCC 164*.

lamp, the mercy seat where God appears as a consuming fire,[16] that is, God the Word made human who became remission for us by appearing in the flesh. The words *mercy seat* mean indeed the place of the remission of sins."

When the brother had finished his exposition of that saying and its commentary, he said, "I am confident that God will forgive me many of my sins because of the remembrance of that just man whose name I just pronounced here before you." All the brothers uttered their admiration for the great knowledge that was in our father Pachomius, until it was time for each of them to return with joy to his cell. LIFE OF PACHOMIUS (BOHAIRIC) 29.[17]

THE ROD OF EQUITY. BEDE: Now the golden urn in the ark holding the manna is the holy soul in Christ that contains in itself all the fullness of divinity.[18] Aaron's rod that budded although cut off from the tree is the invincible power of his priesthood, concerning which the prophet says, "Your royal scepter is a scepter of equity."[19] Even after it seemed for the time being to have been cut off through death, in the dawn of the resurrection morn it was found to have blossomed again all the more vigorously, and it became clear that it would remain forever imperishable and unfading. For "Christ being raised from the dead will never die again; death no longer has dominion over him."[20] The tablets of the covenant in the ark indicate that all knowledge of the Father's secrets and all power of judgment are in Christ. For on the tablets of the covenant were inscribed the faith of the eternal divinity which creates and rules the world, and the commandments through which one ought to serve God, and the discerning judgment with which God rightly condemns those who hate God and with due mercy rewards those who love him. This, then, is the testimony that the Lord gave Moses to be put into the ark. It indicated the truth that we ought to confess in Christ about his flesh, his son, and his word. It showed that after the passion of death the same flesh would be glorified in the resurrection and

lifted up in the eternal dignity of a king and priest. It taught that he alone is privy to the Father's secrets, just as truly as he is the judge of all worlds, of one and the same majesty with the Father. ON THE TABERNACLE 1.4.17.[21]

FROM THE INCORRUPTIBLE WOOD OF HOLY SOULS. BEDE: The ark can also be taken figuratively as the holy church that is constructed from incorruptible wood, that is, from holy souls. Extended throughout the four quarters of the world, with faith in the holy gospel, the church expects from God the eternal crown of life.[22] It contains in itself the tables of the covenant by continual meditation on the law of God. It also contains the golden urn with the manna as a guarantee of the Lord's incarnation, and Aaron's rod that budded as a sharing in the kingship and priesthood of the Lord; for the apostle Peter says, "But you are a chosen race, a royal priesthood."[23] Up above, it has the propitiatory to remind it that every good thing it possesses it has received from the generosity of divine grace. And on the propitiatory it has the glorious cherubim, signifying either the angelic assistance with which it is always aided by a gracious God or the Testaments in which it is taught how it ought to live and in what manner it ought to seek the aid of divine propitiation so that it may live properly. Now the cherubim were set over the propitiatory in this way, just as the city of Christ, that is, the holy church, is said to have been built upon the mountain,[24] that is, upon Christ himself; not that his city can be higher than he but because it derives support from his assistance. The ark has cherubim over the propitiatory because both the angelic ministries and the divine eloquences surely give aid to the church insofar as they themselves stand firm upon the foundation of the highest truth. ON THE TABERNACLE 1.5.20-21.[25]

---

[16]Heb 12:29. [17]CS 45:52-54*. [18]See Col 2:9. [19]Ps 45:6 (44:7 LXX). [20]Rom 6:9. [21]TTH 18:16*. [22]See Jas 1:12. [23]1 Pet 2:9. [24]Cf. Heb 12:22. [25]TTH 18:20-21*.

9:6-7 *Ritual Duties*

THE HIGH PRIEST GOES ONCE A YEAR. OECU-MENIUS: Above the ark there was, so to speak, a certain golden, rectangular table, which was called "seat of propitiation," signifying Christ, who is called our "propitiation" and "redemption."[26] . . . In Exodus, in the passages concerning these things he says that the high priest enters the Holy of Holies twice during the day, as he sacrifices. For it is written as follows: "And Aaron will burn an offering of pleasant mixture of incense on it"—that is, on top of the golden altar which was in the Holy of Holies—"early in the morning. Whenever he trims the lamps, he will burn incense on it, and whenever he lights the lamps in the evening, he will offer a perpetual burning of incense."[27] How then does the blessed apostle say, "the high priest alone enters and that but once a year"? And we say that he enters only once a year with "blood," as he says in the same passage of Exodus, making sacrifice twice that day. For also he says, "Not without taking blood,"[28] that is, with blood, in order that it might be so. For once a year the high priest alone enters with blood, not with the fragrant offering of incense. FRAGMENTS ON THE EPISTLE TO THE HEBREWS 9.5-7.[29]

THIS CURTAIN IS INTERPRETED AS HEAVEN. BEDE: Figuratively, the curtain in the temple represents the same curtain that the apostle declares openly to the Hebrews, in the place where he also explains properly, according to the allegorical sense, the reason that "the priests go continually into the outer tent, performing their ritual duties, but into the second only the high priest goes, and he but once a year, and not without taking blood which he offers for himself and for the errors of the people." This curtain is interpreted as heaven.[30] And the priests entered into the first tabernacle with sacrifices daily throughout the year, which further illustrates the circumstances of this life, in which the saints who serve the Lord as true priests of God and of his Christ cease-lessly atone for the daily errors of their frailty, without which they are by no means able to exist in this life through the daily sacrifices of good works and the daily libations of their own tears. But the apostle understands the high priest who went into the Holy of Holies with the blood of victims once a year to be the great high priest himself, of whom it was said, "You are a priest forever after the order of Melchizedek."[31] He who as both priest and victim had offered himself through his own blood once for our sins entered "into heaven itself, now to appear in the presence of God on our behalf."[32] ON THE TABERNACLE 2.8.71.[33]

BLOOD ONCE FOR ALL. CHRYSOSTOM: And Paul well said, "not without taking blood." . . . He signifies that there shall be a sacrifice, not consumed by fire but rather distinguished by blood. For inasmuch as he called the cross a sacrifice, though it had neither fire nor logs nor was offered many times but had been offered in blood once for all, he shows that the ancient sacrifice also was of this kind, offered "once for all"[34] in blood. ON THE EPISTLE TO THE HEBREWS 15.2.[35]

9:8-10 *The Outer Tent Is Still Standing*

THE PRESENT AGE IS BEFORE CHRIST. CHRYSOSTOM: "This is a symbol for the present age," the apostle says. What does he mean by "the present"? That time before the coming of Christ, for, after the coming of Christ, it is no longer a present age. How could it be, having arrived and being ended? There is something else as well that he indicates when he says, "which is symbolic for the present age," that is, became the type. "Gifts and sacrifices are offered which cannot perfect the conscience of the worshiper." You see now what is the meaning of "The law made nothing perfect,"[36] and "If that first covenant had been

---

[26]1 Jn 2:2; 1 Cor 1:30. [27]Ex 30:7-8. [28]Ex 30:10. [29]NTA 15:465. [30]Heb 9:24. [31]Ps 110:4 (109:4 LXX). [32]Heb 9:24. [33]TTH 18:79. [34]Heb 9:12. [35]NPNF 1 14:439*. [36]Heb 7:19.

faultless."[37] How? As pertaining to "the conscience." For the sacrifices did not put away the defilement from the soul but still were concerned with the body: "after the law of a carnal commandment."[38] On the Epistle to the Hebrews 15.3.[39]

He Does Not Reject the Law as a Whole. Theodoret of Cyr: We are being taught through figures, he is saying, that the law bears of this life and is appropriate for those who still have a moral nature. . . . He also clearly taught us in these words that he does not reject the law as a whole—only the regulations about eating and drinking, menstruation, leprosy, childbirth and periods; they washed themselves and purified themselves with sprinkling, but none of this could make the conscience pure. Now none of these was imposed without reason but to meet some need, specifying which is not relevant at the present time. They were all temporary, however, looking forward to the time of perfection. Interpretation of Hebrews 9.[40]

Models of Clay Until the Time of Correction. Origen: We indeed who are of the church rightly receive Moses and read his writings, believing that he is a prophet who wrote down the future mysteries which God revealed to him in symbols, figures and allegorical forms, which we teach were fulfilled in their own time. But whoever does not receive such an understanding in him, whether one of the Jews or even one of us, certainly cannot teach that he is a prophet. For how will he prove he is a prophet whose writings he asserts to be common, containing no knowledge of the future or anything of a hidden mystery? Whoever thinks thus the divine word censures, saying, "Do you understand what you are reading?"[41]

Therefore, the law and all the things that are in the law are, according to the opinion of the apostle, "imposed until the time of reformation." . . . Those whose craft is to make tokens from copper and to pour statues, before they produce a true work of copper or of silver or of gold, must first form figures from clay to the likeness of the figure image. (The model is necessary only until the work that is principal is completed, for when that work for which that image was made of clay is completed, its use is no longer sought.) [Thus we] understand also something like this in these things which were written or done "in a type" and in a figure of the future in the law and prophets. For the artist and creator of all himself came and transformed "the law which has but a shadow of the good things to come" to "the true form of these realities."[42] But lest perhaps the things we say appear difficult for you to be able to prove, examine them one by one.

First, there was Jerusalem, that great, royal city, where the most renowned temple had been constructed for God. But after that, one who was the true temple of God came and said about the temple of his body, "Destroy this temple,"[43] and began to open the mysteries "of the heavenly Jerusalem."[44] This earthly place was destroyed, and the heavenly became visible, and in the temple "stone" did not remain "upon stone"[45] from the time when the flesh of Christ was made the true temple of God. First there was a high priest who purified the people "by the blood of bulls and goats";[46] but when the true high priest who "sanctifies" believers "through his own blood"[47] came, that first high priest existed no more, and neither was any place left for him. First there was the altar, and sacrifices were being celebrated; but when the true Lamb came who "gave himself up as an offering to God,"[48] all these other, as it were, temporary institutions ceased.

Therefore, does it not seem to you that, according to the figure set forth above, there were some models made from clay, as it were, through which true images were represented? Finally, for this reason, the divine dispensation provided that the city and the temple and all those as well be over-

---

[37]Heb 8:7. [38]Heb 7:16. [39]NPNF 1 14:439**. [40]PG 82:740-41; TCCLSP 2:172-73. [41]Acts 8:30. [42]Heb 10:1. [43]Jn 2:19. [44]Heb 12:22. [45]Mt 24:2. [46]Heb 10:4. [47]Heb 13:12. [48]Eph 5:2.

thrown, lest he who is perhaps still "a child and feeding on milk of the faith"[49] be enraptured by the view itself of the diverse forms, if he should see them standing and be astonished and amazed during the ritual of sacrifices and during the order of the services. But God, watching out for our weakness and desiring his church to be multi-plied, made all these to be overthrown and taken away completely, so that without any hesitation, when those ceased, we might believe these to be true for which the type was contained in advance in them. HOMILIES ON LEVITICUS 10.1.1-4.[50]

[49]See Heb 5:13. [50]FC 83:202-4*.

9:11-28 CHRIST APPEARED AS HIGH PRIEST

[11]*But when Christ appeared as a high priest of the good things that have come,[r] then through the greater and more perfect tent[p] (not made with hands, that is, not of this creation) [12]he entered once for all into the Holy Place, taking[s] not the blood of goats and calves but his own blood, thus securing an eternal redemption. [13]For if the sprinkling of defiled persons with the blood of goats and bulls and with the ashes of a heifer sanctifies for the purification of the flesh, [14]how much more shall the blood of Christ, who through the eternal Spirit offered himself without blemish to God, purify your[t] conscience from dead works to serve the living God.*

[15]*Therefore he is the mediator of a new covenant, so that those who are called may receive the promised eternal inheritance, since a death has occurred which redeems them from the transgressions under the first covenant.[u] [16]For where a will[u] is involved, the death of the one who made it must be established. [17]For a will[u] takes effect only at death, since it is not in force as long as the one who made it is alive. [18]Hence even the first covenant was not ratified without blood. [19]For when every commandment of the law had been declared by Moses to all the people, he took the blood of calves and goats, with water and scarlet wool and hyssop, and sprinkled both the book itself and all the people, [20]saying, "This is the blood of the covenant which God commanded you." [21]And in the same way he sprinkled with the blood both the tent[p] and all the vessels used in worship. [22]Indeed, under the law almost everything is purified with blood, and without the shedding of blood there is no forgiveness of sins.*

[23]*Thus it was necessary for the copies of the heavenly things to be purified with these rites, but the heavenly things themselves with better sacrifices than these. [24]For Christ has entered, not into a sanctuary made with hands, a copy of the true one, but into heaven itself, now to appear in the presence of God on our behalf. [25]Nor was it to offer himself repeatedly, as the high priest enters the Holy Place yearly with blood not his own; [26]for then he would have had to suffer repeatedly since the foundation of the world. But as it is, he has appeared once for all at the end of the age to put away sin by the sacrifice of himself. [27]And just as it is appointed for men to die once, and after that*

comes judgment, [28]*so Christ, having been offered once to bear the sins of many, will appear a second time, not to deal with sin but to save those who are eagerly waiting for him.*

r Other manuscripts read *good things to come*   p Or *tabernacle*   s Greek *through*   t Other manuscripts read *our*   u The Greek word here used means both *covenant* and *will*

Overview: Whereas the levitical high priest does not offer his own blood, Christ offers his own once and for all. A will requires a death to become effective; thus with Christ's death the New Testament became valid. Christ became the mediator by bringing God's words to us and adding his death to them. He is the mediator of the New Testament. A testament is made toward the last day, that is, the day of death. But, because of Christ's death, our dying will be not death but a sleep, for after dying is living. A will also needs witnesses, and we, the apostles and the whole Trinity bear witness to him (Chrysostom, Augustine). A last will and testament is of this character: it makes some heirs and some disinherited (Chrysostom) through the death of the testator (Augustine).

Those things written in the law are "copies" and "forms"[1] of living and true things, which we can perceive with our spiritual senses (Chrysostom, Origen). For instance, the Jewish temple built by people signified the Lord's sacred body (Bede). The tent of meeting in which Christ entered for sacrifice is not a small one made with human hands but a perfect one (Ephrem), the dwelling of grace (Severian). He is robed in perfection (Origen).

The faithful are cleansed by the Lord's blood (Isaac, Chrysostom) and are sanctified (Chrysostom); that cleansing applies to body and soul (Cyril of Jerusalem). Through the sacrifice of Jesus they are granted the ability to conduct saintly lives (Clement of Alexandria) and even to defy death (Chrysostom). Having died once for sin (Photius, Oecumenius), he will appear a second time, not in order to die for sins, for which he has already died, but in order to appear in a new world (Theodore). In this new world there will be no sins in those who in hope expect salvation through him (Ephrem) who granted us entrance into heaven (Chrysostom) and even passage to the throne of God (Origen). However, it is in the eschatological "end of the age," when all sinners are brought to order and sin is no more (Bede), that the salvific work of Christ is fulfilled and perfected (Origen, Chrysostom). Eucharistic sacrifice is a remembrance of Christ's sacrifice as well as the "end of the age" (Chrysostom); and the activity of the Holy Spirit is evident in the sacrifice of the Lord and in the Eucharistic offering (Bede).

9:11 *Priest of the Good Things*

The Future High Priest. Ephrem the Syrian: All these things, as I have said, were performed according to rules by infirm priests up to the time when God made a correction. From that time "Christ" came "as a high priest" not of sacrifices but of "good things." And he entered "the tent"—not a small one "made with hands" but a huge and perfect one, which is not the product of human work—"that is, not of this creation," because it was made out of nothing, unlike that tent which was erected with the spoils of the Egyptians. Commentary on the Epistle to the Hebrews 9.[2]

Not Made with Hands. Theodoret of Cyr: Here he referred to human nature, which Christ the Lord assumed. It was not made in accordance with the law of marriage: the all-holy Spirit was responsible for the tabernacle. Interpretation of Hebrews 9.[3]

---

[1] Cf. 1 Cor 10:6. The Greek *typoi* is translated as "warnings" in RSV. [2] EHA 216-17. [3] PG 82:741; *TCCLSP* 2:173.

THE NEW TABERNACLE OF THE CHURCH.

SEVERIAN OF GABALA: The tent built under Moses was to signify servitude [to the law]. Therefore, the more perfect tent is the dwelling of grace, the body of Christ whose head is Christ himself. FRAGMENTS ON THE EPISTLE TO THE HEBREWS 9.11.[4]

THE ROBE OF PERFECTION.

ORIGEN: It ought to be observed that the priest uses certain clothes while he is in the ministry of sacrifices and other clothes when he goes out to the people. Paul, the wisest of the high priests and the most knowledgeable of the priests, used to do this. When he was in the assembly of the perfect or, as it were, placed in the "Holy of Holies,"[5] having put on the robe of perfection, he used to say, "Among the mature we do impart wisdom, although it is not a wisdom of this age or of the rulers of this age, who are doomed to pass away. But we impart a secret and hidden wisdom of God. . . . None of the rulers of this age understood this; for if they had, they would not have crucified the Lord of glory."[6] But nevertheless, after all these things, "going out to the people,"[7] he changes his robe and puts on another one, greatly inferior to that one. And what does he say? "I decided to know nothing among you except Jesus Christ and him crucified."[8] You see, therefore, how this most learned priest, when he is among the perfect ones as in "the Holy of Holies," uses one robe of doctrine. But when "he goes out" to those who are not capable, he changes the robe of the word and teaches lesser things. And he gives to some "milk" to drink as "children,"[9] to others he gives "solid food," of course, for those who, insofar as they are able, "have their faculties trained to distinguish good from evil."[10] Thus, Paul knew how to change robes and to use one with the people, another in the ministry of the sanctuary.

But the high priest of high priests, and the priest of priests, is our Lord and Savior, about whom the apostle said, "He is a high priest of the good things that have come." Hear how first he did these things and so left them for his disciples to imitate. The Gospel refers to this, saying, "In parables he spoke to the crowds, and without parables he did not speak to them. But separately he explained them to his disciples."[11] You see how he taught that the high priest ought to use certain garments when he went out "to the crowds" and others when he ministered to the experienced and "perfect" in the sanctuary. So we must choose and do, lest Jesus find us so unprepared and bound to the cares of the world that he speaks to us as to the crowds "in parables," that, "seeing, we may not see, and, hearing, we may not hear."[12] Rather, let us be worthy to be found among those to whom he says, "To you it has been given to know the secrets of the kingdom of heaven."[13] HOMILIES ON LEVITICUS 4.6.4-5.[14]

THE BODY AS TABERNACLE VEIL IN HEAVEN.

CHRYSOSTOM: Well did he say, "greater and more perfect tent," since God the Word and all the power of the Spirit dwells therein, "for it is not by measure that he gives the Spirit."[15] "More perfect," as being both without blame and setting right greater things. "That is, not of this creation"—see how it was greater, for it would not have been "of the Spirit," if humankind had constructed it. Nor yet is it "of this creation," that is, not of these created things, but spiritual, of the Holy Spirit.

See how he calls the body tent and curtain and heaven: "Through the greater and more perfect tent." "Through the curtain, that is, through his flesh."[16] And again, "into the inner shrine behind the curtain."[17] And again, "entering into heaven itself, now to appear in the presence of God." Why then does he say this? In accordance with whether one thing or another is signified. I mean, for instance, the heaven is a curtain, for as a curtain it walls off the Holy of Holies; the flesh is a curtain hiding the Godhead; and the tent likewise holds the Godhead. Again, heaven is a tent,

---

[4]NTA 15:350. [5]Ex 30:29. [6]1 Cor 2:6-8. [7]Num 11:24. [8]1 Cor 2:2. [9]1 Cor 3:2. [10]Heb 5:14. [11]See Mt 13:34-37. [12]Mt 13:13. [13]Mt 13:11. [14]FC 83:78-80*. [15]Jn 3:34. [16]Heb 10:20. [17]Heb 6:19.

for the priest is there within. ON THE EPISTLE TO THE HEBREWS 15.4.[18]

THE YEARS TO BUILD THE TEMPLE, THE DAYS TO RAISE IT UP AGAIN. BEDE: "The Jews said, 'It has taken forty-six years to build this temple, and will you raise it up in three days?'"[19] They answered as they understood. But lest we too should perceive our Lord's spiritual word in a carnal way, the Evangelist subsequently explained what temple it was of which he was speaking. . . . This number forty-six of years is most apt for the perfecting of our Lord's physical body. Writers of natural history tell us that the form of the human body is completed within this number of days. During the first six days after conception it has a likeness to milk; during the following nine days it is changed into blood; next, in twelve days it becomes solid; during the remaining eighteen days it is formed into the perfect features of all its members; and after this, during the time remaining until birth, it increases in size. Six plus nine plus twelve plus eighteen make forty-five. If to this we add one, that is the day on which the body, divided into its separate members, begins to grow. We find the same number of days in the building up of our Lord's body as there were years in the construction of the temple.

And because that temple made by human hands[20] prefigured our Lord's most sacred body, which he took from the Virgin, and in like manner pointed to his body which is the church,[21] and to the body and soul of each one of the faithful, as we find in quite a few places in the Scriptures.[22] HOMILIES ON THE GOSPELS 2.1.[23]

9:12-14 Securing an Eternal Redemption

FOR ALL NATIONS. EPHREM THE SYRIAN: Our Lord did not enter yearly like their high priest. After his coming he entered only once, not into the shrine which ceases, like their priesthood, but "into the Holy" of Holies of eternity, and he made a propitiation through his blood for all nations. COMMENTARY ON THE EPISTLE TO THE HEBREWS.[24]

THE REPRESENTATIVE OF HUMANITY. OECUMENIUS: Since he deemed it worthy to be the head of humanity, the apostle says that the things accomplished by us were accomplished by him. FRAGMENTS ON THE EPISTLE TO THE HEBREWS 9.12.[25]

MOUNT ABOVE EARTHLY SENSES. ORIGEN: This is what the letter of the law explains to us, so that, collecting seeds of mysteries from them, we may use them as steps to climb from the lowly to a lofty place, from earthly to heavenly things. Therefore, my hearer, climb up now, if you can, and mount above earthly senses by the contemplation of your mind and by the discernment of your heart. Forget for a while earthly concerns; climb above the clouds and above heaven itself by the tread of your mind. Seek there the tabernacle of God where "Jesus has entered." HOMILIES ON NUMBERS 3.3.[26]

BLOOD OF BULLS, BLOOD OF CHRIST. CHRYSOSTOM: For, he says, if "the blood of bulls" is able to purify the flesh, much more shall the blood of Christ wipe away the defilement of the soul. Because you may not suppose when you hear the word *sanctifies* that it is some great thing, he marks out and shows the difference between each of these purifications and how the one of them is high and the other low. And he says it is so with good reason, since that is "the blood of bulls" and this "the blood of Christ." ON THE EPISTLE TO THE HEBREWS 15.5.[27]

SELF-CONTROL MEANS INDIFFERENCE TO WORKS OF DEATH. CLEMENT OF ALEXANDRIA: We ought to examine not merely one single form of self-control in sexual matters but the other objects which our soul self-indulgently desires,

---

[18]NPNF 1 14:440*. [19]Jn 2:20. [20]Cf. Acts 7:48. [21]Eph 1:22-23; 5:23; Col 1:18, 24. [22]Rom 12:5; 1 Cor 6:15; 12:27; Eph 5:29-30. [23]CS 111:8-9. [24]EHA 217. [25]NTA 15:466. [26]COS 23. [27]NPNF 1 14:440*.

not content with bare necessities but making a fuss about luxury. Self-control means indifference to money, comfort and property, a mind above spectacles, control of the tongue, mastery of evil thoughts. It actually happened that some angels suffered a failure of self-control, were overpowered by sexual desire and fell from heaven to earth.[28] Valentinus in his letter to Agathopus says, "Jesus showed his self-control in all that he endured. He lived in the practice of Godhead. He ate and drank in a way individual to himself without excreting his food. Such was his power of self-control that the food was not corrupted within him, since he was not subject to corruption." So we embrace self-control out of the love we bear the Lord and out of its honorable status, consecrating the temple of the Spirit.[29] It is honorable "to emasculate oneself" of all desire "for the sake of the kingdom of heaven"[30] and "to purify the conscience from dead works to serve the living God." STROMATEIS 3.7.59.[31]

DEAD WORKS DEFILE THE CONSCIENCE. CHRYSOSTOM: "Shall purify your conscience," the apostle says, "from dead works." And well said he "from dead works"; if any man touched a dead body, he was polluted. And here also, if any touch a "dead work," those ones are defiled through their conscience. . . . Here the apostle declares that it is not possible while one has "dead works to serve the living God," for they are both dead and false. ON THE EPISTLE TO THE HEBREWS 15.5.[32]

9:15-17 The Mediator of a New Covenant

HE DIED FOR US. CHRYSOSTOM: How did he become mediator? He brought words from God and brought them to us, conveying what came from the Father and adding his own death. We had offended; we ought to have died. He died for us and made us worthy of the covenant. By this is the covenant secure, in that henceforward it is not made for the unworthy. ON THE EPISTLE TO THE HEBREWS 16.2.[33]

THE DEATH OF THE TESTATOR WAS PREFIGURED. AUGUSTINE: Inasmuch as the apostle says to the Hebrews, "A will takes effect only at the death of the one who made it," he therefore asserts that, with Christ's death for us, the new covenant has become valid. Its likeness was the old covenant, in which the death of the testator was prefigured in the sacrificial victim. Therefore, if one should ask how it is that we, in the words of the same apostle, are "children and heirs of God and fellow heirs with Christ,"[34] since of course the inheritance is made valid by the death of the deceased and since an inheritance cannot be understood in any other way, the answer is this: he himself having in fact died, we have become heirs because we were also called his sons. "The sons of the bridegroom," he says, "do not fast while the bridegroom is with them."[35] Therefore we are called his heirs, for he has left the peace of the Church, a peace which we possess in this life, in our possession through faith in the divine plan of salvation revealed in time. ON EIGHTY-THREE VARIED QUESTIONS 75.1.[36]

WHY A COVENANT? CHRYSOSTOM: It was probable that many of those who were weaker would especially distrust the promises of Christ because he had died. Paul, accordingly, out of a superabundance introduced this illustration, deriving it from common custom. Of what kind is it? He says, "Indeed, on this very account we ought to be of good courage." On what account? Because covenants are established and obtain their force when those who have made them are not living but dead. "Therefore," he says, "he is the mediator of a new covenant." A covenant is made toward the last day, the day of death.

And a covenant is of this character: it makes

---

[28]Gen 6:2. [29]1 Cor 3:16. [30]Mt 19:12. [31]FC 85:292-93*. [32]NPNF 1 14:440*. [33]NPNF 1 14:443**. [34]Rom 8:17. [35]Mt 9:15. "Sons of the bridegroom" is a literal translation; RSV reads "wedding guests." [36]FC 70:191.

some heirs and some disinherited. So in this case also. "I desire that they also," Christ says, "may be with me where I am."[37] And again of the disinherited, hear him saying, "I do not pray for" all, "but for those who believe in me through their word."[38] Again, a covenant has relation both to the testator and to the legatees; so that they have some things to receive, and some to do. So also in this case, for, after having made promises innumerable, he demands also something from them, saying, "A new commandment I give to you."[39] Again, a covenant ought to have witnesses. Hear him again saying, "I bear witness to myself, and the Father who sent me bears witness to me."[40] And again, "he will bear witness to me,"[41] speaking of the Spirit. The twelve apostles too he sent, saying, "Bear witness before God." On the Epistle to the Hebrews 16.1.[42]

9:19-22 Sprinkled with the Blood

The Ashes of a Heifer, the Suffering of Humanity. Theodoret of Cyr: Since the divine nature is immortal, through the blood of the victims he realized the type of death and confirmed the covenant. Since God the Word became man and took a mortal body, there was no longer need of brute beasts as offerings; instead, he confirmed the new covenant with his own blood, the type corresponding to the shadow and the reality to the body. The water was a type of baptism, the blood of brute beasts the saving blood, the heat of the hyssop the grace of the divine Spirit, the scarlet wool the new garment, the piece of cedar (being a wood that does not rot) the impassible divinity, the ashes of a heifer the suffering of humanity. Interpretation of Hebrews 9.[43]

Why Is the Book of the Testament Sprinkled? Chrysostom: "When every commandment of the law had been declared by Moses to all the people, he took the blood of calves and goats, with water and scarlet wool, and hyssop, and sprinkled both the book itself

and all the people, saying, 'This is the blood of the covenant which God commanded you.'" Tell me then, why is the book of the covenant sprinkled and also the people, except on account of the precious blood, figured from the first? Why "with hyssop"? It is close and retentive? And why the "water"? It shows forth also the cleansing by water. And why the "wool"? This also was used, that the blood might be retained. In this place blood and water show forth the same thing, for baptism is his passion. "And in the same way he sprinkled with the blood both the tent and all the vessels used in worship. Indeed, under the law almost everything is purified with blood, and without the shedding of blood there is no forgiveness of sins." Why the "almost"? Why did he qualify it? Because those ordinances were not a perfect purification or a perfect forgiveness of sins, but [they were] half-complete and in a very small degree. But in this case he says, "This is my blood of the covenant, which is poured out for many for the forgiveness of sins."[44]

Where then is "the book"? He purified their minds. They themselves then were the books of the new covenant. But where are "the vessels used in worship"? They are themselves. And where is "the tabernacle"? Again, they are; for "I will live in them," he says, "and move among them."[45] On the Epistle to the Hebrews 16.3-4.[46]

Cleansed by the Lord's Blood. Philoxenus of Mabbug: Vice is a sickness of the soul, and delusion is a loss of truth. Most people who are sick with the disease of vice and delusion proclaim health and are lauded by other people. Unless the soul is cured from vice and is found in the natural state of health with which it was created so that it can be reborn by health of spirit, it is impossible for a person to desire the supernatural things of the Spirit. For so long as the soul is sick

---

[37]Jn 17:24. [38]Jn 17:20. [39]Jn 13:34. [40]Jn 8:18. [41]Jn 15:26. [42]NPNF 1 14:443*. [43]PG 82:744; TCCLSP 2:174-75. [44]Mt 26:28. [45]2 Cor 6:16. [46]NPNF 1 14:444*.

with passions, its senses have no perception of what is spiritual, and it does not even know how to desire it, except from the hearing of the ears and from writings. . . . Those who desire perfection must keep all the commandments, since the working of the commandments heals the powers of the soul. The practice of the commandments is not accomplished simply and by chance, for it is written that "without the shedding of blood there is no forgiveness of sins." Our nature first received renewal through the incarnation of Christ, and it participated in his passion and death. Then, after the renewal of the shedding of blood, our nature was renewed and sanctified and became able to receive his new and perfect commandments. For if the new commandments had been given to humankind before the shedding of the Lord's blood, before our nature was renewed and sanctified, then it is perhaps possible that even the new commandments, like those of old, would have merely cut off vice from the soul but would have been unable completely to pluck out the very root of vice from it. But now it is not so; now there is a secret labor that accompanies the new, spiritual commandments. When the soul keeps these through the circumspection of the fear of God, they renew it, sanctify it and secretly heal all its members. For it is obvious which passion is quietly cured in the soul by each commandment. The operation of the commandments is perceived only by the healer and the healed, after the likeness of the woman who had an issue of blood. LETTER TO ABBA SYMEON OF CAESAREA.[47]

9:23-24 In the Presence of God on Our Behalf

COPIES AND FORM. ORIGEN: Paul, writing to the Hebrews—those, of course, who were indeed reading the law and had meditated on these things[48] and were examining them well but lacked understanding as to how the sacrifices should be understood—says, "For Christ has entered not into a sanctuary made with hands, a copy of the true one, but into heaven itself, now to appear in

the presence of God on our behalf." And again he says about the offerings, "He did this once for all when he offered up himself."[49] But why do we seek testimonies from these one by one? If anyone examines the entire epistle written to the Hebrews—and especially this place, where he compares the high priest of the law with the high priest of the promise, of whom it is written, "You are a priest forever after the order of Melchizedek" —he will find how this entire passage of the apostle shows that those things which were written in the law are "copies" and "forms"[50] of living and true things. HOMILIES ON LEVITICUS 9.2.1.[51]

HEAVEN IS WHAT IS OURS. CHRYSOSTOM: "Thus it was necessary for the copies," he says, "of the heavenly things to be purified with these rites, but the heavenly things themselves with better sacrifices than these." And how are they "copies of the heavenly things"? And what does he mean now by "the heavenly things"? Is it heaven? Or is it the angels? None of these, but what is ours. It follows then that our things are in heaven, and heavenly things are ours, even though they be accomplished on earth; since although angels are on earth, yet they are called "heavenly." The cherubim appeared on earth but yet are heavenly. And why do I say "appeared"? No, rather, they dwell on earth, as indeed in paradise, but this is nothing, for they are heavenly. And "our commonwealth is in heaven,"[52] and yet we live here. "But these are the heavenly things," that is, the philosophy which exists among us, those who have been called to heaven.

"With better sacrifices than these." What is "better" is better than something else that is good. Therefore, "the copies of the heavenly things" have become good, though the copies were not evil; else the things whereof they are copies would also have been evil. If then we are heavenly and have obtained such a sacrifice, let us

---

[47]AHSIS 436. [48]About rites and sacrifices. [49]Heb 7:27. [50]Cf. 1 Cor 10:6. The Greek typoi is translated as "warnings" in RSV. [51]FC 83:178. [52]Phil 3:20.

stand in awe. Let us no longer continue on the earth; for even now it is possible, for him that wishes it, not to be on the earth. For whether one is or is not of the earth is the effect of moral disposition and choice. For instance, God is said to be in heaven. Why? Not because he is confined by space—far from it—nor as having left the earth destitute of his presence, but by his relation to and intimacy with the angels. If then we also are near to God, we are in heaven. For what care I about heaven when I see the Lord of heaven, when I myself am become a heaven? For he says, "We will come," I and the Father, "and make our home with him."[53] Let us then make our soul a heaven. The heaven is naturally bright; for not even in a storm does it become black, for it does not itself change its appearance, but the clouds run together and cover it. Heaven has the Sun; we also have the Sun of Righteousness. ON THE EPISTLE TO THE HEBREWS 16.6-7.[54]

THE HEAVENLY PERSPECTIVE. CHRYSOSTOM: Let us then become heaven. Let us mount up to that height, whence we shall see people differing nothing from ants. I do not speak of the poor only, nor the many, but even if there be a general there, even if the emperor is there, we shall not distinguish the emperor or the private person. We shall not know what is gold or what is silver, what is silken or purple raiment. We shall see all things as if they were flies, if we are seated at that height. There is no tumult there, no disturbance or clamor. . . .

For there is no hindrance, no, not any, but that we may rise above all people, if we have the will. For if we are so successful in arts that are beyond the reach of most people, much more may we rise in that which does not require so great labor. For, tell me, what is more difficult than to walk along a tightrope, as if on level ground, and when walking on high to dress and undress, as if sitting on a couch? Does not the performance seem to us to be so frightful that we are not even willing to look at it but are terrified and tremble at the very sight? And tell me, what is more difficult than to

hold a pole upon your face, and, when you have put up a child upon it, to perform innumerable feats and delight the spectators? And what is more difficult than to play at ball with swords? And tell me, what is harder than thoroughly to search out the bottom of the sea? And one might mention innumerable other arts.

But easier than all these, if we have the will, is virtue and the going up into heaven. For here it is only necessary to have the will, and all the rest follows. For we may not say, I am unable, nor accuse the Creator. For if he made us unable and then commands, it is an accusation against himself. ON THE EPISTLE TO THE HEBREWS 16.8-9.[55]

THE HOLY OF HOLIES IS HEAVEN. ORIGEN: If the ancient custom of sacrifices is clear to you, let us see what these things also contain according to the mystical understanding. You heard that there were two sanctuaries: one, as it were, visible and open to the priests; the other, as it were, invisible and inaccessible. With the exception of the high priest alone, the others were outside. I think this first sanctuary can be understood as this church in which we are now placed in the flesh, in which the priests minister "at the altar of the whole burnt offerings"[56] with that fire kindled about which Jesus said, "I came to cast fire upon the earth, and would that it were already kindled."[57] And I do not want you to marvel that this sanctuary is open only to the priests. For all who have been anointed with the chrism of the sacred anointing have become priests, just as Peter says to all the church, "But you are a chosen race, a royal priesthood, a holy nation."[58] Therefore you are a priestly race, and because of this you approach the sanctuary. . . . Therefore the priesthood is exercised in this way in the first sanctuary and the offerings are offered. And from this sanctuary the high priest, dressed in the sanctified

---

[53]Jn 14:23. [54]NPNF 1 14:444-45*. [55]NPNF 1 14:445-46*. Chrysostom has made it plain in his homilies on Galatians that the will to receive grace is enabled by grace. [56]See Lev 4:10, 25. [57]Lk 12:49. [58]1 Pet 2:9.

garments, proceeds and enters into the interior of the veil just as we already pointed out above in citing the words of Paul, "Christ has entered not into a sanctuary made with hands but into heaven itself, now to appear in the presence of God on our behalf." Therefore, the place of heaven and the throne itself of God are designated by the figure and the image of the interior sanctuary. HOMILIES ON LEVITICUS 9.9.3-5.[59]

INTO HEAVEN ITSELF. PHOTIUS: The statement that "he entered into the heaven itself" must be taken by common agreement as this: "And so that he might not offer himself often, he entered into the very heaven." For it is characteristic of those entering the "antitypes of the true things" to bear sacrifices "often" and "with blood," but not of the one entering "into heaven itself." FRAGMENTS ON THE EPISTLE TO THE HEBREWS 9.24-25.[60]

9:25-26 Once for All at the End of the Age

THE END OF MANY AGES. ORIGEN: But this world, which is itself called an "age," is said to be the end of many ages. Now the holy apostle teaches that in the age that was before this, Christ did not suffer, nor even in the age before that; and I do not know that I am able to enumerate the number of previous ages in which he did not suffer. I will show, however, the statements of Paul from which I have arrived at this understanding. He says, "He has appeared once for all at the end of the age to take away sin by the sacrifice of himself." He says that Christ was made a "sacrifice" once, and "at the end of the ages has appeared to take away sin."[61] Now after this age, which is said to be made for the consummation of other ages, there will be other ages again to follow; for we have clearly learned this from Paul himself, who says, "that in the ages to come he might show the immeasurable riches of his grace in his kindness toward us."[62] He did not say "in the age to come" or "in the two ages to come" but "in the ages to come." I think, therefore, that by

his language many ages are indicated. ON FIRST PRINCIPLES 2.3.5.[63]

WHY "AT THE END OF THE WORLD"? CHRYSOSTOM: In this place he has also veiled over something. "But now once more in the end of the world." Why "at the end of the world"? After the many sins. If it had taken place at the beginning, then no one would have believed. He must not die a second time; otherwise all would have been useless. But since later there were many transgressions, with reason he appeared, which he expresses in another place also, "Where sin increased, grace abounded all the more."[64] "But now once in the end of the world, he has appeared to put away sin by the sacrifice of himself." ON THE EPISTLE TO THE HEBREWS 17.3.[65]

WE OFFER A REMEMBRANCE OF THIS DEATH. CHRYSOSTOM: What then? Do not we offer every day? We offer indeed, but making a remembrance of his death, and this remembrance is one and not many. How is it one, and not many? Inasmuch as that sacrifice was once for all offered and carried into the Holy of Holies. This is a figure of that sacrifice and a remembrance of it. For we always offer the same, not one sheep now and tomorrow another, but always the same thing, so that the sacrifice is one. And yet by this reasoning, since the offering is made in many places, are there many Christs? But Christ is one everywhere, being complete here and complete there also, one body. As then, while offered in many places, he is one body and not many bodies, so also he is one sacrifice. He is our high priest, who offered the sacrifice that cleanses us. That we offer now also, which was then offered, which cannot be exhausted. This is done in remembrance of what was then done. For he says, "Do this in remembrance of me."[66] It is not another sacrifice, as the

[59]FC 83:196-97. [60]NTA 15:648. [61]The Greek text has a plural (*aiōnas*, i.e., ages, eras, times), translated in RSV as "age" but here as "ages." [62]Eph 2:7. [63]ANF 4:273. [64]Rom 5:20. [65]NPNF 1 14:447*. [66]Lk 22:19.

high priest, but we offer always the same, or rather we perform a remembrance of a sacrifice. ON THE EPISTLE TO THE HEBREWS 17.6.[67]

THE WORST SINNER WILL BE BROUGHT INTO ORDER. ORIGEN: By comparing two verses from the apostle, I have often been perplexed as to how this is the "end of the ages" in which Jesus "has appeared once for all . . . to put away sin," if there are to be ages succeeding this one. Here are the two verses. In Hebrews, "But now he has appeared once for all at the end of the ages to put away sin by the sacrifice of himself." And in Ephesians, "That in the coming ages he might show the immeasurable riches of his grace in kindness toward us."[68] If I may hazard a guess at so great a puzzle, I think that, just as the end of the year is the last month, after which the beginning of another month takes place, so perhaps when many ages have been accomplished, as, so to speak, a year of ages, the end is the present age, after which certain ages to come will take place, whose beginning is the age to come. And in those ages to come God will show the riches "of his grace in kindness," since the worst sinner, who has blasphemed the Holy Spirit and been ruled by sin from beginning to end in the whole of this present age, will afterwards in the age to come be brought into order, I know not how. ON PRAYER 27.15.[69]

TYPE, FIGURE AND POWER. CHRYSOSTOM: Do you see again the superabundance of his proofs? This sacrifice, he says, is one. The others were many. Therefore they had no strength, because they were many. For, tell me, what need is there of many, if one had been sufficient? So that their being many and offered "continually," proves that they, the worshipers, were never made clean. For as a medicine, when it is powerful and productive of health and able to remove the disease entirely, effects all after one application—as, therefore, if being once applied, it accomplishes the whole—it proves its own strength in being no more applied, and this is its business, to be no more applied. If

it is applied continually, this is a plain proof of its not having strength. For it is the excellence of a medicine to be applied once and not often. So is it in this case also. Why indeed are they continually cured with the "same sacrifices"? For if they were set free from all their sins, the sacrifices would not have gone on being offered every day. For they had been appointed to be continually offered in behalf of the whole people, both in the evening and in the day, so that there was an arraignment of sins, and not a release from sins; an arraignment of weakness, not an exhibition of strength. For because the first had no strength, another also was offered and, since this effected nothing, again another; so that it was an evidence of sins. The "offering" indeed, then, was an evidence of sins, the "continually," an evidence of weakness. But with regard to Christ, it was the contrary. He was "once offered." The types therefore contain the figure only, not the power; just as in images the image has the figure of the man not the power. The reality and the type partake of one another. For the type is equal to, but no longer possesses the full strength of, the reality. So too also is it in respect of heaven and of the tent, for the figure was equal; there was the Holy of Holies, but the power and the other things were not the same. ON THE EPISTLE TO THE HEBREWS 17.5.[70]

HE PUT AWAY SIN. THEODORET OF CYR: He completely destroyed the force of sin, promising us immortality; sin is incapable of proving a problem to immortal bodies. INTERPRETATION OF HEBREWS 9.[71]

9:27-28 To Save Those Who Wait Eagerly

DYING IS NOT DEATH BUT SLEEP. CHRYSOSTOM: "And as it is appointed for men to die once, and after that comes judgment." He next says why he died once only: because he became a ran-

---

[67]NPNF 14:449*. [68]Eph 2:7. [69]OSW 145-46. [70]NPNF 14:448**. [71]PG 82:745; TCCLSP 2:175.

som by one death. "It is appointed," he says "for men to die once." This then is the meaning of "he died once," for all. What then? Do we no longer die that death? We do indeed die, but we do not continue in it, which is not to die at all. For the tyranny of death, and death indeed, is when he who dies is never more allowed to return to life. But when after dying there is life, indeed a better life, this is not death, but sleep. Since, then, death was to have possession of all, he therefore died that he might deliver us. On the Epistle to the Hebrews 17.4.[72]

He Endured The Things Common to Humankind. Oecumenius: Because he was man along with his being God, he also endured the things common to humankind. For just as people "die one time only, so also Christ died once." Fragments on the Epistle to the Hebrews 9.27.[73]

The Holy Spirit Strengthens. Bede: On the day of atonement the high priest was commanded to expiate the sanctuary and the tabernacle of testimony, together with the altar, the priests as well, and the entire people. John showed clearly who that high priest was and what the expiation was when, as Jesus was coming to his baptism, he spoke, saying, "Behold, the Lamb of God, who takes away the sin of the world."[74] This expiation had been established to be celebrated once during the year because, as the apostle says, "Christ, having been offered once to bear the sins of many, will appear a second time, not to deal with sin but to save those who are eagerly waiting for him." As for the fact that after the high priest went into the sanctuary to make intercession, no other person was permitted to be in the tabernacle until after he came out—this indicates the weakness of the holy church, which was not yet fit to suffer for its faith in him. This was made evident in the case of the apostles themselves, who, when his passion had begun, "all forsook him and fled."[75] When the expiation was completed, the high priest came forth so that an

opportunity might be given to others to go into the tabernacle. When the sacrifice of his passion was over, Christ appeared to his disciples; by giving them the grace of the Holy Spirit he strengthened their heart further for offering to God sacrificial offerings, not only of devoted works and prayer but also of his own blood. I have explained these details about the observance of this festivity under the law so fully in order that you, dear ones, may acknowledge how appropriately the proclamations of new grace took their starting point from it, in which, in so many ways, the working out of this grace and the redemption of the whole world is expressed. Homilies on the Gospels 2.19.[76]

In Order to Appear in a New World. Ephrem the Syrian: "But now once by coming at the end of times" he has suffered, so that through his sacrifice he might destroy sin, which killed the people and all nations together.

In fact "as it is appointed for men to die once" because of their first sin, and "after" death their "judgment" comes, "so Christ too," by coming, was revealed once and "offered" himself for the sins of everybody. Then "he will appear a second time," not in order to die for the sins, for which he has already died once, but in order to appear in a new world, where there will be no sins on the part of those who in hope expect salvation through him. Commentary on the Epistle to the Hebrews.[77]

He Will Be Seen Apart from Suffering. Theodore of Mopsuestia: Christ having now been seen when he gained mastery over sin, took on death that had power because of sin. When sin had been atoned for, as was reasonable, he also will appear apart from suffering. For "without sin"[78] means that when sin no longer has power, so also he himself will be seen apart from all human suffering. Fragments on the Epis-

[72]NPNF 1 14:447*. [73]NTA 15:466. [74]Jn 1:29. [75]Mt 26:56. [76]CS 111:194-95. [77]EHA 218. [78]Heb 4:15.

tle to the Hebrews 9:28.[79]

Christ Became As If a Sinner. Oecumenius: He says that "he bore the sins of many" on the cross, in order that he might quell them, paying the penalty that they deserved.

Now the Father sent him, "having made him sin."[80] For also Christ became as if a sinner, inasmuch as he took on the sins of the whole world and claimed them as his own. But then he paid the penalty that was owed, the punishment belonging to sinners. At last he will come with

his Father's glory, no longer as a sinner, no longer "reckoned among the lawless."[81] Fragments on the Epistle to the Hebrews 9.28.[82]

The Sins of Many, Not All. Theodoret of Cyr: It should be noted, of course, that he bore the sins of many, not of all: not all came to faith, so he removed the sins of the believers only. Interpretation of Hebrews 9.[83]

---

[79]NTA 15:209. [80]2 Cor 5:21. [81]Lk 22:37; Is 53:12. [82]NTA 15:466. [83]PG 82:745; TCCLSP 2:175.

10:1-11 HE ABOLISHES THE FIRST IN ORDER TO ESTABLISH THE SECOND

For since the law has but a shadow of the good things to come instead of the true form of these realities, it can never, by the same sacrifices which are continually offered year after year, make perfect those who draw near. ²Otherwise, would they not have ceased to be offered? If the worshipers had once been cleansed, they would no longer have any consciousness of sin. ³But in these sacrifices there is a reminder of sin year after year. ⁴For it is impossible that the blood of bulls and goats should take away sins.

⁵Consequently, when Christ[v] came into the world, he said,
"Sacrifices and offerings thou hast not desired,
but a body hast thou prepared for me;
⁶in burnt offerings and sin offerings thou hast taken no pleasure.
⁷Then I said, 'Lo, I have come to do thy will, O God,'
as it is written of me in the roll of the book."
⁸When he said above, "Thou hast neither desired nor taken pleasure in sacrifices and offerings and burnt offerings and sin offerings" (these are offered according to the law), ⁹then he added, "Lo, I have come to do thy will." He abolishes the first in order to establish the second. ¹⁰And by that will we have been sanctified through the offering of the body of Jesus Christ once for all.

¹¹And every priest stands daily at his service, offering repeatedly the same sacrifices, which can never take away sins.

v Greek *he*

OVERVIEW: Scripture, like a human being, is comprised of body, soul and spirit (ORIGEN). The law was only a shadow of good things to come (CHRYSOSTOM, OECUMENIUS, ORIGEN, BEDE), those circumcised by the law only a shadow of heavenly things (ORIGEN, SYMEON). Even the gospel might only be understood in part but can be known in full through Christ (ORIGEN). The law cannot guarantee forgiveness of sin through sacrifices offered. It is through the perfect and single sacrificial giving of the body of Christ once and for all that we are sanctified (THEODORET, EPHREM, OECUMENIUS, THEODORE, PHOTIUS, CHRYSOSTOM).

10:1-2 *The Law Has but a Shadow*

THREEFOLD UNDERSTANDING OF SCRIPTURES. ORIGEN: The way which seems right to us for understanding the Scriptures and the investigation of their meaning, we consider to be the following: we are instructed by Scripture itself regarding the ideas that we ought to form of it. In the Proverbs of Solomon we find just such instruction for the examination of holy Scripture. "For your part," he says, "describe these things to yourself in a threefold manner in counsel and knowledge, that you may answer words of truth to those who question you."[1] Each one, then, ought to describe in his own mind, in a threefold manner, the understanding of the divine letters, that is, so that the simple may be edified, so to speak, by the very body of Scripture; for that is what we call the common and historical meaning. But if some have begun to make considerable progress and are able to see something more than that, they may be edified by the very soul of Scripture. And those who are perfect and resemble those of whom the apostle says, "We speak wisdom among them that are perfect, but not the wisdom of this world, nor of the rulers of this world, who are doomed to pass away. But we speak the wisdom of God, hidden in a mystery, which God has decreed before the ages for our glorification."[2] Such people may be edified by the spiritual law[3] which has a shadow of the good things to come, edified as if by the Spirit. For just

as man is said to consist of body, and soul and spirit, so also does sacred Scripture, which has been granted by God's gracious dispensation for the salvation of man. ON FIRST PRINCIPLES 4.2.4 [4.1.11].[4]

THE LAW WAS THE SHADOW OF REVELATION. CHRYSOSTOM: For as in painting, so long as one only draws the outlines, it is a sort of "shadow," but when one has added the bright paints and laid in the colors, then it becomes "an image." Something of this kind also was the law. ON THE EPISTLE TO THE HEBREWS 17.5.[5]

PREFIGUREMENT OF A PREFIGUREMENT. OECUMENIUS: You are able to understand it in this way. It has been said by Gregory in his sacred writings, in his *Apologetics* and in his *To the Governors,* that the present divine mysteries are antitypes of even greater mysteries. And again in his treatise *Concerning the Resurrection* he says, "Let us receive the Passover, now in a typological fashion, but hereafter in a more complete manner. For the Passover under Mosaic law, I dare to say and in fact say it, was a prefigurement of a prefigurement." Gregory said these things in the following sense. The apostle knew among these things "the shadow" and "the image" and "the coming good things," which he also calls "the substance," that is, the true things. For inasmuch as he makes clear what are the true matters—for that is also the truth—by comparing it with the shadow and the image, he first knows the things in the law as the shadow and second our things (those of Christians) as an image, but "the coming good things" and the true "substance" the things in the coming age. For just as the image is not entirely in accord with the truth, so also the shadow is not entirely in accord with the image. For even if the image does not have the very truth, except that it

---

[1]Prov 22:20-21. RSV reads, "Have I not written for you thirty sayings of admonition and knowledge, to show you what is true, that you may give a true answer to those who sent you?" [2]1 Cor 2:6-7. [3]See Rom 7:14. [4]ANF 4:359**. [5]NPNF 1 14:448*.

exists as a visible imitation of the truth by preserving the shape through its surfaces and the proportion of its members and the complexion of the substrate. But the "shadow" is an indistinct appearance of the image, showing none of the things of which it is the image. And I believe that Gregory in his sacred writings has been led forth by these apostolic writings to say what is most likely. And many other fathers say things similar to Gregory. FRAGMENTS ON THE EPISTLE TO THE HEBREWS 10.1.[6]

NARRATIVE AND ALLEGORICAL LEVELS OF SCRIPTURE INTERPRETATION. ORIGEN: That the first "sense," which we have called the literal one, is profitable in that it is capable of imparting edification is witnessed by the multitude of those believers who accept the faith genuinely and simply. But of that interpretation which is referred back to the "soul," there is an illustration in Paul's first epistle to the Corinthians. He says, "You shall not muzzle the mouth of the ox that treads out the grain." Then he adds, "Is it for oxen that God is concerned? Does he not speak entirely for our sake? It was for our sake, no doubt, that this was written: that the plowman should plough in hope, and the thresher thresh in hope of a share in the crop."[7] And there are numerous interpretations adapted to the multitude which are in circulation, and which edify those who are unable to understand the higher meanings, which have something of the same character. But the interpretation is "spiritual" when one is able to show of what heavenly things the Jews "according to the flesh" served as a copy and a shadow, and of what future blessings the law has a shadow.[8] And, speaking generally, we must investigate, according to the apostolic promise, "the wisdom in a mystery, even the hidden wisdom which God ordained before the world for the glory" of the righteous, which "none of the rulers of this world knew."[9] And the same apostle says somewhere, after mentioning certain events from Exodus and Numbers, "that these things happened to them

as a warning, but that they were written down for our instruction, upon whom the end of the ages has come."[10] He also gives hints to show what things these were figures of, when he says, "For they drank of the spiritual Rock that followed them, and that Rock was Christ."[11]

And in another epistle, when outlining the various matters relating to the tabernacle, he used the words: "You shall make everything according to the pattern which was shown you on the mountain."[12] Further, in the epistle to the Galatians, as if reproaching those who think that they are reading the law and yet do not understand it, judging that those do not understand it who do not believe that allegories are contained under what is written, he says: "Tell me, you that desire to be under the law, do you not hear the law? For it is written, Abraham had two sons, one by a slave and one by a free woman. But the son of the slave was born according to the flesh, the son of the free woman through promise. Now this is an allegory: for these women are the two covenants,"[13] and so on. Now we must carefully mark each word spoken by him. He says: "You who desire to be under the law" (not "You that are under the law"), "do you not hear the law?"—"hearing" being understood to mean "understanding" and "knowing."

And in the epistle to the Colossians, briefly epitomizing the meaning of the entire system of the law, he says, "Therefore let no man judge you in questions of food and drink, or with regard to a festival or a new moon or a sabbath. These are only a shadow of things to come."[14] Further, in the epistle to the Hebrews, when discoursing about those who belong to the circumcision, he writes, "They serve a copy and shadow of heavenly things."[15] Now it is probable, from these illustrations, that those who have once admitted that the apostle is divinely inspired will entertain no doubt with respect to the five books of Moses;

---

[6]NTA 15:466-67. [7]1 Cor 9:9-10; cf. Deut 25:4. [8]Cf. Heb 8:5; Rom 8:5. [9]See 1 Cor 2:7-8. [10]1 Cor 10:11. [11]1 Cor 10:4. [12]Heb 8:5; cf. Ex 25:40. [13]Gal 4:21-24. [14]Col 2:16-17. [15]See Heb 8:5.

but they wish to know if the rest of the history also "happened figuratively."[16] We must note, then, the expression in the epistle to the Romans, "I have left to myself seven thousand men, who have not bowed the knee to Baal,"[17] quoted from the third book of Kings. Paul has understood this to stand for those who are Israelites according to election,[18] for not only are the Gentiles benefited by the coming of Christ, but also some who belong to the divine race.[19] On First Principles 4.2.6.[20]

Delivered from the Shadow. Symeon the New Theologian: Those who lived before grace, since they were under the law,[21] found themselves sitting under its shadow. Those who have come after grace and the day have arrived have been delivered from the shadow, the slavery of the law.[22] They have risen above the law, having climbed as it were, the ladder of the life of the gospel. They have been lifted up on high to share the life of the lawgiver and have themselves become lawgivers rather than keepers of the law. Discourse 28.4.[23]

Divine Stumbling Blocks Deepen Scriptural Understanding. Origen: But if in every detail of this outer covering, that is, the actual history, the sequence of the law had been preserved and its order maintained, we should have understood the Scriptures in an unbroken course and should certainly not have believed that there was anything else buried within them beyond what was indicated at a first glance. Consequently the divine wisdom has arranged for certain stumbling blocks and interruptions of the historical sense to be found therein, by inserting in the midst a number of impossibilities and incongruities. [This was done] in order that the very interruption of the narrative might as it were present a barrier to the reader and lead him to refuse to proceed along the pathway of the ordinary meaning. And so, by shutting us out and debarring us from that, [the writers] might recall us to the beginning of another way, and might

thereby bring us, through the entrance of a narrow footpath, to a higher and loftier road and lay open the immense breadth of the divine wisdom. . . . The aim of the Holy Spirit was chiefly to preserve the connection of the spiritual, meaning, both in the things that are yet to be done and in those which have already been accomplished. [Thus] whenever he found that things which had been done in history could be harmonized with the spiritual meaning, he composed in a single narrative a texture comprising both kinds of meaning, always, however, concealing the secret sense more deeply. But wherever the record of deeds that had been done could not be made to correspond with the sequence of the spiritual truths, he inserted occasionally some deeds of a less probable character or which could not have happened at all, and occasionally some that might have happened but in fact did not. Sometimes he does this by a few words, which in their bodily sense do not appear capable of containing truth and at other times by inserting a large number.

This is found to happen particularly in the law, where there are many things that as literal precepts are clearly useful, but also a considerable number in which no principle of utility whatever is disclosed, while sometimes even impossibilities are detected. All this, as we have said, the Holy Spirit supervised, in order that in cases where that which appeared at the first glance could neither be true nor useful we should be led on to search for a truth deeper down and needing more careful examination. And [we] should try to discover in the Scriptures which we believe to be inspired by God a meaning worthy of God.

And not only did the Holy Spirit supervise the writings which were previous to the coming of Christ, but because he is one and the same Spirit and proceeds from the one God, he has acted similarly in regard to the Gospels and

[16]See 1 Cor 10:11. [17]Rom 11:4; cf. 1 Kings 19:18. [18]See Rom 11:5. [19]In the Latin version of the text, the ending reads "the coming of Christ was beneficial not only to the Gentiles but also to the very many of the race of Israel who have been called to salvation." [20]ANF 4:360-62**. [21]Gal 3:23. [22]Cf. Gal 3:23; 4:3. [23]SNTD 297.

the writings of the apostles. For even the narratives that he inspired through them were not woven together without the spell of that wisdom of his, the nature of which we explained above. And so it happens that even in them the Spirit has mingled not a few things by which the historical order of the narrative is interrupted and broken, with the object of turning and calling the attention of the reader, by the impossibility of the literal sense, to an examination of the inner meaning. ON FIRST PRINCIPLES 4.2.9.[24]

LAW AS SHADOW, GOSPEL AS LIGHT. BEDE: The law was indeed given through Moses, and there it was determined by a heavenly rule what was to be done and what was to be avoided, but what it commanded was completed only by the grace of Christ. On the one hand, that law was capable of pointing out sin, teaching justice and showing transgressors what they are charged with. On the other hand, the grace of Christ, poured out in the hearts of the faithful through the spirit of charity,[25] brings it about that what the law commanded may be fulfilled. Hence that which was written, "do not covet,"[26] is the law given through Moses because it is commanded, but grace comes through Christ when what is commanded is fulfilled. Truth came through Christ because "the law has but a shadow of the good things to come, instead of the true form of these realities." And, as the apostle says elsewhere, "These things happened to them as a figure."[27] But in place of a shadow Christ displayed the light of truth, and in place of the figure of the law he displayed the exact image of the things which were prefigured when, with the giving of the grace of the Spirit, he made clear to his disciples the meaning so that they could understand the Scriptures.[28] The law was given through Moses when the people were commanded to be made clean by the sprinkling of the blood of a lamb.[29] The grace and truth which were prefigured in the law came through Jesus Christ when he himself, having suffered on the

cross, "freed us from our sins by his blood."[30] HOMILIES ON THE GOSPELS 1.2.[31]

THE SHADE OF THE WAY. ORIGEN: It is a great thing to have passed from the law to the shadow of Christ. For Christ is the way, Christ is truth and life; and when we come under his shadow we have the shade of the way, are overshadowed by the truth and live in life's shadow. And whereas we have only glimpses of knowledge, like a confused reflection in a mirror,[32] if we follow this way we shall eventually come to see face to face what at first we saw confusedly as a shadow. COMMENTARY ON THE SONG OF SONGS 3.[33]

A MODEL IS NECESSARY BUT NOT REAL. ORIGEN: The law, then, and everything in the law, being inspired, as the apostle says, until the time of amendment, is like those people whose job it is to make statues and cast them in metal. Before they tackle the statue itself, the one they are going to cast in bronze, silver or gold, they first make a clay model to show what they are aiming at. The model is a necessity, but only until the real statue is finished. The model is made for the sake of the statue, and when the statue is ready the sculptor has no further use for the model. Well, it is rather like that with the law and the prophets. The things written in the law and the prophets were meant as types or figures of things to come. But now the artist himself has come, the author of it all, and he has transferred the law, which had only the shadow of the good things to come, to the very image of the things. HOMILIES ON LEVITICUS 10.2.[34]

DRAW NEAR CONTINUALLY. CHRYSOSTOM: Many partake of this sacrifice the Eucharist once in the whole year, others twice, others many times. Our word then is to all, not to those only who are here but to those also who are settled in the desert. For they partake once in the year and

---

[24]OFP 285-87*. [25]Rom 5:5. [26]Deut 5:21; Rom 7:7. [27]1 Cor 10:11. [28]Lk 24:45. [29]Ex 12:7. [30]Rev 1:5. [31]CS 110:13. [32]1 Cor 13:12. [33]GCS 8:182-83; COS 12. [34]FC 83:202-3.

often indeed at intervals of two years. What then? Which shall we approve? Those who receive once in the year? Those who receive many times? Those who receive few times? Neither those who receive once, nor those who receive often, nor those who receive seldom, but those who come with a pure conscience, from a pure heart, with an irreproachable life. Let such draw near continually, but those who are not such, not even once. Why, you will ask? Because they receive to themselves judgment, yea, and condemnation and punishment and vengeance. And do not wonder. For as food, nourishing by nature, if received by a person without appetite, ruins and corrupts all the system and becomes an occasion of disease, so surely is it also with respect to the awful mysteries. Do you feast at a spiritual table, a royal table, and again pollute your mouth with mire? Do you anoint yourself with sweet ointment and again fill yourself with ill savors? Tell me, I ask, when after a year you partake of the communion, do you think that the forty days are sufficient for you for the purifying of the sins of all that time? And again, when a week has passed, do you give yourself up to the former things? Tell me now, if, when you have been well for forty days after a long illness, you should again give yourself up to the food which caused the sickness, have you not lost your former labor too? For if natural things are changed, much more those which depend on choice. As for instance, by nature we see, and naturally we have healthy eyes, but oftentimes from a bad habit of body our power of vision is injured. If then natural things are changed, much more those of choice. You assign forty days for the health of the soul, or perhaps not even forty, and do you expect to propitiate God? Tell me, are you ready for this?

These things I say, not as forbidding you the one and annual coming but as wishing you to draw near continually. ON THE EPISTLE TO THE HEBREWS 17.7.[35]

THE GOSPEL TEACHES A SHADOW. ORIGEN:
We must also know that just as there is a "law"

which contains a "shadow of the good things to come," which have been revealed by the law proclaimed in accordance with truth, so also the gospel, which is thought to be understood by all who read it, teaches a shadow of the mysteries of Christ.

And that which John calls an eternal gospel,[36] which would properly be called a spiritual gospel, clearly presents both the mysteries presented by Christ's words and the things of which his acts were symbols, to those who consider "all things face to face"[37] concerning the son of God himself. COMMENTARY ON THE GOSPEL OF JOHN 1.39-40.[38]

SHADOW, IMAGE AND TRUTH. ORIGEN: Paul
distinguishes three levels in the law: the shadow, the image and the truth. . . . The law contains the shadow of future good things but not the very image of the realities, and this clearly shows that the image of the realities is different from what is designated as the shadow of the law. If anyone can describe the ceremonies of the Jewish worship, let him view the temple as not having had the image of realities but only their shadow. Let him see the altar as a mere shadow, and the rams and the calves brought to sacrifice also as a shadow. According to the Scripture, "our days on the earth are like a shadow."[39]

If someone wishes to go beyond this shadow, let him come to the image of the realities, and let him behold the coming of Christ made flesh. Let him contemplate him in his role as high priest, offering victims to the Father henceforth and in the future; let him understand that all this is an image of spiritual realities and that heavenly functions are denoted by corporeal functions. We employ the term *image* to refer to that which is intelligible at present and which human nature can observe.

If you can penetrate the heavens with your understanding and your mind and follow Jesus, who has penetrated the heavens and who stands

---

[35]NPNF 1 14:449*. [36]Rev 14:6. [37]See Prov 8:9 LXX. Greek is *enōpia*, "face to face." [38]FC 80:42. [39]1 Chron 29:15.

as our intercessor before the face of God, you will find there those good things whose shadow the law contained and whose image Christ revealed through his incarnation. Those good things . . . have been prepared for the blessed, which neither eye has seen nor ear heard, and which no person has ever even imagined or thought of. HOMILIES ON THE PSALMS 38.2.2.[40]

10:3-11 Sacrifices and Offerings

A REMINDER OF SIN. THEODORET OF CYR: He showed both the law's limitations and its usefulness: while it cannot remove sins, it mounts an accusation against them, instills fear and obliges one to have recourse to grace. INTERPRETATION OF HEBREWS 10.[41]

SACRIFICES ABOLISHED THROUGH SACRIFICE. EPHREM THE SYRIAN: If they had become perfect, their priesthood would have ceased, because they should have abstained from their sacrifices. And if their conscience was cleansed from sin, at the same time they would have been cleansed from the impurity of flesh. But "in these sacrifices there is a reminder of sin" every day. "For it is impossible that the blood of bulls and goats should take away sin." Therefore our Lord, who came to this world, said through the mouth of David, "Sacrifices and offerings you have not desired, but a body you have prepared for me,"[42] so that the victims of sacrifices might be abolished through his sacrifice. COMMENTARY ON THE EPISTLE TO THE HEBREWS.[43]

A SACRIFICE FOR ALL SINS. OECUMENIUS: For he says that the sacrifices were offered not only for sins that had taken place, but rather for all sins, on the grounds that the sacrifices that had already taken place could not put the sins away. FRAGMENTS ON THE EPISTLE TO THE HEBREWS 10:4.[44]

HE CHANGES THE TEXT FROM "I WILL ESTABLISH EARS." THEODORE OF MOPSUESTIA: These things have been spoken to those in Baby-

lon who wanted to say to God, "You did not demand sacrifices from me but only to obey you and to do your will." And right away the things pertaining to the quotation have become unambiguous as far as I am concerned. Changing it he speaks in this way about the person of Christ, saying, "I will establish a body" instead of "I will establish ears."[45] FRAGMENTS ON THE EPISTLE TO THE HEBREWS 10.5.[46]

THE OLD TESTAMENT AND THE PREDICTIONS OF CHRIST. PHOTIUS: Christ spoke, "while coming into the world,"[47] not "after he had entered it." But manifestly he was already entering it when he promised David and maintained that he would seat one from the fruit of his loins on his throne until the age would come.[48] Therefore, "while entering into the world" because of the promises made to David, he also says this through him, since "you did not wish for sacrifice and offering, neither were you well pleased"[49] with the rites in the law. And he did not say, "you are not well pleased nor wish," but "you did not want nor were you well pleased," all but saying, "From their very institution and introduction the sacrifices were not entirely satisfactory and well pleasing. But really if any of them were accepted by you, it was accepted owing to the weakness of the one who brought them. Since then I reject these things and 'I prepare a body for myself,' then 'I have come' in order 'to do your will.' For this also is spoken concerning me not in a simple manner and in passing, but as the chief matter and the supposition of the book which foretold about me." And he calls the book the whole Old Testament. For the chief thing and the most noteworthy supposition of the Old Testament are the predictions about Christ. FRAGMENTS ON THE EPISTLE TO THE HEBREWS 10.5-9.[50]

---

[40]PG 12:1402-3; IHEGF 102-3. [41]PG 82:748; TCCLSP 2:176. [42]See Ps 40:6 (39:7 LXX). [43]EHA 218-19*. [44]NTA 15:467. [45]Hebrew and LXX texts have "ears" rather than "body." [46]NTA 15:209. [47]Eiserchomenos is a present participle in Greek. [48]Ps 132:11. [49]Ps 40:7-9. [50]NTA 15:648.

Not Through the Blood of Beasts. Theodoret of Cyr: How could the blood of brute beasts declare guiltless some murderer or parricide? This is the reason blessed David also said, "Had you wanted it, I would have offered sacrifice; you will take no delight in burned offerings."[51] Interpretation of Hebrews 10.[52]

The Lord's Body Is the Common Sacrifice. Chrysostom: Do you see that the law takes its force from the place? And, since the city is gone, there can no longer be a priesthood. There can be no emperor if there are no armies, no crown, no purple robe, none of the other things that weld together an empire. So, too, there can be no priesthood if sacrifice has been destroyed, if offerings are forbidden, if the sanctuary has been trampled into the dust, if everything that constituted it has disappeared. For the priesthood depended on all these things. . . .

That great and wonderful prophet, David . . . made it clear that the one kind of sacrifice would be abolished and another brought in to take its place when he said, "You have multiplied, O Lord my God, your wondrous deeds and your thoughts toward us; none can compare with you! Were I to proclaim and tell of them, they would be more than can be numbered."[53] See how wise the prophet is. He said, "You have multiplied your wondrous deeds," and he stood aghast at God's power to work miracles. But he did not go on to tell us about the creation of the things we see—of heaven, earth, and oceans, of water in Egypt or of any other miracles like those. What did he say were wondrous works? "Sacrifice and offering you do not desire."[54] . . .

David went on to say, "But a body you have fitted to me."[55] By this he meant the Lord's body which became the common sacrifice for the whole world, the sacrifice which cleansed our souls, canceled sin, put down death, opened heaven, gave us many great hopes and made ready all the other things which Paul knew well and spoke of when he exclaimed, "O the depth of the riches and wisdom and knowledge of God! How unsearchable are his judgments and how inscrutable his ways."[56]

David, then, foresaw all this when he said, "Many are the wondrous works you have done, O Lord my God." He went on to say, speaking of the person of Christ, "In holocausts and sin offerings you had had no pleasure," and then continued, "Then I said, 'Lo, I come.' "[57] When was "then"? When the time was ripe for more perfect instructions. We had to learn the less perfect lessons through his servants, but the loftier lessons which surpass the nature of humankind we had to learn from the lawgiver himself. Discourses Against Judaizing Christians 7.2.1-7.[58]

The Abolition of Sacrifice. Chrysostom: Here he does not blame those who offer, showing that it is not because of their wickednesses that he does not accept them, as he says elsewhere, but because the thing itself has been convicted for the future and shown to have no strength or any suitableness to the times. What then has this to do with the "sacrifices" being offered "oftentimes"? Not only from their being "oftentimes" offered, he means, is it manifest that they are weak and that they effected nothing, but also from God's not accepting them, as being unprofitable and useless. And in another place it is said, "If you had desired sacrifice, I would have given it."[59] Therefore by this also he makes it plain that he does not desire it. Therefore sacrifices are not God's will, but the abolition of sacrifices. Wherefore they sacrifice contrary to his will. On the Epistle to the Hebrews 18.1.[60]

He Abolishes the First. Theodoret of Cyr: By "first" he meant the sacrifice of brute beasts, by the "second" the rational one, offered by himself. . . . He brought out clearly that God's will is the salvation of humankind. The Lord also

---

[51]Ps 51:16. [52]PG 82:748; *TCCLSP* 2:176. [53]Ps 40:5 (39:6 LXX). [54]Ps 40:6 (39:7 LXX). [55]RSV reads "but thou has given me an open ear." [56]Rom 11:33. [57]Ps 40:6-7 (39:7-8 LXX). [58]FC 68:182-85*. [59]See Ps 51:16 (50:18 LXX). [60]NPNF 1 14:451*.

said as much, "This is the will of my Father, that everyone who believes in me may not be lost but may have eternal life."[61] INTERPRETATION OF HEBREWS 10.[62]

THE SAME SACRIFICES. PHOTIUS: He calls them "the same sacrifices" because they are always being offered for the same things, since those sacrifices and offerings which have taken place and are taking place are not strong enough to strip away any sin purely and completely. FRAGMENTS ON THE EPISTLE TO THE HEBREWS 10.11.[63]

---

[61]Jn 6:39. [62]PG 82:748; TCCLSP 2:176-77. [63]NTA 15:649.

10:12-25 A NEW COVENANT THROUGH CHRIST

[12]But when Christ[w] had offered for all time a single sacrifice for sins, he sat down at the right hand of God, [13]then to wait until his enemies should be made a stool for his feet. [14]For by a single offering he has perfected for all time those who are sanctified. [15]And the Holy Spirit also bears witness to us; for after saying,

[16]"This is the covenant that I will make with them
after those days, says the Lord:
I will put my laws on their hearts,
and write them on their minds,"

[17]then he adds,

"I will remember their sins and their misdeeds no more."

[18]Where there is forgiveness of these, there is no longer any offering for sin.

[19]Therefore, brethren, since we have confidence to enter the sanctuary by the blood of Jesus, [20]by the new and living way which he opened for us through the curtain, that is, through his flesh, [21]and since we have a great priest over the house of God, [22]let us draw near with a true heart in full assurance of faith, with our hearts sprinkled clean from an evil conscience and our bodies washed with pure water. [23]Let us hold fast the confession of our hope without wavering, for he who promised is faithful; [24]and let us consider how to stir up one another to love and good works, [25]not neglecting to meet together, as is the habit of some, but encouraging one another, and all the more as you see the Day drawing near.

w Greek *this one*

OVERVIEW: After his sacrifice Christ is seated at the right hand of God, for he is no longer a servant and no longer a minister who stands; by his humiliation and poverty he made us rich in grace and worthy of the glory of the kingdom (CHRYSOSTOM). It is according to our faith that

we are allowed the entrance to his own sanctuary and kingdom (EPHREM, CHRYSOSTOM), the
fact that boggles the mind (SYMEON). In the new
covenant he remembers the sins of believers no
more. It is only on the cross that a man dies with
his hands spread out. Thus it was fitting for the
Lord to bear this also and to spread out his
hands, that with one he might draw the ancient
people and with the other those from the Gentiles and unite both in himself (ATHANASIUS).
His death tore the temple curtain and opened us
entrance into heaven (CHRYSOSTOM). He is the
true tabernacle (GREGORY OF NYSSA), the house
of God (OECUMENIUS). In him the faithful are
clothed in the raiment of glory (ISAAC). A person
who has received pardon for sins must refrain
from future sin (CLEMENT OF ALEXANDRIA). Thus
we are encouraged to do good in community
(PHOTIUS). Love is increased by our gathering
together, as the works of love are more powerful
than words, and love is a "highway that leads to
virtue." There is always room for repentance,
but only one cross (CHRYSOSTOM). Chrysostom
encourages faithful living after communion. The
believers are reminded to remember the days of
persecution, when the Hebrews joyfully endured suffering as a community. It is through
suffering that we become strong.

10:12-13 Enemies Underfoot

HE EXECUTED THE PRIESTLY OFFICE ONCE
FOR ALL. CHRYSOSTOM: Do not then, having
heard that he is a priest, suppose that he is always
executing the priest's office. For he executed it
once and thenceforward "sat down." Lest you
suppose that he is standing on high and is a minister, he shows that the matter is part of a dispensation or economy. For as he became a servant, so
also he became a priest and a minister. But as,
after becoming a servant, he did not continue a
servant, so also, having become a minister, he did
not continue a minister. For it belongs not to a
minister to sit but to stand. ON THE EPISTLE TO
THE HEBREWS 13.8.[1]

HIS ENEMIES HIS FOOTSTOOL. THEODORET OF
CYR: In the former case a multitude of priests, a
multitude of victims, and no benefit, whereas in
this case priest and victim are one and the same,
he achieved abolition of sins and needs no further
service; instead, he is seated with the Father who
begot him, awaiting the end of the present life. At
that time, in fact, all the adversaries will adore
him as God and Lord. Among his foes will be,
first, the devil and the mass of the demons, then
those of the Jews and the Gentiles who did not
accept the illumination of the faith, and along
with them the bands of the heretics guilty of the
blasphemies against him. INTERPRETATION OF
HEBREWS 10.[2]

THE RICH PERSON IS ASSAILABLE ON EVERY
SIDE. CHRYSOSTOM: "He sat down at the right
hand of God, then to wait"—why the delay?—
"until his enemies be put under his feet. For by a
single offering he has perfected for all time those
who are sanctified." But perhaps someone might
say, "Why did he not put them under at once?"
For the sake of the faithful who should afterwards be brought forth and born. Whence then
does it appear that they shall be put under? By
the saying "He sat down." He called to mind
again that testimony which says, "until I put the
enemies under his feet."[3] . . . But who are the enemies? All unbelievers. . . . And intimating the
greatness of their subjection, he said not "subjected" but "put under his feet." Let us not therefore be among the number of his enemies. For not
they alone are enemies, the unbelievers and Jews,
but those also who are full of unclean living. "For
the carnal mind is enmity against God, for it is
not subject to the law of God, for neither can it
be."[4] What then, you say? Carnality is not a
ground of blame. Rather, it is very much a ground
of blame. For the wicked person, as long as that
one is wicked, cannot be subject to God's law.
That one can, however, change and become good.

---

[1]NPNF 1 14:430*. [2]PG 82:749; TCCLSP 2:177. [3]Heb 1:13; Ps 110:1
(109:1 LXX). [4]Rom 8:7.

Let us then cast out carnal minds. But what is meant by carnal? Whatever injures the soul even while making the body flourish and do well, as, for instance, wealth, luxury, glory—all these things are of the flesh—carnal love. Let us not then love gain but ever follow after poverty, for this is a great good. But, you say, it makes one humble and of little account. True, for we have need of this, for it benefits us much. "Poverty," it is said, "humbles a man."[5] And again Christ says, "Blessed are the poor in spirit."[6] Do you then grieve because you are upon a path leading to virtue? Do you not know that this gives us great confidence?

But, one says, "the poor man's wisdom is despised."[7] And again another says, "Give me neither poverty nor riches,"[8] and, "Deliver me from the furnace of poverty."[9] And again, if riches and poverty are from the Lord, how can either poverty or riches be an evil? Why then were these things said? They were said under the old covenant, where there was much account made of wealth, where there was great contempt of poverty, where the one was a curse and the other a blessing. But now it is no longer so. But will you hear the praises of poverty? Christ sought after it and said, "But the Son of man has nowhere to lay his head."[10] And again he said to his disciples, "Take no gold, nor silver, nor two tunics."[11] And Paul in writing said, "as having nothing, and yet possessing everything."[12] And Peter said to him who was lame from his birth, "I have no silver and gold."[13] Yes, and under the old covenant itself, where wealth was held in admiration, who were the admired? Was not Elijah, who had nothing save the sheepskin? Was not Elisha? Was not John?

Let none then be humiliated on account of their poverty. It is not poverty which humiliates but wealth, which compels us to have need of many and forces us to be under obligations to many.

And what could be poorer than Jacob, tell me, who said, "If God give me bread to eat and clothing to wear"?[14] Were Elijah and John then wanting in boldness? Did not the one reprove Ahab

and the other Herod? The latter said, "It is not lawful for you to have your brother Philip's wife."[15] And Elijah said to Ahab with boldness, "I have not troubled Israel, but you have, and your father's house."[16] You see that this—poverty—especially produces boldness? For while the rich man is a slave, being subject to loss, and in the power of everyone wishing to hurt him, those who have nothing fear not confiscation nor fine. So if poverty had made people wanting in boldness, Christ would not have sent his disciples in poverty to a work requiring great boldness. For the poor are very strong and have nothing from which they may be wronged or evil entreated. But the rich person is assailable on every side, just as one in the same way would easily catch a man who was dragging many long ropes after him, whereas one could not readily lay hold on a naked person. So here also it falls out in the case of the rich person; slaves, gold, lands, affairs innumerable, innumerable cares, difficult circumstances, necessities make this one an easy prey to all. ON THE EPISTLE TO THE HEBREWS 18.3-4.[17]

10:17-18 He Promised Forgiveness

I WILL REMEMBER SINS NO MORE. THEODORET OF CYR: Now, this happened through the new covenant: we receive also in all-holy baptism the forgiveness of sins. In the life to come, when immortality is granted us, we shall live differently from everyone else, sin no longer capable of troubling those who have become immortal. May it be our good fortune to attain this life. We shall attain it if in the present life we embrace with enthusiasm the effort virtue involves and accept the struggles it requires. The Lord himself, who is the source of the future goods, will work with us. INTERPRETATION OF HEBREWS 10.[18]

---

[5]See Prov 10:4 LXX. [6]Mt 5:3. [7]Eccles 9:16. [8]Prov 30:8. [9]See Is 48:10 LXX. [10]Mt 8:20. [11]Mt 10:9-10. [12]2 Cor 6:10. [13]Acts 3:6. [14]Gen 28:20. [15]Mk 6:18. [16]1 Kings 18:18. [17]NPNF 1 14:452-53*. [18]PG 82:749; TCCLSP 2:177-78.

10:19-21 *The New and Living Way*

THE INNER TABERNACLE IS FAITH. EPHREM
THE SYRIAN: "Therefore, brethren, we have confidence to enter the sanctuary," which is faith. In
his blood he renewed for us the way of faith that
the former priests had already. But since it had
become obsolete among them, he renewed it for
us at that time "through the curtain, that is,
through his flesh." COMMENTARY ON THE EPIS-
TLE TO THE HEBREWS.[19]

COME TO ME! SYMEON THE NEW THEOLOGIAN:
But the people of whom I speak and whom I call
heretics are those who say that there is no one in
our times and in our midst who is able to keep the
gospel commandments and become like the holy
fathers. That is to say, they should believe and
practice, for faith is shown by deeds,[20] just as the
features of the face in a mirror. Further, that they
may be both great contemplatives and see God, by
the illumination and reception of the Holy Spirit,
through whom the Son is perceived together with
the Father. Now those who say that this is impossible have not fallen into one particular heresy, but
rather into all of them, if I may say so, since this
one surpasses and covers them all in impiety and
abundance of blasphemy. Those who make this
claim subvert all the divine Scriptures. I think that
by making this claim this vain person states that
the holy gospel is now recited in vain, that the
writings of Basil the Great and of our other priests
and holy fathers are irrelevant or have even been
frivolously written. If, then, it is impossible for us
to carry out in action and observe without fail all
the things that God says, and all the saints after
first practicing them have left in writing for our
instruction,[21] why did they at that time trouble to
write them down, and why do we read them in
church? Those who make these claims shut up the
heaven that Christ opened for us and cut off the
way to it that he inaugurated for us. God who is
above all[22] stands, as it were, at the gate of heaven
and peers out of it so that the faithful see him.
Through his holy gospel God cries out and says,

"Come to me, all who labor and are heavy laden,
and I will give you rest."[23] But these opponents of
God or, rather, antichrists say, "It is impossible,
impossible!" DISCOURSE 29.4.[24]

THE VEIL OF FLESH IS LIFTED UP. CHRYSOS-
TOM: "For the entrance into the sanctuary." What
does he mean here by "entrance"? Heaven and the
access to spiritual things. "Which he opened,"
that is, which he prepared and which he began.
For the beginning of using is thereafter called the
opening, which he prepared, he means, and by
which he himself passed. "The new and living
way." Here he expresses "the full assurance of
hope." "New," he says. He is anxious to show that
we have all things greater; since now the gates of
heaven have been opened, which was not done
even for Abraham. "The new and living way," he
says, for the first was a way of death, leading to
Hades, but this of life. And yet he did not say, "of
life," but called it indeed "living" namely, that
which persists by God's own command.
"Through the curtain," he says, "of his flesh." . . .
And with good reason did he call the flesh "a curtain." For when it was lifted up on high, then the
things in heaven appeared. ON THE EPISTLE TO
THE HEBREWS 19.2.[25]

**UNITING THE ANCIENT PEOPLE AND THE
GENTILES.** ATHANASIUS: If any of our own people inquire, not from love of debate but from
love of learning, why he suffered death in no
other way save on the cross, let them also be told
that no other way than this was good for us, and
that it was well that the Lord suffered this for
our sakes. For if he came himself to bear the
curse laid upon us, how else could he have
"become a curse" unless he received the death
set for a curse? And that is the cross. For this is
exactly what is written: "Cursed be every one
who hangs on a tree."[26] Again, if the Lord's

---

[19]EHA 219*. [20]See Jas 2:18. [21]See 1 Cor 10:11. [22]Rom 9:5. [23]Mt
11:28. [24]SNTD 312*. [25]NPNF 1 14:454-55*. [26]Gal 3:13; Deut
21:23.

death is the ransom of all, and by his death "the dividing wall of hostility"[27] is broken down, and the calling of the nations is brought about, how would he have called us to him had he not been crucified? For it is only on the cross that a man dies with his hands spread out. Thus it was fitting for the Lord to bear this also and to spread out his hands, that with the one he might draw the ancient people and with the other those from the Gentiles and unite both in himself. For this is what he himself has said, signifying by what manner of death he was ransom to all: "I, when I am lifted up," he says, "will draw all men to myself."[28] For the devil, the enemy of our race, having fallen from heaven, wanders about our lower atmosphere and there, bearing rule over his fellow spirits, as the devil's peers in disobedience, not only works illusions by their means in them that are deceived but tries to hinder them that are going up. About this the apostle says, "Following the prince of the power of the air, the spirit that is now at work in the sons of disobedience,"[29] while the Lord came to cast down the devil and clear the air and prepare the way for us up into heaven, as said the apostle, "Through the curtain, that is to say, his flesh"— and this must be by death. Well, by what other kind of death could this have come to pass than by one which took place in the air, I mean, the cross? For only he that is perfected on the cross dies in the air. Therefore, it was quite fitting that the Lord suffered this death. For thus being lifted up, he cleared the air of the malignity both of the devil and of demons of all kinds, as he says, "I saw Satan fall like lightning from heaven,"[30] and made a new opening of the way up into heaven, as he says once more, "Lift up your heads, O gates, and be lifted up, O ancient doors!"[31] For it was not the Word himself that needed an opening of the gates, being Lord of all; nor were any of his works closed to their maker; but it was we who needed it, whom he carried up by his own body. For as he offered it to death on behalf of all, so by it he once more made ready the way up into the heavens. ON THE INCARNATION 25.[32]

THE NEW WAY IS ALWAYS RECENT. PHOTIUS: He says, "recent,"[33] lest anyone say, "Then if it is recent, it too will cease; for it will age and grow old and it will also be destroyed like that of the old testament." Not in the least, he says. But since it is always recent, it remains new and will be "living," for it never receives death and destruction. FRAGMENTS ON THE EPISTLE TO THE HEBREWS 10.20.[34]

THE HOUSE OF GOD. OECUMENIUS: He calls the faithful "the house of God" in accordance with the passage of Scripture that states, "I will dwell among them and walk in their midst."[35] FRAGMENTS ON THE EPISTLE TO THE HEBREWS 10.21.[36]

THE TRUE TABERNACLE IS CHRIST. GREGORY OF NYSSA: Taking a hint from what has been said by Paul, who partially uncovered the mystery of these things, we say that Moses was earlier instructed by a type in the mystery of the tabernacle that encompasses the universe. This tabernacle would be "Christ who is the power and the wisdom of God," who in his own nature was not made with hands, yet capable of being made when it became necessary for this tabernacle to be erected among us. Thus, the same tabernacle is in a way both unfashioned and fashioned, uncreated in preexistence but created in having received this material composition. LIFE OF MOSES 2.174.[37]

CONVERSING IN ANOTHER FASHION. ISAAC OF NINEVEH: But now, when he has poured out his grace upon the world through his own coming, he has descended not in an earthquake, not in a fire, not in a terrible and mighty sound,[38] but "as the rain upon a fleece and raindrops that fall upon the

---

[27]Eph 2:14. [28]Jn 12:32; cf. Is 65:2. [29]Eph 2:2. [30]Lk 10:18. [31]Ps 24:7. [32]LCC 3:79-80*. [33]RSV translates *prosphatos* as "new" in v. 19. [34]NTA 15:649. [35]2 Cor 6:16; Lev 26:12. [36]NTA 15:467. [37]*GNLM* 98*. [38]See 1 Kings 19:12.

earth,"[39] softly; and he was seen conversing with us after another fashion. This came to pass when, as though in a treasury, he concealed his majesty with the curtain of his flesh and among us spoke with us in that body which his own bidding wrought for him out of the womb of the virgin, even Mary the Theotokos. All this he did so that, on beholding him who was of our race conversing with us, we should not be smitten with terror by the vision of him.

Therefore, every person has put on Christ when he is clothed with the raiment in which the Creator was seen through the body that he put on. For the likeness in which he was seen by his own creation and in which he kept company with it, he willed to put on in his inner man, and to be seen therein by his fellow servants.[40] Instead of a robe of honor and outward glory, he was arrayed in this. When rational and irrational creation beholds any man clad in this likeness, it worships him as master, for the sake of its own master's honor, whom it beheld clad and walking therein. For what creature does not feel reverence at the spectacle of a humble man? And yet until the glory of humility was revealed to all, this vision that is filled with holiness was held in disdain. But now its majesty has dawned on the eyes of the world, and every person honors this likeness in every place where it is seen. In this mediator, creation has been counted worthy of receiving the vision of its Creator and Maker. Thus not even by the enemies of the truth is it despised. Even if he who has acquired it is the most impoverished of all creation, yet by it he is honored as though by the diadem and the purple. ASCETICAL HOMILIES 77.[41]

10:22 Full Assurance of Faith

LET US DRAW NEAR TO FAITH. CHRYSOSTOM: "Let us draw near," he says, "with a true heart." To what should we "draw near"? To the holy things, the faith, the spiritual service. "With a true heart, in full assurance of faith," since nothing is seen, neither the priest henceforward, nor

the sacrifice, nor the altar. And yet neither was the Old Testament priest visible, but stood within, and they all without, the whole people. But here not only has this taken place, that the priest has entered into the Holy of Holies, but that we also enter in. ON THE EPISTLE TO THE HEBREWS 19.2.[42]

WATER PURIFIES, THE SPIRIT SEALS. CYRIL OF JERUSALEM: For since a person's nature is two-fold, compounded of soul and body, the purification is also twofold, incorporeal for the incorporeal part, bodily for the body. For as the water purifies the body, so the Spirit seals the soul, that having our hearts sprinkled and our bodies washed with clean water, we may draw near to God. Therefore, when about to enter the water, do not regard it as mere water, but look for its saving power by the efficacy of the Holy Spirit, for without both you cannot be made perfect. It is not I who say this, but the Lord Jesus, who has the power in this matter, says, "Unless one is born of water and the Spirit, he cannot enter the kingdom of God."[43] Neither does he who is baptized but has not been deemed worthy of the Spirit possess perfect grace; nor will one who acts virtuously, but does not receive the seal by water, enter into the kingdom of heaven. This may appear a bold saying, but it is not mine, for it was Jesus who pronounced it. CATECHETICAL LECTURES 3.4.[44]

10:23-25 Stir Up One Another

WE MUST HOLD OUT IN HOPE. PSEUDO-CLEMENT OF ROME: Let us therefore serve God with a pure heart, and we shall be upright. But if, by not believing in God's promises, we do not serve him, we shall be wretched. For the word of the prophet says, "Wretched are the double-minded, those who doubt in their soul and say, 'We have heard these things long ago, even in our

---

[39]Ps 72:6 (71:6 LXX). [40]See Phil 2:7. [41]AHSIS 382. [42]NPNF 1 14:455*. [43]Jn 3:5. [44]FC 61:110.

fathers' times, and day after day we have waited and have seen none of them.' "[45] You fools! Compare yourselves to a tree. Take a vine: First it sheds its leaves, then comes a bud, and after this, a sour grape, then a ripe bunch. So my people too have had turmoils and troubles; but after that [they] will receive good things. So, my brothers and sisters, we must not be double-minded. Rather must we patiently hold out in hope so that we may also gain our reward. For "he can be trusted who promised" to pay each one the wages due for his work. If, then, we have done what is right in God's eyes, we shall enter his kingdom and receive the promises "what no eye has seen, nor ear heard, nor the heart of man conceived."[46] 2 CLEMENT 11.1-7.[47]

DOING HAS GREATER FORCE FOR INSTRUCTION THAN SPEAKING. CHRYSOSTOM: "For he who promised is faithful." "Promised" what? That we are to depart from here and enter into the kingdom. Do not then be over-curious nor demand reasonings. Our religion needs faith. "And," he says, "let us consider how to stir up one another to love and good works, not neglecting to meet together, as is the habit of some, but encouraging one another, and all the more as you see the day drawing near." And again in other places, "The Lord is at hand; have no anxiety about anything."[48] "For salvation is nearer to us now than when we first believed."[49]

What is, "not neglecting to meet together"? He knew that much strength arises from being together and assembling together. "For where two or three," it is said, "are gathered in my name, there am I in the midst of them";[50] and again, "That they may be one, even as we are";[51] and, "They were of one heart and soul."[52] And not this only, but also because love is increased by our gathering together, and, because love is increased, the things of God must follow. "And earnest prayer," it is said, was "made by" the people.[53] "As is the habit of some." Here he not only exhorted but also blamed them.

"And let us consider," he says, "how to stir up one another to love and good works." He knew

that this also arises from "meeting together." For as "iron sharpens iron,"[54] so also association increases love. For if a stone rubbed against a stone sends forth fire, how much more will soul mingled with soul! But not unto emulation, he says, but "unto the sharpening of love." What is this? It means to love more, and to be loved more. "And good works," that so they might acquire zeal. For if doing has greater force for instruction than speaking, you also have in your number many teachers who effect this by their deeds. ON THE EPISTLE TO THE HEBREWS 19.2-3.[55]

LOVE IS A HIGHWAY THAT LEADS TO VIRTUE. CHRYSOSTOM: This then let us "confirm" toward each other. "For love is the fulfilling of the law."[56] We have no need of labors or of sweatings if we love one another. It is a pathway leading of itself toward virtue. For on the highway, if one finds the beginning, he is guided by it and has no need of one to take him by the hand. So is it also in regard to love. Only lay hold on the beginning, and at once you are guided and directed by it. "Love does no wrong to a neighbor"[57] and "thinks no evil."[58] Let each person consider how he is disposed toward himself. He does not envy himself. He wishes all good things for himself. He prefers himself before all. He is willing to do all things for himself. If then we are so disposed toward others also, all grievous things are brought to an end; there is no enmity; there is no covetousness, for who would choose to overreach himself? No one. On the contrary, we shall possess all things in common and shall not cease assembling together. And if we do this, the remembrance of injuries would have no place, for who would choose to remember injuries against himself? Who would choose to be angry with himself? Do we not make allowances for ourselves most of all? If we were

---

[45]See 2 Pet 3:3-4. [46]1 Cor 2:9; cf. Is 64:4. [47]LCL 1:145-47. [48]Phil 4:5-6. [49]Rom 13:11. [50]Mt 18:20. [51]Jn 17:11. [52]Acts 4:32. [53]Acts 12:5. [54]Prov 27:17. [55]NPNF 1 14:455**. [56]Rom 13:10. [57]Rom 13:10. [58]1 Cor 13:6.

thus disposed toward our neighbors also, there will never be any remembrance of injuries. ON THE EPISTLE TO THE HEBREWS 19.4.[59]

EXERCISE IMPROVES STRENGTH. CHRYSOSTOM: Christ asks nothing impossible, seeing that many have even gone beyond his commands. Who has done this? Paul, Peter, all the company of the saints. Hardly. If I say that they loved their neighbors, I say no great matter, but they have loved their enemies. They have loved them even more than those who would think like themselves. For who would choose for the sake of those like-minded, to go away into hell when he was about to depart for a kingdom? No one. But Paul chose this for the sake of his enemies, for those who stoned him, those who scourged him. What pardon then will there be for us, what excuse, if we shall not show toward our friends even the very smallest portion of that love which Paul showed toward his enemies?

And before him too, the blessed Moses was willing to be blotted out of God's book for the sake of his enemies who had stoned him. David also, when he saw those slain who had stood up against him, said, "I, the shepherd, have sinned, but these, what have they done?"[60] And when he had Saul in his hands, he would not kill him but saved him—and this when he himself would be in danger.[61] But if these things were done under the old covenant, what excuse shall we have who live under the new covenant and do not attain even to the same measure with them? For if, "unless our righteousness exceeds that of the scribes and Pharisees, we will never enter the kingdom of heaven,"[62] how shall we enter when we have even less than they?

"Love your enemies," he says.[63] Love your enemy, therefore, for you are doing good not to your enemy but to yourself. How? You are becoming like God. One whom you love has no great gain, for he is loved by a fellow servant; but you, in loving your fellow servant, have gained much, for you are becoming like God. Do

you see that you are being kind not to him but to yourself? For he appoints the prize not for him but for you.

What if he is evil, you say? So much greater is the reward. You ought to feel grateful to him for his wickedness, even if he continues in his evil despite receiving ten thousand kindnesses. For if he were not exceedingly evil, your reward would not have been exceedingly increased. . . . That he is evil is the very reason for loving him. Take away the contestant, and you take away the opportunity for the crowns. Do you not see how the athletes exercise when they have filled the bags with sand? But there is no need for you to practice this; life is full of things that exercise you and make you strong. Do you not also see that the trees, the more they are shaken by the winds, become ever stronger and firmer? We then, if we are longsuffering, shall also become strong. ON THE EPISTLE TO THE HEBREWS 19.4-5.[64]

THEY DO NOT PERMIT ANY FAULT. PHOTIUS: "Let us stir up one another," concerning those things whose meddlesomeness and inquiry and observation sharpen us in love and edification. And they do this who do not permit any fault concerning one another but receive everything (even whatever things seem to be worse) for the good and the better. FRAGMENTS ON THE EPISTLE TO THE HEBREWS 10.24.[65]

THE COMFORT OF THE ASSEMBLY. PHOTIUS: "But encouraging." Whom?[66] "Their gathering together," that is, one another. For that is how "the gathering together" is commonly understood. And the comfort of the assembly becomes for them a way to be eagerly renewed and in a short space of time. FRAGMENTS ON THE EPISTLE TO THE HEBREWS 10.25.[67]

---

[59]NPNF 1 14:456**. [60]2 Sam 24:17. [61]1 Sam 24; 26:6-25. [62]Mt 5:20. [63]Mt 5:44. [64]NPNF 1 14:456**. [65]NTA 15:649. [66]RSV supplies "one another," which is not present in the Greek. [67]NTA 15:649.

UNITY IS THE WORK OF LOVE. THEODORET OF CYR: It is not separation but assiduous effort at unity that is the work of love. INTERPRETATION

of HEBREWS 10.[68]

[68]PG 82:753; TCCLSP 2:179.

10:26-39 SIN AND JUDGMENT, ENDURANCE AND LIFE BY FAITH

[26]*For if we sin deliberately after receiving the knowledge of the truth, there no longer remains a sacrifice for sins,* [27]*but a fearful prospect of judgment, and a fury of fire which will consume the adversaries.* [28]*A man who has violated the law of Moses dies without mercy at the testimony of two or three witnesses.* [29]*How much worse punishment do you think will be deserved by the man who has spurned the Son of God, and profaned the blood of the covenant by which he was sanctified, and outraged the Spirit of grace?* [30]*For we know him who said, "Vengeance is mine, I will repay." And again, "The Lord will judge his people."* [31]*It is a fearful thing to fall into the hands of the living God.*

[32]*But recall the former days when, after you were enlightened, you endured a hard struggle with sufferings,* [33]*sometimes being publicly exposed to abuse and affliction, and sometimes being partners with those so treated.* [34]*For you had compassion on the prisoners, and you joyfully accepted the plundering of your property, since you knew that you yourselves had a better possession and an abiding one.* [35]*Therefore do not throw away your confidence, which has a great reward.* [36]*For you have need of endurance, so that you may do the will of God and receive what is promised.*

[37]*"For yet a little while,*
and the coming one shall come and shall not tarry;
[38]*but my righteous one shall live by faith,*
and if he shrinks back,
my soul has no pleasure in him."
[39]*But we are not of those who shrink back and are destroyed, but of those who have faith and keep their souls.*

OVERVIEW: There is always room for repentance (OECUMENIUS), but only one cross (CHRYSOSTOM). Chrysostom encourages faithful living after communion. A fear of the upcoming judgment stimulates repentance that helps to escape the judgment (BASIL), although not all people assent to repentance (THEODORE). Chrysostom rebukes those who delay their baptism as they neglect repentance, the second washing, granted to us not by the law but by the gospel (ORIGEN, EPHREM). Struggle and suffering help us to attain self-control and to despise the vanity of wealth and honor; thus, they serve as a medicine for the soul. However, the devil tempts us to respond to the unavoidable sufferings with blasphemy rather than patience (CHRYSOSTOM). All the baptized are called to stand firm as good wrestlers (EPHREM, CHRYSOSTOM). It is the hope of the Lord's second coming that strengthens believers in their struggle and endurance (EUSEBIUS, CHRYSOSTOM, PHOTIUS); that hope is based on faith. The Lord will soon return as the righteous live by faith (THEODORET). The just live by faith, because they believe what they cannot see (AUGUSTINE, EPHREM). The believers are reminded to remember the days of persecution, when the Hebrews joyfully endured suffering as a community. What is closer to your ears than a heart that is penitent and a life founded on faith?

10:26-27 A Fearful Prospect of Judgment

IF WE SIN DELIBERATELY. THEODORET OF CYR: Now, it was not that he was ruling out repentance in these statements; rather, he was claiming there is no second sacrifice: our Lord was immolated for us once and for all. He used the term *deliberately* to emphasize that what is done against our free will enjoys a degree of pardon. INTERPRETATION OF HEBREWS 10.[1]

YET ANOTHER CHANCE OF REPENTANCE. CLEMENT OF ALEXANDRIA: So a person who has received pardon for sins must refrain from future sin. For in the light of the first and only repentance of sins—sins committed earlier in a person's first, pagan life, I mean, a life led in ignorance—repentance is immediately available to those who are called, and it cleanses the region of the soul from anything discordant to provide a foundation for faith. The Lord, "who knows the heart,"[2] and foreknowing all that is going to happen, has a foreknowledge from the very first of human instability and the devil's crooked villainy. [The Lord has knowledge] of how the latter is jealous of the forgiveness of human sins and, by his mischievous calculations to induce them to share in his fall, will introduce other occasions for God's servants to sin.

So in his great mercy he gave yet another chance of repentance to those who, despite their faith, fall into some form of disharmony, so that if anyone should, after their calling, fall into temptation and be forced or tricked into sin, they may have one more chance of "a repentance that brings no regret."[3] "For if we sin deliberately after receiving the knowledge of truth, there no longer remains a sacrifice for sins but a fearful prospect of judgment and a fury of fire which will consume the adversaries." Continual and repeated repentance for sins is no different from those who have once and for all turned away from faith, except alone in the consciousness of sin. I do not know which is worse: deliberate sin, or, after repentance for sin, offending again. . . . To repeat an action repented is a deliberate accomplishment of an action already condemned. STROMATEIS 2.13.56-57.[4]

A MORE WRATHFUL JUDGMENT. BASIL THE GREAT: Each one should conciliate, as far as he is able, anyone at variance with him. He should not hold past wrongs against the repentant sinner but from his heart should pardon him.[5] He who says that he repents of his sin should not only feel remorse for the sin which he has committed but should also bring forth fruits befitting repentance.[6] If he who has been corrected for his first sins and has been deemed worthy of pardon again falls, he prepares for himself a more wrathful judgment. LETTER 22.[7]

NO LONGER REFERS TO CHRIST'S SACRIFICE. CHRYSOSTOM: At this place we are again assailed by those who take away repentance as well as by those who delay to come to baptism. The one says that it is not safe to come to baptism, since there is no second remission. The other asserts that it is not safe to impart the mysteries to those who have sinned, if there is no second remission.

---

[1]PG 82:753; *TCCLSP* 2:179. [2]Acts 15:8. [3]2 Cor 7:10. [4]FC 85:197-98**. [5]2 Cor 2:7. [6]Lk 3:8. [7]FC 13:59.

What shall we say then to them both? The Lord does not thrust away or cast down those who are fallen into despair. Nor does he take away repentance or the propitiation itself through an act of repentance. He is not thus an enemy of our salvation. But what means "no longer"? He takes away the second washing. For he did not say that no more is there repentance or no more is there remission, but "no longer" is there a "sacrifice"; that is, there is no need for a second cross. For this is what he means by sacrifice. "For by a single offering," he says, "he has perfected for all time those that are sanctified,"[8] unlike the Jewish rites. For this reason he has so consistently shown, concerning the sacrifice, that it is one, and one only. This calls us to be more steadfast. ON THE EPISTLE TO THE HEBREWS 20.2.[9]

HE DOES NOT DESTROY THE POSSIBILITY OF REPENTANCE. OECUMENIUS: He did not speak of people who have sinned, but he addressed the reckless and desired to admonish those who wish to remain in sin until the end. Hence it is especially clear that he does not destroy the possibility of repentance. FRAGMENTS ON THE EPISTLE TO THE HEBREWS 10.26.[10]

ONE TAKES NO NOTICE OF STUMBLING. THEODORE OF MOPSUESTIA: Those who have changed from the better to the worse must in the end be handed over to punishment, when they rise from the dead, since they did not allow any repentance in this life. For not merely in the present life does such an individual abolish repentance, but by his inability to assent to repentance he remains content with his fall and takes no notice of his stumbling, accomplishing every sort of sin with much pleasure by a certain lack of reason. FRAGMENTS ON THE EPISTLE TO THE HEBREWS 10.26-27.[11]

10:28-29 Outraging the Spirit of Grace

LAW IN OPPOSITION TO BLOOD AND SPIRIT. THEODORET OF CYR: Once more, note, he brings out the difference under the guise of exhortation, namely, the Son in one case and the slave in the other, those sacrifices of brute beasts in one case and in the other this rational and all-holy sacrifice. To the law he set in opposition not a law but the "blood" and the "Spirit." Through them salvation comes to us. INTERPRETATION OF HEBREWS 10.[12]

A DIFFERENT DISPENSATION. ORIGEN: According to the law, "the adulterer and the adulteress were put to death."[13] They could not say, "We seek repentance and we pray for mercy." There was no place for tears, and no opportunity was granted for any correction, but in every way it was necessary for those who had contravened the law to be punished. This was observed in certain individual offenses for which the death penalty was ascribed. But among Christians, if adultery has been committed, the precept is not that "the adulterer and adulteress" be punished by the destruction of the body. No power was given to episcopal authority to sentence an adulterer to immediate death, as had happened earlier according to the levitical law who gave this power to elders. What does this mean? That while the law of Moses takes adultery seriously enough to punish it unmercifully, the gospel of Christ through gentleness frees the adulterer to go from bad to worse? It is not so. For this reason, we brought forth the word of Paul, saying above, "How much worse punishment will be deserved by one who has spurned the Son of God," etc. Hear, therefore, how neither was the law cruel then, nor does the gospel now appear dissolute because of the abundance of mercy, but in both instances the benevolence of God is held in a different dispensation. HOMILIES ON LEVITICUS 11.2.4.[14]

CONSIDERING THE GOSPEL TO BE EQUAL. EPHREM THE SYRIAN: And who have "outraged

---

[8]Heb 10:14. [9]NPNF 1 14:457**. [10]NTA 15:467. [11]NTA 15:209. [12]PG 82:753; TCCLSP 2:180. [13]Lev 20:10. [14]FC 83:213-14.

the Spirit of grace," which is in us? These are the people who consider the gospel to be equal to the law of Moses. COMMENTARY ON THE EPISTLE TO THE HEBREWS.[15]

OLD REPROACHES RETURN. ORIGEN: But if you sin again, the old reproaches return again against you and all the more so, since it is a much greater crime "to spurn the Son of God and to profane the blood of the covenant" than to neglect the law of Moses. HOMILIES ON JOSHUA 5.6.[16]

10:30-34 A Hard Struggle with Sufferings

THINK LIGHTLY OF WEALTH AND HONOR. CHRYSOSTOM: Knowing then these things, let us be patient when we suffer evil and forthright in offering kindness. This is all the stronger if we think lightly of wealth and honor. He that has stripped himself of those affections is of all people most generous and wealthier even than he who wears the purple. Do you not see how many evils come through money? I do not say how many through covetousness, but merely by our attachment to these things. Just think of one who loses his money and leads a life more wretched than any death. Why do you grieve, my friend? Why do you weep if God has delivered you from excessive watching? Better that you come before God in fear and trembling. Again, if someone might chain you to a treasure, commanding you to sit there perpetually and to keep watch for other people's goods, you are grieved, you are disgusted. But would you, having been bound with these chains, grieve when you yourself are delivered from the slavery? ON THE EPISTLE TO THE HEBREWS 20.5.[17]

THE DEVIL CAUSES LOSSES TO IMPEL US TO BLASPHEMY. CHRYSOSTOM: These things I say to the overreaching, and it is well to say them also to those who are overreached. Bear their overreaching generously; they are ruining themselves, not you. They indeed defraud you of your money, but they strip themselves of the good will and help of God. And he that is stripped of that, though he clothe himself with the whole wealth of the world, is of all people most poor, just as he who is the poorest of all, if he has God's help, is the wealthiest of all. For "the Lord," it is said, "is my shepherd, and I shall lack nothing."[18] Tell me now, if you had had a husband, a great and admirable man, who thoroughly loved you and cared for you, and then you knew that he would live always and not die before you and would give you all things to enjoy in security as your own, would you then have wished to possess anything? Even if you had been stripped of all, would you not have thought yourself the richer for this?

Why then do you grieve? Because you have no property? But consider that you have had the occasion of sin taken away. Or do you grieve because you had property and have been deprived of it? But remember that you have acquired the good will of God. And how have I acquired it, you say? He has said, "Why do you not rather suffer wrong?"[19] He has said, "Blessed are they who bear all things with thankfulness."[20] Consider therefore how great a good you will enjoy, if you show forth those things by your works. For one thing only is required from us, "in all things to give thanks"[21] to God, and then we have all things in abundance. I mean, for instance, have you lost ten thousand pounds of gold? Give thanks unto God, and you have acquired ten times ten thousand, by that word and thanksgiving.

For, tell me, when do you account Job blessed? When he had so many camels and flocks and herds, or when he uttered that saying: "The Lord gave, and the Lord has taken away"?[22] Therefore also the devil causes us losses, not that he may take away our goods only, for he knows that is nothing, but that through them he may compel

---

[15]EHA 220. [16]SC 71:172; COS 38. [17]NPNF 1 14:458-59*. [18]Ps 23:1 (22:1 LXX). [19]1 Cor 6:7. [20]Scriptural source unknown. [21]See Eph 5:20. [22]Job 1:21.

us to utter some blasphemy. So in the case of the blessed Job too, the devil did not strive after this only to make him poor but also to make him a blasphemer. At any rate, when he had stripped him of everything, observe what he says to him through his wife, "Curse God, and die."[23] And yet, O accursed one, you had stripped him of everything. "But," he says, "this is not what I was striving for, for I have not yet accomplished that for which I did it all. I was striving to deprive him of God's help. . . . This is what I wish, the other is nothing. If this be not gained, he not only has not been injured at all, but has even been benefited." Do you see that even that wicked demon knows how great is the loss in this matter? ON THE EPISTLE TO THE HEBREWS 20.7-8.[24]

AFTER DISCOURAGING THEM. EPHREM THE SYRIAN: Then, after he discouraged them from sinning, Paul returned to talk to them about the first topic, that is, that of the joy which was at the beginning of their discipleship. "Recall," he says, "the former days when, after you were enlightened, you endured a hard struggle with sufferings." COMMENTARY ON THE EPISTLE TO THE HEBREWS.[25]

HE DID NOT SAY "TEMPTATIONS" BUT "STRUGGLE." CHRYSOSTOM: The best physicians, after they have made a deep incision and have increased the pains by the wound, soothing the afflicted part and giving rest and refreshment to the disturbed soul, proceed not to make a second incision but rather soothe that which has been made with gentle remedies and such as are suited to remove the violence of the pain. This Paul also did after he had shaken their souls and pierced them with the recollection of hell and convinced them that he who does insult to the grace of God must certainly perish. After he had shown from the laws of Moses that they also shall perish . . . and had said, "It is a fearful thing to fall into the hands of the living God," then, lest the soul, desponding through excessive fear, should be swallowed up with

grief, he soothes them by commendations and exhortation and gives them zeal derived from their own conduct. For, he says, "recall the former days, when, after you had been enlightened, you endured a hard struggle with sufferings." Powerful is the exhortation from deeds already done, for he who begins a work ought to go forward and add to it. It is as if he had said, when you were brought in to the church, when you were in the rank of learners, you displayed such great readiness, such great nobleness. But now it is no longer so. And he who encourages thus especially encourages them from their own example.

And he did not simply say, "you endured a struggle" but a "hard" struggle. Moreover he did not say "temptations" but "struggle," which is an expression of commendation and of very great praise. Then he also enumerates them particularly, amplifying his discourse and multiplying his praise. How? "Sometimes," he says, you are "being publicly exposed to reproaches and affliction." Reproach is a heavy weight and calculated to pervert the soul and to darken the judgment. The prophet remembers those who "say to me continually, 'Where is your God?' "[26] . . . For since the human race is exceedingly vainglorious, it is easily overcome by this. And he did not simply say "by reproaches," but that even with greater intensity, being "publicly exposed." For when a person is reproached alone, it is indeed painful, but far more so when in presence of all. ON THE EPISTLE TO THE HEBREWS 21.1.[27]

SHAME TAKEN AWAY BY BAPTISM. EPHREM THE SYRIAN: Now "exposures to abuse and persecutions" they had to endure, because the law imposed on them the requirement to reveal their sins over their offerings. However, these exposures to abuse discouraged people from revealing their sins. These difficulties, he says, that you had in revealing your sins, and the shames that pre-

---

[23]Job 2:9. [24]NPNF 1 14:459-60*. [25]EHA 221. [26]Ps 42:10 (41:11 LXX). [27]NPNF 1 14:461**.

vented you from revealing them, these fumes of the consciousness, which were like fierce pains and great sufferings of bitterness—all these have been taken away from you through the baptism of the waters and with the single expiation that you received. COMMENTARY ON THE EPISTLE TO THE HEBREWS.[28]

AS NOBLE WRESTLERS YOU STOOD. CHRYSOSTOM: I cannot say, he says, that you suffered these things indeed and were grieved, but you even rejoiced exceedingly. He expressed this by saying, "You became partners with those so treated," and he brings forward the apostles themselves. Not only, he means, were you not ashamed of your own sufferings, but you even shared with others who were suffering the same things. This too is the language of one who is encouraging them. He said not, "Bear my afflictions, share with me," but respect your own.

"You had compassion on those who were bound." You see that he is speaking concerning himself and the rest who were in prison. Thus you did not account "bonds" to be bonds, but you stood as noble wrestlers. For not only did you need no consolation in your own distresses, but you even became a consolation to others. ON THE EPISTLE TO THE HEBREWS 21.2.[29]

10:35-37 Do Not Throw Away Your Confidence

THESE THINGS BESTOW CONFIDENCE ON US. PHOTIUS: "Do not throw away your confidence," your boldness based on your works, based on your faith, based on your periods of testing, based on your endurance. For these things bestow great confidence on us, that we will obtain the promise. FRAGMENTS ON THE EPISTLE TO THE HEBREWS 10.35.[30]

DO NOT FRET OVER LOSING WHAT DOES NOT NEED TO BE HELD FAST. CHRYSOSTOM: In the next place, having praised them, he says, "Therefore do not throw away your confidence,

which has a great reward." What do you mean? He did not say, "you have cast it away, and recovered it." Rather he tended more to strengthen them when he says, "you have it." For to recover again that which has been cast away requires more labor, but not to lose that which is held fast does not. To the Galatians he says the very opposite, "My little children, with whom I am again in travail until Christ be formed in you,"[31] and he says this with good reason, for they were more indifferent and needed a sharper word. These, however, were more faint-hearted, so that they rather needed what was more soothing. "Therefore do not throw away," he says, "your confidence," so that they were in great confidence toward God. "Which has," he says, "a great reward." "And when shall we receive them?" someone might say. "Behold! All things on our part have been done." Therefore he anticipated them on their own supposition, saying in effect, if you know that you have in heaven a better substance, seek nothing here. "For you have need of endurance," not of any addition to your labors, that you may continue in the same state, that you may not throw away what has been put into your hands. You need nothing else but to stand as you have stood, that when you come to the end, you may receive the promise. "For," he says, "you have need of endurance, so that you may do the will of God and receive what is promised." You have need of one thing only, to bear with the delay, not that you should fight again. You are at the very crown, he means. You have borne all the combats of bonds, of afflictions; your goods have been spoiled. What then? Henceforward you are standing to be crowned. Endure this only—the delay of the crown. Oh, the greatness of the consolation! It is as if one should speak to an athlete who had overthrown all and had no antagonist and then was to be crowned but could not show up for the ceremony in which the president of the games comes and places the crown upon him. Instead, he is so impatient that he wishes to go

---

[28]EHA 221. [29]NPNF 1 14:461*. [30]NTA 15:649. [31]Gal 4:19.

out and escape, as though he could not bear the thirst and the heat. He then also says, so as to hint in this direction: "Yet a little while and the coming one shall come and shall not tarry."[32] For lest they should say, "And when will he come?" he comforts them from the Scriptures. For thus also when he says in another place, "salvation is nearer,"[33] he comforts them, because the remaining time is short. And this he says not of himself but from the Scriptures. But if from that time it was said, "Yet a little while and the coming one shall come and shall not tarry," it is plain that now he is even nearer. ON THE EPISTLE TO THE HEBREWS 21.3.[34]

THE WILL OF GOD. PHOTIUS: "The will of God" is to believe sincerely in him and to do virtuous deeds and to contend for them even to the point of blood when the time calls. For such people "receive what is promised."[35] FRAGMENTS ON THE EPISTLE TO THE HEBREWS 10.36.[36]

THE COMING ONE SHALL COME. EUSEBIUS OF CAESAREA: And here it is clearly foretold that that one will come whom prophecy says will come. Who could this be but he who is referred to in the words, "Blessed is he that comes in the name of the Lord, the Lord God also has shone upon us"?[37] With which also Zechariah agrees, when he says, "Behold a man, the Dawn is his name, and he shall rise from below."[38] The same prophet too, noting the time, adds, "At eventide it shall be light. If he delays, wait for him."[39] Instead of this, Aquila reads, "If he tarry expect him, for he that comes will come and will not tarry." And the epistle to the Hebrews has this in mind. . . . But note how clearly the epistle arranges what was obscure in the prophetic writing, because of the inversion of the clauses. For the prophecy says, "He that comes will come and will not tarry," and then adds, "If he shrinks back, my soul has no pleasure in him." Without what follows, this addition would seem absurd. For how could it be said of the just that God takes no pleasure in him? But the placing side by side of

the divided clauses by a change in the arrangement of them preserves the sense. For after "Yet a little while, and the coming one shall come and shall not tarry," it adds next, "but my righteous one shall live by faith." Then what was first in the prophecy it places second, "and if he shrinks back, my soul has no pleasure in him."

For as Scripture has already once foretold through the prophecy that the light promised to all nations by Christ's coming "shall rise late and in the evening, and shall not deceive" (for so Aquila interprets instead of "come to nothing"), it next exhorts to patience, because the coming of the subject of the prophecy is to be late and in the evening, as seen in the words, "If he tarry await him, or if he delay expect him, for he that comes will come and will not tarry." Thus he encourages the hearer to trust the prediction, saying that he that trusts it, shown by his very faith to be just, shall live the life according to God. On the other hand, he that does not trust, drawing back through lack of boldness, and putting no faith in the words "My soul has no pleasure in him." So, then, if we follow this course and place the first clause last and the last first, we shall preserve the sense of the passage, putting "The just shall live by faith" after "For he that comes will come and will not tarry," by transposing the clauses and adding to this, "If he shrinks back, my soul has no pleasure in him." And Aquila agrees with this interpretation, saying, "If he delay, expect him, for he that comes will come and will not tarry. Lo, if he be sluggish, my soul is not true in him, and the just shall live by faith." PROOF OF THE GOSPEL 6.14.[40]

10:38-39 *Live by Faith*

THE RIGHTEOUS SHALL LIVE BY FAITH. THEODORET OF CYR: God has said this through the

---

[32]See Hab 2:3-4. [33]Rom 13:11. [34]NPNF 1 14:462*. [35]Heb 12:4. [36]NTA 15:650. [37]See Hab 2:2-4; cf. Ps 118:26 (117:26 LXX). [38]See Zech 6:12; RSV reads, "Behold, the man whose name is the Branch, for he shall grow up in his place." [39]See Zech 14:7. [40]POG 2:18-20*.

inspired authors, he is saying; and so even when the law was in force, the remedy of faith secured salvation. . . . Through faith we are related to God. Interpretation of Hebrews 10.[41]

The Soul Becomes Just by Sharing in the Better One. Augustine: "Faith working through love,"[42] comes not so much by fearing punishment as by loving justice. Still, as the soul does not become just except by sharing in the better one who justifies the ungodly—for what has it that it has not received?[43]—it ought not to glory as if it had not received it, by attributing to itself what comes from God. That is why it was said to him, "Be not high-minded, but fear." And that fear is also commanded for those who live by faith and are heirs of the new covenant, being "called to freedom." Letter 140.21.[44]

Clad in Justice. Augustine: "No man living is righteous before you,"[45] yet "the righteous one lives by faith." The saints are clad in justice,[46] one more, another less; yet no one lives here without sin. In this also, one more, another less, but he is best who has least sin. Letter 167.13.[47]

Founded on Faith. Augustine: What is closer to your ears than a heart that is penitent and a life founded on faith? Confessions 2.3.5.[48]

The Just Believe What They Cannot See. Augustine: Will there be any of us bold enough to say, "I am just"? I assume, after all, that "I am just" amounts to the same thing as "I am not a sinner." . . . Here we are with people who have been justified from their sins. We can't deny it. There remains, however, the struggle with the flesh, there remains the struggle with the world, there remains the struggle with the devil. When you are struggling, you sometimes hit, sometimes you get hit; sometimes you win, sometimes you're done for; it remains to be seen how you leave the stadium. Because "If we say we have no sin, we deceive ourselves, and the truth is not in us."[49]

Again, if we say we have no justice at all, we are telling a lie about God's gifts. You see, if we have no justice at all, we have no faith either; and if we have not faith, we are not Christians. But if we do have faith, we already have at least some justice. Do you want to know how much that "some" is? The just live by faith. The just, I repeat, live by faith, because they believe what they cannot see. Sermon 158.4.[50]

Until They Are Brought Face to Face. Augustine: This justice is the grace of the New Testament, by which the faithful are just while they live by faith until, by the perfection of justice, they are brought to the face-to-face vision, as they are also equally brought to immortality of the body itself by the perfection of salvation. Hence, in another place the apostle says, "So we are ambassadors for Christ, God making his appeal through us. We beseech you on behalf of Christ, be reconciled to God." And then he adds, "For our sake he made him to be sin who knew no sin"—that is, a sacrifice for sin, for in that law offerings made for sins were called sin—"so that in him we might become the righteousness of God,"[51] that is, in his body, which is the church, of which he is the head, that we may be the justice of God. Letter 140.30.[52]

We Have Faith Instead. Ephrem the Syrian: The just one lives when endurance and faith are found in that one. But if somebody is oppressed by doubts and scruples, because the rewarder did not appear, "my soul has no pleasure in him" on that day.

But we are not victims of scruples, which destroy our path to heaven and "bring us to perdition"; we have faith instead, through which we obtain "the salvation of our soul." Commentary on the Epistle to the Hebrews.[53]

[41]PG 82:756; TCCLSP 2:181. [42]Gal 5:6. [43]1 Cor 4:7. [44]FC 20:101*. [45]Ps 143:2. [46]Job 29:14. [47]FC 30:43*. [48]NPNF 1 1:56*. [49]1 Jn 1:8. [50]WSA 3 5:116. [51]2 Cor 5:20-21. [52]FC 20:122-23. [53]EHA 221-22.

11:1-7 BY FAITH

Now faith is the assurance of things hoped for, the conviction of things not seen. ²For by it the men of old received divine approval. ³By faith we understand that the world was created by the word of God, so that what is seen was made out of things which do not appear.

⁴By faith Abel offered to God a more acceptable sacrifice than Cain, through which he received approval as righteous, God bearing witness by accepting his gifts; he died, but through his faith he is still speaking. ⁵By faith Enoch was taken up so that he should not see death; and he was not found, because God had taken him. Now before he was taken he was attested as having pleased God. ⁶And without faith it is impossible to please him. For whoever would draw near to God must believe that he exists and that he rewards those who seek him. ⁷By faith Noah, being warned by God concerning events as yet unseen, took heed and constructed an ark for the saving of his household; by this he condemned the world and became an heir of the righteousness which comes by faith.

OVERVIEW: This chapter calls the roll of the Old Testament heroes of the faith. Without faith there is no understanding, for faith, which the Greeks think alien and useless, is in fact "the assurance of things hoped for, the conviction of things not seen" (CLEMENT OF ALEXANDRIA). If things are not seen, how can you be convinced that they exist? Where do the things come from, if not from the one whom you cannot see? The reason faith is greatly rewarded is that it does not see and yet believes. Faith does not falter, because it is supported by hope; if you take away hope, faith falters. If, from faith and hope, you withdraw love, what is the point of believing; what is the point of hoping, if you do not love? Indeed, you cannot even hope for anything you do not love (AUGUSTINE). Faith is the foundation of the church, and the faith in the risen Lord sustains many (CYRIL OF JERUSALEM). Faith supersedes human reason, as it penetrates the invisible substance of things. Furthermore, communal faith of the church is superior to individual. Seek God, but not despairingly. For the desperation of our search to see hidden reasons in God's purpose is transcended through simple faith.

The pattern of faith is seen in the history of the patriarchs and primitive heroes who believed God's promise (CHRYSOSTOM). That pattern extends from Abel, who spoke through his faith to Enoch, Moses and even to the woman from Canaan and Paul, all of whom sought God (EPHREM, ATHANASIUS, PACHOMIUS, CHRYSOSTOM). Often the figures and stories are typological allusions to Christ. The figures came first so their fulfillment could follow (LEO THE GREAT). It is only through faith that we join the church through the confession of a creed ("I believe") and thus are released from the bond of sin (BEDE). A sound faith of the church is the foundation of eternal salvation (LEO THE GREAT) as well as of personal morals (CYRIL OF JERUSALEM). Unlike our belief in God, our knowledge about God is limited (CHRYSOSTOM). Noah and Abraham are just two examples of faith that resulted in righteousness through faithful obedience to God's word (EPHREM, CHRYSOSTOM).

11:1-3 The Assurance of Things Hoped For

BECOMING GOD'S FRIENDS THROUGH FAITH.

THEODORET OF CYR: He shows both those before the law and those under the law becoming God's friends through faith and enjoying distinction. In this he achieves two things at the same time: he brings out the power of faith (faith accomplishing what the law did not achieve) and provides encouragement to those dispirited at the insurrections of the adversaries, showing everyone in possession of everlasting repute to have traveled through the same storms. First he teaches the very definition of faith: through it we see what is unseen, and it acts as an eye for discernment of what is hoped for. Faith depicts for us in advance the resurrection of those still lying dead in their tombs and causes the immortality of the dust of our bodies to become evident. INTERPRETATION OF HEBREWS 11.[1]

IF YOU DO NOT BELIEVE, YOU WILL NOT UNDERSTAND. CLEMENT OF ALEXANDRIA:
"Should your springs be scattered abroad, streams of water in the streets?"[2] "The majority do not turn their minds to the sort of things they encounter, and, if they are taught, they do not acquire knowledge, although they think they do." So says the admirable Heraclitus. Do you not realize that he is another critic of nonbelievers? "The righteous shall live by his faith," says the prophet.[3] One of the other prophets remarks, "If you do not believe, you emphatically will not understand either."[4] How could a soul come to the study of these things, itself exceptional, if, deep within, lack of faith over the teaching is fighting against it? Faith, which the Greeks think alien and useless and which they consequently malign, is in fact preconception by the will, an act of consenting to religion and, as the divine apostle puts it, "the assurance of things hoped for, the conviction of things not seen. For by it the men of old received divine approval." Without faith it is impossible to please God. STROMATEIS 2.2.8-9.[5]

JUSTIFICATION BY FAITH. THEODORE OF MOPSUESTIA: He has made use of many proofs, since he knew the Jews especially questioned faith by

means of a certain line of argument. For the Jews were setting forth the law and righteousness by their works, but Christians set forth faith, saying that even if someone should be guilty of ten thousand evils, by only believing in Christ he receives immediately deliverance from all of them, being deemed worthy of justification from him. Therefore, having determined this, then partly to appropriate the things that had been said before and partly to be able to show that faith appeared among all the virtuous men of old, he adds, "by faith the men of old received divine approval." FRAGMENTS ON THE EPISTLE TO THE HEBREWS 11.1-2.[6]

THE DELAY OF SALVATION STRENGTHENED FAITH. LEO THE GREAT: Rejoice that whatever the shadows of the Old Testament used to veil beneath the testimonies of prophets has been brought out into the open through the mystery of the Lord's passion. As a result, the various kinds of sacrifices and the different means of purification have come to a halt. Thus, the precept of circumcision, the distinction between foods, the sabbath rest, and the killing of the paschal lamb have ceased, since "the law was given through Moses, but grace and truth came through Jesus Christ."[7]

Figures came first so that their fulfillment could follow. When the reality which had been announced finally arrived, there was no longer any need for the services of heralds. Reconciliation of the human race was conducted in such a way that the salvation which comes in Christ should have been available to all generations under the same justification. Delaying this salvation was a calculated move. It had the advantage of causing those things which were believed long before they actually took place to be honored without interruption. When the strength of faith has been established in those things that do not lie open to our vision, heavenly doctrine treats us

---

[1]PG 82:757; *TCCLSP* 2:181. [2]Prov 5:16. [3]Hab 2:4. [4]Is 7:9 LXX. [5]FC 85:162. [6]NTA 15:210. [7]Jn 1:17.

more leniently. . . . To help us understand more easily, we benefit from many more prophets and witnesses than former ages. Sermon 69.2.[8]

Scripture Testifies About the Faith.
Ephrem the Syrian: Now our faith is not destroyed by despair because it was made firm by true hope. And there are witnesses who testify about it. In fact, even though faith was hidden from the people of the middle generation, it had nonetheless been revealed to those of the first. And there is a proof that reveals what is not evident. What proof? Certainly the one through which the testimony about the people of the first generation was made, that is, the narrative of scripture, that testified about the faith, through which the ancient fathers were put to test. Commentary on the Epistle to the Hebrews.[9]

Arouse the Reason in Your Heart.
Augustine: If they are not seen, how can you be convinced that they exist? Well, where do these things that you see come from, if not from one whom you cannot see? Yes, of course you see something in order to believe something, and from what you can see to believe what you cannot see. Please do not be ungrateful to the one who made you able to see; this is why you are able to believe what you are not yet able to see. God gave you eyes in your head, reason in your heart. Arouse the reason in your heart, get the inner inhabitant behind your inner eyes on his feet, let him take to his windows, let him inspect God's creation. Sermon 126.3.[10]

A Word to Catechumens About Faith.
Cyril of Jerusalem: "Now faith is the substance of things hoped for, the evidence of things not seen. For by it the elders obtained a good report." Notice how great a dignity the Lord bestows on you in transferring you from the order of catechumens to that of the faithful. The apostle Paul says as much when he affirms, "God is faithful, by whom you were called into the fellowship of his son Jesus Christ."[11] Since God is here

called faithful, you also in receiving this title receive a great dignity. God is called faithful in the same way that he is called good, just, almighty and maker of the universe. Consider therefore to what kind of dignity you are rising, seeing you are to become a partaker of a title of God.

Here, then, it is further required that each of you be found faithful in his conscience: "for a faithful man it is hard to find"[12]—not that you need to reveal to me what is on your conscience, for you are not to be "judged by man's judgment."[13] But you are supposed to show the sincerity of your faith to God, "who tries the reins and hearts"[14] and "knows the thoughts of men."[15] A faithful person is a great thing, being richest of all rich people. For "to the faithful person belongs the whole world of wealth,"[16] in that he disdains and tramples on it. For they who in appearance are rich and have many possessions are poor in soul: since the more they gather, the more they pine with longing for what is still lacking. But the faithful person (a strange paradox, indeed) is rich in poverty. Such a person knows that we only need to have "food and clothing" and, being "content with these,"[17] he has trampled riches under foot. Catechetical Lectures 5.1-2.[18]

Faith Sustains Many. Cyril of Jerusalem: It is not only among those of us who bear the name of Christ that the dignity of faith is great. Rather, all things that are accomplished in the world, even by those who are strangers to the church, are accomplished by faith. By faith the laws of marriage yoke together those who have lived as strangers. Because of the faith in marriage contracts, a stranger is made partner of another stranger's person and possessions. By faith, farmers are also sustained, for the one who does not believe that he shall receive a harvest is not going to endure the work. By faith seafaring men, trusting to the thinnest plank,

---

[8]FC 93:301. [9]EHA 222. [10]WSA 3 4:270-71. [11]1 Cor 1:9. [12]Prov 20:6. [13]1 Cor 4:3. [14]Ps 7:9 (7:10 LXX). [15]Ps 94:11 (93:11 LXX). [16]Prov 17:6 LXX. [17]1 Tim 6:8. [18]NPNF 2 7:29*.

exchange that most solid element, the land, for the restless motion of the waves, committing themselves to uncertain hopes and carrying with them a faith more sure than any anchor. By faith therefore most of men's affairs are held together: and not among us only has there been this belief, but also, as I have said, among those who are outside the church. For if they receive not the Scriptures but bring forward certain doctrines of their own, even these they accept by faith. Catechetical Lectures 5.3.[19]

Prophecy Seen in Long Time Frame. Chrysostom: But I will make the matter more plain by an example. Christ said that Jerusalem should be taken and should be so taken as no city ever was before, and that it should never be raised up, and in fact this prediction came to pass. He said that there should be "great tribulation,"[20] and it came to pass. He said that, as a grain of mustard seed is sown,[21] so should the preaching of the gospel be extended, and every day we see this happening over the world. He said that they who left father or mother or brothers or sisters should have both fathers and mothers,[22] and this we see fulfilled by facts. He said, "In the world you have tribulation, but be of good cheer; I have overcome the world";[23] that is, no one shall get the better of you. And this we see by events has come to pass. He said that "the gates of hell shall not prevail against the church,"[24] even though persecuted, and that no one shall quench the preaching of the gospel; and the experience of events bears witness to this prediction also. And yet, when he said these things, it was very hard to believe him. Why? Because all these were words, and he had not as yet given proof of the things spoken. So that they have now become far more credible. He said that "the gospel will be preached throughout the whole world, then the end will come."[25] Lo! Now you have arrived at the end, for the greater part of the world has been preached to; therefore, the end is now at hand. Let us tremble, beloved. But what, tell me? Are you anxious about the end? It indeed is itself near, but each person's life and death is nearer. For it is said,

"The days of our years are seventy years; but if one be in strength, fourscore years."[26] The day of judgment is near. Let us fear. "A brother does not redeem; shall man redeem?"[27] There we shall repent much, "but in death no man shall praise him."[28] Wherefore he says, "Let us come into his presence with thanksgiving,"[29] that is, his coming. For here in this life indeed, whatever we do has efficacy; but there, no longer. Tell me, if a person placed us for a little while in a flaming furnace, should we not submit to anything in order to escape, even were it necessary to part with our money or to undergo slavery? How many have fallen into grievous diseases and would gladly give up all to be delivered from them, if the choice were offered them? If in this world, then, a disease of short duration so afflicts us, what shall we do yonder, when repentance will be of no avail? On the Epistle to the Hebrews 21.5-6.[30]

Your Hands Are Not Empty. Augustine: When you hope, you do not yet have what you are hoping for, but, by believing it, you resemble someone who does possess it. For faith will eventually take hold, but our very faith stands for the thing itself. I mean, you do not have your hands on anything when you have them on faith, nor are they empty if they are full of faith. The reason faith is greatly rewarded is that it does not see and yet believes. I mean, if it could see, what reward would there be? . . . But faith does not falter, because it is supported by hope. Take away hope, and faith falters. How, after all, when you are walking somewhere, will you even move your feet, if you have no hope of ever getting there? If, though, from each of them, that is from faith and hope, you withdraw love, what is the point of believing; what is the point of hoping, if you do not love? Indeed, you cannot even hope for anything you do not love. Love, you see, kindles

[19]NPNF 2 7:29*. [20]Mt 24:21. [21]Mt 13:31-32; Lk 13:18-19. [22]Mt 19:29. [23]Jn 16:33. [24]Mt 16:18. [25]Mt 24:14. [26]Ps 90:10 (89:10 LXX). [27]See Ps 49:7 (48:8 LXX). [28]Ps 6:5 (6:6 LXX). [29]Ps 95:2 (94:2 LXX). [30]NPNF 1 14:463*.

hope; hope shines through love. But when we attain the things that we have been hoping for while believing in and not seeing them, what faith will there be then to be praised? Considering that "faith is the conviction of things not seen," when we do see, it will not be called faith. After all, you will be seeing, not believing. Sermon 359A.3-4.[31]

Faith Is the Substance. Chrysostom: Oh, what an expression has he used in saying "an evidence of things not seen." For we say there is "evidence" in the case of things that are very plain. Faith then is seeing things not plain, he means, and brings what are not seen to the same full assurance with what are seen. So then neither is it possible to disbelieve in things which are seen, nor, on the other hand, can there be faith unless a person is more fully assured with respect to things invisible than he is with respect to things that are most clearly seen. For since the objects of hope seem to be unsubstantial, faith gives them substantiality or, rather, does not give it, but is itself their substance. For instance, the resurrection has not come, nor does it exist substantially, but hope makes it substantial in our soul. This is the meaning of "the substance of things."

If therefore it is an "evidence of things not seen," why do you wish to see them, so as to fall away from faith and from being just? Since "the just shall live by faith," you, if you wish to see these things, are no longer faithful. You have labored, he says; you have struggled. I too allow this; nevertheless, wait, for this is faith. Do not seek the whole "here." On the Epistle to the Hebrews 21.4.[32]

Our Mutual Faith. Chrysostom: Faith needs a generous and vigorous soul, one rising above all things of sense and passing beyond the weakness of human reasonings. For it is not possible to become a believer otherwise than by raising one's self above the common customs of the world. Inasmuch then as the souls of the Hebrews were thoroughly weakened—though they had begun from faith, yet from circumstances, I mean sufferings, afflictions, they had afterwards become faint-hearted and of little spirit and were shaken from their position—he encouraged them first indeed from these very things, saying, "Recall the former days";[33] next from the Scripture, saying, "But the righteous shall live by faith";[34] afterwards from arguments, saying, "But faith is the substance of things hoped for, the evidence of things not seen." And now again from their forefathers, those great and admirable people, as much as saying, "If, where the good things were close at hand, all were saved by faith, much more are we."

For when a soul finds one that shares its same sufferings, it is refreshed and recovers breath. This we may see both in the case of faith and in the case of affliction, "that we may be mutually encouraged by each other's faith."[35] For people are very distrustful, cannot place confidence in themselves, are fearful about whatever things they think they possess and have great regard for the opinion of the many.

What then does Paul do? He encourages them by the patriarchs. . . . Since faith is slandered as being a thing that cannot be demonstrated and rather a matter of deceit, he shows that the greatest things are attained through faith and not through reasonings. And how does he show this, tell me? It is manifest, he says, that God made the things which are out of things which are not, things which appear out of things which appear not, things which subsist out of things which subsist not. But where is it shown that he did this even "by a Word"? For reason suggests nothing of this kind, but, on the contrary, suggests that the things that appear are formed out of things that appear.

Therefore the philosophers expressly say that "nothing comes out of things that are not being sensual"[36] and trusting nothing to faith. And yet these same people, when they happen to say anything great and noble, are caught entrusting it to

---

[31]*WSA* 3 10:210-11*. [32]NPNF 1 14:462-63*. [33]Heb 10:32. [34]Heb 10:38. [35]Rom 1:12. [36]Jude 18.

faith. For instance: They say that "God is without beginning and unborn"—yet reason does not suggest this, but the contrary. Consider how great their folly, I ask you. They say that God is without beginning, and yet this is far more wonderful than the creation out of things that are not. For to say that he is without beginning, that he is unborn, neither begotten by himself nor by another is more full of difficulties than to say that God made the things which are out of things which are not. For here there are many things uncertain, as that some one made it, that what was made had a beginning, that, in a word, it was made. But in the other case, what? He is self-existing, unborn; he neither had beginning nor time. Tell me, do not these things require faith? But he did not assert this, which was far greater, but the lesser. How does it appear, he would say, that God made these things? Reason does not suggest it. No one was present when it was done. How is it shown? It is plainly the result of faith. "By faith we understand that the world was created." Why "by faith"? Because "the things that are seen were not made of things which do appear." For this is faith. ON THE EPISTLE TO THE HEBREWS 22.1-2.[37]

CREATED BY GOD. THEODORET OF CYR: The body's eye did not recognize the God of all as creator; instead faith instructed us that God, who has always existed, created what did not exist. There is, after all, no example of this among human beings; yet though learning nothing of the kind from nature, we have in faith a teacher of the unexpected. Human beings, of course, make something out of something, whereas the God of all produced what exists out of nothing. INTERPRETATION OF HEBREWS 11.[38]

11:4 Cain and Abel

ABEL TALKS THROUGH HIS FAITH. EPHREM THE SYRIAN: "By faith Abel offered to God a more acceptable sacrifice than Cain," who brought offerings selected without care. The faith

of Abel and the infidelity of Cain were sealed up in their offerings. If Abel had not believed in the promise, he would not have chosen and brought the best offerings. He had actually seen his brother, who picked up everywhere the vile ears [vegetable offerings] with contempt and offered them by laying them on the altar. For that faith Abel "obtained testimony" about himself "that he was righteous" and certainly not from a human being but from God, "who testified of his gifts," so that up to this time Abel talks through his faith, that is, is put to test through it. COMMENTARY ON THE EPISTLE TO THE HEBREWS.[39]

STILL SPEAKING. THEODORET OF CYR: The phrase "he is still speaking" means, To this day he is famous and celebrated and enjoys a good name among all religious people. INTERPRETATION OF HEBREWS 11.[40]

THROUGH FAME, GLORY, MEMORY. OECUMENIUS: "He speaks" by his fame, by his glory and by his memory. FRAGMENTS ON THE EPISTLE TO THE HEBREWS 11.4.[41]

THROUGH IT HE STILL SPEAKS. PHOTIUS: "Although he died, through it he still speaks,"[42] that is, because his very sacrifice furnished his brother with an opportunity for malice and jealousy, and his brother produced murder. Even if "he died," "through it he speaks." For this very reason Abel was always to be remembered and never forgotten. If someone should investigate both matters more accurately, the phrase "through it" (as is commonly understood) applies equally to "dying" and to "he speaks."

He still speaks. He is always to be remembered. He says that Abel's deed done in faith does not allow him to fall into obscurity. FRAGMENTS ON THE EPISTLE TO THE HEBREWS 11.4.[43]

---

[37]NPNF 1 14:465*. [38]PG 82:757; TCCLSP 2:181-82. [39]EHA 222-23. [40]PG 82:757; TCCLSP 2:182. [41]NTA 15:467. [42]RSV supplies "faith." The Greek (di' autēs) simply has the preposition (through) and a personal pronoun (it). [43]NTA 15:650.

11:5-6 God Rewards Those Who Seek God

HE EXISTS AND REWARDS. THEODORET OF CYR: The one who does not believe that this is so does not put up with the hardships of virtue; the farmer would not sustain the sweat of farming unless he believed he would gather the fruits of his labors; likewise the steersman puts up with untold dangers only by keeping his eyes on the harbors. INTERPRETATION OF HEBREWS 11.[44]

PAUL TEACHES US TO SEEK GOD. ATHANASIUS: With the aid of your prayers, I hope to give a true picture of the plans of Paul, that holy man. He was very knowledgeable and skilled in these matters of God, and he knew the power of the Lord's teaching. So he deemed it necessary to teach first about Christ and the mystery of the incarnation. Only then did he point to things in their lives that needed to be corrected. He wanted them first to know the Lord and then to want to do what he told them. For if you don't know the one who leads the people in observing God's commands, you are not very likely to obey them.

Moses, that famous and faithful minister of God, used this method. When he set forth those things having to do with the divine system of laws, he first dealt with the knowledge of God, "Hear, O Israel, the Lord your God is one Lord."[45] Then, after describing God to the people, teaching them about the one in whom they should believe, and informing them concerning the one who is truly God—only then did he tell how a person can please God. Only then did he say, "You shall not commit adultery; you shall not steal," and the other commandments. The reason for this order of teaching is given to us in the apostolic writings. God is sought by godly and righteous acts, as the prophet tells us.[46] FESTAL LETTERS 11.3.[47]

A LIST OF BIBLICAL IRONIES SHOWING WHERE TO SEEK GOD. PACHOMIUS: Become guileless and be like the guileless sheep whose wool is sheared off without their saying a word. Do not go from one place to another, saying, "I will find God here or there." God has said, "Do I not fill heaven and earth?"[48] and again, "When you pass through the waters, I will be with you";[49] and again, "The rivers shall not overwhelm you."[50] My son, be aware that God is within you, so that you may dwell in God's law and commandments. Behold, the thief was on the cross, and he entered paradise; but behold, Judas was among the apostles, and he betrayed his Lord. Behold, Rahab was in prostitution, and she was numbered among the saints; but behold, Eve was in paradise, and she was deceived. Behold, Job was on the dung heap, and he was compared with his Lord; but behold, Adam was in paradise, and he fell away from the commandment. Behold, the angels were in heaven, and they were hurled into the abyss; but behold Elijah and Enoch, who were raised into the kingdom of heaven. "Seek the Lord and his strength, seek his presence continually!"[51] Seek God out like Abraham, who obeyed God and offered his son in sacrifice to God, who called him "my friend." Seek God out like Joseph, who did battle against impurity, so that he was made ruler over his enemies. Seek him out like Moses, who followed his Lord, and God made him lawgiver and let him come to know God's own likeness. Daniel sought God out, and God taught him great mysteries; God saved him from the lions' gullet. The three saints sought God out and found God in the fiery furnace. Job took refuge with God, and God cured him of his sores. Susanna sought God out, and God saved her from the hands of the wicked. Judith sought God out and found God in the tent of Holofernes. All these sought God out, and God delivered them; and God delivered others also. INSTRUCTIONS 1.25.[52]

INTRODUCED AGAIN TO THE HOUSE. EPHREM

---

[44]PG 82:760; TCCLSP 2:182. [45]Deut 6:4. [46]Is 55:6-7. [47]NPNF 2 4:533**. [48]Jer 23:24. [49]Is 43:2. [50]Is 43:2. [51]Ps 105:4 (104:4 LXX). [52]CS 47:23-24*.

THE SYRIAN: "By faith Enoch was taken up and did not taste death." If he had not believed that the observation of the commandment could introduce him again to the place from which the house of Adam had come out because of the transgression, he would not have applied himself to please God for three hundred years. In fact, "without faith," that is, if that person did not believe that the true God exists and "rewards those who seek him," he would have never tried to please and seek him. COMMENTARY ON THE EPISTLE TO THE HEBREWS.[53]

FAITH WAS THE CAUSE OF ENOCH'S PLEASING GOD. CHRYSOSTOM: How was it "by faith" that "Enoch was taken up"? Because his pleasing God was the cause of his being taken, and faith the cause of his pleasing God. For if he had not known that he should receive a reward, how could he have pleased God? But "without faith it is impossible to please" God. How? If a person believes that there is a God and a retribution, that person will have the reward. ON THE EPISTLE TO THE HEBREWS 22.4.[54]

THE WOMAN FROM CANAAN. ATHANASIUS: Jesus continually nourished his believing disciples with his words and gave them life by his closeness. But when the woman from Canaan asked for help, he did not answer her,[55] because she was not yet a believer—even though she desperately needed food from him. He behaved this way not because he despised her; far from it. For the Lord is loving and good to humankind. That is why he went to Tyre and Sidon in the first place. No, it was because she did not believe, because she was an impious woman who had no idea of God's requirements.

What he did was most appropriate, brothers and sisters, because it was not right for her to put her request before faith. Rather, she needed to support her prayer by her faith. For "whoever would draw near to God must believe that he exists and that he rewards those who seek him"; and that "without faith it is impossible to please him." That

is what Paul teaches. FESTAL LETTERS 9.7.[56]

FREEING THEMSELVES FROM THE BONDS OF ORIGINAL GUILT. BEDE: And so that the favors of heavenly condescension might not be lacking to any period of this transitory world, those who lived from the inception of the world up to the time of the giving of circumcision, and those from other countries who lived after the giving of circumcision, also pleased God. [They did so] either by the offering of sacrificial offerings or alternatively by the virtue of faith alone, since they committed their souls and those of their own to the Creator, and so [they] took care to free themselves from the bonds of the original guilt. For "without faith it is impossible to please God." And as it is written in another place, "The just person lives by faith."[57] HOMILIES ON THE GOSPELS 1.11.[58]

THE CREDAL "I BELIEVE." RUFINUS: "I believe," therefore, is placed in the forefront [of the Apostles' Creed], as the apostle Paul, writing to the Hebrews, says, "The one who comes to God must first of all believe that he is, and that he rewards those who believe on him." The prophet also says, "Unless you believe,[59] you shall not understand." In order that the way to understand, therefore, may be open to you, you do the right thing in first of all professing that you believe. For no one embarks upon the sea and trusts himself to the deep and liquid element unless he first believes it is possible that he will have a safe voyage. The farmer does not commit his seed to the furrows and scatter his grain on the earth unless he believes that the showers will come together with the sun's warmth, through whose fostering influence, aided by favorable winds, the earth will produce and multiply and ripen its fruits. In essence, nothing in life can be transacted if there is not first a readiness to believe.

Is it any wonder then that when we come to

[53]EHA 223. [54]NPNF 1 14:467*. [55]Mt 15:22-24. [56]NPNF 2 4:526. [57]Hab 2:4. [58]CS 110:105*. [59]Cf. Dan 12:10; Is 7:9 LXX.

God, we first of all profess that we believe, seeing that, without this, not even common life can be lived? We have premised these remarks at the outset, since the pagans are wont to object to us that our religion, because it lacks reasons, rests solely on belief. We have shown, therefore, that nothing can possibly be done or remain stable unless it is preceded by belief. Finally, marriages are contracted in the belief that children will be born; and children are committed to the care of teachers in the belief that the teaching of these teachers will be transferred to the pupils. In the same way, one person assumes the emblems of empire, believing that peoples and cities and a well-equipped army also will obey him. But if no one enters upon any one of these several undertakings except in the belief that the results spoken of will follow, must not belief be much more requisite if one would come to the knowledge of God? COMMENTARY ON THE APOSTLES' CREED 3.[60]

A SOUND AND UNIFIED FAITH. LEO THE GREAT: A sound faith is a mighty bulwark, a true faith to which nothing has to be added or taken away. Unless it is one, it is no faith, as the apostle says, "one Lord, one faith, one baptism, one God and Father of all, who is above all, and through all, and in us all."[61] Cling to this unity, dearly beloved, with minds unshaken, and "follow after" all "holiness"[62] in faith. Carry out the Lord's commands in faith because "without faith it is impossible to please God." Without faith nothing is holy, nothing is pure, nothing alive: "for the just lives by faith."[63] The one who, by the devil's deception, loses it is dead even though he is living because, as righteousness is gained by faith, so too by a true faith eternal life is gained. This is exactly what our Lord and Savior says, "And this is life eternal, that they may know you, the only true God, and Jesus Christ, whom you have sent."[64] May he make you to advance and persevere to the end, who lives and reigns with the Father and the Holy Spirit, forever and ever. Amen. SERMON 25.6.[65]

FAITH IS THE EYE THAT ENLIGHTENS CONSCIENCE. CYRIL OF JERUSALEM: The lesson also which was read today invites you to the true faith, by setting before you the way in which you also must please God. It affirms that "without faith it is impossible to please him." For when will an individual resolve to serve God, unless he believes that "He is a giver of reward"? When will a young woman choose a virgin life, or a young man live soberly, if they don't believe that for chastity there is "a crown that does not fade away"?[66] Faith is an eye that enlightens every conscience and imparts understanding. The prophet says, "And if you do not believe, you shall not understand."[67] Faith "stops the mouths of lions,"[68] as in Daniel's case, for Scripture says concerning him, "Daniel was brought up out of the den, and he was found to be hurt in no way, because he believed in his God."[69] Is there anything more fearful than the devil? Yet even against him we have no other shield than faith, an impalpable buckler against an unseen foe. For he sends forth various arrows and "shoots down in the dark night"[70] those that are not watching. However, since the enemy is unseen, we have faith as our strong armor, according to the saying of the apostle, "In all things taking the shield of faith with which you shall be able to quench all the fiery darts of the wicked one."[71] A fiery dart of desire to indulge one's baser instincts is often shot from the devil's bow. But faith, suggesting a picture of the judgment, cools down the mind and quenches the dart. CATECHETICAL LECTURES 5.4.[72]

GOD REWARDS THOSE WHO SEEK HIM. CHRYSOSTOM: It is necessary to "believe that God is," not "what God is." If "that God is" needs faith and not reasonings, it is impossible to comprehend by reasoning "what God is." If that "God is a rewarder" needs faith and not reasonings, how is it possible by reasoning to compass God's es-

---

[60]NPNF 2 3:543*. [61]Eph 4:5-6. [62]Cf. Heb 12:14. [63]Hab 2:4. [64]See Jn 17:3. [65]NPNF 2 12:136*. [66]1 Pet 2:4. [67]Is 7:9 LXX. [68]Heb 11:34. [69]Dan 6:23. [70]Ps 11:2 (10:2 LXX). [71]Eph 6:16. [72]NPNF 2 7:29-30*.

sence? For what reasoning can reach this? For some persons say that the things that exist are self-caused. Do you see that, unless we have faith in regard to all things—not only in regard to retribution but also in regard to the very being of God—all is lost to us?

But many ask about where Enoch was translated, and why he was translated, and why he did not die, neither he nor Elijah, and, if they are still alive, how they live, and in what form. But to ask these things is superfluous. For that the one was translated, and that the other was taken up, the Scriptures have said; but where they are, and how they are, they have not added, for they say nothing more than is necessary. For this indeed took place, I mean his translation, immediately at the beginning, the human soul thereby receiving a hope of the destruction of death, and of the overthrow of the devil's tyranny, and that death will be done away; for he was translated, not dead, but "that he should not see death." Therefore, he added, he was translated alive, because he was well pleasing unto God. . . . A father, when he has threatened his son, wishes indeed immediately after he has threatened to relax his threat but endures and continues resolute, that for a time he may chasten and correct him, allowing the threat to remain firm. So also God, to speak, as it were, after the manner of men, did not continue resolute but immediately showed that death is done away. And first God allows death to happen, wishing to terrify the father through the son: For, wishing to show that the sentence is verily fixed, God subjected to this punishment not wicked people at once, but even him who was well-pleasing, I mean, the blessed Abel; and almost immediately after him, God translated Enoch. Moreover, God did not raise the former, lest they should immediately grow bold; but God translated the other being yet alive, having excited fear by Abel, but by this latter giving zeal to be well pleasing unto God. Therefore they who say that all things are ruled and governed of themselves and do not expect a reward are not well pleasing; as neither are the heathen. For "God becomes a rewarder of

them that diligently seek God" by works and by knowledge. ON THE EPISTLE TO THE HEBREWS 22.5.[73]

SEEK GOD BUT NOT DESPAIRINGLY. CHRYSOSTOM: Since then we have "a rewarder," let us do all things that we may not be deprived of the rewards of virtue. For indeed the neglecting of such a recompense, the scorning of such a reward, is worthy of many tears. For as to "those who diligently seek God," God is a rewarder. But to those who do not seek God, the contrary.

"Seek," he says, "and you will find,"[74] but how can we find the Lord? Consider how gold is found, with much labor. "I sought the Lord with my hands," it is said, "by night before God, and I was not deceived,"[75] that is, just as we seek what is lost, so let us seek God. Do we not concentrate our mind thereon? Do we not inquire of every one? Do we not travel from home? Do we not promise money?

For instance, suppose that any one among us has lost a son. What do we not do? What land, what sea do we not make the circuit of? Do we not reckon money and houses and everything else as secondary to finding him? And should we find him, we cling to him, we hold him fast; we do not let him go. And when we are going to seek anything whatever, we busy ourselves in all ways to find what is sought. How much more ought we to do this in regard to God, as seeking what is indispensable; no, rather, not in the same way, but much more! But since we are weak, at least seek God as you seek your money or your son. Will you not leave your home for God? Have you never left your home for money? Do you not busy yourself in all ways? When you have found it, are you not full of confidence?

"Seek," he says, "and you will find." For things sought after need much care, especially in regard of God. For many are the hindrances, many the things that darken, many the things that impede

---

[73]NPNF 1 14:467*. [74]Mt 7:7. [75]Ps 77:2 (76:3 LXX); cf. Ps 76:3 (75:4 LXX).

our perception. For as the sun is manifest and set forth publicly before all, we have no need to seek it; but if, on the other hand, we bury ourselves and turn everything upside down, we need much labor to look at the sun. So truly here also, if we bury ourselves in the depth of evil desires, in the darkness of passions and of the affairs of this life, we look up with difficulty, we raise our heads with difficulty, we see clearly with difficulty. Whoever is buried underground, in whatever degree that one sees upwards, in that degree does that one come towards the sun. Let us therefore shake off the earth; let us break through the mist that lies upon us. It is thick and close and does not allow us to see clearly.

And how, you say, is this cloud broken through? If we draw to ourselves the beams of "the sun of righteousness." "The lifting up of my hands," it is said, "is an evening sacrifice."[76] With our hands let us also lift up our mind. You who have been initiated know what I mean; perhaps too you recognize the expression and see at a glance what I have hinted at. Let us raise up our thoughts on high.

I myself know many people almost suspended apart from the earth, and beyond measure stretching up their hands, and out of heart because it is not possible to be lifted into the air, and thus praying with earnestness. Thus I would have you always praying with earnestness and, if not always, at least very often; and if not very often, at least now and then, at least in the morning, at least in the evening prayers. For tell me, can you not stretch forth the hands? Stretch forth the will, stretch forth as far as you will, yes, even to heaven itself. Even should you wish to touch the very summit, even if you would ascend higher and walk there, it is open to you. For our mind is lighter and higher than any winged creature. And when it receives grace from the Spirit, oh, how swift is it! How quick is it! How does it compass all things! How does it never sink down or fall to the ground! Let us provide these wings for ourselves. By means of them shall we be able to fly even across the tempestuous sea of this present life. The swiftest birds fly unhurt over mountains and woods and seas and rocks in a brief moment of time. Such also is the mind; when it is winged, when it is separated from the things of this life, nothing can lay hold of it; it is higher than all things, even than the fiery darts of the devil. On the Epistle to the Hebrews 22.6-7.[77]

In Faith the Devil Is Disarmed. Chrysostom: The devil is not so good a marksman as to be able to reach this height; he sends forth his darts, indeed, for he is void of all shame, yet he does not hit the mark; the dart returns to him without effect, and not without effect only, but it falls upon his own head. For what is sent forth by him must of necessity strike something. As, then, that which has been shot out by humans either strikes the person against whom it is directed or pierces bird or fence or garment or wood or the mere air, so does the dart of the devil also. It must of necessity strike, and, if it strikes not the one that is shot at, it necessarily strikes the one that shoots it. And we may learn from many instances that, when we are not hit, without doubt the devil is hit himself. For instance, he plotted against Job; he did not hit him but was struck himself. He plotted against Paul; he did not hit him but was struck himself. If we watch, we may see this happening everywhere. For even when he strikes, he is hit—much more then when he does not hit.

Let us then turn the devil's weapons against him, and, having armed and fortified ourselves with the shield of faith, let us keep guard with steadfastness, so as to be impregnable. Now the dart of the devil is evil concupiscence. Anger especially is a fire, a flame; it catches, destroys, consumes; let us quench it, by long-suffering and by forbearance. For as red-hot iron dipped into water loses its fire, so an angry man, falling in with a patient one, does no harm to the patient man but rather benefits him and is himself more thoroughly subdued.

---

[76]Ps 141:2 (140:2 LXX). [77]NPNF 1 14:467-68**.

For nothing is equal to long-suffering. Such a person is never insulted, but, as bodies of the adamant are not wounded, so neither are such souls. For they are above the reach of the darts. The long-suffering person is high and so high as not to receive a wound from the shot. When one is furious, laugh; but do not laugh openly, lest you irritate that one, but laugh mentally on that one's account. For in the case of children, when they strike us passionately, as though thereby they were avenging themselves, we laugh. If then you laugh, there will be as great difference between you and that one as between a child and an adult, but, if you are furious, you have made yourself a child, for the angry are more senseless than children. If one looks at a furious child, does that one not laugh at the child? "The poor-spirited," it is said, "is mightily simple."[78] The simple, then, is a child, and that one "who is long-suffering," it is said, "is abundant in wisdom." Let us then follow after this "abundant wisdom," that we may attain to the good things promised us in Christ Jesus our Lord, with whom to the Father together with the Holy Ghost, be glory, power, honor, now and forever and world without end. Amen. ON THE EPISTLE TO THE HEBREWS 22.7-8.[79]

11:7 Noah Became an Heir of the Righteousness

NOAH RECEIVED A WARNING. EPHREM THE SYRIAN: "By faith Noah was warned by God concerning events as yet unseen," that is, about things which would have happened 120 years after he had received the warning, and [he] "took heed" of those distant threats of punishment [and] "constructed an ark" with great toil "for the saving of his household." By that same faith the world which did not believe was condemned, and that same faith made Noah the heir of the promise. COMMENTARY ON THE EPISTLE TO THE HEBREWS.[80]

FAITH WORKS RIGHTEOUSNESS. CHRYSOSTOM: "Noah became," he says, "an heir of the righteousness which comes by faith." That is, by his believing God, he was shown to be righteous. For this is the part of a soul sincerely disposed toward God and judging nothing more reliable than God's words, just as unbelief is the very contrary. Faith, it is clear, works righteousness. For as we have been warned of God respecting hell, so was Noah. Yet at that time he was laughed at, reviled and ridiculed, but he regarded none of these things. ON THE EPISTLE TO THE HEBREWS 23.1.[81]

---

[78]Prov 14:29. [79]NPNF 1 14:468-69**. [80]EHA 223. [81]NPNF 1 14:469.

11:8-22 ABRAHAM AND THOSE WHO FOLLOW HIM

[8]*By faith Abraham obeyed when he was called to go out to a place which he was to receive as an inheritance; and he went out, not knowing where he was to go.* [9]*By faith he sojourned in the land of promise, as in a foreign land, living in tents with Isaac and Jacob, heirs with him of the same promise.* [10]*For he looked forward to the city which has foundations, whose builder and maker is God.* [11]*By faith Sarah herself received power to conceive, even when she was past the age, since she*

considered him faithful who had promised. ¹²Therefore from one man, and him as good as dead, were born descendants as many as the stars of heaven and as the innumerable grains of sand by the seashore.

¹³These all died in faith, not having received what was promised, but having seen it and greeted it from afar, and having acknowledged that they were strangers and exiles on the earth. ¹⁴For people who speak thus make it clear that they are seeking a homeland. ¹⁵If they had been thinking of that land from which they had gone out, they would have had opportunity to return. ¹⁶But as it is, they desire a better country, that is, a heavenly one. Therefore God is not ashamed to be called their God, for he has prepared for them a city.

¹⁷By faith Abraham, when he was tested, offered up Isaac, and he who had received the promises was ready to offer up his only son, ¹⁸of whom it was said, "Through Isaac shall your descendants be named." ¹⁹He considered that God was able to raise men even from the dead; hence, figuratively speaking, he did receive him back. ²⁰By faith Isaac invoked future blessings on Jacob and Esau. ²¹By faith Jacob, when dying, blessed each of the sons of Joseph, bowing in worship over the head of his staff. ²²By faith Joseph, at the end of his life, made mention of the exodus of the Israelites and gave directions concerning his burial.ˣ

x Greek bones

OVERVIEW: It is through Abraham's faith that previously barren Sarah gave birth (EPHREM, AUGUSTINE), and he became father of many nations, through Christ (CYRIL OF JERUSALEM). This example shows that fulfillment of the faith is worth waiting (GREGORY OF NYSSA). The promise to the descendants of Abraham is not just inheritance of the promised land; rather it is promise of the kingdom to come which they awaited with faith (CHRYSOSTOM, PHOTIUS). Therefore, the saints of the old covenant were citizens of that kingdom yet strangers to the world. Therefore, because of their strong faith, God was not ashamed to be called "their God" (CHRYSOSTOM, ORIGEN). They are in no way inferior to the apostles, and their lives teach us virtue (CHRYSOSTOM). Abraham's faith is the model to be imitated as he did not stagger and never doubted (CHRYSOSTOM, EPHREM, PHOTIUS). The ram caught in the thicket wears a crown of thorns (AUGUSTINE). By sacrificing his own son, Abraham worshiped the Son of God as in faith he foresaw Jesus' coming (ATHANASIUS, ORIGEN, PHOTIUS). Thus, Isaac is a

type of Christ (CHRYSOSTOM, CLEMENT OF ALEXANDRIA). Similarly, Jacob, Esau and Joseph all have christological significance as types of the salvation to come (CHRYSOSTOM, JOHN OF DAMASCUS, PHOTIUS, SEVERIAN).

11:8-10 *Abraham Went Out, Not Knowing Where*

TENTS NOT HOUSES. THEODORET OF CYR: Not even when Abraham arrived in the promised land did he control it. Instead, he himself, his son and grandson lived the life of aliens, in what was their own by promise sojourning as though in a foreign land. Hence, instead of owning houses they spent the time living in tents. Yet they believed the promise to be true, even if not seeing the testimony of fact conforming to their faith. INTERPRETATION OF HEBREWS 11.[1]

ABRAHAM OBEYED. EPHREM THE SYRIAN: "By

[1]PG 82:760; TCCLSP 2:183.

faith Abraham" obeyed and left his father and family "to go" not to his private estate but to "an inheritance" prepared for him. Constantly supporting himself "by faith" through his wanderings, he "sojourned" and lived in the land of promise as in a foreign land, that is, as in a foreign inheritance, "living in tents with Isaac and Jacob, heirs with him of the same promise." Through the promised inheritance, which they did not receive, it became evident that "they looked forward to the city which has foundations, whose builder and maker is God." Commentary on the Epistle to the Hebrews.[2]

To Be Confident Is to Receive. Chrysostom: The metaphor is of persons on shipboard, seeing from afar the longed-for cities. Before they enter, they by their words of greeting already are beginning to occupy. . . . Do you see that they received the promises in this sense, in their already accepting them and being confident respecting them? If then to be confident is to receive the promise, it is in your power also to receive. These faithful did not yet fully enjoy the future blessing but yet by their longing still saw it. Why now do these things happen? That we might be put to shame, in that they indeed, when things on earth were promised them, regarded them not, but sought the future "city." God again and again speaks to us of the city that is above, and yet we seek that which is here. On the Epistle to the Hebrews 23.4.[3]

11:11-12 Sarah Considered God Faithful

She Who Was Barren Gave Birth. Ephrem the Syrian: "By faith Sarah herself received power to conceive, even when she was past the age." She, who was barren gave birth—that is, received the powers and youth that were necessary for conception and bearing—even though her old age was unable to cope with these things. And all this happened to her because, in the midst of the pagan Canaanites, she "considered him faithful who had promised" to give her these things. Com-

mentary on the Epistle to the Hebrews.[4]

How Abraham Fathered Children After Sarah. Augustine: It is written in the epistle to the Hebrews, "Through faith also Sarah herself received strength to conceive seed." For both were old, as the Scripture testifies; but she was also barren and had ceased to menstruate, so that she could no longer bear children even if she had not been barren. Further, if a woman is advanced in years yet still retains the custom of women, she can bear children to a young man but not to an old man, although that same old man can beget, but only of a young woman; as after Sarah's death Abraham could of Keturah, because he met with her in her lively age. This, then, is what the apostle mentions as wonderful, saying, besides, that Abraham's body was now dead; because at that age he was no longer able to beget children of any woman who retained now only a small part of her natural vigor. Of course we must understand that his body was dead only to some purposes, not to all; for if it was so to all, it would no longer be the aged body of a living man but the corpse of a dead one. Although that question, how Abraham begot children of Keturah, is usually solved in this way, that the gift of begetting which he received from the Lord remained even after the death of his wife. Yet I think that solution of the question which I have followed is preferable, because, although in our days an old man of a hundred years can beget children of no woman, it was not so then, when men still lived so long that a hundred years did not yet bring on them the decrepitude of old age. City of God 16.28.[5]

Fulfillment of Faith Is Worth the Wait. Gregory of Nyssa: Let [the one who is waiting for the Lord's second coming] therefore wait for that time then which is, necessarily, in the same time frame as the development of humanity. For even while Abraham and the patriarchs desired to see the promised better things, they did not stop

[2]EHA 223-24. [3]NPNF 1 14:470*. [4]EHA 224*. [5]NPNF 1 2:327.

seeking the heavenly country. This is what the apostle says when he declares that even now they are in a condition of hoping for that grace: "God having provided some better thing for us,"[6] according to the words of Paul, "that they without us should not be made perfect." If those then, who by faith alone and by hope saw the good things "afar off" and "embraced them"—if they bear the delay as the apostle bears witness, and if they place the certainty that they will enjoy the things for which they hoped in the fact that they "judged him faithful who has promised," what should the rest of us do who perhaps do not have a grasp of that better hope from the character of our own lives?

Even the prophet's soul fainted with desire, and in his psalm he confesses this passionate love, saying that his "soul has a desire and longing to be in the courts of the Lord."[7] [He still has this desire] even if he has to be demoted to a place amongst the lowest, since it is a greater and more desirable thing to be last there than to be first among the ungodly tents of this life. Nevertheless he was patient during the delay, considering, indeed, the life there blessed, and accounting a brief participation in it more desirable than "thousands"[of days] of time. For, he says, "one day in your courts is better than thousands."[8] And yet, he did not become dejected at the necessary dispensation concerning existing things. He thought it was sufficient bliss for a person to have those good things even by way of hope. This is why he says at the end of the psalm, "O Lord of hosts, blessed is the man that hopes in you."[9] ON THE MAKING OF MAN 22.7.[10]

ABRAHAM'S FAITH. CYRIL OF JERUSALEM: There is much to tell of faith, and the whole day would not be enough time for us to describe it fully. At present let us be content with Abraham only, as one of the examples from the Old Testament, seeing that we have been made his sons through faith. He was justified not only by works but also by faith: for though he did many things well, yet he was never called the friend of God

except when he believed. Moreover, his every work was performed in faith. Through faith he left his parents, left country and place and home through faith. Therefore, you too should be justified in the same way he was justified. In his body he was already dead in regard to offspring, and Sarah his wife was now old, and there was no hope left of having children. God promises the old man a child, and Abraham, "without being weakened in faith, though he considered his own body now as good as dead," did not look at the weakness of his body but at the power of him who promised because "he counted him faithful who had promised." And so, beyond all expectation, [Abraham] gained the child from bodies already dead, as it were. And when, after he had gained his son, he was commanded to offer him up, although he had heard the word, "In Isaac shall your seed be called," he proceeded to offer up his son, his only son, to God, believing "that God is able to raise up even from the dead." And having bound his son and laid him on the wood, he did in purpose offer him. But he received his son alive through the goodness of God in delivering to him a lamb instead of his child. Being faithful in these things, he was sealed for righteousness "and received circumcision as a seal of the faith which he had while he was in uncircumcision, having received a promise that he should be the father of many nations." CATECHETICAL LECTURES 5.5.[11]

ABRAHAM IS FATHER OF MANY NATIONS THROUGH CHRIST. CYRIL OF JERUSALEM: Let us see, then, how Abraham is the father of many nations. Of Jews he is confessedly the father, through succession according to the flesh. But if we hold to the succession according to the flesh, we shall be compelled to say that the oracle was false. For according to the flesh he is no longer father of us all: but the example of his faith makes us all sons of Abraham. How and in what man-

---

[6]Heb 11:40. [7]Ps 84:3 (83:4 LXX). [8]Ps 84:10 (83:11 LXX). [9]Ps 84:12 (83:12 LXX). [10]NPNF 2 5:412-13*. [11]NPNF 2 7:30*.

ner? With people it is incredible that one should rise from the dead, just as it is also incredible that there should be offspring from aged persons who are as good as dead. But when Christ is preached as having been crucified on the tree, and as having died and risen again, we believe it. By the likeness therefore of our faith we are adopted into the sonship of Abraham. And then, following upon our faith, we receive like him the spiritual seal, being circumcised by the Holy Spirit through baptism, not in the foreskin of the body but in the heart, according to Jeremiah, where he says, "And you shall be circumcised unto God in the foreskin of your heart,"[12] and according to the apostle, "in the circumcision of Christ, having been buried with him in baptism," and the rest.[13] CATECHETICAL LECTURES 5.6.[14]

FROM ONE MAN. THEODORET OF CYR: "From one person"[15] means from Abraham; but if we were to take the "one" to mean both of them [Abraham and Sarah], we would not be wide of the mark: "the two will be one flesh," Scripture says.[16] INTERPRETATION OF HEBREWS 11.[17]

11:13-16 They Greeted the Promise from Afar

STRANGERS AND EXILES. THEODORET OF CYR: The patriarch Abraham spoke in these terms to the Hittites, "I am a stranger and an alien residing among you; give me property among you for a burying place, so that I may bury my dead out of sight."[18] The one in receipt of the promise of the whole earth did not even own a plot three cubits long. INTERPRETATION OF HEBREWS 11.[19]

WHAT KIND OF PROMISES? CHRYSOSTOM: Of what kind of "promises" is he speaking? Isaac and Jacob received the promises of land, but, as to Noah and Abel and Enoch, what kind of promises did they receive? Either then he is speaking concerning these three, or, if concerning those others also, the promise was not this, that Abel should be admired, or Enoch translated, or Noah preserved. These things came to them for their virtue's sake and were a sort of foretaste of things to come. For God from the beginning, knowing that the human race needs much condescension, bestows on us not only the things in the world to come but also those here. For instance, Christ said to the disciples, "Whoever has left houses or brothers or sisters or father or mother shall receive a hundredfold and inherit everlasting life."[20] And again, "Seek the kingdom of God, and all these things shall be yours as well."[21] Do you see that these things are given by him in the way of addition, that we might not faint? Athletes who are engaged in combat have the benefit of careful attention. They live under strict rules. They are not at ease. But after the combat, they enjoy it entirely. So God also does not grant us here to partake of "entire" ease. ON THE EPISTLE TO THE HEBREWS 23.3.[22]

WHAT KIND OF GOOD THINGS? CHRYSOSTOM: For what language, what intellect, can represent that blessedness and virtue, that pleasure, that glory, that happiness, that splendor? "What no eye has seen, nor ear heard, nor the heart of man conceived"[23] (he did not say that they simply surpass what we imagine; but that none has ever conceived) "what God has prepared for those who love him." For of what kind are those good things likely to be, of which God is the preparer and establisher? For if immediately after God had made us, when we had not yet done anything, God freely bestowed so great favors—paradise, familiar intercourse with God's own self, immortality, a life happy and free from cares—what will God not bestow on those who have labored and struggled so greatly and endured on God's behalf? For us God did not spare God's only begotten. For us when we were enemies God gave up God's own son to death.[24] Of what will God not count

---

[12]Jer 4:4. [13]Col 2:11-12. [14]NPNF 2 7:30*. [15]The Greek is *aph' henos,* which literally means "from one." RSV translates this as "from one man." [16]Gen 2:24. [17]PG 82:761; *TCCLSP* 2:183. [18]Gen 23:4. [19]PG 82:761; *TCCLSP* 2:184*. [20]Mt 19:29. [21]Mt 6:33. [22]NPNF 1 14:470*. [23]1 Cor 2:9. [24]Rom 5:8.

us worthy, having become God's friends? What will God not impart to us, having reconciled us to God's own self? On the Epistle to the Hebrews 23.6.[25]

All but Wrapping Themselves in the Promises. Photius: So he says that they believed the promises, "having seen them from afar" through hope, because they also rejoiced in them and embraced them, all but wrapping themselves in them. Fragments on the Epistle to the Hebrews 11.13.[26]

They Called Themselves Strangers. Chrysostom: They called themselves, therefore, "strangers," but Paul said something much beyond this; for not merely did he call himself a stranger, but he said that he was dead to the world and that the world was dead to him. "For the world," he says, "has been crucified to me, and I to the world."[27] But we, both citizens and quite alive, busy ourselves about everything here as citizens. And what righteous people were to the world—"strangers" and "dead"—that we are to heaven. And what they were to heaven—live and acting as citizens—that we are to the world. Therefore we are dead, because we have refused that which is truly life and have chosen this, which is but for a time. Therefore, we have provoked God to wrath, because when the enjoyments of heaven have been set before us, we are not willing to be separated from things on earth, but, like worms, we turn about from the earth to the earth, and again from this to that. And in short [we] are not willing to look up even for a little while or to withdraw ourselves from human affairs, but as if drowned in torpor and sleep and drunkenness, we are stupefied with imaginations. On the Epistle to the Hebrews 24.1.[28]

Belonging to the Far City. Chrysostom: Did they mean that they were "strangers" from the land that is in Palestine? By no means. They were strangers in relation to the whole world. And with reason, for they saw in it none of the

things which they wished for, but everything foreign and strange. They indeed wished to practice virtue, but here there was much wickedness, and things were quite foreign to them. They had no friend, no familiar acquaintance, save only some few. But how were they "strangers"? They had no care for things here. And this they showed not by words but by their deeds. In what way? God said to Abraham, "Leave that which seems your country and come to one that is foreign." And Abraham did not cleave to his kindred but gave it up as unconcernedly as if he were about to leave a foreign land. God said to him, "Offer up your son," and he offered him up as if he had no son; as if he had divested himself of his nature, so he offered him up. The wealth that he had acquired was visible to any passers-by, yet this he accounted as nothing. He yielded the first places to others. He threw himself into dangers. He suffered troubles innumerable. He built no splendid houses, he enjoyed no luxuries, he had no care about dress, which all are things of this world; but he lived in all respects as belonging to the city beyond. He showed hospitality, brotherly love, mercifulness, forbearance, contempt for wealth and for present glory, and for all else.

And his son too was such as himself. When he was driven away, when war was made on him, he yielded and gave way, as being in a foreign land. For foreigners, whatever they suffer, endure it, as not being in their own country. Even when his wife was taken from him, he endured this also as being in a strange land and lived in all respects as one whose home was above, showing sober-mindedness and a well-ordered life. For after he had begotten a son, he had no more intercourse with his wife; and it was when the flower of his youth had passed that he married her, showing that he did it not from passion but in subservience to the promise of God. And what did Jacob do? Did he not seek bread only and raiment, which are asked for by those who are truly strangers, by those that

---

[25]NPNF 1 14:471**. [26]NTA 15:650. [27]Gal 6:14. [28]NPNF 1 14:473-74*.

have come to great poverty? When he was driven out, did he not as a stranger give place? Did he not serve for hire? Did he not suffer afflictions innumerable, everywhere, as a stranger?

And in all these things, he says, they were "seeking" their "own country." Ah, how great is the difference! They indeed were in travail pains each day, wishing to be released from this world and to return to their country. ON THE EPISTLE TO THE HEBREWS 24.4-5.[29]

GOD WAS NOT ASHAMED TO BE CALLED THEIR GOD. CHRYSOSTOM: What sort of "country" was this? Was it that which they had left? By no means. For what hindered them if they wished, from returning again and becoming citizens? But they sought that which is in heaven. Thus they desired their departure, and so they pleased God, for "God was not ashamed to be called their God."

Ah! How great a dignity! God was willing "to be called their God." What do you say? We are speaking of the God of the earth and the God of heaven. Mark it as a great thing that "God is not ashamed to be called their God"? How great and truly great this is. It is a proof of exceeding blessedness. How? Because God is called God of earth and of heaven as of the Gentiles, in that God created and formed them; but God of those holy men, not in this sense, but as some true friend.

And I will make it plain to you by an example. As in the case of slaves in large households, when any of those placed over the household are very highly esteemed and manage everything themselves and can use great freedom toward their masters, the master is called after them, and one may find many so called. But what do I say? As we might say the God, not of the Gentiles but of the world, so we might say "the God of Abraham." But you do not know how great a dignity this is! We do not attain to it. Now God is called the Lord of all Christians, and yet the name goes beyond our deserving. Consider the greatness if God were called the God of one person! He who is called the God of the whole world is "not ashamed to be called" the God of three people,[30] and with good reason. For the saints would turn the scale, I do not say against the world, but against ten thousand worlds. ON THE EPISTLE TO THE HEBREWS 24.5-6.[31]

THE SAINTS WHO PRECEDED JESUS' BODILY SOJOURN. ORIGEN: The saints who preceded Jesus' bodily sojourn, who had a somewhat greater mental grasp than the majority of believers, perceived the mysteries of divinity because the word of God was teaching them even before he became flesh, for he was always working, being an imitator of his Father of whom he says, "My Father is working still."[32]

He says, perhaps to the Sadducees who do not believe in the doctrine of the resurrection, "Have you not read in the book of Moses, in the passage about the bush, how God said to him, 'I am the God of Abraham, and the God of Isaac, and the God of Jacob'? He is not God of the dead, but of the living."[33] If, therefore, God "is not ashamed to be called the God" of these people, and they are numbered among the living by Christ, and all the believers are sons of Abraham,[34] since all the nations are blessed in the faithful Abraham[35] whom God appointed father of the nations,[36] are we hesitant to accept that the living have known the lessons of the living, since they were instructed by Christ, who has existed before the morning star,[37] before he became flesh? COMMENTARY ON THE GOSPEL OF JOHN 6.17-18.[38]

CHANGE BEHAVIOR FROM VIRTUE TO VIRTUE. CHRYSOSTOM: What shall we then do that we may be saved? Let us begin the practice of virtue, as we have opportunity. Let us portion out the virtues to ourselves, as laborers do their husbandry. In this month let us master evil speaking, injuriousness, unjust anger. And let us lay down a law for ourselves and say, "Today let us set this

---

[29]NPNF 1 14:474-75*. [30]Abraham, Isaac, Jacob. [31]NPNF 1 14:475*. [32]Jn 5:17. [33]Mk 12:26-27. [34]Gal 3:7. [35]Gal 3:8. [36]Gen 17:5. [37]Ps 110:3 (109:3 LXX). [38]FC 80:172-73.

right." Again, in this month let us school ourselves in forbearance, and in another, in some
other virtue. And when we have got into the
habit of this virtue let us go to another, just as in
the things we learn at school, guarding what is already gained, and acquiring others.

After this let us proceed to contempt for
riches. First let us restrain our hands from grasp-
ing, and then let us give alms. Let us not simply
confound everything, with the same hands both
slaying and showing mercy. After this, let us go to
some other virtue, and from that, to another. On
the Epistle to the Hebrews 24.9.[39]

He Is Not Ashamed. Theodoret of Cyr: It
was opportune of him to use the phrase "he is not
ashamed." The Lord of the powers, Master of the
angels and Maker of heaven and earth when
asked, "What is your name?" passed over all others and said, "I am the God of Abraham, the God
of Isaac, the God of Jacob. This is my name forever, and how I am to be remembered by generations of generations."[40] Interpretation of
Hebrews 11.[41]

11:17-19 Abraham's Faith

Through Isaac. Theodoret of Cyr: God
promised to bring to light a vast number of Isaac's
offspring like sand on the seashore, and he it was
who bade Isaac become a victim. Beset by the two
conflicting thoughts, then, and with nature tear-
ing at him more harshly than any torturer, the
patriarch easily overcame it all and offered the
sacrifice. He brings out as well the thoughts he
employed in banishing the others, "God was able
to raise men even from the dead." He took issue
with the thought arising in regard to the great
number of offspring, believing that his son, even
if slaughtered, could come back to life, God willing. "Figuratively speaking, he did receive him
back," that is, by way of a symbol and type of the
resurrection. Put to death by his father's zeal, he
came back to life at the word of the one who prevented the slaughter. In him the type of the sav-

ing passion was also prefigured. Hence the Lord
also said to the Jews, "Your father Abraham
rejoiced at the prospect of seeing my day; he saw
it and was glad."[42] Interpretation of Hebrews
11.[43]

**When God's Promise Seemed to Oppose
God's Promise.** Chrysostom: Great indeed
was the faith of Abraham. In the case of Abel,
Noah and Enoch, there was an opposition of
reasonings to be overcome, and it was necessary
to go beyond human reasonings. In the case of
Abraham, however, it was necessary not only to
go beyond human reasonings but to manifest
also something more. For what was of God
seemed to be opposed to what was of God; and
faith opposed to faith, and command opposed to
promise. I mean this: God had said, "Go from
your country and your kindred, and I will give
you this land."[44] But then he said, "He gave him
no inheritance in it, not even a foot's length."[45]
Do you see how what was done was opposed to
the promise? Again, God said, "Through Isaac
shall your descendants be named,"[46] and he
believed, and again God says, "Sacrifice to me
this one, who was to fill all the world from his
seed." Do you see the opposition between the
commands and the promise? He enjoined things
that were in contradiction to the promises, and
yet not even so did the righteous man stagger
nor say he had been deceived. . . . But you
endure nothing except what was promised, and
still you are troubled. On the Epistle to the
Hebrews 25.1.[47]

**Abraham Believed God Could Raise the
Dead.** Ephrem the Syrian: "By faith Abraham,
when he was tested, offered up Isaac" as a victim,
even though he had received this child with the
promise that through him his descendants would
have been named. And Abraham never doubted,

---

[39]NPNF 1 14:477*. [40]Ex 3:15. [41]PG 82:764; TCCLSP 2:184. [42]Jn
8:56. [43]PG 82:764; TCCLSP 2:185*. [44]Gen 12:1, 7. [45]Acts 7:5.
[46]Gen 21:12. [47]NPNF 1 14:477*.

not even when he was about to kill him, that through him his descendants would have been named.

He decided in his mind and accepted the idea that "God is able to raise men even from the dead; hence, figuratively speaking, he did receive him back," that is, so that in him he might come to know the resurrection of the dead, and in him might know the children of the spirit whom he would have had. COMMENTARY ON THE EPISTLE TO THE HEBREWS.[48]

THE RAM WAS CROWNED WITH THORNS.

AUGUSTINE: The apostle says, "He who did not spare his own Son but gave him up for us all."[49] This explains why Isaac himself, just like the Lord carrying his cross, carried to the place of sacrifice the wood on which he was to be placed. . . . Note that when Abraham first saw the ram, it was caught by its thorns in a thicket of briers. This surely is a symbol of Jesus, crowned with thorns by the Jews before he was immolated. CITY OF GOD 16.32.[50]

IN HARMONY WHEN VIEWED BY FAITH.

CHRYSOSTOM: He heard the opposite of the promises from the one who had made them, and yet he was not disturbed but did them as if they had been in harmony. For they were in harmony, being opposed indeed according to human calculations, but in harmony when viewed by faith. And how this was, the apostle himself has taught us, saying, "accounting that God was able to raise him up, even from the dead." By the same faith, he means, by which he believed that God gave what was not and raised up the dead, by the same was he persuaded that God would also raise him up after he had been slain in sacrifice. For it was similarly impossible—to human calculation, I mean—for a womb which was dead and grown old and already become useless for childbearing to give a child, and to raise again one who had been slain. But his previous faith prepared the way for things to come. ON THE EPISTLE TO THE HEBREWS 25.2.[51]

ABRAHAM BELIEVED IN A RESURRECTION THAT HAD NOT YET HAPPENED.

ORIGEN: Give me your attention, you who have approached God, who believe yourselves to be faithful. Consider diligently how the faith of the faithful is proved from these words that have been read to us. "After these things," the text says, "God tested Abraham and said to him, 'Abraham, Abraham.' And he said, 'Here I am.' "[52] Observe each detail that has been written. For, if one knows how to dig into the depth, one will find a treasure in the details. Perhaps also the precious jewels of the mysteries lie hidden where they are not esteemed.

This man was previously called Abram. Nowhere do we read that God called him by this name or said to him, "Abram, Abram." For God could not call him by a name that was to be abolished, but he calls him by this name which God gave; and not only does God call him by this name, but he also repeats it. And when he had responded, "Here I am," God says to him, "Take your dearest son Isaac, whom you love, and offer him to me. Go," the text says, "into the high land, and there you shall offer him for a holocaust upon one of the mountains which I shall show you."[53]

Why God gave him this particular name and called him Abraham, he himself has interpreted. "Because," the text says, "I have made you a father of many nations."[54] God gave him this promise when he had his son Ishmael, but it is promised him that the promise will be fulfilled in a son who will be born of Sarah. He had kindled his soul, therefore, in love for his son not only because of posterity but also in the hope of the promises.

But this son, in whom these great and marvelous promises have been made, this son, I say, on whose account his name is called Abraham, "he is ordered to offer for a holocaust to the Lord on one of the mountains."

What do you say to these things, Abraham? What kind of thoughts are stirring in your heart?

---

[48]EHA 224-25. [49]Rom 8:32. [50]FC 14:546*. [51]NPNF 1 14:478*. [52]Gen 22:1. [53]Gen 22:2. [54]Gen 17:5.

A word has been uttered by God that is such as to shatter and try your faith. What do you say to these things? What are you thinking? What are you reconsidering? Are you thinking, are you turning over in your heart that, if the promise has been given to me in Isaac, but I offer him for a holocaust, it remains that that promise holds no hope? Or rather do you think of those well-known words, and say that it is impossible, for him who promised, to lie;[55] be that as it may, the promise shall remain?

But I, because "I am the least,"[56] am not able to examine the thoughts of such a great patriarch nor can I know what thoughts the voice of God which had proceeded to test him stirred in him, what feeling it caused, when he was ordered to slay his only son. But since "the spirit of prophets is subject to the prophets,"[57] the apostle Paul, who, I believe, was teaching by the Spirit what feeling, what plan Abraham considered, has revealed it when he says, "By faith Abraham did not hesitate, when he offered his only son, in whom he had received the promises, thinking that God is able to raise him up even from the dead."

The apostle, therefore, has reported to us the thoughts of the faithful man, that the faith in the resurrection began to be held already at that time in Isaac. Abraham, therefore, hoped for the resurrection of Isaac and believed in a future that had not yet happened. How, then, are they "sons of Abraham"[58] who do not believe what has happened in Christ, which Abraham believed was to be in Isaac? No, rather, that I may speak more clearly, Abraham knew himself to prefigure the image of future truth; he knew the Christ was to be born from his seed, who also was to be offered as a truer victim for the whole world and was to be raised from the dead. HOMILIES ON GENESIS 8.1.[59]

GOD TESTED ABRAHAM TO MAKE HIS PROMISE KNOWN TO ALL. CHRYSOSTOM: And he shows another thing too, by saying that "God tempted Abraham."[60] What then? Did not God know that the man was noble and approved? Why

then did God tempt him? Not that God might learn but that God might show to others and make his fortitude manifest to all. And here also he shows the cause of trials, that they may not suppose they suffer these things as being forsaken of God. ON THE EPISTLE TO THE HEBREWS 25.2.[61]

IN OFFERING HIS SON HE WORSHIPED THE SON OF GOD. ATHANASIUS: Here is a man of true faith, for when the Lord asked him to sacrifice Isaac, his only son, he was willing to do so. By faith he offered up the one through whom the Lord had given him the promise of a nation of descendants. And in offering his son he worshiped the Son of God. When the Lord held him back from sacrificing Isaac, Abraham saw the Messiah in the ram that was ultimately offered as the sacrifice to God.[62]

We see, then, that the patriarch was tested by means of Isaac—not that Isaac was sacrificed but rather the one who was pointed out in Isaiah, "He shall be like a lamb that is led to the slaughter, and like a sheep that before its shearers is dumb."[63] He was, in truth, tested by him who took away the sin of the world.

That is why Abraham was held back from laying his hand on the boy. If he had sacrificed Isaac, the Jews might very well have rejected all the prophecies concerning the Savior. Undoubtedly they would have especially rejected such prophecies given by the psalmist as, "You have not wanted sacrifice and offering; for you have prepared a body for me."[64] They would have referred all such prophecies to the son of Abraham.

Thus the sacrifice was not for the sake of Isaac but of Abraham, who was tested by being called upon to make this offering. And of course, God accepted his intentions, but God prevented him from slaying Isaac. The death of Isaac would not buy freedom for the world. No, that could be

[55]Heb 6:18. [56]1 Cor 15:9. [57]1 Cor 14:32. [58]Jn 8:37. [59]FC 71:136-37*. [60]Gen 22:1. [61]NPNF 1 14:478*. [62]See Gen 22:13. [63]Is 53:7. [64]Ps 40:6 (39:7 LXX).

accomplished only by the death of our Savior, by whose stripes we are all healed.[65] He alone picked up the falling, healed the sick, satisfied those who were hungry and filled the poor. Above all else, he alone raised us all from the dead, and having abolished death, he has brought us from sorrow and sighing to the rest and gladness of this feast. That, dear friends, is a joy that reaches heaven! FESTAL LETTERS 6.8.[66]

NOT OF GRACE BUT OF DEBT. CHRYSOSTOM: Afterwards, that no one may suppose he does this in despair, and in consequence of this command had cast away that faith, but may understand that this also was truly of faith, he says that he retained that faith also, although it seem to be at variance with this. But it was not at variance. For he did not measure the power of God by human reasonings but committed all to faith. And hence he was not afraid to say that God was "able to raise him up, even from the dead."

"From this also he received him in a figure," that is in idea, by the ram, he means. How? The ram having been slain, he was saved, so that by means of the ram, he received him again, having slain it in his stead. But these things were types, for here it is the Son of God who is slain. And observe, I beseech you, how great is God's loving-kindness. For inasmuch as a great favor was to be given to humanity, God, wishing to do this, not by favor but as a debtor, arranges that a man should first give up his own son on account of God's command. God does this in order that God might seem to be doing nothing great in giving up God's own Son, since a man had done this before God, so that God might be supposed to do it not of grace but of debt. We do kindness to those we love. We may seem to give all when they have first received something little. We boast more of the receiving than of the giving. We do not say, "We gave him this," but, "We received this from him." "From this also" are his words, "he received him in a figure," that is, as in a riddle, for the ram was, as it were, a figure of Isaac or as in a type. For since the sacrifice had been completed and Isaac

slain in purpose, therefore he gave him back to the patriarch. ON THE EPISTLE TO THE HEBREWS 25.3.[67]

ISAAC IS A TYPE. CLEMENT OF ALEXANDRIA: Isaac is a type of the infant Lord as son, and, in fact, Isaac was the son of Abraham as Christ is of God, victim as was the Lord. But he was not cut down like the Lord; no, Isaac only carried the wood of the sacrifice, as the Lord did his cross. He laughed mystically by way of prophesying that the Lord fills us with joy, we who have been redeemed by his blood. He did not suffer but left to the Logos, as is fitting, the first fruits of suffering. What is more, because he was not immolated, he signifies also the divinity of the Lord. For after his burial, Jesus was raised up, thus leaving suffering behind, just as Isaac had escaped the sacrifice. CHRIST THE EDUCATOR 1.5.23.1-2.[68]

HE SUFFERED NOTHING UNDER DEATH'S POWER. THEODORE OF MOPSUESTIA: He obtained it in accordance with his faith. For believing in the resurrection, he received him who had died symbolically. For the fact that he suffered nothing, although he fully expected to die, was a symbol of the one who would truly rise, inasmuch as, "having tasted death for a short time,"[69] he rose, having suffered nothing under death's power. For this was done "in a parable" instead of in symbols. FRAGMENTS ON THE EPISTLE TO THE HEBREWS 11.19.[70]

ABRAHAM RECEIVED ISAAC IN A FIGURATIVE WAY. PHOTIUS: One can understand the statement "hence, figuratively speaking, he did receive him back" in the following sense: "Abraham received Isaac in a figurative way." For, as he says, since he showed some untold obedience and a faith that conquers even the laws of nature itself, he received his son again, not merely because he offered his son but because he offered him with

---

[65]Is 53:5. [66]NPNF 2 4:522**. [67]NPNF 1 14:478-79**. [68]ANF 2:215; *IHEGF* 87-88*. [69]Heb 2:9. [70]NTA 15:210.

great assent and his worthy faith. For Abraham received Isaac, who bore a figure and likeness to the Son of God and God himself. For such faith can set matters aright. But if you understand "in a figurative way" to apply to Abraham and Isaac, in that Abraham acted as a type of the Father and as a figure and likeness of him, while Isaac acted as a type of the Son, this interpretation would accord well with the understanding we have already stated. Abraham's faith brought him such a gain, he says, because after offering him he received him back with great addition. What sort of addition? That he would receive him again "in a figurative manner" and likeness of the action with the Father and the Son, that is, he received his son with so great profit, since both became a type of the offering with which the Father thought it good to be completed in his Son.

Or one can understand it as follows. God "in a figurative way received" Isaac, that is, because of the faith and zeal of Abraham. To be sure, later a ram was offered, and even then it was not brought out of Abraham's flock but was also provided by God. Nonetheless, God received the sacrifice in this way, as if Abraham had offered Isaac himself albeit in a symbolic manner and through the substitution of the ram. Therefore he says, "He received him," namely, Isaac, "in a figurative way" and substitution[71] of the ram, that is, the intended and fulfilled purpose of Abraham and the desire of his faith. Thus God received the sacrifice of Abraham in this manner. FRAGMENTS ON THE EPISTLE TO THE HEBREWS 11.19.[72]

THE METAPHOR OF THE BALL. CHRYSOSTOM: Do you see that what I am constantly saying is shown in this case also? When we have proved that our mind is made perfect and have shown that we disregard earthly things, then earthly things also are given to us, but not before, lest, being bound to them already, we receiving them should be bound still. Loose yourself from your slavery first, he says, and then receive, so that you may receive no longer as a slave but as a master. Despise riches, and you shall be rich. Despise

glory, and you shall be glorious. Despise avenging yourself on your enemies, and then you shall attain it. Despise repose, and then you shall receive it, that in receiving you may receive not as a prisoner or as a slave but as a free person.

For as with little children, when the child eagerly desires childish playthings, as a ball, for instance, and such things, we hide them from the child with much care, that the child may not be hindered from necessary things. But when the child thinks little of them and no longer longs for them, we allow them fearlessly, knowing that no harm can come to the child from them, because the desire no longer has strength enough to draw the child away from things necessary. So God also, when God sees that we no longer eagerly desire the things of this world, henceforth permits us to use them. For we possess them as free people, not as children. ON THE EPISTLE TO THE HEBREWS 25.4.[73]

11:20-22 Esau, Jacob, Joseph

HUMAN AND DIVINE ORDERS. SEVERIAN OF GABALA: "By faith Isaac invoked future blessings on Jacob and Esau." First he gave it to Jacob, then to Esau, not according to the sequence of their birth but according to the order of spiritual blessing. FRAGMENTS ON THE EPISTLE TO THE HEBREWS 11.20[74]

JACOB FIRST PREFIGURED THE CROSS. JOHN OF DAMASCUS: The tree of life that was planted by God in paradise prefigured this honorable cross, for, since death came by a tree, it was necessary for life and the resurrection to be bestowed by a tree. It was Jacob who first prefigured the cross, when he adored the top of the rod of Joseph.[75] And when he blessed Joseph's sons with his hands crossed,[76] he most clearly described the sign of the cross. Then there was the rod of

---

[71]The text has *karenthēkē* but is read as *parenthēkē*. [72]NTA 15:650-51. [73]NPNF 1 14:479**. [74]NTA 15:351. [75]See Gen 47:31. [76]See Gen 48:13-15.

Moses which struck the sea with the form of a cross and saved Israel while causing Pharaoh to be swallowed up;[77] his hands stretched out in the form of a cross and put Amalek to flight;[78] the bitter water being made sweet by a tree,[79] and the rock being struck and gushing forth streams of water.[80] Further, the rod of Aaron miraculously confirmed the dignity of the priesthood,[81] a serpent was raised in triumph upon a tree, as if dead, with the tree preserving those who with faith beheld the dead enemy,[82] even as Christ was nailed up in flesh of sin but which had not known sin.[83] . . . May we who adore this attain to the portion of Christ the crucified. Amen. ORTHODOX FAITH 4.11.[84]

BOWING IN WORSHIP. PHOTIUS: Thereupon he not only spoke but he also was bold to demonstrate it to coming generations by his action. For since another king would arise from Ephraim, for this very reason he says, "and Jacob bowing in worship over the head of his staff," that is, being an old man, he bowed down to Joseph, showing the obeisance of the whole people that would take place for him. And this has already come to pass, when the brothers bowed down to him, and it was about to come to pass later through the ten tribes. FRAGMENTS ON THE EPISTLE TO THE HEBREWS 11.21.[85]

THE RIGHTEOUS PEOPLE KNEW ALL THE THINGS TO COME. CHRYSOSTOM: "Many prophets and righteous men," it is said, "longed to see what you see, and did not see it; and to hear what you hear and did not hear it."[86] Did then those righteous people know all the things to come? Yes, most certainly. For if, because of the weakness of those who were not able to receive him, the Son was not revealed, he was with good reason revealed to those conspicuous in virtue. This Paul also says, that they knew "the things to come," that is, the resurrection of Christ.

Or he does not mean this, but that "by faith, concerning things to come" means not concerning the world to come but "concerning things to come" in this world. For how, except by faith, could a man sojourning in a strange land, give such blessings?

On the other hand, he obtained the blessing and yet did not receive it. You see that what I said with regard to Abraham may be said also of Jacob, that he did not fully enjoy the blessing. The blessings went to his posterity, while he himself obtained the "things to come." For we find that his brother rather enjoyed the blessing. For Jacob spent all his time in servitude, working as a hireling amid dangers and plots and deceits and fears; when asked by Pharaoh, he says, "Few and evil have my days been,"[87] while the other lived in independence and great security and afterwards was an object of terror to Jacob. Where then did the blessings come to their accomplishment, save in the world to come?

Do you see that from the beginning the wicked have enjoyed things here, but the righteous the contrary? Not all, however, for behold, Abraham was a righteous man, and he enjoyed things here as well, though with affliction and trials, for indeed wealth was all he had, seeing all else relating to him was full of affliction. For it is impossible that the righteous man should not be afflicted, though he be rich, for when he is willing to be overreached, to be wronged, to suffer all other things, he must be afflicted. So while he may enjoy wealth, it is still not without grief. . . . "By faith," he says, "Isaac blessed Jacob and Esau concerning things to come." Esau was the elder; but he puts Jacob first for his excellence. Do you see how great his faith was? How did he promise to his sons so great blessings? Entirely from his having faith in God.

"By faith, Jacob, when dying, blessed both the sons of Joseph." Here we ought to set down the blessings entirely, in order that both his faith and his prophesying may be made manifest. "And worshiped leaning," he says, "upon the top of his

[77]Ex 14:16ff. [78]Ex 17:9-13. [79]Ex 15:25. [80]Ex 17:6. [81]Num 17:8. [82]See Num 21:9. [83]See Deut 28:66. [84]FC 37:352. [85]NTA 15:651. [86]Mt 13:17. [87]Gen 47:9.

staff." Here, he means, he not only spoke but was even so confident about the future things as to show it also by his act. For inasmuch as another king was about to arise from Ephraim, therefore it is said, "And he bowed himself upon the top of his staff." That is, even though he was now an old man, "he bowed himself" to Joseph, showing the obeisance of the whole people which was to be directed to him. And this indeed had already taken place, when his brethren "bowed down" to him, but it was afterwards to come to pass through the ten tribes. Do you see how he foretold the things which were to be afterwards? Do you see the great faith they had, and how they believed "concerning the things to come"? On the Epistle to the Hebrews 26.1-2.[88]

The Things That Concern Joseph Are of Faith Only. Chrysostom: For some of the things here, the things present, are examples of patience only and of enduring ill treatment and of receiving nothing good, as, for instance, what is mentioned in the case of Abraham and Abel. But others are examples of faith, as in the case of Noah, that there is a God, that there is a recompense. . . . And the things that concern Joseph are also of faith only. Joseph heard that God had made a promise to Abraham, that God had engaged God's word, "to you and to your seed will I give this land"; and, though in a strange land and not yet seeing the engagement fulfilled, he never faltered even so, but believed so as even to "speak of the exodus and to give directions concerning his burial." He then not only believed himself but led the rest also to faith, that, having the exodus always in mind—for he would not have "given directions concerning his burial" unless he had been fully assured of this—they might look for

their return to Canaan.

On hearing this, some people say, "See! Even righteous people had care about their sepulchers." Let us reply to them that it was for this reason—that he knew that "the earth is the Lord's and all that is therein."[89] He could not indeed have been ignorant of this, who lived with such great love of wisdom, who spent his whole life in Egypt. And yet if he had wished, it was possible for him to return and not to mourn or vex himself. But when he had taken up his father, why did he enjoin them to carry up then his own bones also? Evidently for this same reason.

Tell me, are not the bones of Moses himself laid in a strange land? And those of Aaron, of Daniel, of Jeremiah? And as to those of the apostles, we do not know where those of most of them are laid. For of Peter, indeed, and Paul and John and Thomas, the sepulchers are well known, but those of the rest, being so many, have nowhere become known. Let us not therefore lament at all about this or be so little-minded. For wherever we may be buried, "the earth is the Lord's and all that is in it."[90] Certainly what must take place does take place. Inordinately to mourn, however, and lament and bewail the departed arises from littleness of mind. On the Epistle to the Hebrews 26.2.[91]

Directions Concerning His Burial. Theodoret of Cyr: Joseph would not have given directions about his remains if he had not believed the divine promises. Interpretation of Hebrews 11.[92]

---

[88]NPNF 1 14:481-82**. [89]Ps 24:1 (23:1 LXX). [90]Ps 24:1 (23:1 LXX). [91]NPNF 1 14:482-83*. [92]PG 82:765; TCCLSP 2:185.

11:23-31 MOSES

^{23}*By faith Moses, when he was born, was hid for three months by his parents, because they saw that the child was beautiful; and they were not afraid of the king's edict.* ^{24}*By faith Moses, when he was grown up, refused to be called the son of Pharaoh's daughter,* ^{25}*choosing rather to share ill-treatment with the people of God than to enjoy the fleeting pleasures of sin.* ^{26}*He considered abuse suffered for the Christ greater wealth than the treasures of Egypt, for he looked to the reward.* ^{27}*By faith he left Egypt, not being afraid of the anger of the king; for he endured as seeing him who is invisible.* ^{28}*By faith he kept the Passover and sprinkled the blood, so that the Destroyer of the first-born might not touch them.*

^{29}*By faith the people crossed the Red Sea as if on dry land; but the Egyptians, when they attempted to do the same, were drowned.* ^{30}*By faith the walls of Jericho fell down after they had been encircled for seven days.* ^{31}*By faith Rahab the harlot did not perish with those who were disobedient, because she had given friendly welcome to the spies.*

OVERVIEW: The miraculous acts and lives of the Old Testament saints are a work of God's grace granted to them according to their faith. For instance, Moses refused the palace of the pharaoh because of his faith in the kingdom of God and was rewarded accordingly (CHRYSOSTOM). In this passage Paul uses an economy of words to present great things through simple acts in Israel's history. Chrysostom refers to the sprinkling of blood in the exodus: "Although what was done was nothing, what was achieved was great. For what was done was blood, but what was achieved was salvation and the stopping and preventing of destruction. The angel feared the blood, for he knew of what it was a type; he shuddered, thinking on the Lord's death; therefore he did not touch the doorposts. Thus the hearer is to be confident." Moses is a type of Christ; as Moses brought his people out of Egypt, a place deprived of faith (EPHREM), so Christ brought us through suffering from death to eternal life (PHOTIUS). Faith can do all things and transcends human reasoning.

Rahab is a type of the church (GREGORY OF ELVIRA) as through her faith she received those

who signify the Trinity (IRENAEUS) and was saved according to her faith (CHRYSOSTOM, EPHREM). Moreover, everyone in her home was saved because of the scarlet rope that signifies the blood of Christ as well as his passions (JUSTIN, HILARY). Salvation of the former harlot calls all of us to repentance (ORIGEN).

11:23-28 Moses' Faith

THOSE OTHERWISE OBSCURE. CHRYSOSTOM: Joseph did not say, "God did not give the land to me in my lifetime, nor to my father or my grandfather, whose excellence too ought to have been reverenced. Will God give to these wretched people what God did not give to them?" He said nothing like this, but by faith he both conquered and went beyond all these things. The apostle has named Abel, Noah, Abraham, Isaac, Jacob, Joseph—all illustrious and admirable men. But then he makes the encouragement greater by bringing the matter down to ordinary persons. For that the admirable should feel thus is nothing wonderful, and to appear inferior to them is nothing dreadful; but to show oneself inferior even to people without names, this is awesome.

He begins with the parents of Moses, obscure persons who had nothing so great as their son had. Then he goes on to increase the strangeness of what he says by enumerating even women who were harlots and widows. For "by faith," he says "the harlot Rahab did not perish with them that believed not, for she had received the spies with peace." And he mentions the rewards not only of belief but also of unbelief, as in the case of Noah.

But at present we must speak of the parents of Moses. Pharaoh gave orders that all the male children should be destroyed, and none had escaped the danger. How did these expect to save their child? By faith. What sort of faith? "They saw," he says, "that the child was beautiful." The very sight of him drew them on to faith. Thus from the beginning—yes, from the very swaddling clothes—great was the grace that was poured out on that righteous man, this being not the work of nature. For observe, the child immediately on its birth appears fair and not disagreeable to the sight. Whose work was this? Not that of nature but of the grace of God, which also stirred up and strengthened that barbarian woman, the Egyptian, and took and drew her on. On the Epistle to the Hebrews 26.3.[1]

Moses Refused the Palace. Chrysostom: Paul says, "By faith Moses, when he was grown up, refused to be called the son of Pharaoh's daughter, choosing rather to suffer ill treatment with the people of God than to enjoy the fleeting pleasures of sin; considering abuse suffered for the Christ greater wealth than the treasures of Egypt; for he looked to the reward." It is as though Paul had said to them, "No one of you has left a palace, yes a splendid palace, or such treasures. None of you, when you might have been a king's son, has despised this. But Moses did." And he did not simply leave it there. He further expressed it by saying, "he refused," that is, he hated, he turned away. For when heaven was set before Moses, it was superfluous to admire an Egyptian palace.

And see how admirably Paul has put it. He did not say, "Esteeming heaven and the things in heaven," "greater wealth than the treasures of Egypt," but what? "Abuse suffered for the Christ." For he accounted being abused for the sake of Christ better than being thus at ease; and this itself by itself was reward.

"Choosing rather," he says, "to suffer ill treatment with the people of God." For you indeed suffer on your own account, but Moses "chose" to suffer for others and voluntarily threw himself into so many dangers, when it was in his power both to live religiously and to enjoy good things, rather "than," he says, "to enjoy the fleeting pleasures of sin." He called unwillingness "to suffer ill treatment with" the rest "sin." This, he says, Moses accounted to be "sin." If then he accounted it "sin" not to be ready to "suffer ill treatment with" the rest, it follows that the suffering ill treatment must be a great good, since he threw himself into it from the royal palace. On the Epistle to the Hebrews 26.4.[2]

Moses Considered Christ. Ephrem the Syrian: "By faith Moses, when he was grown up, refused to be called a son of Pharaoh's daughter." If he had not believed in the promise of Abraham, he would have not refused to be corrupted by sin, nor would he have chosen to share ill treatment with the people of God. He considered the emulation of Christ, about whom he indeed wrote, to be more important than the wealth of the Egyptians, which he would have received, because in his expectation "he was looking ahead to the reward." Commentary on the Epistle to the Hebrews.[3]

The Reproaches of Christ. Theodoret of Cyr: What was a type of Christ, the similarity to the reproaches of Christ, was committed against religion by the adversaries. Interpretation of Hebrews 11.[4]

---

[1]NPNF 1 14:483**. [2]NPNF 1 14:483-84**. [3]EHA 225. [4]PG 82:765; TCCLSP 2:186*.

ABUSE SUFFERED FOR CHRIST. PHOTIUS:
What is the "abuse suffered for the Christ"? It is
bearing the reproach of such things, while revealing the reproach that Christ endured. Or it can
mean that Moses endured reproach because of
Christ—for "the rock was Christ"[5]—since it was
likely that Moses was vilified when he heard,
"You don't wish to kill me in the same way that
you killed the Egyptian yesterday, do you?"[6] That
is the "abuse suffered for the Christ," namely, to
suffer ill until one's end and last draught of
breath, just as Christ himself was reviled and
heard, "If you are the Son of God, come down
from the cross."[7] For both were reviled by their
very own countrymen for whom they were doing
good works. FRAGMENTS ON THE EPISTLE TO THE
HEBREWS 11.26.[8]

HE DID NOT RUN FAR AWAY. OECUMENIUS:
He did not fear lest Pharaoh's wrath be so great
so as to investigate him as he fled. Therefore he
did not run far away, but from where he could
return.[9] And that was done by faith. FRAGMENTS
ON THE EPISTLE TO THE HEBREWS 11.4.[10]

LIKE MOSES, WE TOO WILL LOVE GOD.
CHRYSOSTOM: If then we too always see God
with our mind, if we always think in remembrance of God, all things will appear endurable to
us, all things tolerable. We shall bear them all easily. We shall be above them all. If you see one
whom you love, or remember that one, you are
reawakened in spirit and elevated in thought and
you bear all things easily while delighting in the
remembrance. Then when will one who has in
mind the one who has promised to love us
indeed, remembering that one, either feel anything painful or dread anything fearful or danger-
ous? When will he be of cowardly spirit? Never.
ON THE EPISTLE TO THE HEBREWS 26.6.[11]

**BY THE LAMB SLAIN, GOD HAS BROUGHT US
FROM EGYPT.** CHRYSOSTOM: Paul wants to establish many things incidentally and is very full of
thoughts. For such is the grace of the Spirit. He
does not comprehend a few ideas in a multitude
of words but includes great and manifold thought
in brevity of expressions. Observe at least how, in
the midst of exhortation and when discoursing
about faith, he reminds us of the source of the reality as seen in its type and mystery. "By faith," he
says, "he kept the Passover and the sprinkling of
blood, lest he that destroyed the first-born should
touch them."

But what is the "sprinkling of blood"? A lamb
was slain in every household, and the blood was
smeared on the doorposts, and this was a means of
warding off the Egyptian destruction. If then the
blood of a lamb preserved the Jews unhurt in the
midst of the Egyptians, and under so great a
destruction, much more will the blood of Christ
save us, who have had it sprinkled not on the doorposts but in our souls. For even now also the
Destroyer is going about in this depth of night, so
let us be armed with that sacrifice. . . . For God has
brought us out from Egypt, from darkness, from
idolatry. Although what was done was nothing,
what was achieved was great. For what was done
was blood, but what was achieved was salvation
and the stopping and preventing of destruction.
The angel feared the blood, for he knew of what it
was a type. He shuddered, thinking on the Lord's
death; therefore he did not touch the doorposts.
Moses said, "Smear," and they smeared and were
confident. And you, having the blood of the Lamb
himself, are you not confident? ON THE EPISTLE
TO THE HEBREWS 27.1.[12]

A PREMONITION OF THE LORD'S BLOOD. THE-
ODORET OF CYR: How would he, without faith,
have believed that death would be prevented by
the blood of a sheep? He recognized in advance
the reality in the type and had a premonition of
the power of the Lord's blood. INTERPRETATION
OF HEBREWS 11.[13]

---

[5]1 Cor 10:4. [6]Ex 2:14. [7]Mt 27:40. [8]NTA 15:651. [9]Ex 2:15. [10]NTA
15:467. [11]NPNF 1 14:484*. [12]NPNF 1 14:487**. [13]PG 82:765;
TCCLSP 2:186.

11:29 As If on Dry Land

Everywhere Faith Goes Beyond Human Reasonings. Chrysostom: Again he compares one whole people with another, lest they should say, "We cannot be as the saints." "By faith," he says, "they passed through the Red Sea as if by dry land, which the Egyptians were drowned in trying to do." Here he leads them also to a recollection of the sufferings in Egypt. How "by faith"? Because they had hoped to pass through the sea, and therefore they prayed, or rather it was Moses who prayed. Do you see that everywhere faith goes beyond human reasonings and weakness and lowliness? Do you see that at the same time they both believed and feared punishment, both in the blood on the doors and in the Red Sea? And he made it clear that it was really water, through those that fell into it and were choked. He made it clear that it was not a mere appearance. Rather it was, as in the case of the lions, those who were devoured proved the reality of the facts; and in the case of the fiery furnace, those who were burned. Here also you see that the same things become to the one a cause of salvation and glory, and to the other of destruction.

So great a good is faith. When we fall into perplexity, then are we delivered, even though we come to death itself, even though our condition is desperate. For what else was left for them? They were unarmed, surrounded by the Egyptians and the sea. They must either be drowned if they fled, or fall into the hands of the Egyptians. But nevertheless God saved them from impossibilities. That which was spread under the one as land overwhelmed the others as sea. In the former case, it forgot its nature; in the latter, it actually armed itself against them.[14] On the Epistle to the Hebrews 27.2.[15]

The Egyptians Were Without Faith. Ephrem the Syrian: "By faith they crossed the Red Sea." In fact, the people who entered into it believed and crossed it as if on dry land. On the other hand, the Egyptians went into it without faith and received the reward for their crimes in the midst of it. Commentary on the Epistle to the Hebrews.[16]

11:30 The Walls of Jericho

Faith Can Do All Things. Chrysostom: "By faith, the walls of Jericho fell down, after they had been encircled for seven days." For assuredly the sound of trumpets cannot throw down stones, even if one blows for ten thousand years, but faith can do all things.

Do you see that in all cases it is not by natural sequence, nor yet by any law of nature, that it was changed, but all is done contrary to expectation? Accordingly, in this case also, all is done contrary to expectation. For since he had said again and again that we ought to trust to future hopes, he again introduced all this argument with good reason, showing that not now only, but even from the beginning, all the miracles have been accomplished and achieved by means of it. On the Epistle to the Hebrews 27.3.[17]

11:31 Rahab's Faith

Faith Covered the Wounds of Sin. Theodoret of Cyr: Lawlessness of life did not prevent salvation; faith covered the wounds of sin. Now, it is worth admiring the apostle's wisdom—or, rather, we ought sing the praises of the activity of the divine Spirit in associating a foreign woman and prostitute with Moses, Abraham, Noah, Enoch, and the other saints so as to establish the power of faith and repress the Jews' conceit. After all, six hundred thousand of them were consumed in the desert on account of lack of faith, as they gained no benefit from the way of life of the law. She on the contrary, though removed from kinship with Abraham, living outside the way of life of the law and spending most

---

[14]Cf. Wis 19:20. [15]NPNF 1 14:487**. [16]EHA 225-26. [17]NPNF 1 14:487*.

of her time in licentious behavior, through faith reaped salvation and foreshadowed in type the church. Just as she with faith gave admission to the spies, so the church did to the apostles. And as she was given the scarlet cord as a sign of salvation, so the church through the Lord's blood enjoyed the eternal goods. INTERPRETATION OF HEBREWS 11.[18]

RAHAB ALONE WAS PRESERVED. CHRYSOSTOM: It would be disgraceful, if you should appear more faithless even than a harlot. Yet she merely heard what the men related and then believed. Thereupon the end also followed, for, when all perished, she alone was preserved. She did not say to herself, "I shall be with my many friends." She did not say, "Can I possibly be wiser than these judicious men who do not believe—and shall I believe?" She said no such thing, but [she] believed what had taken place, which it was likely that they would suffer. ON THE EPISTLE TO THE HEBREWS 27.3.[19]

FAITH THROUGH THE RUMORS. EPHREM THE SYRIAN: Indeed, through the rumors about the miracles which had happened in Egypt and the desert, she believed that they would have possessed the land of Canaan, as God had said to Abraham. The apostle also added some words about the "explorers," who "were received by her in peace," because he wanted to show that they came out of her house in purity and honesty. In fact, they had not entered that place for the sake of fornication. COMMENTARY ON THE EPISTLE TO THE HEBREWS.[20]

SHE RECEIVED THE TRINITY. IRENAEUS: So also did Rahab the harlot, while condemning herself because she was a Gentile, receive the three speculators who were spying out the land—which three were doubtless the Father, the Son and the Holy Spirit—and hid them in her home. And when the entire city in which she lived fell to ruins at the sounding of the seven trumpets, Rahab and all her house were preserved, through

faith in the scarlet sign. So the Lord declared to those who did not receive the Lord—the Pharisees, that is—and to those who despised the scarlet thread, which signified the Passover and the redemption and the exodus from Egypt, that "the publicans and the harlots go into the kingdom of heaven before you."[21] AGAINST HERESIES 4.20.12.[22]

THE BLOOD OF CHRIST. JUSTIN MARTYR: The red rope, which the spies sent by Joshua, son of Nun, gave to Rahab the harlot in Jericho, instructing her to tie it to the same window through which she lowered them down to escape their enemies, was a symbol of the blood of Christ. By [this blood] those of every nationality who were once fornicators and sinful are redeemed, receiving pardon of their past sin and avoiding all sin in the future. DIALOGUE WITH TRYPHO 111.[23]

THE CHURCH RECEIVES THE LAW AND PROPHETS. HILARY OF POITIERS: This episode in the Old Testament is a series of important types [*sacramenta*] of future spiritual events. The harlot takes into her house the two spies sent by Jesus [Joshua] to survey the land. The church, which was a sinner, receives the law and the prophets, sent to spy out the faith of men, and acknowledges that "God is in heaven above and on the earth beneath." She receives from these same spies the scarlet sign of salvation, a color which is manifestly the color of royalty when considered as a dignity, and, when looked at, the color of blood. Both these features were found in the passion—the Lord was clothed in scarlet, and blood flowed from his side. Manasseh[24] also received scarlet as a sign. The dwellings in Egypt marked with blood were spared, and with blood the book of the covenant was sprinkled and the people sanctified. Every member of the family

[18]PG 82:765, 768; *TCCLSP* 2:186. [19]NPNF 1 14:488*. [20]EHA 226. [21]Mt 21:31. [22]ANF 1:492. [23]FC 6:320. [24]Hilary may have meant Zerah (Gen 38:30).

found outside the house was guilty—a lesson that those apart from those called are responsible for their own death. TRACTATE OF THE MYSTERIES 2.9.154-56.[25]

OUTSIDE THE CHURCH THERE IS NO SALVATION. ORIGEN: She who was formerly a harlot receives this injunction: All who shall be found in your house shall be saved. . . if anyone wishes to be saved, let him come into the house of her that was a harlot. Even if anyone of this people [the Jews] wishes to be saved, let him come into this house to obtain salvation. Let him come into this house in which the blood of Christ is the sign of redemption. Let there be no mistake, let no one deceive himself: outside this house, that is outside the ecclesia, there is no salvation. If anyone does go forth, he is the cause of his own death.[26] HOMILIES ON JOSHUA 3.5.[27]

RAHAB IS A TYPE OF THE CHURCH. GREGORY OF ELVIRA: Rahab, who is a type of the church, suspended the scarlet thread from her window as a sign of salvation, to show that the nations would be saved through the Lord's passion. . . . The house of Rahab and all those with her were saved through the scarlet sign when Jericho was destroyed and burned and its king, a type of the devil, slain. So when this world is destroyed by fire and the devil who now has dominion over the world is overthrown, no one will be preserved for eternal salvation if that one is not found inside the house of the ecclesia which is marked with the scarlet sign, that is, with the blood of Christ. Or again, as in the flood, no one escaped the drowning of the world save those who were preserved in the ark of Noah, which is a type of the church. ORIGEN'S TRACTATE ON THE BOOKS OF HOLY SCRIPTURE 139.[28]

EVERY ONE OF US WAS THE HARLOT. ORIGEN: Our Jesus [Joshua] sent his spies to the king of Jericho. There they are welcomed by a harlot. But this harlot who received the spies sent by Jesus did so that she might no longer be a harlot. The soul of every one of us was that harlot when we lived in the desires and lusts of the flesh. But our souls received the messengers of Jesus, the angels, whom he has sent before his face to prepare his ways. Every soul who receives them with faith, lodges them not in unworthy and inferior places but in those which are more elevated, because we do not receive Jesus from low and earthly places but as coming forth from the Father and descending from heaven. HOMILIES ON JOSHUA 1.4.[29]

---

[25]FSTR 255*; cf. 246. [26]This is an early attestation of the tradition that "outside the church there is no salvation." [27]PG 12:841-42; FSTR 250-51. [28]FSTR 259*. [29]PG 12:829-30; FSTR 252.

11:32-40 SUMMARY OF THE ACTS OF THE FAITHFUL

[32]*And what more shall I say? For time would fail me to tell of Gideon, Barak, Samson, Jephthah, of David and Samuel and the prophets—*[33]*who through faith conquered kingdoms, enforced justice, received promises, stopped the mouths of lions,* [34]*quenched raging fire, escaped the edge of the sword, won strength out of weakness, became mighty in war, put foreign armies*

to flight. [35]*Women received their dead by resurrection. Some were tortured, refusing to accept release, that they might rise again to a better life.* [36]*Others suffered mocking and scourging, and even chains and imprisonment.* [37]*They were stoned, they were sawn in two,[y] they were killed with the sword; they went about in skins of sheep and goats, destitute, afflicted, ill-treated—*[38]*of whom the world was not worthy—wandering over deserts and mountains, and in dens and caves of the earth.*

[39]*And all these, though well attested by their faith, did not receive what was promised,* [40]*since God had foreseen something better for us, that apart from us they should not be made perfect.*

y Other manuscripts add *they were tempted*

OVERVIEW: Some find fault with Paul, because he puts Barak, Samson and Jephthah in these places of honor. Nevertheless, as is the case with Rahab, Paul is not concerned with the rest of their lives but only whether they did or did not believe (CHRYSOSTOM). Faith is tested in the adversity that Abraham, Isaac, Jacob, Daniel and the prophets suffered. For this is faith: when things are turning out adversely, then we ought to believe that nothing adverse is done but all is in order. Even as all the heroes of faith did not see the promise but had faith, we, believing in the promise having come also, need to wait in faith, even in suffering, for the final consummation (EPHREM, CHRYSOSTOM, SEVERIAN). The wonderful qualities of faith are two; it accomplishes great things and suffers great things and counts itself to suffer nothing (CHRYSOSTOM). We are called to imitate that faith (CLEMENT OF ROME, JEROME, BASIL). The martyrdom of Isaiah signifies Christ (JUSTIN). The saints of the Old Covenant will share their reward with us in the second coming (CHRYSOSTOM, AUGUSTINE, THEODORE), the day of retribution and resurrection (EPHREM, ORIGEN).

11:32-40 *Time Would Fail Me*

TIME FIT FOR AN EPISTLE. OECUMENIUS: "The time," he says, namely, the amount of time that would be fit for an epistle and of such sort to be in due proportion. FRAGMENTS ON THE EPISTLE TO THE HEBREWS 11.32.[1]

THEY ACCOMPLISHED ALL BY FAITH. CHRYSOSTOM: "And what shall I more say? For time would fail me to tell." After this Paul no longer puts down the names, but, having ended with a harlot and put them to shame by the quality of the person, he no longer enlarges on the histories, lest he should be thought tedious. However, he does not set them aside but runs over them, doing both very judiciously, avoiding satiety without spoiling the closeness of the argument. He was neither altogether silent, nor did he speak so as to annoy, for he effected both points. For when a person is contending vehemently in argument, if he persists in contending, he wears out the hearer, annoying him when he is already persuaded and gaining the reputation of vain ambitiousness. For he ought to accommodate himself to what is expedient. "And what more do I say?" he says. "For time would fail me to tell of Gideon, Barak, Samson, Jephthah, of David and Samuel and the prophets."

Some find fault with Paul because he puts Barak, Samson and Jephthah in these places. What do you say? After having introduced the harlot, shall he not introduce these? For do not tell me of the rest of their life but only whether they did not believe and shine in faith. "And the prophets," he says, "who through faith conquered kingdoms." Do you see that he does not here testify to their life as being illustrious, for this was not the point in question; the inquiry thus far was about their faith. For tell me whether they

---

[1]NTA 15:467.

did not accomplish all by faith?

"By faith," he says, "they conquered kingdoms"—those with Gideon. "Enforced justice." Who? The same. Plainly, he here means kindness. I think it is of David that he says "they received promises." But of what sort were these? Those in which the Lord said that his "sons shall sit upon" his "throne."[2]

"Stopped the mouths of lions, quenched raging fire, escaped the edge of the sword." See how they were in death itself, Daniel encompassed by the lions, the three children abiding in the furnace, the Israelites, Abraham, Isaac, Jacob, in diverse temptations; and yet not even so did they despair. For this is faith. When things are turning out adversely, then we ought to believe that nothing adverse is done but all things in due order.

"Escaped the edge of the sword." I think that he is again speaking of the three children.

"Won strength out of weakness." Here he alludes to what took place at their return from Babylon. For "out of weakness" is out of captivity. When the condition of the Jews had now become desperate, when they were no better than dead bones, who could have expected that they would return from Babylon, and not return only but also "become mighty" and "put foreign armies to flight"? "But to us," someone says, "no such thing has happened." But these are figures of "the things to come." "Women received their dead by resurrection." He here speaks of what occurred in regard to the prophets Elisha and Elijah, for they raised the dead. ON THE EPISTLE TO THE HEBREWS 27.4.[3]

THESE THINGS CONCERN DAVID. PHOTIUS: I suppose he says these things concerning David. And he calls his benevolence "righteousness."[4] FRAGMENTS ON THE EPISTLE TO THE HEBREWS 11.3.[5]

THEY REMAINED IN FAITH. EPHREM THE SYRIAN: In order not to repeat all the details in his review of the works of faith, Paul stopped relating the stories of these ancient fathers, deciding not to describe their actions in their different aspects.

However, he did not omit other cases, which he included in a short account, . . . that is, about the faith of Gideon, who defeated ten thousand Midianites with three thousand soldiers, and Barak, who by his faith destroyed the army of Sisera; and Samson, who by his faith killed one thousand men with the jaw of an ass; and Jephthah, who by his faith conquered twenty-two cities of the sons of the Ammonites; and David, who by his faith beat and killed Goliath; and Samuel, who by his faith prevailed among the Philistines; "and about the other prophets, who by faith conquered kingdoms" (in prophecy, not in the sword), "enforced justice" (that is, through the revenges and punishments that they inflicted on the impious), "received promises" (like Elisha, who went into ecstasy), "stopped the mouths of lions" (like the house of Daniel), "quenched raging fire" (like the house of Hananiah),[6] "escaped the edge of the sword" (like those whom the Chaldaeans tried to slay together with the wise men of Babylon, and also Uriah and Elijah, and other prophets), "won strength out of weakness" (like King Hezekiah and Elisha), "became mighty in war" (like Abraham, Lot, Moses and Joshua), and "put foreign armies to flight" (like Samson, Barak, David and his companions, who were mentioned above).

"Women received their dead by resurrection," like Silomaea and Zarephath, who had them from Elijah and his disciple.[7] Others, however, who were given to death despised their own life, like the seven brothers together with their mother.[8] Even though they did not do what their companions had done in faith, they nevertheless desired death in their expectation and believed that they would have deserved to obtain "a better resurrection."

"Others had trial of mocking and scourging," like Elisha, or "were imprisoned and chained," like Jeremiah and Micah.

"They were stoned," like Moses and Naboth;

---

[2]Ps 132:12 (131:12 LXX). [3]NPNF 1 14:488*. [4]RSV translates *dikaiosynē* ("righteousness") as "justice." [5]NTA 15:651. [6]Hananiah was renamed Shadrach by Nebuchadnezzar's chief eunuch (Dan 1:7). [7]1 Kings 17:17-24; 2 Kings 4:18-37. [8]2 Macc 7.

"sawn in two," like Zechariah and Isaiah; "tempted" in different manners, like Job; and "killed with the sword" like Micah, Uriah and John. "They went about in the skins of sheep and goats," like Elijah and Elisha. "They were destitute, afflicted and ill-treated—of whom the world was not worthy," like the prophets whom Obadiah hid and nourished with food. "They wandered in deserts, in mountains, in dens and caves of the earth," and when Jezebel heard about the reputation of those hiding, she looked for them, but Obadiah made them run away and take refuge in other places.

Their great afflictions testify before everybody that they remained in faith "and did not even receive their promises." COMMENTARY ON THE EPISTLE TO THE HEBREWS.[9]

THEY DIED BY THEIR WILLINGNESS TO DIE. CHRYSOSTOM: After he said, "They were put to death by the sword, and others were tortured," after he recounted many and different modes of martyrdom, he went on to say, "Therefore, since we are surrounded by so great a cloud of witnesses, let us also lay aside every weight and run with perseverance."[10] Do you see that he called Abel a martyr, as well as Noah, Abraham, Isaac and Jacob? For some of these died for God's sake in the same way that Paul spoke of when he said, "I die daily";[11] they died not by dying but only by their willingness to die. DISCOURSES AGAINST JUDAIZING CHRISTIANS 8.8.3.[12]

THINGS CLOSEST TO HOME. CHRYSOSTOM: "Others suffered mocking and scourging, and even chains and imprisonment." He ends with these, things that come nearer home. For these examples especially bring consolation when the distress is from the same cause, since even if you mention something more extreme, yet unless it arises from the same cause, you have effected nothing. Therefore, he concluded his discourse with this, mentioning "chains, imprisonments, scourges, stonings," alluding to the case of Stephen, also to that of Zechariah. ON THE

EPISTLE TO THE HEBREWS 27.5.[13]

TWO QUALITIES OF FAITH. CHRYSOSTOM: Some "escaped the edge of the sword," and some "were killed with the sword." What is this? Which do you praise? Which do you admire? The latter or the former? No, he says. The former, indeed, is appropriate to you. The latter, because faith was strong even unto death itself, were a type of things to come. For the wonderful qualities of faith are two; it both accomplishes great things and suffers great things, treating suffering as if it were nothing. ON THE EPISTLE TO THE HEBREWS 27.5.[14]

IN SKINS OF SHEEP AND GOATS. CLEMENT OF ROME: You see, dear friends, the kind of example we have been given. . . . If the Lord humbled himself in this way, what should we do who through him have come under the yoke of his grace? Let us be imitators even of those who wandered around "in the skins of sheep and goats" and preached the coming of the Christ. We refer to the prophets Elijah and Elisha—yes, and Ezekiel, too—and to the heroes of old as well. 1 CLEMENT 16.17-17.2.[15]

THE STORY ABOUT ISAIAH SAWN IN TWO. ORIGEN: Whatever they feared might bring blame upon the elders, rulers and judges they kept from the knowledge of the people. But some of these things have been preserved in the apocryphal books.[16] For an example we shall give the story about Isaiah, witnessed by the epistle to the Hebrews but not written in any of the canonical books of the Old Testament. LETTER TO AFRICANUS 9.[17]

"CUT IN TWO" SYMBOLIZED CHRIST'S JUDGMENT OF ISRAEL. JUSTIN MARTYR: The words describing the death of Isaiah, whom you Jews sawed in half with a wooden saw, were expunged from the Scriptures. This incident was a symbol

---

[9]EHA 226-227. [10]Heb 12:1. [11]1 Cor 15:31. [12]FC 68:235*. [13]NPNF 1 14:488-89*. [14]NPNF 1 14:489*. [15]LCC 1:51-52; LCL 1:37-39. [16]E.g., Martyrdom of Isaiah, Ascension of Isaiah. [17]PG 11:65; COS 36.

of Christ, who is going to cut your nation in two, to admit the worthy half into God's eternal kingdom with the holy patriarchs and prophets. But the rest, he has said, he will condemn to the undying flames of hell, together with all those of all nations who are likewise disobedient and unrepentant. DIALOGUE WITH TRYPHO 120.[18]

SHARE IN THE LOT OF CHRIST. JUSTIN MARTYR: Notice how the Lord makes the same promises to Isaac and Jacob. Here are the Lord's words to Isaac: "By your descendants all the nations of the earth shall be blessed."[19] And to Jacob: "By you and your descendants shall all the families of the earth be blessed."[20] But the Lord does not address this blessing to Esau or to Rueben or to any other, but only to them from whom Christ was to come through the Virgin Mary in accordance with the divine plan of our redemption. If you were to think over the blessing of Judah, you would see what I mean, for the seed is divided after Jacob and comes down through Judah and Perez and Jesse and David. Now, this was a sign that some of you Jews would certainly be children of Abraham and at the same time share in the lot of Christ, but that others, also children of Abraham, would be like the sand on the beach, which, though vast and extensive, is barren and fruitless, not bearing any fruit at all, but only drinking up the water of the sea. DIALOGUE WITH TRYPHO 120.[21]

CALAMITIES AND HUNGER. JEROME: Moses and the prophets went about in goatskins, wandering in their caves and in holes in the ground. They were poor men just like Lazarus, and they suffered calamities and endured hunger. ON LAZARUS AND DIVES 86.[22]

THE NARROW AND CLOSE WAY. BASIL THE GREAT: Here is the narrow and close way that leads to life.[23] Here are the teachers and prophets, "wandering in deserts, mountains, caves and holes in the earth." Here are the apostles and evangelists . . . living as citizens of the desert. LETTER 42.[24]

MARTYRDOM AS SERVICE TO YOUR PEOPLE. SEVERIAN OF GABALA: "Of whom the world was not worthy." . . . He does not say this about everyone but about the latter ones whom he sees as martyrs, witnesses of faith. He reminds us that these put foreign armies to flight and through their service to their people received grace. FRAGMENTS ON THE EPISTLE TO THE HEBREWS 11.38.[25]

THEY ARE WAITING FOR YOU. CHRYSOSTOM: What then is the reward of so great a change? What is the recompense? They have not yet received it but are still waiting; and after thus dying in so great tribulation, they have not yet received it. They gained their victory so many ages ago but have not yet received their reward. And you who are yet in the conflict, are you vexed?

Do you also consider what a thing it is, and how great, that Abraham should be sitting and the apostle Paul waiting till you have been perfected, so that they may then be able to receive their reward? For the Savior has told them before that, unless we also are present, he will not give it to them, just as an affectionate father might say to sons who were well approved and had accomplished their work that he would not give them to eat unless their siblings came. And are you vexed that you have not yet received the reward? What then shall Abel do, who was victor before all and is sitting uncrowned? Or Noah? Or those who lived in those early times, seeing that they wait for you and those after you? Do you see that we have the advantage of them? For "God," he says, "has provided some better thing for us." In order that they might not seem to have the advantage over us of being crowned before us, God appointed one time of crowning for all; and he that gained the victory so many years before will receive his crown with you. Do you see God's

---

[18]FC 6:334. [19]Gen 26:4. [20]Gen 28:14. [21]FC 6:332-33*. [22]FC 57:205-6. [23]Mt 7:14. [24]FC 13:110. [25]NTA 15:351.

tender mercy? And he did not say, "that they without us might not be crowned" but "that apart from us they should not be made perfect," so that at that time they appear perfect also. They were before us as regards the conflicts but are not before us as regards the crowns. God did not wrong them; God honored us. For they also wait for the siblings, for, if we are "all one body," the pleasure becomes greater to this body when it is crowned altogether and not part by part. For the righteous are also worthy of admiration in this, that they rejoice in the welfare of their siblings, as in their own, and, for themselves also, it is according to their wish to be crowned along with their own members. To be glorified all together is a great delight. ON THE EPISTLE TO THE HEBREWS 28.2.[26]

FOLLOWING AFTER UNSEEN REWARDS. AUGUSTINE: Now this would be no praise for faith, nor would it be faith at all, if people were in believing to follow after rewards that they could see—in other words, if the reward of immortality were bestowed on believers in this present world. ON THE MERITS AND FORGIVENESS OF SINS AND ON INFANT BAPTISM 2.50.[27]

THE PEOPLE BEFORE CHRIST'S COMING. THEODORE OF MOPSUESTIA: It is also clear from the passage that when he says, "the dead in Christ will rise first,"[28] he does not mean to neglect the just who died before Christ's coming. Otherwise, how could he explicitly say in the epistle to the Hebrews, "And all these, though well attested by their faith, did not receive what was promised, since God had foreseen something better for us, that apart from us they should not be made perfect." COMMENTARY ON 1 THESSALONIANS 4.16-17.[29]

A SINGLE DAY OF RETRIBUTION. EPHREM THE SYRIAN: Even though we come later in the test of temptations, it was previously promised to us that "apart from us they should not be made perfect." In fact it does not happen that, since our

brothers lived before, they will have their reward before. There is a single day of retribution for all the afflictions which people endured and endure. COMMENTARY ON THE EPISTLE TO THE HEBREWS.[30]

ONE BODY RISES FROM THE DEAD IN JUDGMENT. ORIGEN: For indeed, even the apostles have not yet received their joy, but they also wait that I may be a partaker of their joy. For the saints, when they leave this place, do not immediately obtain the whole rewards of their merits. They also wait for us, though we delay, even though we remain. For they do not have perfect delight as long as they grieve for our errors and mourn for our sins. Perhaps you do not believe me when I say this. For who am I that I am so bold to confirm the meaning of such a doctrine? But I produce their witness about whom you cannot doubt. For the apostle Paul is "a teacher of the Gentiles in faith and truth."[31] Therefore, in writing to the Hebrews, after he had enumerated all the holy fathers who were justified by faith, he adds after all that, "all these, though well attested by their faith, did not receive what was promised, since God had foreseen something better for us, that apart from us they should not be made perfect." You see, therefore, that Abraham is still waiting to obtain the perfect things. Isaac waits, and Jacob and all the prophets wait for us, that they may lay hold of the perfect blessedness with us.

For this reason, therefore, that mystery of the delayed judgment is also kept until the last day. For there is "one body"[32] that is waiting to be justified. There is "one body" that is said to rise from the dead in judgment. "As it is, there are many parts, yet one body. The eye cannot say to the hand, 'I have no need of you.'"[33] HOMILIES ON LEVITICUS 7.2.8-9.[34]

---

[26]NPNF 1 14:492*. [27]NPNF 1 5:65*. [28]1 Thess 4:16. [29]TEM 2:31; COS 241*. [30]EHA 227. [31]1 Tim 2:7. [32]See Rom 12:5. [33]1 Cor 12:20-21. [34]FC 83:136-37*.

NOT APART FROM OTHERS. THEODORET OF CYR: Their trials, then, were of this kind and number, but they did not yet receive their crowns. The God of all is waiting for the trials of the others so that, with the stadium no more, he may award acclaim to all the victors together. INTERPRETATION OF HEBREWS 11.[35]

[35]PG 82:769; TCCLSP 2:188.

12:1-13 THAT WE MAY SHARE GOD'S HOLINESS

Therefore, since we are surrounded by so great a cloud of witnesses, let us also lay aside every weight, and sin which clings so closely, and let us run with perseverance the race that is set before us, [2]looking to Jesus the pioneer and perfecter of our faith, who for the joy that was set before him endured the cross, despising the shame, and is seated at the right hand of the throne of God.

[3]Consider him who endured from sinners such hostility against himself, so that you may not grow weary or fainthearted. [4]In your struggle against sin you have not yet resisted to the point of shedding your blood. [5]And have you forgotten the exhortation which addresses you as sons?—

"My son, do not regard lightly the discipline of the Lord,

nor lose courage when you are punished by him.

[6]For the Lord disciplines him whom he loves,

and chastises every son whom he receives."

[7]It is for discipline that you have to endure. God is treating you as sons; for what son is there whom his father does not discipline? [8]If you are left without discipline, in which all have participated, then you are illegitimate children and not sons. [9]Besides this, we have had earthly fathers to discipline us and we respected them. Shall we not much more be subject to the Father of spirits and live? [10]For they disciplined us for a short time at their pleasure, but he disciplines us for our good, that we may share his holiness. [11]For the moment all discipline seems painful rather than pleasant; later it yields the peaceful fruit of righteousness to those who have been trained by it.

[12]Therefore lift your drooping hands and strengthen your weak knees, [13]and make straight paths for your feet, so that what is lame may not be put out of joint but rather be healed.

OVERVIEW: Appealing to this great cloud of witnesses, that is, the heroes of the faith, the author of Hebrews now turns to the present persecutions and sufferings of contemporary Christians and calls for a patient striving in the Lord that is active in faith and long in endurance (THEODORE, EPHREM, CHRYSOSTOM). The early writers recognized the call for striving and holiness in this pericope while insisting on the priority of the gift of faith. "The author and finisher of our faith has put faith within us. . . . He put the beginning into us, he will also put on the end" (CHRYSOSTOM,

Oecumenius). He is the beginning and completion of our faith (Augustine). It is his death and resurrection that give us faith and endurance to reach the glory of the eternal life (Chrysostom, Gregory of Nyssa). The life of faith and virtue is not unlike the contest in the arena in which we are to demonstrate strength, endurance (Chrysostom, Jerome, Severian), and discipline (Chrysostom, Oecumenius).

The early writers were conscious not only of the first coming of Christ but a second as well, far more glorious than the first. Suffering thus had meaning and value and it was not to be regretted; nor were people to lose confidence amid temptation (Ephrem). Augustine argues that power is handed over to the demons for a while in persecutions. Basil argues that tribulations are, for those well prepared, like certain foods and exercises for athletes that lead the contestant to glory. Origen points out that the compassion and the loyalty of the good God is experienced by us as God's jealousy for our good and anger toward sin.

12:1 So Great a Cloud of Witnesses

Witnesses Who Testified for Our Faith. Theodore of Mopsuestia: He did not simply say that there is one time of repayment for all—for this was not his intention—but he said this to show that also those who had done such things and suffered such things through faith might still await the payment of the things promised. Not bearing it with ill grace, they are brought with us of the later generation. Thus he showed their even greater endurance, if indeed they still await after death those who ought to contend likewise with them so that with them we may obtain the enjoyment of all the good. And therefore he speaks of "witnesses," not of the things suffered but of the things testified for our faith. Fragments on the Epistle to the Hebrews 12.1.[1]

The Weight of Sin. Severian of Gabala: Let us lay aside every weight. "Weight" is a sin of

the enjoyment of the flesh, a form in which the "sin which clings so closely" is born. It clings closely to us as it surrounds us with pleasure and subdues us to its own will. Fragments on the Epistle to the Hebrews 12.1.[2]

Sin Clings. Theodoret of Cyr: The models of godliness are set before us on all sides, he is saying, in such vast numbers as to resemble a cloud in density and testify to the power of faith. Accordingly, let us keep our eyes on them, be light on our feet and rid ourselves of the burden of unnecessary worries, in this way being able also to avoid sin that is easy to contract. Before everything else we need perseverance to succeed in the course ahead of us. He said sin "clings" because it is easily contracted and committed: the eye is fascinated, the ear charmed, touch titillated, tongue easily loosened and thought quickly directed to the worst. Interpretation of Hebrews 12.[3]

A Cloud of Sad Afflictions. Ephrem the Syrian: "Therefore, since we are surrounded by so great a cloud of witnesses" about the weight of our life, that is, about the fact that we have ahead of us a cloud of sad afflictions, which lead many who trust in Christ and die for him to honor, "let us lay aside everything" from us.... And "let us run with perseverance the race that is set for us" not only by our persecutors but by the devil himself. Commentary on the Epistle to the Hebrews.[4]

12:2 The Pioneer and Perfecter of Our Faith

The Savior's Joy Is the Salvation of Human Beings. Theodoret of Cyr: He could have avoided suffering, he is saying, had he so chosen; but he put up with the suffering for the benefit of all. The Savior's joy is the salvation of human beings; for it he endured the suffering,

---

[1]NTA 15:210. [2]NTA 15:351. [3]PG 82:768; TCCLSP 2:188. [4]EHA 228.

and after the suffering he is seated with the Father who begot him. Interpretation of Hebrews 12.[5]

He Is Able to Reward You. Oecumenius: "For the joy that was set before him" can be understood also as Gregory says: although it was possible for him to remain in his own personal glory and divinity, he not only humbled himself to the very point of the form of a slave, but he also endured the cross and despised its shame.[6]

Therefore he says that he is able to reward you for all your afflictions for his sake. For not only was he crucified, but also he sat down at "the right hand of God,"[7] the right hand and the throne giving him the same honor. Fragments on the Epistle to the Hebrews 12.2.[8]

Learn to Run Well. Chrysostom: As in all arts and games, we impress the art upon our mind by looking to our masters, receiving certain rules through our sight, so here also, if we wish to run and to learn to run well, let us look to Christ, even to Jesus, "the author and finisher of our faith." What is this? He has put the faith within us. For he said to his disciples, "You did not choose me, but I chose you";[9] and Paul too says, "But then shall I understand, even as I have been fully understood."[10] He put the beginning into us; he will also put on the end. On the Epistle to the Hebrews 28.4.[11]

An Arena of Struggle and Endurance. Jerome: God has entered us as contestants in a racecourse where it is our lot to be always striving. This place, then, a valley of tears, is not a condition of peace, not a state of security, but an arena of struggle and of endurance. Homilies on the Psalms 16 (Psalm 83).[12]

All Things Are Twofold in Our Lord Jesus Christ. Cyril of Jerusalem: We preach not one coming of Christ but a second as well, far more glorious than the first. The first gave us a spectacle of his patience; the second will bring with it the crown of the kingdom of God. In general all things are twofold in our Lord Jesus Christ. His birth is twofold, one of God before the ages and one of a virgin in the consummation of the ages. His descent is twofold, one lowly, "like the rain upon the fleece,"[13] and a second, his manifest coming, which is yet to be. In his first coming he was wrapped in swaddling clothes in the manger; in his second he will be "robed in light as with a cloak."[14] In his first coming he "endured the cross, despising the shame"; in his second he will come in glory, attended by a host of angels. We do not rest, therefore, in his first coming, but we look also for his second. Just as we said of his first coming, "Blessed is he who comes in the name of the Lord,"[15] so we shall repeat the same at his second. Catechetical Lectures 15.1.[16]

Given Faith by the One Who Made Christ. Augustine: Our being born again by water and the Spirit is not a recompense for any merit but is freely given. And if faith has led us to the bath of regeneration, we ought not for that reason to think that we have first given something, so that our saving regeneration might be given us in return. For that one has made us believe in Christ who made for us the Christ in whom we believe. That one made in humans the beginning and the completion of their faith in Jesus who made the human Jesus "the author and finisher of the faith," for this is what he is called, as you know, in the Epistle to the Hebrews. Predestination of the Saints 31.[17]

He Finished It Through the Cross. Ephrem the Syrian: Let us look not toward human beings for the perfection of our faith. In fact, among them one is good for something, but the other is not. Rather let us look into "Jesus

---

[5]PG 82:769, 772; TCCLSP 2:188. [6]Phil 2:6-8. [7]Ps 100:1. [8]NTA 15:467-68. [9]Jn 15:16. [10]1 Cor 13:12. [11]NPNF 1 14:493*. [12]FC 48:123. [13]See Ps 72:6 (71:6 LXX). [14]See Ps 104:2 (103:2 LXX). [15]Mt 21:9. [16]FC 64:53*. [17]NPNF 1 5:513; FC 86:255-56*.

Christ, the pioneer of faith," who was made our leader and "the perfecter" of our faith, because he began from the Jordan the fight against the enemy, then continued it in the desert, and finished it in Jerusalem through the cross, which was erected by the persecutors on Golgotha. COMMENTARY ON THE EPISTLE TO THE HEBREWS.[18]

UNDER NO NECESSITY OF BEING CRUCIFIED. CHRYSOSTOM: "Who," he says, "for the joy that was set before him endured the cross, despising the shame." That is, it was in his power not to suffer at all, if he so willed. For "he committed no sin; no guile was found on his lips";[19] as he also says in the Gospels, "the ruler of this world is coming, and he has no power over me."[20] It lay then in his power, if so he willed, not to come to the cross. For "I have power," he says, "to lay down my life; and I have power to take it again."[21] If then he who was under no necessity of being crucified was crucified for our sake, how much more is it right that we should endure all things nobly! "Who for the joy that was set before him," he says, "endured the cross, despising the shame." But what is "despising the shame"? He chose, he means, that ignominious death. For suppose that he died, some wonder why he should die so ignominiously? For no other reason than to teach us to make no account of glory from the human sphere. Therefore, though under no obligation, he chose death, teaching us to be bold against it and to make it as nothing. Why did the apostle say not "pain" but "shame"? Because it was not with pain that he bore these things. ON THE EPISTLE TO THE HEBREWS 28.4.[22]

THE FLAME OF HIS LIFE. GREGORY OF NYSSA: A fire that lies in wood hidden below the surface is often unobserved by the senses of those who see or even touch it but is manifest when it blazes up. So too, at his death (which he brought about at his will, who separated his soul from his body; who said to his own Father, "Into your hands I commit my spirit";[23] who, as he says, "had power

to lay it down and had power to take it again"[24]) he—who, because he is the lord of glory, despised that which is shame among men—having concealed, as it were, the flame of his life in his bodily nature, by the dispensation of his death, kindled and inflamed it once more by the power of his own Godhead, fostering into life that which had been brought to death. Having infused with the infinity of his divine power that humble firstfruits of our nature, he made it also to be that which he himself was—making the servile form to be Lord, and the human born of Mary to be Christ, and him who was crucified through weakness to be life and power, and making all that is piously conceived to be in God the Word to be also in that which the Word assumed. Thus these attributes no longer seem to be in either nature by way of division, but the perishable nature, being, by its commixture with the divine, made anew in conformity with the nature that overwhelms it, participates in the power of the Godhead, as if one were to say that mixture makes a drop of vinegar mingled in the deep to be sea, by reason that the natural quality of this liquid does not continue in the infinity of that which overwhelms it. This is our doctrine. AGAINST EUNOMIUS 5.5.[25]

WHAT IS SUPERFLUOUS, DO WITHOUT. CHRYSOSTOM: Why do I trifle in saying these things to people who do not even choose to disregard riches but hold fast to them as though they were immortal, and, if they give a little out of much, think they have done all? This is not almsgiving, for almsgiving is that of the widow, who emptied out "her whole living."[26] But if you do not go on to contribute so much as the widow, at least contribute the whole of your superfluity. Keep what is sufficient, not what is superfluous. But there are none who contribute even their superabundance. For so long as you have many servants and garments of silk, these things are all superfluities.

---

[18]EHA 228. [19]1 Pet 2:22. [20]Jn 14:30. [21]Jn 10:18. [22]NPNF 1 14:493**. [23]Lk 23:46. [24]Jn 10:18. [25]NPNF 2 5:181*. [26]Mk 12:44.

Nothing is indispensable or necessary, without which we are able to live. These things are superfluous and are simply superadded. Let us then see, if you please, what we cannot live without. If we have only two servants, we can live. For, whereas some live without servants, what excuse have we, if we are not content with two? We can also have a house built of brick of three rooms, and this is sufficient for us. For are there not some with children and wife who have but one room? Let there be also, if you will, two serving boys.

And how is it not a shame, you say, that a gentlewoman should walk out with only two servants? It is no shame that a gentlewoman should walk along with two servants, but it is a shame that she should go forth with many. Perhaps you laugh when you hear this. Believe me, it is a shame. Do you think it a great matter to go out with many servants, like dealers in sheep or dealers in slaves? This is pride and vainglory; the other is love of wisdom and respectability. For a gentlewoman ought not to be known from the multitude of her attendants. For what virtue is it to have many servants? This belongs not to the soul, and whatever is not of the soul does not show gentility. When she is content with a few things, then is she a gentlewoman indeed; but when she needs many, she is a servant and inferior to slaves.

Tell me, do not the angels go to and fro about the world alone and need not anyone to follow them? Are they then on this account inferior to us? Are they who need no attendants inferior to us, who need them? If, then, not needing an attendant at all is angelic, who comes nearer to the angelic life—she who needs many, or she who needs few? Is not this a shame? For a shame it is to do anything out of place. On the Epistle to the Hebrews 28.9-10.[27]

Conspicuous Consumption. Chrysostom: Tell me, who attracts the attention of those who are in the public places, she who brings many in her train or she who brings but few? And is not she who is alone less conspicuous even than she who is attended by few? Do you see that this is a shame? Who attracts the attention of those in the public places, she who wears beautiful garments or she who is dressed simply and artlessly? Again, who attracts those in the public places, she who is borne on mules and with trappings ornamented with gold, or she who walks out simply and, as it may be, with propriety? Perhaps we do not even look at this latter, if we even see her; but the multitudes not only force their way to see the other but ask, "Who is she, and where from?" And I do not say what great envy is hereby produced. Tell me, then, is it disgraceful to be looked at or not to be looked at? When is the shame greater, when all stare at her, or when no one does? When they inform themselves about her, or when they do not even care? Do you see that we do everything, not for modesty's sake, but for vainglory?

However, since it is impossible to draw you away from that, I am content for the present that you should learn that this is no disgrace. Sin alone is a disgrace, which no one thinks to be a disgrace, but everything rather than this. . . .

But my discourse is not addressed to women only but also to men. For the rest of the things that we have are all superfluous; only the poor possess no superfluities, and perhaps they from necessity, since, if it had been in their power, even they would not have abstained from them. Nevertheless, "whether in pretense or in truth,"[28] so far they have no superfluities. On the Epistle to the Hebrews 28.10-11.[29]

12:3 *He Endured Such Hostility*

Tension Within the Soul. Ephrem the Syrian: "Consider him who," for our love, "showed such" patience toward sinners, not toward those with whom he was in hostility but toward those who, because of their disbelief, appeared to be in tension within their own souls. Do not regret your afflictions, and do not lose

---

[27] NFPF 1 14:495. [28]Phil 1:18. [29]NPNF 1 14:495-96*.

your confidence amid the hour of your temptation. Commentary on the Epistle to the Hebrews.[30]

12:4 Your Struggle Against Sin

You Have Suffered No Great Thing.
Chrysostom: There are two kinds of consolation, apparently opposed to one another but yet contributing great strength each to the other, both of which the apostle has here put forward. The one is when we say that persons have suffered much. For the soul is refreshed when it has many witnesses of its own sufferings, and this he introduced above, saying, "Recall the former days, when, after you were enlightened, you endured a hard struggle with sufferings."[31]

The other is when we say, "You have suffered no great thing." The former, when the soul has been exhausted, refreshes it and makes it recover breath; the latter, when it has become indolent and supine, turns it again and pulls down pride. Thus, so that no pride may spring up in them from that testimony, see what he does. "In your struggle against sin," he says, "you have not yet resisted to the point of shedding your blood." ... This he says also in writing to the Corinthians, "No temptation has overtaken you that is not common to man,"[32] that is, small. For this is enough to arouse and set right the soul, when it considers that it has not risen to the whole trial and encourages itself from what has already befallen it. On the Epistle to the Hebrews 29.1.[33]

Illustrious and Honored Citizens.
Augustine: For short periods and at prescribed times, power has been given to the demons to incite people whom they control to exercise a tyrannical hostility to the City of God. Thus, they are able not only to receive sacrifice from those who offer it and to seek it from those who are well disposed but also to extort it violently from the unwilling by means of persecutions. However, this power is not a menace to the church but rather an advantage, since it helps to fill up the number of its martyrs.[34] And these the City of God esteems as its most illustrious and honored citizens, just because they have resisted the impious so valiantly, even "to the shedding of blood, striving against sin." City of God 10.21.[35]

Resist Sin Even to Death. Evagrius Ponticus: Do not think you have attained to virtue until first you have fought to the shedding of blood. One must resist sin even to death—manfully and irreproachably, as the divine apostle tells us. Chapters on Prayer 136.[36]

12:5-6 The Discipline of the Lord

Tribulations Leading Us on to Glory.
Basil the Great: In truth, tribulations are, for those well prepared, like certain foods and exercises for athletes which lead the contestant on to the hereditary glory, if, when reviled, we bless; if when maligned, we entreat; if ill-treated, we give thanks; if afflicted, we glory in our afflictions.[37] It is indeed shameful for us to bless on propitious occasions but be silent on dark and difficult ones. On the contrary, we must bless even more at that time, knowing that "the Lord disciplines him whom he loves and chastises every son whom he receives." Homilies on the Psalms 16.1 (Psalm 33).[38]

Whipping the Sins. Origen: "I will punish with the rod" your saints; "I will visit with a whip their sins."[39] Why? So that "I may not take my mercy from them."[40] For when he leaves someone, he no longer punishes or whips them, since he does not whip everyone, but "every son the Lord receives." Selections from Exodus 127.[41]

---

[30]EHA 228-29. [31]Heb 10:32. [32]1 Cor 10:13. [33]NPNF 1 14:499*. [34]See Rev 6:11. [35]FC 14:154. [36]CS 4:77. [37]See 1 Cor 4:12-13. [38]FC 46:249-50. [39]Ps 89:32 (88:33 LXX). [40]Ps 89:33 (88:34 LXX). [41]PG 12:292-93; COS 30.

WE MUST PASS THROUGH AFFLICTION.
CHRYSOSTOM: "The Lord disciplines him whom he loves and chastises every son whom he receives." You cannot say that any righteous person is without affliction; even if that one appears to be so, we do not know that person's other afflictions. Of necessity every righteous person must pass through affliction. For it is a declaration of Christ that the wide and broad way leads to destruction but the straight and narrow one to life.[42] If then it is possible to enter into life by that means and no other, then all have entered in by the narrow way, as many as have departed unto life. ON THE EPISTLE TO THE HEBREWS 29.2.[43]

THE MERCY OF THE GOOD GOD. ORIGEN: Therefore, if this "jealous God" asks for you and wishes your soul to cleave to him, if he keeps you from sin, if he corrects and chastises you, if he is indignant, if he is angry and uses a kind of jealousy against you, know that this is your hope of salvation. . . . See the compassion and loyalty of the good God. When he wishes to have mercy, he says he is indignant and angry. HOMILIES ON EXODUS 8.5.[44]

LED TO HOPE THAT DOES NOT DISAPPOINT.
BASIL THE GREAT: Not in the amount of money, not in the pride of power, not in the height of glory is victory gained, but the Lord freely gives his help to those who seek him through excessive affliction. Such was Paul,[45] who made his afflictions his boast. Therefore he was able to say, "When I am weak, then I am strong."[46] "Give us therefore, O Lord, help from trouble," since "suffering produces endurance, and endurance produces character, and character produces hope, and hope does not disappoint."[47] Do you see where affliction leads you? To hope that does not disappoint. Are you ill? Be of good cheer, because "the Lord disciplines him whom he loves." HOMILIES ON THE PSALMS 20.5 (PSALM 59).[48]

COMPLETE JOY. BEDE: At this point we might

consider and commit more actively to memory how almighty God allows God's chosen ones and beloved servants—those God has predestined to life and the eternal kingdom—to be so stricken in this life by the persecution of the wicked and to be wasted by so many kinds and such fierce punishments and deaths. This is so that when we have viewed the sufferings of the maturely faithful, we may grieve less over the adversities that perhaps have happened to us and learn instead to esteem it complete joy when we fall into various kinds of struggles,[49] keeping in mind that "the Lord disciplines him whom he loves and chastises every son whom he receives." HOMILIES ON THE GOSPELS 2.23.[50]

THE WRONG SENSE IS INFERRED FROM HUMAN HABITS. CASSIODORUS: The anger of the Lord is cited in two senses. First, when the Lord punishes to save, as in the passage, "For he chastises every son whom he receives," and second, when the Lord consigns to eternal fire, of which another psalm says, "Lord, rebuke me not in your anger, nor chastise me in your wrath."[51] The wrong sense is inferred from human habits, for when we punish some guilt we are angry at wicked deeds; but God judges all things in tranquility, for God need not tolerate any confusion of emotion. EXPOSITION OF THE PSALMS 58.14.[52]

12:7-10 God Treats You as Offspring

FATHERS DESPISE ILLEGITIMATE CHILDREN.
THEODORET OF CYR: Fathers are in the habit of disciplining their true children, and if they see them caned by the teachers, they do not worry; they see the fruit coming from the discipline. But they despise illegitimate children and do not accord them equal attention. So if you also avoid discipline, you are of the number of the illegitimate. INTERPRETATION OF HEBREWS 12.[53]

---

[42]Mt 7:13-14. [43]NPNF 1 14:499**. [44]FC 71:327-28*. [45]Rom 5:3. [46]2 Cor 12:10. [47]Rom 5:3-5. [48]FC 46:340*. [49]Jas 1:2. [50]CS 111:237*. [51]Ps 6:1. [52]ACW 52:59*. [53]PG 82:772; TCCLSP 2:189.

FROM THIS SUFFERING YOU MAY BE CONFIDENT. CHRYSOSTOM: "You endure discipline," he says, not for punishment or for vengeance or suffering. See, it is from these sufferings from which they supposed they had been deserted, he says, that they may be confident that they have not been deserted. It is as if he had said, "Because you have suffered so many evils, do you suppose that God has left you and hates you?" If you did not suffer, then it would be right to suppose this. For if "he chastises every son whom he receives," then he who is not chastised perhaps is not a son. What then, you say, do not bad men suffer distress? They suffer indeed. How then? He did not say, "Every one who is chastised is a son" but "every son is chastised." ON THE EPISTLE TO THE HEBREWS 29.2.[54]

CORRECTED FROM SIN. AUGUSTINE: Here discipline is spoken of in reference to those evils that anyone suffers for his sins in order that he may be corrected. ON THE TRINITY 14.1.1.[55]

DISCIPLINE THAT MAKES US PERFECT. OECUMENIUS: For human fathers do not always prevail to discipline us so that they can render us perfect, but God always disciplines us and makes us perfect. For the process of discipline stops when the father dies or the child comes of age. FRAGMENTS ON THE EPISTLE TO THE HEBREWS 12.9.[56]

NOT FOR THEIR OWN INTERESTS. CHRYSOSTOM: He reasons from their own experiences, from what they themselves suffered. For, as he says above, "Recall the former days,"[57] he says here also, "God is treating you as sons," and you could not say, "We cannot bear it." Yes, "as sons" tenderly beloved. For if they reverence their "fathers of the flesh," how shall you not reverence your heavenly Father? However, the difference arises not from this alone, nor from the persons, but also from the cause itself, and from the fact. For it is not on the same grounds that he and they impose discipline. They did it with a view to "what seemed good to them," that is, fulfilling

their own pleasure oftentimes and not always looking to what was expedient. But here that cannot be said, for the Lord does this not for any interest of the Lord's own but for you and for your benefit alone. They did it that you might be useful to themselves, often without reason; but here there is nothing of this kind. Do you see that this also brings consolation? For we are most closely attached to those when we see that they either command or advise us not for any interests of their own, when their earnestness is, wholly and solely, on our account. For this is genuine love, and love in reality, when we are beloved though we be of no use to the one who loves us— not so that one may receive but so that one may impart. God chastens, God does everything, God uses all diligence, that we may become capable of receiving God's benefits. ON THE EPISTLE TO THE HEBREWS 29.3.[58]

TAKE AWAY WHAT IS SUPERFLUOUS. CHRYSOSTOM: Do you wish to nourish the body? Take away what is superfluous, and give what is sufficient, as much as can be digested. Do not load it, lest you overwhelm it. A sufficiency is both nourishment and pleasure. For nothing is so productive of pleasure as food well digested, nothing so productive of health, nothing so productive of acuteness of the faculties, nothing tends so much to keep away disease. For a sufficiency is nourishment, pleasure and health, but excess is injury, unpleasantness and disease. For what famine does, satiety does also—or rather more grievous evils. For the former indeed within a few days carries a person off and sets that one free; but the other, eating into and putrefying the body, gives it over to long disease and then to a most painful death. But we, while we account famine a thing greatly to be dreaded, yet run after satisfaction, which may be more distressing than famine. What is this disease? What this madness? I do not say that we should waste ourselves away but

---

[54]NPNF 1 14:499-500*. [55]NPNF 1 3:183*. [56]NTA 15:468. [57]Heb 10:32. [58]NPNF 1 14:500**.

that we should eat as much food as also gives us pleasure that is really pleasure and can nourish the body and furnish it to us well ordered and adapted for the energies of the soul, well joined and fitted together. But when it comes to be waterlogged by luxury, it cannot in the flood wave keep fast the bolts themselves, one might say, and the joints which hold the frame together. For when the flood wave comes in, the whole breaks up and scatters. ON THE EPISTLE TO THE HEBREWS 29.7.[59]

12:11 *Painful Rather Than Pleasant*

THEIR REWARD IS JUSTICE. EPHREM THE SYRIAN: They gain a profit from it: their reward is justice. Paul said this in order to prove that even though they gain a profit through discipline, their reward and grace is constituted by justice. COMMENTARY ON THE EPISTLE TO THE HEBREWS.[60]

A GREAT ABUNDANCE OF FRUITS. CHRYSOSTOM: They who drink bitter medicines first submit to some unpleasantness and afterwards feel the benefit. For such is virtue, such is vice. In the latter, there is first the pleasure, then the despondency; in the former, first the despondency, and then the pleasure. But there is no equality; for it is not the same to be first grieved and afterwards pleased and to be first pleased and afterwards grieved. How so? Because, in the latter case, the expectation of coming despondency makes the present pleasure less, but, in the former, the expectation of coming pleasure cuts away the violence of present despondency. The result is that, in the one instance, we never have pleasure; in the latter, we never have grief. . . .

From this Paul then undertakes to console them and again takes up the common judgment of people, which no one is able to stand against or to contend with the common decision, when one says what is acknowledged by all.

You are suffering, he says. For such is chastisement; such is its beginning. "For the moment all discipline seems painful rather than

pleasant." He said well, "seems." Discipline, he means, is not grievous but "seems" so. "All discipline" . . . means both human and spiritual. Do you see that he argues from our common notions? "Seems painful," he says, so that it is not really so. For what sort of pain brings forth joy? So neither does pleasure bring forth despondency.

Nevertheless, "later it yields the peaceful fruits of righteousness to those who have been trained by it."[61] Not "fruit" but "fruits," a great abundance.

"To those," he says, "who have been trained by it." That is, to those who have endured for a long while and been patient. And he uses an auspicious expression; so then, discipline is exercise, making the athlete strong and invincible in combats, irresistible in conflicts. ON THE EPISTLE TO THE HEBREWS 30.1.[62]

12:12-13 *What Is Lame May Be Healed*

THE DISCIPLINE IS OF LOVE. CHRYSOSTOM: Do not wonder if discipline, being itself hard, has sweet fruits; since in trees also the bark is almost destitute of all quality and rough, but the fruits are sweet. . . . Why, after you have endured the painful, are you despondent as to the good? The distasteful things that you had to endure you endured. Do not then become despondent when you are rewarded. He speaks as to runners and boxers and warriors. Do you see how he arms them, how he encourages them? "Walk straight," he says. Here he speaks with reference to their thoughts; that is to say, not doubting. For if the discipline be of love, if it begin from loving care, if it end with a good result (and this he proves both by facts and by words, and by all considerations), why are you dispirited? For such are they who despair, who are not strengthened by the hope of the future. "Walk straight," he says, that your lameness may not be increased but brought back

---

[59]NPNF 1 14:502**. [60]EHA 229. [61]RSV uses "fruit" in the singular. [62]NPNF 1 14:503*.

to its former condition. For he that runs when he is lame galls the sore place. Do you see that it is in our power to be thoroughly healed? On the Epistle to the Hebrews 30.1.[63]

Repentance for Those Who Have Sinned. Theodore of Mopsuestia: Where are those who say that the apostle in this epistle precludes repentance by saying, "It is impossible to renew again thereafter to repentance those once enlightened"?[64] How then do they understand these words: "Therefore lift your drooping hands and strengthen your weak knees"? What sort of healing of the lame does this apostle, who allegedly does not believe in a repentance for those who have sinned, wish to take place? It is clear he writes these things to believers in that he says to them: "Recall the former days when, after you were enlightened, you endured a hard struggle with sufferings."[65] Fragments on the Epistle to the Hebrews 12.12-13.[66]

You Who Are Cast Down. Origen: Nevertheless, since Jesus recites the law to you and reveals to your hearts its spiritual meaning, do not remain "proselytes," that is, catechumens, any longer, but hurry to receive fully the grace of God.... And you "children," "do not be children in your thinking; be babes in evil, but in thinking be mature."[67] As the apostle says to the Hebrews, "Let us leave the elementary doctrines of Christ and go on to maturity."[68] But you, too, who under the title *women* are weak, cast down and tired, you are exhorted to "lift your drooping hands and strengthen your weak knees." Homilies on Joshua 9.9.[69]

Lameness of Transgression. Ephrem the Syrian: "Therefore lift your drooping hands and strengthen your weak knees," that is, "make straight paths for your feet" throughout the afflictions caused by your persecutors, so that they may not slip. [Do this] "so that what is lame," that is, those who transgressed through the denial of faith, "may not be put out of joint" and increase the power of sin "but rather be healed," so that, through his healing, sin may be affected by sickness. Commentary on the Epistle to the Hebrews 12.[70]

---

[63]NPNF 1 14:503*. [64]Heb 6:4-6. [65]Heb 10:32. [66]NTA 15:210-11. [67]1 Cor 14:20. [68]Heb 6:1. [69]FC 105:106. [70]EHA 229.

12:14-29 WARNING AGAINST REFUSING GOD

[14]*Strive for peace with all men, and for the holiness without which no one will see the Lord.* [15]*See to it that no one fail to obtain the grace of God; that no "root of bitterness" spring up and cause trouble, and by it the many become defiled; [16]that no one be immoral or irreligious like Esau, who sold his birthright for a single meal. [17]For you know that afterward, when he desired to inherit the blessing, he was rejected, for he found no chance to repent, though he sought it with tears.*

[18]*For you have not come to what may be touched, a blazing fire, and darkness, and gloom, and a tempest, [19]and the sound of a trumpet, and a voice whose words made the hearers entreat that no further messages be spoken to them. [20]For they could not endure the order that was given, "If even*

a beast touches the mountain, it shall be stoned." [21]*Indeed, so terrifying was the sight that Moses said, "I tremble with fear."* [22]*But you have come to Mount Zion and to the city of the living God, the heavenly Jerusalem, and to innumerable angels in festal gathering,* [23]*and to the assembly[z] of the first-born who are enrolled in heaven, and to a judge who is God of all, and to the spirits of just men made perfect,* [24]*and to Jesus, the mediator of a new covenant, and to the sprinkled blood that speaks more graciously than the blood of Abel.*

[25]*See that you do not refuse him who is speaking. For if they did not escape when they refused him who warned them on earth, much less shall we escape if we reject him who warns from heaven.* [26]*His voice then shook the earth; but now he has promised, "Yet once more I will shake not only the earth but also the heaven."* [27]*This phrase, "Yet once more," indicates the removal of what is shaken, as of what has been made, in order that what cannot be shaken may remain.* [28]*Therefore let us be grateful for receiving a kingdom that cannot be shaken, and thus let us offer to God acceptable worship, with reverence and awe;* [29]*for our God is a consuming fire.*

z Or angels, and to the festal gathering and assembly

OVERVIEW: In the midst of suffering, the early writers counsel the faithful to pray and avoid isolation (CHRYSOSTOM). Faith and hope in the mercy of God strengthen us in our pursuit of virtue (ORIGEN, BASIL, BEDE). We are to strive for peace that results in the absence of vengeance that is the result of mutual forgiveness and the encouraging of that peace that is the very condition of our seeing God (AUGUSTINE). The ultimate goal of our struggle is the joy of the heavenly kingdom (BEDE), healing from sin and suffering through the love of God (CHRYSOSTOM, ORIGEN, EPHREM) and sanctification (JEROME). Ministers of the church are especially expected to be holy (BASIL). There are many characteristics of Christianity, but more than all and better than all is love toward one another (CHRYSOSTOM) and peace, as quarrel blocks the light of God (GREGORY THE GREAT). Thus no one is to be left behind from grace in the community of faith (CHRYSOSTOM).

Esau counted his birthright as worthless and could not repent, but for us who have faith in Christ the door is always open (CHRYSOSTOM, THEODORE, OECUMENIUS). Esau is guilty of the thirst of control and pride (EPHREM). We are called to remember our sins for the sake of humil-

ity. In mutual forgiveness, bitterness does not develop. God was formerly revealed through wonderful and awesome things: the temple, the Holy of Holies, fire, darkness, gloom, and tempest.

The new covenant, however, has been given in simple discourse by God incarnate. We now have heard a voice not through darkness but the flesh. "Now what is sin to heaven?" (CHRYSOSTOM). Now we have come to the city of the living God. Jerusalem can be understood as the community of the faithful in heaven and on earth and the soul of every holy and faithful person (EUSEBIUS). The new Jerusalem, the city of God (BASIL), is built with living stones (AMBROSE), that is, made up of a myriad of angels, the baptized and the spirits of those made perfect by the God of the just. This God spoke more graciously with the blood of Jesus than Abel, for Abel's blood cried out for vengeance but Christ's for pardon (ATHANASIUS). The Lord Jesus offered his own self, that is, the firstlings of his own body (AMBROSE); thus we are called to imitate his sacrificial love and mercy (CHRYSOSTOM). Proclamation of the gospel shook the earth, yet God's kingdom cannot be shaken (THEODORE, OECUMENIUS, SEVERIAN, GREGORY OF NAZIANZUS). The end of the pericope, which portrays God as a consuming fire, was interpreted by the Fathers spiritually and figuratively (OECUMENIUS, ORIGEN, THEODORE).

12:14 *Strive for Peace*

THE HELPLESSNESS OF ISOLATION. CHRYSOSTOM: Earlier he had spoken of "not neglecting to meet together,"[1] and here he hints at it again. For nothing so especially makes persons easily vanquished and subdued in temptations as isolation. For scatter a phalanx in war, and the enemy will have no trouble but will take them prisoners, coming on them separately and thus the more helpless. ON THE EPISTLE TO THE HEBREWS 30.2.[2]

WITHOUT HOLINESS NO ONE WILL SEE THE LORD. AUGUSTINE: Many careful precepts have been given us, such as those concerning mutual forgiveness and the encouraging of that peace which is the very condition of our seeing God. One has only to recall the fearsome command given to the servant to pay the debt of ten thousand talents, from which he had been released, because he had not released his fellow servant from the debt that he owed of one hundred pence. When the Lord had proposed this parable, he added the words, "So also my heavenly Father will do to every one of you, if you do not forgive your brother from your heart."[3] CITY OF GOD 15.6.[4]

THE INWARD PERSON ALONE IS ABLE TO SEE GOD. AUGUSTINE: It is better, then, that we affirm that concerning which we have no doubt—that God shall be seen by the inward person which alone is able, in our present state, to see that love in commendation of which the apostle says, "God is love."[5] This inward person alone is able to see "peace and holiness, without which no one shall see the Lord." For no fleshly eye now sees love, peace and holiness, and such things. Yet all of them are seen, so far as they can be seen, by the eye of the mind, and the purer [the mind] is,

the more clearly it sees. Therefore we may, without hesitation, believe that we shall see God. LETTER 148.18.[6]

CHRIST IS THAT SANCTIFICATION WITHOUT WHICH NO ONE SHALL SEE GOD. JEROME: The disciple of Christ must do more for the attainment of spiritual glory than the philosopher of the world, than the venal slave of flying rumors and the people's whims. It is not enough for you to despise wealth unless you follow Christ as well. And only the one who follows Christ forsakes his sins and walks hand in hand with virtue. We know that Christ is wisdom. He is the treasure which in the Scriptures a man finds in his field.[7] He is the peerless gem which is bought by selling many pearls.[8] But if you love a captive woman, that is, worldly wisdom, and if no beauty but hers attracts you, make her bald and cut off her alluring hair, that is to say, her adornments and pare away her dead nails.[9] Wash her with the soap of which the prophet speaks,[10] and then take your ease with her and say, "Her left hand is under my head, and her right hand embraces me."[11] Then shall the captive bring to you many children; from a Moabitess she shall become an Israelite woman. Christ is that sanctification without which no one shall see the face of God. Christ is our redemption, for he is at once our redeemer and our ransom.[12] Christ is everything, so that the one who has left everything for Christ may find one in place of everything and may be able to proclaim freely, "the Lord is my portion."[13] LETTER 66.8.[14]

EXPECTATION OF HOLINESS FOR MINISTERS. BASIL THE GREAT: I am much distressed that the canons of the Fathers have fallen through and that the exact discipline of the church has been banished from among you. I am apprehensive lest, as

---

[1]Heb 10:25. [2]NPNF 1 14:503*. [3]Mt 18:35. [4]FC 14:423. [5]1 Jn 4:8.
[6]NPNF 1 1:503*. [7]See Mt 13:44. [8]Mt 13:45. [9]Cf. Deut 21:11-12.
[10]Jer 2:22. [11]See Song 2:6. [12]Cf. 1 Cor 1:30. [13]Ps 73:26 (72:26 LXX).
[14]NPNF 2 6:138.

this indifference grows, the affairs of the church should, little by little, fall into confusion. According to the ancient custom observed in the churches of God, ministers in the church were received after careful examination. The whole of their life was investigated; an enquiry was made as to their being neither partiers nor drunkards, not quick to quarrel, keeping their youth in subjection, so as to be able to maintain "the holiness without which no man shall see the Lord." This examination was made by presbyters and deacons living with them. Then they brought them to the *chorepiscopi;* and the *chorepiscopi,* after receiving the suffrages of the witnesses as to the truth and giving information to the bishop, so admitted the minister to the sacerdotal order. Now, however, you have quite passed me over; you have not even had the grace to refer to me and have transferred the whole authority to yourselves. Furthermore, with complete indifference, you have allowed presbyters and deacons to introduce unworthy persons into the church, just any one they choose, without any previous examination of life and character, by mere favoritism, on the score of relationship or some other tie. The consequence is that in every village there are many who are considered ministers but not one single person worthy of the service of the altars. Of this you yourselves supply proof from your difficulty in finding suitable candidates for election. LETTER 54.[15]

QUARRELS BLOCK THE LIGHT OF THE SOUL. GREGORY THE GREAT: It is written, "Follow peace with all men, and holiness, without which no man shall see God." For in quarrels the very light of the soul, the light of good intent, is blocked. This is why the psalmist says, "My eye is troubled because of anger."[16] And what good works remain in us if we lose peace from the heart without which we cannot see the Lord? Therefore, act in such a way that you garner your reward even from those who through strife might have caused it to perish. May almighty God guard your love with heavenly grace and grant you to bear much fruit from those who are com-

mitted to you so that your measure may overflow with eternal joys. LETTER 46.[17]

LOVE TOWARD ONE ANOTHER. CHRYSOSTOM: There are many things characteristic of Christianity, but more than all and better than all, love towards one another, and peace. Therefore Christ says, "My peace I give to you,"[18] and again, "By this all men will know that you are my disciples, if you have love for one another."[19] Therefore Paul too says, "Strive for peace with all men, and for the holiness," that is, purity, "without which no one will see the Lord." ON THE EPISTLE TO THE HEBREWS 31.1.[20]

STRIVE FOR HOLINESS. THEODORET OF CYR: By "holiness" he referred to self-control. It is possible even for those in wedlock to achieve it. INTERPRETATION OF HEBREWS 12.[21]

12:15 Obtain the Grace of God

NO ONE LEFT BEHIND. CHRYSOSTOM: As if they were traveling together on some long journey, in a large company, he says, "Take heed that no one be left behind: I do not seek this only, that you should arrive yourselves, but also that you should look diligently after the others." "That no one," he says, "fails to obtain the grace of God." He means the good things to come, the faith of the gospel, the best course of life, for they all are of "the grace of God." Do not tell me, "It is only one that perishes." Even for one Christ died. Have you no care for him "for whom Christ died"?[22] ON THE EPISTLE TO THE HEBREWS 31.1.[23]

12:16-17 So That No One Is Immoral

ESAU'S BIRTHRIGHT. CHRYSOSTOM: He says, "strive after holiness, that no one be immoral or irreligious like Esau," that is, gluttonous, without

---

[15]NPNF 2 8:157*. [16]Ps 6:8 (6:9 LXX). [17]NPNF 2 13:68*. [18]Jn 14:27. [19]Jn 13:35. [20]NPNF 1 14:506*. [21]PG 82:773; TCCLSP 2:190. [22]1 Cor 8:11. [23]NPNF 1 14:506*.

self-control, worldly, selling away things spiritual. "Who sold his birthright for a single meal," who through his own slothfulness sold this honor which he had from God and, for a little pleasure, lost the greatest honor and glory. This was suitable to them, the conduct of an abominable, of an unclean person. So not only is the fornicator unclean, but also the glutton, the slave of his belly, for he also is a slave of a different pleasure. He is forced to be overreaching, to be rapacious, to behave himself unseemly in ten thousand ways, being the slave of that passion, and oftentimes he blasphemes. So he accounted "his birthright" to be worth nothing. That is, while providing for temporary refreshment, he even sacrificed his "birthright." On the Epistle to the Hebrews 31.2.[24]

Not Because of Hunger. Ephrem the Syrian: Scripture thus shows that Esau did not sell his birthright because of hunger, since it says that after he ate, "Esau rose and went away and despised his birthright."[25] He did not sell it because of hunger, therefore, but because he indeed considered it to be worthless and sold it for nothing. Commentary on Genesis 23.2.[26]

Esau Wanted to Gain Control. Ephrem the Syrian: Even if the door is closed before him, it is not closed in the same manner before us. "Know that afterward, when he desired to inherit the blessing, he was rejected, for he found no chance to repent." Moreover, Esau's repentance and his tears did not mean that he wanted to be blessed more than his brother but that he wanted to gain control over his brother. "Even though he sought the blessing with tears," it was not conceded to him. He did not demand blessing, as I said, but the right of the firstborn. In fact, if he had demanded to be superior to his brother in the kingdom of heaven, this would have not been denied to him. But, since he neglected what was useful to his soul and asked for an estate more fertile than that of his brother, he did not receive the blessing that he begged and

was deprived of those things that Jacob, by prevailing on him, received through his faith. Commentary on the Epistle to the Hebrews.[27]

He Found No Chance to Repent. Theodoret of Cyr: Esau wept but did not repent; instead he envied his brother's prosperity.... The divine apostle also suggested this in what he said: "for he found no chance to repent," that is, he did not take the way to repentance, nor did he lament his evil intentions; instead, he grieved not for his sin but for Jacob's success.... It was not without purpose that the divine apostle cited the story of Esau: it was to emphasize that, although the firstborn, he was stripped of the blessing for gluttony and depravity. Jews too, by honoring the firstborn and being enslaved to the obsolete requirements of the law through gluttony, lost their claim to salvation, whereas the Gentiles, the new people, of whom Jacob was a type, gained the privileges of the firstborn. So he urges the believers from Jews not to imitate the lawlessness of the firstborn but to participate in the blessing of the newer people. Interpretation of Hebrews 12.[28]

He Does Not Wish to Preclude Repentance. Theodore of Mopsuestia: Through these words he does not wish to preclude the chance of repentance, but to teach that it is not possible for those who do not receive correction at the present time to receive it later.... For he has not been eager to say contradictory things, especially in so close proximity. And anyone could figure this out from the example that he uses. For first he made mention of Esau, who partly was disheartened when he did not obtain the blessing, but partly abided the decision even after this event owing to the malice of his character. Then when he repented of his assent to sin, he did not obtain the blessing.[29] For he was not asking for repentance, but for the blessing that had been given to his brother in accordance with the wor-

[24]NPNF 1 14:506*. [25]Gen 25:34. [26]TOB 359. [27]EHA 230-31*. [28]PG 82:776; TCCLSP 2:191**. [29]Gen 27:34-35; 41:1.

thiness of his character. It was impossible that the blessing would again be taken away and given to him again. Also, however, it is possible to discover that his tears were not altogether unprofitable.[30] His father seems to have grieved thereafter for his careless son and seems to have given him some blessings. So he does not wish to preclude repentance through these words. FRAGMENTS ON THE EPISTLE TO THE HEBREWS 12.17.[31]

SEEKING THE BLESSING WITH TEARS? OECUMENIUS: Some interpret "and yet seeking the blessing with tears" as a time during which "he did not find an opportunity for repentance." FRAGMENTS ON THE EPISTLE TO THE HEBREWS 12.17.[32]

REMEMBRANCE OF OUR SINS. CHRYSOSTOM: If you keep your sins continually in remembrance, you will never bear in mind the wrongs of your neighbor. I do not say, if you are persuaded that you are yourself a sinner; this does not avail so to humble the soul, as sins themselves, taken by themselves and examined specifically. You will have no remembrance of wrongs done you, if you have these things continually in remembrance; you will feel no anger, you will not revile, you will have no high thoughts, you will not fall again into the same sins, you will be more earnest toward good things. Do you see how many excellent effects are produced from the remembrance of our sins? Let us then write them in our minds. I know that the soul does not endure a recollection that is so bitter, but let us constrain and force it. ON THE EPISTLE TO THE HEBREWS 31.6-7.[33]

12:18-21 You Have Not Come to What May Be Touched

TERRIBLE THINGS. CHRYSOSTOM: Wonderful indeed were the things in the temple, the Holy of Holies; awful were those things that occurred at Mount Sinai, "a blazing fire, and darkness, and gloom, and a tempest." For, it says, "God appeared in Sinai,"[34] and long ago were these things celebrated. The new covenant, however, was not given with any of these things but has been given in simple discourse by God. See then how he makes the comparison in these points, putting them afterward with good reason. For when he had persuaded them by innumerable arguments, when he had also shown the difference between each covenant, then afterwards, the one having been already condemned, he easily begins on these points. And what says he? "For you have not come to what may be touched, a blazing fire, and darkness, and gloom, and a tempest." . . . These things, he means, are terrible, and so terrible that they could not even bear to hear them, that not even "a beast" dared to go up. But things that come hereafter are not such, for what is Sinai to heaven? And what is the "blazing fire" to God who cannot be touched? For "God is a consuming fire." For it is said, "You speak to us, and we will hear; but let not God speak to us, lest we die."[35] "And so fearful was that which was commanded, 'Though even a beast touch the mountain, it shall be stoned,'[36] Moses said, 'I tremble with fear.'"[37] What wonder as respects the people? He himself who entered into "the darkness where God was"[38] says, "I tremble with fear." ON THE EPISTLE TO THE HEBREWS 32.1.[39]

OBJECTS OF SENSE AND SIGHTS AND SOUNDS. CHRYSOSTOM: Fearful were those things, but these are far more admirable and glorious. For here there is not "darkness" or "gloom" or "tempest." It seems to me that by these words he hints at the obscurity of the Old Testament and the overshadowed and veiled character of the law. And, besides, the giver of the law appears in fire terrible and apt to punish those who transgress.

But what are "the sounds of the trumpet"? Probably it is as though some king were coming. This at all events will also be at the second coming. "At the last trumpet"[40] all must be raised, but

---

[30]Gen 27:39. [31]NTA 15:211. [32]NTA 15:468. [33]NPNF 1 14:508*. [34]See Deut 33:2. [35]Ex 20:19. [36]Ex 19:12-13. [37]See Deut 9:19. [38]Ex 20:21. [39]NPNF 1 14:510*. [40]1 Cor 15:52.

it is the trumpet of his voice which effects this. At that time then all things were objects of sense and sights and sounds. Now all are objects of the understanding and invisible. On the Epistle to the Hebrews 32.3.[41]

So Terrifying Was the Sight. Theodoret of Cyr: While he brought out the fearsome things, he did not reveal the fruit springing from them. He did not say he "appeared," because what they saw was not the God of all in person but some impression of the divine coming. Interpretation of Hebrews 12.[42]

12:22-24 You Have Come to the City of the Living God

Jesus Instead of Moses. Chrysostom: Instead of "Moses," Jesus. Instead of the people, "innumerable angels." Of what "firstborn" does he speak? Of the faithful. "And to the spirits of just men made perfect." On the Epistle to the Hebrews 32.2.[43]

The Church Established by Christ. Eusebius of Caesarea: Zion and Jerusalem that have the good news told them[44] the apostle knew to be heavenly, when he said, "But the Jerusalem above is free, and she is our mother,"[45] and, "You have come to Mount Zion and to the city of the living God, the heavenly Jerusalem, and to innumerable angels." Zion might also mean the church established by Christ in every part of the world, and Jerusalem the holy constitution that, once established of old time among the ancient Jews alone, was driven into the wilderness by their impiety and then again was restored far better than before through the coming of our Savior. Therefore the prophecy says, "Break forth together into singing, you waste places of Jerusalem; for the Lord has comforted his people, he has redeemed Jerusalem."[46]

Nor would you be wrong in calling Zion the soul of every holy and godly person, so far as it is lifted above this life, having its city in heaven, see-ing the things beyond the world. For it means "a watchtower." And insofar as such a person remains calm and free from passion, you could call that one Jerusalem—for Jerusalem means "vision of peace." Proof of the Gospel 6.24.[47]

You Have Heard a Voice Through Flesh. Chrysostom: From the first, therefore, the Isra-elites were themselves the cause of God's being manifested through the flesh. Let Moses speak with us, and "Let not God speak with us."[48] They who make comparisons elevate the one side more that they may show the other to be far greater. In this respect also our privileges are more gentle and more admirable. For they are great in a two-fold respect, because, while they are glorious and greater, they are more accessible. This he says also in the epistle to the Corinthians, "with un-veiled face,"[49] and "not as Moses put a veil over his face."[50] They, he means, were not counted worthy as we are. For of what were they thought worthy? They saw "darkness, gloom"; they heard "a voice." But you also have heard a voice, not through darkness but through flesh. You have not been disturbed, neither troubled, but you have stood and held discourse with the Mediator.

And in another way, by the "darkness" he shows the invisibleness. "And darkness," it says, "was under his feet."[51] Then even Moses feared, but now no one. . . . The Son is near to God, but not as Moses. There was a wilderness, here a city.

"And to innumerable angels." Here he shows the joy, the delight, in place of the "darkness" and "gloom" and "tempest." "And to the assembly and church of the firstborn who are enrolled in heaven, and to a judge who is God of all." They did not draw near but stood afar off, even Moses, but "you have come near." Here he makes them stand in awe by saying, "And to a judge who is God of all," not of the Jews alone and the faithful,

---

[41]NPNF 1 14:511*. [42]PG 82:776; *TCCLSP* 2:191. [43]NPNF 1 14:510*. [44]Eusebius comments here on the interpretation of "Jerusa-lem" in Is 52:7. [45]Gal 4:26. [46]Is 52:9. [47]*POG* 2:45-46*. [48]Ex 20:19. [49]2 Cor 3:18. [50]2 Cor 3:13. [51]Ps 18:9 (17:10 LXX).

but even of the whole world. "And to the spirits of just men made perfect." He means the souls of those who are approved. On the Epistle to the Hebrews 32.3-4.[52]

Jerusalem Built of Living Stones.

Ambrose: The Lord says, "Then let those who are in Judea flee to the mountains."[53] Mount Zion is there, and so is the city of peace, Jerusalem, built not of earthly stones but of living stones, with ten thousand angels and the church of the firstborn and the spirits of those made perfect and the God of the just, who spoke better with his blood than Abel. For one cried out for vengeance,[54] but the other for pardon. The one was a reproach to his brother's sin. The other forgave the world's sin; the one was the revelation of a crime, the other covered a crime according to what was written, "Blessed is he whose transgression is forgiven."[55] Flight from the World 5.31.[56]

Jerusalem Is Besieged by Christ.

Ambrose: But because we ought always to be anxious, always attentive, and because the Word of God leaps forth like the gazelle or the young stag,[57] let the soul who searches after the Christ and longs to possess Christ always be on watch and maintain its senses. "Upon my bed at night I sought him whom my soul loves,"[58] as if Christ had stolen in upon her. Let one who seeks carefully seek while in his bed; let him seek at night. Let there be neither nights nor holiday, let no time be free from service, and if one does not find Christ at first, let him persevere in searching after Christ. And so the soul says, "I will rise now and go about the city, in the streets and in the squares."[59] And perhaps [the soul] still does not find Christ, because it sought in the public places, where there are court cases, in the streets, where there are markets with goods for sale; for Christ cannot be obtained for any amount of money. . . . That soul searches for Christ who seeks after Christ with tranquility and peace. It searches at night because Christ spoke through parables[60]—"he

made darkness his covering around him,"[61] and "night to night declares knowledge"[62]—and also because "the things we say in our heart we ought also to be sorry for on our beds."[63] But [the soul] does not find Christ in this way, and so it says, "I am a strong city, a city besieged."[64] The city is besieged through Christ; the city is that heavenly Jerusalem, in which there are interpreters of God's law and people skilled in doctrine in great abundance; through them one seeks the Word of God. Isaac or the Soul 5.38-39.[65]

Your Ancient Fathers.

Ephrem the Syrian: In it there are the firstborn, that is, the first ones and the most excellent, and "the spirits of just men," that is, of your ancient fathers who accomplished perfection. Commentary on the Epistle to the Hebrews.[66]

Seek What Pertains to the City of God.

Basil the Great: Some give the definition that a city is an established community, administered according to law. And the definition that has been handed down of the city is in harmony with the celestial city, Jerusalem above. For there it is a community of the firstborn who have been enrolled in heaven, and this is established because of the unchanging manner of the life of the saints, and it is administered according to the heavenly law. Therefore, it is not the privilege of human nature to learn the arrangement of that city and all its adornment. Those are the things "no eye has seen, nor ear heard, nor the heart of man conceived, what God has prepared for those who love him,"[67] but there are myriads of angels there, an assembly of saints and a church of the firstborn that are enrolled in heaven. Concerning that, David said, "Glorious things are spoken of you, O city of God."[68] To that city through Isaiah God has promised, "I will make you majestic for-

---

[52]NPNF 1 14:511*. [53]Mt 24:16. [54]Gen 4:10. [55]Ps 32:1 (31:1 LXX). [56]FC 65:305. [57]Song 2:9. [58]Song 3:1. [59]Song 3:2. [60]Mt 13:13; Ezek 20:49. [61]Ps 18:11. [62]Ps 19:2. [63]See Ps 4:4 (4:5 LXX). [64]Is 27:3 LXX. [65]FC 65:32-33. [66]EHA 231. [67]1 Cor 2:9. [68]Ps 87:3.

ever, a joy from age to age. Devastation and destruction shall no more be within your borders; you shall call your walls Salvation."[69] Therefore, having raised the eyes of your soul, seek, in a manner worthy of things above, what pertains to the city of God. What could anyone consider as deserving of the happiness in that city which the river of God makes joyful and of which God is the craftsman and creator? HOMILIES ON THE PSALMS 18.4 (PSALM 45).[70]

JESUS CAME TO RAISE ADAM. AMBROSE: The Lord Jesus came to raise up Adam; Abel also was raised up, for his offerings were pleasing to God. The Lord Jesus offered his own self, that is, the firstlings of his own body,[71] in the sprinkling of blood that speaks better than the blood of Abel spoke upon the earth. THE PRAYER OF JOB AND DAVID 4.9.32.[72]

HIS BLOOD DOES NOT CRY OUT FOR VENGEANCE. ATHANASIUS: The prophet Nahum proclaimed the good news of what was to come, "Behold, on the mountains the feet of him who brings good tidings, who proclaims peace."[73] Then he went on to tell them, "Keep your feasts, O Judah; fulfill your vows. For they shall no more go to that which is old; it is finished; it is taken away. He is gone up who breathed upon the face and delivered you from affliction."[74]

Now who is he who went up? Notice, by the way, that the one who went up went to the Jews, so there is no way they can ignore the end of those practices that foreshadowed his coming. And the prophet did say, "It is finished." But as I asked, who was he? It would be absurd to say that he was Moses, because when he was with Israel they had not even entered the land in which these sacrificial rites were to be carried out. Or suppose that he was Samuel or some other one of the prophets. That would not do either, because, while they were around, the sacrifices were being made and Jerusalem was still standing. Thus it was none of these men who went up.

But if you want to know the truth . . . look to

our Savior, who went up and who "breathed on them, and said to them, 'Receive the Holy Spirit.'"[75] As soon as these things were done, all the old things came to an end. The altar was broken; the veil of the temple was torn from top to bottom. And although the city was not yet sacked and destroyed, its time was coming. As the prophecy foretold,[76] the abomination of desolation was soon to rest upon the temple and the city. The consummation of the ancient ceremonies was at hand.

Thankfully, then, we have come far beyond these shadows of reality, having turned to the Lord himself. And we know that "the Lord is the Spirit, and where the Spirit of the Lord is, there is freedom."[77] Therefore, as the ears of our hearts hear the call of the priestly trumpet, we do not look with our physical eyes and see an animal lamb slain, but we see the true Lamb, our Lord Jesus Christ. For as Isaiah said, he "was led as a lamb to the slaughter, and like a sheep that before its shearers is dumb."[78]

We are purified by his precious blood, which cleanses us from sin. His blood does not cry out for vengeance as did the blood of Abel. FESTAL LETTER 1.8-9.[79]

MERCY SPEAKS A BETTER WORD THAN THE BLOOD OF ABEL. CHRYSOSTOM: The work of mercy is, as it were, a most excellent art and a protector of those who labor at it. For it is dear to God and ever stands near God, readily asking favor for whomsoever it will, if only it be not wronged by us. . . . So, if it is pure, it gives great confidence to those who offer it up. It intercedes even for those who have offended, so great is its power, even for those who have sinned. It breaks the chains, disperses the darkness, quenches the fire, kills the worm, drives away the gnashing of teeth. The gates of heaven open to it with great security. And as, when a queen is entering, none

---

[69]Is 60:15, 18. [70]FC 46:302-3*. [71]See Gen 4:4. [72]FC 65:416. [73]Nahum 1:15. [74]Nahum 1:15 (2:1 LXX). [75]Jn 20:22. [76]Dan 11:31; Mt 24:15. [77]2 Cor 3:17. [78]Is 53:7. [79]NPNF 2 4:509.

of the guards stationed at the doors dares to inquire who she is, but all straightway receive her, so also indeed with mercifulness. For she is truly a queen indeed, making humans like God, for, he says, "Be merciful, as your Father is merciful."[80] She is winged and buoyant, having golden pinions, with a flight which greatly delights the angels. There, it is said, are "the wings of a dove covered with silver, its pinions with green gold."[81] As some dove, golden and living, she flies, with gentle look and mild eye. Nothing is better than that eye. The peacock is beautiful, but, in comparison with her, is a jackdaw. So beautiful and worthy of admiration is this bird. She continually looks upwards; she is surrounded abundantly with God's glory. She is a virgin with golden wings, decked out, with a fair and mild countenance. She is winged and buoyant, standing by the royal throne. When we are judged, she suddenly flies in and shows herself and rescues us from punishment, sheltering us with her own wings. God would rather have her than sacrifices. Much does God discourse concerning her, God loves her so. "He upholds," it is said, "the widow" and "the fatherless"[82] and the poor. God wishes to be called by her. "The Lord is gracious and merciful, slow to anger and abounding in steadfast love,"[83] and true. The mercy of God is over all the earth. She has saved the race of humankind,[84] for, unless she had pitied us, all things would have perished. "While we were enemies,"[85] she "reconciled" us, she wrought innumerable blessings; she persuaded the Son of God to become a slave and to empty himself of his glory.[86]

Let us earnestly emulate her by whom we have been saved; let us love her, let us prize her before wealth and apart from wealth; let us have a merciful soul. Nothing is so characteristic of a Christian as mercy. There is nothing that both unbelievers and all people so admire as when we are merciful. For often we are ourselves also in need of this mercy and say to God, "Have mercy upon us, according to your steadfast love."[87] Let us begin first ourselves, or rather it is not we that begin first, for God has already shown his mercy toward us. At least let us follow second. For if people have mercy on a merciful person, even if that person has done innumerable wrongs, so much more does God. ON THE EPISTLE TO THE HEBREWS 32.7.[88]

SPEAKS MORE GRACIOUSLY THAN THE BLOOD OF ABEL. THEODORET OF CYR: There you find dread, he is saying, here on the contrary festival and assembly. The former happens on earth, the latter in heaven; there thousands of people, here tens of thousands of angels. There unbelievers and lawbreakers, here church of the firstborn enrolled in heaven and spirits of the just who have been made perfect; there an old covenant, here a new one; there a slave as mediator, here a Son; there blood of brute beasts, here blood of a rational lamb. The phrase "speaks more graciously than the blood of Abel" means communicating through deeds and betraying its own activity: while the blood of Abel is celebrated, this blood is responsible for the salvation of human beings. INTERPRETATION OF HEBREWS 12.[89]

12:25-27 What Cannot Be Shaken

"ON EARTH" AND "FROM HEAVEN." PHOTIUS: "The one who warned them on earth" can be understood to mean the one promising them earthly things that will pass away: the land flowing with milk and honey, the conquest of enemies, goodly offspring and long life. But from heaven speaks the one who promises heaven itself as an inheritance, who graciously bestows the enjoyment of that unspeakable and eternal glory. Or "warned them on earth" can be said to mean that bodily purifications pervaded nearly everything of the law given through Moses. But the giving of the law that took place through Christ is

---

[80]Lk 6:36. [81]Ps 68:13 (67:14 LXX). [82]Ps 146:9 (145:9 LXX). [83]Ps 145:8 (144:8 LXX). [84]See Ps 145:9 (144:9 LXX). [85]Rom 5:10. [86]Phil 2:7. [87]Ps 51:1 (50:1 LXX). [88]NPNF 1 14:513**. [89]PG 82:777; TCCLSP 2:192**.

a cleansing and illumination of the soul for us. Then "on earth" are the things proclaimed, because they are lowly and applied to the body made of dirt; and the things of the New Testament are "from heaven" because they are divine and exalted and cleanse the soul in a truly divine manner and bear it up into heaven. FRAGMENTS ON THE EPISTLE TO THE HEBREWS 12.25.[90]

THE STEADFASTNESS TO COME. THEODORE OF MOPSUESTIA: Quite rightly on the basis of the prophetic verse[91] does he establish the instability of the present order and the steadfastness of the things which shall be later. For the "shaking" shows that he is proclaiming the alteration of the present order exactly as it will be. And by adding the word *once* he shows that what will be afterwards cannot be changed. COMMENTARY ON HEBREWS 12.26.[92]

SHAKINGS OF THE EARTH. GREGORY OF NAZIANZUS: There have been two remarkable transformations of the human way of life in the course of the world's history. These two are called two "covenants" and, so famous was the business involved, two "shakings of the earth." The first was the transition from idols to the law;[93] the second, from law to gospel.[94] The gospel also tells of the third "shaking," the change from this present state of things to what lies unmoved, unshaken, beyond. An identical feature occurs in both covenants. The feature? There was nothing sudden involved in the first movement to take their transformations in hand. We need to know why. It was so that we should be persuaded, not forced. The unspontaneous is the impermanent—as when force is used to keep stems or plants in check. The spontaneous both lasts longer and is more secure. It belongs to despotic power to use force; it is a mark of God's reasonableness that the issue should be ours. ON THE HOLY SPIRIT, THEOLOGICAL ORATION 5(31).25.[95]

"TO SHAKE" "ONCE AND FOR ALL." THEODORE OF MOPSUESTIA: Based on the voice of the prophet he proves both the change from the things that now exist and the establishment of the things that follow. For the promise "to shake"[96] makes clear that they will change altogether in the future. By the addition of the word "once and for all" he shows clearly that thereafter they will be unchangeable. FRAGMENTS ON THE EPISTLE TO THE HEBREWS 12.26.[97]

YET ONE MORE SHAKING. OECUMENIUS: The phrase "yet once more"[98] makes clear that another "one time" would be added after the second. For the world was shaken for the first time when the law was given on Sinai: "For the earth shook,"[99] David said. Again the earth was shaken during the sojourn in the flesh: "For all Jerusalem was shaken"[100] and "the idols of Egypt built by human hands."[101] And he calls an earthquake that which was heard of the proclamation, through which people were shaken from their old condition in error and brought into a new condition. So says Cyril.[102] He speaks of yet one more occasion, namely, at his second coming with glory, when he will alter and change creation. For then creation will especially be shaken with a real shaking and crash—a more drastic change than of people who were corrupt at the time turning from evil to good. FRAGMENTS ON THE EPISTLE TO THE HEBREWS 12.27.[103]

COMING OF THE ETERNITY. SEVERIAN OF GABALA: That is why Paul says elsewhere, "For the form of this world is passing away."[104] So that the temporary may pass away and the eternal may come. FRAGMENTS ON THE EPISTLE TO THE HEBREWS 12.27.[105]

12:28-29 A Kingdom That Cannot Be Shaken

---

[90]NTA 15:651. [91]Hag 2:6. [92]PG 66:968; COS 234. [93]Ex 20:3-5. [94]Mt 27:51; Heb 9:3-15; Gal 2:14. [95]FGFR 292. [96]Hag 2:6. [97]NTA 15:211. [98]Hag 2:6. [99]Ps 68:9. [100]Mt 21:10. [101]Is 19:1. [102]*On the Gospel of John* 3.415. [103]NTA 15:468. [104]1 Cor 7:31. [105]NTA 15:351.

AWE OR ENCOURAGEMENT? OECUMENIUS:
Either he wishes to scare them not to be ungrateful and not to grumble about their tribulations,
lest somehow, he says, you chance upon God in
his wrath and vengeance; or he wishes to encourage them, as if he had said, "We will give thanks
for our afflictions, for we have a Lord able to
destroy those opposed to him." FRAGMENTS ON
THE EPISTLE TO THE HEBREWS 12.29.[106]

OUR GOD IS A CONSUMING FIRE. ORIGEN: In
sacred language God is called a fire, as when
Scripture says, "Our God is a consuming fire."
Concerning the substance of the angels, it also
speaks as follows: "Who makes his angels spirits
and his ministers a burning fire."[107] And in
another place, "The angel of the Lord appeared
in a flame of fire in the bush."[108] In addition, we
have received a command to be "fervent in
spirit"[109] by which expression undoubtedly the
word of God is shown to be hot and fiery. The
prophet Jeremiah also hears from him who gave
him oracles, "Behold, I am making my words in
your mouth a fire."[110] As God, then, is a "fire"
and the angels are "flames of fire" and all the
saints are "fervent in spirit," so, on the contrary,
those who have fallen away from the love of God
are undoubtedly said to have cooled in their
affection for God and to have become cold. ON
FIRST PRINCIPLES 2.8.3.[111]

GOD'S JUDGMENT AS A FIRE. THEODORE OF
MOPSUESTIA: The apostle did not think it possible to describe God's judgment sufficiently in any
other way than through an analogy from our
experience, and for this reason he did not hesitate
to call God "fire." COMMENTARY ON JOHN 1.1.1.[112]

GOD'S ESSENCE. ORIGEN: Many have produced
lengthy discussions of God and God's essence.
Some have even said that God has a bodily nature
that is composed of fine particles and is like ether.
Others have said that God is incorporeal and is of

a different essence that transcends bodies in dignity and power. For this reason it is worthwhile
for us to see if we have resources from the divine
Scriptures to say something about God's essence.
In John 4:24 it is stated as if God's essence were
spirit, for it says, "God is spirit." But in the law, it
is instead as if God's essence were fire, for it is
written, "Our God is a consuming fire."[113] In
John, however, it is stated as if God were light, for
John says, "God is light, and in him is no darkness at all."[114] If, then, we should listen to these
words literally, making no inquiry beyond the letter, we would have to say that God is a body. . . .
But because we do not see the consequences if we
attribute a body to God when we say, even on the
basis of Scripture, that God is some such body as
spirit, or consuming fire, or light, unless we
accept the conclusions that necessarily follow
these assertions, we will disgrace ourselves as
foolish and contradicting the obvious. For every
fire is subject to extinction because it needs fuel;
and every spirit, even if we take the spirit to be
simple, because it is a body, admits of change to
what is coarser in its own nature. In these matters, then, we must either accept so many absurd
and blasphemous things about God in preserving
the literal meanings, or, as we also do in many
other cases, examine and inquire what can be
meant when it is said that God is spirit or fire or
light. First we must say that just as when we find
it written that God has eyes, eyelids, ears, hands,
arms, feet, and even wings, we change what is
written into an allegory, despising those who
bestow on God a form resembling humans; and
we do this with good reason. So also must we act
consistently with our practice in the case of the
names mentioned above. COMMENTARY ON THE
GOSPEL OF JOHN 13.123-131.[115]

---

[106]NTA 15:469. [107]Heb 1:7. [108]Ex 3:2. [109]Rom 12:11. [110]Jer 5:14.
[111]ANF 4:287-88**. [112]CSCO 115-116:12. [113]Cf. Deut 4:24. [114]1 Jn
1:5. [115]FC 89:93-95**.

13:1-7 LET BROTHERLY LOVE CONTINUE

Let brotherly love continue. [2]*Do not neglect to show hospitality to strangers, for thereby some have entertained angels unawares.* [3]*Remember those who are in prison, as though in prison with them; and those who are ill-treated, since you also are in the body.* [4]*Let marriage be held in honor among all, and let the marriage bed be undefiled; for God will judge the immoral and adulterous.* [5]*Keep your life free from love of money, and be content with what you have; for he has said, "I will never fail you nor forsake you."* [6]*Hence we can confidently say,*

"The Lord is my helper,

I will not be afraid;

what can man do to me?"

[7]*Remember your leaders, those who spoke to you the word of God; consider the outcome of their life, and imitate their faith.*

OVERVIEW: In this pericope the theme of mutual love in the community is reinforced, especially hospitality. One was not expected to give up everything, but "superfluities" were to be discouraged (CHRYSOSTOM, AUGUSTINE) as we should practice self-discipline (CLEMENT OF ALEXANDRIA). Marriage and childbearing are worthy of honor (EPHREM, EUSEBIUS). We are to remember our leaders, that is, the ones who preach the word to us (DIDACHE, THEODORE). Faith is validated by steadfastness (CHRYSOSTOM).

13:1-2 Hospitality to Strangers

PAUL ENJOINS THEM TO PRESERVE WHAT THEY HAVE. CHRYSOSTOM: See how he enjoins them to preserve what they had; he does not add other things. He did not say, "Be loving as brothers," but "Let brotherly love continue." And again, he did not say, "Be hospitable," as if they were not, but "Do not neglect to show hospitality," for this neglect was likely to happen, due to their afflictions.

Therefore, he says, "Some have entertained angels unawares." Do you see how great was the honor, how great the gain!

What is "unawares"? They entertained them without knowing it. Therefore, the reward also was great, because he entertained them, not knowing that they were angels. If he had known it, it would have been nothing wonderful. Some say that he here alludes to Lot also. ON THE EPISTLE TO THE HEBREWS 33.1.[1]

HOSPITALITY IS LOVE OF STRANGERS. CHRYSOSTOM: If others have plundered your property, display your hospitality out of such things as you have. What excuse, then, shall we have, when they, even after the spoiling of their goods, were thus admonished? And he did not say, "Do not neglect" to entertain strangers, but "to show hospitality"; that is, do not merely entertain strangers, but do it with love for the strangers. Moreover, he did not speak of the recompense that is future and in store for us, lest he should make them more supine, but of that already given. For "thereby some," he says "have entertained angels unawares." ON THE EPISTLE TO THE HEBREWS 33.4-5.[2]

13:4 *Marriage Held in Honor*

---

[1]NPNF 1 14:514*. [2]NPNF 1 14:516*.

GOD JUDGES THE IMMORAL AND ADULTER-ERS. AUGUSTINE: Sometimes people who commit this sin treat it lightly out of heaven knows what kind of perversity. They hunt about for heaven knows what null and worthless proofs in their support, and say, "God does not mind the sins of the flesh." Well, what about what we have heard today, "God will judge the immoral and adulterous"? So there you are, pay attention, any of you afflicted with this sort of disease. Listen to what God is saying, not to what your own prejudice is saying in favor of your sins, or to your friend, perhaps, chained with the same shackles of wickedness as yourself—though in fact he is more your enemy and his own. SERMON 82.11.[3]

IS THE MARRIAGE BED HELD IN HONOR? EPHREM THE SYRIAN: A further interpretation of "he knew her not until she had borne a son"[4] is that this holiness was of necessity, even though they both willingly shared in it. But the holiness they observed after the birth of our Lord was of their own free will.

The Evangelist defined the nature of this necessity and showed us concerning its limit, that it was "until." . . . Should it be deduced from this therefore that he did not live with her chastely after she had given birth, since it is indicated "until"? But "until" is not the end limit. For he said, "The Lord said to my Lord, Sit at my right hand, until I put your enemies under your feet."[5] Therefore, when his enemies were put beneath his feet, did he stand up? Another interpretation of "he knew her not" follows. Is not marriage pure, according to the testimony of the apostle, "The fruit of their womb is pure"? But, if one were to say, "See, the brothers of our Lord are named in the Gospel," I would reply, "Because our Lord entrusted his mother Mary to John,[6] it is clear that these are not her sons, nor is Joseph her husband." For how could he who said, "Honor your father and your mother,"[7] have separated Mary from her sons and entrusted her to John instead? COMMENTARY ON TATIAN'S DIATESSARON 10-11.[8]

CHILDREN ARE NOT FORBIDDEN. EUSEBIUS OF CAESAREA: According to the laws of the new covenant, the producing of children is certainly not forbidden, but the provisions are similar to those followed by the ancient men of God. "Now a bishop," says the Scripture, "must be the husband of one wife."[9] Yet it is fitting that those in the priesthood and occupied in the service of God should abstain after ordination from the intercourse of marriage. To all who have not undertaken this wondrous priesthood, Scripture almost completely gives way, when it says, "Let marriage be held in honor, and let the marriage bed be undefiled, for God will judge the immoral and adulterous." PROOF OF THE GOSPEL 1.9.[10]

13:5 Be Content with What You Have

HE FORBADE NOT POSSESSIONS. THEODORET OF CYR: He forbade not possessions but the love of money, from which greed springs. INTERPRETATION OF HEBREWS 13.[11]

SEEK NOT SUPERFLUITIES. CHRYSOSTOM: And having first set down, "Let marriage be held in honor among all, and let the marriage bed be undefiled," he shows that he rightly added what follows. For if marriage has been conceded, justly is the fornicator punished, justly does the adulterer suffer recompense. . . .

He did not say again, "Let no one be a fornicator"; but, having said it once for all, he then went on as with a general exhortation, and not as directing himself against them. "Be content with what you have," he says. He did not say, "Possess nothing," but "be content with what you have"; that is, let it show forth the philosophical character of your mind. And it will show it, if we do not seek superfluities, if we keep only to what is necessary. For he says above also, "you joyfully accepted the plundering of your goods."[12] He

---

[3]WSA 3 3:375-76. [4]Mt 1:25. [5]Ps 110:1 (109:1 LXX). [6]Jn 19:27. [7]Mk 10:19. [8]ECTD 65. [9]1 Tim 3:2. [10]POG 1:53-54. [11]PG 82:780; TCCLSP 2:193. [12]Cf. Heb 10:34.

gives these exhortations that they might not be covetous. On the Epistle to the Hebrews 33.2.[13]

Release Your Heart from Money. Augustine: So keep a moderate amount of money for temporal uses; treat it as journey money, with the end in view stated in the text. Notice above all what he put first: "Free from love of money," he says, put your hand in the purse in such a way that you release your heart from it. Sermon 177.3.[14]

Self-Discipline Is God's Greatest Gift. Clement of Alexandria: We must join in disciplining ourselves to beware of all that is subject to the passions. We must, like true philosophers, escape from any foods that arouse sexual desire, from a dissolute relaxation in bed, from luxury and all the passions that make for luxury. We realize that others find this a grievous struggle. It is no longer so for us, since self-discipline is God's greatest gift. He has said, "I will never forsake you or abandon you,"[15] who have judged you worthy by a decision that is wholly genuine. In this way, as we carefully strive to go to him, the Lord's "easy yoke"[16] will receive us. . . . There is, according to Hippocrates of Cos, a discipline of the soul as well as of the body, "a state of health which does not shrink from hardship and cannot have enough nourishment." Stromateis 2.20.126.[17]

13:7 Remember Your Leaders

Remember the One Who Preaches. Didache: My child, day and night "you should remember him who preaches God's word to you,"

and honor him as you would the Lord. For where the Lord's nature is discussed, there the Lord is. Every day you should seek the company of saints to enjoy their refreshing conversation. You must not start a schism but reconcile those at strife. Didache 4.1-3.[18]

"Faith" Means Steadfastness. Chrysostom: By "faith" he means steadfastness. How so? Because they believe in the things to come. For they would not have shown forth a pure life if they were troubled with questions about the things to come, if they had doubted. On the Epistle to the Hebrews 33.3.[19]

Leaders Long Dead. Theodoret of Cyr: He referred to the saints long dead—Stephen the protomartyr, James the brother of John, James called Just; many others as well were done away with by the Jews' fury. By having an eye to them, he is saying, and acquainting yourselves with their praiseworthy lifestyle, emulate their faith. Interpretation of Hebrews 13.[20]

Leaders Who Were Killed. Theodore of Mopsuestia: "The leaders" are those who have proclaimed the word of godliness among them and were killed by the Jews on the spot. And there were many, not only Stephen[21] and James who was killed by the sword,[22] but also James, brother of our Lord, and very many others handed over in silence. Fragments on the Epistle to the Hebrews 13.7.[23]

---

[13]NPNF 1 14:514-15*. [14]WSA 3 5:281. [15]Deut 31:6. [16]Mt 11:30. [17]FC 85:239-40. [18]LCC 1:173*. [19]NPNF 1 14:515*. [20]PG 82:781; TCCLSP 2:194. [21]Acts 7:54-60. [22]Acts 12:2. [23]NTA 15:211.

13:8-19 HE SUFFERED OUTSIDE THE CAMP

[8]*Jesus Christ is the same yesterday and today and for ever.* [9]*Do not be led away by diverse and strange teachings; for it is well that the heart be strengthened by grace, not by foods, which have not benefited their adherents.* [10]*We have an altar from which those who serve the tent[a] have no right to eat.* [11]*For the bodies of those animals whose blood is brought into the sanctuary by the high priest as a sacrifice for sin are burned outside the camp.* [12]*So Jesus also suffered outside the gate in order to sanctify the people through his own blood.* [13]*Therefore let us go forth to him outside the camp, and bear the abuse he endured.* [14]*For here we have no lasting city, but we seek the city which is to come.* [15]*Through him then let us continually offer up a sacrifice of praise to God, that is, the fruit of lips that acknowledge his name.* [16]*Do not neglect to do good and to share what you have, for such sacrifices are pleasing to God.*

[17]*Obey your leaders and submit to them; for they are keeping watch over your souls, as men who will have to give account. Let them do this joyfully, and not sadly, for that would be of no advantage to you.*

[18]*Pray for us, for we are sure that we have a clear conscience, desiring to act honorably in all things.* [19]*I urge you the more earnestly to do this in order that I may be restored to you the sooner.*

a Or *tabernacle*

OVERVIEW: In the passage "Jesus Christ is the same yesterday and today and forever," the early writers saw a witness to the humanity and divinity of Christ, "God by nature even when incarnate, truly, not purely man like us, remaining what he was even when he had become flesh." As such, he is the mediator of our salvation (CYRIL OF ALEXANDRIA). As God he is one and the same Son of the Father (THEODORET). Although the titles of Christ are many, he is the same in the incarnation and in the Spirit forever (GREGORY OF NAZIANZUS). "Today" signifies the present age or this life, while "yesterday" points out the past age (ORIGEN), yet Jesus Christ is always the same as there is no other to come (CHRYSOSTOM, AMBROSE). "Strange teachings" and diverse practices do not benefit those who hold them (CHRYSOSTOM, EPHREM).

The cross turns everything inside out. Since Jesus was crucified outside the city (PHOTIUS), Christians are always called upon to be on the outside of society to live with less and to bear abuse. "The cross of Christ would be the altar not of the temple but of the world" (LEO THE GREAT). It is through separation from worldly things that the Christian ascetical ideal is fulfilled (ISAAC). However, Ephrem points out that we are also called into the world, but only for the purpose of preaching Christ's gospel.

Our sacrifice to God is thankfulness and perseverance; they bring us closer to God (CHRYSOSTOM). Mercy is another sacrifice pleasing to God (AUGUSTINE). According to Chrysostom, even wicked leaders should be obeyed with regard to civic matters, as anarchy is evil, yet with regard to the matters of faith such obedience is deadly. The commandments of the Lord must be obeyed; preaching them is a great and grave responsibility (EPHREM, AUGUSTINE). We are to be good to one another and know that mercy is the true sacrifice. We have a mutual need for one another's prayers. If the apostles used to ask for prayers on their behalf, how much more does it behoove us to do so (AUGUSTINE)? A good conscience is a consequence of righteous living (EPHREM).

13:8 Yesterday, Today, Forever

ETERNAL EXISTENCE. THEODORET OF CYR: This, too, he does not simply put down, but he fits it to the argument that has been interrupted, teaching that he was crucified by the Jews. And he also demonstrates his eternal existence, for he calls the human nature "yesterday and today" and names the divinity "forever." And he says that the two are the same, since the only begotten and the firstborn are one and the same Son. INTERPRETATION OF HEBREWS 13.8.[1]

NO BROKENNESS IN WHAT IS THE SAME.
CYRIL OF ALEXANDRIA: The natural properties of the Word who came forth from the Father were maintained even when he became flesh. It is foolish therefore to dare to introduce a breach. For the Lord Jesus Christ is one[2] and through him the Father created all things.[3] He is composed of human properties and of others that are above the human, yielding a kind of middle term. He is, in fact, a mediator between God and humankind, according to the Scriptures,[4] God by nature even when incarnate, truly, not purely man like us, remaining what he was even when he had become flesh. For it is written, "Jesus Christ is the same yesterday and today and forever." ON THE INCARNATION 709.[5]

THE SAME YESTERDAY? CYRIL OF ALEXANDRIA: How then could he be the same in the past when he had not yet assumed generation according to the flesh? . . . It is of Jesus Christ and not just of the Word that the text affirms that he is the same today, yesterday and forever, but how could the human nature possess immutability and unaltered identity when it is subject to movement and, above all, to that movement that made it pass from nothingness to being and to life? . . . In virtue of the union with flesh that is proper to

him, it is still he himself who is described as existing yesterday and as preexistent. ON THE INCARNATION.[6]

REMAINING WHAT HE WAS AND ALWAYS WILL BE. CYRIL OF ALEXANDRIA: The Son of God, assuming our likeness and becoming human,[7] not taking up what he was but taking on what he was [i.e., the divine condition] effects our salvation. For he remains, as Paul put it, the same yesterday and today and forever, without undergoing any change in his divinity by reason of his incarnation, but remaining what he was and will always be. EASTER HOMILY 1.6.[8]

TITLES OF THE SON. GREGORY OF NAZIANZUS: These names—righteousness, sanctification, redemption, resurrection . . . are still common to the one who is above us and to the one who came for our sake. But others are peculiarly our own and belong to that nature which he assumed. So he is called man, not only that through his body he may be apprehended by embodied creatures, whereas otherwise this would be impossible because of his incomprehensible nature; but also that by himself he may sanctify humanity and be, as it were, a leaven to the whole lump. Then, by uniting to himself that which was condemned, he may release it from all condemnation, becoming for all people all things that we are, except sin—body, soul, mind, and all through which death reaches. Thus he became man, who is the combination of all these; God in visible form, because he retained that which is perceived by mind alone. He is son of man both on account of Adam and of the Virgin from whom he came, from the one as a forefather, from the other as his mother, both in accordance with the law of generation and apart from it. He is Christ because of his Godhead. For this is the anointing of his manhood and does not, as is the case with all other anointed ones, sanctify by its action but by the

[1]PG 82:781; COS 304. [2]See 1 Cor 8:6. [3]See Jn 1:1-3. [4]1 Tim 2:5. [5]SC 97:286. [6]SC 97:288-91; COS 353. [7]Phil 2:5-7. [8]PG 77:424.

presence in his fullness of the anointing one; the effect of which is that that which anoints is called human and makes that which is anointed God. He is the way, because he leads us through himself; the door as letting us in; the shepherd, as making us dwell in a place of green pastures and bringing us up by waters of rest, and leading us there and protecting us from wild beasts, converting the erring, bringing back that which was lost, binding up that which was broken, guarding the strong, and bringing them together in the fold beyond, with words of pastoral knowledge. The sheep, as the victim; the lamb, as being perfect; the high priest as the offerer; Melchizedek, as without mother in that nature which is above us and without father in ours; and without genealogy above for who, it says, shall declare his generation?[9] and, moreover, as king of Salem, which means peace, and king of righteousness, and as receiving tithes from patriarchs, when they prevail over powers of evil.[10] They are the titles of the Son. Walk through them, those that are lofty in a godlike manner; those that belong to the body in a manner suitable to them; or rather, altogether in a godlike manner, that you may become a god, ascending from below, for his sake who came down from on high for ours. In all and above all keep to this, and you shall never err, either in the loftier or the lowlier names. Jesus Christ is the same yesterday and today in the incarnation, and in the Spirit forever and ever. Amen. On the Son, Theological Oration 4(30).21.[11]

"Today" Signifies This Life. Origen: The "today" signifies this life; for it says, "Jesus Christ yesterday and today and forever" and again "while it is called today." Selections from the Psalms 94.8.[12]

The Age Which Is Past. Origen: And if "today" is the whole of this age, probably "yesterday" is the age which is past. We suppose that this is what it means in the psalm and in Paul's epistle to the Hebrews. In the psalms it says, "a

thousand years in your sight are but as yesterday when it is past."[13] This is the famous millennium which is compared with "yesterday" and distinguished from "today." And the apostle writes, "Jesus Christ is the same yesterday and today and forever." There is nothing surprising in God's reckoning the whole age as the span of one of our days, and I think that it is even less in his sight. On Prayer 27.13.[14]

Another Will Not Come. Chrysostom: In these words, "Jesus Christ the same yesterday and today and forever," "yesterday" means all the time that is past; "today," the present; "forever," the endless which is to come. That is to say, "You have heard of a high priest, but not a high priest who fails." He is always the same. As though there were some who said, "He is not, another will come," he says this, that he who was "yesterday and today," is "the same also forever." On the Epistle to the Hebrews 33.3.[15]

Promise and Fulfillment. Ambrose: The words of Scripture include all days in two days, yesterday and today, as in the words, "Imitate their faith in Jesus Christ; he is the same yesterday and today and forever." The promise is made the first day; the following day it is fulfilled. Letter 50.[16]

13:9 Strange Teachings

By Faith All Things Are Pure. Chrysostom: Not "with strange teachings" only, but neither with "diverse ones." "For it is well that the heart be strengthened by grace, not by foods, which have not benefited their adherents." Here he gently hints at those who introduce the observance of "foods." For by faith all things are pure. There is need then of faith, not of "foods." On the Epistle to the Hebrews 33.3.[17]

---

[9]Is 53:8. [10]Heb 7:1-10; 8:1. [11]LCC 3:192-93. [12]PG 12:1556; COS 25. [13]Ps 90:4 (89:4 LXX). [14]PG 11:517; COS 26; OSW 144-45*. [15]NPNF 1 14:515*. [16]FC 26:268-69. [17]NPNF 1 14:515*.

STRANGE DOCTRINES ARE OF NO BENEFIT.
EPHREM THE SYRIAN: That is, the doctrines of
the [levitical] priests and their offerings. "It is
well that the heart is strengthened by grace," that
is, is made firm by the new gospel, not by the
restrictions of the priests about food. Those who
practiced this way of life obtained no profit in
these rules; that is, those who observed them
were not purified nor had eternal life in them.
COMMENTARY ON THE EPISTLE TO THE
HEBREWS.[18]

GRACE EMBRACED BY GOOD WORKS. CHRY-
SOSTOM: Who . . . can preserve grace by prideful
conduct? How then will grace, that is, good pleasure or the energy of the spirit, be with you,
unless you embrace it by good deeds? Indeed, the
very cause of all good things is our constant abiding in the grace of the Spirit, for he guides us to
everything. ON THE EPISTLE TO THE HEBREWS
34.6.[19]

PERSEVERE IN THE TEACHINGS OF GRACE.
THEODORET OF CYR: By "strange teachings" he
referred to what was at variance with the evangelical teachings. So he bids them persevere in the
teaching of grace and abandon the observances of
the law: No one reaped any benefit from them.
INTERPRETATION OF HEBREWS 13.[20]

13:11-14 Outside the Camp

HE SUFFERED OUTSIDE THE GATE. PHOTIUS:
This is spoken to those who would still be at a
loss, asking, "How do you say, 'you have an altar'?
For what was offered on it?" It is Christ himself
whom you neglect above and below and fail to see
that he was sacrificed, since his sacrifice and
offering took place for the world, although he
himself has not been sacrificed on your altar. For
it is manifest that "he suffered outside" the city of
Jerusalem. Therefore he says to them, "Yes, he
suffered outside, but through this very fact it has
rather been accomplished that 'we have an altar.'
For even among you 'the bodies' of the sacrificial

victims 'are burned' not on the altars themselves,
but 'outside the camp.' And still for this reason 'he
suffered outside the gate,' so that he might sanctify all and not merely the priests. And if the sacrifice took place for all, how could it not have
been an altar?" But the statement "in order to
sanctify the people" gives a different interpretation. He says, "I said that 'those serving the temple do not have authority to eat' from our altar,
not because this is impossible for them, but
because in their opinion they reject themselves as
unworthy, since—due to the mercy of Christ—
not only is it not forbidden, but for this very reason he once suffered." He says, " 'He suffered outside the gate to sanctify the people,' not this
people or that one but all the people and to grant
them to have the authority to eat also from this
altar." FRAGMENTS ON THE EPISTLE TO THE
HEBREWS 13.10-13.[21]

THE CROSS IS THE ALTAR OF THE WORLD.
LEO THE GREAT: "Christ, our paschal lamb, has
been sacrificed,"[22] as the apostle says. Offering
himself to the Father as a new and real sacrifice of
reconciliation, he was crucified—not in the temple whose due worship is now completed, nor
within the enclosure of the city which was to be
destroyed because of its crime, but "outside the
camp." That way, as the mystery of the ancient
sacrifices was ceasing, a new victim would be put
on a new altar, and the cross of Christ would be
the altar not of the temple, but of the world. SER-
MON 59.5.[23]

OUTSIDE THE CAMP. THEODORET OF CYR:
"Outside the camp" means, Let our way of life be
beyond the law, and let us bear the reproaches for
the one who saved us. INTERPRETATION OF
HEBREWS 13.[24]

JESUS CALLS US AWAY FROM THE WORLD.

---

[18]EHA 232. [19]NPNF 1 14:521*. [20]PG 82:781; TCCLSP 2:194.
[21]NTA 15:652. [22]1 Cor 5:7. [23]FC 93:257. [24]PG 82:784; TCCLSP
2:195.

ISAAC OF NINEVEH: The Lord Redeemer very rightly commanded whoever would follow him to strip himself and leave the world, for a person ought first to cast off from himself the causes of slackness and then approach the work. When the Lord himself began to wage war with the devil, he fought him in the arid desert. Paul exhorts those who take up the cross of Christ to go forth also from the city, saying, "Let us go forth unto him outside the city and take up his reproach, for he suffered outside the city." For by setting himself apart from the world and what pertains to it, a person speedily forgets his former habits and his mode of life, and he will not struggle long with these. But if he should draw near to the world and its possessions, he will speedily enfeeble the strength of his mind. Therefore, one must know that separation from the worldly greatly aids one and guides him on the way of progress in the fierce and saving struggle. It is proper, then, and helpful in this struggle if a monk's cell be in a poor and mean condition and if his cell be empty and devoid of everything that could incite in him the desire of ease. For, when the causes of slackness are distant from a man, he is not endangered by the twofold warfare, that is, the one which is both inward and outward. See how much easier is the struggle when a man desires things that are afar off than when the very things themselves are close at hand and by their sight inflame the thoughts; for the struggle in the latter case is twofold. ASCETICAL HOMILIES 37.[25]

JESUS CALLS US INTO THE WORLD. EPHREM THE SYRIAN: The body of the beasts was an example for our Lord, and our Lord is an example for us, so that "we may go forth outside the camp," that is, go out and become evangelists of his preaching, "and bear the abuse he endured." COMMENTARY ON THE EPISTLE TO THE HEBREWS 13.[26]

THE BLOOD OF A RED HEIFER. THEODORET OF CYR: Look at the type, compare it with the reality and perceive the similarity. The law required a red heifer to be sacrificed, and the high priest to take some of its blood and sprinkle the mercy seat seven times with his finger. Burning the heifer itself outside the camp, they took the ashes and with them purified those people called impure. This acted as a type of the saving passion. The word *red* here means the body from Adam in the Hebrew language.[27] He was fixed to the cross outside the gate. His blood purifies our souls; in place of the dust we have the life giving body. INTERPRETATION OF HEBREWS 13.[28]

WE HAVE NO LASTING CITY. THEODORET OF CYR: So let us despise things of this life and look forward to those that are stable and permanent. INTERPRETATION OF HEBREWS 13.[29]

13:15-16 Continually Offer a Sacrifice of Praise

BEAR ALL THINGS THANKFULLY. CHRYSOSTOM: Let us bear all things thankfully, be it poverty, be it disease, be it anything else whatever, for God alone knows the things expedient for us, "for we do not know how to pray as we ought."[30] We, then, who do not know even how to ask for what is fitting unless we have received of the Spirit, let us take care to offer up thanksgiving for all things, and let us bear all things nobly. Are we in poverty? Let us give thanks. Are we in sickness? Let us give thanks. Are we falsely accused? Let us give thanks. When we suffer affliction, let us give thanks. This brings us near to God. ON THE EPISTLE TO THE HEBREWS 33.8.[31]

BEING CONCERNED ABOUT FELLOW BELIEVERS. THEODORE OF MOPSUESTIA: He calls it "doing good" in order to praise what takes place and "fellowship"[32] because they are concerned about their fellow believers . . . and so with zeal

---

[25]AHSIS 169. [26]EHA 232. [27]See Num 19:2. The Hebrew *'adummah* is read to suggest *'adam.* [28]PG 82:781; TCCLSP 2:194-95. [29]PG 82:784; TCCLSP 2:195. [30]Rom 8:26. [31]NPNF 1 14:517*. [32]RSV translates *koinōnia* ("fellowship") as "to share what you have."

they seek to meet their needs. FRAGMENTS ON THE EPISTLE TO THE HEBREWS 13.16.[33]

MERCY IS THE TRUE SACRIFICE. AUGUSTINE: In the words of the prophet Micah, a distinction is clearly drawn between the fact that God does not require sacrifices as they are in themselves and the fact that God does desire the offerings that are symbolized by these sacrifices.[34] . . . That is why the words "For I desire mercy and not sacrifice"[35] must be understood to mean that one sacrifice is to be preferred to another, since what is commonly called a sacrifice is merely a symbol of the true sacrifice. For, mercy is the true sacrifice. Hence, "such sacrifices are pleasing to God." CITY OF GOD 10.5.[36]

HYMNS ONLY THROUGH HIM. THEODORET OF CYR: Hymn singing offered to God is of no benefit to us apart from faith in the Son. Since it was to the Hebrews he wrote, who were in the habit of honoring the Father alone, he felt he had to add "through him." INTERPRETATION OF HEBREWS 13.[37]

SHARE WHAT YOU HAVE. THEODORET OF CYR: He brought out the sacrifice of praise that is pleasing to God. To it he linked also that of doing good, which he was right to refer to as sharing. . . . Elsewhere the divine apostle says, "Our abundance supplies for their need so that their abundance may be for your need for a balance to be achieved."[38] Sharing, then, is also repayment: one person gives money, another returns a blessing, and the person in need is in the stronger position. INTERPRETATION OF HEBREWS 13.[39]

13:17 Obey Your Leaders

IT IS BETTER TO BE LED BY NO ONE THAN BY ONE WHO IS EVIL. CHRYSOSTOM: Anarchy is an evil and the occasion of many calamities and the source of disorder and confusion. For as, if you take away the leader from a chorus, the chorus will not be in tune and in order. If from a pha-

lanx of an army you remove the commander, the evolutions will no longer be made in time and order. If from a ship you take away the helmsman, you will sink the vessel. So too, if from a flock you remove the shepherd, you have overthrown and destroyed all.

Anarchy, then, is an evil and a cause of ruin. But no less an evil is disobedience of rulers, for it comes again to the same. For a people not obeying a ruler is like one which has none, and perhaps even worse. For, in the former case, they have at least an excuse for disorder but no longer in the latter, but are punished.

But perhaps someone will say that there is also a third evil, when the ruler is bad. I myself know it, and no small evil it is, but even a far worse evil than anarchy. It is better to be led by no one than to be led by one who is evil, for the former indeed are sometimes saved and sometimes in peril, but the latter will be altogether in peril, being led into the pit of destruction. . . .

What then, you say, when he is wicked—should we obey? Wicked? In what sense? If in regard to faith, flee and avoid him, whether he is a man or an angel come down from heaven. But if in regard to life, be not overcurious. And this instance I do not allege from my own mind but from the divine Scripture, for hear Christ saying, "The scribes and the Pharisees sit on Moses' seat."[40] Having previously spoken many fearful things concerning them, he then says, "So practice and observe whatever they tell you but not what they do."[41] They have, he means, the dignity of office but are of unclean life. Attend not to their life but to their words. For as regards their characters, no one thus would be harmed. How is this? Both because their characters are manifest to all, and also because, though a ruler were ten thousand times as wicked, he would not be teaching wickedness. But in matters of faith if the wicked ruler is teaching evil, the evil is harder to recognize. ON

[33]NTA 15:211. [34]Mic 6:6-8. [35]Hos 6:6. [36]FC 14:125*. [37]PG 82:784; TCCLSP 2:195. [38]2 Cor 8:14. [39]PG 82:784; TCCLSP 2:195*. [40]Mt 23:2. [41]Mt 23:3.

THE EPISTLE TO THE HEBREWS 34.1.[42]

RESPECT THOSE RULES THAT BELONG TO CHRIST. EPHREM THE SYRIAN: Leave behind the rules which belong to the law, and respect those which belong to Christ. "They will give account" and a reply to God if they fail to guide you. Therefore, obey them, so that they may give account "with joy" and not with afflictions and tears. COMMENTARY ON THE EPISTLE TO THE HEBREWS 13.[43]

TO GIVE AN ACCOUNT OF YOU. AUGUSTINE: In all my sermons I am presenting you with a mirror. These are not my sermons, anyway; I only speak at the Lord's command. It is only dread of him that stops me from keeping quiet. I mean to say, who would not much rather keep quiet and not have to give an account of you? But it is quite a time since I accepted this burden, and now I neither can nor should shrug it off my shoulders. You heard, my brothers and sisters, when the letter to the Hebrews was being read. SERMON 82.15.[44]

13:18 Pray for Us

CLEAR CONSCIENCE. THEODORET OF CYR: Paul had been misrepresented to them as preaching the opposite of the law; so he impresses on them that he acted for no other reason than obedience to the divine word—hence his calling his conscience to witness. INTERPRETATION OF HEBREWS 13.[45]

RECIPROCAL PRAYERS ARE ENLIVENED BY CHARITY. AUGUSTINE: We have mutual need of one another's prayers, for those reciprocal prayers are enkindled by charity and—like a sacrifice offered on the altar of piety—are fragrant and pleasing to the Lord. If the apostles used to ask for prayers on their own behalf, how much more does it behoove me to do so? SERMON 305A.10.[46]

A GOOD CONSCIENCE. EPHREM THE SYRIAN: And so we are confident that you will have "a good conscience," that is, a perfect opinion on everything. We must live righteously in everything which concerns us. But I invite you to do more, "that is, to encourage us to this task." COMMENTARY ON THE EPISTLE TO THE HEBREWS 13.[47]

---

[42]NPNF 1 14:518-19*. [43]EHA 232. [44]WSA 3 3:378. [45]PG 82:784; TCCLSP 2:195. [46]WSA 3 3:332. [47]EHA 233.

13:20-25 BENEDICTION OR JESUS THE GREAT SHEPHERD

[20]*Now may the God of peace who brought again from the dead our Lord Jesus, the great shepherd of the sheep, by the blood of the eternal covenant,* [21]*equip you with everything good that you may do his will, working in you[b] that which is pleasing in his sight, through Jesus Christ; to whom be glory for ever and ever. Amen.*

[22]*I appeal to you, brethren, bear with my word of exhortation, for I have written to you briefly.* [23]*You should understand that our brother Timothy has been released, with whom I shall see you if*

he comes soon. [24]*Greet all your leaders and all the saints. Those who come from Italy send you greetings.* [25]*Grace be with all of you. Amen.*

b Other ancient authorities read *us*

OVERVIEW: In the final exhortation Paul preaches good works according to the gospel, not the customs of the law (EPHREM). Both righteous life and right faith are required for perfection, which is pleasing in the sight of God. The final benediction emphasizes the great value of peace and concordance. Paul prays for his readers as the epistle ends (CHRYSOSTOM).

13:20-22 *That Which Is Pleasing*

YOU WILL BE EQUIPPED WITH EVERYTHING GOOD. EPHREM THE SYRIAN: "The blood of the eternal covenant," not through that which passes away but through the one which remains forever, that is, Jesus Christ our Lord. "He will equip you with everything good," and away from the covenant of the law, which you have now, "that you may do his will" in everything and not in accordance with the weak observations of the law. "I appeal to you, brethren, bear with my words of exhortation"—I wrote and proved that all those traditional customs on which you pride yourselves are only traces of this new gospel which was preached to you through Christ. "I have written to you briefly," in accordance with your strength; if you are just adequate to your task, I will write to you more, but if you have reached perfection, you do not need any of these words. COMMENTARY ON THE EPISTLE TO THE HEBREWS.[1]

GOD WORKS IN US WHAT IS WELL PLEASING. CHRYSOSTOM: Do you see how he shows that virtue is born neither wholly from God nor yet from ourselves alone? First, by saying, "make you perfect in every good work," he means you have virtue indeed but need to be made complete. What is "good work and word"?[2] So as to have both life and doctrines right, "according to his will, work-ing in you that which is pleasing in his sight." ON THE EPISTLE TO THE HEBREWS 34.6.[3]

PAUL PRAYS FOR THEM AT THE END. CHRYSOSTOM: Therefore, having first asked their prayers, he then himself also prays for all good things on them: "Now may the God of peace," he says; do not therefore be at variance one with another. "Who brought again from the dead the great shepherd of the sheep." This is said concerning the resurrection. . . . Again he confirms to them even to the end, his discourse concerning the resurrection: "by the blood of the eternal covenant, our Lord Jesus Christ." "Make you perfect in every good work to do his will, working in you that which is pleasing in his sight." Again he bears high testimony to them, for that is made "perfect" which, having a beginning, is afterwards completed. And he prays for them, which is the act of one who yearns for them. And, while in the other epistles he prays in the prefaces, here he does it at the end. "Working in you," he says, "that which is pleasing in his sight, through Jesus Christ, to whom be glory forever and ever. Amen." ON THE EPISTLE TO THE HEBREWS 34.4.[4]

13:25 *Grace Be with You All*

SING PRAISES. THEODORET OF CYR: He appended the usual conclusion, invoking on them a share in grace. As for us, let us sing the praises of the giver of old laws and new. And let us pray to receive grace from him so that by observing the divine laws we may attain the promised goods, in Christ Jesus our Lord, to whom with the Father and the all-holy Spirit be glory, now and forever, for ages of ages. Amen. INTERPRETATION OF HEBREWS 13.[5]

---

[1]EHA 233. [2]2 Thess 2:17. [3]NPNF 1 14:520*. [4]NPNF 1 14:520*. [5]PG 82:785; TCCLSP 2:196.

Appendix

Early Christian Writers and the Documents Cited

The following table lists all the early Christian documents cited in this volume by author, if known, or by the title of the work. The English title used in this commentary is followed in parentheses with the Latin designation and, where available, the Thesaurus Linguae Graecae (=TLG) digital references or Cetedoc Clavis numbers. Printed sources of original language versions may be found in the bibliography of works in original languages.

Ambrose

Concerning Repentance (*De paenitentia*)	Cetedoc 0156
Flight from the World (*De fuga saeculi*)	Cetedoc 0133
Isaac, or the Soul (*De Isaac vel anima*)	Cetedoc 0128
Letters (*Epistulae*)	Cetedoc 0160
On Paradise (*De paradiso*)	Cetedoc 0124
On the Christian Faith (*De fide libri v*)	Cetedoc 0150

Arethas of Caesarea

Fragments on the Epistle to the Hebrews
    (*Fragmenta in epistulam ad Hebraeos [in catenis]*)

Athanasius

Deposition of Arius (*Deposition Arii in De decretis Nicaenae synodi*)	TLG 2035.003
Festal Letters (*Epistulae festales*)	TLG 2035.x01
Four Discourses against the Arians (*Orationes tres contra Arianos*)	TLG 2035.042
Letter, To Maximus (*Epistula ad Maximum*)	TLG 2035.051
Letter to the Bishops of Egypt (*Epistula ad episcopos Aegypti et Libyae*)	TLG 2035.041
Life of St. Anthony (*Vita sancti Antonii*)	TLG 2035.047
On the Incarnation (*De incarnatione verbi*)	TLG 2035.002

Augustine

City of God (*De civitate Dei*)	Cetedoc 0313
Confessions (*Confessionum libri tredecim*)	Cetedoc 0251
Letters (*Epistulae*)	Cetedoc 0262
On Eighty-three Varied Questions	
(*De diversis quaestionibus octoginta tribus*)	Cetedoc 0289
On Faith and the Creed (*De fide et symbolo*)	Cetedoc 0293
On Genesis, Against the Manicheans (*De Genesi contra Manichaeos*)	Cetedoc 0265
On the Literal Interpretation of Genesis	
(*De Genesi ad litteram libri duodecim*)	Cetedoc 0266

On the Merits and Forgiveness of Sins and on Infant Baptism
    (*De peccatorum meritis et remissione et de baptismo parvulorum*)   Cetedoc 0342
On the Trinity (*De Trinitate*)   Cetedoc 0329
Predestination of the Saints (*De praedestinatione sanctorum*)   Cetedoc 0354
Sermons (*Sermones*)   Cetedoc 0284

Basil the Great
Homilies on the Psalms (*Homiliae super Psalmos*)   TLG 2040.018
Letters (*Epistulae*)   TLG 2040.004
On the Spirit (*De Spiritu Sancto*)   TLG 2040.003

Bede
Homilies on the Gospels (*Homiliarum evangelii libri ii*)   Cetedoc 1367
On the Tabernacle (*De tabernaculo et vasis eius ac vestibus
    sacerdotum libri iii*)   Cetedoc 1345

Braulio of Saragossa
Letters (*Epistulae*)

Cassian, John
Conferences (*Collationes*)   Cetedoc 0512
On the Incarnation of the Lord against Nestorius
    (*De incarnatione Domini contra Nestorium*)   Cetedoc 0514

Cassiodorus
Expositions of the Psalms (*Expositio Psalmorum*)   Cetedoc 0900

Clement of Alexandria
Christ the Educator (*Paedagogus*)   TLG 0555.002
Exhortation to the Greeks (*Protrepticus*)   TLG 0555.001
Stromateis (*Stromata*)   TLG 0555.004

Clement of Rome
1 Clement (*Epistula i ad Corinthios*)   TLG 1271.001

Cyprian
Letters (*Epistulae*)   Cetedoc 0050

Cyril of Alexandria
Apology for the Twelve Anathematisms against Theodoret
    (*Apologeticus contra Theodoretum pro XII capitibus in
    Concilium universale Ephesenum anno 431*)   TLG 5000.001
Commentary on Hebrews (*Fragmenta in sancti Pauli epistularum ad Hebraeos*)   TLG 4090.006
Easter Homilies (*Epistulae paschales sive Homiliae paschales [epist. 1-30]*)   TLG 4090.032
Letter to Pulcheria and Eudoxia (*In Concilium universale Ephesenum anno 431*)   TLG 5000.001

On the Incarnation (*De incarnatione unigeniti*)   TLG 4090.026
On the Unity of Christ (*Quod unus sit Christus*)   TLG 4090.027
Second Letter to Nestorius (*In Concilium universale Ephesenum anno 431*)   TLG 5000.001

Cyril of Jerusalem
Catechetical Lectures (*Catecheses ad illuminandos 1-18*)   TLG 2110.003
Mystagogical Lectures (*Mystagogiae 1-5 [Sp.]*)   TLG 2110.002
Didache (*Didache xii apostolorum*)   TLG 1311.001

Didymus the Blind
Fragments on the Epistle to the Hebrews
    (*Fragmenta in epistulam ad Hebraeos [in catenis]*)

Ephrem the Syrian
Commentary on Genesis (*Commentarii in Genesim*)
Commentary on Tatian's Diatessaron (*In Tatiani Diatessaron*)
Commentary on the Epistle to the Hebrews (*Srboyn Ep'remi Matenagrowt'iwnk'*)

Epiphanius of Salamis
Panarion 4, Against Mechizedekians (*Panarion [Adversus haereses]*)   TLG 2021.002

Eusebius of Caesarea
Ecclesiastical History (*Historia ecclesiastica*)   TLG 2018.002
Proof of the Gospel (*Demonstratio evangelica*)   TLG 2018.005

Evagrius of Pontus
Chapters on Prayer (*De oratione*)   TLG 4110.024

Gregory of Elvira
Origen's Tractate on the Books of Holy Scripture
    (*Tractatus Origenis de libris Sanctarum Scripturarum*)

Gregory of Nazianzus
On the Birth of Christ, Oration 38 (*In theophania*)   TLG 2022.046
On the Holy Spirit, Theological Oration 5 (31) (*De Spiritu Sancto*)   TLG 2022.011
On the Son, Theological Oration 3 (29), (*De filio*)   TLG 2022.009
On the Son, Theological Oration 4 (30), (*De filio*)   TLG 2022.010
On Theology, Theological Oration 2(28) (*De theologia*)   TLG 2022.008

Gregory of Nyssa
Against Eunomius (*Contra Eunomium*)   TLG 2017.030
Life of Moses (*De vita Mosis*)   TLG 2017.042
On Perfection (*De perfectione Christiana ad Olympium monachum*)   TLG 2017.026
On the Faith (*Ad Simplicium de fide*)   TLG 2017.004
On the Making of Man (*De opificio hominis*)   TLG 2017.079

Gregory the Great
Letters (*Registrum epistularum*)   Cetedoc 1714

Hilary of Poitiers
Tractate of the Mysteries (*Tractatus mysteriorum*)

Hippolytus
Against Noetus (*Contra haeresin Noeti*)   TLG 2115.002

Ignatius of Antioch
Letter to the Magnesians (*In Epistulae vii genuinae [recensio media]*)   TLG 1443.001

Irenaeus
Against Heresies (*Adversus haereses*)   Cetedoc 1154

Isaac of Nineveh
Ascetical Homilies (*De perfectione religiosa*)

Jerome
Hebrew Questions on Genesis (*Liber quaestionum hebraicarum in Genesim*)   Cetedoc 0580
Homilies on the Psalms (*Tractatus lix in psalmos*)   Cetedoc 0592
Homilies on the Psalms, Alternate Series (*Tractatuum in psalmos series altera*)   Cetedoc 0593
Letters (*Epistulae*)   Cetedoc 0620
On Lazarus and Dives (*Homilia in Lucam, de Lazaro et Divite*)   Cetedoc 0596

John Chrysostom
Discourses Against Judaizing Christians (Adversus Judaeos [orationes 1-8])   TLG 2062.021
On the Epistle to the Hebrews (*In epistulam ad Hebraeos*)   TLG 2062.168

John of Damascus
Orthodox Faith (*Expositio fidei*)   TLG 2934.004

Justin Martyr
Dialogue with Trypho (*Dialogus cum Tryphone*)   TLG 0645.003
First Apology (*Apologia*)   TLG 0645.001

Lactantius
Epitome of the Divine Institutes (*Epitome divinarum institutionum*)   Cetedoc 0086

Leo the Great
Sermons (*Tractatus septem et nonaginta*)   Cetedoc 1657

Marius Victorinus
On the Necessity of Accepting Homoousios (*De homoousio recipiendo*)   Cetedoc 0097

Maximus the Confessor

The Lord's Prayer (*Expositio orationis dominicae*)   TLG 2892.111

Nestorius

First Sermon Against the Theotokos (*Erster Sermon gegen des theotokos*
   genannt Anfang des Dogmas)

Oecumenius

Fragments on the Epistle to the Hebrews (*Fragmenta in epistulam ad Hebraeos [in catenis]*)

Origen

Against Celsus (*Contra Celsum*)	TLG 2042.001
Commentary on the Gospel of John	
(*Commentarii in evangelium Joannis [lib. 1, 2, 4, 5, 6, 10, 13]*)	TLG 2042.005
(*Commentarium in evangelium Joannis [lib. 19, 20, 28, 32]*)	TLG 2042.079
Commentary on the Song of Songs (*Commentarium in Canticum canticorum*)	Cetedoc 0198
Exhortation to Martyrdom (*Exhortatio ad martyrium*)	TLG 2042.007
Homilies on Exodus (*Homiliae in Exodum*)	TLG 2042.023
Homilies on Genesis (*Homiliae in Genesim*)	TLG 2042.022
Homilies on Joshua (*In Jesu nave*)	
Homilies on Leviticus (*Homiliae in Leviticum*)	TLG 2042.024
Homilies on Numbers (*In Numeros homiliae*)	Cetedoc 0198
Homilies on the Gospel of Luke (*Homiliae in Lucam*)	TLG 2042.016
Homilies on the Psalms (*Homiliae in Selecta in Psalmos [dub.]*)	
Letter to Julius Africanus (*Epistula ad Africanum*)	TLG 2042.045
On First Principles (*De principiis*)	TLG 2042.002
On Prayer (*De oratione*)	TLG2042.008
Selections from Exodus (*Selecta in Exodum*)	TLG 2042.050
Selections from the Psalms (*Selecta in Psalmos [dub.]*)	TLG 2042.058

Pachomius

Instructions (*Catecheses*)
Life of Pachomius (Bohairic) (*Vita Pachomii*)

Philoxenus of Mabbug

Letter to Abba Symeon of Caesarea
   (In *Isaac of Nineveh, Hapanta ta heurethenta asketika*)

Photius

Fragments on the Epistle to the Hebrews
   (*Fragmenta in epistulam ad Hebraeos [in catenis]*)

Pseudo-Clement of Rome

2 Clement (*Epistula ii ad Corinthios [Sp.]*)   TLG 1271.002

Pseudo-Dionysius
Celestial Hierarchy (*De caelestine hierarchia*)   TLG 2798.001
Ecclesiastical Hierarchy (*De ecclesiastica hierarchia*)   TLG 2798.002

Rufinus of Aquileia
Commentary on the Apostles' Creed (*Expositio symboli*)   Cetedoc 0196

Severian of Gabala
Fragments on the Epistle to the Hebrews
   (*Fragmenta in epistulam ad Hebraeos [in catenis]*)

Symeon the New Theologian
Discourse (*Catecheses*)

Tertullian
Against All Heresies (*Adversus omnes haereses [dub.]*)   Cetedoc 0034
The Chaplet (*De corona*)   Cetedoc 0021

Theodore of Mopsuestia
Catechetical Homilies
Commentary on Ephesians (*In epistolam beati Pauli ad Ephesios*)
Commentary on 1 Thessalonians (*In epistolam b. Pauli ad Thessalonicenses I*)
Commentary on John (*Commentarius in evangelium Johannis Apostoli*)
Fragments on the Epistle to the Hebrews
   (*Fragmenta in epistulam ad Hebraeos [in catenis]*)   TLG 4135.018
Fragments on the Treatise on the Incarnation
   (*Ex libris de incarnatione filii Dei*)
Treatises Against Apollinaris (*Ex tertio libro contra Apollinarium*)

Theodoret of Cyr
Apology for the Twelve Anathematisms Against Theodoret
   (*Apologeticus contra Theodoretum pro XII capitibus*
   in Concilium universale Ephesenum anno 431)   TLG 5000.001
Dialogue (*Eranistes*)   TLG 4089.002
Interpretation of Hebrews (*In Interpretatio in xiv epistulas sancti Pauli*)   TLG 4089.030
Letters (*Epistulae: Collectio Sirmondiana*)   TLG 4089.006

Biographical Sketches &
Short Descriptions
of Select Anonymous Works

This listing is cumulative, including all the authors and works cited in this series to date.

Acacius of Beroea (c. 340-c. 436). Syrian monk known for his ascetics. He became bishop of Beroea in 378, participated in the council of Constantinople in 381, and played an important role in mediating between Cyril of Alexandria and John of Antioch; however, he did not take part in the clash between Cyril and Nestorius.

Acacius of Caesarea (d. c. 365). Pro-Arian bishop of Caesarea in Palestine, disciple and biographer of Eusebius of Caesarea, the historian. He was a man of great learning and authored a treatise on Ecclesiastes.

Adamnan (c. 624-704). Abbot of Iona, Ireland, and author of the life of St. Columba. He was influential in the process of assimilating the Celtic church into Roman liturgy and church order. He also wrote *On the Holy Sites*, which influenced Bede.

Alexander of Alexandria (fl. 312-328). Bishop of Alexandria and predecessor of Athanasius, on whom he exerted considerable theological influence during the rise of Arianism. Alexander excommunicated Arius, whom he had appointed to the parish of Baucalis, in 319. His teaching regarding the eternal generation and divine substantial union of the Son with the Father was eventually confirmed at the Council of Nicaea (325).

Ambrose of Milan (c. 333-397; fl. 374-397). Bishop of Milan and teacher of Augustine who defended the divinity of the Holy Spirit and the perpetual virginity of Mary.

Ambrosiaster (fl. c. 366-384). Name given by Erasmus to the author of a work once thought to have been composed by Ambrose.

Ammonius (c. fifth century). An Aristotelian commentator and teacher in Alexandria, where he was born and of whose school he became head. Also an exegete of Plato, he enjoyed fame among his contemporaries and successors, although modern critics accuse him of pedantry and banality.

Amphilochius of Iconium (b. c. 340-345, d.c. 398-404). An orator at Constantinople before becoming bishop of Iconium in 373. He was a cousin of Gregory of Nazianzus and active in debates against the Macedonians and Messalians.

Andreas (c. seventh century). Monk who collected commentary from earlier writers to form a catena on various biblical books.

Antony (or Anthony) the Great (c. 251-c. 356). An anchorite of the Egyptian desert and founder of Egyptian monasticism. Athanasius regarded him as the ideal of monastic life, and he has become a model for Christian hagiography.

Aphrahat (c. 270-350; fl. 337-345). "The Persian

Sage" and first major Syriac writer whose work survives. He is also known by his Greek name Aphraates.

Apollinaris of Laodicea (310-c. 392). Bishop of Laodicea who was attacked by Gregory of Nazianzus, Gregory of Nyssa and Theodore for denying that Christ had a human mind.

Aponius/Apponius (fourth–fifth century). Author of a remarkable commentary on Song of Solomon (c. 405-415), an important work in the history of exegesis. The work, which was influenced by the commentaries of Origen and Pseudo-Hippolytus, is of theological significance, especially in the area of Christology.

Apostolic Constitutions (c. 381-394). Also known as *Constitutions of the Holy Apostles* and thought to be redacted by Julian of Neapolis. The work is divided into eight books, and is primarily a collection of and expansion on previous works such as the *Didache* (c. 140) and the *Apostolic Traditions*. Book 8 ends with eighty-five canons from various sources and is elsewhere known as the *Apostolic Canons*.

Arethas of Caesarea (c. 860-940) Byzantine scholar and disciple of Photius. He was a deacon in Constantinople, then archbishop of Caesarea from 901.

Arius (fl. c. 320). Heretic condemned at the Council of Nicaea (325) for refusing to accept that the Son was not a creature but was God by nature like the Father.

Arnobius the Younger (fifth century). A participant in christological controversies of the fifth century. He composed *Conflictus cum Serapione*, an account of a debate with a monophysite monk in which he attempts to demonstrate harmony between Roman and Alexandrian theology. Some scholars attribute to him a few more works, such as *Commentaries on Psalms*.

Athanasius of Alexandria (c. 295-373; fl. 325-373). Bishop of Alexandria from 328, though often in exile. He wrote his classic polemics against the Arians while most of the eastern bishops were against him.

Athenagoras (fl. 176-180). Early Christian philosopher and apologist from Athens, whose only authenticated writing, *A Plea Regarding Christians*, is addressed to the emperors Marcus Aurelius and Commodius, and defends Christians from the common accusations of atheism, incest and cannibalism.

Augustine of Hippo (354-430). Bishop of Hippo and a voluminous writer on philosophical, exegetical, theological and ecclesiological topics. He formulated the Western doctrines of predestination and original sin in his writings against the Pelagians.

Babai (c. early sixth century). Author of the Letter to Cyriacus. He should not be confused with either Babai of Nisibis (d. 484), or Babai the Great (d. 628).

Babai the Great (d. 628). Syriac monk who founded a monastery and school in his region of Beth Zabday and later served as third superior at the Great Convent of Mount Izla during a period of crisis in the Nestorian church.

Basil of Seleucia (fl. 444-468). Bishop of Seleucia in Isauria and ecclesiastical writer. He took part in the Synod of Constantinople in 448 for the condemnation of the Eutychian errors and the deposition of their great champion, Dioscurus of Alexandria.

Basil the Great (b. c. 330; fl. 357-379). One of the Cappadocian fathers, bishop of Caesarea and champion of the teaching on the Trinity propounded at Nicaea in 325. He was a great administrator and founded a monastic rule.

Basilides (fl. second century). Alexandrian heretic of the early second century who is said to have believed that souls migrate from body to body and that we do not sin if we lie to protect the body from martyrdom.

Bede the Venerable (c. 672/673-735). Born in Northumbria, at the age of seven he was put under the care of the Benedictine monks of Saints Peter and Paul at Jarrow and given a broad classical education in the monastic tradition. Considered one of the most learned men of his age, he is the author of *An Ecclesiastical History of the English People*.

Benedict of Nursia (c. 480-547). Considered the most important figure in the history of Western monasticism. Benedict founded many monasteries, the most notable found at Montecassino, but his lasting influence lay in his famous Rule. The Rule outlines the theological and inspirational foundation of the monastic ideal while also legislating the shape and organization of the cenobitic life.

Besa the Copt (5th century). Coptic monk, disciple of Shenoute, whom he succeeded as head of the monastery. He wrote numerous letters, monastic catecheses and a biography of Shenoute.

Book of Steps (c. 400). Written by an anonymous Syriac author, this work consists of thirty homilies or discourses which specifically deal with the more advanced stages of growth in the spiritual life.

Braulio of Saragossa (c. 585-651). Bishop of Saragossa (631-651) and noted writer of the Visigothic renaissance. His *Life* of St. Aemilianus is his crowning literary achievement.

Caesarius of Arles (c. 470-543). Bishop of Arles renowned for his attention to his pastoral duties. Among his surviving works the most important is a collection of some 238 sermons that display an ability to preach Christian doctrine to a variety of audiences.

Callistus of Rome (d. 222). Pope (217-222) who excommunicated Sabellius for heresy. It is very probable that he suffered martyrdom.

Cassia (b. c. 805, d. between 848 and 867). Nun, poet and hymnographer who founded a convent in Constantinople.

Cassian, John (360-432). Author of the *Institutes* and the *Conferences,* works purporting to relay the teachings of the Egyptian monastic fathers on the nature of the spiritual life which were highly influential in the development of Western monasticism.

Cassiodorus (c. 485-c. 580). Founder of the monastery of Vivarium, Calabria, where monks transcribed classic sacred and profane texts, Greek and Latin, preserving them for the Western tradition.

Chromatius (fl. 400). Bishop of Aquileia, friend of Rufinus and Jerome and author of tracts and sermons.

Clement of Alexandria (c. 150-215). A highly educated Christian convert from paganism, head of the catechetical school in Alexandria and pioneer of Christian scholarship. His major works, *Protrepticus, Paedagogus* and the *Stromata,* bring Christian doctrine face to face with the ideas and achievements of his time.

Clement of Rome (fl. c. 92-101). Pope whose *Epistle to the Corinthians* is one of the most important documents of subapostolic times.

Commodian (probably third or possibly fifth century). Latin poet of unknown origin (possibly Syrian?) whose two surviving works suggest chiliast and patripassionist tendencies.

Constitutions of the Holy Apostles. See Apostolic Constitutions.

Cyprian of Carthage (fl. 248-258). Martyred bishop of Carthage who maintained that those baptized by schismatics and heretics had no share in the blessings of the church.

Cyril of Alexandria (375-444; fl. 412-444). Patriarch of Alexandria whose extensive exegesis, characterized especially by a strong espousal of the unity of Christ, led to the condemnation of Nestorius in 431.

Cyril of Jerusalem (c. 315-386; fl. c. 348). Bishop of Jerusalem after 350 and author of *Catechetical Homilies.*

Cyril of Scythopolis (b. c. 525; d. after 557). Palestinian monk and author of biographies of famous Palestinian monks. Because of him we have precise knowledge of monastic life in the fifth and sixth centuries and a description of the Origenist crisis and its suppression in the mid-sixth century.

Diadochus of Photice (c. 400-474). Antimonophysite bishop of Epirus Vetus whose work *Discourse on the Ascension of Our Lord Jesus Christ* exerted influence in both the East and West through its Chalcedonian Christology. He is also the subject of the mystical *Vision of St. Diadochus Bishop of Photice in Epirus.*

Didache (c. 140). Of unknown authorship, this text intertwines Jewish ethics with Christian liturgical practice to form a whole discourse on the "way of life." It exerted an enormous amount of influence in the patristic period and was especially used in the training of catechumen.

Didymus the Blind (c. 313-398). Alexandrian exegete who was much influenced by Origen and admired by Jerome.

Diodore of Tarsus (d. c. 394). Bishop of Tarsus and Antiochene theologian. He authored a great scope of exegetical, doctrinal and apologetic works, which come to us mostly in fragments because of his condemnation as the predecessor of Nestorianism. Diodore was a teacher of John Chrysostom and Theodore of Mopsuestia.

Dionysius of Alexandria (d. c. 264). Bishop of Alexandria and student of Origen. Dionysius actively engaged in the theological disputes of his day, opposed Sabellianism, defended himself against accusations of tritheism and wrote the earliest extant Christian refutation of Epicureanism. His writings have survived mainly in extracts preserved by other early Christian authors.

Dorotheus of Gaza (fl. c. 525-540). Member of Abbot Seridos's monastery and later leader of a monastery where he wrote *Spiritual Instructions*. He also wrote a work on traditions of Palestinian monasticism.

Ephrem the Syrian (b. c. 306; fl. 363-373). Syrian writer of commentaries and devotional hymns which are sometimes regarded as the greatest specimens of Christian poetry prior to Dante.

Epiphanius of Salamis (c. 315-403). Bishop of Salamis in Cyprus, author of a refutation of eighty heresies (the *Panarion*) and instrumental in the condemnation of Origen.

Epiphanius the Latin. Author of the late fifth-century or early sixth century Latin text *Interpretation of the Gospels*, with constant references to early patristic commentators. He was possibly a bishop of Benevento or Seville.

Epistle of Barnabas. See Letter of Barnabas.

Eucherius of Lyons (fl. 420-449). Bishop of Lyons c. 435-449. Born into an aristocratic family, he, along with his wife and sons, joined the monastery at Lérins soon after its founding. He explained difficult Scripture passages by means of a threefold reading of the text: literal, moral and spiritual.

Eugippius (b. 460). Disciple of Severinus and third abbot of the monastic community at Castrum Lucullanum, which was made up of those fleeing from Noricum during the barbarian invasions.

Eunomius (d. 393). Bishop of Cyzicyus who was attacked by Basil and Gregory of Nyssa for maintaining that the Father and the Son were of different natures, one ingenerate, one generate.

Eusebius of Caesarea (c. 260/263-340). Bishop of Caesarea, partisan of the Emperor Constantine and first historian of the Christian church. He argued that the truth of the gospel had been foreshadowed in pagan writings but had to defend his own doctrine against suspicion of Arian sympathies.

Eusebius of Emesa (c. 300-c. 359). Bishop of Emesa from c. 339. A biblical exegete and writer on doctrinal subjects, he displays some semi-Arian tendencies of his mentor Eusebius of Caesarea.

Eusebius of Gaul, or Eusebius Gallicanus (c. fifth century). A conventional name for a collection of seventy-six sermons produced in Gaul and revised in the seventh century. It contains material from different patristic authors and focuses on ethical teaching in the context of the liturgical cycle (days of saints and other feasts).

Eusebius of Vercelli (fl. c. 360). Bishop of Vercelli who supported the trinitarian teaching of Nicaea (325) when it was being undermined by compromise in the West.

Eustathius of Antioch (fl. 325). First bishop of Beroea, then of Antioch, one of the leaders of the anti-Arians at the council of Nicaea. Later, he was banished from his seat and exiled to Thrace for his support of Nicene theology.

Euthymius (377-473). A native of Melitene and influential monk. He was educated by Bishop Otreius of Melitene, who ordained him priest and placed him in charge of all the monasteries in his diocese. When the Council of Chalcedon (451) condemned the errors of Eutyches, it was greatly due to the authority of Euthymius that most of the Eastern recluses accepted its decrees. The empress Eudoxia returned to Chalcedonian orthodoxy through his efforts.

Evagrius of Pontus (c. 345-399). Disciple and teacher of ascetic life who astutely absorbed and creatively transmitted the spirituality of Egyptian and Palestinian monasticism of the late fourth century. Although Origenist elements of his writings were formally condemned by the Fifth Ecumenical Council (Constantinople II, A.D. 553), his literary corpus continued to influence the tradition of the church.

Eznik of Kolb (early fifth century). A disciple of Mesrob who translated Greek Scriptures into Armenian, so as to become the model of the classical Armenian language. As bishop, he participated in the synod of Astisat (449).

Facundus of Hermiane (fl. 546-568). African bishop who opposed Emperor Justinian's *post mortem* condemnation of Theodore of Mopsuestia, Theodoret of Cyr and Ibas of Edessa at the fifth ecumenical council. His written defense, known as "To Justinian" or "In Defense of the Three Chapters," avers that ancient theologians should not be blamed for errors that became obvious only upon later theological reflection. He continued in the tradition of Chalcedon, although his Christology was supplemented, according to Justinian's decisions, by the theopaschite formula *Unus ex Trinitate passus est* ("Only one of the three suffered").

Fastidius (c. fourth-fifth centuries). British author of *On the Christian Life*. He is believed to have written some works attributed to Pelagius.

Faustinus (fl. 380). A priest in Rome and supporter of Lucifer and author of a treatise on the Trinity.

Faustus of Riez (c. 400-490). A prestigious British monk at Lérins; abbot, then bishop of Riez from 457 to his death. His works include *On the Holy Spirit*, in which he argued against the Macedonians for the divinity of the Holy Spirit, and *On Grace*, in which he argued for a position on salvation that lay between more categorical views of free-will and predestination. Various letters

and (pseudonymous) sermons are extant.

The Festal Menaion. Orthodox liturgical text containing the variable parts of the service, including hymns, for fixed days of celebration of the life of Jesus and Mary.

Filastrius (fl. 380). Bishop of Brescia and author of a compilation against all heresies.

Firmicus Maternus (fourth century). An anti-Pagan apologist. Before his conversion to Christianity he wrote a work on astrology (334-337). After his conversion, however, he criticized paganism in *On the Errors of the Profane Religion*.

Fructuosus of Braga (d. c. 665). Son of a Gothic general and member of a noble military family. He became a monk at an early age, then abbot-bishop of Dumium before 650 and metropolitan of Braga in 656. He was influential in setting up monastic communities in Lusitania, Asturia, Galicia and the island of Gades.

Fulgentius of Ruspe (c. 467-532). Bishop of Ruspe and author of many orthodox sermons and tracts under the influence of Augustine.

Gaudentius of Brescia (fl. 395). Successor of Filastrius as bishop of Brescia and author of twenty-one Eucharistic sermons.

Gennadius of Constantinople (d. 471). Patriarch of Constantinople, author of numerous commentaries and an opponent of the Christology of Cyril of Alexandria.

Gerontius (c. 395-c.480). Palestinian monk, later archimandrite of the cenobites of Palestine. He led the resistance to the council of Chalcedon.

Gnostics. Name now given generally to followers of Basilides, Marcion, Valentinus, Mani and others. The characteristic belief is that matter is a prison made for the spirit by an evil or ignorant creator, and that redemption depends on fate, not on free will.

Gregory of Elvira (fl. 359-385). Bishop of Elvira who wrote allegorical treatises in the style of Origen and defended the Nicene faith against the Arians.

Gregory of Nazianzus (b. 329/330; fl. 372-389). Cappadocian father, bishop of Constantinople, friend of Basil the Great and Gregory of Nyssa, and author of theological orations, sermons and poetry.

Gregory of Nyssa (c. 335-394). Bishop of Nyssa and brother of Basil the Great. A Cappadocian father and author of catechetical orations, he was a philosophical theologian of great originality.

Gregory Thaumaturgus (fl. c. 248-264). Bishop of Neocaesarea and a disciple of Origen. There are at least five legendary *Lives* that recount the events and miracles which led to his being called "the wonder worker." His most important work was the *Address of Thanks to Origen*, which is a rhetorically structured panegyric to Origen and an outline of his teaching.

Gregory the Great (c. 540-604). Pope from 590, the fourth and last of the Latin "Doctors of the Church." He was a prolific author and a powerful unifying force within the Latin Church, initiating the liturgical reform that brought about the Gregorian Sacramentary and Gregorian chant.

Hesychius of Jerusalem (fl. 412-450). Presbyter and exegete, thought to have commented on the whole of Scripture.

Hilary of Arles (c. 401-449). Archbishop of Arles and leader of the Semi-Pelagian party. Hilary incurred the wrath of Pope Leo I when he removed a bishop from his see and appointed a new bishop. Leo demoted Arles from a metropolitan see to a bishopric to assert papal power over the church in Gaul.

Hilary of Poitiers (c. 315-367). Bishop of Poitiers and called the "Athanasius of the West" because of his defense (against the Arians) of the common nature of Father and Son.

Hippolytus (fl. 222-245). Recent scholarship places Hippolytus in a Palestinian context, personally familiar with Origen. Though he is known chiefly for *The Refutation of All Heresies,* he was primarily a commentator on Scripture (especially the Old Testament) employing typological exegesis.

Horsiesi (c. 305-c. 390). Pachomius's second successor, after Petronius, as a leader of cenobitic monasticism in Southern Egypt.

Ignatius of Antioch (c. 35-107/112). Bishop of Antioch who wrote several letters to local churches while being taken from Antioch to Rome to be martyred. In the letters, which warn against heresy, he stresses orthodox Christology, the centrality of the Eucharist and unique role of the bishop in preserving the unity of the church.

Irenaeus of Lyons (c. 135-c. 202). Bishop of Lyons who published the most famous and influential refutation of Gnostic thought.

Isaac of Nineveh (d. c. 700). Also known as Isaac the Syrian or Isaac Syrus, this monastic writer served for a short while as bishop of Nineveh before retiring to live a secluded monastic life. His writings on ascetic subjects survive in the form of numerous homilies.

Isho'dad of Merv (fl. c. 850). Nestorian bishop of Hedatta. He wrote commentaries on parts of the Old Testament and all of the New Testament, frequently quoting Syriac fathers.

Isidore of Seville (c. 560-636). Youngest of a family of monks and clerics, including sister Florentina and brothers Leander and Fulgentius. He was an erudite author of comprehensive scale in matters both religious and sacred, including his encyclopedic *Etymologies.*

Jacob of Nisibis (d. 338). Bishop of Nisibis. He was present at the council of Nicaea in 325 and took an active part in the opposition to Arius.

Jacob of Sarug (c. 450-c. 520). Syriac ecclesiastical writer. Jacob received his education at Edessa. At the end of his life he was ordained bishop of Sarug. His principal writing was a long series of metrical homilies, earning him the title "The Flute of the Holy Spirit."

Jerome (c. 347-420). Gifted exegete and exponent of a classical Latin style, now best known as the translator of the Latin Vulgate. He defended the perpetual virginity of Mary, attacked Origen and Pelagius and supported extreme ascetic practices.

John Chrysostom (344/354-407; fl. 386-407). Bishop of Constantinople who was noted for his orthodoxy, his eloquence and his attacks on Christian laxity in high places.

John of Antioch (d. 441/42). Bishop of Antioch, commencing in 428. He received his education together with Nestorius and Theodore of Mopsuestia in a monastery near Antioch. A supporter of Nestorius, he condemned Cyril of Alexandria, but later reached a compromise with him.

John of Apamea (fifth century). Syriac author of the early church who wrote on various aspects of the spiritual life, also known as John the Solitary. Some of his writings are in the form of dialogues. Other writings include letters, a treatise on baptism, and shorter works on prayer and silence.

John of Damascus (c. 650-750). Arab monastic and theologian whose writings enjoyed great influence in both the Eastern and Western Churches. His most influential writing was the *Orthodox Faith*.

John the Elder (c. eighth century). A Syriac author who belonged to monastic circles of the Church of the East and lived in the region of Mount Qardu (northern Iraq). His most important writings are twenty-two homilies and a collection of fifty-one short letters in which he describes the mystical life as an anticipatory experience of the resurrection life, the fruit of the sacraments of baptism and the Eucharist.

John the Monk. Traditional name found in *The Festal Menaion*, believed to refer to John of Damascus. *See* John of Damascus.

Josephus, Flavius (c. 37-c. 101). Jewish historian from a distinguished priestly family. Acquainted with the Essenes and Sadducees, he himself became a Pharisee. He joined the great Jewish revolt that broke out in 66 and was chosen by the Sanhedrin at Jerusalem to be commander-in-chief in Galilee. Showing great shrewdness to ingratiate himself with Vespasian by foretelling his elevation and that of his son Titus to the imperial dignity, Josephus was restored his liberty after 69 when Vespasian became emperor.

Julian of Eclanum (c. 385-450). Bishop of Eclanum in 416/417 who was removed from office and exiled in 419 for not officially opposing Pelagianism. In exile, he was accepted by Theodore of Mopsuestia, whose Antiochene exegetical style he followed. Although he was never able to regain his ecclesiastical position, Julian taught in Sicily until his death. His works include commentaries on Job and parts of the Minor Prophets, a translation of Theodore of Mopsuestia's commentary on the Psalms, and various letters. Sympathetic to Pelagius, Julian applied his intellectual acumen and rhetorical training to argue against Augustine on matters such as free will, desire and the locus of evil.

Justin Martyr (c. 100/110-165; fl. c. 148-161). Palestinian philosopher who was converted to Christianity, "the only sure and worthy philosophy." He traveled to Rome where he wrote several apologies against both pagans and Jews, combining Greek philosophy and Christian theology; he was eventually martyred.

Lactantius (c. 260-c. 330). Christian apologist removed from his post as teacher of rhetoric at Nicomedia upon his conversion to Christianity. He was tutor to the son of Constantine and author of *The Divine Institutes*.

Leander (c. 545-c. 600). Latin ecclesiastical writer, of whose works only two survive. He was instrumental in spreading Christianity among the Visigoths, gaining significant historical influence in Spain in his time.

Leo the Great (regn. 440-461). Bishop of Rome whose *Tome to Flavian* helped to strike a balance between Nestorian and Cyrilline positions at the Council of Chalcedon in 451.

Letter of Barnabas (c. 130). An allegorical and typological interpretation of the Old Testament with a decidedly anti-Jewish tone. It was included with other New Testament works as a "Catholic epistle" at least until Eusebius of Caesarea (c. 260/263-340) questioned its authenticity.

Letter to Diognetus (c. third century). A refutation of paganism and an exposition of the Christian life and faith. The author of this letter is unknown, and the exact identity of its recipient, Diognetus, continues to elude patristic scholars.

Lucifer (d. 370/371). Bishop of Cagliari and vigorous supporter of Athanasius and the Nicene Creed. In conflict with the emperor Constantius, he was banished to Palestine and later to Thebaid (Egypt).

Luculentius (fifth century). Unknown author of

a group of short commentaries on the New Testament, especially Pauline passages. His exegesis is mainly literal and relies mostly on earlier authors such as Jerome and Augustine. The content of his writing may place it in the fifth century.

Macarius of Egypt (c. 300-c. 390). One of the Desert Fathers. Accused of supporting Athanasius, Macarius was exiled c. 374 to an island in the Nile by Lucius, the Arian successor of Athanasius. Macarius continued his teaching of monastic theology at Wadi Natrun.

Macrina the Younger (c. 327-379). The elder sister of Basil the Great and Gregory of Nyssa, she is known as "the Younger" to distinguish her from her paternal grandmother. She had a powerful influence on her younger brothers, especially on Gregory, who called her his teacher and relates her teaching in *On the Soul and the Resurrection*.

Manichaeans. A religious movement that originated circa 241 in Persia under the leadership of Mani but was apparently of complex Christian origin. It is said to have denied free will and the universal sovereignty of God, teaching that kingdoms of light and darkness are coeternal and that the redeemed are particles of a spiritual man of light held captive in the darkness of matter (*see* Gnostics).

Marcellus of Ancyra (d. c. 375). Wrote a refutation of Arianism. Later, he was accused of Sabellianism, especially by Eusebius of Caesarea. While the Western church declared him orthodox, the Eastern church excommunicated him. Some scholars have attributed to him certain works of Athanasius.

Marcion (fl. 144). Heretic of the mid-second century who rejected the Old Testament and much of the New Testament, claiming that the Father of Jesus Christ was other than the Old Testament God (*see* Gnostics).

Marius Victorinus (b. c. 280/285; fl. c. 355-363). Grammarian of African origin who taught rhetoric at Rome and translated works of Platonists. After his conversion (c. 355), he wrote against the Arians and commentaries on Paul's letters.

Mark the Hermit (c. sixth century). Monk who lived near Tarsus and produced works on ascetic practices as well as christological issues.

Martin of Braga (fl. c. 568-579). Anti-Arian metropolitan of Braga on the Iberian peninsula. He was highly educated and presided over the provincial council of Braga in 572.

Martyrius. *See* Sahdona.

Maximus of Turin (d. 408/423). Bishop of Turin. Over one hundred of his sermons survive on Christian festivals, saints and martyrs.

Maximus the Confessor (c. 580-662). Palestinian-born theologian and ascetic writer. Fleeing the Arab invasion of Jerusalem in 614, he took refuge in Constantinople and later Africa. He died near the Black Sea after imprisonment and severe suffering, having his tongue cut off and his right hand mutilated. He taught total preference for God and detachment from all things.

Methodius of Olympus (d. 311). Bishop of Olympus who celebrated virginity in a *Symposium* partly modeled on Plato's dialogue of that name.

Minucius Felix (second or third century). Christian apologist who was an advocate in Rome. His *Octavius* agrees at numerous points with the *Apologeticum* of Tertullian. His birthplace is believed to be in Africa.

Montanist Oracles. Montanism was an apocalyptic and strictly ascetic movement begun in the latter half of the second century by a certain Montanus in Phrygia, who, along with certain of his followers, uttered oracles they claimed were inspired by the Holy Spirit. Little of the authentic oracles remains and most of what is known of Montanism comes from the authors who wrote against the movement. Montanism was formally condemned as a heresy before by Asiatic synods.

Nemesius of Emesa (fl. late fourth century). Bishop of Emesa in Syria whose most important work, *Of the Nature of Man*, draws on several theological and philosophical sources and is the first exposition of a Christian anthropology.

Nestorius (c. 381-c. 451). Patriarch of Constantinople (428-431) who founded the heresy which says that there are two persons, divine and human, rather than one person truly united in the incarnate Christ. He resisted the teaching of *theotokos*, causing Nestorian churches to separate from Constantinople.

Nicetas of Remesiana (fl. second half of fourth century). Bishop of Remesiana in Serbia, whose works affirm the consubstantiality of the Son and the deity of the Holy Spirit.

Nilus of Ancyra (d. c. 430). Prolific ascetic writer and disciple of John Chrysostom. Sometimes erroneously known as Nilus of Sinai, he was a native of Ancyra and studied at Constantinople.

Novatian of Rome (fl. 235-258). Roman theologian, otherwise orthodox, who formed a schismatic church after failing to become pope. His treatise on the Trinity states the classic western doctrine.

Oecumenius (sixth century). Called the Rhetor or the Philosopher, Oecumenius wrote the earliest extant Greek commentary on Revelation. Scholia by Oecumenius on some of John Chrysostom's commentaries on the Pauline Epistles are still extant.

Olympiodorus (early sixth century). Exegete and deacon of Alexandria, known for his commentaries that come to us mostly in catenae.

Origen of Alexandria (b. 185; fl. c. 200-254). Influential exegete and systematic theologian. He was condemned (perhaps unfairly) for maintaining the preexistence of souls while purportedly denying the resurrection of the body. His extensive works of exegesis focus on the spiritual meaning of the text.

Pachomius (c. 292-347). Founder of cenobitic monasticism. A gifted group leader and author of a set of rules, he was defended after his death by Athanasius of Alexandria.

Pacian of Barcelona (c. fourth century). Bishop of Barcelona whose writings polemicize against popular pagan festivals as well as Novatian schismatics.

Palladius of Helenopolis (c. 363/364-c. 431). Bishop of Helenopolis in Bithynia (400-417) and then Aspuna in Galatia. A disciple of Evagrius of Pontus and admirer of Origen, Palladius became a zealous adherent of John Chrysostom and shared his troubles in 403. His *Lausiac History* is the leading source for the history of early monasticism, stressing the spiritual value of the life of the desert.

Paschasius of Dumium (c. 515-c. 580). Translator of sentences of the Desert Fathers from Greek into Latin while a monk in Dumium.

Paterius (c. sixth-seventh century). Disciple of Gregory the Great who is primarily responsible for the transmission of Gregory's works to many later medieval authors.

Paulinus of Milan (late 4th-early 5th century). Personal secretary and biographer of Ambrose of Milan. He took part in the Pelagian controversy.

Paulinus of Nola (355-431). Roman senator and distinguished Latin poet whose frequent encounters with Ambrose of Milan (c. 333-397) led to his eventual conversion and baptism in 389. He eventually renounced his wealth and influential position and took up his pen to write poetry in service of Christ. He also wrote many letters to, among others, Augustine, Jerome and Rufinus.

Paulus Orosius (b. c. 380). An outspoken critic of Pelagius, mentored by Augustine. His *Seven Books of History Against the Pagans* was perhaps the first history of Christianity.

Pelagius (c. 354-c. 420). Contemporary of Augustine whose followers were condemned in 418 and 431 for maintaining that even before Christ there were people who lived wholly without sin and that salvation depended on free will.

Peter Chrysologus (c. 380-450). Latin archbishop of Ravenna whose teachings included arguments for adherence in matters of faith to the Roman see, and the relationship between grace and Christian living.

Peter of Alexandria (d. c. 311). Bishop of Alexandria. He marked (and very probably initiated) the reaction at Alexandria against extreme doctrines of Origen. During the persecution of Christians in Alexandria, Peter was arrested and beheaded by Roman officials. Eusebius of Caesarea described him as "a model bishop, remarkable for his virtuous life and his ardent study of the Scriptures."

Philo of Alexandria (c. 20 B.C.-c. A.D. 50). Jewish-born exegete who greatly influenced Christian patristic interpretation of the Old Testament. Born to a rich family in Alexandria, Philo was a contemporary of Jesus and lived an ascetic and contemplative life that makes some believe he was a rabbi. His interpretation of Scripture based the spiritual sense on the literal. Although influenced by Hellenism, Philo's theology remains thoroughly Jewish.

Philoxenus of Mabbug (c. 440-523). Bishop of Mabbug (Hierapolis) and a leading thinker in the early Syrian Orthodox Church. His extensive writings in Syriac include a set of thirteen *Discourses on the Christian Life*, several works on the incarnation and a number of exegetical works.

Photius (c. 820-891). An important Byzantine churchman and university professor of philosophy, mathematics and theology. He was twice the patriarch of Constantinople. First he succeeded Ignatius in 858, but was deposed in 863 when Ignatius was reinstated. Again he followed Ignatius in 878 and remained the patriarch until 886, at which time he was removed by Leo VI. His most important theological work is Address on the Mystagogy of the Holy Spirit, in which he articulates his opposition to the Western filioque, i.e., the procession of the Holy Spirit from the Father and the Son. He is also known for his Amphilochia and Library (Bibliotheca).

Poemen (c. fifth century). One-seventh of the sayings in the *Sayings of the Desert Fathers* are attributed to Poemen, which is Greek for shepherd. Poemen was a common title among early Egyptian desert ascetics, and it is unknown whether all of the sayings come from one person.

Polycarp of Smyrna (c. 69-155). Bishop of Smyrna who vigorously fought heretics such as the Marcionites and Valentinians. He was the leading Christian figure in Roman Asia in the middle of the second century.

Potamius of Lisbon (fl. c. 350-360). Bishop of Lisbon who joined the Arian party in 357, but later returned to the Catholic faith (c. 359?). His works from both periods are concerned with the larger Trinitarian debates of his time.

Primasius (fl. 550-560). Bishop of Hadrumetum in North Africa (modern Tunisia) and one of the few Africans to support the condemnation of the Three Chapters. Drawing on Augustine and Tyconius, he wrote a commentary on the Apocalypse, which in allegorizing fashion views the work as referring to the history of the church.

Procopius of Gaza (c. 465-c. 530). A Christian exegete educated in Alexandria. He wrote numerous theological works and commentaries on Scripture (particularly the Hebrew Bible), the latter marked by the allegorical exegesis for which the Alexandrian school was known.

Prosper of Aquitaine (c. 390-c. 463). Probably a lay monk and supporter of the theology of Augustine on grace and predestination. He collaborated closely with Pope Leo I in his doctrinal statements.

Prudentius (c. 348-c. 410). Latin poet and hymn-writer who devoted his later life to Christian writing. He wrote didactic poems on the theology of the incarnation, against the heretic Marcion and against the resurgence of paganism.

Pseudo-Clementines (third-fourth century). A series of apocryphal writings pertaining to a conjured life of Clement of Rome. Written in a form of popular legend, the stories from Clement's life, including his opposition to Simon Magus, illustrate and promote articles of Christian teaching. It is likely that the corpus is a derivative of a number of Gnostic and Judeo-Christian writings. Dating the corpus is a complicated issue.

Pseudo-Dionysius the Areopagite (fl. c. 500). Author who assumed the name of Dionysius the Areopagite mentioned in Acts 17:34, and who composed the works known as the *Corpus Areopagiticum* (or *Dionysiacum*). These writings were the foundation of the apophatic school of mysticism in their denial that anything can be truly predicated of God.

Pseudo-Macarius (fl. c. 390). An anonymous writer and ascetic (from Mesopotamia?) active in Antioch whose badly edited works were attributed to Macarius of Egypt. He had keen insight into human nature, prayer and the inner life. His work includes some one hundred discourses and homilies.

Quodvultdeus (fl. 430). Carthaginian bishop and friend of Augustine who endeavored to show at length how the New Testament fulfilled the Old Testament.

Rufinus of Aquileia (c. 345-411). Orthodox Christian thinker and historian who nonetheless translated and preserved the works of Origen, and defended him against the strictures of Jerome and Epiphanius. He lived the ascetic life in Rome, Egypt and Jerusalem (the Mount of Olives).

Sabellius (fl. 200). Allegedly the author of the heresy which maintains that the Father and Son are a single person. The patripassian variant of this heresy states that the Father suffered on the cross.

Sahdona (fl. 635-640). Known in Greek as Martyrius, this Syriac author was bishop of Beth Garmai. He studied in Nisibis and was exiled for his christological ideas. His most important work is the deeply scriptural *Book of Perfection* which ranks as one of the masterpieces of Syriac monastic literature.

Salvian the Presbyter of Marseilles (c. 400-c. 480). An important author for the history of his own time. He saw the fall of Roman civilization to the barbarians as a consequence of the reprehensible conduct of Roman Christians. In *The Governance of God* he developed the theme of divine providence.

Second Letter of Clement (c. 150). The so-called *Second Letter of Clement* is an early Christian sermon probably written by a Corinthian author, though some scholars have assigned it to a Roman or Alexandrian author.

Severian of Gabala (fl. c. 400). A contemporary of John Chrysostom, he was a highly regarded preacher in Constantinople, particularly at the imperial court, and ultimately sided with Chrysostom's accusers. He wrote homilies on Genesis.

Severus of Antioch (fl. 488-538). A monophysite theologian, consecrated bishop of Antioch in 522. Born in Pisidia, he studied in Alexandria and Beirut, taught in Constantinople and was exiled to Egypt.

Shenoute (c. 350-466). Abbot of Athribis in Egypt. His large monastic community was known for very strict rules. He accompanied Cyril of Alexandria to the Council of Ephesus in 431, where he played an important role in deposing Nestorius. He knew Greek but wrote in Coptic, and his literary activity includes homilies, catecheses on monastic subjects, letters, and a couple of theological treatises.

Shepherd of Hermas (second century). Divided into five *Visions*, twelve *Mandates* and ten *Similitudes*, this Christian apocalypse was written by a former slave and named for the form of the second angel said to have granted him his visions. This work was highly esteemed for its moral value and was used as a textbook for catechumens in the early church.

Sulpicius Severus (c. 360-c. 420). An ecclesiastical writer from Bordeaux born of noble parents. Devoting himself to monastic retirement, he became a personal friend and enthusiastic disciple of St. Martin of Tours.

Symeon the New Theologian (c. 949-1022). Compassionate spiritual leader known for his strict rule. He believed that the divine light could be perceived and received through the practice of mental prayer.

Tertullian of Carthage (c. 155/160-225/250; fl. c. 197-222). Brilliant Carthaginian apologist and polemicist who laid the foundations of Christology and trinitarian orthodoxy in the West, though he himself was later estranged from the catholic tradition due to its laxity.

Theodore of Heraclea (d. c. 355). An anti-Nicene bishop of Thrace. He was part of a team seeking reconciliation between Eastern and Western Christianity. In 343 he was excommunicated at the council of Sardica. His writings focus on a literal interpretation of Scripture.

Theodore of Mopsuestia (c. 350-428). Bishop of Mopsuestia, founder of the Antiochene, or literalistic, school of exegesis. A great man in his day, he was later condemned as a precursor of Nestorius.

Theodore of Tabennesi (d. 368) Vice general of the Pachomian monasteries (c. 350-368) under

Horsiesi. Several of his letters are known.

Theodoret of Cyr (c. 393-466). Bishop of Cyr (Cyrrhus), he was an opponent of Cyril who commented extensively on Old Testament texts as a lucid exponent of Antiochene exegesis.

Theodotus the Valentinian (second century). Likely a Montanist who may have been related to the Alexandrian school. Extracts of his work are known through writings of Clement of Alexandria.

Theophanes (775-845). Hymnographer and bishop of Nicaea (842-845). He was persecuted during the second iconoclastic period for his support of the Seventh Council (Second Council of Nicaea, 787). He wrote many hymns in the tradition of the monastery of Mar Sabbas that were used in the *Paraklitiki*.

Theophilus of Antioch (late second century). Bishop of Antioch. His only surviving work is *Ad Autholycum*, where we find the first Christian commentary on Genesis and the first use of the term *Trinity*. Theophilus's apologetic literary heritage had influence on Irenaeus and possibly Tertullian.

Theophylact of Ohrid (c. 1050-c. 1108). Byzantine archbishop of Ohrid (or Achrida) in what is now Bulgaria. Drawing on earlier works, he wrote commentaries on several Old Testament books and all of the New Testament except for Revelation.

Valentinus (fl. c. 140). Alexandrian heretic of the mid-second century who taught that the material world was created by the transgression of God's Wisdom, or Sophia (*see* Gnostics).

Valerian of Cimiez (fl. c. 422-439). Bishop of Cimiez. He participated in the councils of Riez (439) and Vaison (422) with a view to strengthening church discipline. He supported Hilary of Arles in quarrels with Pope Leo I.

Verecundus (d. 552). An African Christian writer, who took an active part in the christological controversies of the sixth century, especially in the debate on Three Chapters. He also wrote allegorical commentaries on the nine liturgical church canticles.

Victorinus of Petovium (d. c. 304). Latin biblical exegete. With multiple works attributed to him, his sole surviving work is the *Commentary on the Apocalypse* and perhaps some fragments from *Commentary on Matthew*. Victorinus expressed strong millenarianism in his writing, though his was less materialistic than the millenarianism of Papias or Irenaeus. In his allegorical approach he could be called a spiritual disciple of Origen. Victorinus died during the first year of Diocletian's persecution, probably in 304.

Vincent of Lérins (d. before 450). Monk who has exerted considerable influence through his writings on orthodox dogmatic theological method, as contrasted with the theological methodologies of the heresies.

Timeline of Writers of the Patristic Period

Location / Period	British Isles	Gaul	Spain, Portugal	Rome* and Italy	Carthage and Northern Africa
2nd century				Clement of Rome, fl. c. 92-101 (Greek)	
				Shepherd of Hermas, c. 140 (Greek)	
				Justin Martyr (Ephesus, Rome), c. 100/110-165 (Greek)	
		Irenaeus of Lyons, c. 135-c. 202 (Greek)		Valentinus the Gnostic (Rome), fl. c. 140 (Greek)	
3rd century				Marcion (Rome), fl. 144 (Greek)	
				Callistus of Rome, regn. 217-222 (Latin)	Tertullian of Carthage, c. 155/160- c. 225 (Latin)
				Minucius Felix of Rome, fl. 218-235 (Latin)	
				Hippolytus (Rome, Palestine?), fl. 222-235/245 (Greek)	Cyprian of Carthage, fl. 248-258 (Latin)
				Novatian of Rome, fl. 235-258 (Latin)	
				Victorinus of Petovium, 230-304 (Latin)	

*One of the five ancient patriarchates

Alexandria* and Egypt	Constantinople* and Asia Minor, Greece	Antioch* and Syria	Mesopotamia, Persia	Jerusalem* and Palestine	Location Unknown
Philo of Alexandria, c. 20 B.C. – c. A.D. 50 (Greek)				Flavius Josephus (Rome), c. 37-c. 101 (Greek)	
Basilides (Alexandria), 2nd cent. (Greek)	Polycarp of Smyrna, c. 69-155 (Greek)	*Didache* (Egypt?), c. 100 (Greek)			
Letter of Barnabas (Syria?), c. 130 (Greek)		Ignatius of Antioch, c. 35–107/112 (Greek)			
Theodotus the Valentinian, 2nd cent. (Greek)	Athenagoras (Greece), fl. 176-180 (Greek)	Theophilus of Antioch, c. late 2nd cent. (Greek)			*Second Letter of Clement* (spurious; Corinth, Rome, Alexandria?) (Greek), c. 150
Clement of Alexandria, c. 150-215 (Greek)	*Montanist Oracles*, late 2nd cent. (Greek)				
Sabellius (Egypt), 2nd–3rd cent. (Greek)					Pseudo-Clementines 3rd cent. (Greek)
			Mani (Manichaeans), c. 216-276		
Letter to Diognetus, 3rd cent. (Greek)	Gregory Thaumaturgus (Neocaesarea), fl. c. 248-264 (Greek)				
Origen (Alexandria, Caesarea of Palestine), 185-254 (Greek)					
Dionysius of Alexandria, d. 264/5 (Greek)					
	Methodius of Olympus (Lycia), d. c. 311 (Greek)				

Timeline of Writers of the Patristic Period

Location	British Isles	Gaul	Spain, Portugal	Rome* and Italy	Carthage and Northern Africa
Period					
4th century				Firmicus Maternus (Sicily), fl. c. 335 (Latin)	
		Lactantius, c. 260- 330 (Latin)		Marius Victorinus (Rome), fl. 355-363 (Latin)	
				Eusebius of Vercelli, fl. c. 360 (Latin)	
			Hosius of Cordova, d. 357 (Latin)	Lucifer of Cagliari (Sardinia), d. 370/371 (Latin)	
		Hilary of Poitiers, c. 315-367 (Latin)	Potamius of Lisbon, fl. c. 350-360 (Latin)	Faustinus (Rome), fl. 380 (Latin)	
				Filastrius of Brescia, fl. 380 (Latin)	
			Gregory of Elvira, fl. 359-385 (Latin)	Ambrosiaster (Italy?), fl. c. 366-384 (Latin)	
			Prudentius, c. 348-c. 410 (Latin)	Faustus of Riez, fl. c. 380 (Latin)	
			Pacian of Barcelona, 4th cent. (Latin)	Gaudentius of Brescia, fl. 395 (Latin)	Paulus Orosius, b. c. 380 (Latin)
				Ambrose of Milan, c. 333-397; fl. 374-397 (Latin)	
				Paulinus of Milan, late 4th early 5th cent. (Latin)	
5th century				Rufinus (Aquileia, Rome), c. 345-411 (Latin)	
	Fastidius (Britain), c. 4th-5th cent. (Latin)	Sulpicius Severus (Bordeaux), c. 360-c. 420/425 (Latin)		Aponius, fl. 405-415 (Latin)	Quodvultdeus (Carthage), fl. 430 (Latin)
				Chromatius (Aquileia), fl. 400 (Latin)	
		John Cassian (Palestine, Egypt, Constantinople, Rome, Marseilles), 360-432 (Latin)		Pelagius (Britain, Rome), c. 354-c. 420 (Greek)	Augustine of Hippo, 354-430 (Latin)
				Maximus of Turin, d. 408/423 (Latin)	Luculentius, 5th cent. (Latin)
		Vincent of Lérins, d. 435 (Latin)		Paulinus of Nola, 355-431 (Latin)	
		Valerian of Cimiez, fl. c. 422-449 (Latin)		Peter Chrysologus (Ravenna), c. 380-450 (Latin)	
		Eucherius of Lyons, fl. 420-449 (Latin)		Julian of Eclanum, 386-454 (Latin)	

*One of the five ancient patriarchates

Alexandria* and Egypt	Constantinople* and Asia Minor, Greece	Antioch* and Syria	Mesopotamia, Persia	Jerusalem* and Palestine	Location Unknown
Antony, c. 251-355 (Coptic /Greek)	Theodore of Heraclea (Thrace), fl. c. 330-355 (Greek)	Eustathius of Antioch, fl. 325 (Greek)	Aphrahat (Persia) c. 270-350; fl. 337-345 (Syriac)	Eusebius of Caesarea (Palestine), c. 260/263-340 (Greek)	Commodius, c. 3rd or 5th cent. (Latin)
Peter of Alexandria, d. c. 311 (Greek)	Marcellus of Ancyra, d.c. 375 (Greek)	Eusebius of Emesa, c. 300-c. 359 (Greek)			
Arius (Alexandria), fl. c. 320 (Greek)	Epiphanius of Salamis (Cyprus), c. 315-403 (Greek)	Ephrem the Syrian, c. 306-373 (Syriac)	Jacob of Nisibis, fl. 308-325 (Syriac)		
Alexander of Alexandria, fl. 312-328 (Greek)	Basil (the Great) of Caesarea, b. c. 330; fl. 357-379 (Greek)				
Pachomius, c. 292-347 (Coptic/Greek?)	Macrina the Younger, c. 327-379 (Greek)				
Theodore of Tabennesi, d. 368 (Coptic/Greek)	Apollinaris of Laodicea, 310-c. 392 (Greek)				
Horsiesi, c. 305-390 (Coptic/Greek)	Gregory of Nazianzus, b. 329/330; fl. 372-389 (Greek)	Nemesius of Emesa (Syria), fl. late 4th cent. (Greek)		Acacius of Caesarea (Palestine), d. c. 365 (Greek)	
Athanasius of Alexandria, c. 295-373; fl. 325-373 (Greek)	Gregory of Nyssa, c. 335-394 (Greek)	Diodore of Tarsus, d. c. 394 (Greek)		Cyril of Jerusalem, c. 315-386 (Greek)	
Macarius of Egypt, c. 300-c. 390 (Greek)	Amphilochius of Iconium, c. 340/345- c. 398/404 (Greek)	John Chrysostom (Constantinople), 344/354-407 (Greek)			
Didymus (the Blind) of Alexandria, 313-398 (Greek)	Evagrius of Pontus, 345-399 (Greek)	Apostolic Constitutions, c. 375-400 (Greek)			
		Didascalia, 4th cent. (Syriac)			
	Eunomius of Cyzicus, fl. 360-394 (Greek)	Theodore of Mopsuestia, c. 350-428 (Greek)		Diodore of Tarsus, d. c. 394 (Greek)	
	Pseudo-Macarius (Mesopotamia?), late 4th cent. (Greek)	Acacius of Beroea, c. 340-c. 436 (Greek)		Jerome (Rome, Antioch, Bethlehem), c. 347-420 (Latin)	
	Nicetas of Remesiana, d. c. 414 (Latin)				
Palladius of Helenopolis (Egypt), c. 365-425 (Greek)	Nestorius (Constantinople), c. 381-c. 451 (Greek)	Book of Steps, c. 400 (Syriac)	Eznik of Kolb, fl. 430-450 (Armenian)	Jerome (Rome, Antioch, Bethlehem), c. 347-419 (Latin)	
		Severian of Gabala, fl. c. 400 (Greek)			
Cyril of Alexandria, 375-444 (Greek)	Basil of Seleucia, fl. 440-468 (Greek)	Nilus of Ancyra, d.c. 430 (Greek)		Hesychius of Jerusalem, fl. 412-450 (Greek)	
	Diadochus of Photice (Macedonia), 400-474 (Greek)			Euthymius (Palestine), 377-473 (Greek)	

Timeline of Writers of the Patristic Period

Location / Period	British Isles	Gaul	Spain, Portugal	Rome* and Italy	Carthage and Northern Africa
5th century (cont.)		Hilary of Arles, c. 401-449 (Latin)		Leo the Great (Rome), regn. 440-461 (Latin)	
		Eusebius of Gaul, 5th cent. (Latin)			
		Prosper of Aquitaine, c. 390-c. 463 (Latin)		Arnobius the Younger (Rome), fl. c. 450 (Latin)	
		Salvian the Presbyter of Marseilles, c. 400-c. 480 (Latin)			
		Gennadius of Marseilles, d. after 496 (Latin)			
6th century		Caesarius of Arles, c. 470-543 (Latin)	Paschasius of Dumium (Portugal), c. 515-c. 580 (Latin)	Epiphanius the Latin, late 5th–early 6th cent. (Latin)	Fulgentius of Ruspe, c. 467-532 (Latin)
			Leander of Seville, c. 545-c. 600 (Latin)	Eugippius, c. 460- c. 533 (Latin)	Verecundus, d. 552 (Latin)
				Benedict of Nursia, c. 480-547 (Latin)	Primasius, fl. 550-560 (Latin)
			Martin of Braga, fl. 568-579 (Latin)	Cassiodorus (Calabria), c. 485-c. 540 (Latin)	Facundus of Hermiane, fl. 546-568 (Latin)
7th century				Gregory the Great (Rome), c. 540-604 (Latin)	
				Gregory of Agrigentium, d. 592 (Greek)	
			Isidore of Seville, c. 560-636 (Latin)	Paterius, 6th/7th cent. (Latin)	
			Braulio of Saragossa, c. 585-651 (Latin)		
	Adamnan, c. 624-704 (Latin)		Fructuosus of Braga, d.c. 665 (Latin)		
8th-12th century	Bede the Venerable, c. 672/673-735 (Latin)				

*One of the five ancient patriarchates

Alexandria* and Egypt	Constantinople* and Asia Minor, Greece	Antioch* and Syria	Mesopotamia, Persia	Jerusalem* and Palestine	Location Unknown
Ammonius of Alexandria, c. 460 (Greek) Poemen, 5th cent. (Greek) Besa the Copt, 5th cent. Shenoute, c. 350-466 (Coptic)	Gennadius of Constantinople, d. 471 (Greek)	John of Antioch, d. 441/2 (Greek) Theodoret of Cyr, c. 393-466 (Greek) Pseudo-Victor of Antioch, 5th cent. (Greek) John of Apamea, 5th cent. (Syriac)		Gerontius of Petra c. 395-c.480 (Syriac)	
Olympiodorus, early 6th cent.	Oecumenius (Isauria), 6th cent. (Greek)	Philoxenus of Mabbug (Syria), c. 440-523 (Syriac) Severus of Antioch, c. 465-538 (Greek) Mark the Hermit (Tarsus), c. 6th cent. (4th cent.?) (Greek)	Jacob of Sarug, c. 450-520 (Syriac) Babai the Great, c. 550-628 (Syriac) Babai, early 6th cent. (Syriac)	Procopius of Gaza (Palestine), c. 465-530 (Greek) Dorotheus of Gaza, fl. 525-540 (Greek) Cyril of Scythopolis, b. c. 525; d. after 557 (Greek)	Pseudo-Dionysius the Areopagite, fl. c. 500 (Greek)
	Maximus the Confessor (Constantinople), c. 580-662 (Greek)	Sahdona/Martyrius, fl. 635-640 (Syriac)	Isaac of Nineveh, d. c. 700 (Syriac)		(Pseudo-) Constantius, before 7th cent.? (Greek) Andreas, c. 7th cent. (Greek)
		John of Damascus (John the Monk), c. 650-750 (Greek)			
	Theophanes (Nicaea), 775-845 (Greek) Cassia (Constantinople), c. 805-c. 848/867 (Greek) Arethas of Caesarea (Constantinople/Caesarea), c. 860-940 (Greek) Photius (Constantinople), c. 820-891 (Greek) Symeon the New Theologian (Constantinople), 949-1022 (Greek) Theophylact of Ohrid (Bulgaria), 1050-1126 (Greek)		John the Elder of Qardu (north Iraq), 8th cent. (Syriac) Isho'dad of Merv, d. after 852 (Syriac)		

Bibliography of Works
in Original Languages

This bibliography refers readers to original language sources and supplies Thesaurus Linguae Graecae (=TLG) or Cetedoc Clavis (=Cl.) numbers where available. The edition listed in this bibliography may in some cases differ from the edition found in TLG or Cetedoc databases.

Ambrose. "De fide libri v." In *Sancti Ambrosii opera*. Edited by Otto Faller. CSEL 78. Vienna, Austria: Hoelder-Pichler-Tempsky, 1962. Cl. 0150.

———. "De fuga saeculi." In *Sancti Ambrosii opera*. Edited by Karl Schenkl. CSEL 32, pt. 2, pp. 161-207. Vienna, Austria: F. Tempsky; Leipzig, Germany: G. Freytag, 1897. Cl. 0133.

———. De Isaac vel anima." In *Sancti Ambrosii opera*. Edited by Karl Schenkl. CSEL 32, pt. 1, pp. 639-700. Vienna, Austria: F. Tempsky; Leipzig, Germany: G. Freytag, 1897. Cl. 0128.

———. *De paenitentia*. Edited by R. Gryson. SC 179. Paris: Éditions du Cerf, 1971. Cl. 0156.

———. "De paradiso." In *Sancti Ambrosii opera*. Edited by Karl Schenkl. CSEL 32, pt. 1, pp. 263-336. Vienna, Austria: F. Tempsky; Leipzig, Germany: G. Freytag, 1897. Cl. 0124.

———. "Epistulae; Epistulae extra collectionem traditae." In *Sancti Ambrosii opera*. Edited by Otto Faller and M. Zelzer. CSEL 82. Vienna, Austria: F. Tempsky; Leipzig, Germany: G. Freytag, 1968-1990. Cl. 0160.

Arethas of Caesarea. "Fragmenta in epistulam ad Hebraeos (in catenis)." In *Pauluskommentare aus der griechischen kirche: Aus Katenenhandschriften gesammelt und herausgegeben*. Edited by Karl Staab. NTA 15, pp. 653-61. Münster in Westfalen: Aschendorff, 1933.

Athanasius. "De incarnatione verbi." In *Sur l'incarnation du verbe*. Edited by C. Kannengiesser. SC 199, pp. 258-468. Paris: Éditions du Cerf, 1973. TLG 2035.002.

———. "Deposition Arii." In "De decretis Nicaenae synodi." In *Athanasius Werke*. Vol. 2.1, pp. 1-45. Edited by Hans-Georg Opitz. Berlin: De Gruyter, 1940. TLG 2035.003.

———. "Epistula ad episcopos Aegypti et Libyae." In Opera omnia. PG 25, cols. 537-93. Edited by J.-P. Migne. Paris: Migne, 1857. TLG 2035.041.

———. "Epistula ad Maximum." In *Opera omnia*. PG 26, cols. 1085-89. Edited by J.-P. Migne. Paris: Migne, 1887. TLG 2035.051.

———. "Epistulae festalis." In *Opera omnia*. PG 26, cols. 1351-444. Edited by J.-P. Migne. Paris: Migne, 1887. TLG 2035.014.

———. "Orationes tres contra Arianos." In *Opera omnia*. PG 26, cols. 813-920. Edited by J.-P. Migne. Paris: Migne, 1887. TLG 2035.042.

———. "Vita sancti Antonii." In *Opera omnia*. PG 26, cols. 835-976. Edited by J.-P. Migne. Paris: Migne, 1857. TLG 2035.047.

Augustine. *Confessionum libri tredecim*. Edited by L. Verheijen. CCL 27. Turnhout, Belgium: Brepols, 1981. Cl. 0251.

———. *De civitate Dei*. 2 vols. Edited by Bernhard Dombart and Alphons Kalb. CCL 47-48. Turnhout, Belgium: Brepols, 1955. Cl. 0313.

———. "De diversis quaestionibus octoginta tribus." In *Aurelii Augustini opera*. Edited by Almut Mutzenbecher. CCL 44A, pp. 11-249. Turnhout, Belgium: Brepols, 1975. Cl. 0289.

————. "De fide et symbolo." In *Sancti Aureli Augustini opera*. Edited by J. Zycha. CSEL 41, pp. 3-32. Vienna, Austria: F. Tempsky, 1900. Cl. 0293.

————. "De Genesi ad litteram libri duodecim."In *Sancti Aureli Augustini opera*. Edited by J. Zycha. CSEL 28.1, pp. 3-435. Vienna, Austria: F. Tempsky, 1894. Cl. 0266.

————. "De Genesi contra Manichaeos." In *Opera omnia*. PL 34, cols. 173-220. Edited by J.-P. Migne. Paris: Migne, 1845. Cl. 0294.

————. "De peccatorum meritis et remissione et de baptismo parvulorum." In *Sancti Aureli Augustini opera*. Edited by C. F. Urba and J. Zycha. CSEL 60, pp. 3-151. Vienna, Austria: F. Tempsky, 1913. Cl. 0342.

————. "De praedestinatione sanctorum." In *Opera omnia*. PL 44, cols. 959-92. Edited by J.-P. Migne. Paris: Migne, 1861. Cl. 0354.

————. "De Trinitate." In *Aurelii Augustini opera*. Edited by W. J. Mountain. CCL 50-50A. Turnhout, Belgium: Brepols, 1968. Cl. 0329.

————. "Epistulae." In *Sancti Aurelii Augustini opera*. Edited by A. Goldbacher. CCL 34, pts. 1, 2. Turnhout, Belgium: Brepols, 1895. Cl. 0262.

————. "Sermones." In *Augustini opera omnia*. PL 38 and 39. Edited by J.-P. Migne. Paris: Migne, 1844-1865. Cl. 0284.

Basil the Great. *De Spiritu Sancto*. Edited by Benoit Pruche. SC 17. Paris: Éditions du Cerf, 2002. TLG 2040.003.

————. "Epistulae." In *Saint Basil: Lettres*. Edited by Yves Courtonne. Vol. 2, pp. 101-218; vol. 3, pp. 1-229. Paris: Les Belles Lettres, 1961-1966. TLG 2040.004.

————. "Homiliae super Psalmos." In *Opera omnia*. PG 29, cols. 209-494. J.-P. Migne. Paris: Migne, 1886. TLG 2040.018.

Bede. "De tabernaculo et vasis eius ac vestibus sacerdotum libri iii." In *Bedae opera*. Edited by D. Hurst. CCL 119A, pp. 5-139. Cl. 1345.

————. "Homiliarum evangelii." In *Bedae opera*. Edited by D. Hurst. CCL 122, pp. 1-378. Turnhout, Belgium: Brepols, 1956. Cl. 1367.

Braulio of Saragosa. "Epistulae." In *Scriptorum ecclesiasticorum, opera omnia*. PL 80, cols. 649-700. Edited by J.-P. Migne. Paris: Migne, 1864.

Cassian, John. "Collationes xxiii." Edited by Michael Petshenig. CSEL 13. Vienna, Austria: F. Tempsky, 1886. Cl. 0512.

————. "De incarnatione Domini contra Nestorium." In *Johannis Cassiani*. Edited by Michael Petschenig. CSEL 17, pp. 233-391. Vienna, Austria: F. Tempsky; Leipzig, Germany: G. Freytag, 1888. Cl. 0514.

Cassiodorus. *Expositio Psalmorum*. 2 vols. Edited by Marcus Adriaen. CCL 97 and 98. Turnhout: Brepols, 1958. Cl. 0900.

Clement of Alexandria. "Paedagogus." In *Le pédagogue [par] Clement d'Alexandrie*. 3 vols. Translated by Mauguerite Harl, Chantel Matray and Claude Mondésert. Introduction and notes by Henri-Irénée Marrou. SC 70, 108, 158. Paris: Éditions du Cerf, 1960-1970. TLG 0555.002.

————. "Protrepticus." In *Clément d'Alexandrie. Le protreptique*. 2nd ed. Edited by C. Mondésert. SC 2, pp. 52-193. Paris: Éditions du Cerf, 1949. TLG 0555.001.

————. "Stromata." In *Clemens Alexandrinus*. Vol. 2, 3rd ed., and vol. 3, 2nd ed. Edited by Otto Stählin, Ludwig Früchtel and Ursula Treu. GCS 15, pp. 3-518, and GCS 17, pp. 1-102. Berlin: Akademie-Verlag, 1960-1970. TLG 0555.004.

Clement of Rome. "Epistula i ad Corinthios." In *Clément de Rome: Épître aux Corinthiens*. Edited by Annie Jaubert. SC 167. Paris: Éditions du Cerf, 1971. TLG 1271.001.

Cyprian. *Epistulae.* Edited by G. F. Diercks. CCL 3B, 3C. Turnhout, Belgium: Brepols, 1994-1996. Cl. 0050.

Cyril of Alexandria. "Apologeticus contra Theodoretum pro XII capitibus." In *S. P. N. Cyrilli Opera omnia.* PG 76, cols. 385-452. Edited by J.-P. Migne. Paris: Migne, 1863.

———. "De incarnatione unigeniti." In *Cyrille d'Alexandrie: Deux dialogues christologiques.* Edited by G. M. de Durand. SC 97, pp.188-300. Paris: Éditions du Cerf, 1964.TLG 4090.026.

———. "Epistulae." In *Concilium universale Ephesenum.* Edited by E. Schwartz. Berlin: Walter De Gruyter, 1927. TLG 5000.001.

———. "Fragmenta in sancti Pauli epistularum ad Hebraeos." In PEP 3, pp. 362-423. Edited by P. E. Pusey. Oxford: Clarendon Press, 1872. Reprint, Brussels: Culture et Civilization, 1965. TLG 4090.006.

———. "Homiliae Paschales." In *S. P .N. Cyrilli Opera omnia.* PG 77, cols. 401-982. Edited by J.-P. Migne. Paris: Migne, 1864. TLG 4090.032.

———. "Quod unus sit Christus." In *Cyrille d'Alexandria. Deux dialogues christologiques.* Edited by G. M. de Durand. SC 97, pp. 302-514. Paris: Éditions du Cerf, 1964. TLG 4090.027.

Cyril of Jeruslaem. "Catecheses ad illuminandos 1-18." In *Cyrilli Hierosolymorum archiepiscopi opera quae supersunt omnia,* 1:28-320; 2:2-342. 2 vols. Edited by W. C. Reischl and J. Rupp. Munich: Lentner, 1860. Reprint, Hildesheim: Olms, 1967. TLG 2110.003.

———. "Mystagogiae 1-5 (Sp.)." In *Cyrille de Jérusalem: Catéchèses, mystagogigues.* 2nd edition. SC 126, pp. 82-174. Edited by Auguste Piédagnel. Paris: Éditions du Cerf, 1988. TLG 2110.002.

Didache xii apostolorum. In *Instructions des Apôtres,* pp. 226-42. Edited by J. P. Audet. Paris: Lecoffre, 1958. TLG 1311.001.

Didymus the Blind. "Fragmenta in epistulam ad Hebraeos (in catenis)." In *Pauluskommentare aus der griechischen kirche: Aus Katenenhandschriften gesammelt und herausgegeben.* Edited by Karl Staab. NTA 15, pp. 83-112. Münster in Westfalen: Aschendorff, 1933.

Ephrem the Syrian. *Sancti Ephraem Syri in Genesim et in Exodum Commentarii.* Edited by R. M. Tonneau. CSCO 152 (Scriptores Syri 71), Louvain, Belgium: Impremarie Orientaliste L. Dubecq, 1955.

———. In Tatiani Diatessaron. In Saint Éphrem: Commentaire de l'Évangile Concordant – Text Syriaque (Ms Chester-Beatty 709), vol. 2. Edited by Louis Leloir. Leuven and Paris: Peeters Press, 1990.

———. *Srboyn Ep'remi Matenagrowt'iwnk',* vol. 3. 4. Venetik, Armenia: S. Ghazar, 1836.

Epiphanius of Salamis. "Panarion." In *Epiphanius.* 2 vols. Edited by Karl Holl. GCS 25, 31. Leipzig: Hinrichs, 1915-1922.

Eusebius of Caesarea. "Demonstratio evangelica." In *Eusebius Werke.* Vol 6. Edited by Ivar A. Heikel. GCS 23, pp. 1-492. Leipzig: Hinrichs, 1913. TLG 2018.005.

———. "Historia ecclesiastica." In *Eusèbe de Césarée. Histoire ecclésiastique.* 3 vols. Edited by G. Bardy. SC 31, pp. 3-215; SC 41, pp. 4-231; SC 55, pp. 3-120. Paris: Éditions du Cerf, 1952-1958. TLG 2018.002.

Evagrius of Pontus. "De oratione." (Pseudo-Nilus of Ancyra) In *Opera omnia.* PG 79, cols. 1165-200. Edited by J.-P. Migne. Paris: Migne, 1865. TLG 4110.024.

Gregory of Elvira. "Tractatus Origenis de libris Sanctarum Scripturarum." In *Gregorii Iliberritani episcopi quae supersunt.* Edited by Vincentius Bulhart. CCL 69, pp. 1-146. Turnhout, Belgium: Brepols, 1967. Cl. 0546.

Gregory of Nazianzus. "De filio (orat. 29)." In *Gregor von Nazianz. Die fünf theologischen Reden,* pp. 128-68. Edited by J. Barbel. Düsseldorf, Germany: Patmos-Verlag, 1963. TLG 2022.009.

———. "De filio (orat. 30)." In *Gregor von Nazianz. Die fünf theologischen Reden,* pp. 170-216. Edited by J. Barbel. Düsseldorf, Germany: Patmos-Verlag, 1963. TLG 2022.010.

———. "De spiritu sancto (orat. 31)." In *Gregor von Nazianz. Die fünf theologischen Reden*, pp. 218-76. Edited by J. Barbel. Düsseldorf, Germany: Patmos-Verlag, 1963. TLG 2022.011.

———. "De theologia (orat. 28)." In *Gregor von Nazianz. Die fünf theologischen Reden*, pp. 62-126. Edited by J. Barbel. Düsseldorf, Germany: Patmos-Verlag, 1963. TLG 2022.008.

———. "In theophania (orat. 38)." In *Opera omnia*. PG 36, cols. 312-33. Edited by J.-P. Migne. Paris: Migne, 1858. TLG 2022.046.

Gregory of Nyssa. "Ad Simplicium de fide." In *Gregorii Nysseni opera*. Vol. 3.1, pp. 61-67. Edited by F. Mueller. Leiden: Brill, 1958. TLG 2017.004.

———. "Contra Eunomium." In *Gregorii Nysseni opera*. Vol. 1.1, pp. 3-409; vol. 2.2, pp. 3-311. Edited by W. Jaeger. Leiden: Brill, 1960. TLG 2017.030.

———. "De opificio hominis." In *Opera S. Gregorii*. PG 44, cols. 124-256. Edited by J.-P. Migne. Paris: Migne, 1863. TLG 2017.079.

———. "De perfectione Christiana ad Olympium monachum." In *Gregorii Nysseni opera*. Vol. 8.1, pp. 173-214. Edited by W. Jaeger. Leiden: Brill, 1963. TLG 2017.026.

———. "De vita Mosis." In *Grégoire de Nysse. La vie de Moïse*. 3rd ed. Edited by J. Daniélou. SC 1, pp. 44-326. Paris: Éditions du Cerf, 1968. TLG 2017.042.

Gregory the Great. *Registrum epistularum*. Edited by Dag Norberg. CCL 140-140A. Turnhout, Belgium: Brepols, 1982. Cl. 1714.

Hilary of Poitiers. *Tractatus mysteriorum*. Edited by Jean-Paul Brisson. SC 19. Paris: Éditions du Cerf, 1967.

Hippolytus. "Contra haeresin Noeti." In *Hippolytus of Rome. Contra Noetum*, pp. 43-93. Edited by R. Butterworth. London: Heythrop College (University of London), 1977. TLG 2115.002.

Ignatius of Antioch. "Epistulae vii genuinae." In *Ignace d'Antioche: Polycarpe de Smyrne: Lettres: Martyre de Polycarpe*. 4th ed. Edited by P. T. Camelot. SC 10, pp. 56-154. Paris: Éditions du Cerf, 1969. TLG 1443.001.

Irenaeus. "Adversus haereses [liber 3]." In *Irénée de Lyon. Contre les heresies, livre 3*, vol. 2. Edited by Adelin. Rousseau and Louis Doutreleau. SC 211. Paris: Éditions du Cerf, 1974. Cl. 1154.

[Isaac of Nineveh]. *Mar Isaacus Ninivita: De perfectione religiosa*. Edited by Paul Bedjan. Paris, 1909.

Jerome. *Epistulae*. Edited by I. Hilberg. CSEL 54, 55 and 56. Vienna, Austria: F. Tempsky; Leipzig, Germany: G.F. Freytag, 1910-1918. Cl. 0620.

———. "Homilia in Lucam, de Lazaro et Divite." In *S. Hieronymi Presbyteri opera*. Edited by Germain Morin. CCL 78, pp. 507-16. Turnhout, Belgium: Brepols, 1958. Cl. 0596.

———. "Liber quaestionum hebraicarum in Genesim." Edited by Paul de Lagarde. CCL 72, pp. 1-56. Turnhout, Belgium: Brepols, 1959. Cl. 0580.

———. "Tractatus lix in psalmos." In *S. Hieronymi Presbyteri opera*. Edited by Germain Morin. CCL 78, pp. 3-352. Turnhout, Belgium: Brepols, 1958. Cl. 0592.

———. "Tractatus lix in psalmos, series altera." In *S. Hieronymi Presbyteri opera*. Edited by Germain Morin. CCL 78, pp. 355-447. Turnhout, Belgium: Brepols, 1958. Cl. 0593.

John Chrysostom. "Adversus Judaeos (orationes 1-8)." In *Opera omnia*. Edited by J.-P. Migne. PG 48, cols. 843-942. Paris: Migne, 1862. TLG 2062.021.

———. "In epistulam ad Hebraeos (homiliae 1-34)." In *Opera omnia*. Edited by J.-P. Migne. PG 63, cols. 9-236. Paris: Migne, 1862. TLG 2062.168.

John of Damascus. "Expositio fidei." In *Die Schriften des Johannes von Damaskos*, vol. 2, pp. 3-239. Edited by B. Kotter. PTS 12. Berlin: De Gruyter, 1973. TLG 2934.004.

Justin Martyr. "Apologia." In *Die ältesten Apologeten*, pp. 26-77. Edited by E. J. Goodspeed. Göttingen, Germany: Vandenhoeck & Ruprecht, 1915. TLG 0645.001.

————. "Dialogus cum Tryphone" In *Die ältesten Apologeten*, pp. 90-265. Edited by E. J. Goodspeed. Göttingen, Germany: Vandenhoeck & Ruprecht, 1915. TLG 0645.003.

Lactantius. "Epitome divinarum institutionum." In *L. Caeli Firmiani Lactanti Opera omnia*. Edited by Samuel Brandt. CSEL 19, pp. 673-761. Vienna, Austria: F. Tempsky; Leipzig, Germany: G. Freytag, 1890. Cl. 0086.

Leo the Great. *Tractatus septem et nonaginta*. Edited by Antonio Chavasse. CCL 138 and 138A. Turnhout, Belgium: Brepols, 1973. Cl. 1657.

Marius Victorinus. "De homoousio recipiendo." In *Marii Victorini Opera*. Edited by Paul Henry and Pierre Hadot. CCL 83.1, pp. 278-84. Turnhout, Belgium: Brepols, 1971. Cl. 0097.

Maximus the Confessor. "Expositio orationis dominicae." In *Maximi confessoris opuscula exegetica duo*. Edited by Peter van Deun. CCG 23, pp. 27-73. Turnhout, Belgium: Brepols, 1991. TLG 2892.111.

Nestorius. "Erster Sermon gegen des *theotokos* genannt Anfang des Dogmas." In *Nestoriana: Die Fragmente des Nestorius*, pp. 252-53. Edited by Friedrich Loofs. Halle: Max Niemeyer, 1905.

Oecumenius. "Fragmenta in epistulam ad Hebraeos (in catenis)." In *Pauluskommentare aus der griechischen kirche: Aus Katenenhandschriften gesammelt und herausgegeben*. Edited by Karl Staab. NTA 15, pp. 423-69. Münster in Westfalen: Aschendorff, 1933.

Origen. "Commentarii in evangelium Joannis (lib. 1, 2, 4, 5, 6, 10, 13)." In *Origene. Commentaire sur saint Jean*, 3 vols. Edited by Cécil Blanc. SC 120, 157, 222. Paris: Éditions du Cerf, 1966-1975. TLG 2042.005.

————. "Commentarii in evangelium Joannis (lib. 19, 20, 28, 32)." In *Origenes Werke*. Vol. 4. Edited by Erwin Preuschen. GCS 10, pp. 298-480. Leipzig: Hinrichs, 1903. TLG 2042.079.

————. "Commentarium in Canticum Canticorum." In *Origenes Werke*. Vol. 8. Edited by W. A. Baehrens. GCS 33, pp. 61-241. Leipzig: Teubner, 1925. Cl. 0198/TLG 2042.026.

————. "Contra Celsum." In *Origène Contre Celse*, 4 vols. Edited by M. Borret. SC 132, 136, 147 and 150. Paris: Éditions du Cerf, 1967-1969. TLG 2042.001.

————. "De oratione." In *Origenes Werke*. Vol. 2. Edited by Paul Koetschau. GCS 3, pp. 297-403. Leipzig: Hinrichs, 1899. TLG 2042.008.

————. "De principiis." In *Origenes vier Bücher von den Prinzipien*, pp. 462-560, 668-764. Edited by Herwig Görgemanns and Heinrich Karpp. Darmstadt, Germany: Wissenschaftliche Buchgesellschaft, 1976. TLG 2042.002.

————. "Epistula ad Africanum." In *Opera omnia*. PG 11, cols. 48-85. Edited by J.-P. Migne. Paris: Migne, 1857. TLG 2042.045.

————. "Exhortatio ad martyrium." In Origenes Werke. Vol. 1. Edited by Paul Koetschau. GCS 2, pp. 3-47. Leipzig: Hinrichs, 1899. TLG 2042.007.

————. "Homiliae in Exodum." In *Origenes Werke*, vol. 6. Edited by W. A. Baehrens. GCS 29, pp. 217-30. Leipzig: Teubner, 1920. Cl. 0198/TLG 2042.023.

————. "Homiliae in Genesim." In Origenes Werke. Vol. 6. Edited by W. A. Baehrens. GCS 29, pp. 23-30. Leipzig: Teubner, 1920. Cl. 0198/TLG 2042.022.

————. "Homiliae in Leviticum." In *Origenes Werke*. Vol. 6. Edited by W. A. Baehrens. GCS 29, pp. 332-34, 395, 402-7, 409-16 Leipzig: Teubner, 1920. TLG 2042.024.

————."Homiliae in Lucam." In *Opera omnia*. PG 13, cols. 1799-1902. Edited by J.-P. Migne. Paris: Migne, 1862. TLG 2042.016.

————. "Homiliae." In "Selecta in Psalmos (dub.)." In *Opera omnia*. PG 12, cols. 1319-70. Edited by J.-P. Migne. Paris: Migne, 1862.

————. "In Jesu nave." In *Homélies sur Josué*. Edited by Annie Jaubert. SC 71. Paris: Éditions du Cerf, 1960.

———. "In Numeros homiliae." In *Origenes Werke*. Vol. 7. Edited by W. A. Baehrens. GCS 30, pp. 3-285. Leipzig: Teubner, 1921. Cl. 0198.

———. "Selecta in Exodum." In *Opera omnia*. PG 12, cols. 281-97. Edited by J.-P. Migne. Paris: Migne, 1862. TLG 2042.050.

———. "Selecta in Psalmos (dub.)." TLG 2042.058. In *Opera omnia*. PG 12, cols. 1053-320, 1368-69, 1388-89, 1409-685. Edited by J.-P. Migne. Paris: Migne, 1862. TLG 2042.058.

Pachomius. "Catecheses." In *Oeuvres de s. Pachôme et de ses disciples*. Edited L.T. Lefort. CSCO 159, pp. 1-26. Louvain: Imprimerie Orientaliste, 1956.

———. "Vita Pachomii." *Le corpus athénien de saint Pachome*, pp. 11-72. Edited by F. Halkin. Cahiers d'Orientalisme 2. Genève: Cramer, 1982.

Philoxenus of Mabbug. *See* Isaac of Nineveh. *Hapanta ta heurethenta asketika*. Leipzig: 1770. Edited by Nikephorus Hieromonachus. Reprint, Athens: Ch. Spanos, 1895.

Photius. "Fragmenta in epistulam ad Hebraeos (in catenis)." In *Pauluskommentare aus der griechischen kirche: Aus Katenenhandschriften gesammelt und herausgegeben*. Edited by Karl Staab. NTA 15, pp. 470-652. Münster in Westfalen: Aschendorff, 1933.

Pseudo-Clement of Rome. "Epistula ii ad Corinthios (Sp.)" In *Die apostolischen Väter*, pp. 71-81. 3rd edition. Edited by Karl Bihlmeyer and W. Schneemelcher. Tübingen: Mohr, 1970. TLG 1271.002.

Pseudo-Dionysius. "De caelestine hierarchia." In *Denys l'Aréopagite: La hiérarchie céleste*. Edited by R. Roques, G. Heil and M. de Gandillac. SC 58, pp. 70-225. Paris: Éditions du Cerf, 1958. Reprint, 1970. TLG 2798.001.

———. "De ecclesiastica hierarchia." In *Corpus Dionysiacum II*. Edited by Gunter Heil and Adolf Martin Ritter. Patristische Texte und Studien, pp. 61-132. Berlin: de Gruyter, 1991.

Rufinus of Aquileia. "Expositio symboli." In *Opera*. Edited by Manlio Simonetti. CCL 20, pp. 125-82. Turnhout, Belgium: Brepols, 1961. Cl. 0196.

Severian of Gabala. "Fragmenta in epistulam ad Hebraeos (in catenis)." In *Pauluskommentare aus der griechischen kirche: Aus Katenenhandschriften gesammelt und herausgegeben*. Edited by Karl Staab. NTA 15, pp. 213-351. Münster in Westfalen: Aschendorff, 1933.

Symeon the New Theologian. Catecheses 1-5. Edited by Basil Krivochéine and Joseph Paramelle. SC 96. Paris: Éditions du Cerf, 1963.

Tertullian. "Adversus omnes haereses (dub.)." In *Opera omnia*. Edited by E. Kroymann. CCL 2, pp. 1401-10. Turnhout, Belgium: Brepols, 1954. Cl. 0034.

———. "De corona." In *Opera omnia*. Edited by E. Kroymann. CCL 2, pp. 1039-65. Turnhout, Belgium: Brepols, 1954. Cl. 0021.

Theodore of Mopsuestia. *Commentarius in evangelium Johannis Apostoli*. 2 vols. Edited by J. M. Vosté. CSCO 115, 116. Paris: Typographeo Reipublicae, 1940.

———. "Ex libris de incarnatione filii dei." In *TEM* 2, pp. 290-312. Cambridge: Cambridge University Press, 1882.

———. "Ex tertio libro contra Apollinarium." In *TEM* 2, pp. 312-23. Cambridge: Cambridge University Press, 1882.

———. "Fragmenta in epistulam ad Hebraeos (in catenis)." In *Pauluskommentare aus der griechischen kirche: Aus Katenenhandschriften gesammelt und herausgegeben*. Edited by Karl Staab. NTA 15, pp. 113-212. Münster in Westfalen: Aschendorff, 1933. TLG 4135.018.

———. "In epistolam b. Pauli ad Thessalonicenses I." In *TEM* 2, pp. 1-40. Cambridge: Cambridge University Press, 1882.

———. "In epistolam beati Pauli ad Ephesios." In *TEM* 1, pp. 112-96. Cambridge: Cambridge University Press, 1880.

[Theodore of Mopsuestia]. *Les Homélies Catéchétiques de Théodore de Mopsueste*. Edited by Raymond Tonneau and Robert Devreesse. Reproduction phototypique du ms. Mingana Syr. 561 (Selly Oak Colleges' Library, Birmingham). Studi e testi 145. Città del Vaticano: Biblioteca apostolica vaticana, 1949.

Theodoret of Cyr. "Ad eos qui in Euphratesia et Osrhoena regione, Syria, Phoeni." In PG 83, cols. 1416-33. Edited by J.-P. Migne. Paris: Migne, 1859. TLG 4089.034.

———. "Apologeticus contra Theodoretum pro XII capitibus." In *Concilium universale Ephesenum anno 431*. Edited by E. Schwartz. Berlin: Walter De Gruyter, 1927. TLG 5000.001.

———. "Interpretatio in xiv epistulas sancti Pauli." In *Theodoretus*. PG 82, cols. 36-877. Edited by J.-P. Migne, 1864. TLG 4089.030.

Bibliography of Works
in English Translation

Ambrose. *Hexameron, Paradise, and Cain and Abel*. Translated by John J. Savage. FC 42. Washington, D.C.: Catholic University of America Press, 1961.

———. *Letters*. Translated by Mary Melchior Beyenka. FC 26. Washington, D.C.: Catholic University of America Press, 1954.

———. *Select Works and Letters*. Translated by H. De Romestin. NPNF 10. Series 2. Edited by Philip Schaff and Henry Wace. 14 vols. 1886-1900. Reprint, Peabody, Mass.: Hendrickson, 1994.

———. *Seven Exegetical Works*. Translated by Michael P. McHugh. FC 65. Washington, D.C.: Catholic University of America Press, 1972.

Athanasius. "On the Incarnation." In *Christology of the Later Fathers*, pp. 55-110. Translated by Archibald Robertson. LCC 3. Philadelphia: Westminster Press, 1954.

———. *Selected Works and Letters*. Translated by Archibald Robertson. NPNF 4. Series 2. Edited by Philip Schaff and Henry Wace. 14 vols. 1886-1900. Reprint, Peabody, Mass.: Hendrickson, 1994.

Augustine. *Anti-Pelagian Works*. Translated by Peter Holmes and Robert Ernest Wallis. NPNF 5. Series 1. Edited by Philip Schaff. 14 vols. 1886-1889. Reprint, Peabody, Mass.: Hendrickson, 1994.

———. *City of God, Christian Doctrine*. Translated by Marcus Dods and J. F. Shaw. NPNF 2. Series 1. Edited by Philip Schaff. 14 vols. 1886-1889. Reprint, Peabody, Mass.: Hendrickson, 1994.

———. *The City of God: Books VIII-XVI*. Translated by Gerald G. Walsh and Grace Monahan. FC 14. Washington, D.C.: Catholic University of America Press, 1952.

———. *The City of God: Books XVII-XXII*. Translated by Gerald G. Walsh and Daniel J. Honan. FC 24. Washington, D.C.: Catholic University of America Press, 1954.

———. *The Confessions and Letters of Augustine, with a Sketch of His Life and Work*. Translated by Philip Schaff, J. G. Pilkington, and J. G. Cunningham. NPNF 1. Series 1. Edited by Philip Schaff. 14 vols. 1886-1889. Reprint, Peabody, Mass.: Hendrickson, 1994.

———. *Eighty-three Different Questions*. Translated by David L. Mosher. FC 70. Washington, D.C.: Catholic University of America Press, 1977.

———. *Four Anti-Pelagian Writings: On Nature and Grace, On the Proceedings of Pelagius, On the Predestination of the Saints, On the Gift of Perseverance*. Translated by John A. Mourant and William J. Collinge. FC 86. Washington, D.C.: Catholic University of America Press, 1992.

———. *Letters*. Translated by Sister Wilfrid Parsons. FC 20 and 30. 2 vols. Washington, D.C.: Catholic University of America Press, 1953-1955.

———. *The Literal Meaning of Genesis*. Translated by John Hammond Taylor. ACW 42. New York: Newman Press, 1982.

———. *On Genesis, Two Books on Genesis Against the Manichees, and On the Literal Interpretation of Genesis: An Unfinished Book*. Translated by Roland J. Teske, S.J. FC 84. Washington, D.C.: Catholic University of America Press, 1991.

———. *On the Holy Trinity, Doctrinal Treatises, Moral Treatises*. Translated by Arthur West Haddan, et al. NPNF 3. Series 1. Edited by Philip Schaff. 14 vols. 1886-1889. Reprint, Peabody, Mass.: Hendrickson, 1994.

————. *Sermons.* 5 vols. Translated by Edmund Hill. WSA 3, 4, 5, 6, and 10. Part 3. Edited by John E. Rotelle. New York: New City Press, 1991-1995.

————. *Treatises on Marriage and Other Subjects.* Translated by Charles T. Wilcox et al. FC 27. Washington, D.C.: Catholic University of America Press, 1955.

————. *The Trinity.* Translated by Stephen McKenna. FC 45. Washington, D.C.: Catholic University of America Press, 1962.

Basil the Great. *Exegetic Homilies.* Translated by Agnes C. Way. FC 46. Washington, D.C.: Catholic University of America Press, 1963.

————. *Letters.* Translated by Agnes C. Way. 2 vols. FC 13 and 28. Washington, D.C.: Catholic University of America Press, 1951-1955.

————. *Letters and Select Works.* Translated by Blomfield Jackson. NPNF 8. Series 2. Edited by Philip Schaff and Henry Wace. 14 vols. 1886-1900. Reprint, Peabody, Mass.: Hendrickson, 1994.

Bede the Venerable. *Homilies on the Gospels.* 2 vols. Translated by Lawrence T. Martin and David Hurst. CS 110 and 111. Kalamazoo, Mich.: Cistercian Publications, 1991.

————. *On the Tabernacle.* Translated with notes and introduction by Arthur G. Holder. TTH 18. Liverpool: Liverpool University Press, 1994.

Braulio of Saragossa. "Letters." In *Iberian Fathers, Volume 2: Braulio of Saragossa, Fructuosus of Braga*, pp. 15-112. Translated by Claude W. Barlow. FC 63. Washington, D.C.: Catholic University of America Press, 1969.

Cassian, John. *Conferences.* Translated by Colm Luibheid. The Classics of Western Spirituality. New York: Paulist Press, 1985.

————. "Incarnation of the Lord, Against Nestorius." In *Sulpitius Severus, Vincent of Lerins, John Cassian*, pp. 547-621. Translated by Edgar C. S. Gibson. NPNF 11. Series 2. Edited by Philip Schaff and Henry Wace. 14 vols. 1886-1900. Reprint, Peabody, Mass.: Hendrickson, 1994.

Cassiodorus. *Explanation of the Psalms.* Translated by P. G. Walsh. 2 vols. ACW 51 and 52. New York: Newman Press, 1990-1991.

Clement of Alexandria. *Fathers of the Second Century: Hermas, Tatian, Athenagoras, Theophilus, and Clement of Alexandria.* Translated by F. Crombie et al. ANF 2. Edited by Alexander Roberts and James Donaldson. 10 vols. 1885-1887. Reprint, Peabody, Mass.: Hendrickson, 1994.

————. *Stromateis: Books 1-3.* Translated by John Ferguson. FC 85. Washington, D.C.: Catholic University of America Press, 1991.

Clement of Rome. "First Letter to Corinthians." In *The Apostolic Fathers*, pp. 9-58. Translated by Francis X. Glimm, et al. FC 1. New York: Christian Heritage, Inc., 1947.

————. "The Letter of the Church of Rome to the Church of Corinth, Commonly Called Clement's First Letter." In *Early Christian Fathers*, pp. 33-73. Translated by Cyril C. Richardson. LCC 1. Philadelphia: Westminster Press, 1953.

Cyprian. "Letter." In *Fathers of the Third Century: Hippolytus, Cyprian, Caius, Novatian, Appendix*, pp. 275-420. Arranged by A. Cleveland Coxe. ANF 1. Edited by Alexander Roberts and James Donaldson. 10 vols. 1885-1887. Reprint, Peabody, Mass.: Hendrickson, 1994.

Cyril of Alexandria. *Passim* in Rowan A. Greer, *The Captain of Our Salvation: A Study in the Patristic Exegesis of Hebrews.* Tübingen, Germany: Mohr, 1973.

————. "Second Letter to Nestorius." *Passim* in Richard A. Norris Jr., *The Christological Controversy.* Philadelphia: Fortress, 1980.

Cyril of Jerusalem. "Catechetical Lectures." In *Cyril of Jerusalem and Nemesius of Emesa*, pp. 64-199. Edited by William Telfer. LCC 4. Philadelphia: Westminster Press, 1955.

————. "Catechetical Lectures." In *S. Cyril of Jerusalem, S. Gregory Nazianzen*, pp. 1-202. Translated by

Edward Hamilton Gifford et al. NPNF 7. Series 2. Edited by Philip Schaff and Henry Wace. 14 vols. 1886-1900. Reprint, Peabody, Mass.: Hendrickson, 1994.

[Cyril of Jerusalem]. *The Works of Saint Cyril of Jerusalem.* Translated by Leo P. McCauley and Anthony A. Stephenson. 2 vols. FC 61 and 64. Washington, D.C.: Catholic University of America Press, 1969-1970.

Didache. "A Church Manual." In *Early Christian Fathers*, pp. 171-79. Translated by Cyril C. Richardson. LCC 1. Edited by Cyril C. Richardson. Philadelphia, Westminster Press, 1953.

Ephrem the Syrian. "Commentary on Genesis." In *St. Ephrem the Syrian: Selected Prose Works*, pp. 67-213. Translated by Edward G. Mathews Jr. and Joseph P. Amar. FC 91. Edited by Kathleen McVey. Washington, D.C.: Catholic University of America, 1994.

———. "Commentary on Genesis." *Passim* in James L. Kugel, *Traditions of the Bible: A Guide to the Bible as It Was at the Start of the Common Era.* Cambridge, Mass.: Harvard University Press, 1998.

———. *Saint Ephrem's Commentary on Tatian's Diatessaron: An English Translation of Chester Beatty Syriac MS 709.* Journal of Semitic Studies Supplement 2. Oxford: Oxford University Press for the University of Manchester, 1993.

[Epiphanius of Salamis]. *The Panarion of Epiphanius of Salamis.* Translated by Frank Williams. Nag Hammadi and Manichaean Studies 36. Leiden and New York: E. J. Brill, 1994.

Eusebius of Caesarea. *Ecclesiastical History.* 2 vols. Translated by Roy J. Defarrari. FC 19, 29. Washington, D.C.: Catholic University of America Press, 1953-1955.

———. *Ecclesiastical History.* Translated by Kirsopp Lake and J. E. L. Oulton. 2 vols. LCL 153, 265. Cambridge, Mass.: Harvard University Press, 1926-1932.

———. *Proof of Gospel.* 2 vols. Translated by W. J. Ferrar. London: SPCK, 1920. Reprint, Grand Rapids, Mich.: Baker, 1981.

Evagrius Ponticus. *The Praktikos and Chapters on Prayer.* Translated by John Eudes Bamberger. CS 4. Kalamazoo, Mich.: Cistercian Publications, 1970.

Gregory of Elvira. "Origen's Tractate on the Books of Holy Scripture." *Passim* in Jean Danielou, *From Shadows to Reality: Studies in the Biblical Typology of the Fathers.* London: Burns & Oates, 1960.

Gregory of Nazianzus. "Orations." In *Cyril of Jerusalem, Gregory Nazianzen.* Translated by Charles Gordon Browne et al. NPNF 7. Series 2. Edited by Philip Schaff and Henry Wace. 14 vols. 1886-1900. Reprint, Peabody, Mass.: Hendrickson, 1994.

———. "The Theological Orations." In *Christology of the Later Fathers*, pp. 128-214. Translated and edited by Edward Rochie Hardy. LCC 3. Philadelphia: Westminster, 1954.

[Gregory of Nazianzus]. *Faith Gives Fullness to Reasoning: The Five theological Orations of Gregory Nazianzen.* Introduction and commentary by Frederick W. Norris. Translated by Lionel Wickham and Frederick Williams. Leiden and New York: E. J. Brill, 1991.

Gregory of Nyssa. *The Life of Moses.* Translated by A. J. Malherbe and E. Ferguson. The Classics of Western Spirituality. New York: Paulist Press, 1978.

———. "On Perfection." In *Saint Gregory of Nyssa: Ascetical Works*, pp. 93-124. Translated by Virginia Woods Callahan. FC 58. Washington, D.C.: Catholic University of America Press, 1967.

[Gregory of Nyssa]. *Select Writings and Letters of Gregory, Bishop of Nyssa.* Translated by William Moore and Henry Austin Wilson. NPNF 5. Series 2. Edited by Philip Schaff and Henry Wace. 14 vols. 1886-1900. Reprint, Peabody, Mass.: Hendrickson, 1994.

Gregory the Great. "Letter." In *Gregory the Great, Ephraim Syrus, Aphraha*, pp. 1-111. Translated by James Barmby. NPNF 13. Series 2. Edited by Philip Schaff and Henry Wace. 14 vols. 1886-1900. Reprint, Peabody, Mass.: Hendrickson, 1994.

Hilary of Poitiers. "Tractate of the Mysteries." *Passim* in Jean Danielou, *From Shadows to Reality: Studies in the Biblical Typology of the Fathers.* London: Burns & Oates, 1960.

Hippolytus. *Contra Noetum*. Heythrop Monographs 2. Edited and translated by Robert Butterworth. London: Heythrop College, 1977.

Ignatius of Antioch. "Letter to the Magnesians." In *The Apostolic Fathers: Volume I*, pp. 165-279. Translated by Kirsopp Lake. LCL 1. London: William Heinemann, 1912.

Irenaeus. "Against Heresies." In *The Apostolic Fathers with Justin Martyr and Irenaeus*, pp. 315-567. Edited by Alexander Roberts and James Donaldson. Arranged by A. Cleveland Coxe. ANF 1. Edited by Alexander Roberts and James Donaldson. 10 vols. 1885-1887. Reprint, Peabody, Mass.: Hendrickson, 1994.

[Isaac of Nineveh]. *The Ascetical Homilies of Saint Isaac the Syrian*. Translated by the Holy Transfiguration Monastery. Boston: Holy Transfiguration Monastery, 1984.

Jerome. *Hebrew Questions on Genesis*. Translated with introduction and commentary by C. T. R. Hayward. Oxford Early Christian Studies. Oxford: Clarendon Press, 1995.

———. *Letters and Select Works*. Translated by W. H. Fremantle. NPNF 6. Series 2. Edited by Philip Schaff and Henry Wace. 14 vols. 1886-1900. Reprint, Peabody, Mass.: Hendrickson, 1994.

[Jerome]. *The Homilies of Saint Jerome*. Translated by Marie Liguori Ewald. 2 vols. FC 48 and 57. Washington, D.C.: Catholic University of America Press, 1964-1966.

John Chrysostom. *Discourses Against Judaizing Christians*. Translated by Paul W. Harkins. FC 68. Washington, D.C.: Catholic University of America Press, 1979.

———. "On the Epistle to the Hebrews." In *Chrysostom: Homilies on the Gospel of Saint John and the Epistle to the Hebrew*, pp. 335-524. Translated by Frederic Gardiner. NPNF 14. Series 1. Edited by Philip Schaff. 14 vols. 1886-1889. Reprint, Peabody, Mass.: Hendrickson, 1994.

John of Damascus. "Orthodox Faith." In *Writings*, pp. 165-406. Translated by Frederic H. Chase. FC 37. Washington, D.C.: Catholic University of America Press, 1958.

Justin Martyr. "Dialogue with Trypho." In *The Apostolic Fathers with Justin Martyr and Irenaeus*, pp. 194-270. Arranged by A. Cleveland Coxe. ANF 1. Edited by Alexander Roberts and James Donaldson. 10 vols. 1885-1887. Reprint, Peabody, Mass.: Hendrickson, 1994.

———. "Dialogue with Trypho." In *Writings of Saint Justin Martyr*, pp. 147-366. Translated by Thomas B Fallis. FC 6. New York: Christian Heritage, Inc., 1948.

———. "First Apology." In *Early Christian Fathers*, pp. 242-89. Translated by Edward Rochie Hard. LCC 1. Edited by Cyril C. Richardson. Philadelphia, Westminster Press, 1953.

Lactantius. "The Epitome of the Divine Institutes." In *Lactantius, Venantius, Asterius, Victorinus, Dionysius, Apostolic Teaching and Constitutions, 2 Clement, Early Liturgies*, pp 224-58. Translated by William Fletcher. ANF 7. Edited by Alexander Roberts and James Donaldson. 10 vols. 1885-1887. Reprint, Peabody, Mass.: Hendrickson, 1994.

Leo the Great. *Sermons*. Translated by Jane P. Freeland and Agnes J. Conway. FC 93. Washington, D.C.: Catholic University of America Press, 1957.

[Leo the Great]. "The Letters and Sermons of Leo the Great, Bishop of Rome." In *Leo the Great, Gregory the Great*. Translated by Charles Lett Feltoe. NPNF 12. Series 2. Edited by Philip Schaff and Henry Wace. 14 vols. 1886-1900. Reprint, Peabody, Mass.: Hendrickson, 1994.

Marius Victorinus. "On the Necessity of Accepting *Homoousios*." In *Marius Victorinus: Theological Treatises on the Trinity*, pp. 305-14. Translated by Mary T. Clark. FC 69. Washington, D.C.: Catholic University of America Press, 1978.

Nestorius. "First Sermon Against the *Theotokos*." *Passim* In Richard A. Norris Jr., *The Christological Controversy*. Philadelphia: Fortress, 1980.

Origen. "Against Celsus." In *Tertullian (IV); Minucius Felix; Commodian; Origen (I and III)*, pp. 395-669. Translated by Frederick Combie. ANF 4. Edited by Alexander Roberts and James Donaldson. 10 vols. 1885-1887. Reprint, Peabody, Mass.: Hendrickson, 1994.

————. *Commentary on the Gospel According to John, Books 1-10 and 13-32*. Translated by Ronald E. Heine. FC 80 and 89. 2 vols. Washington, D.C.: Catholic University of America Press, 1989-1993.

————. *An Exhortation to Martyrdom, Prayer and Selected Works*. Translated by Rowan A. Greer. The Classics of Western Spirituality. New York: Paulist Press, 1979.

————. *Homilies on Genesis and Exodus*. Translated by Ronald E. Heine. FC 71. Washington, D.C.: Catholic University of America Press, 1982.

————. "Homilies on Joshua." In Jean Danielou, S.J., *From Shadows to Reality: Studies in the Biblical Typology of the Fathers*," pp. 229-86. London: Burns & Oates, 1960.

————. *Homilies on Joshua*. Translated by Cynthia White. FC 105. Washington, D.C.: Catholic University of America Press, 2002.

————. *Homilies on Leviticus: 1-16*. Translated by Gary Wayne Barkley. FC 83. Washington, D.C.: Catholic University of America Press, 1990.

————. *Homilies on Luke; Fragments on Luke*. Translated by Joseph T. Lienhard. FC 94. Washington D.C.: Catholic University of America Press, 1996.

————. *Passim* in Rowan A. Greer, *The Captain of Our Salvation: A Study in the Patristic Exegesis of Hebrews*. Tübingen, Germany: Mohr, 1973.

————. "Homilies on the Psalms." *Passim* in Bertrand de Margerie, *An Introduction to the History of Exegesis I: The Greek Fathers*. Petersham, Mass.: Saint Bede's Publication, 1993.

————. *On First Principles*. Translated by G. W. Butterworth. London: SPCK, 1936. Reprint, Gloucester, Mass.: Peter Smith, 1973.

————. "On First Principles." In *Tertullian (IV); Minucius Felix; Commodian; Origen (I and III)*, pp. 221-669. Translated by Frederick Crombie. ANF 4. Edited by Alexander Roberts and James Donaldson. 10 vols. 1885-1887. Reprint, Peabody, Mass.: Hendrickson, 1994.

Pachomius. *Pachomian Koinonia*. Vols. 1 and 3. Translated by Armand Veilleux. CS 45 and 47. Kalamazoo, Mich.: Cistercian Publications, 1980, 1982.

Philoxenus of Mabbug. "Letter to Abba Symeon of Caesarea." In *The Ascetical Homilies of Saint Isaac the Syrian*, pp. 427-48. Translated by The Holy Transfiguration Monastery. Boston: Holy Transfiguration Monastery, 1984.

[Pseudo-Clement of Rome]. "2 Clement." In *The Apostolic Fathers 1*, pp. 125-63. Translated by Kirsopp Lake. LCL 1. London: William Heinemann, 1925.

[Pseudo-Dionysius]. *Pseudo-Dionysius: The Complete Works*. Translated by Colm Luibheid. The Classics of Western Spirituality. New York: Paulist, 1980.

Rufinus of Aquileia. "Commentary on the Apostles' Creed." In *Theodoret, Jerome, Gennadius, Rufinus: Historical Writings, etc.*, pp. 541-63. Translated by William Henry Fremantle. NPNF 3. Series 2. Edited by Philip Schaff and Henry Wace. 14 vols. 1886-1900. Reprint, Peabody, Mass.: Hendrickson, 1994.

Symeon the New Theologian. *The Discourses*. Translated by C. J. de Catanzaro. The Classics of Western Spirituality. New York: Paulist, 1980.

Tertullian. "The Chaplet." In *Tertullian: Disciplinary, Moral and Ascetical Works*, pp. 231-67. Translated by Rudolph Arbesmann, Sister Emily Joseph Daly and Edwin A. Quain. FC 40. Washington, D.C.: Catholic University of America Press, 1959.

[Tertullian]. *Latin Christianity: Its Founder, Tertullian*. Translated by S. Thelwall et al. ANF 3. Edited by Alexander Roberts and James Donaldson. 10 vols. 1885-1887. Reprint, Peabody, Mass.: Hendrickson, 1994.

Theodore of Mopsuestia. *Passim* in Rowan A. Greer, *The Captain of Our Salvation: A Study in the Patristic Exegesis of Hebrews*. Tübingen, Germany: Mohr, 1973.

Theodoret of Cyr. "Interpretation of Hebrews." In *Theodoret of Cyrus: Commentary on the Letters of St.*

Paul, vol. 2, pp. 136-207. Translated and edited by Robert Charles Hill. Brookline, Mass.: Holy Cross Orthodox Press, 2001.

[Theodoret of Cyr]. "The Ecclesiastical History, Dialogues, and Letters of Theodoret." In *Theodoret, Jerome, Gennadius, Rufinus: Historical Writings, etc*, pp. 1-348. Translated by Blomfield Jackson. NPNF 3. Series 2. Edited by Philip Schaff and Henry Wace. 14 vols. 1886-1900. Reprint, Peabody, Mass.: Hendrickson, 1994.

Subject Index

Aaron
  appointment of, 70-71
  blessed by Melchizedek, 104
  bones of, 196
  branch of, 133
  Christ and, 70, 93, 116-17
  death and, 48
  duty of, 135
  as forebear of priests, 121
  Melchizedek and, 95
  priesthood of, 105
  as priestly representation, 114-15
  rest and, 57
  rod of, 134, 195
Abednego, 98
Abel
  Cain and, 177
  Christ and, 224-26
  death of, 181
  divine promises to, 187
  example of, 196
  faith of, 177, 197
  fame, glory, memory of, 177
  reason and, 190
  result of sacrifice of, 177
  still speaks, 177
  waiting for us, 206
  willing to die, 205
Abraham
  children after Sarah and 185
  citizen of far city, 188
  commands and promises to, 190
  example of, 197
  faith and obedience of, 184-85, 186, 190-92, 197
  father of nations, 186-87
  God of, 189
  God speaks to, 4, 201

God's appearances to, 4-5
God's promise to, 92-93
heaven not opened for, 159
Isaac figuratively received by, 193-94
Isaac, Jacob and, 52, 103, 112, 204
Jacob and, 195
Jews and, 206
Melchizedek and, 95-97, 99-101, 104, 108, 111
Rebekah and, 107
righteousness of, 98
Sarah and, 187
seed of, 47, 48
seek God like, 178
Shem and, 106
as stranger/exile, 187
testing of, 192-93
waiting for us, 206
willing to die, 205
woman associated with, 200
abuse, 199
Adam
  Christ and, 76
  fall of, 178
  God's appearances to, 5
  red heifer and, 236
  under sentence of death, 122
  Seth and, 113
  Son of God and, 233
adoption, 37, 44
adultery, 230
adversity, 50
advice, 56
affliction(s), 50, 209, 214, 228. *See also* suffering; tribulations
Agathopus, 141
age(s), 7-8, 145-46, 234
age to come, 84
Ahab, 158
aid, 89
Alcuin, xix
Alexandrian tradition, xix-xx
allegory, xx
almsgiving, 211-12
Amalek, 195
Ambrosiaster, xviii
Ammonites, 204
Amraphel, 99
anarchy, 237

angels
  being aware of, 30-31
  Christ and, 18-19, 28
  definition of, 24
  description of, 22-23
  good and evil, 30
  guardian, 30
  hierarchy of, 22
  humans and, 22, 29-30
  incorporeality of, 22
  law given by, 32
  ministry/service of, 24, 124-25
  mysteries transmitted by, 30-31
  nature of, 22
  present with elect, 30
  salvation and, 28-29
  Sodom and, 32
  Son of God and, 19
  as spirit and fire, 22
  were created, 28
  work for our sake, 29
  work of, 29
anger, 182-83, 214
Anthony, 9
Antiochene tradition, xix-xx
Apollos, xviii
apostles, 127
apostolic preaching, 1
Aquila, 170
archangels, 22
Arian controversy, xviii
Arians, xxv, 12
Arioch, 99
Arius, 14, 24
ark of the covenant, 134
Arpachshad, 99
ascents, 22
assembly, 163
Assyrians, 97
Athanasius, 25
Athenians, 77
Baal, 151
Babylon, 127, 154, 204
ball, 194
baptism
  of children, 109
  confidence and, 57
  crucifixion and, 85
  death and, 45, 87
  description of ritual of, 82

forgiveness of sins and, 85-86, 158
limit of, 84
result of, 44
a second, 85
shame removed by, 168-69
sin and, xvii
under the law, 81
Barak, 203-4
Barnabas, 1
Baruch, 121
Basil the Great, 159
belief, 173, 179-80
bishop(s), 53-54
blasphemy, 167-68
blood
  of beasts, 155
  of Christ and Abel, 226
  of red heifer, 236
  sprinkling of, 142
  See also blood of Christ
blood of Christ, 140, 142-43, 226
body, 62, 139-40, 215-16
bread, 56
bulls, 140
Cain, 5, 177
Caleb, 57
Calvin, John, xviii
Canaan, Canaanites, 107, 179, 196, 201
canonization, xvii-xx
carnality, 157-58
Chaldeans, 204
Chedorlaomer, 99
cherubim, 133
children, 109, 230
Christian life, xxii
christology, xix
church, 123, 139, 202
common arts, 6
comparison, xxi, xxii
confidence, 57, 169, 185, 215
conscience, 238
consensual interpretation, xxiv
consolation, 213
Constantine Augustus, 9
Cornelius, 29
Council of Carthage, xviii
covenant, 141-42
covetousness, 230-31
Cozbi, 100